The
Utilization
Management
Guide
Third
Edition

URAC
PROMOTING QUALITY HEALTH CARE

Acknowledgments

Executive Editor: Garry Carneal, JD, MA

Managing Editors: David H. Reiter, Esq. and Howard Burde, Esq.

Assistant Editor: Jacquelyn A. Lombos

The Utilization Management Guide, Third Edition, is the product of a cumulative effort from a host of writers, editors, research assistants, and support staff. No book of this scope could possibly be published without such outstanding support. In addition to the dedicated individuals whose biographies appear in this Guide, we would be remiss to not only mention but also express our eternal thanks to this special group of individuals.

Our first thanks go out to the staff at URAC, especially to Jackie Lombos, Brigitte Schnorr, and Regina Xerez-Burgos, whose superlative efforts saw this project through from beginning to end by coordinating, organizing, drafting, editing, and laying out this entire Guide. We greatly thank URAC's accreditation reviewers Claire Barrett, Chris Brown, Christine Leyden, Donna Merrick, Sue Ohr, Susan Stern, and Bonnie Sturges for their assistance as well.

Mr. Burde wishes to personally extend his thanks as well to Myra Callahan and Dawn Bachetti of Blank Rome who typed and copy edited many sections of this Guide provided by Blank Rome and were most diplomatic in their grammatical criticism. Of course, we also extend our appreciation to several law students and young lawyers who assisted with this Guide's research, including Mandara Meyers, Holly Fernandez, Penelope Jones, Leasa Woods, and Michael Lorelli. Finally, Mr. Burde wishes to greatly thank all his partners at Blank Rome who willingly, if not always knowingly, contributed the firm's resources to this effort.

Important Note to Readers:

In this Guide, URAC has attempted to survey, analyze, and summarize all the state laws and regulations that pertain to both health utilization management and workers' compensation utilization management. In addition, this publication also includes a chapter on such federal programs as Medicaid and Medicare. While URAC has tried to address all facets of this material, by design this publication does not cover every state and federal utilization review or utilization management provision. Nor for this matter should this publication be used as a substitute for a review of the actual laws and regulations of each state. URAC recommends consulting the state laws and the appropriate government officials for definitive answers to questions of a regulatory nature. Please note that the views expressed in the *The Utilization Management Guide* are those of the individual authors. They do not necessarily represent the views and positions of URAC.

©2005 URAC
1220 L Street, Suite 400, Washington, D.C. 20005
☎ (202) 216-9010 🖨 (202) 216-9006
💻 www.urac.org

About URAC

URAC, an independent, nonprofit organization, is a well-known leader in promoting health care quality through its accreditation and certification programs. As a nonprofit industry neutral organization, URAC's Certificate of Accreditation serves as a seal of approval to assure both regulators and consumers a health care provider is meeting a superior standard of quality care. Through its broad-based governance structure and an inclusive standards development process, URAC ensures that all stakeholders are represented in establishing meaningful quality measures for the entire health care industry.

Since its inception in 1990, URAC has accredited over 2,700 office and Internet sites doing business in all 50 states and three foreign countries. URAC-accredited organizations provide health care services to over 150 million Americans. Currently, URAC offers over 18 different accreditation and certification programs. These programs cover a wide range of health care operations ranging from integrated health plan offerings to specialty carve out services such as utilization management and other medical management functions to include the following:

Clinical Accreditation and Certification Programs:
➤ Case Management
➤ Claims Processing
➤ Consumer Education and Support
➤ Core
➤ Credentials Verification Organization
➤ Disease Management
➤ Health Call Center
➤ Health Network
➤ Health Plan
➤ Health Provider Credentialing
➤ Health Utilization Management
➤ Independent Review
➤ Vendor Certification
➤ Workers' Compensation Utilization Management

Health IT Accreditation Programs:
➤ Health Web Site
➤ HIPAA Privacy – for Covered Entity or Business Associate
➤ HIPAA Security – for Covered Entity or Business Associate

Other URAC Quality Benchmarking Programs:
➤ Consumer Satisfaction Commendation

Because of URAC's broad-based standards and rigorous accreditation process, purchasers and consumers look to URAC accreditation as an indication that a health care organization has the necessary structures and processes to promote high quality care and preserve patient rights. In addition, regulators in 35 states and three federal agencies recognize URAC's accreditation standards in the regulatory process.

Along with their mission to promote and maintain quality health care for the general public, URAC is engaged in several research projects to assess and identify new approaches to improve performance measurement in a variety of health care settings. In addition, URAC also authors many cutting-edge publications on health care delivery systems, HIPAA Privacy and Security regulations, and offers over 40 days of educational conferences, workshops, and seminars annually on issues ranging from accreditation to best practices.

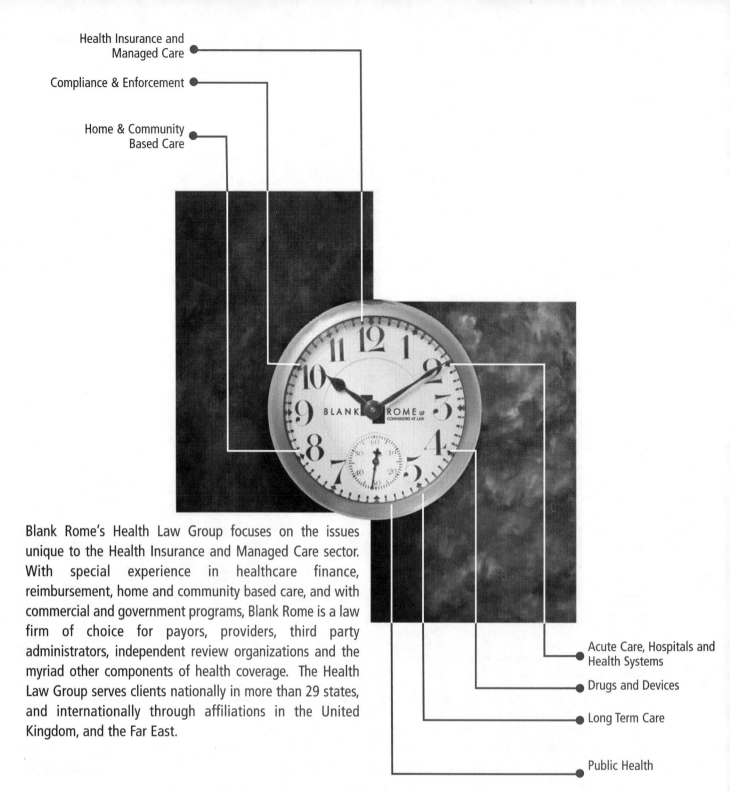

Health Insurance and Managed Care

Compliance & Enforcement

Home & Community Based Care

Acute Care, Hospitals and Health Systems

Drugs and Devices

Long Term Care

Public Health

Blank Rome's Health Law Group focuses on the issues unique to the Health Insurance and Managed Care sector. With special experience in healthcare finance, reimbursement, home and community based care, and with commercial and government programs, Blank Rome is a law firm of choice for payors, providers, third party administrators, independent review organizations and the myriad other components of health coverage. The Health Law Group serves clients nationally in more than 29 states, and internationally through affiliations in the United Kingdom, and the Far East.

BLANK ROME LLP
COUNSELORS AT LAW

Howard A. Burde

Washington, DC: 202.772.5988 • Fax 202.572.8484 • Philadelphia: 215.569.5724 • Fax 215.832.5724 • Burde@BlankRome.com

www.BlankRome.com

About the Authors

David H. Reiter, J.D.
Legislative Counsel for Government Policy and Legal Affairs, URAC
David H. Reiter currently serves as URAC's Legislative Counsel for Government Policy and Legal Affairs. For 14 years, Mr. Reiter practiced trial law in the District of Columbia and Maryland state and federal court systems. During this period he also provided Of Counsel work regarding internal and external litigation matters for a national and international patent and trademark law firm in Washington, D.C. In the year 2000, he left private practice for a position with Cable and Wireless, U.S.A., an International Internet Technology company, where he assisted with their ISO audit of their international data center. Immediately prior to his coming to URAC, Mr. Reiter worked at both The Center for Biologics Evaluation and Research, and The Center for Drug Evaluation and Research with the U.S. Food and Drug Administration. Mr. Reiter received his B.A. in Economics from the George Washington University Columbian College in Washington, D.C., and his J.D. from Suffolk School of Law in Boston, MA. He is also an active member of the American Health Lawyers Association.

Howard A. Burde, J.D.
Partner, Blank Rome LLP
Howard A. Burde is Chair of the Health Law Group of Blank Rome LLP. His practice includes providing advice on complex health, health insurance and managed care law issues to institutional providers, health insurers, managed care organizations and governments.

Prior to joining Blank Rome, Mr. Burde served as Deputy General Counsel to Governors Tom Ridge and Mark Schweiker, where he served as legal counsel for Commonwealth of Pennsylvania responsible for the Departments of Health, Public Welfare and Aging, as well as for the Health Related Professional Boards, the Medical Professional Liability Catastrophe Loss Fund, and all managed care, health insurance, and health and human service issues. Mr. Burde is Editor in Chief and primary author of The Health Laws of Pennsylvania (PBI, 2000) as well as numerous peer reviewed articles. Mr. Burde is on the Boards of the Journal of Health Law and The BNA Health Law Reporter. Mr. Burde is a frequent speaker on health law topics to audiences including the American Health Lawyers Association, the Utilization Review Accreditation Commission, the Health Care Financial Management Association, and the Milbank Memorial Fund.

Mr. Burde graduated from Duke University, B.A. magna cum laude, 1984 and was a Baccalaureate Speaker at the Duke University Graduation. He received his J.D. degree in 1988 from the University of Virginia School of Law and was a founder of the Virginia Health Law Forum.

Garry Carneal, JD, MA
Garry Carneal is a leading expert in health care quality, including issues pertaining to the quality and regulation of health care and medical management operations. Since 1996, Mr. Carneal has served as President & CEO of URAC, a non-profit, independent organization. Currently, URAC offers 16 accreditation programs in both the clinical and health information technology arenas. Previously, Mr. Carneal has served as the Vice President of Legal and State Affairs at the American Association of Health Plans (AAHP) and Legislative Counsel for Health Policy for the National Association of Insurance Commissioners (NAIC).

Karen L. Cavalli, Esquire
Karen L. Cavalli is Senior Counsel with Independence Blue Cross in Philadelphia, Pennsylvania and concentrates her practice in the areas of managed care, health and insurance law. She received her B.A. from Muhlenburg College and her J.D. from the Widener University School of Law, where she served as president of the Health Law Society and managing editor of the Society of Healthcare Attorneys of the Hospital Association of Pennsylvania's Health law Newsletter. While in law school, she studied international health law at the Padua International Law Institute in Padua, Italy. She has authored numerous articles and lectured on managed care topics, such as regulatory compliance and utilization review. In 2002, she served on the Blue Cross Blue Shield Association's Utilization Management Task Force and was a featured speaker on the topic of extraterritorial considerations for state utilization review laws, at the Blue Cross Blue Shield Association's 36th Annual Lawyers Conference.

Guy D'Andrea
Mr. D'Andrea has worked in health care policy for over 12 years. He is the founder of Discern LLC, a consulting firm focusing on health care compliance and project management. For seven years, Mr. D'Andrea led product development and government affairs for URAC, a private accreditation organization. Prior to joining URAC, Mr. D'Andrea held positions in health care policy and legislation at the American Association of Health Plans (now AHIP), the American Managed Care and Review Association, and the Maryland Association of HMO's.

Mr. D'Andrea is a frequent speaker on the topic of health care quality and oversight, and has authored numerous articles on accreditation and compliance issues. He received his undergraduate degree from Cornell University and is currently working towards dual Masters of Business Administration degrees from Columbia University and the London Business School.

Pam Foster

Pam Foster has worked in the managed health care industry since 1986. Her most recent work with AdvancePCS, purchased by Caremark in January 2004, included responsibility for drug prior authorization and appeals' profitability as well as for product regulatory compliance. She served on the DMAA (Disease Management Association of America) Board for three years and led the AdvancePCS disease management programs to full NCQA compliance in 2002. She is a Master's prepared nurse, graduated from Johns Hopkins University, who prior to joining AdvancePCS, worked for three large managed care companies directing utilization, case management, network development and disease management activities. Ms. Foster is an active NCQA surveyor with a strong commitment to quality healthcare delivery.

Liza Greenberg, RN, MPH

Liza Greenberg, RN, MPH, is a health care consultant with a special interest in patient safety, quality, prevention and public health. She formerly was Vice President of Research and Quality Initiatives at URAC, a nonprofit national accreditation organization for health care. Ms. Greenberg's responsibilities at URAC included development of new research initiatives on performance measurement and health improvement for managed care organizations. She also staffed development of URAC's case management and disease management accreditation standards. Ms. Greenberg received her BA and BSN from the University of Pennsylvania, and an MPH from the Johns Hopkins University School of Hygiene and Public Health.

Lori Harris-Stevens, RN, MHA

Lori Harris-Stevens is Vice President of Accreditation for URAC. Ms. Harris-Stevens joined URAC in 1997 as an Accreditation Reviewer. In addition to her accreditation reviewer responsibilities, Ms. Harris-Stevens was the primary URAC staff person assigned to the development and implementation of the Health Call Center Standards. Ms. Harris-Stevens is a Registered Nurse with over 20 years of experience in health care, 14 of which were in the managed care arena. Before working in the managed care industry, Ms. Harris-Stevens had extensive experience in both the public and private health care sectors. Ms. Harris-Stevens has a Masters degree in Health Administration.

Valerie Nosek, RN, BSN, CPHQ

Valerie Nosek has over five years' experience as an Accreditation Reviewer at URAC for accreditation programs including Health Utilization Management, Workers' Compensation Utilization Management, Case Management, Health Provider Credentialing, Credentials Verification Organization and Claims Processing. Her career in managed care includes seven years of varied experience in the development and management of utilization management, case management and quality programs for general health and workers' compensation programs, during which time she coordinated successful URAC Health Utilization Management Accreditation. Additional experience includes two years in HMO quality management, focusing on provider quality issues and consumer grievance resolution.

Susan Prest, MA, LP

Susan Prest is president of Prest & Associates, Inc., a Madison, Wisconsin based, URAC accredited independent review organization specializing in the independent review of psychiatric, addictions medicine and behavioral health care cases. Ms. Prest is the current president of the National Association of Independent Review Organizations (NAIRO). She is a graduate of the University of California at Berkeley, a licensed psychologist with twenty-six years of experience as an administrator and clinician specializing in mental health and substance abuse managed care. Ms. Prest is a nationally recognized expert on independent review and managed care.

John D. Shire

John D. Shire practices with the Health Law Group of Blank Rome LLP. Mr. Shire concentrates his practice in health care transactions, health care regulatory matters, health care operations, health information compliance, and technology contracts. Mr. Shire represents hospital systems, physician practices, managed care organizations, imaging centers, and private equity investors in health care-related businesses. Mr. Shire is a co-author of *How Government and Industry Pharma Compliance Guidance Impacts Attorney Advice For All Health Care Clients*, Health Lawyers News, Vol. 7 No. 8 (August 2003), and has contributed as an author and researcher for two major health care resources, *The Guide to Medical Privacy and HIPAA* (Thompson Publishing Group, 2002) and *The Health Laws of Pennsylvania* (PBI Press 2000). Mr. Shire is a graduate of the Dickinson School of Law, where he was an associate editor of the *Dickinson Law Review*. He received his B.A. degree, cum laude, from Bucknell University. Mr. Shire is admitted to practice in Pennsylvania, New Jersey, and Maryland.

Patricia M. Wagner

Patricia M. Wagner is an associate with Epstein Becker & Green, where she practices in the firm's National Health Law Practice. Ms. Wagner counsels clients on a full range of legal and regulatory issues. Ms. Wagner's experience includes advising clients on a variety of health regulatory matters including issues related to compliance with: the HIPAA Privacy Rule; HIPAA portability provisions; ERISA claims regulations; and other state and federal regulatory requirements. Ms. Wagner also has experience with litigation of federal and state healthcare antitrust matters.

The Utilization Management Guide: 3rd Edition

Table of Contents

Foreword

During the past 30 years, utilization management (UM) has been instrumental in assisting heath plans, insurers, the government, health providers, and others in determining what care is medically necessary and appropriate for patients. UM accomplishments include the improvement of medial practice protocols and the reduction of unnecessary medical expenses, to name just a few benefits. In today's medical management system, UM services are often integrated into a more dynamic "care coordination" approach, which may utilize case management and disease management services as well.

The current edition of *The Utilization Management Guide* details many of the business, legal, and regulatory forces directly impacting the medical management system. In addition, the publication continues to serve as the definitive text detailing how regulatory and business trends are impacting UM programs. This resource guide:

➤ Provides a detailed description of current state health and workers' compensation UM regulations;

➤ Overviews federal UM requirements including Medicare, Medicaid, ERISA and the Department of Labor guidelines;

➤ Analyzes recent trends in the UM field including an assessment of how the medical management system is changing;

➤ Provides a legal update on how recent court decisions are impacting UM operations;

➤ Highlights how independent or external review laws are impacting the medical management process;

➤ Overviews how URAC accreditation standards support and improve the UM process; and

➤ Showcases other topics such as how pharmacy benefit management (PBM) services and patient safety indicators can improve the medical management system.

As a result of its extensive subject matter, this book remains a must read for those health care professionals, compliance staff, benefit administrators, consumers, government officials and others who require a better understanding of the UM process.

In closing, URAC expresses its sincerest gratitude to all those regulators who peer reviewed the enclosed state UM summaries, and the guest authors who have contributed to this book. We are truly indebted to these individuals for their efforts. URAC also would like to extend a special thank you to Howard Burde, a senior health care attorney at Blank Rome, for his many hours of volunteering in the researching, writing and editing significant portions of this book. I also would like to express my gratitude to URAC's staff, especially Jackie Lombos and David Reiter, for their efforts in putting this book together.

Garry Carneal, JD, MA
President & CEO
URAC

1.0: Executive Summary

Garry Carneal, JD, MA

On behalf of URAC, its President, Board of Directors, and its entire dedicated staff we are pleased to present this Third Edition of *The Utilization Management Guide*. This publication provides helpful guidance to the reader and includes several insightful articles by a number of leading authorities on various aspects of utilization review (UR), and utilization management (UM). The book also presents a comprehensive state-by-state survey analyses on UM laws and regulations.

Utilization management has become an accepted and integral component of today's American health care system. While the prominence of UM may rise and fall inversely with the cost of health care, it still remains an essential vehicle for making informed medical necessity determinations and for distributing health care resources. A prime example of the importance and sensitivity associated with UM interventions can be observed by the vast number of laws both new and old, and pending legislation that address and oversee the UM process. In addition to the state laws governing the application of utilization management, federal programs (such as the Medicare and Medicaid programs, and the U.S. Department of Labor Claims Benefit Regulations) and many state workers compensation programs also have adopted guidelines directly impacting UM operations.

Beginning in the late 1980's and throughout the 1990's, most states adopted enabling legislation governing how UM should be conducted in most managed settings. While the number of new state UM laws may have lessened in recent years, these laws continue to be refined by the state legislatures and their respective regulatory agencies. On the federal level, since the year 2000 the Medicare program has twice significantly changed its utilization management requirements (through the Benefits Improvement and Protection Act of 2000 (BIPA) and the Medicare Prescription Drug, Improvement and Modernization Act of 2003 – also known as the Medicare Modernization Act, hereinafter, MMA). The end result is that any health care entity involved in, or associated with, UM activities will be obligated to comport their activities to the appropriate jurisdictions' standards. Not an easy task.

The purpose of *The Utilization Management Guide* is to provide a comprehensive reference manual detailing the UM process and its current applicable regulations. A primary goal is to create an invaluable resource for both new and experienced health care practitioners in the UM field. To accomplish this aim, the Guide is divided into two distinct sections. Part I provides an introduction to utilization management on the state and federal levels and the unique issues that surround it. Part II provides an in-depth summary of state UM laws and URAC accreditation standards. Indeed, *The Utilization Management Guide: Third Edition* should be the starting point for any questions regarding this subject.

In Section 2.0, "An Overview of Business Trends", Garry Carneal, JD, MA, URAC's President and Chief Executive Officer, offers an overview of utilization management. Mr. Carneal draws upon his 15 years of experience in the health care field and also the experiences of URAC's accreditation review team. The analysis details the evolution of utilization review as well as recent trends that include the integration of utilization, case and disease management services. With his eye to the future, Mr. Carneal concludes his section by offering his predictions about what changes are in store for utilization management and medical management systems going forward.

Sections 3.0 through 6.0 deal with the many levels of regulations a health care entity must face when embarking on the path of UM. From the numerous variations of state UM laws to those required on the federal level, these chapters demonstrate that UM practitioners must walk a careful line in terms of complying with all applicable regulations.

Both Howard Burde and Karen Cavalli team up in Section 3.0 to provide an "Overview of State Health UM Regulation." In it the reader is not only presented with the definition of UM, but its specific regulatory components. Consisting of such aspects as benefit determinations, criteria review, qualifications of benefit reviewers, decision timeframes, and appeals processes, UM is not just a single process but also a series of processes that is most often governed by an array of statutory and administrative regulations. This Section should be read in conjunction with the guide's Appendix B, the state survey on UM laws.

In Section 4.0, "The Landscape of Utilization Review Programs for Workers' Compensation Programs," Trish Wagner with the law firm of Epstein Becker & Green reports that the UM requirements within workers' compensation arrangements continue to be a constantly shifting landscape. To combat the rising costs associated with workers' compensation insurance, more and more states are turning to utilization management as a viable solution. As Ms. Wagner explains, UM not only controls costs but also promotes more effective treatment protocols for injured employees. This Section should be read in conjunction with the guide's Appendix C, the state survey on workers' compensation UM laws completed by the law firm of Blank Rome.

Looking next to the federal level, Mr. Burde provides his insights on UM's role in Medicaid and Medicare in Section 5.0. This chapter focuses on the role of state UM laws and regulations and their relationship to Medicare and Medicaid. As Burde theorizes, while Medicare and Medicaid laws do not directly regulate the content of utilization management, the statues and regulations applicable to each provide detailed guidelines for UM conducted under the variety of different Medicare and Medicaid programs.

In Section 6.0 "Utilization Management under ERISA Plans" both Mr. Burde and Guy D'Andrea, Clinical Program Consultant for URAC, narrow UM's focus on the federal level to ERISA plans. With most of the attention regarding ERISA devoted to preemption issues, ERISA regulations governing utilization management are often ignored. The 2003 implementation of the ERISA Claims Procedure Regulation has significantly altered the regulatory environment for utilization management. Self-insured plans – which had previously been exempt from most state oversight, and therefore most UM regulation – now have to comply with UM requirements. In addition, health care benefit arrangements – which fall under the purview of ERISA and are offered through insured plans - - must now reconcile federal and state regulations in each state where they operate.

In Section 7.0, David Reiter, Esq., Legislative Counsel for URAC, and John Shire, an attorney with the law firm of Blank Rome, cover a wide range of legal issues impacting UM and managed care. Among the other cases and legal issues involving managed care, this chapter overviews a major landmark ruling by the U.S. Supreme Court in 2004 that will impact significantly health plan operations. In Aetna Health Inc. v. Davila, and Cigna Healthcare of Texas Inc. v. Calad, the Supreme Court decisively addressed the legal liability issues caused by UM's sometimes overlapping functions of medicine and insurance where treatment and benefit decisions are often intermixed. The situation is inherent in managed care where treatment and benefit decisions are often overseen by plan administrators or reviewers who may not be doctors. Despite this major ruling by the Supreme Court, the issue is one that still rages between health plans and their participants and is not likely to be settled soon.

In Section 8.0, "Pharmacy Benefit Management: Drug Utilization Review," Pam Foster, the former AVP of Medical Affairs at CareMark, Inc., provides an insightful overview on how pharmacy benefit management (PBM) services are being eyed as a more prominent tool in managed care. For example, the White House Office of Management and Budget (OMB) now estimates that the actual cost of the Medicare prescription drug program will be between $530 and $540 billion dollars over the next 10 years. Because of such a staggering figure it is more than likely that the government will be looking to PBMs to help manage the new benefit scheduled to begin for seniors in 2006.

Since the last edition of *The Utilization Management Guide*, the UM system has been dramatically impacted by new requirements at the state level that require independent review of UM denials. In Section 9.0, Susan Prest M.A., L.P. provides an informative overview on the new external review practices carried out by independent review organizations (IRO's), and the relationship of IRO's to the UM process. Ms. Prest is a leading expert on the subject. She is also president of Prest & Associates, Inc., a URAC accredited independent review organization specializing in the independent review of psychiatric, addictions medicine, and behavioral healthcare cases. Additionally, Ms. Prest is the current president of the National Association of Independent Review Organizations (NAIRO).

Turning to operational issues in Section 10.0, Lori Harris-Stevens, RN, MHA, URAC's Vice President of Accreditation, and Valerie Nosek, RN, BSN, one of URAC's most senior and experienced accreditation reviewers, discuss the fundamentals of a successful UM program. In "URAC Health Utilization Management Standards: Pathways to Building a UM Program," Ms. Harris-Stevens and Ms. Nosek provide practical advice on how URAC's standards relate to establishing and operating a utilization management program.

In Section 11.0, "Promoting Patient Safety through Medical Management," Liza Greenberg, RN, MPH, and Health Project and Management Consultant for URAC, turns our discussion to recent findings of a RWJ-funded survey that examines how medical management programs can contribute to making the health care system safer for patients. The study concludes that UM systems can assume an important role in protecting patients from medical errors and adverse outcomes. Ms. Greenberg notes that automated UM systems have the capability of flagging unexpected events that may be indicators of a quality problem, including unexpected readmissions or other medical complications.

Last and certainly not least we have included a lengthy Appendices Section that most readers should find very useful. Appendix A "Methods," explains how the URAC's state-by-state surveys of both health UM and worker's compensation were conducted in Appendices B and C[1]. Within Appendices D and E, you will find the current versions of URAC's Health Utilization Management Standards and Workers Compensation Utilization Management Standards. In Appendix F, you will find a list of "State Regulatory Contacts;" and in Appendix G, URAC has included a chart summarizing those states that recognize URAC as part of the regulatory process. Finally, Appendix G provides instructions on how to access a current list of utilization management organizations accredited by URAC.

In closing, we once again thank all those who have contributed to this book, and extend URAC's very best wishes to all our readers as they begin their journey into the area of utilization management.

---

1   As any such survey is as authoritative as the law remains current, we feel we must caution all readers that each state's legislature's web site should always be checked for any changes in the law, and the information obtained in these surveys is for reference use only and does not constitute the rendering of legal, financial, or other professional advice on the part of URAC.

2.0: Recent Trends in Utilization Management[1]

Garry Carneal, JD, MA

2.1 Introduction

Historically, no function has assumed a more central and dynamic role in the evolution of managed care than utilization review (UR) and utilization management (UM).[2] Over the years, utilization management has become the single most important activity in supporting virtually all forms of managed care. This includes health maintenance organizations (HMO's), preferred provider organizations (PPO's), managed indemnity programs, third party administrator (TPA) offerings, workers' compensation programs, and various medical management organizations.

Utilization management tools and techniques have continually evolved in response to the changing demands and circumstances in health care. This section highlights many of the recent trends impacting UM programs, including how medical, technological, and social scientific advancements are accelerating change in UM and medical management systems across the country.

2.2 The Value Equation

For over 30 years, UM processes have assisted heath plans, providers, and others to help determine what care is medically necessary and appropriate. Some of these UM accomplishments have included the improvement of medial practice patterns, the reduction of unnecessary medical expenses, and the elimination of long term hospital stays, to name just a few benefits.

Yet, some of the value originally tied to UM has diminished over the years. For example, studies looking at the impact of prospective and concurrent UM have shown a net savings in total per capital medical expenditures of about 5 percent.[3] Others studies have demonstrated a low denial rate for UM interventions.[4] The lower potential "return on investment" (ROI) in UM systems is explained in part because most of the costs have been squeezed out of the system, and best practice treatment patterns have been identified and implemented for most routine care.

In order to increase the value of UM, medical directors along with other staff running such programs are pulling back from applying rigid precertification and concurrent requirements in order to create more fluid care coordination model. The ability of health care organizations to use a more flexible approach to medical management has occurred as a result of more data becoming available and the implementation of sophisticated health IT systems to analyze health care and utilization trends. These advancements have led to the expansion of more intensive care management services which often concentrate on high dollar medical cases.

The scaling back of authorization requirements is occurring in many health care settings including large group offerings. UM oversight for outpatient care has dissipated dramatically in recent years, and UM oversight for inpatient care has been scaled back as well. This has been accomplished in part by shifting the responsibility of UM decisions to the treating providers who are often profiled on the back end to assess their treatment patterns. However, these trends are less apparent in some coverage options such as small group arrangements where traditional UR processes are often still the norm. And in most settings, drug UR programs still require specific clinical criteria to be met and adherence to a designated formulary before a prescription order is authorized.

The need to limit UM interventions for routine care may be partially driven by a lower ROI in today's market due to higher salary costs stemming from the short supply of licensed and experienced nurses. As a result, UM nurses are typically now detailed to higher cost procedures. For example, in some hospital settings "onsite" concurrent UR reviews have come back in vogue to help improve care coordination and monitor providers and hospital staff that have become more savvy over the years in soliciting UM approvals (especially on the West Coast). In addition, utilization review is often used along with claims data analysis to help identify patients who need more intense case management (CM) and disease management (DM) services.

A few years ago, many industry experts were predicting that UM services would fade away as the medical management system evolved toward case management and disease management interventions. This did not turn out to be true. Notwithstanding the comments above, most medical management systems still utilize some form of UM to help control how health care is delivered. While the focus of UM may be changing, it still serves an important function within the health care system. A good example of UM's continued survival is the fact that URAC continues to see at least a dozen new UM accreditation applications annually.[5]

2.3 Integration or Segmentation

The core UM functions that survive today often become the foundation for enhanced medical management interventions which include CM and DM services. At first, most health care organizations kept these functions separate. Then over time, many medical management programs began to integrate UM, CM, and DM services both at the functional and personnel levels. Yet, understanding the best way to coordinate care through these various medical management techniques is easier said than done. In fact, health care organizations currently are experimenting with different ways to integrate UM, CM, and DM services –- some with better results than others.

Due to medical management integration, the role of UR nurses have expanded in various health plans and managed care settings. Today UR nurses sometimes serve as health care facilitators and consultants, as well as coordinating UM reviews. UM by design is more focused on a particular intervention or procedure to assess the medical appropriateness of care and the cost. Whereas CM interventions focus on the chronic conditions for a particular patient over a continuum of time with an emphasis on coordinating care. In addition, nurses may be called on to not only serve as case managers, but also be either asked or required to negotiate reimbursement rates or benefit coverage levels.

These new responsibilities generate a number of new business and ethical challenges for clinical staff. Potential conflict of interests must be addressed proactively, and other precautions must be taken to ensure the ongoing integrity of the medical management system. Challenges include the following scenarios:

➢ The requirement that a UR-trained nurse carry out complex case management responsibilities;

➢ The need for a case manager nurse to make medical necessity determinations without access to traditional programs supporting UM rights and appeals; and

➢ The difficulty for any single health professional to make both the benefits and clinical determination.[6]

Clearly, it is often hard and sometimes inappropriate to wear more than one hat at once without clearly delineated responsibilities and access to appropriate resources. Training, inter-departmental cooperation and conflict of interest protocols become important stepping stones to ensure the success of an integrated medical management system.

Interestingly, the integration of various medical management service functions was a major trend identified in the last edition of *The Utilization Management Guide*. Since then, however, URAC's accreditation reviewers report that in some settings, medical management programs are intentionally keeping UM services separated from CM and DM interventions.

In addition to addressing the concerns of clinicians wearing too many hats, the UM siloed approach continues due to several factors including:

➢ Continued payor/purchaser demand to apply traditional UM interventions especially precertifications to reduce health care costs. (The demand goes even higher if health care inflation is on the rise or if the economy is struggling);

➢ The ability of UM services to verify coding, length of stay (LOS) patterns, and other data elements required for quality improvement initiatives;

➢ The ability for UM services to be used as a tool to pre-screen patients for certain CM and DM interventions;

➢ The failure of the hybrid or care coordination approach to clearly document ROI or patients outcomes;

➢ The operational confusion that is sometimes generated when UM, CM and/or DM services overlap, in contrast to a stand-alone UM program or a siloed approach;

➢ Increased public and provider trust due to the implementation of regulatory external review requirements (as highlighted in Section 9).

As a result, UM programs are now both segmented and integrated into different medical management solutions. UM services will continue to be offered through a full array of platforms, ranging from traditional, standalone UM services to the hybrid approach (utilizing various medical management techniques including UM, CM and DM). In fact, one of the factors that will ensure the continued growth and success of UM is the ability of health maintenance organizations (HMO's), preferred provider organizations (PPO's), utilization management organizations (UMO's), third party administrators (TPA's), insurance carriers and other organizations to customize their UM products and services as they are doing now.

2.4 Health Information Technology

Health information technology (IT) applications are having a profound impact on medical management programs, which for the most part is positive. Prior to the mid-1990's, most UM personnel relied on paper-based manuals. Health IT resources during this period were very basic. By the year 2000, most UM clinical processes and support guidelines were automated through various computer-based applications. In addition, the Internet can now link the primary stakeholders in the UM process (including patients, physicians, other providers, facilities, and reviewers) through the electronic transfer of data and related

Defining the Elements of Care Management

To fully understand the UM process in today's rapidly changing medical management model, we need to understand the basic terms of care management in various health care settings, especially how managed care is carried out. Here are some definitions of the basic components:

A.   Utilization Management/Utilization Review

URAC defines "Utilization Management" as the "(e)valuation of the medical necessity, appropriateness, and efficiency of the use of health care services, procedures, and facilitates under the auspices of the applicable health benefit plan; sometime called 'utilization review.'"[7]

There are 3 basic time intervals when UM can occur:

➢ Prospective review. UM conducted prior to a patient's admission, stay, or other service or course of treatment, sometimes called "precertification review."

➢ Concurrent review. UM conducted during a patient's hospital stay or course of treatment, sometimes called "continued stay review."

➢ Retrospective review. Review conducted after the services have been provided to the patient.[8]

Most state laws define "utilization review" to include prospective, concurrent, and retrospective reviews. However, some states define UR to include only retrospective review (see Sections 3.0 and 4.0 for a detailed overview of state health and workers' compensation UM laws) and others include prospective and concurrent review, but not retrospective review.

B.   Case Management

URAC defines "Case Management" as "(a) collaborative process that assesses, plans, implements, coordinates, monitors, and evaluates options and services to meet a client's health needs through communication and available resources to promote quality, cost-effective outcomes."[9]

C.   Independent (External) Review

URAC defines "Independent Review" as a "process, independent of all affected parties, to determine if a healthcare service is medically necessary and medically appropriate or experimental/investigational. *Independent review* typically (but not always) occurs after all appeals mechanisms available within the *health benefits plan* have been exhausted. *Independent review* can be voluntary or mandated by law."[10]

D.   Demand Management

URAC defines "Demand Management" as "The use of self-management and decision support systems to education and enable people to improve their health and make appropriate use of medical care."[11]

E.   Disease Management

Within URAC's Disease Management Accreditation Standards v 1.0, URAC defines "disease management" as:

"(A) system of coordinated health care interventions and communications for populations with conditions in which patient self-care efforts are significant. Disease management: supports the physician or practitioner/patient relationship and plan of care, emphasizes prevention of exacerbations and complications utilizing *evidence*-based practice guidelines and patient empowerment strategies, and evaluates clinical, humanistic, and economic outcomes on an on-going basis with the goal of improving overall health. Disease management components include: population identification processes; evidence-based practice guidelines; collaborative practice models to include physician and support-service providers; patient self-management education (may include primary prevention, behavior modification programs, and compliance/surveillance); process and outcomes measurement, evaluation, and management; routine reporting/feedback loop (may include communication with patient, physician, health plan and ancillary providers, and practice profiling."[12]

UM information. In recent years, the UM process has been enhanced further through the development of information support and data base services.

Health IT systems have made the UM process faster, more consistent, and increased the level of integration within the medical management process. Health IT benefits include:

➢ Electronic monitoring of the UM process, including screening devices and reminder alarms for sentinel events.

➢ Windows-based software programs that now allow for multiple screen applications, creating a seamless environment. With just a mouse click or two, UM personnel can verify enrollment status and benefit coverage when available, track the medical necessity determination process, monitor a patient's electronic health record, and review clinical guidelines/pathways.

➢ Enhanced communication links through eHealth transactions. These improvements allow for a more robust exchange of clinical information or criteria, real time updates for providers who can track the status of their requests via the Internet or wireless applications, the elimination of routine phone calls (and the "phone tag" experience) and facsimile exchanges, and better inter-departmental coordination within a health care organization.[13]

➤ The integration of medical management data into electronic health records (EHR) and data warehousing tools that includes health care organizations formalizing their computer system disaster recovery plans, including off-site backup storage capabilities.

➤ Computerized support systems which promote and integrate new administrative efficiencies into the UM process. Today some UM programs through their Health IT systems allow selected providers to skip the preauthorization requirements based upon the providers historic medical practice patterns that promote quality outcomes. In some respects, this is a reward for the provider by reducing the hassle factor. Yet, the same systems will still monitor claims on the back end to identify any changes in the provider's practice patterns.

While all the above is true, some hurdles must be overcome to fully optimize Health IT applications supporting UM systems. These challenges include the need to:

➤ Improve interoperability due to the fragmented health care system with the goal of increasing IT system functionality both within and between companies/individuals;

➤ Clearly establish the ROI on technology investments;

➤ Ensure privacy and security of protected health information (e.g., HIPAA);

➤ Identify best Health IT practices and then share those practices with others;

➤ Balance IT versus human-based UM interventions. UM scripted screening can be used without clinical oversight as long as the criteria are well established for routine care decisions (but not for denials or in situations where clinical judgment may be required);

➤ Draft new policies and procedures that address the expanding intersection of clinical and IT operations;

➤ Digest and integrate literally thousands of journal articles and other medical published content that is published annually.

2.5 The Patient Safety Factor[14]

Since the release five years ago of the Institute of Medicine's (IOM) report, *To Err is Human*, the issue of patient safety has become a major public policy issue.[15] Moreover, a recent study by URAC has concluded that UM systems can assume an important role in protecting patients from medical errors and adverse outcomes (see Section 11.0 for additional details).[16] Automated UM systems have the capability of flagging unexpected events that may be indicators of a quality problem, including unexpected readmissions or other medical complications. Findings by URAC generally show that medical management organizations possess untapped resources that may be mobilized to promote patient safety. Such capabilities include:

➤ Overseeing clinical patient encounters;

➤ Promoting more direct patient contacts through CM and DM interventions;

➤ Detailing discharge responsibilities and follow-up;

➤ Improving data resources and infrastructure;

➤ Expanding use of clinical staff;

➤ Implementing guidelines and algorithms that can be used to identify unanticipated events; and

➤ Expanding use of electronic health record systems.

As a result, in a UM setting these capabilities could be applied to help improve patient safety by:

➤ Identifying specific safety indicators relevant to medical management processes;

➤ Staff training;

➤ Promoting regular and systematic use of flags, triggers and protocols;

➤ Tracking and trending safety indicators through the provider or facility; and

➤ Reporting and collaborating with purchasers, providers and other stakeholder regarding the selected safety indicators.[17]

2.6 The Role of Clinical Guidelines

Clinical guidelines are based upon evidence-based research to promote and support medical management systems, among other applications. Documented clinical protocols are often established through the grading of available evidence. The protocols are then folded into some sort of compendium or tool that documents and describes how to promote efficient care through an optimal level of resources. The ultimate goal is to standardize the delivery of care.

In the early years of managed care, "cookbook" medicine was a pejorative label sometimes attached to manage care. This was due in part to the rigid coverage and payment requirements based upon clinical guidelines such as specific length of stay (LOS) protocols. It has not been the case in recent years where clinical guideline usage has become more widely accepted as a result of improvements in the way the guidelines are developed, tested, implemented, and updated (e.g., reliance on the evidence-based medicine movement). However, the interface between UM processes and the clinical guidelines supporting the actual medical necessity determinations is still not well understood in some circles.[18] As a result, some have argued that further study is warranted on how clinical criteria can support UM programs, especially the scientific basis for some criteria and the effect on outcomes. Generally speaking, UR criteria have become more focused on specialized procedures (e.g., gastric bypass surgery) and non-routine procedures (e.g., transplants).

2.6.1 Standardization vs. Customization

Many health organizations with UM programs are moving away from using in-house, proprietary clinical criteria and instead using commercially available guidelines such as the clinical protocols published by Milliman, InterQual, and Reeds. The consolidation around commercial criteria is being spurred in part by the desire to mitigate potential legal concerns and malpractice exposure when medical management systems rely solely on in-house criteria. On the positive side, this trend promotes increased standardization and is being used by many organizations across the country as an effective risk management strategy. On the downside, UM personnel may have less flexibility to customize clinical treatment decisions based upon a particular set of facts. Moreover, some states require participation by network physicians or medical directors in developing, approving or validating clinical criteria. To fill in any potential or existing gaps, some UM organizations are drafting new medical policies and procedures (P&P's) as an adjunct to the commercial criteria to further detail what care is medically necessary and appropriate, and what level or type of care will be paid for. UM personnel will frequently supplement "off the shelf" criteria by using committees to draft protocols for procedures not included in national guidelines and to periodically update both commercial and in-house criteria in a timely manner when new advances are made in technology or medical practice.

2.6.2 Pre-Review Screening

With more regularity medical management programs are implementing pre-review scripted clinical screening tools to help guide coverage decisions based upon established algorithms for routine care. Under these programs intake staff who are not clinically trained are permitted to authorize some routine medical services such as length of stay for a normal childbirth delivery through scripted screening. However, clinically-licensed staff must still authorize non-routine services based upon clinical criteria. All services that do not meet routine clinical criteria should be referred to physician advisors or other appropriate peer reviewers before any denial of care is made.

The URAC Health UM Accreditation Standards, v. 4.2 address the issue of scripted screening through the following definition and standards:

Pre-Review Screening: Automated or semi-automated screening of requests for authorization that may include: (1) collection of *structured clinical data* (including diagnosis, diagnosis codes, procedures, procedure codes); (2) asking scripted clinical questions; (3) accepting responses to scripted clinical questions; and (4) taking specific action (*certification* and assignment of length of stay explicitly linked to each of the possible responses). It excludes: (1) applying clinical judgment or interpretation; (2) accepting unstructured clinical information; (3) deviating from script; (4) engaging in unscripted clinical dialogue; (5) asking clinical follow-up questions; and (6) issuing non-*certifications*.

Standard UM 13: For *pre-review* screening, the *organization limits* use of *non-clinical administrative staff* to:

a) Performance of *"review of service requests"* for completeness of information;

b) Collection and transfer of non-clinical data;

c) Acquisition of *structured clinical data*; and

d) Activities that do not require evaluation or interpretation of clinical information.

Standard UM 14: All scripts or algorithms used for *pre-review screening* are:

a) Approved by the *medical director* or *clinical director* (or designate); and

b) Reviewed (and updated if necessary) no less than annually.

Standard UM 15: Licensed health professionals monitor non-clinical administrative staff performing pre-review screening.

Standard UM 16: The organization does not issue non-certifications based on pre-review screening.

2.7 Evidence-Based Medicine

UM programs are becoming more dynamic and objective due to the rise of the evidence-based medicine movement. Evidence-based medicine is often defined as the "conscientious, explicit and judicious use of current best evidence in making decisions about the care of individual patients."[19] As one expert notes, to "satisfy employer demands for appropriate care and lower costs, health plans are transitioning from managed utilization to evidence-based care management."[20] He also observes:

> Coverage and denial management is a pivotal area for application of evidence-based guidelines and presents an opportunity to clearly demonstrate that a plan's rulings are evidence-based. Coverage is allowed when evidence is strong that a given treatment is effective for a given condition but disallowed in favor of more cost-effective options when evidence is not strong.[21]

Of course, medical management decision-making becomes much more difficult when there is no evidence or limited data to make an assessment or evaluation of care.

2.8 Predictive Modeling

Predictive modeling is now being used in conjunction with medical management services to identify and stratify high cost patient cases. The predictive modeling process applies rule-based clinical logic to help grapple with mountains of health care data and make decisions about what to do to lower costs and promote the best outcomes. As a result, most predictive modeling applications are implemented through integrated medical management systems where a wide array of data and departmental resources can be used to support the system.

Traditional CM and DM programs typically focus on patients who previously have been diagnosed with specific high-cost conditions in an attempt to control utilization and improve care for specific disease states. In contrast, predictive modeling casts a wider net as it focuses on population-based health issues by identifying statistical relationships between "current" and "future" demographic data, medical use patterns, and various outcomes. The result is predictive information that can be used to identify specific patients who are at risk to incur high medical costs in the future.

Health plans can use predictive information to develop outreach programs for patients identified using UM data for the purpose of offering preventative services and disease management. Predictive modeling tools can be used to:

➤ Promote sound risk management strategies;

➤ Compare physician practice patterns;

➤ Calculate ROI on specific interventions;

➤ Determine product pricing;

➤ Help deliver information to patients; and

➤ Improve the quality of care.[22]

While UM data can play a supporting role in predictive modeling programs, by definition it can never become the sole determining factor. Claims data and other basic forms of utilization information can generate some of the data points needed for a dynamic, predictive health care analysis, but usually not all of it. Furthermore, the comparison of demographic data with treatment patterns is not the same as the science of generating a prediction through a statistical and rule-based analysis.

2.9 Outcomes

In recent years, more pressure has been applied by health care purchasers (e.g., employers) to demonstrate positive business and health outcomes when investments are made in medical management services. In a recent white paper, a panel of disease management experts made the following observation:

> Rigorous evaluations, which may have once been undertaken for pure academic research, are now beginning to be adapted by those studying DM outcomes. This new rigor is considered more essential for business, due to the keen interest of public and private sector purchasers in the evaluation of program effectiveness and to determine if the intervention is truly able to bring about positive, desirable outcomes in a specified population.[23]

The need to document outcomes for medical management interventions is paramount in today's marketplace. Of course, expectations may vary depending on whether the health plan is just employing traditional UR services or using a combination of UM, CM and DM services. Regarding UR or UM interventions, baseline outcomes expectations would include things such as reduced lengths of stays, lower admission or re-admission rates, timely and appropriate specialty referrals, reduced costs for a particular procedure, and so on. With an advanced care coordination approach, outcome assessments would not only focus those indicators but also attempt to document the actual improved health of patients and the over-all reduction of health care costs. No matter what the medical management intervention being measured, methodological challenges will need to be grappled with to clearly establish the ROI. This includes the need to:

Table 1: Medical Management State and Federal Regulatory Provisions

Function[25]	State Law	State Regulations	Federal Law	Federal Regulations
Case Management	1,869	5,253	120	95
Disease Management	88	119	6	1
Utilization Management	1,771	2,863	25	113
Grand Total				12,203

> Clearly identify the cause and effect relationship between the intervention and the outcome (e.g., the need to actually touch the patient). Understanding and controlling for confounding variables is critical to establish statistically significant results.

> When appropriate, establish a control group for comparison purposes, or analyze the same group over a period of time (i.e. both before and after a specified intervention). Among other benefits, this helps account for the natural regression to the mean which typically occurs over time for most population-based groups.

> Clearly differentiate between "process" and "actual" health outcomes (e.g., an improved immunization rate for a defined population is a process outcome; a drop in the incidence of Lyme disease for the same population represents an improved health outcome).

2.10 Regulatory Changes

As highlighted in Table 1, over 12,000 regulatory provisions have been adopted impacting UM, CM and DM services. UM has over 4,700 statutory and regulatory provisions when compared to 7,300 for CM and 214 for DM.[26] Although CM services have the highest number of regulatory provisions that apply, UM functions have the most comprehensive and intense oversight because states have adopted more licensure and certification requirements for utilization management organizations (UMOs).[27] Detailed summaries of current UM regulation can be found in Sections 3 and 4 (see also Appendices B & C). In addition, medical management functions are more regulated at the state level than at the federal level.28

2.10.1 DOL Regulations

The regulatory environment for UM changed significantly with the implementation of the U.S. Department of Labor's (DOL) claims procedure regulation beginning in 2002.[29] These regulations, issued under authority created by Employee Retirement Income Security Act of 1974 (ERISA), are the federal government's first major entry into the oversight of medical management processes (outside of Medicare and Medicaid). Self-insured plans -- which previously had been exempt from most state oversight requirements -- now have to comply with the federal UM requirements. In addition, insured plans must now reconcile federal and state regulations in each state where they operate. Understanding and implementing the DOL regulation is an essential component of any effective UM compliance program.

Similar in many ways to state laws, the DOL requirements address the following aspects of the utilization management process:

> Time frames for prospective, concurrent, and retrospective claims review determinations, as well as for appeals processes;

> Processes to follow when the health plan needs additional information to conduct a review;

> The contents of adverse determination notices (both initially and on appeal);

> The qualifications of reviewers that conduct appeal considerations. (However, the DOL regulations are silent on the qualifications of reviewers issuing initial adverse determinations.)

While the DOL regulations cover many of the same issues as state UM laws, the perspective and approach is somewhat different. For example, while some states have tried to protect consumers by allowing more levels of appeal (i.e., internally and/or externally), federal regulations assert that a health plan may not require more than 2 levels of appeal of an adverse determination before a claimant brings an action for civil enforcement.[30]

The DOL is very specific in some areas where state laws tend to be general, and vice versa. These differing approaches can often create inconsistencies between the federal and state requirements. In most case, any inconsistencies are resolved in favor of the federal regulation (i.e., the DOL regulations contain a clause preempting any state law that prevents application of the federal requirement). However, state laws that do not conflict with the DOL rule still apply. In some cases, this issue of preemption cannot be clearly resolved between state and federal requirements. For example, state laws that require a third level of appeal, internally or externally, may be preempted by the DOL rule.

2.10.2 Independent (External) Review

Perhaps one of the most dramatic changes in the UM field during the past several years is the adoption of independent (or external) review requirements in the majority of states (see Section 9 for details). Fueled in part by the backlash against managed care, external review requirements have altered the UM process by adding an additional layer of review by independent third parties.

Presently, many states adopted external appeal requirements to serve as a safety net for medical necessity and benefit determinations. In the past, existing internal and expedited appeal rights within most UM programs were considered too insular by many and ineffective by some. As a result, policymakers agreed that an outside independent opinion was needed to serve as a peer review mechanism in order to protect against any wrongful denials of care. Despite this agreement, it should be noted that there are significant variations between the external review regulatory requirements between each state.[31]

2.10.3 HIPAA Privacy and Security

With the move towards more electronic health transactions, concerns over the privacy and security of health care information have expanded in recent years. Although UM interventions are typically carried outside of the point of care for the patient, the need to maintain the privacy and security of health UM systems has been heightened by the adoption of the Health Insurance Portability & Accountability Act of 1996 (HIPAA).

Companies that engage in UM, CM, and DM services are likely to be either covered entities (i.e., health care providers, health plans, and clearing houses) or business associates under HIPAA. In both cases medical management companies must take certain precautions to protect personal health information (PHI). Health care providers and health plans must give the patient a copy of its written notice of privacy practices. This notice serves to explain how a patient's PHI will be used to help carry out the treatment, payment or health care operations. The federal regulation explicitly references UR as a *payment* function and implies that UM is also a *health care operation*, which makes them activities covered under HIPAA.[32]

UM personnel must be more vigilant about protecting PHI used for UM decision-making not only because of HIPAA regulations, but also due to state privacy laws, corporate professional liability underwriting requirements, accreditation standards, purchasing requirements (e.g., requests for proposals – RFP's), and new case law rulings.[33]

2.10.4 Same-State Licensure

15 states have either adopted laws or issued regulations limiting the ability of out-of-state UM staff to participate in the UM process.[34] While some states require the medical director to be licensed in the state where the patient resides, others require nurse reviewers or

physicians who make or validate an adverse determination, to be licensed in the applicable state. A byproduct of these requirements is the restriction of the ability of UM programs to administer and manage care on an interstate basis.[35]

2.11 Other Contributions

In reviewing the evolution of UM systems in general, several other trends can be noted. Table 2 highlights the evolution of the health utilization review process over the past 2 decades. As the table indicates, UM systems now have the ability to:

➢ **Become more consistent.** UM systems can promote greater inter-rater reliability from one case to the next in part due the support of Health IT systems that can analyze and profile treatment patterns.

➢ **Promote efficiency.** Many UM systems are now authorizing admissions or treatments within an hour or two of the provider's request for care. UM systems are moving to more real time applications. Also, staffing allocations are becoming more efficient and in some cases UM reviewers are providing basic case management services (sometimes referred to as "mini-case management").

➢ **Customize operations.** UM systems can now be adapted and more focused on particular needs of purchasers, payors, providers, patients, and other stakeholders.

➢ **Promote consumer involvement.** Consumers are becoming more involved in the management of their health conditions. This is due in part to the rise of CM and DM programs that actively promote patient education and involvement with their care. In addition, the Internet is driving this trend by allowing patients to have access to more medical information and treatment protocols. This movement is being driven by new benefit packages that are designed around "consumer-directed health care" choices such as health savings accounts.

➢ **Integrate health call center services.** Health call center operations appear to be on the rise around the country. Among their other duties, they often serve as the front door to a company's medical management system.

➢ **Promote quality.** Through URAC accreditation, regulation, contracting requirements and other sources, quality oversight mechanisms are becoming more integrated into and supportive of UM services. The investment in quality not only improves patient outcomes but makes medical necessity determinations more efficient. UM personnel can now assess utilization patterns and systematically analyze customer service issues such as caller wait times. As a result, UM programs can modify or reallocate resources to improve medical management procedures.

2.12 The Conceptual Challenges

UM services often deal with the challenges associated with determining what is or is not medically necessary in a particular case and overseeing how that care is rendered with limited resources. As a result, URAC accreditation standards, regulatory requirements, and purchasing guidelines help UMO's follow established guidelines and enforce certain procedures to ensure the integrity of the UM process. However, as highlighted throughout this book, UM interventions are complex and always undergoing a constant state of change. Therefore, it is helpful to raise a series of questions periodically about the efficacy and true benefits of UM interventions. These questions include the following:

➤ **What is the ROI on UM interventions?** As has been previously mentioned, some studies have documented a very low denial rate for UM interventions. Therefore, what are the quantifiable benefits of using traditional UM interventions as review criteria becomes more focused and specialized, and as advanced care coordination techniques continue to expand? In fact, the ROI on UM interventions can be established in most cases, but the actual benefits will vary from one setting to the next.

➤ **Is a decision to deny care a medical necessity or benefits determination?** The basis for a denial of care may not always be clear. The rationale or justification for some denials or non-certification decisions can be ambiguous. In any particular circumstance, a bright line may not exist to justify the decision based upon a clinical versus administrative determination – both of which supports different processes and of appeal rights. Clinical denials should normally be coordinated through the UM program.

➤ **When is a delay in the UM process effectively a denial?** At what point in time does a non-determination become a constructive denial? When is a request for additional information, a demand for a second opinion, or a recommendation of an alternative course of treatment effectively a denial as well? The UM process should not result in default determinations based upon the failure to complete the relevant analysis. Ideally, UM decisions should be made by the application of evidence in a particular case to the relevant clinical criteria. Often medical exigencies make the timing of a determination extremely important. To that end, virtually all UM laws require an expedited process for making determinations in cases of a medical emergency.

➤ **How should clinical guidelines be used within the UM process?** The merging between the UM process and clinical guidelines or pathways is an interesting one. How much latitude should UM programs be afforded in developing their own customized clinical protocols? Should there be more scientific testing and open discussion providing input on how commercially available criteria is developed? What is the best process to integrate in-house and commercially available criteria?

➤ **Is the patient or provider aware of their appeal rights?** Although URAC standards, state laws, and DOL regulations afford patients and providers certain appeal rights when a denial is made, it is not always apparent to the parties what their rights appeal or grievance rights are. In some instances, the complexity of the health care system itself creates a chilling effect thereby preventing the patient from getting a meaningful reconsideration.

➤ **Is UM decision-making reliable?** A few studies have demonstrated some variability in how UM decisions are processed and made within the same company.[36] The need for reliability is akin to the goal of accountability.

How can standardized UM reporting and analysis be promoted? Many purchasers, payors, regulators and consumers would like to have information on UM approval and denial rates, as well as on UM process and clinical outcome indicators. However, the reporting and analysis of UM programs is complicated by the diverse procedures that may be reviewed (e.g., some companies only review inpatient care, while others may review outpatient services or high cost procedures). Variations in the UM process itself also can complicate the goal of establishing standard reporting criteria (e.g., some plan sponsors require the UMO to apply UR criteria very strictly, while others might prefer to approve most procedures as a strategy to promote patient/employee satisfaction).

Timeframe	UM Activity	Mode of Communication	Explanatory Notes
1970's	➤ Emphasis on retrospective review.	➤ Claims.	➤ UR emerged from examining/evaluating utilization costs after medical services had been rendered.
Early 1980's	➤ Majority of UR decisions still retrospective, but some programs begin to rely on prospective (i.e., precertification) and concurrent reviews.	➤ Claims. ➤ Phone.	➤ With the introduction of phone-based communications, some UR decisions were now being made prior to or concurrent with medical treatment.
Mid-1980's	➤ General expansion of UR programs.	➤ Claims. ➤ Phone. ➤ Some facsimiles and letters (used typically for notifications).	➤ In part, the emphasis on precertification requirements was spread from HMOs to an industry-wide platform.
Late 1980's	➤ State legislatures begin to pass laws to regulate UR ➤ Industry convenes several meetings through the American Managed Care Review Association (AMCRA) to consider establishing a voluntary accreditation program.	➤ Phone usage expands.	➤ Concerns are expressed about the integrity of some UR programs. As a result, several states pass UR/UM legislation (i.e., Arkansas, Connecticut, Iowa, Louisiana, Maryland, and North Carolina).[48]
Early 1990's	➤ Continued growth of precert and concurrent reviews. ➤ URAC incorporated in 1990, adopts first set of UR Standards in 1991 (version 1.0). ➤ Additional states pass UR laws. ➤ Introduction of case management (CM) by managed care, especially for catastrophic, high cost cases.	➤ Continued use of claims, phone, facsimiles, and letters. ➤ Health call centers or demand management services employed as well.	➤ Although case management (CM) has been used in other fields such as workers' compensation and behavioral health for some time, the introduction of CM into the managed care system did not occur until the early to mid 1990's. Traditionally, managed care organizations maintained two separate departments for UR and CM. ➤ Length-of-stay rates drop due to UR. ➤ URAC requires that non-cert decisions be communicated in a timely fashion via facsimile or letter.
Mid-1990's	➤ UR offerings on more advanced information systems (IS) or information technology (IT) platforms thrive. ➤ Use of CM services expands in many managed care settings. ➤ Some MCO's begin to integrate UR/CM functions. ➤ URAC revises UR standards (version 2.0). ➤ UM/CM integration expands, departments are sometimes consolidated. ➤ NAIC adopts Utilization Review Model Act.	➤ Some companies begin using e-mail as a supplementary mode of communication.	➤ Mid-1990's marks the beginning point of rapid evolution in the UR field. The previous 10 years did not experience drastic change (compared to late 1990's). ➤ Access to data relating to clinical outcomes, patient records, and other information increases dramatically. ➤ URAC's revised UR standards emphasize clinical oversight of UR process. ➤ E-mail transmissions begin to shorten approval times for medical necessity approvals. ➤ "Utilization Management" (UM) becomes preferred term over "Utilization Review" (UR) by many. UM denotes a more comprehensive approach to medical necessity review determinations including quality oversight assurance monitoring.
Late 1990's	➤ URAC revises UM Standards (version 3.0). ➤ Disease management also introduced by some MCO's as a way to improve medical management. ➤ External Review requirements added to the UM process in many states. ➤ URAC adopts CM Standards (version 1.0). ➤ The interaction between UM and CM better understood leading to more focused CM applications. ➤ Increasing interest in identifying better outcomes by managing specific disease states through disease management (DM) programs.	➤ Although phone calling still common, e-mail transmissions expand. ➤ Telephonic dial-in capabilities allow automated precert for some medical treatments. ➤ New Internet communication links under development. ➤ UM program personnel begin communicating with providers and other stakeholders via Internet-based software applications. ➤ Sophisticated phone/IT systems employed to track abandonment rate and wait times.	➤ The efficiency of the medical necessity determination process continues to improve. ➤ URAC's revised UR standards recognize limited use of "scripted clinical reviews" by administrative staff. IT/IS systems provide support. ➤ URAC requires that non-cert decisions be communicated in a timely fashion via facsimile, letter, or electronically (e.g., e-mail). ➤ Many MCO's begin to offer web-enabled communication links that have potential for real time approval and denials. ➤ Population-based disease management expands. ➤ Medical management approach customizes services for each client.
2000 – 2004	➤ In the spring of 2000, URAC adopts External Review Organization Standards (v 1.0) (Name changed later to "Independent Review". ➤ Scripted screening rises to help automate UM systems. ➤ Precertification and concurrent reviews drop off significantly for routine procedures. ➤ UM is customized into various medical management applications which include both integrated care coordination models and traditional siloed UR applications – but UM interventions typically focus on high cost cases. ➤ URAC amends Health UM Standards to integrate DOL Claims requirements.	➤ Most communication links described above still are in use ➤ Web-enabled communications links gain momentum supporting UM systems.	➤ Medical management model more appropriately utilizes the various UM/CM/DM services available, and is able to customize application to individual patient. ➤ Consumer empowerment movement begins ➤ Greater reliance on evidence-based medicine, predictive modeling and outcomes reporting. ➤ Offshore operations for certain managed care functions are launched (e.g., staffing for health call centers, claims processing).
2005 – 2010	➤ The care coordination approach becomes more dominant with UM, CM and DM each having defined (and sometimes over-lapping) roles. ➤ UM interventions include patient safety indicators. ➤ UM services regularly generate performance and quality outcomes data (where appropriate). ➤ URAC develops care coordination accreditation standards and standards impacting Health IT operations.	➤ Wireless technologies will eventually overtake hard-wired applications. ➤ Some traditional modes of communication such as fax transmissions begin to drop off significantly.	➤ The goal of inter-operability between medical management systems continues to be a challenge. ➤ Marriage of UM data with electronic health record (EHR) application will eventually create a seamless data stream for health care organizations, providers and patients. ➤ Efforts continue to link the UM process with objective evidence-based treatment protocols. ➤ The ROI of UM interventions will continue to be an issue, but UM programs will gain additional support in the future through the introduction of new business and clinical outcome indicators.

Table 2: Evolution of Health Utilization Review Process[39]

> **What is the effect of UM on practice patterns overall?** Some observers of the UM field speculate that the presence of UM programs has changed provider behavior through direct and indirect means. This suggests that UM has an influence well beyond that which can be calculated through rates of approvals and denials.

> **Does the hybrid "care coordination" approach provide opportunities to game the system?** With the influx of CM and DM interventions, care treatment plans can be manipulated in such a way that the UM appeal rights afforded by regulatory requirements or URAC standards can be avoided. Among other approaches, this can be done by folding or converting the traditional UM process into the new care coordination paradigm, which is more fluid and manages care over a period of time. This makes it more difficult for the patient to determine when a specific denial of care has taken place since care is being "re-routed" through a case manager.

> **Can an over-reliance on technology compromise UM services?** A watchful eye is required as eHealth transactions become more common in UM systems. Pre-review scripted screening applications could over-reach the proper latitude granted to certify routine procedures or be possibly used as a subterfuge to deny care. The role of clinical oversight should not be compromised through technological advancements.

> **Can economic forces compromise the UM process?** Several URAC accredited companies have received a lower accreditation status (e.g., "conditional" accreditation) or have lost their accreditation altogether in recent years because they are forced to underbid their contracts with large employer groups to stay competitive. In such cases, quality can be comprised. Although there is a lot of lip service given to quality by large employers, it is not uncommon to have an RFP really just focus on cost.

> **How can nurse resources best be used in medical management programs?** When UM nurses are carrying out UR reviews but are then asked to case manage or make benefit coverage determinations for the same patient, this can become a potential recipe for disaster by creating confusion and compromising patient care. Certain precautions must be taken to avoid any perceived or real conflicts of interest. Also, what are the proper roles for LPN's within the UM process?

> **Is UM the practice of medicine?** In addition to some state laws, several state medical boards have argued

that making UM medical necessity determinations is the practice of medicine.[49] Where such a position takes hold, UM programs are significantly restricted in the ability to manage care. However, in most states UM is not considered to be the practice of medicine and therefore allowing traditional medical reviews to continue. This debate will likely continue for years to come.

> **How can UM deal with the realities of limited health resources?** Perhaps the greatest UM challenge or conundrum can be best characterized as follows:

> UM can play an important role in rationalizing care and enhancing efficiency, but it cannot, and should not, be asked to do what the public and politicians so far have not been unable to do.[50]

2.13 Conclusion

Traditional UR systems that emphasize fairly rigid certification requirements are becoming outmoded. A common UM model today is to rely on a more fluid approach supported by sophisticated health IT applications. Medical management services can vary from one setting to the next through a combination of integrated and sometimes siloed approaches. Generally speaking, a new medical management model is emerging that emphasizes cost efficiencies, quality monitoring, evidence-based research, predictive modeling, and improved patient health outcomes.

Although some health care experts predicted the demise of traditional UR and UM services, this does not appear to be the case. UM interventions will continue to assume a critical role in most health care coverage decisions, albeit for more non-routine and specialized high cost cases. In addition, UM programs will play a key supportive role in advanced care coordination systems that are driven by CM and DM interventions.

UM and other medical management services will continue to undergo constant change as clinical and information advancements are made. This makes it difficult to predict exactly what UM will look like in the future – in part due the fact that there is so much flexibility and customization that occurs today. Despite this uncertainty the core function of UM systems will continue to play a critical role in health care decision-making by asking what care is medically necessary and appropriate given the facts of the case, the available resources, and the clinical treatment alternatives.

1   Much of the research for this article was completed through a series of face-to-face interviews with URAC's accreditation reviewers, who annually visit hundreds of medical management organizations. Interviews took place in May and June of 2004. Special thanks to the following URAC staff who provided their insights and perspectives on how the medical management system is changing: Claire Barrett, Iskla Brown; Guy D'Andrea, Liza Greenberg, Lori Harris-Stevens; Christine Leyden; Donna Merrick; Val Nosek; Sue Ohr; Susan Stern; Bonnie Sturges, and Annette Watson.

2   The terms "utilization management" (UM) and "utilization review" (UR) are used interchangeably within this chapter. See side bar in this chapter on how various terms associated with UM and UR are defined. Historically the term UR was used first. Then the term UM caught on in the mid-1990's as UR systems became more complex, which included a quality improvement component (e.g., See URAC UM Standards, v. 4.2, Appendix D).

3   Wickizer TM and Lesser D. "Utilization Management: Issues, Effects and Future Prospects," Annu. Rev. Public Health, 2002 23:233-254.

4   Wickizer, Lessler, Boyd-Wickizer, Effects of Health Care Cost-Containment Programs on Patterns of Care and Readmissions Among Children and Adolescents American Journal of Public Health: Sept. 1999, pages 1353-1358.

5   As of September 1, 2004, URAC has accredited 193 health organizations in 320 sites across the nation pursuant to URAC's Health UM Standards, v. 4.2; and 36 workers' compensation organizations in 67 sites pursuant to URAC's WC UM Standards, v. 3.0.

6   The last example depends on the circumstances as non-clinical and nursing personnel do check for benefits/coverage, forwarding the "gray areas" to a medical director who may also have to make a medical necessity decision as part of a benefit determination. The frequency depends in part upon how well the certificate of coverage is written.

7   URAC Health Utilization Management Standards, version 4.2.

8   Id.

9   URAC Case Management Organization Standards, version 1.1.

10   URAC Independent Review Organization Standards, version 2.0.

11   URAC Health Call Center Standards, version 2.0.

12   See also, www.DMAA.org.

13   Recently, Medicine on the Net analyzed and rated 23 different web sites offering clinical guidelines and practice resources: 2003, Vol. 9, no. 9, pages 13-28.

14   Greenberg, L. and Schloss, S. Patient Safety Capabilities of UM Programs: 2003, URAC Report, 52 pages (Funded in part by a grant by the Robert Wood Johnson Foundation).

15   The report, and a follow-up report by the IOM, Crossing the Quality Chasm, highlighted the widespread prevalence of errors in the health care, and declared that systemic, rather than individual flaws were at the root most of these errors. The reports called upon all sectors in the health care system, from health plans, to hospitals, to providers, to accrediting organizations, to examine their role in promoting systematic approaches to improving patient safety.

16   "Promoting Patient Safety Through Medical Management:" 2004 URAC White Paper.

17   In 2004, URAC was assessing whether or not it should develop specific patient safety standards for UM programs. As of the September 2004, no specific decision had been made. Some concerns have been raised about whether UM customers (e.g., health plan sponsors) would support the costs associated with such an upgrade in UM services to cover patient safety issues at this point in time.

18   URAC's UM Standards have relatively little to say on what types of clinical guidelines can best support a UM system, nor do the standards have specific quality benchmarks addressing how clinical criteria should be developed and maintained.

19   Definition used by the Centre for Evidence-Based Medicine, University Health Network, see www.cebm.utronto.ca/glossary/.

20   Keckly, Paul "Evidence-based Medicine in 2006: A Survey of Health plan Leaders Identifies Current and Emerging Strategies," April 2004 – Healthcare Informatics (See www.ebm.vanderbilt.edu).

21   Id.

22   "Looking Beyond DM for Uses of Predictive Modeling" Disease Management News (February 25, 2004, page 5).

23   "Principles for Assessing Disease Management Outcomes," Disease Management Association of America (DMAA) White Paper: April 2004, 25 pages.

24   URAC has developed accreditation programs for all three medical management functions covered in this table.

25   Carneal, G. "Government Oversight of Case Management: 2002 Survey," Chapter 4, Case Management Trends: An Overview of Recent Industry and Regulatory Developments. URAC 2002, 494 pages.

26   State UM regulatory requirements have been actively enforced in recent years. For example, several accreditation reviewers have observed that regulators recently have assumed a more active role (e.g., levying fines) overseeing UM operations in states like California, Maryland, Ohio, Texas and other jurisdictions.

27   This survey did not look at the "purchasing" requirements that federal agencies require when coordinating care for federal employees and military personnel.

28   29 CFR 2650.503-1 (July 9, 2001).

29   29 CFR §2560.503-1(c)(2).

30   Note that the National Association of Insurance Commissioners (NAIC) may be revising its existing model law on external/independent review to promote more standardization in this area. See also, URAC's Independent Review Accreditation Standards, v. 2.0.

31   Utilization review is considered a "payment" activity under HIPAA's privacy protections and maybe considered a "health care operation" pursuant to 65 CFR 164.501 (December 28,2000).

32   See URAC's HIPAA Handbook series for more details on how HIPAA impacts UM operations.

33   See Section 3 and Appendix B for details on the 15 states.

34   See state attorney general opinions: 1993 WL 207359 (Miss. A.G.); 60 N.C. Opinion Attorney General 100; Kan. Opinion Attorney General 90-130 (11/28/90).

35   Wickizer and Lessler, "Utilization Management: Issues, Effects, and Future Prospects," Annu. Rev. Public Health, 2002, 23:233-254.

36   National Association of Insurance Commissioners, Utilization Review Model Act (Appendix 73-13), Model Regulation Service (1999).

37   Murphy v. Arizona Bd. Of Med. Examiners rev. denied, N. CV97-0381-(R (Ariz. Jan. 21, 1998); Texas Medical Board Report, Vol. 18, No. 2 (Spring 1987); Medical Board of California Action Report, p. 5 (April 1996).

38 Wickizer and Lessler, "Utilization Management: Issues, Effects, and Future Prospects," Annu. Rev. Public Health, 2002, 23:233-254.

39 The evolution of UR/UM sometimes varies from one geographic region to another, and from one delivery system to another. The information presented in Table 2, represents an aggregate summary of how the UM industry has evolved based upon a collection of URAC's experiences and opinions from experts in the field.

3.0: An Overview of State Health UM Regulation

Howard A. Burde and Karen L. Cavalli

3.1 Introduction

Section 2 discusses the evolution of Utilization Management (UM). As UM has emerged and developed, it has been identified by lawmakers and regulators as the tool by which health care organizations determine the type and intensity of services for which their subscribers (e.g., the patients) receive coverage. By regulating the utilization management process, states and federal governments are able to limit perceived abusive or overly restrictive practices and create a rubric through which patients obtain their benefits. Today utilization management applies in virtually all health coverage contexts.

In this Section, we review the various state health UM laws and regulations. The review focuses on several key components of these regulations, including: the definition of utilization management; the structure of utilization management regulations; the applicability, scope and content of health utilization management regulation at the state level; jurisdictional considerations; regulatory recognition of URAC accreditation; and, finally, enforcement.

3.2 Definition of Utilization Management

The National Association of Insurance Commissioners model law on Utilization Review and Benefit Determination defines UM as a set of formal techniques designed to monitor the use of, or evaluate the medical necessity, appropriateness, efficacy, or efficiency of, health care services, procedures, or settings. Techniques may include ambulatory review, prospective review, second opinion, certification, concurrent review, case management, discharge planning or retrospective review.[1] Most states adhere to some paraphrase of this definition.

Any entity involved with utilization management must examine all relevant state and federal laws and regulations so a determination can be made whether or not the organization's activities are covered by the regulations. However, though the differences between each state's laws can be profound, the effect of such definitional differences is minimal, except to the extent that certain practices may be excluded from the definition like retrospective review. The exception is for state laws that apply to behavioral health as they focus on treatment plans and treatment objectives.[2] These definitions differ in the focus of the utilization activity and the requirements for the utilization process differ as well. Therefore, entities engaged in utilization management for behavioral health services should review the applicability of state laws unique to those services.

3.3 The Structure and Process of UM Regulation

Examining the "processes" and "systems" associated with UM operations fits well into the common methodology employed to oversee and regulate a wide array of health care services. As Avedis Donabedian described over twenty years ago, any assessment of the quality of health care comes down to measurable aspects of structure, process, and outcomes.[3] Virtually all health care regulations and accreditation standards are built on these concepts.

Structure is the availability of resources, including human, physical, and financial resources, as well as the system design. While structure is critically important to the provision of quality care, structural surveys give very little current information about the quality of health care.

Process is a normative behavior. It is derived from medical science or from societal ethics. It is what the actors in the system do. The advantages of using a process-based method of assessment are that procedures are well-documented, accessible, timely, and permit specific attribution of responsibility for success or failures. One can usually tell whether a process is followed irrespective of any benefits gained.

When the causal connection between certain procedures and outcomes is weak, normative validity, or general acceptance of the use of certain procedures in certain circumstances, may be the best way to evaluate quality of care. Examples of *process measures* include credentialing requirements, utilization review and complaint and grievance systems.

Donabedian describes the term *outcome* as a change in a patient's current and future health status that can be attributed to antecedent health care. Outcomes are, or should be, the best result of appropriate structure and effective processes. In terms of the structure and process of UM, it is not necessarily important that outcomes will be achieved, but rather that health plan subscribers have both an opportunity and forum to seek access to the benefits afforded by their plan.

UM regulation is composed of both structure and process requirements. In the absence of a capacity to assure the outcome of care inherent in health coverage, utilization management is able to provide needed standards for the process by which subscribers can seek health benefits available under their plans and the structure of who makes these decisions.

Before describing the components of UM laws, it is important to understand that the UM process is intended to provide the rules by which health plan benefits are received. If benefits are not available under a benefit plan, they are not available through a UM process (at least ordinarily). However, there are occasions when benefits that are not included in a plan may be obtained but the laws governing UM are not intended to provide the tools for procuring such benefits.

3.4 Components of UM Regulation

3.4.1 Applicability

The first level of analysis of UM regulation is the determination of whether and to what extent the law may apply to the activity of a given organization. State laws differ. In most cases UM regulations apply to utilization review organizations as well as to health plans, insurers, medical management companies, and others that perform UM on their behalf of other organizations. UM criteria may also apply to limited or full benefit plans.

There are cases where a few states regulate UM functions and UM functions for health plan operations separately. Yet, even in these states health plans still remain responsible for the UM processes they provide, whether internally or by subcontract for the purpose of the administration of their benefits. In many states where a health plan is already subject to state licensure as an HMO or other health care organization, a separate licensure for the performance of UM activities for subscribers is not required.[4] Conversely, where a separate UM entity is performing UM activities on behalf of a plan, the subcontracted UM entity is often subject to UM licensure for such activities.

3.4.2 Scope and Content

UM regulations, regardless of the jurisdiction or program type, provide guidelines with respect to the necessary components of utilization management programs. UM regulation typically includes the following components:

a) Medical Necessity Determinations

What conditions, diagnoses or proposed treatments are subject to a medical necessity determination under the benefit plan and in what time frame (e.g. prior to services being provided)? Do certain procedures need to be evaluated prior to their performance (e.g. elective inpatient procedures)? Who has the responsibility under the plan benefits to make the request, that is, is it the responsibility of the provider or the subscriber?

b) Benefit Determinations

What is determined? Health plans govern the definition and application of medical necessity, appropriateness, health care setting, level of care and effectiveness. Moreover, certain types of care may be exempted from certain types of reviews. For example, emergency care or urgent care services are generally exempted from precertification or preservice review. These exceptions can be objective when there is an existence of a physical condition requiring immediate treatment, or subjective when a reasonably prudent person would believe that a condition requires immediate medical attention.

c) Criteria for Review

While no jurisdiction dictates the selection of a particular set of criteria for UM processes, all UM processes require the use of objective third-party or internally professionally developed clinically evidence-based and consistently applied criteria to decisions regarding benefit determination. The use of medical necessity criteria based on clinically credible evidence for this process is viewed as able to promote a balanced access to quality care, medically appropriate utilization, and coverage determinations based on the benefits available under a subscriber's benefit plan.

d) Reviewer Qualifications

The qualifications of individuals who may or may not make the ultimate decision regarding utilization have been, and remain, a controversial topic. Some states require that reviewers with the ultimate authority to deny coverage be a physician. Many states require that the health care professional making the denial decision to be Board certified, or have experience in the same or similar specialty as the treating provider. While the regulations for each state may vary, at a minimum all states require that any health care intervention that is subject to a medical necessity review be done by healthcare professionals such as nurses (although some exceptions exist for "scripted screening" as discussed in Section 2.0).

In an effort to protect the patient even further, some states require that UR nurses and physicians be licensed in the same state where the medical services are being provided. For example, states such as Arizona, Connecticut, Kentucky, Mississippi and Oklahoma[5] require that a state-licensed physician or health care professional make, approve or oversee adverse determinations. However, most states only require that the clinical reviewers hold and maintain an appropriate clinical license in the United States for the period during which they are performing reviews. The level of training, experience or certification beyond state licensure will dictate the conformity of a plan or UM entity to the state law in question. Additionally, virtually every state, federal law and national managed care accrediting organization such as URAC, implicitly or explicitly prohibits compensation or other financial incentives to utilization reviewers based on coverage denial decisions or limitation of care.

e)   Timeframes for UM Determinations

The timeframes for processing UM decisions are regulated with specificity in all statutes. Virtually all states regulating UM, the federal government and national health care organization accrediting entities such as URAC provide for specific timeframes in which such review must be performed, often by the category of review. Most timeframes begin either with the actual date of the request for the medical intervention being reviewed, or upon receipt of all the information necessary to make the determination.

The time period for making a UM decision depends on the type of medical service performed. For the performance of non-urgent medical services (e.g., precertification and preservice reviews), the review must usually be completed within a few days of the request. Reviews that occur during a hospital stay (e.g., concurrent reviews), or reviews of urgently needed services typically must be completed within one day of the request. Some states mandate that reviews of services requested following stabilization from emergency treatment be reviewed within hours of the request. Reviews occurring after services have been performed (e.g., retrospective or post-service reviews) are usually afforded the most time for review since the subscriber has received the service. Unfortunately, these timeframes as well as the categories for review may differ among individual states although they are in general conformance with federal law, such as the Department of Labor's (DOL's) Final Claims Rule, or URAC standards (See Section 6.0 for additional details on the DOL requirements).

f)   Communication of Determinations

How and when a UM decision is communicated to the appropriate parties depends on a variety of factors and differs depending on the type of review performed and the benefit plan design. For example, precertification and concurrent reviews are generally subject to more rapid communication requirements than retrospective reviews. Likewise, the method of communication and content of the review determination are also regulated. Generally, review decisions communicated verbally must be confirmed in writing to the requesting provider and/or the subscriber within prescribed timeframes. Denials or adverse determination decisions must usually contain the clinical rationale for the denial and outline the appeal mechanism.

g)   Adverse Determinations/Denials

The NAIC Model Act defines an *adverse determination* as a:

> determination by a health carrier or its designee utilization review organization that, based upon the information provided, a request for a benefit under the plan, upon application of utilization review does not meet the health carrier's requirements for medical necessity, appropriateness, health care setting, level of care or effectiveness or is determined to be experimental or investigational and the requested benefit is therefore denied, reduced or terminated, or payment is not provided or made, in whole or in part, for the benefit.

Some states and accreditation agencies such as URAC require that providers be afforded the opportunity to speak with the physician reviewer making an adverse determination. Often referred to as a peer-to-peer discussion, this opportunity allows provider input prior to, or immediately after, issuing the adverse determination. Generally, the clinical rationale or criteria upon which the determination was made must be disclosed. In addition, an opportunity must be granted to either the attending provider or the subscriber to appeal the adverse decision.

h)   Grievances and Appeals

In addition to designated timeframes to process a UM decision, UM laws usually provide for one or more internal appeals and then an external review for adverse determinations. Grievance and appeal rights typically allow a provider to engage in peer-to-peer discussions as referenced above. This includes the availability of an informal dispute resolution and the ability of the attending provider to make his or her case for the patient either prior to an adverse determination or as part of the pre-appeal process. For example, some states including Pennsylvania and Maryland require a managed care plan provide for an appeals process for adverse determinations that contains two internal levels of appeal and a third external level which is handled by the state Department of Health.

Physicians involved in the UM appeal process must be of a similar specialty as the requesting provider and may not be the same physician who rendered the initial adverse determination. Similarly, a different physician or panel of physicians must be used at each subsequent level of appeal. Health plans will sometimes contract with state-licensed utilization review entities for such matched-specialty peer reviewers, as a result of direct employment. However, both arrangements need a sufficient number of physicians in various specialties and can be administratively and financially prohibitive.

In addition to the factors listed above, the laws governing grievance and appeals processes may address some or all of the following issues: (1) informal review, usually between the subscriber's provider and the plan's assigned provider (as discussed above); (2) continuity of care during the determination process (obviously this is more relevant for preservice and concurrent review than for retrospective review); (3) the right to be represented during the process by a third party or by the treating provider; (4) prohibition on retaliation against a subscriber who uses the review process or a participating provider who advocates on behalf of a subscriber; (5) the role of prior decision makers in an appellate process; (6) the confidentiality of information and timing of requests for additional information; (7) the method and content of information provided to the patient; (8) written notification of and explanations for the appeal decisions; (9) the right to pursue external appeal; (10) the selection and neutrality of an external reviewer; (11) the cost of the external review; and (10) the right to challenge a final determination beyond the external review or other last step in the process through a court of competent jurisdiction.

How a subscriber or provider accesses the benefit plan's grievance and appeal system will depend on how and when the denial for a medical procedure or treatment is made. In some cases the right to file a UM grievance or appeal may be limited by the specific benefit plan coverage. An adverse determination may include or exclude certain determinations, such as partial payment, partial approval (e.g., approving the general service requested but denying the level or frequency of the service requested), length of stay (LOS) limitations, and so on. In these cases, the health plan's obligations and subscriber's opportunities may differ. Of course, UM regulatory requirements will control if the benefit plan documents differ from the state or federal laws.

In addition to the laws summarized in this Section, other UM regulatory requirements exist through laws governing worker's compensation coverage, self-funded plans, Medicare and Medicaid plans, and auto coverage. Grievance and appeal rights may differ significantly based upon what regulatory and benefit plan coverage requirements apply. It is essential for the relevant party to determine which rules apply, or if such a determination is not possible to understand the conflict and determine how to proceed.

i) *External Review*

Utilization management regulations create rules that permit enrollees to obtain those benefits which are medically necessary under their respective plans. However, these determinations even on a first or second level of appeal remain within the plan's control. Since health plans remain in control of initial and secondary appeals, thirty-eight states have sought to provide enrollees with an additional right to appeal to a neutral third party arbiter once the participant has exhausted all their internal appeals. This external reviewer may be selected by the state, the plan, or the plan in conjunction with the enrollee. These external reviewers and the process of external review are subject to the significant level of state scrutiny and provide for an important counterbalance in the utilization process.

3.5 General Jurisdictional Considerations

Within the last decade, many states have attempted to expand their regulatory jurisdiction over UM activities beyond those occurring within their borders as discussed in more detail below. Likewise, the application of state UM regulation to ERISA plans and Medicare/Medicaid plans[6] creates the potential for redundancy, confusion and expense on the part of benefit administrators, providers, subscribers, regulators, and other stakeholders as to which rules apply and in what circumstances.

The majority of state UM laws are drafted broadly and require licensure and oversight for entities performing utilization review. Where the UM entity is certified in one state but performs its operations in another state, an interstate legal analysis is often required to determine which state laws apply in a given circumstance. As an example, the UM entity may be domiciled and licensed in one state, the health insurance policy issued in another, and the treatment under review may take place in a third state. In these cases the determination of which state UM laws apply can be difficult to ascertain. When a state attempts to extend its jurisdiction over UM activities occurring outside its borders, or to utilization review entities certified in other states (sometimes referred to as "Foreign UM entities"), the rationale is based on the state's authority to protect the interests of its residents.[7] With national employers and states sharing borders, it is not uncommon for one state's residents to be covered by policies issued and delivered in another state or to seek services from providers in another state. This cross border activity raises issues regarding which state's laws have jurisdiction over the activity.

Compounding the issue of interstate regulation are the multi-jurisdictional lines of state law, federal law and regulations, including the DOL's Final Claims Rule[8] issued in 2000. In addition, UM standards issued by national accreditation entities and by various employers through RFP requirements further add to the complexity of which UM rules should be applied.

As a result of the jurisdictional issues raised by UM activities, many local and regional health care organizations seek to engage utilization review entities that have national reputations, sufficient staff, multi-state capacity, and are empowered by the states to issue UM certifications where UR licensure is required. In fact, some states, including Florida and Arizona, specifically require that health plans subcontract with utilization review entities that are licensed in their respective states.[9]

3.6 Application of State UM Regulations

To the extent a utilization review entity conducts business in or performs UM activities in a particular state, its UM activities may be subject to that state's regulatory jurisdiction irrespective of where the policy was actually issued. This occurs when the utilization review entity is incorporated in the state or the sponsoring health plan providing the services is licensed within the state. A particular state UM law will equally apply when the clinical and administrative personnel performing the utilization review activities are located within the same state as the patient.

When the UM activities are performed outside the state and where care is being rendered to a patient by a foreign UM entity licensed in another state, the need for an interstate jurisdictional analysis comes into play. Often the only contact the utilization review entity has with a state's residents and/or providers is through telephone requests for clinical information, and the mailing of decision letters to the insured individuals and providers. In these situations, the requirements as well as the regulatory authority to enforce them remain less clear. A valid question arises as to whether this de minimus contact is sufficient to be considered performing utilization management within the state. Of the states that require UM certification for utilization review entities, there are no specific out-of-state exemptions offered to foreign UM entities whose utilization management activities are performed in their state of domicile.

States such as Maryland have attempted to regulate UM activities performed by foreign entities outside of it's borders if the utilization review is conducted on services provided to a its residents.[10] In these cases states try to regulate UM entities when the provider of services is located out of the state and the policy for which the utilization review is being performed is issued in another state. Other states will attempt to regulate UM activities that review a provider's services located inside the state regardless of the residency of the individual, or the location of the UM entity's activities. A good example is Florida where its UM law requires UM certification based on the location of the services being performed. Of the states that require UM certification 14 states appear to base their requirements on the state residency of the individual, or the health care services subject to the review being provided in the state.[11] Such laws have the potential to impact not only UM organizations having minimal contact with the state, but also out-of-state licensed insurers and health plans that perform utilization review on behalf of their members residing or reviewing services in a contiguous state.

3.7 UM Certification Exemptions for ERISA Plans

While some states exempt self-funded employer group health plans (i.e. ERISA plans)[12] from UM certification, the exemption generally applies only to the plan itself, and does not extend to an independent utilization review entity which performs utilization review activities on that plan's behalf. Some states like Illinois make this clear distinction in their statute while others do not.[13] Pennsylvania is one state that sets itself apart by its managed care reform law applying to self-funded plans only to the extent that such regulations are not preempted by ERISA.[14] Normally a state's UM appeal requirements will be preempted by ERISA as these requirements apply to self-funded plans offering the coverage.

3.8 Regulatory Accreditation Recognitions

Many states now recognize the significance and value of a UM accreditation by a nationally recognized accrediting organization such as URAC. Presently, 35 states either require URAC certification for their state-licensure or deem URAC accreditation as sufficient evidence of a utilization review entity's meeting the state utilization requirements. (See Summary Chart at the end of Section 3.0) In the states where accreditation is recognized, accredited entities are deemed in compliance with the state's standards and need only file evidence of accreditation to receive exemption from the state UM certification requirements.[15] In other states, including Connecticut, URAC accreditation is deemed as satisfying some of the state's many criteria for UM certification.

3.9 Extraterritorial Enforcement

To this date, a state's extraterritorial enforcement of its UM laws against a foreign UM entity remains untested in the courts. The question of whether a UM entity is engaged in the business of insurance also remains unresolved in those states that do not regulate UM. Depending on the specific facts of a case and the degree of contact a foreign UM entity has with a given state, extraterritorial enforcement of a state's utilization review laws, if asserted, could be challenged by a foreign UM entity on a number of grounds, including ERISA preemption and preclusion under the Federal Commerce Clause. Plans and UM entities need to carefully evaluate the nature and extent of the contracted UM services they provide on behalf of insurers and health plans and the degree of contact they will have with a state which requires UM certification. Until such time as all states requiring UM certification deem URAC accreditation as meeting state UM certification standards or a federal law for uniform regulation of utilization management is enacted, state variations in UM certification requirements and extraterritorial enforcement of utilization review laws will continue to be an evolving area.

3.10 Conclusion

The evolution of state utilization management laws has reached a point of maturity. While every state regulates health plans, most states, either through regulating utilization management entities, or through regulating utilization management by health plans, regulate utilization management. Indeed, from a consumer perspective, the states and federal governments have passed these laws to address enrollee concerns. The current problem is not a lack of regulation, but the coordination of the regulations but coordinating them in a manner that provides results for enrollees. The is to coordinate them in a manner that permits compliance with the law without effectively mandating a cost structure that makes health coverage unaffordable.

The redundancy that occurs in this system is unlikely to change given the vested interest of state governments and the federal government in protecting the rights of enrollees. From a political perspective, absent the imposition of strong preemption language in ERISA and the Social Security Act, plans that provide services will be subject to both federal and state laws. Likewise, absent any significant amendments to federal law governing jurisdictional disputes among states with respect to the applicability of utilization review law, plans will remain subject to the laws of each state in which they have enrollees.

---

1   Utilization Review and Benefit Determination Model Act, Section 3(BB), NAIC Model Laws, Regulations and Guidelines I:73-5 (2003).

2   See Hawaii's utilization review law, CODE HAW. R. §16-16-2 (2004).

3   See generally, Avedis Donabedian, Explorations in Quality Assessment and Monitoring: The Definition of Quality and Approaches to Its Assessment, (Griffith, et al., eds, Health Administration Press, 1980).

4   See PA. STAT. ANN. tit. 40 §991.2151 (2004).

5   Arizona: For denials of precertification and the medical director overseeing UM activities must be state licensed (ARIZ. REV. STAT. ANN. § 20-2510(B) (2003)); Connecticut: Final adverse determinations for services within the state must be made by physician/ nurse/ licensed

health professional under the authority of state licensed physician/ nurse/ health professional (CONN GEN. STAT. § 38a-226c(6) (2003)); Kentucky: denial of chiropractor or optometrist services must be made by a state-licensed chiropractor or optometrist (KY. REV. STAt. ANN. § 304.17A-607 (1)(b) (2003)); Mississippi: state-licensed physician must review and concur with all adverse determinations (MISS. CODE ANN. § 41-83-31(a) (2003)); Oklahoma: UM entities must have a sufficient number of state-licensed physicians/ heath care professionals overseeing UM activities (OKLA. STAT. tit. 36, § 6558 (2003)).

6   We address Medicare and Medicaid jurisdictional issues in Section 5.0.

7   See Georgia and Maryland.

8   29 CFR Part 2560.

9   Florida: "No insurer shall knowingly contract with or utilize a private review agent which has failed to register as required by this section or which has had a registration revoked by the agency [Agency for Health Care Administration] FLA. STAT. ANN § 395.0199(7) (2004). Arizona: "A health care insurer that proposes to provide coverage of …medical benefits…for residents of this state with utilization review of those benefits shall meet at least one of the following requirements: 1. have a [UR] certificate issued pursuant to this chapter…3. contract with a utilization review agent that has a [UR] certificate issued pursuant to this chapter…" ARIZ. REV. STAT. ANN. § 20-2510 A (2004).

10   MD. CODE ANN. [Ins.] § 15-10B-03(a) (2004).

11   Arizona, Alabama, Connecticut, Florida, Georgia, Illinois, Kansas, Louisiana, Maryland, Nebraska, Oklahoma, Rhode Island, Tennessee, Texas, Virginia and Vermont (for mental health only).

12   ERISA UM Standards, specifically the U.S. Department of Labor's Final Claims rule at 29 CFR Part 2560, are addressed in detail in Section 6.0.

13   "The provisions of this section [utilization review licensure] do not apply to: ...(2) self-insured health plans under the ERISA; however, this section does apply to persons conducting UR programs on behalf of these health plans." 215 ILCS 134/85(c).

14   This tautology is known as the "it's preempted by ERISA if its preempted by ERISA" provision. See PA. STAT. ANN. tit. 40 §991.2193 (2004).

15   "A person is exempt from the provisions of this article if the person is accredited by the utilization review accreditation commission, the national committee for quality assurance or any other nationally recognized accreditation process recognized by the director." ARIZ. REV. STAT. ANN. § 20-2510 A (2004).

Summary Chart of State Utilization Management Requirements

States	Provision of State Law or Regulation (Regulation of standalone URO's, if blank or other entities to which applicable)	Licensure registration or certification required	UR laws apply to retrospective reviewer	UR laws apply to HMOs (All states have HMO act that may apply additional UR requirements)	Number of years that license or certificate is valid	Requirements for clinical review criteria	Prohibitions against financial incentives	Quality assurance program required	Provisions for oversight of delegated functions	Physicians or clinical peers must approve adverse determinations	Medical director required	Same-state licensure requirement	Criteria for adverse determination available	Appeals process required	External appeals process required	Recognition of URAC's Health UM Standards
AK		√	√	√						√		√		√	√	
AL	√	√			1	√		√		√			√	√	√	√a
AR	√	√	√	√	2	√		√	√					√	√	√
AS																
AZ	√	√	√	√	3	√	√		√	√	√	√b	√	√	√	√
CA	√		√	√		√	√	√	√	√	√	√b		√	√	
CO				√			√			√c						
CT	√	√		√	1	√	√		√			√	√	√	√	
DC																
DE		√		√	1	√d	√	√d		√	√	√b		√	√	
FL	√	√	√		1		√			√e				√	√	
GA	√	√		√	2	√		√	√	√e			√	√	√	√
GU																
HI				√		√	√	√		√			√	√	√	√
IA	√f			√		g				√			√	√		
ID	√			√		√				√			√	√h	√	√
IL	√	√	√	√	2	√	√	√d	√	√			√	√	√	√
IN	√	√	√		1	√	√		√	√			√	√	√d	√
KS	√	√	√		1	√	√		√	√	√		√	√	√	√
KY	√	√	√		2	√		i		√	√	√j	√	√	√	√k
LA	√	√l		√m	2	√	√n		√	√	√	√		√	√	
MA	√	√	√	√m		√	√	√	√	√	√		√	√	√	
MD	√	√	√	√	2	√	√		√	√	√		√	√	o	
ME	√	√	√	√	1	√			√	√	√			√	√	
MI			√	√y												
MN	√	√	√	√	2	√	√	√	√	√			√	√	√	
MO	√	√	√	√	1	√	√	√m	√	√	√	√b	√	√	√	
MS	√	q	√	√	2	√								√	p	
MT	√	√				√		r						√	√	
NC	√	√	√	√		√	√		√		√	√b	√	√	√	
ND	√	√	√	√	1	√	√		√	√	√		√	√	√	
NE	√	√	√	√	2	√	√s	m		√		√b	√	√	m	
NH		√t		√	1	√		√			√	√b	√	√	√	
NJ	√			√		√		d			√	√b		√	√	
NM			√			√		d		√				√	√	√

Summary Chart of State Utilization Management Requirements

States	Provision of State Law or Regulation (Regulation of standalone URO's, if blank or other entities to which applicable)	Licensure registration or certification required	UR laws apply to retrospective reviewer	UR laws apply to HMOs (All states have HMO act that may apply additional UR requirements)	Number of years that license or certificate is valid	Requirements for clinical review criteria	Prohibitions against financial incentives	Quality assurance program required	Provisions for oversight of delegated functions	Physicians or clinical peers must approve adverse determinations	Medical director required	Same-state licensure requirement	Criteria for adverse determination available	Appeals process required	External appeals process required	Recognition of URAC's Health UM Standards
NV	✓	✓	✓		1				✓		✓u				✓v	
NY	✓	✓	✓	✓	2	✓	✓		✓	✓	✓		✓	✓	✓	
OH	✓	w	✓	✓	1	✓	✓	✓	✓				✓	✓	✓	✓
OK	✓	✓	✓	✓	1	✓									✓	
OR	✓	✓	✓	✓		✓	✓	d	✓	✓		✓	✓	✓	✓	
PA	✓	✓			3	✓	✓		✓	✓		✓		✓		
PR	✓															✓
RI	✓	✓	✓	✓	2	✓	✓	✓	✓	✓			✓	✓	✓	
SC	✓	✓	✓	✓	2	✓		✓		✓			✓	✓		
SD	✓	✓	✓	✓	1	✓	✓	✓m	✓	✓	✓		✓	✓	✓	
TN	✓	✓		x	1	✓				✓				✓		✓
TX	✓	✓	✓	✓	2	✓	✓		✓	✓	✓		✓	✓	✓	
UT	✓	✓	✓			✓								✓	✓	
VA	✓	✓	✓	✓	2	✓			✓	✓			✓	✓	✓	
VI																
VT	✓	✓	✓	✓	2	✓	✓		✓				✓	✓	✓	
WA	✓	✓	✓	✓		✓					✓	✓	✓	✓		
WI																
WV	✓					✓		✓	✓	✓			✓	✓		✓
WY																

UM CHART ENDNOTES

a. Licensure fee waived for URAC accredited companies.
b. For Medical Directors
c. Must be familiar with standards of care in CO.
d. For HMO's.
e. Panel of 3 must consist of at least 1 physician and 1 Medical Director.
f. Any third party payor.
g. No provision. However, for certification compliance must use most recent URAC UR standards.
h. MCO's must have internal grievance system.
i. For MCO's

j. For denial of service for chiropractor or optometrist.
k. In lieu of disclosing a UR plan, PRA may submit evidence of URAC accreditation.
l. Requires accreditation.
m. For all health carriers.
n. For external review entities.
o. Patient may file with insurance commissioner who may consult with an IRO.
p. Allows for judicial appeals.
q. No license but must file review plans.
r. Insurers must routinely assess their UR programs.
s. Does not apply to in network HMO and PPO referrals.

t. HMO's, ODS's and carriers that include UM must be licensed by the Department of Banking Insurance (assumed risk), or certified by the Department of Health and Senior Services (no assumed risk).
u. For Dental Services Medical Director must be a dentist.
v. External Review Organizations must be certified.
w. Must file an annual certificate of compliance.
x. HMO's have their own UM requirements.
y. Michigan does not currently regulate utilization review organizations. However, In Michigan "health carriers" are subject to the "Patient's Right to Independent Review Act."

4.0: The Landscape of Utilization Review Programs for Workers' Compensation Programs

Patricia Wagner, JD, PhD

4.1 Introduction

Utilization Management (UM)[1] requirements within state workers' compensation laws exist within a constantly shifting landscape. As employers attempt to control the rising costs of workers' compensation insurance, and promote more effective treatment protocols for injured employees, an increasing number are evaluating and experimenting with providing or regulating workers' compensation insurance through managed care arrangements.[2] The range of these managed care arrangements varies both in terms of the managed care being provided to injured employees, and the arrangements states allow for managing that care.

4.2 Workers' Compensation Insurance

All 50 states and the District of Columbia require that employers offer workers' compensation coverage. This traditionally covers medical care required for employee work related injuries, and is generally obtained by an employer from 1 of 3 sources: a state fund; private insurance (including managed care arrangements); or self-insurance (which can also utilize managed care arrangements).

Workers' compensation insurance was originally set up as a fee-for-service system in which employers were required to pay 100% of an injured employee's medical costs[3] While employers are still required to provide workers' compensation benefits, as medical costs continue to increase more and more states have implemented or allowed some type of managed care arrangement for workers' compensation services.[4] Currently less than half of all states manage a state-funded insurance program, and even those states with state-funded products recognize that employers may opt for different coverage options, such as self-insurance or private insurance.[5]

4.3 Workers' Compensation Managed Care Fundamentals

Managed care offers an integrated or more specialized set of interventions to more effectively treat employees' work-related injuries or illnesses and to help return these employees to work in a more cost-effective and meaningful manner.

Although traditional workers' compensation coverage arrangements have utilized claims adjustors to review and monitor the injured employee's progress, managed care offers a higher level of assessment through utilization management (UM) and case management (CM). Under a workers' compensation UM program, assessments are made by clinically trained staff to determine the most appropriate treatment regimen. In the same vein, clinically trained staff can help coordinate over a period of time a wide range of medical and administrative issues while the injured employee prepares to return to work.

Another advantage in providing workers' compensation through a managed care arrangement is the ability to negotiate rates with participating providers. In addition, in many states an injured employee is required to visit a network physician for the first visit.[6] While this may seem unremarkable from a traditional managed care experience, given that workers' compensation has traditionally been fee-for-service, and driven by the right of the injured employee to receive full payment for treatment for the applicable injury, such a requirement can have a significant impact on controlling workers' compensation costs, for carriers, and ultimately for employers. Minnesota exemplifies this changing role, as employers that contract with a certified managed care organization can require employees receive in-network care through the managed care organization procedures. However, if the employer chooses to contract with a managed care organization which is not certified by the state as a workers' compensation managed care arrangement, the employer cannot require injured employees to receive in-network care.[7]

4.4 Rising Costs

States continue to struggle with the rising costs associated with workers' compensation insurance. Workers' compensation managed care arrangements have received a lot more attention from state regulators, employers and others in recent years. Managed care interventions such as UM, CM, and network-based programs have demonstrated the ability to reduce workers' compensation costs by approximately 20%.[8] As a result, more states and employers are apt to encourage the use of managed care services to improve the efficiency and effectiveness of workers' compensation coverage. As the shift toward managed care continues for workers' compensation, tracking workers' compensation claims will become even more prevalent and significant. As noted above, one of the key strategies that managed care organizations use to control costs of providing care is utilization management.[9] Therefore, it is not unreasonable to expect that UM and CM interventions will play an even bigger role in workers' compensation insurance as employers and states struggle to control spiraling costs.

A recent publication from the state of California reporting on workers' compensation costs noted that the total costs of medical care payments and wage replacement benefits in the California Workers' Compensation system had more than doubled between 1995 and 2002.[10] The report outlined several strategies for managing workers' compensation costs, including the use of managed care services such as UM.[11] In that regard, many states have begun to assess the impact of utilization review and managed care on workers' compensation arrangements through the study and evaluation of their control on costs. In fact, New York State recently extended its Treatment Utilization Pilot Program—a program designed to assess the effect of higher reimbursement rates on reducing utilization in workers' compensation care.[12] The State of Florida also published a recent study evaluating the effect of managed care on workers' compensation outcomes.[13] This study noted that not only did the use of managed care in workers' compensation decrease average medical costs, it also noted that injured workers remained generally satisfied with the care they received.[14]

4.5 Regulatory Oversight

All workers' compensation benefits offered to either private or public employees are regulated by each individual state. For these types of entities no federal regulation applies. States will generally regulate workers' compensation benefits through their respective Departments of Workers' Compensation. In some states where workers' compensation benefits are offered through managed care arrangements, the arrangements also may be regulated by the state's Department of Insurance.

About 31 states directly regulate workers' compensation managed care. These laws tend to focus on both clinical criteria and appellate processes with such requirements as a second opinion, and the utilization of employer designated providers. Moreover, workers' compensation regulators tend to be integrated in the dispute resolution process, and workers' compensation appeals serve a quasi-judicial state function whose health UM equivalent is external review. Other states, although a small minority, regulate indirectly through reference to state laws regarding managed care. A broader picture of these different state statutes can be found in Appendix C of this Guide which provides the reader with a state-by-state breakdown of the existing workers' compensation UM laws.

4.5.1 Workers' Compensation Managed Care

States have adopted a variety of models for managed care arrangements for workers' compensation insurance. In Pennsylvania, any entity providing managed care workers'

compensation must become certified as a Coordinated Care Organization.[15] Once certified, a Coordinated Care Organization performs much like a traditional managed care organization, and is required to provide both UM and CM services.[16] If the Coordinated Care Organization makes a decision to contract with outside organizations to perform UM or CM, the Coordinated Care Organization must receive the approval of the arrangement by the Department of Labor and Industry. Attaining the Department of Labor and Industry's approval must be accomplished before the outside organization can perform these services.[17]

Like Pennsylvania, the State of Connecticut has similarly adopted legislation that allows provider networks the use of care managers and coordinators for workers' compensation care.[18] These arrangements, established as "Medical Care Plans" must be certified by the state. Once established, a plan's decision related to the necessity and appropriateness of health care services provided to an injured employee is not subject to review by the Connecticut Workers' Compensation Commissioner until the injured employee has exhausted the plan's utilization review and dispute resolution.[19] Furthermore, any decision made by the plan under these arrangements is reviewed under a standard that requires modification only if the decision by the plan is found to be unreasonable, arbitrary and capricious.[20] Nevertheless, Connecticut mandates that entities providing UM be licensed by the Commissioner of Insurance as a utilization review company.[21]

In Ohio, participation in a managed care organization in the Health Partnership Program (HPP) is mandatory for state fund employers. Those employers may either choose a managed care organization or have one assigned to them.[22] If the employer has selected a managed care organization, an injured employee may select either a managed care organization panel provider, a non-panel provider who is certified by the Bureau of Workers' Compensation (but the managed care organization still manages the treatment), or a non-managed care organization, non-Bureau certified provider (in which case the managed care organization manages the initial treatment or emergency care only; further treatment, if not authorized by employee's managed care organization is paid for by the employee).[23] Interestingly, if an employee selects a Bureau-certified provider who has not selected to participate on the managed care organization's provider panel, the Bureau-certified provider may still provide treatment to the injured employee under the HPP. Under this arrangement it is understood the provider agrees to submit to the managed care organization's medical management of the employee's care.[24] In addition, the Bureau of Worker's Compensation requires all managed care organizations in the HPP to have URAC certification.

In terms of providing workers' compensation benefits through a managed care arrangement, Florida is an example of one state which allows such procedures and officially designates the relationship as a "Workers' Compensation Managed Care Arrangement."[25] Just as in Connecticut and Pennsylvania, Florida provides a number of specific requirements on the Workers' Compensation Managed Care Arrangement including that the entity provide for utilization review of requests for services, and that the utilization review performed meet nationally recognized written criteria. In contrast to these states, Montana's workers' compensation arrangements are more provider driven as a health care provider, group of medical service providers, or an "entity with a managed care organization" can apply to provide workers' compensation managed care.[26] Interestingly, the statutory language prohibits the application by an organization formed, owned, or operated by a workers' compensation insurer or a self-insured employer.

The regulations in North Carolina further demonstrate the effect a state's insurance department can have on such managed care arrangements. Under North Carolina law, the Industrial Commission promulgates rules for workers' compensation managed care organizations, but the Department of Insurance is the "primary" regulator. Thus, a managed care organization must first be approved by the Department of Insurance, and then the Industrial Commission provides the organization with a letter which allows the organization to enter into workers' compensation contracts.[27]

All the above examples illustrate that as states adopt or encourage managed care arrangements for providing injured workers with covered services, the type of these arrangements will vary tremendously. Irrespective of any form, the fundamental concept of managed care through utilization review still remains an integral step in all cases. Thus, as more states adopt or encourage these arrangements for workers compensation, the more prevalent the role UM will take in those arrangements.

4.5.2 Workers' Compensation Utilization Management

As with traditional health UM, organizations that perform utilization review for workers' compensation claims, and regulating the utilization review process itself can occur through a state's Health department or Insurance department. In addition, under some state regulatory schemes, workers' compensation UM is directly regulated through the state's workers' compensation regulatory body.[28] However, even those states which mandate that an employer or managed care arrangement can conduct

utilization review still do not regulate the utilization review process further.[29] As managed care becomes more the norm for workers' compensation, utilization review organizations and the UM process will become more closely scrutinized by state regulators.

A. Defining UR/UM

Given the various types of workers' compensation managed care arrangements, it comes as no surprise that the extent of regulation of workers' compensation UR and UM programs varies by state as well. This variation is illustrated by how each state defines the term "utilization review" or "utilization management" in their statutes. Alabama distinguishes the two as follows:

➢ UM is a "comprehensive set of integrated components including: pre-certification review, admission review, continued stay review, retrospective review, discharge planning, bill screening and individual medical case management as required"; and

➢ UR is a "determination of medical necessity for medical and surgical in-hospital, outpatient, and alternative setting treatments for acute and rehabilitation care. It includes pre-certification for elective treatments, concurrent review and, if necessary, retrospective review for emergency cases".[30]

In contrast to Alabama, California defines UR as "a system used to manage costs and improve patient care and decision making through case-by-case assessments of the frequency, duration, level and appropriateness of medical care and services to determine whether medical treatment is or was reasonably required to cure or relieve the effects of the injury."[31] Connecticut exercises additional control over the utilization review by requiring both review and appeal procedures, including a requirement to make determinations on requests for services within 2 days of receiving the request.[32] Given the variation in the definitions of UR and UM between each state it is to be expected that the regulation of other aspects of the process varies as well.

B. Initial Determinations

Similar to the review of traditional medical claims, many states regulate the timing of the initial determination process when making a medical necessity decision in a workers' compensation coverage arrangement, although the timing may vary from state to state. Connecticut requires that the utilization reviewer make initial determinations of requests for services within 2 days of receiving all necessary information to evaluate the request.[33] In contrast, Florida only requires that decisions related to the utilization review of care (or precertification) be provided in a timely manner.[34]

C. Appeals

In addition to the initial benefit determination, states also regulate (as is true for traditional health UM) the appeals processes within workers' compensation coverage arrangements. Again, the level of regulation and the time frames that apply will vary depending on the particular jurisdiction. There are states that require after the exhaustion of the internal appeal process, that utilization review agents complete the appeals process by filing with the appropriate agency[35] no later than twenty days after the date the injured worker files his/her appeal.[36] On the other hand, the State of Minnesota perhaps best demonstrates how the workers' compensation managed care is still evolving from traditional fee-for-service workers' compensation. While Minnesota allows employers to contract directly with certified managed care organizations and their utilization review process[37], it does not mandate utilization review of appeals. Instead it requires that disputed determinations be first addressed within the plan at no cost to the employee and that the process be complete within 30 days after a review request is made. If the dispute is not resolved between the plan and the injured employee at that time, the parties may request an administrative conference with the Commissioner of Workers' Compensation or a hearing with the Division of Workers' Compensation.[38]

D. Reviewer Qualifications

States can also regulate the qualifications of reviewers who perform UM. Kentucky requires that utilization reviewers be "appropriately qualified" and is defined as someone who has the:

> education, training, and experience necessary for evaluating the clinical issues and services under review. A physician, registered nurse, licensed practical nurse, medical records technician or other personnel, who through training and experience is qualified to issue decisions on medical necessity or appropriateness, shall issue the initial utilization review approval.[39]

However, Kentucky further provides that any issuance of an adverse determination must be made by an appropriately licensed physician.[40] The state even requires that individuals conducting review of the medical bills "have the education, training or experience necessary for evaluating medical bills and statements."[41]

In contrast to Kentucky, Georgia mandates specific requirements indirectly, by requiring that the reviewer satisfy the State Workers' Compensation Board's requirements for peer review, which require that a majority of the reviewers be in the same discipline as the care that is being reviewed.[42]

4.5.3 Oversight Through Traditional Insurance Regulation

While some states have separately designated processes for workers' compensation UM or have mandated that UR take place for workers' compensation claims, other states rely on regulatory provisions that fall under traditional insurance and health UM laws.

Louisiana mandates that any employer or insurance carrier providing workers' compensation perform UM on injured workers' claims for services.[43] On the other hand, Louisiana does not regulate Utilization Review Organizations that perform those services.[44] While Arkansas mandates utilization review of workers' compensation claims and requires the Utilization Review Organization to be accredited by the state[45], it does not distinguish between those Utilization Review Organizations performing workers' compensation claims review and those Utilization Review Organizations performing traditional medical claims review.[46] There are some states that do not require that entities providing workers' compensation coverage perform UM, but do regulate the process if the employer or carrier chooses to perform utilization review (or chooses to contract for those services). In those instances, the organization performing the review must be licensed as a Utilization Review Organization in the state.[47]

While there are some states that provide for the regulation of UM within worker's compensation regulations, the reader should be aware that there are some states that explicitly exclude the regulation of UM or UR for workers' compensation by statute. For example, Kansas explicitly excludes workers' compensation from its utilization review statutes, but instead "directs" utilization review through the Director of Workers' Compensation.[48] Finally, it is important to note that while some states may not regulate workers' compensation UM, they may consider utilization review to be the adjustment of a claim (particularly when claims are reviewed retrospectively) and therefore require the licensure of the entity as a claims adjuster and/or independent bill reviewer.[49]

4.6 Conclusion

As one solution to controlling the rising costs of workers' compensation insurance, managed care alternatives offer established mechanisms to manage the cost of care provided to injured employees. In recognition of this fact, many states have adopted statutes and regulations that allow employers to offer workers' compensation benefits through a managed care arrangement. As managed care is relatively new to workers' compensation, the various states have adopted a wide variety of models for these managed care arrangements, presumably in an attempt to transition the change as smoothly and effectively as possible. The result is a legislative environment surrounding workers' compensation care in flux.

States that regulate managed care arrangements have adopted a wide variety of regulatory mechanisms. As a consequence, managed care arrangements are regulated differently among the various states. This is true even to the way in which a state regulates the appeals processes and reviewer qualifications. As more and more states encourage managed care arrangements, the role of UM and UR in these arrangements is also bound to increase. The probable end result will be that the regulation of the utilization process within these arrangements will continue to shift as well.

1   Throughout this section and the rest of the book, the terms utilization management (UM) and utilization review (UR) are used interchangeably.

2   9 No. 7 HEALTH LAWYER 16 (1997); For a discussion of the various types of managed care arrangements in various states *see* Dana Baroni & Amy Lee, *An Analysis of Managed Care Network Standards in Other State Workers' Compensation Systems*, RESEARCH AND OVERSIGHT COUNCIL ON WORKERS' COMPENSATION (July 2002).

3   *See*, Lisa Krause, *Managed Care and Workers' Compensation*, 33 Tort & Ins. L. J. 849 (1998).

4   *Id.*

5   3 LARSON'S WORKERS' COMPENSATION, § 150.

6   *See*, e.g., 452 CODE MASS. REGS. § 6.03(1).

7   MINN. STAT. § 176.1351.

8   33 TORT & INS. L. J. 849, 851 (1998).

9   Department of Justice & Federal Trade Commission Report, *Improving Health Care: A Dose of Competition* at 12; Chapter 1 at 4 (July 2004).

10 Commission on Health & Safety and *Workers Compensation, Workers' Compensation Medical Care in California: Costs* (August 2003).

11 *Id.*

12 State of New York Workers' Compensation Board, Letter to Insurance Carriers, et.al, (Nov. 17, 2003).

13 Florida Workers' Compensation, *How Has Managed Care Affected Workers' Compensation Outcomes?*, (2000).

14 *Id.* At 57.

15 34 PA. CODE §§ 122.603, 122.608 (2004).

16 34 PA. CODE §§ 122.611. Note that part of the requirements of utilization review require that decisions on pretreatment certification be made within 7 days of the request.

17 34 PA. CODE §§ 122.626.

18 CONN. AGENCIES REGS. § 31-279-10(f) (2004).

19 *Id.*

20 *Id.*

21 CONN. AGENCIES REGS. § 31-279-10(h)(7).

22 OHIO ADMIN. CODE § 4123-6-052 (2004). Employers becoming self-insured after October 1993 must do so through a Qualified Health Plan (QHP). Employers using a QHP may require employees to receive care from network providers, although the employee has freedom of choice of providers within QHP network, however, if an employee is dissatisfied with QHP care, the employee may switch to a non-network Bureau certified provider upon notifying the QHP and Bureau. All care still must be managed by the QHP. OHIO ADMIN. CODE § 4123-6-056 (2004).

23 OHIO ADMIN. CODE § 4123-6-042, -062, -12.

24 OHIO ADMIN. CODE § 4123-6-026(F).

25 FLA. STAT. § 440.134(6)(c)(9) (2004).

26 MONT. CODE ANN. § 39-71-1105 (2004).

27 N.C. ADMIN CODE tit. 4, r. 10D.0105 (2004).

28 *See*, e.g., ALA. ADMIN. CODE r. 480-5-5-.06 (2004)(regulation of utilization review by the Department of Health); CONN. GEN. STAT. § 38a-226c & d; CONN. AD. REG. § 31-278-10 (2004) (regulation by the Department of Insurance); and 34 PA. CODE §§ 127.401(b), 127.651-127.670 (regulation by the Department of Labor and Industry).

29 *See*, e.g., ALA. ADMIN. CODE r. 480-5-5-.06; OKLA. ADMIN. CODE 365:10-15-3 (2004); 28 TEX. ADMIN. CODE § 19.2004 (2004).
30 ALA ADMIN. CODE r. 480-5-5.02(67).

31 CAL. CODES REGS. tit 8, § 9792.6(a)(5) (2003).

32 CONN. AGENCIES REGS. § 31-279-10(e).

33 CONN. AGENCIES REGS. § 31-279-10(e).

34 FLA. STAT. § 440.134(6)(c)(9); FLA. ADMIN. CODE r. 59A-23.004(8) (2004).

35 MASS. REGS. CODE tit. 452, §§ 1.07; 6.04(5) (2004).

36 MASS. REGS. CODE tit. 452, § 6.04(4)(c)(1).

37 MINN. R. 5128.0250 (2004).

38 MINN. R. § 5218.0700.

39 803 KY ADMIN. REGS. 25:190 § 6(1) (2004).

40 803 KY ADMIN. REGS. 25:190 § 6(2).

41 803 KY ADMIN. REGS. 25:190 § 6(3).

42 GA. COMP. R & REGS. r. 208(g)(1) (2004).

43 LA. ADMIN. CODE tit 40:I§ 2703 (2004).

44 *Id.*

45 ARK. CODE ANN. § 20-9-902 et. seq. (2004).

46 *Id.*

47 *See* NEV. REV. STAT. 683A.375 – .379 (2004); NEV. ADMIN. CODE ch. 683A, § 280 - § 295 (2004)(utilization not required, but if performed, the organization must be registered as a utilization review agent in the state).

48 KAN. STAT. ANN. § 40-1-41 (2004).

49 HAW. REV. STAT. § 431:9-222.5; -243 (2004).

5.0: Utilization Review in the Medicare and Medicaid Programs
Howard Burde, JD

5.1 Introduction

In other sections of this book we analyze utilization management (UM) regulation under state health and insurance laws, ERISA, and state worker's compensation laws. By contrast, this section focuses on the role of state and federal governments as payors and purchasers of UM services for Medicare and Medicaid.

Medicare and Medicaid include both fee-for-service and managed care programs. Given the role of government as purchaser rather than regulator in this context, the rules governing Medicare and Medicaid UM were originally not very prescriptive. With the identification of UM as a potential source of abuse and due to the rising costs of health care, the law has evolved to become more specific. Examples of this evolution include the Benefits Improvement and Protection Act of 2000 (BIPA)[1] and the Medicare Prescription Drug, Improvement and Modernization Act of 2003 (colloquially the Medicare Modernization Act, hereinafter, MMA). These laws provide detailed requirements for initial determinations, reconsiderations and appeals processes for the Medicare program. Indeed, these requirements, like those which apply to Medicaid managed care, create redundant systems for challenging benefits determinations for beneficiaries.

5.2 Medicare

The Medicare Act states that no payment shall be made for services that are not "reasonable and necessary for the diagnosis or treatment of illness or injury or to improve the functioning of a malformed body member."[2] Carriers and intermediaries are required to reject or adjust claims if the carrier or intermediary determines that the services furnished or proposed to be furnished were not reasonable, not medically necessary, or not furnished in the most appropriate setting; or if the claim does not properly reflect the kind and amount of services furnished.[3] Based upon this statute, Medicare carriers and intermediaries, (which shall be replaced by Medicare Administrative Contractors (MAC) under the MMA),[4] have the responsibility and authority to conduct utilization review. In addition, the Medicare program also provides for external UM through quality improvement organizations and Medicare managed care plans.

5.3 Quality Improvement Organizations- External Utilization Review

The Peer Review Improvement Act of 1982—part of the Tax Equity and Fiscal Responsibility Act of 1982 (TEFRA)—provided for the establishment of a utilization and quality control peer review program. The program was to be administered by private contractors named Peer Review Organizations (PROs). In 2002, the Centers for Medicare and Medicaid Services (CMS) changed the name of PRO's to "Quality Improvement Organizations" (QIO). Pursuant to both CMS contracts and memoranda of understanding with providers and Medicare+Choice organizations, QIO's are responsible for determining whether health care services under the Medicare program are reasonable and medically necessary. QIO's must also meet professionally accepted quality standards, and be provided in the most effective and economic setting.[5] In addition to their responsibilities for UM, QIO's must perform mandatory reviews of medical necessity determinations referred by regional offices which originate with intermediaries or carriers, review clinical data abstraction centers and certain referrals by Medicare+Choice organizations, as well as denial notices issued by hospitals, beneficiary complaints about the quality of services received, allegations of antidumping violations, and assistants at surgery requests for cataract operations.[6]

Medicare regulations contain very specific language regarding the application of UM processes by QIO's. Medicare UM is more specifically delineated than most state laws. For example, prior to reaching an initial determination, QIO's must promptly notify both the provider and the patient's attending physician of the proposed determination. They must also afford the provider or attending physicians the opportunity to discuss the matter with the QIO physician advisor to explain the nature of the patient's need for health care services.[7] The right of providers to discuss a patient's care with a QIO physician prior to the determination is consistent with most state laws, though plans need to be mindful of the impact of such discussions on mandatory time frames.

The QIO regulations contain detailed descriptions of the timing and content of denial determination notices. Notice must be delivered to beneficiaries, the physician, facility and fiscal intermediary and/or carrier, within the following timeframes: (i) for admission, on the first working day after the initial denial determination; (ii) for continued stay, by the first working day after the initial denial determination if the beneficiary is still in the facility and within 3 working days; (iii) for pre-procedure review, before the procedure is performed; (iv) for preadmission review, before admission; (v) if identification as a

Medicare program patient has been delayed, within three working days of identification; (vi) for retrospective review, within 3 working days of the initial denial determination; and (vii) for post-procedure review, within 3 working days of the initial denial determination.[8]

The regulations also addresses the content of the notice, including: (i) the reason for the initial denial determination or change; (ii) for day outliers in hospitals, the day on which the stay or services in the facility will not be approved as being reasonable and medically necessary or appropriate to the patients heath care needs; (iii) a statement regarding the right and location for a request for reconsideration and the deadline for filing.[9]

Like most state UM laws, Medicare QIO regulations mandate reviewer qualifications and participation. Only licensed physicians or dentists with active staff privileges in the QIO area can make initial denial determinations about services furnished, or proposed to be furnished, by a licensed physician or dentist, respectively. On the other hand, health care practitioners other than physicians may review services furnished by other practitioners in the same professional field. Initial denial determinations may not be made by anyone whose family member: (i) participated in developing or executing the beneficiary's treatment plan; (ii) is a member of the beneficiary's family; or (iii) is a governing body member, officer, partner, five percent or more owner, or managing employee in the health care facility where the services were or are to be furnished.[10]

In assessing the necessity and appropriateness of treatment or proposed treatment, the QIO must use national, or where appropriate, regional clinical guidelines and must consult with peers of practitioners who furnish services.

Should a beneficiary, provider or practitioner be dissatisfied with a QIO initial denial determination, they have a right to request reconsideration by the QIO that made the initial denial determination.[11] Requests for expedited reconsideration must be submitted within 3 days after the receipt of the notice of the initial denial determination. Other requests must be received within 60 days of receipt of notice of the initial determination.[12] Providers, beneficiaries and practitioners must have the opportunity to examine the material upon which a denial is based, but the QIO may not provide the record of the QIO deliberation, the identity of the QIO reviewers or consultants.[13]

The reconsideration reviewer must be qualified under the regulations to perform the initial review and must be a specialist in the type of services under review[14], but must not be the individual who made the initial denial

determination. When reconsidering the merits of the initial determination, the reviewer may consider the information that led to the initial determination, new information found in the medical records, or additional evidence submitted by a party.[15]

The reconsidered determination must be completed and the beneficiary notified:

➢ Within 3 working days after the QIO receives the request for reconsideration if (i) the beneficiary is still in the hospital and the reconsideration involves length of stay (LOS); or (ii) the reconsideration involves preadmission requests;

➢ Within 10 working days regarding a skilled nursing facility (SNF) LOS if the beneficiary is no longer in the SNF; and

➢ Within 30 working days if the request for reconsideration involves ambulatory or non-institutional services, (ii) the beneficiary is no longer a hospital or SNF inpatient for the stay in question, or (iii) the beneficiary does not request reconsideration in a timely manner.[16]

The notice of the reconsidered determination must contain the basis for the reconsidered determination, a detailed rational for the reconsidered determination, a statement explaining the Medicare payment consequences of the reconsidered determination, and a statement informing the parties of their appeal rights.[17]

> The QIO reconsidered determination is binding upon all parties to the reconsideration unless a hearing is requested or it is later reopened under the QIO's audit responsibilities.[18] If the amount in controversy is at least $200, a beneficiary (but not a provider or practitioner) who is dissatisfied with a QIO reconsidered determination may obtain a hearing by an administrative law judge on the following issues: (i) the reasonableness of the services; (ii) the medical necessity of the services; or (iii) the appropriateness of the setting in which the services were furnished.[19]

QIO determinations apply to Part A and Part B determinations. A different set of rules apply to utilization review under Medicare managed care programs.

5.4 Medicare Modernization Act
The MMA clarified the application of state law to Medicare Advantage Plans (formerly Medicare+Choice Plans) and consequently to Medicare managed care. The MMA amended the Medicare statute to provide that the Medicare managed care standards "shall supersede any state law or regulation (other than state licensing laws or state laws relating to plan solvency) with respect to

Medicare Advantage plans…"[20] This amendment replaced prior language which specifically provided that the Medicare law specifically superseded state laws governing "…coverage determinations (including related appeals and grievance processes)."[21] Arguably, the repealed language limited the application of state UM laws because the Medicare statute contained specific language providing for plan determinations.[22]

With the changes instituted by the MMA, it appears that the Medicare Advantage plan organization determination process as well as other medical necessity determinations might be subject to state rules governing UM, depending upon the meaning of "state licensing laws." This apparent redundancy is familiar to Medicaid plans. It means that Medicare Advantage Plans must be prepared to comply with both state and Medicare mandated UM processes. To further confuse the situation, for Regional Medicare Advantage Plans (which will cover more than one state) initial licensure will not be required for all states in a region. Moreover, the regional Medicare Advantage Plans will be in the same position as multi-state ERISA plans, with respect to the application of state law.

The following section summarizes the UM requirements for Medicare Advantage Plans.

5.4.1 Organization Determinations

Each Medicare Advantage plan must establish and maintain procedures for:

➤ Standard and expedited organization determinations;

➤ Standard and expedited appeals; and

➤ Grievances.

Medicare Advantage organizations must also provide written notification to their enrollees regarding the Medicare Advantage organization's available grievance and appeal procedures upon an adverse organization determination.[23]

The Act defines adverse determination to be whenever the Medicare Advantage organization decides not to provide or pay for a requested service, in whole or in part.[24] Organization determinations are any decisions (i.e., an approval or denial) made by the Medicare Advantage organization, or its delegated entity, with respect to the following:

➤ Payment for temporarily out of the area renal dialysis services;

➤ Payment for emergency services, post-stabilization care, or urgently needed services;

➤ Denial, refusal to authorize or reduction of payment for any other health services furnished by a provider (other than the Medicare Advantage organization), that the enrollee believes: (a) are covered under Medicare; (b) if not covered under Medicare, should have been furnished, arranged for, or reimbursed by the Medicare Advantage organization; (c) should be furnished or arranged by the organization at the level requested;

➤ Discontinuation of a service that the enrollee believes should be continued because they believe the service to be medically necessary; and

➤ Failure of the Medicare Advantage organization to approve, furnish, arrange for, or provide payment for health care services in a timely manner, or to provide the enrollee with timely notice of an adverse determination, such that a delay would adversely affect the health of the enrollee.[25]

Each Medicare Advantage organization must establish procedures for making timely organization determinations regarding the benefits an enrollee is entitled to receive under a Medicare Advantage plan including basic benefits, mandatory and optional supplemental benefits and the amount, if any, that the enrollee is required to pay for a health service.[26]

Once an organization determination has occurred, the appeals process is triggered when an enrollee believes the Medicare Advantage organization's decision is unfavorable. If a Medicare Advantage enrollee disputes the organization determination, the case would be handled using the federally mandated appeals process, though, as discussed above, even the Department of Health and Human Services has not determined whether or not state UM laws will apply under the MMA. If an enrollee complains about any other aspect of the Medicare Advantage organization (e.g. the manner in which care was provided), the Medicare Advantage organization must address the issue through the separate grievance process.[27]

5.4.2 Standard Time Frames for Organization Determinations

When an enrollee has made a request for a service, the Medicare Advantage organization must notify the enrollee of its determination as expeditiously as the enrollee's health condition requires, but no later than 14 calendar days after the date the organization receives the request for a standard organization determination. The Medicare Advantage organization may extend the time frame up to 14 calendar days. This extension is allowed if the enrollee requests the extension or if the organization justifies a need for additional information and documents how the delay is in the interest of the enrollee (e.g., the receipt of additional medical evidence from non-contract providers may change a Medicare Advantage organization's decision to deny). When the Medicare Advantage organization grants itself an extension to the deadline, it must notify the enrollee, in writing, of the reasons for the delay, and inform the enrollee of the right to file a grievance if he or she disagrees with the Medicare Advantage organization's decision to grant an extension. The Medicare Advantage organization must notify the enrollee, in writing, of its determination as expeditiously as the enrollee's health condition requires, but no later than the expiration of any extension that occurs, in accordance with the federal requirements.[28]

5.4.3 Written Notification by Medicare Advantage Organizations

If the Medicare Advantage organization decides to deny, in whole or in part, the services or payments, that is, issue an adverse organization determination, then it must give the enrollee a written notice of its determination. If the beneficiary has a representative, the representative must be sent a copy of the notice.

The written notice must include:

The specific reason for the denial that takes into account the enrollee's presenting medical condition, disabilities, and special language requirements, if any;

1) Information regarding the enrollee's right to a standard or expedited reconsideration and the right to appoint a representative to file an appeal on the enrollee's behalf (as mandated by 42 C.F.R. §§ 422.570 and 422.566(b)(3));

2) For service denials, a description of both the standard and expedited reconsideration processes and time frames, including conditions for obtaining an expedited reconsideration, and the other elements of the appeals process;

3) For payment denials, a description of the standard reconsideration process and time frames, and the rest of the appeals process; and

4) The beneficiary's right to submit additional evidence in writing or in person.[29]

5.4.4 Expediting Determinations

An enrollee or any physician (regardless of whether the physician is affiliated with the Medicare Advantage organization) may request that a Medicare Advantage organization expedite a medical necessity determination when the enrollee or his/her physician or the Medicare Advantage organization believes that waiting for a decision under the standard time frame could place the

enrollee's life, health, or ability to regain maximum function in serious jeopardy.[30]

Expedited determinations may not be requested for cases in which the only issue involves a claim for payment for services that the enrollee has already received. However, if a case includes both a payment denial and a pre-service denial, the enrollee has a right to request an expedited appeal for the pre-service denial.

When requesting an expedited determination, the enrollee or a physician must submit either an oral or written request directly to the organization, or if applicable, to the entity responsible for making the determination. A physician may also provide oral or written support for an enrollee's own request for an expedited determination.

Once such a request is made, the Medicare Advantage organization must automatically provide an expedited determination to any request made or supported by a physician. The physician must indicate, either orally or in writing, that applying the standard time for making a determination could seriously jeopardize the life or health of the enrollee or the enrollee's ability to regain maximum function. The physician need not be appointed as the enrollee's authorized representative in order to make the request.

For expedited requests made by an enrollee, the Medicare Advantage organization must expedite the review of a determination if the organization finds that the enrollee's health, life, or ability to regain maximum function may be jeopardized by waiting for a standard organization determination. If the Medicare Advantage organization decides to expedite the request, it must render a decision as expeditiously as the enrollee's health condition might require, but no later than 72 hours after receiving the enrollee's request.[31]

5.4.5 Defining the Medical Exigency Standard

The medical exigency standard requires a Medicare Advantage organization and CMS's independent review entity to make decisions as "expeditiously as the enrollee's health condition requires."[32] This standard requires that the Medicare Advantage organization or the independent entity apply, at a minimum, established, accepted standards of medical practice in assessing an individual's medical condition. Evidence of the individual's condition can be demonstrated by indications from the treating provider or from the individual's medical record (including such information as the individual's diagnosis, symptoms, or test results).

The medical exigency standard was established by regulation to ensure that Medicare Advantage organizations would develop a system for determining the urgency of both standard and expedited requests for services, triage incoming requests against pre-established criteria, and then give each request priority according to that system. That is, Medicare Advantage organizations must treat every case in a manner that is appropriate to its medical particulars or urgency. Medicare Advantage organizations should not systematically take the maximum time permitted for service-related decisions.[33]

5.4.6 Action Following Denial for Expedited Review

If a Medicare Advantage organization denies a request for an expedited organization determination, it must automatically transfer the request to the standard time frame and make a determination within 14 calendar days (the 14-day period starts when the request for an expedited determination is received by the Medicare Advantage organization), give the enrollee prompt oral notice of the denial including the enrollee's rights, and subsequently deliver to the enrollee, within 3 calendar days, a written letter of the enrollee's rights that:

1) Explains that the organization will automatically transfer and process the request using the 14-day time frame for standard determinations;

2) Informs the enrollee of the right to file an expedited grievance if he or she disagrees with the organization's decision not to expedite the determination;

3) Informs the enrollee of the right to resubmit a request for an expedited determination and that if the enrollee gets any physician's support indicating that applying the standard time frame for making determinations could seriously jeopardize the life or health of the enrollee or the enrollee's ability to regain maximum function, the request will be expedited automatically; and

4) Provides instructions about the expedited grievance process and its time frames.[34]

5.4.7 Action on Expedited Determinations

If an organization grants a request for an expedited determination, the determination must be made in accordance with the following requirements:

➤ A Medicare Advantage organization that approves a request for expedited determination must make the determination and notify the enrollee and the physician involved, as appropriate, of its decision. Whether the decision is adverse or favorable, the Medicare Advantage organization must make its decision as expeditiously as the enrollee's health condition requires, but no later than 72 hours after receiving the request.

➤ The Medicare Advantage organization will extend the 72-hour time frame by up to 14 calendar days if the

enrollee requests the extension. The Medicare Advantage organization also may extend the time frame by up to 14 calendar days if the organization justifies a need for additional information and documents how the delay is in the interest of the enrollee. The Medicare Advantage organization must notify the enrollee of its determination as expeditiously as the enrollee's health condition requires, but no later than the expiration of the extension.

➤ If the Medicare Advantage organization first notifies the enrollee of its expedited determination orally, it then must mail written confirmation to the enrollee within 72 hours of the oral notification.[35]

5.4.8 Notification of the Result of an Expedited Organization Determination

The Medicare+Choice Manual provides a standardized denial notice form, written in a manner that is understandable to the enrollee and provides:

➤ The specific reason for the denial that takes into account the enrollee's presenting medical condition, disabilities, and special language requirements, if any;

➤ Information regarding the enrollee's right to a standard or expedited reconsideration and the right to appoint a representative to file an appeal on the enrollee's behalf;

➤ A description of both the standard and expedited reconsideration processes should include conditions for obtaining an expedited reconsideration, and the other elements of the appeals process; and

The beneficiary's right to submit additional evidence in writing or in person.[36]

5.5 Appeals

An adverse organization determination by a Medicare Advantage Plan triggers the beneficiary's right to up to 5 appeals. The levels need only be sequentially followed if the original denial continues to be upheld at each level by the reviewing entity. These levels of appeal are a:

1) Reconsideration of an adverse organization determination by the Medicare Advantage organization;

2) Reconsideration of an adverse organization determination by the independent review entity;

3) Hearing by an Administrative Law Judge (ALJ), if at least $100 is at issue;

4) Review by Departmental Appeals Board (DAB); and

5) Judicial Review, if at least $1000 is at issue.

5.6 Reconsideration

Denial notices sent by Medicare Advantage organizations are required to inform the enrollee of the right to reconsideration, and the right to be represented by an attorney or other representative in the reconsideration process. Instructions on how and where to file a request for reconsideration must also be included. The reconsideration consists of a review of an adverse organization determination or termination of services decision, the evidence and findings upon which it was based, and any other evidence that the parties submit or that is obtained by the Medicare Advantage organization, the QIO, or the independent review entity.[37]

5.6.1 Good Cause Extension

If a party shows good cause, the Medicare Advantage organization may extend the time frame for filing a request for reconsideration.[38]

5.6.2 Opportunity to Submit Evidence

The Medicare Advantage organization must provide the parties to the reconsideration reasonable opportunity to present evidence and allegations of fact or law related to the issues in dispute. Parties must be allowed but are not required to present additional evidence in person or in writing.[39] The Medicare Advantage organization must use the evidence in the reconsideration process. In addition, the Medicare Advantage organization must, upon an enrollee's request, provide the enrollee with a copy of the contents of the case file, including but not limited to, a copy of supporting medical records and other pertinent information used to support the decision. Moreover, HIPPA and other federal and state privacy laws apply.[40]

5.6.3 Reconsideration- Reviewer and Clinical Standards

The Medicare Advantage organization must designate someone other than the person involved in making the initial organization determination to review the adverse organization determination upon reconsideration. If the original denial was based on a lack of medical necessity, then the reconsideration must be performed by a physician with expertise in the field of medicine that is appropriate for the services at issue.[41] The reconsidering physician need not, in all cases, be of the same specialty or subspecialty as the treating physician but must have the training and expertise necessary to evaluate the necessity of the service.[42]

In cases involving emergency services, the Medicare Advantage organization must apply the prudent layperson standard when making the reconsideration determination.[43]

5.6.4 Time Frames for Reconsiderations

a) *Standard Reconsideration.* The Medicare Advantage Organization must make its reconsidered determination as expeditiously as the enrollee's health condition requires. This must be no later than 30 calendar days from the date the Medicare Advantage organization receives the request for a standard reconsideration.[44]

b) *Expedited Reconsiderations.* If the Medicare Advantage organization approves a request for an expedited reconsideration, then it must complete the expedited reconsideration and give the enrollee (and the physician involved, as appropriate) notice of its decision as expeditiously as the enrollee's health condition requires, but no later than 72 hours after receiving the request. If the request is made or supported by a physician, the Medicare Advantage organization must grant the expedited reconsideration request when the physician indicates that the life or health of the enrollee, or the enrollee's ability to regain maximum function could be jeopardized by applying the standard time frame in the processing of the reconsideration request.[45]

5.7 Reconsideration by Independent Review Entity

If upon reconsideration, the Medicare Advantage organization affirms, in whole or in part, its adverse organization determination, the issues that remain in dispute must be reviewed and resolved by an independent, outside entity that contracts with CMS. The independent outside entity must conduct the review as expeditiously as the enrollee's health condition requires.[46]

5.7.1 Forwarding Adverse Reconsiderations to the Independent Review Entity

The Medicare Advantage organization must forward the enrollee's case file within the following time frames:

➢ **For standard requests for service,** the Medicare Advantage organization must forward an enrollee's case file to the independent review entity as expeditiously as the enrollee's health condition requires. This must be completed no later than 30 calendar days from the date the Medicare Advantage organization receives the enrollee's request for reconsideration (or no later than upon the expiration of an extension).

➢ **For expedited reconsiderations,** the Medicare Advantage organization must forward the enrollee's case file to the independent review entity as expeditiously as the enrollee's health condition requires, but no later than within 24 hours of affirmation of its adverse expedited organization determination.

affirmation of its adverse expedited organization determination.

> **For requests for payment,** the Medicare Advantage organization must forward the enrollee's case file to the independent review entity no later than 60 calendar days from the date it receives the request for a standard reconsideration.[47]

The independent review entity must conduct the reconsideration as expeditiously as the enrollee's health condition requires and should observe the same time frames as required for Medicare Advantage organizations. When the independent review entity completes its reconsidered determination, it is responsible for notifying all the parties of the reconsidered determination, and for sending a copy of the reconsidered determination to the appropriate CMS Regional Office. This notice must include:

1) Specific reasons for the entity's decisions;

2) Notice of the parties right to an ALJ hearing if the amount in controversy is $100 or more, and; if the decision is adverse (any reconsideration decision short of complete reverse the organization's adverse determination); and

3) Procedures that the parties must follow to obtain an ALJ hearing.[48]

5.8 Administrative Law Judge (ALJ) Hearings

If the amount remaining in controversy is $100 or more, any party to the reconsideration (with the exception of the Medicare Advantage organization) dissatisfied with the reconsidered determination has a right to a hearing before an ALJ.[49]

The parties to an ALJ hearing are the same as those for the reconsideration, and also include the Medicare Advantage organization and any other person or entity whose rights with respect to the reconsideration may be affected by the hearing, as determined by the ALJ. Although the Medicare Advantage organization does not have a right to request an ALJ hearing, it must be made a party to the hearing. Fees for services provided by the Medicare Advantage organization representative are not subject to regulations at 20 C.F.R. § 404.1720, which govern appointment of representatives and payment of fees to representatives at the ALJ hearing level of appeal.

5.8.1 Determination of Amount in Controversy

The ALJ determines whether the amount remaining in controversy (for both Part A and Part B services) is $100 or more. For cases involving denied services, the projected value of the services is used to determine whether the amount in controversy is $100 or more. For cases involving optional or supplemental benefits, but not employer-sponsored benefits limited to employer group members, the projected value of those benefits is used to determine whether the amount in controversy is $100 or more.

The Medicare Advantage organization is expected to cooperate with the ALJ and assist in the computation of the amount in controversy. The hearing may be conducted on more than one claim at a time (i.e., the enrollee may have several claims involving several issues). The enrollee may combine claims to meet the $100 limitation, if the following requirements are met: (i) the claims must belong to the same beneficiary; (ii) the claims must each have received a determination through the independent review entity reconsideration process; (iii) the 60-day filing time limit must be met for all claims involved; and (iv) the hearing request must identify all claims.

If, after a hearing is initiated, the ALJ finds that the amount in controversy is less than $100, the hearing will be discontinued and no ruling will be made on the substantive issues raised in the appeal. Any party may request a review of the a hearing dismissal action through the Departmental Appeals Board (DAB) review.[50]

5.9 Departmental Appeals Board (DAB) Review

Any party dissatisfied with the ALJ hearing decision (including the Medicare Advantage organization) may request that the DAB review the ALJ's decision or dismissal. Regulations located at 20 C.F.R. §§ 404.967 through 404.984 regarding Appeals Council Review apply to DAB review for matters addressed in this chapter.[51]

5.10 Judicial Review

Any party, including the Medicare Advantage organization (upon notifying all the other parties), may request judicial review of an ALJ decision if: (i) the DAB denied the parties request for review; and (ii) the amount in controversy is $1,000 or more.[52] In addition, any party, including the Medicare Advantage organization (upon notifying all the other parties), may request judicial review of a DAB decision if: (i)The DAB denied the parties request for review; or (ii) it is the final decision of CMS; and (iii) the amount in controversy is $1,000 or more.[53]

The enrollee may combine claims to meet the $1,000 amount in controversy requirement. To meet the requirement:

1) All claims must belong to the same enrollee;

2) The DAB must have acted on all the claims;

3) The enrollee must meet the 60-day filing time limit for all claims; and

4) The requests must identify all claims.

A party may not obtain judicial review unless the DAB has acted on the case - either in response to a request for review or on its own motion.[54]

A party must file a civil action in a district court of the United States in accordance with § 205(g) of the Act (*see* 20 C.F.R. § 422.210 for a description of the procedures to follow in requesting judicial review). The action should be initiated in the judicial district in which the enrollee lives or where the Medicare Advantage organization has its principal place of business. If neither the organization nor the member is in such judicial district, the action should be filed in the United States District Court for the District of Columbia.[55]

5.11 Notice of Discharge and Medicare Appeal Rights (NODMAR)

Medicare Advantage organizations that make adverse organization determinations regarding a discharge from a hospital must provide the enrollee with a Notice of Discharge and Medicare Appeal Rights (NODMAR)[56] (and hospitals that have been delegated responsibility by a Medicare Advantage organization to make the discharge/noncoverage decision) will distribute the NODMAR only when the:

➢ Enrollee expresses dissatisfaction with his or her impending discharge; or

➢ Medicare Advantage organization (or the hospital that has been delegated the responsibility) is not discharging the individual, but no longer intends to continue coverage of the inpatient stay.

The Medicare Advantage organization (or hospital that has been delegated the responsibility) is not required to issue the NODMAR if the enrollee dies while in an inpatient hospital setting.[57]

5.11.1 Requesting Immediate Quality Improvement Organization (QIO) Review of Inpatient Hospital Care

An enrollee remaining in the hospital that wishes to appeal the Medicare Advantage organization's discharge decision that inpatient care is no longer necessary must request immediate QIO review of the determination in accordance with this section's requirements. An enrollee will not incur any additional financial liability if the:

➢ Enrollee remains in the hospital as an inpatient;

➢ Enrollee submits the request for immediate review to the QIO that has an agreement with the hospital;

➢ Request is made either in writing, by telephone or fax; and

➢ Request is received by noon of the first working day after the enrollee receives written notice of the

Medicare Advantage organization's determination that the hospital stay is no longer necessary.[58]

5.12 Medicaid[59]

The Medicaid program is a joint federal and state undertaking whose purpose is to help with medical costs for some people with low incomes and limited resources and/or who are disabled. Under federal law, a Medicaid state plan must provide for UR to safeguard against unnecessary utilization and to assure that payments are consistent with efficiency, economy, and quality of care.[60] The program must include specific requirements for the control of institutional services and outpatient drug use. A state may meet its UR requirements by assuming direct responsibility for assuring the review requirements are met or the requirements may be deemed met if the state contracts with a PRO to perform the review.[61]

5.12.1 Medicaid Fee-for-Service

Under Medicaid regulations, states must establish and use written criteria for evaluating the appropriateness and quality of Medicaid services.[62] In addition, each state Medicaid agency must have an agreement with the state health agency or other appropriate state medical agency to establish a plan for the review by professional health personnel of the appropriateness and quality of Medicaid services.[63] States must have in place a post-payment review process that allows for development and review of utilization profiles, provider services profiles, and criteria to identify exceptions. This enables the state to correct inappropriate utilization practices of recipients and providers.[64]

5.12.2 Inpatient Services

A state's UR program must provide for a review and/or screening for admissions to any hospital, intermediate care facility for the mentally retarded (ICF/MR), or hospital for mental diseases. The criteria for these admissions are to be established by impartial medical and other professional personnel.[65] For cases in which payment for inpatient hospital services, services in an ICF/MR, or inpatient mental hospital services is made under the state plan, a physician (or, in the case of skilled nursing facility services or intermediate care facility services, a physician, nurse practitioner, or clinical nurse specialist who is not an employee of the facility) must certify and periodically recertify that services are or were required to be provided on an inpatient basis.[66]

For inpatient hospital services, recertifications are required at least every 60 days. In the case of services in an ICF/MR, recertifications are required at least 60 days after the date of initial certification and then at 180 days, at 12 months, at 18 months, and at 24 months after the date of initial certification. Recertifications are required at

12-month intervals for inpatient stays beyond 24 months after the date of initial certification.[67]

Those services that are provided must be furnished under a plan established, periodically reviewed, and evaluated by a physician, or, in the case of skilled nursing facility services or intermediate care facility services, a physician, or a nurse practitioner or a clinical nurse specialist who is not an employee of the facility.[68]

Federal Medicaid law prohibits federal financial participation for Medicaid payments for hospital care unless the hospital has in effect a UR plan that meets the Medicare requirements (set forth above). However, HHS may waive this requirement if the state has UR requirements superior in effectiveness to those for Medicare.[69]

5.12.3 Drug Use Review

States must provide a Medicaid outpatient drug use review (DUR) program to assure that prescriptions are appropriate, medically necessary, and unlikely to cause adverse medical results.[70] Each state must provide for the establishment of the DUR board of health care professionals with specified expertise to assist in implementing the DUR program.

Each state's DUR program must provide for:

➢ *Prospective review* of drug therapy before each prescription is filled or delivered to a beneficiary to screen for potential duplication, drug-disease contradictions, or drug-drug interactions;

➢ *Retrospective review* of claims and data, through mechanized claims processing or otherwise, to identify patterns of waste, fraud, abuse, gross overuse, or inappropriate or medically unnecessary care among physicians, pharmacists, and beneficiaries;

➢ *Assessment of usage* against predetermined standards on indicators such as therapeutic appropriateness, under-utilization, over-utilization, duration of treatment, etc.; and

➢ *Education of practitioners* on common drug therapy problems.[71]

5.13 Medicaid Managed Care

Many states use managed care as a vehicle for providing health coverage to eligible populations while controlling the cost of providing Medicaid services. Federal law currently provides little guidance regarding the conduct of UR under Medicaid managed care programs.

The federal regulations governing Medicaid managed care carefully straddle the Utilization Management conundrum. State contracts with Medicaid managed care organizations must require that services be provided "in

an amount, duration, and scope" that is "no less than the amount, duration and scope for the same services in a fee for service setting." At the same time, the state contract with a Medicaid managed care organization "may place appropriate limits on a service…on the basis of medical necessity…for the purpose of utilization control."[72]

Under the regulations, MCO's are required to provide services as expeditiously as an enrollee's health requires, but within time frames established by the states, which may not exceed 14 days after a request for the services is made.[73] This section applies to both state and federal laws to the Medicaid managed care organizations utilization management process. If a physician indicates or the MCO determines that following the ordinary time frame could seriously jeopardize the enrollee's life or health or ability to regain maximum function, the MCO must expedite the determination within 3 working days after receipt of the request.[74]

MCO's must also generally resolve grievances as expeditiously as an enrollee's health requires, but no later than 30 days after the Medicaid managed care organization receives the grievance.[75] Further, MCO's must have a process for the expedited resolution of grievances as an enrollee's health requires, but generally no later than 3 working days after the Medicaid managed care organization receives the grievance.[76] Standard grievances must be resolved within 90 days or some shorter state time frame.[77] The grievance process must be conducted using impartial individuals who were not involved in the initial decision. In the case of a denial based on medical necessity, the individual must be a physician with appropriate expertise in the field relevant to the enrollee's condition or disease.[78]

A state must either permit an enrollee to request a fair hearing on a grievance at any time, or provide for a fair hearing following an MCO adverse decision on a grievance.[79] The regulation would prohibit MCO's from compensating individuals or entities conducting utilization management in a manner that provides incentives for the individual or entity to deny, limit, or discontinue medically necessary services to any enrollee.[80]

Often states apply both state UM processes and the Medicaid mandated processes, offering enrollees separate opportunities to file grievances.

5.14 Conclusion

Over the last four decades, both Medicare and Medicaid have gradually adopted certain aspects of utilization management. Under these two programs the statues and regulations applicable to each have been amended to provide detailed guidelines for the process of utilization management.

1   Section 521 of BIPA contained significant structural and procedural changes to the existing claims appeals process. Due to budgetary limitations, CMS declined to implement many of the changes. CMS Ruling No. 02-1, 10/01/2002.

2   42 U.S.C. § 1395y(a)(1).

3   42 C.F.R. § 421.200(a)(2) for carriers and 42 C.F.R. § 421.100(a)(2) for intermediaries.

4   SSA § 1874A.

5   42 U.S.C. § 1320c-3(a)(1); 42 C.F.R. § 476.72.

6   Quality Improvement Organization Manual § 4070, summarizing statutory requirements.

7   42 C.F.R. § 476.93.

8   42 C.F.R. § 476.94(a).

9   42 C.F.R. § 476.94(b).

10   42 C.F.R. § 476.98.

11   42 C.F.R. § 478.16.

12   42 C.F.R. § 478.20.

13   42 C.F.R. § 478.24.

14   42 C.F.R. § 478.28.

15   42 C.F.R. § 478.30.

16   42 C.F.R. § 478.32.

17   42 C.F.R. § 478.34.

18   42 C.F.R. § 478.38.

19   42 C.F.R. § 478.40.

20   2242 U.S.C. § 1395w-26(b)(3)(B).

21   42 U.S.C. § 1395w-26(b)(3)(B)(iii) REPEALED.

22   The Department of Health and Human Services acknowledges that the breadth of preemption remains unclear and indicated that it will both consult with state agencies and accept public comment on this issue. 69 FR 46926-7.

23   42 C.F.R. § 422.588.

24   42 C.F.R. § 422.588.

25   42 C.F.R. § 422.566(b).

26   42 C.F.R. § 422.566(a).

27   Medicare+Choice Manual § 30.

28   42 C.F.R. § 422.568.

29   42 C.F.R. § 422.568(e); Medicare+Choice Manual § 2.2.1.

30   42 C.F.R. § 422.570(c)(2).

31   42 C.F.R. § 422.572; Medicare+Choice Manual § 50.

32   This standard is set forth in regulation at 422.568(a) (standard organization determination), 422.572(a) (expedited organization determination), 422.5 90(a) (standard reconsideration), 422.590(d)(l) (expedited reconsideration) and 422.592(b) (for reconsidered determination by independent review entity), 422.618(a) (Medicare Advantage organization effectuating standard reconsidered determination), 422.61 8(b)(1) (effectuation requirements for reversals by the independent review entity), 422.618(c) (effectuation requirements for reversals by the ALJ or higher levels of appeal), 422.6 19 (effectuation requirements for expedited reconsidered determinations), 422.619(a) (Medicare Advantage organization effectuating expedited reconsidered determinations), 422.6 19(b) (effectuation requirements for reversals by the independent review entity for expedited reconsidered determinations), 422.6 19(c) (effectuation requirements for reversals by the ALJ or higher levels of appeal for expedited reconsidered determinations).

33   Medicare+Choice Manual § 50.2.1.

34   42 C.F.R. § 570(d).

35   42 C.F.R. § 572(a).

36   42 C.F.R. § 422.572(e); Medicare+Choice Manual § 50.5.

37   42 C.F.R. § 422.580.

38   42 C.F.R. § 422.582(c).

39   42 C.F.R. § 422.586.

40   Medicare+Choice Manual § 70.5.

41   42 C.F.R. § 422.590(g).

42   Medicare+Choice Manual § 70.6.1.

43   Medicare+Choice Manual § 70.6.

44   42 C.F.R. § 422.590(a); Medicare+Choice Manual § 70.7.1.

45   42 C.F.R. § 422.590(d).

46   42 CFR §422.592.

47   Medicare+Choice Manual § 80.4.

48   Medicare+Choice Manual § 90.

49   42 C.F.R. § 422.600.

50   42 C.F.R. § 422.602; Medicare+Choice Manual § 100.

51   42 .C.F.R § 422.608.

52   42 C.F.R. § 422.612(a).

53   42 C.F.R. § 422.612(b).

54   Medicare+Choice Manual § 120.

55   42 C.F.R. § 422.612; Medicare+Choice Manual § 120.1.

56   42 C.F.R. § 422.620.

57 Medicare+Choice Manual § 150.2.

58 42 C.F.R. § 422.622.

59 The description of the Medicaid section is based, in part, on Marc Joffe's contribution on the subject to the UM Guide Second Edition (2000).

60 Section 1902(a)(30) of the Social Security Act, 42 U.S.C. § 1396a(a)(30) (2004).

61 42 C.F.R. § 456.2.

62 42 C.F.R. § 456.5.

63 42 C.F.R. § 456.6.

64 42 C.F.R. § 456.23.

65 Section 1902(a)(30)(B) of the Social Security Act, 42 U.S.C. § 1396a(a)(30) (2000).

66 Section 1902(a)(44)(A) of the Social Security Act, 42 U.S.C. § 1396a(a)(44)(A) (2000).

67 Section 1903(g)(6)(A) and (B) of the Social Security Act, 42 U.S.C. § 1396b(g)(6)(A) and (B).

68 Section 1902(a)(44) of the Social Security Act, 42 U.S.C. § 1396a(a)(44).

69 Section 1903(i)(4) of the Social Security Act, 42 U.S.C. § 1396b(i)(4).

70 Section 1927(g) of the Social Security Act, 42 U.S.C. § 1396r-8(g).

71 Section 1927(g)(2) of the Social Security Act, 42 U.S.C. § 1396r-8(g)(2).

72 42 C.F.R § 438.210(a).

73 42 C.F.R § 438.210(d).

74 42 C.F.R. § 438.210.

75 42 C.F.R. § 438.228.

76 42 C.F.R. § 438.408.

77 42 C.F.R. § 438.408(b).

78 63 Fed. Reg. 42022 (to be codified at 42 C.F.R. § 438.406).

79 63 Fed. Reg. 52022 (to be codified at 42 C.F.R. § 438.402(d)).

80 63 Fed. Reg. 52022 (to be codified at 42 C.F.R. § 438.410(e)).

6.0: Utilization Management Under ERISA Plans

Howard Burde, JD, and Guy D'Andrea

6.1 Introduction

Over 60% of health plans in the United States are governed by The Employee Retirement Income Security Act of 1974[1] (ERISA). With attention on ERISA devoted mostly toward preemption issues, the ERISA regulations governing utilization management are often ignored. Yet, most health plans are subject to ERISA regulations governing Utilization Management found in the ERISA Benefit Claims Procedure Regulation.[2]

The U.S. Department of Labor's (DOL) ERISA's new Benefit Claims Procedure Regulation[3] (DOL Regulation), which implements UM standards under ERISA for the first time, applies to all "group health plans," defined as DOL, those plans which cover expenses related to the "diagnosis, cure, mitigation, treatment or prevention of disease."[4] As a result, employer-sponsored health plans are subject to the DOL Regulation irrespective of whether the health care arrangement is self-funded by the employer or underwritten by a third party insurer.[5]

The January 1, 2003 implementation of the DOL Regulation significantly altered the UM regulatory environment for all employer-sponsored plans. Prior to the new federal regulation, most UM regulation existed at the state level for commercially-insured arrangements (and for the Medicare and Medicaid programs). Self-insured plans were exempted from most of these requirements, but now have to comply with the DOL Regulation. For those employer-sponsored plans that are underwritten by an insurance company, these plans now must comply with the applicable state laws and the DOL Regulation. In these cases, the plans must reconcile the regulations in each state where they operate with the new federal requirements.[6]

6.2 Background on ERISA

ERISA covers both pension plans and welfare benefit plans. ERISA defines welfare benefit plan to include employment based medical, dental, vision, and hospitalization benefits:

> …any plan, fund, or program, which was heretofore or is hereafter established or maintained by an employer or by an employee organization, or by both, …for the purpose of providing for its participants or their beneficiaries, through the purchase of insurance or otherwise, medical, surgical, or hospital care or benefits, or benefits in the event of sickness, accident, disability, death…[7]

ERISA applies to group health plans that are sponsored by employers, unions and jointly administered funds; and ERISA covers both self-insured and fully-insured arrangements. ERISA does not apply to non-group or individual health coverage arrangements.

ERISA requires that each employee benefit plan describe: (1) procedures for the allocation of responsibilities for the financing operation and administration of the plan; (2) the administrators of the plan; and (3) eligibility criteria.

6.3 Fiduciary Status

The individuals or entities responsible for the administration of an ERISA welfare benefit plan are called fiduciaries. ERISA defines fiduciary as any person or entity that:

> (E)xercises discretionary authority or control regarding management of the plan, exercises any authority or control involving management or disposition of its assets, and has discretionary authority or responsibility in the administration of the plan.[8]

A fiduciary status can depend on whether the functions are discretionary or ministerial. According to the DOL, however, a fiduciary status will not arise from conducting tasks within the framework of policies, interpretations, rules, practices, and procedures made by others such as determining eligibility, calculating service credits or benefits, or simply by processing claims.[9]

DOL regulations provide that a party with authority to review and decide upon denied claims is a fiduciary for purposes of the ERISA claims review requirements.[10] Therefore, a person or party conducting UM will be deemed an ERISA fiduciary and will be subject to federal regulatory requirements.

Being defined as having fiduciary status is relevant with respect to the entity's responsibility for the plan and any associated liability. This is especially true for the duties required for claims determinations. ERISA fiduciaries are required to act:

➤ Solely in the interest of the participants and beneficiaries;

➤ For the exclusive purposes of providing benefits to participants and their beneficiaries and defraying reasonable expenses of administering the plan[11]; in accordance with the documents and instruments governing the plan insofar as such documents and instruments are consistent with ERISA, and without any conflict of interest. This is referred to under the law as the "exclusive purpose" rule and it is designed to ensure that fiduciaries acting on behalf of the plan do not have competing loyalties. The most common violation of the exclusive purpose rule occurs when a fiduciary acts to benefit a third party, such as a plan sponsor, to the detriment of a plan participant. If the UM provider acts on behalf of the managed care organization, it could be viewed as a breach of fiduciary responsibility.

➤ With a "care, skill, procedure and diligence that a prudent man, acting in a like capacity and familiar with such matters, would use."[12] This provision, known as the "Prudent Expert" rule, provides the basis for determining who may act as a reviewer of a claim for benefits under an ERISA plan.

6.4 ERISA Claims Procedure

Any entity or person performing UM is a fiduciary under ERISA. In this case, the health care organization or individual must act in the best interest of the person covered by the plan, for the purpose of providing benefits and defraying the cost of the plan; and must act as a "prudent expert." The prudent expert rule can be interpreted in the UM context as requiring the appropriate licensure and credentialing of physicians and UM reviewers who make medical necessity determinations.

To implement these statutory provisions, the DOL has promulgated the DOL Regulations in a manner similar to (if not more descriptive than) most state UM Laws. The 2 main components of the regulations mandate that every employee benefit plan shall:

➤ Provide adequate notice in writing to any participant or beneficiary whose claim for benefits under the plan has been denied, setting forth the reasons for such denial, written in a manner calculated to be understood by the participant; and

➤ Afford a reasonable opportunity to any participant whose claim for benefits has been denied for a full and fair review by the appropriate named fiduciary of the decision denying the claim.[13]

The DOL Regulations, which were effective for all covered benefit plans by January 1, 2003, provide detailed guidance for plans to develop claims and UM processes. These regulations set out the minimum requirements for the filing of benefit claims, and the notification of adverse benefit determinations and their method of appeal. In November of 2000, the DOL published final regulations revising the minimum requirements for benefit claims procedures. The DOL Regulations changed rules that

were in effect since 1977. Indeed, the 1977 era regulation still remains applicable for pension plans and other plans that are not either group health or disability plans. The new DOL Regulation substantially changed and expanded the requirements for claims benefits processing to include shorter timeframes for decision-making, new procedural standards for appeal of denied claims, and full disclosure to claimants.

The DOL Regulation ensures the prompt approval of health and disability claims that otherwise would have been wrongly denied.[14] The stated rationale for the Claims Regulation was to improve health care quality by averting harmful inappropriate delays and denials of health benefits, thereby yielding substantial social benefits such as the delivery of more beneficial healthcare which will improve health benefit claimants' health overall, productivity and quality of life and possibly also reduce the need for health care later in life.[15] Optimistically, the DOL concluded that these regulations would create standardization and therefore "more efficient labor and insurance outlets," which should facilitate more and better health and disability coverage.[16] The specific elements of this regulation are discussed in more detail below.

The DOL Regulation provides minimum procedure requirements for the filing of benefit claims, notification of benefit determinations and appeals of adverse benefit determinations. In doing so, it addresses the same issues covered by most state UM laws, namely: definition of determinations; criteria for review; reviewer qualifications, notifications; timelines; and appeals. The nomenclature, however, differs. Additionally, these procedures differ for health and disability benefits. This discussion below focuses solely on health UM services.

6.4.1 Claims for Benefits

While state UM laws often refer to "benefit determinations," and the Medicare Managed Care Regulations refer to the same decisions as an "organization determinations," ERISA refers to the decisions as "adverse benefit determinations." Under ERISA requests for benefits are called "claims for benefits" and are defined as follows:

> …a request for a plan benefit or benefits made by a claimant in accordance with a plan's reasonable procedure for filing benefit claims. …Claims for benefits include pre-service claims…and post-service claims…[17]

To expand on this definition, a claim for benefit is simply a request for benefits within a plan's procedures which meet the minimum standards of the regulations. These procedures must appear in the summary plan description that is distributed to participants and beneficiaries.[18]

Naturally, the existence of a claims procedure acknowledges that plans will deny some claims for benefits. Under ERISA, such a denial is known as an "adverse benefit determination,"[19] which may include a denial of a benefit, the termination of a benefit (i.e., during the course of treatment), the reduction of a benefit or the failure to provide or approve a benefit in whole or in part, or the failure to make payment in whole or in part, for a benefit.[20]

There are many legitimate reasons for a plan to issue an adverse benefit determination, including but not limited to:

➤ Lack of coverage of the benefit in the plan;

➤ Exhaustion of the plan's maximum benefit;

➤ Lack of eligibility for plan benefits or limitations on coverage; and

➤ Lack of medical necessity.

It is determinations related to "lack of medical necessity" with which we are most concerned in a UM context.

6.4.2 Reasonable Claims Procedures

For a plan's claims procedures to be "reasonable," they may not contain any provision that unduly inhabits or hampers the initiation or processing of claims for benefits."[21] Unreasonable provisions or practices are those that would hamper or unduly inhibit the initiation or processing of a benefit claim, such as requiring the payment of a fee or costs as a condition of making a claim, or a fee for appealing an adverse determination. Other unreasonable practices include denying a claim for failure to obtain prior approval when the circumstances would make a prior approval impossible in an emergency, or when the claimant is unconscious and in need of immediate care.[22]

6.4.3 Initial Determinations

All claims benefit reviews involve some form of initial determination. The time period permitted for making an initial claim decision or request for authorization depends on the nature of that claim.

Obviously, the DOL Regulations require that urgent care claims be handled differently. Urgent care claims occur when the normal application and decision time period could jeopardize the life or health of the claimant, or, in the opinion of the claimant's physician, subject the claimant to severe pain which cannot be adequately managed without the disputed treatment. Initial determinations with respect to an urgent care pre-service claim must be made as soon as possible but not later than 72 hours after the request for authorization.[23]

Moreover, the timeframes for claims for benefits under a group health plan will also differ depending on whether the claim is "pre-service" or "post-service." If a claim is filed pre-service, the fiduciary must notify the claimant of the determination within a reasonable timeframe based on medical circumstances but not later than 15 days of the receipt of the initial claim. Post-service claims are subject to a 30-day limit for initial determinations. For concurrent care, the plan must provide sufficient notice, at least 24 hours, before a reduction or termination of an ongoing course of treatment. Any reduction or termination of an ongoing course of treatment will be considered an adverse benefit determination regardless of whether or not an additional claim is filed.

6.4.4 Timeframes, Delays, Additional Information

Under DOL Regulation, a plan must make an initial claim determination within the specified time period even if it hasn't received all of the information necessary to make that determination. The initial determination period concerning a pre- or post-service claim may be extended up to 15 days if circumstances beyond the plan's control prevent it from making a determination within the mandated time period. Should this occur, the plan must notify the claimant of both the reason for the extension and provide a date by which it expects to reach a decision. This notification must be accomplished prior to the expiration of the period for making its initial determination. A claimant may also voluntarily agree to extend the applicable time period for the plan to make its initial determination.

Should a claimant not provide the needed information in order to make a determination, the plan can either deny the claim or give the claimant at least 45 days to provide that information. If the plan elects to give the claimant additional time to file the required information, the time period for issuing a decision is suspended while awaiting that information. The time period will be reduced by the elapsed time from the date the plan receives the incomplete claim and the date it notifies the claimant of the need for additional information.

A notice of time extension must include a warning that the claim will be denied if the information is not provided within the specified time period. If the claimant fails to properly submit a pre-service or urgent claim or fails to provide complete information, the plan must notify the claimant within 5 days for a pre-service claim and within 24 hours after receiving an urgent care claim. The plan must permit the claimant 48 hours to provide information required to make a decision concerning an urgent claim and then render its decision within 48 hours after receiving that information. The regulations, therefore, provide an additional 24 hours to review new information, even regarding an urgent care claim.[24]

6.5 Notices of Claims Determinations

The DOL regulations are as prescriptive as any state law regarding the manner and content of the notice of claims determinations. A notice of claims determination must explain why a claim was denied, identify the relevant plan provision used as the basis for the denial, and outline the plan's appeal procedure. The notice of an adverse claim determination must also include a copy or reference to rules, guidelines, protocols, and limitations in the plan which provided a basis for that determination.

More specifically, the DOL regulations state that the notification of an adverse determination must set forth the following:

➤ Specific reason or reasons for the adverse determination;

➤ Specific plan provisions on which the adverse determination is based;

➤ Description of any additional information or material necessary to perfect the claim and an explanation of why such material is necessary;

➤ Description of the plan's review procedures and time limits, including a statement regarding a claimant's right to bring a civil action;

➤ Identification of any intended rule, guideline, protocol or criterion relied upon in making the determination;

➤ If the adverse determination is based on medical necessity or experimental treatment or similar exclusion or limit, an explanation of the scientific or clinical judgment for the determination or a statement that such an explanation will be provided; and

➤ Description of the expedited review process for adverse determinations involving urgent claims.[25]

6.6 Appeals of Claims Determinations

Each plan must have an appeals process that provides at least one level (and may provide 2 levels) of internal appeal. For group health claim determinations, claimants must be given at least 180 days to file an appeal.[26] Other determinations must be appealed within 60 days of an adverse benefit determination. Claimants must be given the opportunity to submit written comments regarding the adverse determination, as well as any documents, records, and other information relating to the claim for benefits.[27] Upon request and free of charge, claimants must be provided reasonable access to and copies of all

documents, records and other information relevant to a claim for benefits.[28] A document shall be considered relevant to an adverse determination if the document:

➤ Was relied upon in making the benefit determination;

➤ Was considered, or generated in the course of the benefit determination whether or not it was actually relied upon in the adverse determination;

➤ Demonstrates compliance with the administrative processes and safeguards required under the appeals regulations; or

➤ Constitutes a statement of policy or guidance with respect to the plan concerning the denied treatment option or benefit for the claimant's diagnosis.[29]

Any review of a claimant's appeal must be conducted by a new reviewer and not by the individual who made the adverse benefit determination. Nor can it be made by a subordinate of that individual.[30]

If the adverse determination is based in whole or in part on a medical judgment, including whether a particular treatment, drug or other item is experimental, investigational or not medically necessary or appropriate, the fiduciary named to conduct the appeal must consult with a health care professional who has appropriate training and experience in the field of medicine involved in the medical judgment.[31] This provision hearkens back to the statutory requirement that the fiduciary be a "prudent expert" as discussed above. It is insufficient for a fiduciary conducting the appeal to merely use common lay sense. The regulation mandates medical expert input. The regulation also mandates that the expert involved in the adverse determination be identified, regardless of whether or not the advice was followed.[32] This requirement is similar to the requirements in many state laws and the Medicare program.

Urgent care adverse determinations require an expedited review process. This process may be initiated either orally or in writing by the claimant and all necessary information, including the plan's benefit determination, must be transmitted by the plan to the claimant by telephone fax or other "expeditious method."[33]

6.6.1 Timelines for Appeals

The plan must notify the claimant of its decision on appeal, known as a "plan benefit determination on review," in accordance with a strict time line. With respect to urgent care claims, the plan administrator must notify the claimant of the plan's benefit determination on review as soon as possible, taking into account the medical exigencies, but not later than 72 hours after receipt of the request for a review of the adverse benefit determination.[34]

With respect to pre-service claims, the regulation distinguishes between plans that provide a single appeal and those that provide two levels of appeal of adverse determinations. For plans that provide one appeal, notification of the plan's benefit determination on review must occur within a reasonable time period appropriate to the medical circumstances, but not later than 30 days after receipt of the adverse benefit determination. If the plan provides for 2 appeals of an adverse determination, notification must be provided with respect to any level of appeal not later than 15 days after receipt by the plan of the claimant's request for review.[35]

For post service claims, the plan administrator must notify the claimant within a reasonable period of time, but not later than 60 days after receipt of the appeal. If the plan has 2 levels of appeals, the timeframe for notification is not later than 30 days after either appeal.[36]

6.6.2 Manner and Content of Notification of Benefit Determination on Review

Notification to a claimant of a plan's benefit determination on review can be made either in writing or electronically. In the case of an adverse determination, the notification must set forth:

➤ The specific reason or reasons for the adverse determination;

➤ Reference to the specific plan provisions on which the benefit determination is based;

➤ A statement that the claimant is entitled to receive upon request and free of charge, reasonable access to, and copies of, all documents, records and other information relevant to the claim for benefits; and

➤ A statement describing the voluntary appeal procedures including the right to bring an action under section 502(a) of ERISA, regarding fiduciary duties and enforcement.[37]

Additionally, the plan must provide:

➤ Any specific internal rule, guideline, protocol or other similar criterion relied upon in making the determination;

➤ An explanation of the medical, clinical or scientific judgment applied in the decision; and

➤ A statement regarding the availability of alternative dispute resolution.[38]

6.7 Remedies

Finally, because UM is considered a fiduciary function and involves an administrative process for seeking a remedy for breaches of the rules, claimants must exhaust all designated appeal procedures before filing a civil action

for benefits under ERISA. DOL Section 502(a) of ERISA provides what some would argue as the sole statutory remedy for plan participants. The DOL regulation provides the mandatory administration process which claimants must exhaust prior to seeking relief under ERISA section 502(a). Specifically, section 502(a) allows a participant or beneficiary to bring a civil action only to recover benefits under the terms of a plan or to enforce rights under the plan or to enjoin any act or practice which violates the terms of the plan or to obtain other equitable relief.

The exclusive remedy under ERISA does not provide for the non-economic damages which drive the state court cases. It is important to note the DOL Regulation provides for dual non-preemption: nothing in the regulation is construed to supercede any provision of state law that regulates insurance except to the extent that such state law prevents the application of the ERISA claims scheme; and just because a state has a law that establishes an external review procedure to evaluate and resolve disputes involving adverse benefit determinations does not automatically prevent application of the DOL Regulations.[39]

6.8 Preemption Issues

As noted in the introduction to this section, most utilization management regulatory oversight before the implementation of the DOL regulation was at the state level. Consequently, the cases which considered whether ERISA preempted UM laws did so prior to the federal regulatory scheme. While the newer federal rules change the regulatory environment for UM, this does not mean that the UM and independent review requirements adopted in most states are no longer relevant. The DOL regulation provides specific language[40] that addresses the interaction of the federal and state laws. The language provides that state laws remain intact and applicable, except "to the extent that such law prevents the application of a requirement" of the DOL regulation.

This approach complicates compliance programs, because it means that the federal rule does not necessarily provide a single consistent national standard for claims processes. Organizations subject to both the federal and state regulations will need to conduct an analysis to ensure compliance with both sets of requirements. Only in cases where the state requirement prevents adherence to the federal rule would the state law be preempted. These occurrences should be fairly rare, as both state and federal regulators have similar goals in setting standards. However, there are cases where the federal and state perspectives seem to vary, and these may invoke the preemption language. For example, most state UM laws require a *minimum* number of appeal levels, on the theory that more appeals provide more rights for consumers. The federal law, however, sets a *maximum* limit on the number of appeals, apparently on the theory that appeals may be used to delay consumers from pursuing their rights through the courts. Because of these differences, health plans will do well to analyze possible conflicts with the federal law, and to monitor court decisions that may have a bearing on preemption issues.

6.9 Conclusion

The DOL regulations are a watershed event for enrollees in ERISA group health plans. The DOL regulations provide group health plans and their enrollees with a process for benefit determinations and appeals. However, plan compliance with both the DOL regulations and state UM laws remains a challenge.

It is possible that a plan can meet the terms of both the DOL Regulations and state external review laws. Such dual compliance may defeat the uniformity of ERISA plans across state lines. It is also possible that an ERISA plan could develop a claims and appeal procedure that contains one or more levels of internal review followed by an external review and would thereby provide sufficient process that state preemption would be less likely.

1   29 U.S.C. §§ 1101-1461 (2004).

2   Administration and Enforcement Under The Employee Retirement Income Security Act of 1974, 29 C.F.R. §§ 2560.503-1 et seq. (2004).

3   Id.

4   29 C.F.R. § 2560.503-1(m)(6).

5   Several aspects of the regulations also apply to disability plans, but are not addressed herein.

6   We address the issues of preemption in Section 7 of *The Utilization Management Guide.*

7   29 C.F.R. §§ 2560.503-1 et seq.

8   29 U.S.C. § 1002(21)(A) (2004).

9   Interpretive Bulletins Relating To The Employee Retirement and Income Security Act of 1974, 29 C.F.R. § 2509.75-8 (2004).

10 29 C.F.R. § 2650.503-1.

11 29 U.S.C. § 1104(a)(1)(A) (2004).

12 29 U.S.C. §1104(a)(1)(B). The Section is entitled the "Prudent Man Standard of Care."

13 29 USC § 1133.

14 Employee Retirement Income Security Act of 1974, Rules And Regulations For Administration And Enforcement, Claims Procedure, 65 Fed. Reg. 70246-70259 (Nov. 21, 200).

15 65 Fed. Reg. at 70259.

16 65 Fed. Reg. at 70256.

17 29 C.F.R. § 2560.503-1(e).

18 29 C.F.R. § 2560.503-1(b).

19 While state UM laws often refer to "benefit determinations," and the Medicare Managed Care Regulations refer to the same decisions as "organization determinations," ERISA refers to these decisions as "adverse benefit determinations."

20 29 C.F.R. § 2560.503-1(m)(4).

21 29 C.F.R. § 2560.2503-1(b)(3).

22 29 C.F.R. § 2560.5031(b)(3).

23 29 C.F.R. § 2560.503-1(c)(1)(i).

24 29 C.F.R. § 2560-503-1(f)(2)(I).

25 29 C.F.R. § 2560.503-1(g).

26 29 C.F.R. § 2560.503-1(h)(3)(i).

27 29 C.F.R. § 2560.503-1(h)(2)(ii).

28 C.F.R. § 2560.503-1(h)(2)(iii).

29 C.F.R. § 2560.503-1(m)(8).

30 C.F.R. § 2560.503-1(h)(3)(ii).

31 29 C.F.R. § 2560.503-1(h)(3)(iii).

32 29 C.F.R. § 2560-1(h)(3)(iv).

33 29 C.F.R. § 2560-1(h)(3)(vi).

34 29 C.F.R. § 2560-1(i)(2)(i).

35 29 C.F.R. § 2560-1(i)(2)(ii).

36 29 C.F.R. § 2560-1(i)(2)(iii).

37 29 C.F.R. § 2560-1(j).

38 29 C.F.R. §2560-1(j)(5).

39 29 C.F.R § 2560-1(k).

40 29 C.F.R. § 2560.503-1(k).

7.0: Utilization Management Legal Update: An Overview of the ERISA Preemption Issue

David H. Reiter, JD, and John D. Shire, JD

7.1 Introduction

Employer-sponsored health plans like most other health coverage arrangements were originally indemnity plans. As more and more health plans began to incorporate the process of utilization management (UM), the courts also began to recognize UM's merging of provider and payor functions. As health plans were originally not set up to engage in UM, they could not be considered, nor were they held by the courts, to be engaged in treatment decisions. Consequently, when adverse medical events occur involving UM determinations, courts are confronted with the issue of health plan and/or provider culpability.

While the direct liability of providers for treatment decisions was traditionally available under the jurisdiction of state law, due to ERISA[1] preemption issues the question was not so clear if allegations of negligent UM determinations were made against the health plan directly. Concurrent with the development of this type of health plan direct liability, is the recognition that there should be some type of responsibility for negligent UM practices. However, as plan participants found, the remedies available for this harm are limited due to the principle of ERISA preemption.

7.2 UM Liability

Virtually all health plans engage in some form of UM to provide or pay for medically appropriate and cost effective care. However, UM interventions that control the access or provision of health care can create a certain exposure to liability. Typically, a health plan functions as both a benefits and medical management administrator. In this instance the health plan oversees how and when treatments and payments are authorized. As a result, a health plan has the inherent option to refuse the authorization of treatments, limit services that are not medically necessary, or limit services that otherwise fall outside the scope of the coverage arrangement (i.e., limitations for out-of-network care). The health plan may also authorize an alternative treatment approach pursuant to approved clinical review criteria. To the extent that denials of or alternations to the proposed treatment plans result in an injury to the patient, health care organizations may be held accountable under an array of legal liability theories which include breach of contract, negligence, bad faith, fraud, tortuous interference with healthcare decision-making, and vicarious liability over those who provide care.[2]

Two of the early health plan liability cases that resulted in success occurred in the late 1980's early 1990's in the state of California. In both cases of Wickline v. State of California,[3] and Wilson v. Blue Cross of Southern California[4], these cases specifically addressed whether the type of liability that arose our of managed care negligence was either direct or indirect.

7.2.1 The Wickline Case

In Wickline v. State of California, the plaintiff sued her managed health care plan for refusing to approve an extended hospital stay after major vascular surgery. Despite the recommendation by all the plaintiff's treating physicians that her hospitalization be extended, she was released after her managed health care plan approved only 4 of the 8 requested inpatient days. Within days of her release, the plaintiff experienced severe medical complications whereby she was readmitted and subsequently had her leg amputated. In weighing the liability of all the parties (the treating physicians and the plaintiff's health care provider), the Wickline court held that if a patient is injured by the failure of providing medical care that in fact should have been provided, a patient can recover from those responsible for any injuries suffered. This would include not only a patient's treating physicians, but also her employer-sponsored health care provider. Although Wickline ruled that a third party payor of health care could be found liable for medically inappropriate decisions that result from a defect in implementing cost containment mechanisms, the same court held that ultimately it was the patient's physician who was responsible for that particular individual's care. A treating physician, in other words, could not point to a health care payor as a scapegoat whenever the doctor's medical decisions go wrong.[5]

7.2.2 The Wilson Case

Even though the court's ruling in Wickline stated that a patient's physician was still ultimately responsible for a patient's care,[6] health plans still retained a viable argument against direct liability. This argument lost some of its force when the same California court four years later decided Wilson v. Blue Cross Blue Shield of California.[7] In Wilson, a health plan denied a 30-day inpatient hospitalization stay for an anorexic patient who thereafter committed suicide. Declaring Wickline's holding that the ultimate responsibility for the patient rested with the patient's physician as being dicta, the Wilson court found that UM decisions were directly involved in a patient's care. The California court ruled that so long as either the physician or the health plan's negligent conduct was a "substantial factor" in bringing about the patient's harm, both parties could be held liable for the harm caused.[8] In short, a health plan could not claim that it was the provider's ultimate responsibility for clinical decision-making in order to shield it from liability for harm caused by utilization management decisions.

While both the Wickline and Wilson initially led to findings for health plan liability based on utilization decisions, most state law actions that followed against employer-sponsored health plans were still preempted by ERISA which limited plaintiffs to federal-based legal reimbursement claims. This started to change through the middle 1990's when a steady erosion of ERISA preemption took place until the recent Supreme Court decision in Aetna Health, Inc. v. Davila and Cigna Healthcare of Texas, Inc. v. Calad,[9] discussed in more detail in this article.

7.3 Introduction to the ERISA Preemption Issue

In order to fully understand the recent developments in ERISA preemption, it is important to understand the statute's history. Established by Congress to create a uniform set of federal standards to protect employee pension plans from fraud and mismanagement, ERISA covers not only employee pension plans, but also health plans, and all other benefit plans established by private sector employers, companies, and employee work organizations such as unions. ERISA does not apply to health and other benefit plans administered by the federal, state, and local government sectors.[10]

There are several instances where ERISA's requirements may or may not supersede state provisions. Section 542 of ERISA explicitly supersedes or "preempts" state laws that "relate to" employee benefit plans.[11] This is known as *substantive or conflict preemption*. On the other hand, under section 514 (also known as ERISA's *savings clause*), ERISA does not preempt state laws that regulate insurance, banking or securities.[12] This savings clause is subject to a *deemer clause* which mandates that states not arbitrarily deem ERISA plans to be insurance companies, banks or trusts in order to subject such health plans to state law.[13]

7.4 The Preemption Analysis Regarding Direct Agency and Vicarious Liability Claims

Until the mid-1990s, U.S. Supreme Court decisions routinely upheld ERISA preemption of state laws related to health plans. In early holdings, actions brought by employees to recover benefits due under a plan covered by ERISA, or to enforce rights under such a plan, were subject to complete substantive preemption and removable to federal court even if they were brought in

the form of a state law tort claim. In cases such as Metropolitan Life Insurance v. Taylor[14], the Court held that it was Congress' intent to completely oversee the regulation of ERISA plans by providing for an exclusive civil remedies under section 502(a) of the act. Any state claim which involved issues of benefit recovery, or the enforcement or clarification of participant rights was deemed to be characterized under ERISA as a federal cause of action.[15] The Supreme Court had also held that ERISA even preempted state laws that specifically related to employee benefit plans either covered by ERISA, or have a significant financial and administrative impact on them.[16]

Despite The Supreme Court's decision in Metropolitan Life Insurance v. Taylor, there were still lawsuits having some success against being removed from state court. Over time, the federal courts took a more varied approach to rulings based upon vicarious liability claims against employer-sponsored health plans. Some circuits viewed claims of vicarious liability asserting negligent hiring and supervision, breach of fiduciary duty, and intentional infliction of emotional distress as having no relation to claims covered by ERISA preemption and not available for removal to federal court.[17] These cases often based themselves on either agency or vicarious claims based on a theory of *respondeat superior*[18] which focused on the individual physician's negligence. In contrast, other circuits ruled that vicarious liability suits other than ones alleging *respondeat superior* did not involve interpretation of plans under ERISA, but alleged negligence against a plan's UM program for the denial of benefits, and were preempted under ERISA's section 514(a).[19]

Subsequently in 1995, an attempt was made by the Third Federal Circuit Court to more clearly differentiate between state law actions that are, and are not, preempted by ERISA. In Dukes v. U.S. Healthcare[20], the court reviewed past decisions on preemption and determined that a difference exists between claims attacking the *quality* of ERISA benefits received, and those attacking the *right to receive* benefits. The Third Circuit held that state law actions could be brought against health plans for the quality of benefits received while actions regarding plan benefits could not. The court based its reasoning on the fact that claims asserting the poor quality of benefits received are not claims under section 502(a)(1)(B) (i.e., ERISA's civil enforcement provisions) to either recover plan benefits due under the terms of the plan, or to enforce rights under the plan or to clarify rights to future benefits.[21]

7.5 The U.S. Supreme Court Narrows ERISA Preemption

By the year 1995 The U.S. Supreme Court more directly addressed the language of the ERISA statute. In a unanimous decision authored by Justice David Souter, the Supreme Court found that a broad and unchallenged interpretation of ERISA'S preemption was not just unhelpful, but "counterproductive." In New York State Conference of Blue Cross Blue Shield Plans v. Travelers Insurance Company (Travelers)[22], the Supreme Court refused to interpret the preemptive provisions of ERISA as displacing all state laws effecting costs and charges on the theory they indirectly relate to ERISA plans. The Court held that if ERISA preempted laws only "indirectly related" to ERISA plans, the result would be to effectively read the limiting language in section 514(a) out of the statute, because the extent of relatedness was ultimately infinite. In the opinion of Justice Souter, by giving effect to the preemption language of section 514 without recognizing the language of the saving clause would violate basic principles of statutory interpretation. Further, it would be inconsistent with another Supreme Court's decision that held preemption would not occur if the state law had only a tenuous, remote, or peripheral connection with a covered plan.[23] Laws, therefore, with only an indirect economic effect on relative costs of various health insurance packages in a given state are a far cry from those conflicting directives from which Congress meant to insulate ERISA plans.[24] In the eyes of the Court, nothing in ERISA's language or in the context of its passage indicated that Congress chose to displace general health care regulation which has historically been a matter for the states.[25] This decision did not address the meaning of "health care regulation" and whether or not that traditionally state regulated function includes utilization management regulation. This would latter be addressed in the Kentucky Association of Health Plans case.

7.6 "Any Willing Provider" Actions

While the "treatment" vs. "coverage" decisions became determinative factors in ERISA preemption, the next logical issue was by what, and how much, authority states themselves could regulate employee benefit health plans. It was this issue that framed the Supreme Court's decision in Kentucky Ass'n of Health Plans, Inc. v. Miller.[26]

In Kentucky Association of Health Plans, the health plans involved sought ERISA preemption of Kentucky's "Any Willing Provider" law. Any Willing Provider laws prohibit network-based health plans from discriminating against any provider "willing" to meet the insurer's requirements for participation in the health plan. In ruling that Kentucky's Any Willing Provider laws were not subject to preemption due to ERISA's savings clause, the Supreme Court modified its previous test in McCarran-Ferguson later used in Metropolitan Life Ins. Co. v. Massachusetts[27] that identified those laws regulating the business of insurance. Under the McCarran-Ferguson test, what constitutes the business of insurance was determined by whether the practice had an effect of transferring or spreading a policy holder's risk, whether the practice was an integral part of the policy relationship between the insurer and the insured, and whether the practice was limited to entities within the insurance industry.[28] In short, the Court held that laws regulating insurance must be specifically directed toward the insurance industry. For a state law to regulate insurance, the law must be specifically directed toward entities engaged in insurance, and the law must substantially affect the risk pooling arrangement between the insurer and the insured.[29] Any Willing Provider laws met the McCarran-Ferguson test because they were directed to insurance plans, and they prevented insurance plans from selectively choosing providers who could participate. While The Supreme Court's decision in Kentucky Association of Health Plans created a new test for whether ERISA preempted state laws related to insurance, it failed to clarify the issue further.

7.7 ERISA Preemption of Tort Claims

Noting the U.S. Supreme Court's preemption analysis in Travelers, and its subsequent decisions in California Division of Labor Standards Enforcement v. Dillingham Construction, N.A., Inc.,[30] and DeBuono v. NYSA-ILA Medical and Clinical Services Fund,[31] by the late 90's state courts began to show less inclination towards removal actions against health benefit plans to federal court. As a result of this shift, the Pennsylvania State Supreme Court in Papas v. Asbel,[32] used the same analysis as the U.S. Supreme Court in Travelers to hold that ERISA did not preempt state law tort claims brought against an employee benefit plan pursuant to 29 U.S.C. § 1002(1). Although the Pennsylvania Court acknowledged federal court precedent that supported ERISA preemption of state claims against HMO's, it went on to hold that most of these cases predated the U.S. Supreme Court's decision in Travelers. In addition, it found the Supreme Court's decisions against ERISA preemption were too persuasive to ignore.[33]

As in Travelers, the Papas court similarly found that negligence claims against health maintenance organizations did not "relate to" ERISA employee benefit plans, as there was no congressional intent to preempt state laws concerning regulations for the provision of safe medical care.[34] Negligence laws, the court explained, have only a tenuous connection with ERISA employee benefit plans.[35] On remand the Pennsylvania Supreme Court not only reaffirmed that that there was no ERISA preemption of state laws regulating the provision of medical care, but narrowed the preemption exception further by holding that ERISA also does not preempt mixed eligibility treatment decisions under the U.S. Supreme Court ruling in the Pegram v. Herdich.[36]

With the Supreme Court's decision in Pegram v. Herdich[37] came additional confusion concerning the ERISA and UM preemption. In Pegram the plaintiff suffered a ruptured appendix when her physician, rather than ordering an immediate ultrasound, chose to wait some eight days in order to admit the plaintiff in an ultrasound facility staffed by the HMO physicians. The HMO was operated by the plaintiff's physician and her partners, and an essential element to the plaintiff's negligence claim was that the HMO rewarded its physicians for limiting medical care.[38] Asserting preemption under ERISA, the HMO in Pegram was granted removal to federal court whereupon the federal court dismissed the two state law fraud counts. Although the federal court dismissed the state claims, the plaintiff was allowed to amend her complaint to assert that the HMO's incentive plan was a breach of a fiduciary duty due under ERISA and not state law.[39] Although the District Court dismissed the ERISA fiduciary duty claim, the Court of Appeals for the Seventh Circuit reversed stating that the HMO was acting as a fiduciary when its physicians made challenged decisions.[40] Finding this issue worthy for review the Supreme Court granted certiorari to determine whether treatment decisions made by a health maintenance organization, acting through its physician employees, are fiduciary acts within the meaning of ERISA.[41]

7.7.1 Mixed Eligibility Determinations: Treatment versus Administrative Decisions

Once again writing for a unanimous court, Justice Souter in Pegram concluded that treatment decisions made by health maintenance organizations acting through physician employees were not fiduciary acts within the meaning of ERISA.[42] The Court used the opportunity to define the unique roles HMO physicians play in the treatment of their individual patients. It held that HMO physicians play dual roles under employee benefit plans. The physicians can either act in an administrative role when they decide whether a particular medical treatment or condition is covered by the plan (an eligibility decision), or as a provider when they decide what specific medical treatment a patient will receive (a treatment decision).[43] There are even times when a physician can act as both an administrator and a provider. The Supreme Court termed these types of decisions as *mixed eligibility*. Mixed eligibility decisions are those that cannot be untangled from a physician's decision regarding reasonable medical treatment. It was this type of decision the plaintiff in Pegram faced.[44]

To the Supreme Court, the proper venue for mixed eligibility decisions was not one of a fiduciary claim covered by ERISA, but of a claim covered by state malpractice law.[45] While the Supreme Court in Travelers may have held that ERISA does not a preempt state law that regulates the provisions of adequate medical treatment, Pegram's significance lies in the Court's premise that mixed eligibility decisions by HMO's implicate state law malpractice claims and are not causes of action covered by ERISA.[46] This analysis appeared to subvert the plain language of ERISA regarding utilization and benefit determinations as fiduciary functions.

7.8 ERISA Preemption Revisited

Recently, in a decision greatly anticipated by all parties in the health care field, the Supreme Court in Aetna Health Care, Inc. v. Davila (and Cigna of Texas v. Calad)[47] attempted to clarify its stance in its prior decisions on the issue of ERIA preemption. In doing so, it upheld the supremacy of ERISA preemption and its remedial scheme for state law causes actions alleging failure of ordinary care by MCO's in the handling benefit coverage decisions.[48]

In Davila, an employee, Juan Davila, received his health insurance coverage from a predecessor of Aetna Health, Inc. ("Aetna") pursuant to an ERISA plan sponsored by Davila's employer.[49] The agreement between Aetna and Davila's employer provided that Aetna would contract with participating physicians who were independent contractors and solely responsible for health services rendered to covered patients. Under this agreement, Aetna had complete authority to review all claims for covered benefits, including discretionary authority to determine whether and to what extent eligible individuals and beneficiaries were entitled to coverage and construe any disputed or doubtful terms under the group plan agreement.[50] Benefits had to be "medically necessary" in order to be deemed covered benefits, Aetna had the authority to determine whether any benefit provided under the plan was medically necessary. The term "medically necessary" was defined as a service or supply that was no more costly than an equally effective service or supply in satisfying certain standards of medical efficacy.[51] More significantly, the agreement also provided that its coverage of benefits would not restrict a plan member's ability to receive health care benefits that were not covered benefits.[52]

In April 2000 although Davila's physician prescribed Vioxx for Davila's arthritis, Aetna refused to pay for the prescription.[53] Aetna informed the physician that under the terms of its formulary policy, Aetna would cover Davila for Vioxx only if he had a diagnosis of osteoarthritis or acute pain and has a contraindication, intolerance, allergy to or a documented trial of at least two other covered drugs.[54] Consequently Davila began taking one of these other drugs which allegedly led to his hospitalization for bleeding ulcers and a near heart attack.[55] Following his hospitalization, Davila sued Aetna in Texas state court for violations of the Texas Health Care Liability Act (THCLA). The THCLA required managed care organizations exercise ordinary care when making health care treatment decisions. It also imposed liability for damages resulting from harm proximately caused by an MCO's failure to exercise such care. Davila alleged that Aetna's formulary policy regarding the use of Vioxx amounted to a failure to use ordinary care in making a health treatment decision that ultimately affected the quality of the treatment Davila received.[56] Davila also sought punitive damages, alleging that Aetna knew that its policy involved a risk of serious injury or death.

Aetna removed the Davila action to federal court under the "complete preemption" doctrine recognized under Metropolitan Life Insurance Co. v. Taylor.[57] The doctrine provided that a state-law claim that falls within the scope of the civil enforcement provisions of ERISA section 502(a), 29 U.S.C. section 1132(a), is deemed to be a federal claim subject to removal.[58] Aetna argued that Davila's state-law claims were within the scope of section 502(a) because they were based on Aetna's alleged wrongful conduct of denying a benefit under the plan. Davila filed a motion to remand the case to state court, which the district court denied. The district court reasoned that while ERISA would not completely preempt a claim challenging the quality of medical care received, the claim at issue challenged the administration of health benefits under an ERISA plan. Because Davila elected not to re-file his state-based claims as ERISA claims, the district court dismissed his state-based claims with prejudice.[59]

In Calad, the plaintiff Ruby Calad was a member of CIGNA Health Care's (CIGNA) HMO through an ERISA plan sponsored by her husband's employer.[60] Under the terms of that plan, hospital benefits were not authorized in excess of the number of days certified through a pre-admission certification (PAC) or continued stay review (CSR). In September 1999, Calad was admitted to a hospital for a hysterectomy. CIGNA allegedly informed Calad that it would authorize only one day of hospitalization following the procedure. On the second day after the surgery, CIGNA informed Calad that they would not extend her hospital stay unless she had hemorrhaging, fever, or high blood pressure. Absent any of these symptoms, Calad would have to pay the cost of an extended hospitalization.[61] Following her discharge from the hospital, Calad experienced complications causing her to return to the hospital emergency room.[62] Calad then

sued CIGNA in state court under the THCLA for failing to use ordinary care in its medical decisions, alleging that CIGNA's medical necessity criteria disqualified her from continued hospital care following her hysterectomy. CIGNA removed the action to federal court under the complete preemption doctrine. The district court denied Calad's motion to remand and dismissed her state law claims with prejudice. The reason for the dismissal was that Calad elected not to amend her pleading to incorporate an ERISA claim.[63]

The United States Court of Appeals for the Fifth Circuit consolidated both appeals filed by Davila and Calad and reversed the district courts' refusal to remand their claims to state court.[64] The Fifth Circuit ruled the removal improper because the claims were not covered by the relevant provisions of section 502(a) authorizing a suit for breach of fiduciary duty or a claim for benefits.[65] Specifically, the court determined that the claims were not within section 502(a)(3) of ERISA, 29 U.S.C. section 1132(a)(3), which authorizes suits to enjoin or redress violations of ERISA.[66] The court concluded further that the claims were not within the scope of section 502(a)(2) of ERISA, which authorizes a plan participant, beneficiary, or fiduciary or the Secretary to obtain appropriate relief to the plan against a fiduciary who breaches ERISA duties, because AETNA and CIGNA were not acting as plan fiduciaries when denying medical treatment.[67]

In another part of its decision, the Fifth Circuit concluded that the claims by Davila and Calad did not fall within the scope of section 502(a)(1)(B) of ERISA, which authorizes a suit by a plan participant or beneficiary to recover benefits due to him under the terms of his plan, to enforce rights under the terms of the plan, or to clarify his rights to future benefits under the terms of the plan.[68] In this case, Davila and Calad asserted tort claims and had not sued their ERISA plan administrator or challenged its interpretation of the plan.[69] The court reasoned that section 502(a)(1)(B) creates a cause of action for breach of contract whereby patients can sue for benefits when a plan administrator incorrectly interprets the plan to deny benefits but does not provide a tort remedy. Therefore, ERISA would not preempt state tort remedies.

On appeal, the Supreme Court thoroughly rejected the Fifth Circuit's analysis. In its unanimous decision, the Court reversed and ruled that the causes of action were completely preempted and removable from state to federal court.[70] This decision held that the Texas Healthcare Liability Act created a tort remedy in the guise of an insurance regulation. Under the Supreme Court's analysis, the Texas tort remedy is merely an alternative remedy for coverage denial. Because any injury caused by the plan's utilization determination was not a treatment decision, it must be subject to the ERISA remedy under section 502 of that Act and that ERISA section 502 independently preempted all other remedies. The Court also noted that a state characterizing its tort remedy as insurance regulation was inadequate to evade ERISA preemption.

Finally, in a less studied aspect of <u>Davila</u>, the Supreme Court distinguished its decision in <u>Pegram</u> in which it rejected the idea that physicians in a physician owned and operated HMO who made utilization decisions were fiduciaries. Additionally, the decision in <u>Davila</u> clarified the problematic fiduciary analysis under <u>Pegram</u> by holding that ERISA plan administrators are "fiduciaries" with respect to coverage decisions. In <u>Davila</u>, the Court limited the <u>Pegram</u> analysis to cases in which utilization decisions are made by physicians in a physician owned and operated HMO. Following this analysis to a logical conclusion, only those HMO's which are owned and operated by physicians would be subject to direct or vicarious liability under state malpractice law for utilization decisions, while other plans would be protected from state tort liability by ERISA. Further, the Court referenced the Department of Labor ERISA Benefit Claims Process (BCP) Regulations, its internal claims appeals procedures, and external claims review followed by judicial review as furthering the scope of preemption under ERISA.

7.9 Conclusion

The Supreme Court's decision in <u>Davila</u> clarified the issue of ERISA preemption, and its applicability to a plan member's recourse against his managed care organization. The decision, however, did not clarify the multitude of other outstanding questions raised by the past decade of ERISA jurisprudence. The Court has yet to clarify its <u>Pegram</u> decision with respect to UM as a fiduciary function.

Another important issue that remains unresolved is whether all forms of "make whole" relief are foreclosed by ERISA. The Court declined to rule on this issue in Davila, and it did not foreclose this possibility.[71] In other words, the door to state court relief had not been totally shut. It should also be noted that both Davila and Calad failed to pursue any form of ERISA based claim.[72] Looking to the future, there is still a possibility that the Davila case will engender litigation seeking damages under section 502 of ERISA, a concept endorsed by the court in footnote 7 of the <u>Davila</u> decision and in Justice Ginsburg's concurrence. One can expect further ERISA decisions by the courts until Congress does what the federal courts have been requesting for years: clarify the ERISA preemption provision.

1   Employee Retirement Security Act of 1974.

2   In addition to liability for utilization management activities, managed care organizations may also have liability for negligent selection and retention of providers, inappropriate financial incentives for limiting medically necessary care, or misrepresentation.

3   239 Cal. Rptr. 810 (Cal. App. 1986).

4   271, Cal. Rprtr. 876 (Cal. App. 1990).

5   <u>Id.</u> 192 Cal. App. 3d at 1645, 239 Cal. Rptr. At 819.

6   <u>Id.</u>

7   <u>Wilson v. Blue Cross Blue Shield of California</u>, 222 Cal. App. 3d 660, 271 Cal. Rptr. 876 (1990).

8   <u>Id.</u> 222 Cal. App. 3d at 672-673, 271 Cal. Rptr. at 884, citing, Rest. 2d Torts § 431.

9   Collectively cited at 124 S.Ct. 2488 (2004).

10   29 U.S.C. § 1002(1)(B).

11   29 U.S.C. § 1144(a).

12   29 U.S.C. § 1144(b).

13   29 U.S.C. § 1144(b).

14   <u>Metropolitan Life Insurance Co. v. Taylor, 481</u> U.S. 58, 66-67 (1987).

15   <u>Id.</u> at 64.

16   <u>Shaw v. Delta Airlines</u>, 463 U.S. 85 (1983); <u>Metropolitan Life Insurance Co. v. Massachusetts,</u> 471 U.S. 724 (1985); <u>Alassi v. Raybestos-Manhattan</u>, 451 U.S. 504 (1981).

17   <u>Lupo v. Human Affairs International, Inc.,</u> 28 F. 3d 269, 272 (2nd Cir. 1994).

18   Respondeat superior is Latin for "let the master answer." The phrase is used in the law of agency. It provides that an employer is and/or can be held responsible for the actions of his/her/its agent (employee) during their course of employment.

19   <u>Jass v. Prudential Health Care Plan, Inc.</u> 88 F.3d 1482 (7th cir. 1996)(A determination of not providing certain coverage by a utilization review nurse was determined to be literally a denial of benefits under ERISA).

20   <u>Dukes v. U.S. Healthcare, Inc.</u>, 57 F.3d 350 (3rd Cir.), cert. denied, 516 U.S. 1009 (1995).

21   <u>Dukes,</u> 57 F.3d at 356 n. 10.

22   <u>New York State Conference of Blue Cross Blue Shield Plans v. Travelers Insurance Company,</u> 514 U.S. 645, 657 (1995).

23   <u>Id.</u> at 662, citing, <u>D.C. v. Greater Washington Board of Trade,</u> 506 U.S. 125, 130 (1992).

24   <u>Id.</u> 514 at 663.

25   <u>Id.</u> at 661.

26   <u>Kentucky Ass'n of Health Plans, Inc. v. Miller</u>, 123 S.Ct. 1471 (2003).

27   Metropolitan Life Ins. Co. v. Massachusetts, 471 U.S. 724 (1985).

28   <u>Id.</u> at 743.

29 Kentucky Ass'n of Health Plans, 123 S. Ct. at 1475.

30 California Division of Labor Standards Enforcement v. Dillingham Construction, N.A., Inc.,519 U.S. 316 (1997).

31 DeBuono v. NYSA-ILA Medical and Clinical Services Fund, 520 U.S. 806 (1997).

32 Papas v. Asbel, 555 Pa. 342, 724 A. 2d 889 (1996)

33 Id. at 351, 893.

34 Id.

35 Id. at 352, 894.

36 Pappas, 564 Pa. 407, 417, 768 A.2d 1089, 1095 (2001).

37 Pegram v. Herdich, 530 U.S. 211 (2000).

38 Id. at 216.

39 Id. (§502(a)(2) allows benefit plan participants to sue for appropriate relief for fiduciary breach).

40 Id. at 217.

41 Id. at 218.

42 Id. at 211.

43 Id. at 227-228.

44 Id. at 229.

45 Id. at 236-237.

46 Papas, 546 Pa. at 417, 768 at 1095.

47 Aetna Health Care, Inc. v. Davila (and Cigna of Texas v. Calad), Nos. 02-1845 and 03-83, 2004 U.S. LEXIS 4571, at *7 (2004),

48 Id., at *7-8.

49 Id., at *8.

50 Id.

51 Brief for Respondants at 6, Aetna Health Care, Inc. v. Davila (and Cigna of Texas v. Calad), Nos. 02-1845 and 03-83, 2004 U.S. LEXIS 4571, at *7 (2004).

52 Id., at 6-7.

53 2004 U.S. LEXIS 4571, at *8.

54 Brief for the United States as Amicus Curiae supporting Petitioners at 3, Aetna Health Care, Inc. v. Davila (and Cigna of Texas v. Calad), Nos. 02-1845 and 03-83, 2004 U.S. LEXIS 4571, at *7 (2004).

55 2004 U.S. LEXIS 4571, at *8.

56 Id., at *9.

57 Id.

58 Taylor, 481 U.S. at 65-67.

59 2004 U.S. LEXIS 4571, at *9-10.

60 Id., at *8.

61 Brief for Respondants at 5, Aetna Health Care, Inc. v. Davila (and Cigna of Texas v. Calad), Nos. 02-1845 and 03-83, 2004 U.S. LEXIS 4571, at *7 (2004),

62 2004 U.S. LEXIS 4571, at *9.

63 Id., at *10.

64 Roark v. Humana, Inc., 307 F.3d 298, 312 (5th Cir. 2002).

65 Id.

66 Id., at 310-311.

67 Id.

68 Id.

69 Id.

70 2004 U.S. LEXIS 4571, at *7.

71 2004 U.S. LEXIS 4571, at *36, n.7.

72 Id.

8.0: Pharmacy Benefit Management: Drug Utilization Review

Pam Foster, RN, MS

8.1 Introduction

There are approximately 10,000 prescription drugs currently available on the market today and that number is growing every year. In addition, the number of new drug approvals has been increasing steadily from 1991 when 63 drugs were approved to a record number of 131 in 1996. Besides approvals, in 2002 there were 152 expanded uses for already approved drugs and 13 over-the-counter (OTC) drugs or Rx to OTC switches. The responsibility of regulating all these medicines falls on the U.S. Food and Drug Administration (FDA). It is a daunting task and it comes as no surprise that the FDA's Center for Drug Evaluation and Research (CDER), a division of FDA since 1994, is the largest component of the agency.

2002	FDA Data[1]	2003
78	New drugs	72
z17	New molecular entities	21
8	Orphan new drugs	10
384	Generic equivalents	362

In addition to the growth in the number of drugs available, the United States has experienced a concomitant growth of both drug costs and spending. As was noted in TIME magazine:

"(W)hile health care spending rose 9.3% in 2002, the largest increase in 11 years-prescription drug costs rose 14%. Although prescriptions represented only 10.5% of total health-care costs in the US in 2002, they accounted for 23% of out-of-pocket costs for the consumer - Americans spent $162.4 billion on prescription drugs in 2002.[2,3]

Americans pay for prescription drug costs in ways other than at their local pharmacy counter. The Washington Post reported in March of 2004 that "for each mid-size DaimlerChrysler AG builds at one of its U.S. plants, the company pays about $1,300 to cover employee health costs…when it builds an identical car in Canada, the health care cost is negligible."[4]

Based on the volumes and increasing costs of pharmaceuticals facing ordinary Americans, it is easily apparent why physicians, payors, and consumers can all benefit from help in managing the explosion of information and escalating costs of these potentially life-saving and life extending products.

8.2 What are Pharmacy Benefit Managers (PBM's)?

The late 1980's saw a marked rise in prescription drug prices, and by the year 1989 Pharmacy Benefit Managers or PBM's oversaw pharmacy benefits for 60 million people. This trend has continued and today there are currently 60 PBM's with more than 130 million members. PBM's are fiscal intermediaries who specialize in the administration and management of prescription drug benefit programs. A primary objective is to provide high-quality pharmaceutical care at the lowest possible cost. PBM's contract with employers, unions, HMO's and other health plans to coordinate payment of prescriptions for employees and covered members.[5] They help managed care organizations, employer groups, state and federal payors and other stakeholders manage prescription drugs and their costs. They do this in part by pooling payor purchasing power, and negotiating with pharmaceutical companies.

PBM's can also can manage the enormous volume of drug information to support the provision of complete and safe pharmacy coverage to members. In addition to paying pharmacy claims, PBM's can provide information to clients on new drugs, new uses of drugs, drug safety issues, and drugs pending FDA approval; PBM's facilitate safety, planning and efficiency of drug benefits as well as the appropriateness of drug utilization.

PBM Ownership	
Independent companies	Owned by Managed Care Organizations or pharmacy chains
Caremark (ADVP)	Anthem Prescription
ExpressScripts	Eckerd
Medco Health Solutions	Walgreens
	Wellpoint
	Prime Therapeutics

PBM ownership can be an important issue when considering the mission and role of PBM's. PBM's owned by pharmaceutical companies, for example, have in the past been targeted for evidence that their interest in promoting certain drugs could out-weigh therapeutic and cost considerations; this type of ownership/management relationship constitutes a conflict of interest in pharmaceutical management. Independent PBM's may also be subjected to pressure from pharmaceutical companies who use their enormous financial power to attempt to influence the direction of presenting"their" drugs favorably.

8.3 Need for PBM's

What needs do PBM's fill? The goal of pharmacy management is not to reduce utilization but rather to make sure that use is appropriate. In many cases, PBM disease management programs strive to increase appropriate use of outpatient pharmaceuticals in order to manage chronic disease states and diseases/conditions such as hypertension, elevated cholesterol, blood sugar and symptoms of persistent asthma, so that the quality of life and length of life are enhanced. Physicians cannot be expected to keep up with the constant volume of new drug information (in addition to new medical advances and recommendations) introduced to the market every year. As a result, physicians not only rely on pharmacists and pharmaceutical manufacturers, but on PBM's for support regarding FDA indications, dosage protocols, and drug interaction information. PBM's are able to provide this information through the employment of pharmacists, content specialists in drug use issues, and physicians with special expertise in pharmaceuticals.

The Evolution of PBM's within Health Plans

Before the existence of co ntemporary PBM's, HMO's developed their own pharmacy benefit management programsEmployer groups never had the internal resources to develop and operate their own pharmacy benefit, and they obtained their pharmacy program through their health benefits insurer or through a PBM.An MCO's decision whether to develop and operate an internal pharmacy program or to contract with an external PBM depends on many factors but essentially the MCO must determine if it can build'or.if it is more efficient to buy'Even though MCO's have the option of building or buying pharmacy management services, they often decide to take advantage of both options through a hybrid program. Thus, it is quite common for an HMO to build an internal pharmacy management program and also use a PBM for specific resource intensive operational services that take advantage of PBM's economies of scale."[6]

Robert P. Navarro

Filtering the massive volume of pharmaceutical information is just one of the niche roles PBM's play, along with managing the pharmaceutical claims and applying safety protocols. PBM data has enormous value in supporting the effective management of health care conditions both at the individual patient and population-based levels. Compared to medical data, it is often more consistently formatted, and it is timelier. PBM's generate and manage information that can help identify patients who need access to a certain drug therapies or need a change to their current prescription regimen. In addition, PMB's can be used to monitor compliance, implement

safety screening for drug interactions, and safeguard against prescription and dosage errors.

8.4 PBM Services

PBM's use a number of services to influence drug costs both from the supply and demand side. On the supply side, PBM's may implement formularies and initiate disease management programs. On the demand side, they may institute higher co-pays for brand name drugs.[7]

Generally speaking, PBM's provide the following services:

➤ Provide drug information

➤ Negotiate price discounts and rebates with drug manufacturers

➤ Process pharmacy claims

➤ Negotiate price discounts with retail pharmacies

➤ Operate mail-order pharmacies

➤ Deliver disease management services or information

➤ Provide pharmaceutical care management

➤ Develop formularies

➤ Offer specialty pharmacy

➤ Conduct clinical pharmacy management programs

1) POS DUR (Point of service drug utilization review)

2) prior authorization

3) appeals management

4) step therapy

5) quantity limits

6) therapeutic interchange and generic substitution

7) fraud and abuse programs

8.5 Formulary Development

A "formulary" is a list of drugs chosen for use in treating patients and meant to cover all their pharmacological needs. The development of the formulary is based first upon clinical considerations and then on financial considerations. The formulary strategy is based upon a dynamic system that combines both the current body of pharmaceutical knowledge and medical community practice standards in the health care setting it serves. Formularies are regularly evaluated by a committee of experts, primarily physicians and pharmacists, working within that health care setting. This committee is most often called the P&T (Pharmacy and Therapeutics) committee.[8] The goal of formulary use is to provide all available remedies in the most cost effective formulas, (i.e.

generics and lower cost brand names). Sources used to develop formularies include, but not limited to:

➤ Drug labeling approved by the Food and Drug Administration (FDA),

➤ Input from physicians and pharmacists

And when available:

➤ Peer-reviewed literature

➤ Recognized compendia

➤ Practice Guidelines

➤ Other publications of the National Institutes of Health (NIH)

➤ Agency for Healthcare Research and Quality (AHRQ)

➤ Other organizations or government agencies

One way that a Pharmacy &Therapeutics Committees may consider new drugs for formulary inclusion is depicted below. The committee evaluates the drug clinically and selects one of three possible categories for the new drug:

Therapeutically unique"– The drug exhibits significant clinical benefit over existing formulary drugs. These drugs are automatically added to the formulary.

Therapeutically similar"– The drug is considered to be clinically equivalent to similar drugs already on the formulary in efficacy or safety.

Therapeutically inferior"– The drug is not added to the formulary and receives a non-formulary designation. This designation indicates that the P&T Committee believes that there is currently insufficient information to determine its appropriate clinical role, or that questions remain regarding the drug's safety or effectiveness.

The standard list of drugs available through a PBM is sometimes referred to as a "closed formulary." As a result, those drugs that are excluded from the normal formulary are not paid for unless they qualify for an exception. Although closed formularies have been fairly common in the past, an ever increasing consumer demand for drug choice has lead to the development and growth of "tiered formularies" where most drugs are available to consumers but with additional cost for drugs that reside on the second or third tiers.

8.6 PBM Utilization Tools

To pursue the goal of providing all available remedies through the most cost effective formulas, PBM's often use four available utilization methods.

The first method called "Point-Of-Service drug utilization review" (POS DUR) is a concurrent online editing system that evaluates prescription drug claims for several types of potential adverse drug interactions (e.g., drug-drug, drug-age, drug-gender interactions). When any of these issues is detected, warning messages are transmitted to the dispensing pharmacy to provide an opportunity for the pharmacist to evaluate and determine the need for intervention. These systems are on-line, real-time and all of the participating PBM's pharmacies are linked to the same system for consistent review. The larger a PBM's network of pharmacies, the more data it has on users and therefore create a better safety net it can provide.

The second method of drug utilization is called "Prior Authorization" (PA). Prior Authorization is a form of prospective drug utilization review used to promote safe and effective drug therapy; it is intended to promote appropriate prescribing, and to control costs by application of clinically based guidelines for selected drugs. PA requires a drug's prescribed use be evaluated against a predetermined set of criteria before the prescription is dispensed. At point of sale, a message is displayed to the pharmacy that the drug requested requires prior authorization. This initiates communication with the physician, and dialogue with the PBM pharmacist regarding the criteria for use.

Prior Authorization can decrease drug expenses by shifting utilization to less expensive, more clinically appropriate agents. It can impact safety by avoiding coverage for drugs prescribed for non-approved uses. PA ensures that drugs are dispensed appropriately according to labeling indications, national guidelines or peer reviewed clinical literature. In its July/August 2001 issue, *The Journal of Managed Care Pharmacy* published an article on outcomes measured in six prior authorization studies. All six studies documented drug cost savings from the PA programs. Of the three studies that measured the effect of the PA program on non-drug costs, none found a significant increase in costs elsewhere in the health care system.[9]

A third type of utilization tool for PBM is realized by establishing "drug benefit limits." In this method, the PBM establishes a quantity of certain drugs that will be covered over a specified period. The limit may be expressed in terms of quantity dispensed, days supply dispensed, or number of prescription claims for the drug. When a claim exceeds the established limit for the drug, the claim will reject. Messaging is provided to the dispensing pharmacy advising when the drug benefit has been exceeded, or that prior authorization is required for coverage of additional drug quantities.

Benefits of Prior Authorization:

Quality
  ➢ Provides standard clinically appropriate criteria
  ➢ Addresses safety concerns, reducing patient risk
  ➢ Promotes appropriate prescribing for select drugs by ensuring adherence
    to approved treatment protocols

Cost Control
  ➢ Improves management of drug costs by shifting utilization to higher value clinically appropriate drugs
  ➢ Helps avoid inappropriate dispensing
  ➢ Offers flexible drug coverage controls

Example of Prior Authorization Process:

Anabolic Steroids

FDA-approved Indications

  ➢ Anemia: Anemia caused by deficient red cell production, acquired or congenital aplastic anemia, myelofibrosis and hypoplastic anemias due to the administration of a cytotoxic drug. (oxymetholone)
  ➢ Hereditary angioedema: Prophylactic use may decrease frequency and severity of attacks. (stanozolol only)
  ➢ Adjunctive therapy: Promote weight gain after weight loss following extensive surgery, chronic infections, or severe trauma, and in some patients who, without definite pathologic reasons, fail to gain or maintain normal weight; to offset the protein catabolism associated with the administration of corticosteroids; for the relief of bone pain frequently accompanying osteoporosis. (oxandrolone only)

Sample (Actual) Prior Authorization Questions

Does the patient have the diagnosis of anemia (hematocrit <30%)?

Does the patient have the diagnosis of hereditary angioedema?

Did the patient have weight loss following extensive surgery, chronic infection or severe trauma? Sample

Yes to any of the above yields approval

Drug Limitations restrict coverage of drugs over a defined time period to a specific amount.

➢ Drug limits may be set to express benefit limits such as for life style drugs like those for erectile dysfunction.

➢ They may be set as a result of clinical guidelines for appropriate drug use:

Example: Toradol limited to a 5 days supply.
Reason: Significant increased risk of gastrointestinal bleeding with longer than 5 day use.

A fourth utilization tool for PBMs is sometimes referred to as "Step Therapy" (ST). ST simply requires the use of one or more prerequisite drugs that meet specific conditions prior to the use of another drug or drugs. It defines how and when a particular drug or drug class should be used based on a patient's drug history.

> **Example:** Require use of NSAIDs (Motrin) before allowing the use of COX-2 inhibitors. (Celebrex)

Pharmaceutical utilization management generates the same concerns about abuse that medical utilization management has since "managed care" first became a part of our health care delivery system. Who is deciding what care is necessary? What rights do consumers have if they or their physicians do not agree with utilization decisions? For this reason, regulation of the utilization processes in PBM's, like those for MCO's, is important. Companies like URAC and NCQA with their accreditation/certification processes require adherence to levels of protection that assure appeals rights, rigor in the criteria development process and inter-rater reliability documentation that address these concerns. Many states categorize PBM utilization management in the same way as medical utilization management; accordingly they require licensure and or certification. However, to date, PBM utilization management is not uniformly regulated and that gap needs to be closed.

8.7 The Relationship of Pharmacy UM and Medical UM

When searching for any similarities between pharmacy-based UM (sometimes referred to as drug UR) and traditional health UM in today's healthcare environment one encounters a surprising result. The relationship between the two fields at this time is slight. Although the terminology of both pharmacy and medical UM is often the same, despite what one would expect, there is very little integration between the two fields. Professionals who do pharmacy UM are usually pharmacists while professionals who do medical UM are usually doctors and nurses. The documentation systems between the two groups are almost always different as well. In addition, the claims payment systems differ. Although the lack of coordination may not be an optimal situation, it is just another prime example of how health care lags behind other industries in how services are coordinated through the use of interoperable computerized systems.

8.8 PBM Regulation

Currently, depending upon the individual state, there can be up to three agencies that regulate services performed by PBM's as well as several federal agencies. PBM activities may be overseen locally by such entities as the departments of health, insurance, welfare, consumer protection agencies, and state personnel agencies if state employees are covered under the PBM. Moreover, federal agencies including the Drug Enforcement Agency, Food and Drug Administration, the Department of Health and Human Services, and the Justice Department can play a role in regulating PBM activities.[10] State regulations can even require that the PBM acquire a Utilization Review (UR) accreditation issued by a nationally recognized accreditation organization. With so many possible avenues for regulation, inconsistencies are inevitable.

In 2003, 22 states introduced bills impacting PBM operations. The bills under consideration provide for licensing and inspection of PBM's, fiduciary standards, mandatory disclosure of financial terms with manufacturers, and require any pass-through savings to consumers. Most provide oversight by the state insurance commissioner."[11]

8.9 The Future

As a greater share of the American population nears retirement age, future drivers of the PBM industry will likely fall into two categories: managing cost and promoting health care quality.

The White House Office of Management and Budget (OMB) now estimates that the actual cost of the Medicare prescription drug program will be between $530 and $540 billion dollars over the next 10 years. The baby boomer generation, a growing group of empowered consumers, is now looming on the health care radar screen. They are more than likely to be high utilizers of health care services due to the following statistics:

➢   78% have at least one chronic condition

➢   32% have four or more conditions and account for 78% of Medicare costs

➢   20% have five or more conditions and

  1)   fill 49 prescriptions/year

  2)   have 37 physician visits/year

  3)   See 14 different physicians

  4)   Utilize 7000 hospital days/1000 people[12]

These worrisome figures have led to a growing emphasis on outcomes and quality of care delivery including the documentation of the true value of pharmaceutical-based and disease-focused interventions in regards to overall costs of care. Employers too are acutely concerned with the need to reduce costs and increase worker productivity.[13] In some circles it is thought that increased pharmacy expenditures for drug therapy can coincide with decreased hospital admissions and fewer days in the hospital, but that assertion has yet to have more documented support. What is certain is that PBM

operations will continue to be closely monitored by state and federal regulatory agencies and other interested parties.

1   See also, www.fda.gov/cder/index.html.

2   Donald L. Barlett & James B. Steele, Why We Pay So Much for Drugs, TIME Magazine February 2, 2004.

3   Donald L. Barlett & James B. Steele, Why We Pay So Much for Drugs, TIME Magazine February 2, 2004.

4   Kirstin Downey, A HEFTIER DOSE TO SWALLOW; Rising Cost of Health Care in U.S. Gives Other Developed Countries an Edge in Keeping Jobs, The Washington Post, March 6, 2004.

5   Pharmacy Benefit Managers, OLR Research Report, December 24, 2003 2003-R-0908.

6   Robert P. Navarro, Managed Care Pharmacy Practice, Aspen Publication 1999, pgs. 230-238.

7   Pharmacy Benefit Management and Pharmacy Benefit Managers (PBMs), Resource Document; Approved by the Assembly, May 2002, Approved by the Board of Trustees, June 2002.

8   Robert P. Navarro, Managed Care Pharmacy Practice.

9   JMCP Journal of Managed Care Pharmacy Volume seven •number four July/August 2001.

10   Id.

11   White Paper –PBM Activities Already Appropriately Regulated.

12   Presentation by Margaret O'Kane, President NCQA House Ways & Means Committee, 2004.

13J MCP Journal of Managed Care Pharmacy Volume eight •number 2 March/April.

9.0: Independent Review[1]

Susan Prest, M.A., L.P.

9.1 Introduction

Independent medical review has become both an important and integral part of our health care system. Independent review's emergence upon the American health care scene is one of the most important developments in patient and consumer protection in the past decade. Physicians, health plans, employers, state and federal regulators, patient and consumer advocacy groups all agree that independent review, and not lawsuits, is the best means of resolving health care disputes.

In the year 2000 the overwhelming majority, or 92%, of all insured employees were in managed care plans; up from 54% in 1993.[2] With the dramatic increase in consumers who receive their health care through managed care plans has come an increase in number of disagreements over what services the health plans[3] would or should cover. In response to these rising concerns about the impartiality of health plan benefit coverage decisions, coupled with the lack of progress with a Patients' Bill of Rights at the federal level, 44 states and the District of Columbia have

enacted independent review laws. As shown in Figure 1, there are only 6 states that have still not yet enacted independent review laws (Idaho, Mississippi, Nebraska, North Dakota, South Dakota and Wyoming).

In March of 2002, The Henry J. Kaiser Family Foundation commissioned a study prepared by the Georgetown University Institute for Health Care Research and Policy[4] whose subject included one of the first comprehensive analyses of state independent review programs. The study found that independent review was becoming widely recognized as an important mechanism for consumer protection. It also demonstrated extensive state activity in the area of independent review and its success in resolving disputes between individuals and their health plans. In fact, independent review organizations (IRO's) are currently receiving high marks for quality, performance, and integrity. Yet, with all of the activity, optimism, and widespread support for independent review, the programs are used infrequently. There are only about

Figure 1. Independent Review Laws By State

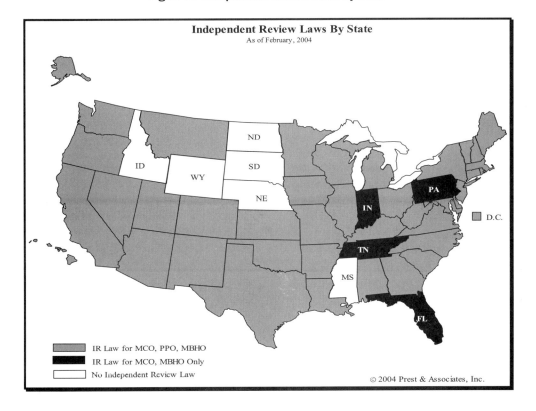

4,000 documented requests for an independent review annually. Thus, careful attention needs to be paid in order to preserve the integrity and viability of independent review and to take advantage of its full potential.

9.2 What Is Independent Review?

URAC defines independent review, also called external review, as a process, independent of all affected parties, to determine if a health care service is medically necessary, medically appropriate, experimental, or investigational.[5] It is a formal and unbiased process for the resolution of disputes involving adverse medical benefit determinations and is usually conducted by a medical expert or panel of medical experts who are not affiliated with the health plan. These expert medical reviewers must be qualified to perform the review and are usually associated with an independent review organization approved by the state. It may typically (but not always) occur after all utilization management and benefit appeal mechanisms available within the health benefits plan have been exhausted.

A primary goal of an independent review is to assure the patient, attending physician, and other treating clinicians that after a treatment recommendations and coverage decisions will be reviewed by a qualified and truly independent expert medical reviewer. In most cases the independent review process has the power to overrule the health plan's denial of benefits. However, the laws vary on whether the decisions are binding although they are binding in most states. Recent data shows that approximately 50% of the coverage disputes at the state level result in a finding on behalf of the insured.[6]

9.2.1 Background

In 1978, Michigan became the first state to establish an independent review program. Subsequently throughout the 1990's a large number of states began to enact patient protection legislation in earnest. By March 2000, 33 states had either legislated or enacted independent review laws. In that same year, URAC began its formal accreditation program for external review organizations (ERO's now IRO's) by accrediting the first 5 independent review organizations. The standards employed by URAC, both then and now, address a consumer's concerns that insurance appeal decisions are based on financial considerations or poor medical judgment, rather than what is best for the patient. Currently, 22 independent review organizations are fully accredited by URAC.[7]

Today independent review organizations operate in all the 50 states and their performance is earning them excellent ratings. Despite this fact the debate over patient protections still continues. In fact, most health care consumers are unaware of independent review laws and how to access the appeals process.

Founded in 2001 by the majority of URAC accredited independent review organizations, the National Association of Independent Review Organizations (NAIRO) is a trade association dedicated to protecting the integrity of independent medical review. Recognizing both legislative growth in this area, and in furtherance of their objectives, NAIRO, has called for the preservation of the integrity and viability of independent review.[8]

9.2.2 Independent Review Organizations

An independent review organization (IRO) is an entity that conducts independent external reviews of adverse health care determinations. Independent review organizations maintain panels of licensed, credentialed, and board-certified physicians who are experts in their areas of review. By design, independent review organizations are fully independent from all parties involved with an appeal. In light of their purpose IRO's should not have any financial, professional or contractual ties with the involved health plans, hospitals, providers, patients or manufacturers.

Generally independent review organizations usually contract with state regulatory agencies to conduct impartial reviews of disputed denials of health care benefits. Depending on the particular state, IRO's are subject to not only the rules and regulations set by the contracting agencies, but may be required by the state to be accredited by a nationally recognized accrediting body. URAC accredits independent review organizations by using standards that assure IRO's: are free from conflicts of interest; maintain established qualifications for physician reviewers; address medical necessity and experimental treatment issues; have reasonable time periods for standard and expedited reviews; and maintain an appeals processes. A URAC IRO accreditation means the organization provides a fair and impartial review process that benefits to both patients and physicians who have grievances with their MCO.[9]

9.2.3 The Independent Review Process

Independent review laws provide insureds with a process to challenge adverse medical determinations made by their health plans. While health plans are required to establish internal formal grievance procedures, it is usually after all the health plan's internal appeal mechanisms are exhausted that the insured or enrollee can proceed through the state independent review process, if one is available. There are exceptions to this rule. Sometimes requests for an independent review may be made before the internal appeal process has been exhausted if the request involves life threatening conditions, or the health plan waives the exhaustion requirement.

There is a great deal of variation among the states regarding legislation, and which state administrative agency is responsible for regulating independent review.as (*See* Table 1).

In general, despite the many variations between states, the independent review process usually follows several basic steps. First, the enrollee must file a written request with the specific state agency that regulates independent or external review. The filing must be accomplished within a specific time period that follows the date of receiving notice of a health plan's final adverse determination. At that point the state governing authority determines if the case is either a *standard review* or an *expedited review* and if the request for an independent review is appropriate. Once that decision is made, the case is then assigned to an independent review organization.

Second, after filing for an independent review the state may chose either an IRO, or compose a panel of physicians to conduct the appeal review. While Hawaii offers appeal by IRO, Vermont's Department of Insurance offers a review panel by maintaining an internally selected panel of in-state psychiatrists to review psychiatric and addictions medicine state level appeals. In New Mexico the Superintendent of Insurance compiles and maintains a list of physicians available to perform independent reviews. Some states will also add an additional requirement that an external independent review organization be certified by the state in order to provide independent reviews.

Third, IRO decision time frames are determined by whether the appeal falls under a standard, expedited, or experimental or investigational review. A standard review must be completed within 30 days of the date that the request for the review is filed with the state regulating department. An expedited review may be requested if the patient has a medical condition where waiting for the completion of a standard review would jeopardize the life or health of the patient or would interfere with the patient's ability to regain maximum function or if the patient has not been discharged from inpatient care. Expedited review decisions normally must be completed within 24 to 72 hours from the time the review is requested. If an adverse determination is made by a health plan on the basis that the recommended care is considered experimental or investigational, the enrollee may request an independent review as well. The enrollee's treating physician must certify that standard treatments have not been effective, or are not appropriate, or that there is no available standard treatment covered by the health plan that is more beneficial than the recommended treatment.

In addition to notification and time frame requirements, IRO's are required to provide toll-free telephone access for consumers and providers. Upon receipt of an independent review request, the organization will screen the case to determine if a conflict of interest exists for either the expert medical reviewer or the independent review organization. This will also determine whether the case is a standard or an expedited review, whether the case relates to a clinical or administrative issue, whether the case refers to medical necessity or experimental/investigational treatment, and whether the issue may be appropriately resolved through the independent review process. Independent review organizations also will require that their reviewers do no accept any type of compensation based on the reviewer's opinion or the outcome of the review.

Each IRO establishes and implements procedures for the selection and credentialing of reviewers following either the applicable state requirements, URAC standards, or both. A medical expert or panel of medical experts who are considered to be peers of the attending provider and who have the proper scope of licensure and professional experience to complete the review are selected. The organization provides these medical reviewers with a file containing the necessary information to complete the review. This documentation normally includes the patient's medical records, the attending health care professional's recommendation, applicable clinical review criteria, medical and scientific evidence determined to be relevant and appropriate to the case, terms of coverage, consulting reports, and any other relevant documentation. Any decisions made will be criteria or evidence-based using both scientific and medical evidence. When more than one reviewer is used, IRO's will provide an opportunity for the reviewers to discuss the case. In these circumstances, the majority decision prevails.

For every IRO decision made by the IRO, each reviewer must provide a written opinion to the independent review organization. In reaching their opinion, the reviewer is not bound by any decisions or conclusions reached during the health plan's internal review process. The report must contain a description of the reason for the review request, the date that the review request was received from the state regulator, the date the review was conducted, the principal reasons, and rationale for the determination and references or practice guidelines considered in reaching the decision.

After a final decision, a written notice to either uphold or reverse the health plan's adverse determination is sent to the appropriate parties as designated by the state statutes or regulations. With the exception of three jurisdictions (i.e., the District of Columbia, Oklahoma, and Oregon), independent review decisions are binding on the health plan and the enrollee to the extent that the parties have other remedies available under applicable federal or state

Table 1: State Departments* Regulating Independent Review

As of February, 2004

Department of Insurance		Department of Health	Other State Department	No Independent Review Organization
Alaska	Nevada	Alabama	California, Department of Managed Care (HMO's only)	Idaho
Arizona	New Hampshire	Delaware		Mississippi
Arkansas	New Mexico	District of Columbia		Nebraska
California	New York	Florida		North Dakota
Colorado	North Carolina	Georgia		South Dakota
Connecticut	Ohio	Massachusetts		Wyoming
Hawaii	Oregon	Minnesota		
Illinois	South Carolina	Montana		
Indiana	Tennessee	New Jersey		
Iowa	Texas	Oklahoma		
Kansas	Utah	Pennsylvania		
Kentucky	Vermont	Rhode Island		
Louisiana	Virginia			
Maine	Washington			
Maryland	West Virginia			
Michigan	Wisconsin			
Missouri				

* The term "department" is used to refer to agencies, commissions, administrations or other such terms. ©2004 Prest & Associates, Inc.

law. In some states the health plan or the enrollee may appeal by seeking judicial or administrative review of the binding independent review decision. For example, in Alaska the person who is aggrieved by a final decision at the state level may appeal the decision to the superior court. In Iowa, the enrollee or the enrollee's treatment provider acting on behalf of the enrollee may appeal the review decision by the independent review organization by filing a petition for judicial review.

In terms of who pays for the independent review process, it is the health plan against whom a request for an independent review is filed that usually pays the costs consistent with the fee schedule of the independent review organization. These fees vary widely and are dependent upon a number of factors including the number of reviewers that are used to review a case, state fee cap requirements, and complexity of the medical review. The fees are reported to range from a low of $350 to a high of $2000 with the median cost of a review of $700 to $900.

9.3 Legal and Regulatory Challenges

During the last few years independent review has survived most of its major legal challenges. One of these was a 5 to 4 decision by the U.S. Supreme Court in Rush Prudential HMO Inc., v Moran. In Rush the Supreme Court found that an Illinois HMO Act which called for mandated independent review was not preempted by the Employee Retirement Income Security Act of 1974 (ERISA).[10] As the Court explained, external review laws regulate insurance and therefore are not preempted by ERISA. Rush is significant because it means that patients in employer-sponsored health plans who live in the 42 states with external review laws can obtain an independent physician review of treatment denials. Unfortunately, the ruling did not apply to the large number of employees who are

covered under "self-insured" plans. "Self-insured" plans do not have to comply with state insurance regulations.[11] Moreover, the facts in Rush preceded the effective date of the ERISA claims benefit regulations and, therefore, future decisions may hold that a specific reduced legal scheme preempts state independent review laws.

According to a National Committee for Quality Assurance (NCQA) study,[12] as of July 31, 2003, most health plans are subject to state independent review laws to varying degrees. But, as shown in Table 1, the fact is that these state independent review laws apply inconsistently across managed care products such as managed care organizations (MCO's), preferred provider organizations (PPO's), and managed behavioral healthcare organizations (MBHO's).

9.4 Benefits of Independent Review

According to an American Association of Health Plans (AAHP) report titled *Independent Medical Review of Health Plan Coverage Decisions: A Framework for Excellence*, "(f)or the consumers of American health care, the widespread enactment of independent medical review is perhaps the most important development of the past decade."[13] Although once lobbied against by most health plans, independent review has gained a wide range of acceptance as ultimately benefiting both members and health plans together. Some examples of these benefits are:

1) *Reduction of costly litigation.* As reported by The New York Times, states with mandatory independent review laws can expect reduced litigation. When an external review sides with the patient, plans almost always back down and are unwilling to bear the legal risk of continuing to deny coverage for the disputed treatment. On the other hand, few patients or their

lawyers wish to waste both the time and the money by going to court and arguing against a plan that has won approval from independent physicians.[14] According to Terese Giorgio, Senior Director, Corporate Programs for IPRO, Inc., a New York based URAC accredited independent review organization, independent review will continue to offer a fair and impartial venue for enrollees and insurers to resolve their disputes without seeking expensive and time-consuming legal recourse.

2) *Enhanced health plan credibility.* Health plans welcome the opportunity to restore the public's faith in the health plans appeal process that independent review can provide. Health plans are aware that the public holds generally negative views about managed care and independent review is credited with enhancing health plans creditability.

3) *Consumer satisfaction.* Independent review gives consumers the accountability they want. It addresses their concerns that appeal decisions are sometimes based on financial considerations or poor medical judgment, rather than what is truly best for the patient.

4) *Quality Improvement.* Independent review shows the promise of improving medical care. As Winifred S. Hayes, Ph.D., President of HayesPlus, a URAC accredited independent review organization based in Lansdale, PA has communicated to the author, the role of independent (medical) review has grown as health plans and hospitals recognize its value in enhancing quality of care, addressing health outcome problems and medical errors, and developing and applying medical policy.

9.5 Independent Review Issues to be Resolved

1) *Lack of public awareness.* Consumers enrolled in health plans are generally unfamiliar with their plan's internal review process and are unaware of any independent review program available in their states. Even though all but six states have enacted laws requiring independent review, the number of such reviews being requested is small and infrequent. The Kaiser Family Foundation in a report released in March 2002[15] demonstrated that consumers were granted relief through independent review 50% of the time they chose to use the process. Even so, very few consumers have turned to independent review.

2) *Lack of standardization and consistency of independent review between states.* Independent reviews vary considerably between states. There is variation in the types of disputes that are accepted, the process, time frames and whether to allow access to specialty expert

medical review panels such as behavioral health care independent review organizations. For example, in some states independent review requirements apply to all types of health plans while in other states they apply only to some types of health plans. Creating consistency in the application of important standards across the nation with uniform and standardized independent review processes would protect the viability and integrity of independent review. In response to this concern Steven B. Larsen, Esq., former Commissioner of Insurance for the State of Maryland, in his article, *It's Time to Fix State External Review Laws*[16] recommends the creation of a uniform right to external review to ensure that health plans and their members are subject to a more predictable and equitable process. He also calls for some form of administrative review of external review decisions to ensure compliance with statutory standards.

3) *State licensing or domicile requirement for reviewers.* Same-state licensure limits the range of medical expertise available to the client/patient. It limits an IRO's ability to be competitive in certain marketplaces as not all IRO's have sufficient reviewers available for coverage in all 50 states.

4) *Lack of statutory immunity for independent review organizations and their reviewers for review activities conducted in good faith.* According to Dr. Hayes, "The biggest threat to independent review is litigation, especially in those states that do not indemnify the IRO and its' reviewers."

5) *Exclusion of certification of specialty behavioral health independent review organizations.* 12 of the 44 states that certify independent review organizations exclude the certification of specialty behavioral health independent review organizations. The primary reason given by states for this exclusion is clerical. They say it interferes with the state's process of assigning cases by rotation among independent review organizations.[17] Many states have solved this clerical problem without compromising patient protection and patient rights. Other states only certify one or a limited number of independent review organizations. These states do not include specialty behavioral health independent review organizations on their restricted panels. Only Vermont and Minnesota have separate review panels for mental illness and substance abuse.

In consideration of these and other issues requiring attention and resolution the National Association of Independent Review Organizations (NAIRO) recommended ten key elements for inclusion in any

Patients' Bill of Rights legislation or regulation concerning independent review as discussed in more detail below.[18]

9.6 Recommendations for Independent Review

NAIRO recommends the following ten key elements for inclusion in Patients' Bill of Rights legislation or state laws and regulations concerning independent review.

1) A reviewer's opinions should be supported by best available scientific evidence and nationally recognized clinical guidelines and consensus statements.

2) Standardization of external review processes, timeframes, methods, and credentialing requirements throughout the U.S. using a private standard setting organization (i.e., adopt URAC standards, including a minimum of 72 hours for expedited reviews, except in extreme emergencies).

3) Require reviewers to hold an unrestricted license to practice medicine or other clinical discipline in one of the 50 US states (no same-state licensing or domiciliary requirements for the reviewers).

4) Guarantee anonymity of the reviewers.

5) Provide statutory immunity for IRO's and reviewers for review activities conducted in good faith.

6) Do not exclude single-service IRO's.

7) Conflict of interest standards should be case-specific.

8) Upon request, the patient has the right to see the reviewer's original reports.

9) Review outcomes that are binding on the plan. Member must go through the external review process before litigating.

10) Fund a plan to educate the patient regarding his/her rights to external review.

9.7 Conclusion

Independent review is in a unique position to dramatically improve the quality of health care available to all Americans for many years to come. It has gained wide recognition as a successful tool to resolve disputes involving denial of medical benefits. It is now one of the most actively regulated areas impacting health plan and managed care operations. Although there are many issues that still require attention in order to preserve the viability and integrity of independent review, there is general agreement by qualified physicians that independent review is here to stay and should be the accountability cornerstone in any patient protection proposal.

Currently there is important work being done in both the private and public sector by organizations such as the America's Health Insurance Plans (AHIP), the Department of Labor (DOL), the National Association of Health Underwriters (NAHU), the National Association of Insurance Commissioners (NAIC), the National Association of Independent Review Organizations (NAIRO), the National Committee for Quality Assurance (NCQA), URAC, The Henry J. Kaiser Family Foundation, Georgetown University Institute for Health Care Research and Policy, Congress, the courts and other organizations in the area of independent review. With the unique cooperation evident among these organizations it appears that independent review will continue to take its place as an important national and state patient and consumer protection.

---

1 The term "independent review" as used in this article refers to independent medical review which is also referred to as external review, external independent review, and other similar terms.

2 *Patient's Rights*, The Henry J. Kaiser Family Foundation, 2003.

3 The term "health plan" as used in this article refers to array of managed care programs and insurers providing health care insurance or benefits coverage.

4 *Assessing State External Review Programs and the Effects of Pending Federal Patients' Rights Legislation*, prepared for The Henry J. Kaiser Family Foundation by Georgetown University, Institute for Health Care Research and Policy, March, 2000, Revised May, 2002 [hereinafter "Kaiser report"].

5 URAC, *Accredited Independent Review Organizations*, March 1, 2004, www.urac.org/prog_accred_orgs.asp [hereinafter "URAC website"].

6 Kaiser report at 3.

7 URAC, *Independent Review Organization, Accreditation Standards Summary, Accreditation Overview*, March 1, 2004, www.urac.org/prog_accred_IRO.

8 *Preserving the Integrity and Viability of Independent Medical Review*, National Association of Independent Review Organizations (NAIRO), 2001 [hereinafter "NAIRO white paper"].

9 URAC *Core Standards, Version 1.1* and *Independent Review Standards, Version 2.0*.

10 Rush Prudential HMO, Inc. v Moran, 230 F.3d 5959 (7th cir. 2000), cert. granted, 121S.Ct. 2598 (U.S. June 29, 2001)(No. 00-1021).

11 Jay Fisher, *U.S. Supreme Court rules in Rush Prudential Inc. v. Moran case*, The Academy of Orthopaedic Surgeons Bulletin, Vol. 5, No. 4, August 2002.

12 *External Review (IRO) Laws By State*, NCQA, July 31, 2003, www.ncqa.org

13 *Independent Medical Review of Health Plan Coverage Decisions: A Framework for Excellence*, an American Association of Health Plans (AAHP) survey, April, 2001.

14 Michael M. Weinstein, *Will Patients' Rights Fix The Wrongs?* The New York Times, June 24, 2001, Section 4 at 1.

15 Kaiser report at 3.

16 Steven B. Larsen, Esq., and Saul Ewing, LLP, *It's Time to Fix State External Review Laws,* HMO & Health Plans, January, 2004.

17 The state of Washington wrote, "Yes, we certify IROs to operate in Washington State. However, our laws, specifically require that an IRO be able to perform "a full range" of reviews, so no specialty IRO's are allowed." The state of Oregon simply states that they are following the Washington state law. The state of Indiana wrote, "Indiana HMO's are required to rotate through a list of IRO's certified by the Department of Insurance. In order for the rotation process to work efficiently Indiana is choosing to certify only full-service review organizations."

18 NAIRO white paper at 5.

10: URAC Health Utilization Management Standards: Pathways to Building a UM Program

Lori Harris-Stevens, RN, MHA, and Valerie Nosek, RN, BSN, CPHQ

Designing and maintaining an effective utilization management (UM) program is a considerable challenge. Companies may take many pathways towards developing an efficient UM program. There are many useful methods a company may consider as it strives to create a highly defined and well integrated product for customers.

An important first step in developing a successful UM program is to incorporate URAC's Health Utilization Management Standards as a foundation to establish and refine the processes and structure of the program. By drafting and implementing policies and procedures as recommended in the URAC Health UM Standards Program Guide, companies can create the foundation for a comprehensive, efficient and effective UM program. As it is absolutely necessary to have a full understanding of the Health UM Standards, it is advised that any organization that wishes to attempt this goal send at least one representative to a URAC Standards Workshop. The workshops are taught by experienced reviewers who can discuss the intent and rationale for each standard, as well as provide helpful hints on how to apply the applicable standards.

10.1 Establish a Utilization Management Program Model

When establishing a UM program model, an organization must define its life cycle process for handling utilization review requests from initiation to final determination then followed by the effective notification of the decision. Organizations need to establish a process flow comprised of how information will be collected, how the information will be collected and evaluated, and the qualifications of staff responsible for each review function. The typical UM program model uses non-clinical administrative personnel, first level clinical reviewers, and peer clinical reviewers. Organizations will discover that creating flowcharts at this stage provides a blueprint detailing the process flow of a request for a procedure or services.

10.1.1 Non-clinical Administrative Staff

Non-clinical administrative staff, often referred to as "intake staff," provide an important first contact with the UM organization. Their duties include screening calls to determine if a request requires a medical necessity determination. If it does, the reviewers will "set up" these cases on the computer system for later clinical review. A request for a procedure or service for medical necessity determination is referred to as a "case" or "episode of care."

Most UM companies limit the role of their non-clinical administrative staff to collecting demographic information, verifying benefits, and establishing a case or episode of care in a computer database. However, URAC's Health UM Standards allow for non-clinical administrative staff to collect structured clinical data over the phone, and perform scripted clinical screening that does not require evaluation or any interpretation of clinical data. If non-clinical administrative staff cannot complete the request based on the scripted clinical screening questions, the staff must then promptly transfer the caller to a clinically-trained health professional. URAC Health UM Standards require all screening scripts to be developed and reviewed at least annually. The review must be done by the appropriate actively practicing physicians or other providers.

Many UM companies use non-clinical administrative staff to increase the efficiency of clinical staff resources. Non-clinical administrative staff will often have a "call center" background or basic health care and medical terminology training.

In addition, some organizations also are using web-based products for pre-authorization. The benefits of web-based products are that they allow physicians or their staff to enter data via a secure web page. Typically, in these web-based pre-authorization products the system prompts the user to enter demographic and basic clinical data such as a diagnosis. Through a series of algorithms, the program will either authorize the treatment or refer the case to a first level reviewer for additional clinical data.

10.1.2 Initial Clinical Reviewers

The next step in the UM process often involves a clinical reviewer who decides whether a procedure or service meets established clinical review criteria. Initial clinical reviewers are usually health professionals who have undergone formal training and have a valid license or certificate in a specific health care field. The URAC Health UM Standards also require first level reviewers to have professional experience in providing direct patient care. The vast majority of UM companies employ nurses as first level reviewers who may be either licensed practical nurses (LPN's) or registered nurses (RN's). Specialty review organizations may employ clinicians with a specific expertise (e.g., licensed social workers for behavioral health review).

10.1.3 Peer Reviewers

If a procedure or service does not meet the medical necessity criteria, the case is forwarded to a peer reviewer. In URAC's Health UM Standards, only peer reviewers have the authority to make a decision not to certify or deny treatment or services. Peer reviewers are usually physicians. However, if the utilization management company is limited to a single specialty, practitioners from other health care disciplines may be used as peer reviewers. An example of this practice is a chiropractic specialty review organization that uses chiropractors for peer reviews.

Companies may choose to establish a process where the peer reviewer speaks to the attending physician or other ordering provider before making a decision not to certify or deny for medical necessity. Although this system can contain more up-front costs, there are many benefits to this UM model. Often once additional clinical information is obtained telephonically, the procedure or service can then be certified. This will likely decrease the number of appeals the UM company will conduct and in doing so will decrease overall costs. This type of system also promotes provider education and in turn may decrease future inappropriate admissions or service requests. It also allows for the negotiation of days or services with the attending provider. This is essential for UM companies seeking to eliminate adverse relationships with providers.

Other considerations UM organizations may want to examine are whether to employ or use independent contract peer reviewers, and whether to have peer reviewers perform their respective job functions onsite (in the UM office) or off-site (out of the UM offices). If the choice is to use peer reviewers onsite, scheduling a telephonic discussion between the peer reviewer and attending provider allows for more efficient use of the peer reviewer's time in the office. Another advantage to using peer reviewers on site includes the availability to perform clinical rounds with first level reviewers.

Whether using onsite or off-site peer reviewers, the UM company must decide whether the peer reviewer will document their review decisions in the computer database. Having peer reviewers enter their own decisions and clinical rationale into the database eliminates any concerns regarding interpretation of information from the initial clinical reviewer. If a remote access system is used, special precautions must be taken to ensure the information is collected and transmitted in a confidential manner.

UM companies must also decide whether to establish a panel of physicians to conduct peer reviews or delegate all or part of peer review function to a company that specializes in third-party independent reviews. If the decision is to delegate peer or appeal reviews to another organization, choosing a URAC accredited organization is recommended. A choice of a URAC accredited organization significantly decreases the amount of delegation oversight required when the primary UM company seeks URAC accreditation as well. Many health plans in The United States contract with URAC-accredited Independent Review Organizations (IRO's) for UM peer and appeal review services.

10.1.4 Appeal Reviewers

The last process to establish in a UM model is an appeals mechanism. With the initial non-certification decision process, UM companies must decide whether to establish a panel of physicians to conduct appeal reviews or contract with a company that specializes in appeal reviews. Again, if the UM company decides to delegate appeals to another organization, it is recommended that the company performing the appeal reviews be accredited by URAC as this decreases the amount of required delegation oversight. Under URAC's Health UM Standards, the primary difference between initial non-certification peer reviewers and appeal peer reviewers are that the appeal peer reviewer: 1) cannot be a subordinate of the initial non-certification peer reviewer or the same reviewer who made the original decision; and 2) should be board-certified (if a physician) in a same or similar specialty.

10.2 Select Clinical Review Criteria:

The next step in developing a UM program is deciding what clinical review criteria will be used to guide the medical necessity decision making process. Several national companies develop and license clinical review criteria, including Interqual and Milliman. These companies develop and revise criteria based upon feedback from actively practicing health care practitioners. UM companies may also develop proprietary criteria. If a choice is made to development one's own proprietary criteria, it is prudent to first consult with your legal department. Under some circumstances, legal counsel may recommend using nationally licensed criteria due to risk management concerns. URAC's Health UM Standards require that clinical review criteria be developed along side the involvement from appropriate actively practicing physicians or other providers. Clinical review criteria should be annually evaluated and updated as necessary.

10.3 Select UM Software

Once a choice as to what UM model and clinical criteria will be used, the next step is to decide on the appropriate software. Technology investments at the outset of a UM program provide multiple benefits for attracting and retaining customers. UM software guides the process flow, createsefficiencies, and accommodates customer reporting and claims processing requirements. The software program should preferably be windows-based and include appropriate fields for the collection of UM and quality management data. It should have the ability to collect quality management data including quantitative UM review results, results of internal quality auditing on a case-by-case basis, clinical quality issues, and a means to record and tabulate complaints and grievances.

One important factor in choosing UM software is the ability of the system to generate efficient notification of review determinations. Because URAC Health UM Standards require all denial letters to contain principal reasons for the denial, many companies have developed a list of common principal reasons for non-certification and post these reasons in their database. Based on the case under review, a principal reason can be customized as needed to provide an accurate explanation for the denial determination.

UM software should contain the ability to develop management reports during the early phases of UM program development. These reports ensure URAC Standards are being monitored and met. Continual analysis of computer data is also essential to the management of resources. Software that allows for flexible querying of data is especially valuable in environments where customers frequently request ad hoc queries and reports.

In choosing a software product, the need for security of electronic data is essential. Documentation accompanying a software system should include mechanisms for maintaining data integrity, confidentiality and security, as well as storage, maintenance, and destruction of documentation. A disaster recovery plan will be considered a necessary component of such a system, and helps to ensure minimum disruption to operations under adverse circumstances.

If an organization is planning to develop a case management or disease management program in the future, the organization's staff may want to assess whether the software program can easily be adapted to a case management model. Often programs that work very well for a UM program are not useful for a case management model. Additionally, the UM software program should easily communicate with internal and external claims systems. If an organization performs UM in more than one state, they should consider a software program that alerts users to state-specific requirements. This is especially useful in workers' compensation UM programs. If using licensed criteria, most organizations offer web-based programs, or can imbed a program into the organization's existing software program.

URAC currently recognizes three McKesson medical management software programs under its Vendor Certification Program- CareEnhance Care Manger, CareEnhance Review Manager Enterprise (CERME), and CareEnhance Disease Monitor.

10.4 Develop Job Descriptions

Once a UM process is established, the next step is to develop job descriptions for all staff involved in the UM review process. Job descriptions should include the individual's scope of responsibilities, educational and licensure requirements, professional competencies, reporting supervisor, and physical requirements. Job descriptions for licensed staff can address whether restricted or unrestricted licensure is accepted and in which state(s) licensure/certification is required. If it is a company's policy to accept restricted licensure, the organization's staff must develop a written procedure that outlines the support of this policy. It is a best practice to require staff to notify management immediately upon any changes in licensure or certification. In order to meet the URAC standards for appeal reviewers, the description needs to specify a board certification by the Advisory Board of Osteopathic Specialists (ABOS) or the American Board of Medical Specialties (ABMS) of those clinical peers performing appeals.

10.5 Develop Policies and Procedures

Following the development of job descriptions, a UM organization must next document its UM program process flow. Most companies begin this process by generating policies and procedures. Establishing a standard format for a company's policies should at a minimum include the company name, policy effective date, last review and revision date, and a title that identifies the document as a policy and procedure. In addition, a place for signature approvals for each policy and procedure should be incorporated into each document. If policies and procedures are maintained electronically, it is advantageous to make available at least one hard copy of the policy and procedure manual. Additionally, it is helpful to develop a global policy and procedure on the organization's policies and procedures. This is especially true if the organization has more than one person involved in the development of its policies and procedures. Ideally, the global policy and procedure will incorporate a sample template, detail how policies and procedures are maintained, how often policies and procedures are reviewed and by whom, and other key elements to ensure the integrity of how various policies and procedures are developed, implemented and revised. Creating a master list of policies and procedures will assist in annual review and update efforts.

10.5.1 UM Review Process

URAC recommends documentation of at least the following core review processes:

➢ prospective/precertification review;

➢ concurrent/continued stay review;

➢ retrospective review;

➢ second opinion;

➢ onsite review;

➢ lack of information (administrative non-certification);

➢ non-certification;

➢ peer-to-peer conversations (formerly called "reconsiderations");

➢ accessibility, hours of operation, callbacks;

➢ expedited (urgent) appeals; and

➢ standard appeals.

Ideally, each procedure will describe all required functions, identify staff responsible for these functions, and explain the time frames for task completion. As an example, precertification review would include the time frames for verbal and written notification. These timeframes are outlined in the URAC Health UM Standards.

When developing any policies and procedure, it is important to obtain input from staff members. Staff members provide valuable input on the accuracy and clarity of the procedure and can correct any technical errors. Remember: the purpose of documenting a company's operations in a written procedure is to have a living document describing how things are to be done and defining time frames for task completion.

10.5.2 Confidentiality and Conflict of Interest

Policies addressing confidentiality of protected health information (PHI) are essential for a UM program. Each UM company that applies for URAC Health UM accreditation must implement a confidentiality policy that protects against inappropriate uses and disclosures of PHI. It is an industry standard to require each employee or contracted person involved with the UM process to sign a confidentiality statement on hire that attests to the fact they understand the confidentiality policy. Moreover,

having employees review and sign a confidentiality statement annually is considered a best practice. Issues to address in the confidentiality policy include compliance with state and federal laws, how the information gathered during the UM process is used and shared internally, and how information will be disclosed to parties external to the organization. Additionally, staff must understand the issues surrounding potential or actual conflicts of interest during the UM process. Organizations often address conflicts of interest through "Code of Business Conduct" training.

10.6 Delegation – Yes or No?

Delegation is a process that establishes a written contract with another entity to perform UM services that a company would otherwise perform. For example, many health insurance companies delegate behavioral health reviews. Delegation arrangements must be outlined in writting the role and responsibilities of the delegating entity and subcontractor. The delegation agreement also must clearly define which entity is responsible for various aspects of the review process (i.e., telephonic notification, denial letters, etc.).

To establish compliance with the URAC Standards, if a UM company delegates any part of the review process, the delegation agreement must outline the responsibilities of the delegee and must include a statement that requires the subcontractor to perform services in accordance with the organization's requirements and URAC Standards. If the subcontractor is not URAC accredited, more extensive oversight of the delegated functions is required. In addition, a delegation policy and procedure is required that addresses specifics regarding the oversight process.

10.7 Develop Orientation and Training Program Descriptions

Essential to any UM organization is a structured orientation program for all staff and consultants who support or participate in the UM review process. An orientation outline for each staff position involved in the UM process will be necessary. Orientation outlines may include an overview of the URAC Standards and pre and post tests to assess UM staff knowledge. Some companies develop an attestation statement for staff and consultants to sign that verifies they understand the URAC Standards, and how the standards relate to their job function. In conjunction with the development of a training program, it is recommended that each position type have a training manual. If an organization develops a general training manual, it typically includes sections specific to each role or job function. Training manuals may include policies and procedures, computer database information, customer-specific requirements, and other references needed to function in their role. Online training materials provide staff with easy access to this information for ready reference.

Part of developing any orientation program is to establish early on how to communicate process changes to all staff. E-mail messages are a beneficial mode of information exchange. However, an organization must not rely solely on e-mail messages to communicate changes. Weekly or monthly face-to-face staff meetings to discuss changes in operations are crucial. Annual all-staff meetings that take place at the beginning of each calendar year are also useful to review the URAC standards, policies and procedures, changes in client services, and criteria updates. Meeting minutes are useful for referencing previous issues addressed in meetings and are helpful for those that were absent. Many UM companies post meeting minutes on their intranet along with their policies and procedures to provide a ready resource for staff.

It is essential that UM companies provide and promote continuing training and education to enhance staff development. An increasing number of states are requiring clinicians to attend continuing education programs to maintain licensure or certification. Many UM companies meet with clinicians weekly or bi-monthly to discuss interesting or challenging cases. Monthly or quarterly clinical inservices on a specific medical topic help clinicians maintain a current knowledge base. Pharmaceutical companies and local hospitals are often good resources for clinical inservices. It is important that the organization document efforts to provide ongoing training and education to staff by using sign-in sheets and maintaining copies of continuing education certificates/credits for personnel files.

10.8 Develop Quality Management Program

Quality management (QM) programs are essential to the success of a UM program. Quality management monitors and evaluates the effectiveness of a UM organization's policies, practices, and progress. URAC UM Standards require each UM organization to maintain and document a quality management program that monitors and evaluates UM processes. For a quality management program to be effective, it is necessary to have support from the executive staff. Staff training on the general principles of quality management will enhance the understanding of QM concepts and the operationalization of processes that support these concepts.

10.8.1 QM Program Description-

Developing a QM program begins by documenting a formal program description or plan that describes scope and objectives, program organization, monitoring and oversight mechanisms, and evaluation and organizational improvements of clinical review services. Key

components in a detailed QM program description for UM program include:

➤ *Quality Management Committee (QMC) Structure* — Address committee membership, frequency of meetings, organizational chart of committees, and guidelines for meeting minutes.

➤ *Composition of Quality Management Department* — Include qualifications of quality managers/coordinators and an organizational chart that outlines reporting structure.

➤ *Performance Standards or Benchmarks* — Establishes performance standards and key indicators and the methodology for measuring performance of audit processes, automatic call distribution system, verbal and written notification of UM decisions, appeals processes, and complaint/grievance processes. Performance standards should be measurable. For example, a performance standard for prospective review would be the expected timeframe for completing the review, as measured from receipt of request to issuance of a UM decision.

➤ *System for Tracking Complaints and Grievances* — How complaints are routed in an organization for resolution, a feedback mechanism for complainants, and how complaints are tracked, trended, and reported to the QMC is necessary.

➤ *Action Plans for Improvement* — Adopt a process to establish corrective action plans when areas of improvement are identified.

➤ *Auditing Process* — Address sampling methodology, audit tools, frequency of audits, and identify which staff conduct audits. In addition, address the feedback mechanism of audit results to individuals and aggregate reports to the QMC.

➤ *Satisfaction Surveys* — Patient, provider, or client satisfaction survey results provide external feedback for the quality improvement process.

➤ *Quality Improvement Projects* — When quality monitoring reveals a process that requires improvement for optimal operations, document formal efforts in the improvement process.

10.8.2 Annual Quality Improvement Initiatives

At the beginning of each calendar year, UM organizations need to focus on areas in the UM program that require improvement in the coming year. This behavior includes establishing objectives and measurable goals for each quality indicator as well as outlining the process to be used to meet these goals. Following these periodic written or verbal reports tracking the progress in meeting the identified goals, this information should be reviewed and discussed by organization's quality committee. It should be noted that quality initiatives can always be added or modified throughout the year and if deficiencies are found corrective action plans can be instituted. A corrective action plan need not always include an entire department, it may be a piloted project with a select number of individuals. At the end of each year, the UM organization can evaluate the indicators to determine if goals were met, and analyze any barriers in meeting those goals. If necessaryt, these goals can be redefined.

10.8.3 Auditing Process

All persons involved with the UM review process must be evaluated for adhering to the policies, criteria, and guidelines established by the organization. This includes not only non-clinical staff and initial clinical reviewers, but also peer reviewers and the Medical Director if he/she performs UM reviews. Most companies perform this process monthly or quarterly. Audits performed less than quarterly may not be frequent enough to implement timely interventions to correct problems. If an organization introduces new criteria, a new computer system, or new procedures, more frequent auditing may be necessary to confirm that staff is accurately and consistently implementing the changes. New employees may receive more intensive auditing than experienced staff. Many companies place new employees on a sliding scale auditing process during the probationary period to validate comprehension of the UM process, role and responsibilities.

Auditing tools, usually developed internally, typically address the specific level of review and may include adherence to clinical and procedural guidelines. Each indicator may be assigned points to develop a quantitative tool, and certain areas or indicators may be weighted more heavily than others (i.e., clinical indicators may be weighted more heavily than procedural indicators). Sharing the audit tool with employees during orientation will clearly communicate the areas in which staff will be evaluated. Quality audit summary reports are another example of an auditing tool that can be shared with the QMC as it allows for input and closes the feedback loop on this process.

10.9 Regulatory Compliance

UM organizations may operate in a single state or several states. An organization must be aware of, and comply with, all state and federal regulations that govern the UM business. This can be a major undertaking when beginning UM operations. Companies may assign dedicated staff to oversee regulatory compliance but depending on the size of the organization this is not always necessary. Companies must not only be able to

track applicable laws and regulations to their processes, but must also have a mechanism to ensure compliance with these laws.

10.10 Conclusion

Implementing a UM program for any health care organization is a considerable challenge. However, whether establishing a new UM program or redesigning an established UM program, the use of URAC's Health UM Standards can provide a valuable roadmap that can point to an efficient and effective review program. By structuring an organization's UM program along URAC guidelines, an organization also will gain a strong foundation towards accreditation and regulatory compliance with numerous states UM laws.

Onsite Utilization Management: Enhancing Provider Relations and Promoting Patient Safety

Valerie Nosek, RN, BSN, CPHQ, Lori Harris-Stevens, RN, MHA, and Christine Leyden, RN, MSN, A-CCC

After years of noting a decline in onsite (facility-based) UM activities, URAC has begun to see a trend in the re-emergence of onsite UM. While it may not be practical for all UM organizations to perform onsite utilization management, companies may want to still consider the feasibility of this practice. Onsite UM not only provides a mechanism to enhance relationships between managed care organizations (MCO's) and providers, it also helps facilitate positive outcomes for patients. As medical management programs; increase their focus on supporting consumers who require a high level of medical services during and after their hospitalization, onsite review services can be of extraordinary use.

Enhancing communications and improving provider relations with hospital staff.

Facility-based medical management review complements the relationships involved in managed care. It provides a ready resource for hospital staff and attending physicians by promptly addressing and resolving utilization and benefit issues. Further, active participation by a medical management company at the site of services outwardly demonstrates a dedication to patient care outcomes. Reviewers can share information regarding the managed care organization's clinical guidelines and provide timely information on alternative and/or appropriate medical settings and levels of care. In addition, a managed care company's willingness to collaborate on patient care issues with hospital staff and provide rationales for utilization decisions improves relations between the two and ultimately results in enhanced productivity for both hospital and managed care staff.

Those companies who perform onsite review are able to experience a decrease in administrative denials, which are benefit denials due to lack of information. Onsite reviewers are able to accomplish this by having the capability to access enrollees' medical records in order to collect necessary clinical information, especially after physicians have conducted "inpatient rounds." The ability to reduce administrative denials can benefit both the MCO and the treatment facilities by eliminating the bureaucracy associated with these denials. The end result is that those burdens associated with issuing administrative denials such as subsequent appeals and the need to submit clinical information are avoided.

Promoting patient safety through enhanced communication and effective discharge planning.

Utilization management programs that provide effective and collaborative onsite UM help to promote patient safety. Facility-based UM also provides an opportunity for onsite clinical reviewers to educate consumers and providers on available network resources as well as provide authorizations for timely transfers or post-discharge services. Onsite reviewers have a distinct advantage over telephonic reviewers in that they possess familiarity with the local network resources. This lends itself to more timely and effective outcomes for the patient. The onsite reviewers become active participants in enrollee discharge planning rounds. This creates a

tremendous resource for the facilities, social workers and discharge planners. By participating in the authorization of services such as durable medical equipment, home care, inpatient rehabilitation, or hospice, authorization delays typically encountered by the facilities are avoided. In addition, onsite reviewers who initiate personal contact with the patient and their family provide an atmosphere of increased trust that leads to an increased understanding of the medical management process. The reviewers become the "face" of the organization for the patient and family members.

An example of a best practice by utilization management companies that enhances patient safety is the performance of post-discharge follow-up. After discharge to the patient's home, facility-based MCO reviewers often conduct follow-up telephonic contact with consumers to evaluate the transition to home care. This allows the medical management organization to assess the effectiveness of discharge planning and to modify the plan as needed. Typically, the follow-up call includes verification of: 1) follow-up appointment with the primary physician or specialist; 2) prescriptions filled; 3) confirmation of delivery of any durable medical equipment; and 4) arrival of home health services. In addition, the MCO staff can assist the consumer in arranging for follow up appointments with health care providers and thus promote a continuity of care. By assuring the consumer has received the necessary services prescribed for discharge some companies are reporting a reduction in unplanned readmissions and ER visits.

Onsite review staff can also provide referrals for patients who possibly may benefit from participation in case management or disease management programs. Onsite hospital utilization review is an excellent way to identify these particular patients. Case management and disease management programs have the ability to assist consumers in navigating the health care system and in turn promote health and wellness through this ongoing communication and service coordination.

Implementing a facility-based onsite UM program.
1) Selecting the hospitals

Selecting a facility in which to perform onsite UM should be based on certain criteria. The criteria most often used by managed care companies are high volume and high claims network facilities. Other criteria may include facilities with lacking provider relations, or unique patient service needs such as inpatient rehabilitation facilities. Often this is done through an analysis of claims and/or UM data. Many organizations perform this analysis annually to ensure that these targeted facilities continue to meet the criteria for facility-based utilization management. Once the criteria for onsite utilization management is chosen, the next logical step is to address specific legal issues with the facility which may or may not include a review of the facility's network contract if one is present, or the development of a new contract between the managed care organization and facility.

2) Selecting the onsite UM nurse

The role of the onsite UM reviewer is one of educator, liaison, diplomat, independent decision-maker and resource person. Many organizations recruit people who have lived and worked in a targeted community for several years. This often provides a solution to one of the biggest obstacles in health care, that is, assisting patients in navigating the health care system and understanding available resources.

In addition to UM experience, many organizations look for persons who have a background in case management, home care, or discharge planning as these roles are often intertwined in the onsite UM process. Once hired, it is essential that an onsite reviewer receive in-house orientation. Items normally addressed during this orientation can include: 1) review of the organization's UM policies and procedures, including skillful communication techniques; 2) information on in-network and out-of-network providers and benefits offerings available to patients; 3) explanation of company policies on travel reimbursement; 4) training on company UM software programs, and 4) information technology support (i.e., laptop computers and cellular telephones).

3) Meet with facility UM department administrators

Prior to starting an onsite UM program, a meeting should be conducted between the administrator of the hospital UM department and the managed care organization. Participants from the managed care organization may include the UM director or manager, the medical director, and an onsite reviewer. This meeting provides the managed care organization with an opportunity to share utilization management philosophy, discuss UM criteria and onsite policies, and explain the role of an onsite reviewer. Copies of managed care organizations onsite policies and UM criteria should also be provided. In addition, the facility staff can discuss facility policies, including identification and security requirements and bring up any issues or concerns regarding the onsite review process. To further enhance both communication and understanding between organizations, these meetings should be held on an annual basis or more often if necessary. The frequency of the meeting is based on provider relation needs.

4) Provide a Technology Interface

An MCO's commitment to technology helps achieve optimal productivity and efficiency during onsite review. Companies typically provide either a laptop or handheld device in which the onsite reviewer documents the findings of the review. The reviewer also has ready access to the MCO's clinical guidelines. Some companies have a designated area at the facility for utilizing wireless devices or internet access via a Virtual Private Network (VPN). This allows streamlined communication between the onsite reviewer and the MCO, including the MCO's peer review staff as needed.

5) Establish a Feedback Mechanism

While the primary contact with the facility is the UM nurse, it is also helpful to identify an MCO manager to serve as an alternate contact person to assist if the facility nurse is unavailable, or to log a complaint or compliment. This additional communication mechanism provides a tool for the MCO to not only collect feedback on facility satisfaction with the onsite review process, but also in measuring its staff performance as well.

Conclusion

The use of onsite Utilization Management is increasing in part due to its many advantages over typical telephonic UM. Onsite UM provides for more timely review of patient progress and eliminates the occurrence of administrative denials for lack of information. The end result is a win-win-win solution for the managed care organization, facility, and the patient. In addition, onsite UM's timely assessment of both patient health care status and needs facilitates safe and effective discharge planning. The managed care organization is able to collect a more thorough assessment of patient needs and can facilitate more targeted services through functions such as case management and disease management. For patients, the benefit from having an onsite reviewer is improved coordination of health care benefits, close monitoring of appropriate levels of care, and targeted coordination of services based on their medical needs. This promotes continuity of care and can avoid future admissions for same or similar health care issues. Onsite review enhances communication among providers, medical management organizations, and consumers resulting in a dedicated team committed to the optimal health of consumers.

11.0 Promoting Patient Safety Through Medical Management[1]

Liza Greenberg, RN, MPH

"All health care settings should establish comprehensive patient safety programs operated by trained personnel within a culture of safety. These programs should encompass (1) case finding – identifying system failures, (2) analysis – understanding the factors that contribute to system failures, and (3) system redesign – making improvements in care processes to prevent errors in the future. Patient safety programs should invite the participation of patients and their families and be responsive to their inquiries."

From: *Patient Safety: Achieving a New Standard For Care*, Institute of Medicine Committee on Data Standards for Patient Safety
National Academies Press, 2004

11.1 Medical Management Has a Role in Patient Safety

11.1.1 The Environment

In 2003, URAC convened a Patient Safety Advisory Committee whose members included patient safety experts, representatives from URAC accredited companies, and industry stakeholders. The purpose of the Committee was to explore the development of standards that could encourage medical management programs, particularly Case Management, Disease Management, Utilization Management, Health Call Center, and Independent Review organizations, to become engaged in ongoing efforts to improve patient safety. The Committee recommended that URAC create standards to help medical management organizations establish systematic approaches to improving patient safety. A systems approach would build on the core capabilities of medical management programs, use approaches documented in the patient safety literature, and focus on high priority areas.

The Patient Safety Advisory Committee reviewed major patient safety initiatives to attain guidance in the current direction of patient safety efforts. In addition, URAC's staff conducted surveys, interviews, and focus groups. In the spring of 2004, the Committee met with national patient safety leadership organizations to discuss medical management patient safety strategies. The specific participants in this meeting included the Institute of Medicine (IOM), the National Quality Forum, the Agency for Healthcare Research and Quality, the Centers for Medicare and Medicaid Services, and the Centers for Disease Control and Prevention. These organizations were able to establish a number of far reaching initiatives to improve quality and safety[2]. Their recommendations included:

- Implementation of data standards to more effectively understand and capture patient safety events;

- Increased use of automated systems to augment human efforts to create safer patient care;

- Establishment of patient safety "systems" that include leadership, policies, priority setting, training, and data collection; and

- Routine use of quality indicators to analyze adverse events and potential events to identify preventive systems improvements.

11.1.2 Potential Patient Safety Roles For Medical Management Programs

Medical management programs play an important role in the administration and oversight of the health care system. Medical management programs also contribute to the coordination of health care ; an area the IOM singled out as a significant need. While medical management programs do not specifically provide patient care, they possess ability to use the information they collect to enhance the safety of health care systems and improve care coordination in a collaborative, partnership role.

Medical Management Includes:

- Utilization Management

- Case Management

- Disease Management

- Telephone Triage and Health Information

- External Review

Medical management opportunities that can influence patient safety may include:

- Prevention

- Intervention

- Education

- Reporting

- Tracking

- Authorizing

- Collaboration

Medical management programs can bring capabilities to the table that could be applied to patient safety as well. These include:

➢ Evidence-based guidelines;

➢ Decision support tools;

➢ Automated algorithms to guide staff;

➢ Clinical professionals;

➢ Multi-disciplinary care coordination;

➢ Direct patient and provider interaction (for some);

➢ Patient reported and automated data access and linkages;

➢ Routine use of CPT and ICD9 codes to classify activities;

➢ Patient assessment; and

➢ Patient education

Both the Patient Safety Advisory Committee and the national patient safety leaders who attended the spring 2004 meeting recognized that these capabilities represent unique strengths. Medical management organizations, particularly when supported by sophisticated information technology systems, are able to provide a basis of support for safer health care.

11.2 The Role of Health Information Technology

The Institute of Medicine along with other experts recently highlighted the importance of health information technology (Health IT) in managing and resolving patient safety problems in a variety of settings. The highlights included a particular emphasis on hospital systemsthe to which the IOM recommended the adoption of standardized data elements in order to facilitate the implementation of

safer systems. Not only can Health IT be a vital tool of medical management, it can also be tailored to support safety functions more seamlessly.

Example: UM-identified patient safety concerns:

➢ Delay in inpatient testing or treatment;

➢ Failure of provider to deliver standardized treatment; and

➢ A pattern of adverse events linked to a facility that cause extended length of stay.

When technology that supports medical management decisions linked to other available information such as claims, pharmacy, patient-reported, and lab data, medical errors and adverse events can be prevented. These types of medical management information technology tools can be designed to routinely and seamlessly support identification of quality of care and patient-safety issues. Medical management processes supported by Health IT can be enhanced to address patient safety concerns through systematic identification, analysis, intervention, reporting, and evaluation. The results of these efforts may provide a return on investment through the prevention of error and improved outcomes. URAC encourages that medical management leaders become a part of national efforts to define data elements in order to create more unified information systems.

Example: CM-identified patient safety concerns:

➢ Potential adverse medication interaction due to multiple providers and prescriptions;

➢ Failure of patient or provider follow through plan of care; and

➢ Unsafe home environment.

Medical Management Practice Example: Patient Safety Systems at Work			
System component	**Utilization Management**	**Case Management**	**Disease Management**
1. Standard assessment protocols are used in medical management process to collect and enter patient data in an automated system	UM reviews the case of a patient admitted for fracture. Standard medication and clinical history assessment indicates that the patient has congestive heart failure (CHF) and has been prescribed NSAIDS while hospitalized	Standard assessment of a patient referred for case management after a transplant indicates that the patient is taking St. John's Wort	A patient is identified for disease management due to coronary artery disease (CAD). The initial standard assessment indicates that the patient is taking nitrates and Viagra
2. Automated algorithm is used to identify specific clinical issues	The patient has a history of CHF which NSAIDS can worsen	St. John's Wort may lower the level of anti-rejection medications in the patient's blood	Nitrates and Viagra can cause harm when taken together
3. An automated system flags safety issues and alerts medical management staff	When data is entered in the care management decision support system, an alertis issued and communicated to the provider or member	A flag is issued for the case manager to communicate with the provider or member regarding a possible interaction	An alert is issued and communicated to the provider and/or member indicating a serious interaction
Note: These are examples of how medical management programs could identify potential unsafe practices that could lead to adverse events. Medical management programs need to identify specific priority indicators feasible and relevant for their eligible populations. ActiveHealth Management developed the initial concept for this model.			

The National Quality Forum (NQF) Safe System Components	How Medical Management Could Implement Safer Systems Initiatives
Prioritize patient safety events and situations that should be reported	Define high priority patient safety events that might be captured by the organization Build systems for identifying, investigating and reporting events that identify: Specific patient safety opportunities and potential responses Clinical triggers for non-routine safety assessment Protocols for routinely incorporating safety into patient assessments Processes analyzing and reporting patient safety events The range of interventions with providers and triggers for provider contacts Define the process for evaluating the return on investment specific to the organization
Analyze the patient safety events and situations that are reported	Develop a tracking and reporting process by provider, facility, or payer that includes policies for: Routine and non-routine reporting to staff and external parties such as payers Disclosure of safety concerns or errors to providers and professional boards Aggregate and patient specific reporting
Verify that the remedial actions identified through analysis of reported patient safety events are implemented and effective and do not cause unintended adverse consequences	Develop quality management processes to complement patient safety indicators Monitor medical management indicators that could be affected by patient safety initiatives
Ensure that organizational leadership is kept knowledgeable about patient safety issues present within the organization and continuously involved in processes to assure that the issues are appropriately addressed and patient safety is improved	Engage and inform the organization's leaders Develop policies and procedures for all aspects of the patient safety program that include a role for the organization's leaders
Provide oversight and coordination of patient safety activities	Identify an accountable unit and individual for patient safety, and designate resources to safety initiatives
Provide feedback to frontline healthcare providers about lessons learned	Establish internal feedback loops between quality management processes, line medical management staff and the organization's leadership, with a defined performance improvement component
Publicly disclose implementation of or compliance with all NQF endorsed safe practices applicable to the facility	Inform purchasers and regulators of initiatives to enhance medical management's contribution to patient safety Comply with state, professional, regulatory requirements for reporting
Train all staff in techniques of teamwork-based problem solving and management	Provide staff training on the organization's priority safety indicators and how staff are expected to respond to safety concerns.
Other (non National Quality Forum)	Collaborate with community based patient safety initiatives to position medical management as a partner for safety Implement automated tracking and decision support tools that support safety priorities.

The model developed by ActiveHealth Management, illustrates how data collected in the medical management process can be used to improve quality and safety. In the model, automated algorithms compare data entered during the medical management transaction to evidence-based protocols and lists of contraindications. Flags are generated to alert staff of the need for action to prevent a potential safety or quality breach. The use of automated algorithms to identify safety concerns of commission or omission augments the effectiveness of medical management and enhances the value of medical management care coordination. URAC believes that safer medical management through information technology-driven approaches should be expanded and disseminated throughout the industry.

11.3 Next Steps: A Systems Based Approach for Patient Safety

As part of its findings the URAC Patient Safety Advisory Committee concluded that the next step for the medical management industry is to define a specific agenda for patient safety. The agenda should be based on core medical management capabilities, and focusing on high priority clinical conditions. Medical management programs should also adopt a system-based approach that maximizes their contribution to patient safety. An example of such a systematic approach includes measuring the impact of patient safety efforts to show purchasers the value of patient safety initiatives.

One model for a systems-based approach to medical management has been developed by the National Quality Forum, a national consensus driven organization. This particular model defines characteristics of patient safety systems that could be customized for implementation by any type of health care program. The following table illustrates how medical management programs could be designed consistently with National Quality Forum Safer System Components.

11.4 Looking Ahead

The URAC Patient Safety Advisory Committee concluded that medical management programs can make a significant contribution in making the health care system safer for patients. Current URAC Core Standards for accreditation require an organization to have a mechanism for responding to urgent issues affecting safety of patients. The next generation of URAC standards will likely define patient safety responses more explicitly, building on core medical management capabilities. In fact, in September, 2004 URAC released "Informational" Patient Safety Standards as a model for the medical management community. The informational standards will accompany URAC's mandatory standards, but will not be evaluated and scored. It is hoped that the standards will provide a template for development of patient safety systems embedded in medical management programs.

URAC also encourages Case Management, Utilization Management, Disease Management, and other medical management programs to begin the process of embracing and adopting a patient safety role. Medical management programs should review their own operations against systems capabilities defined by the Institute of Medicine and other organizations, to identify patient safety opportunities. These programs can be part of the solution to providing safer and better quality care through evidence-based practices and information-driven systems.

11.5 Resources for Patient Safety

The Institute of Medicine inspired the current national focus on patient safety through the release of two seminal publications, *To Err is Human*, and *Crossing the Quality Chasm*. The IOM has also described 20 clinical priority areas for improving the quality of health care. In 2004, the IOM produced *Patient Safety: Achieving a New Standard for Care*, which serves as a road map for developing a data infrastructure to improve patient safety. The IOM Web site is www.iom.edu. IOM reports can be purchased or viewed online at http://www.nap.edu/books/0309090776/html/

The Agency for Healthcare Research and Quality (AHRQ), a federal agency, has supported a number of critical research projects and policy reports and has made funding available for patient safety research. AHRQ has developed a set of "Patient Safety Indicators," derived from hospital data to identify trends in adverse events occurring during hospitalization. The AHRQ Web site is www.ahrq.gov.

The American College of Medical Quality (ACMQ), a national organization that provides leadership in health care quality management, has produced an excellent brief summary of key IOM reports. ACMQ's Web site is www.acmq.org.

The Joint Commission on Accreditation of Healthcare Organizations (JCAHO), a national accreditation organization, has redesigned its accreditation standards and performance reporting requirements for hospitals to increase emphasis on patient safety. The JCAHO Web site is www.jcaho.org.

The Leapfrog Group, a consortium of employers that have agreed to promote safety in their health care offerings, has embraced three evidence-based approaches to improving patient safety. Leapfrog's Web site is www.leapfroggroup.org.

The National Patient Safety Foundation (NPSF), an offshoot of the American Medical Association, has developed a national agenda for educating and informing providers and patients about safety issues in a collaborative manner. NPSF can be found on the Web at www.npsf.org.

The National Quality Forum (NQF) has developed several consensus reports on patient safety. *Safe Practices for Better Health Care* offers a recommended list of safe practices for hospital settings. The NQF Web site is www.qualityforum.org, which includes an executive summary of the *Safe Practices* report.

URAC issued a report in fall 2003, *Patient Safety Capabilities of UM Organizations*. The report and other patient safety information for medical management, including brief case studies of disease management patient safety practices, can be retrieved at www.urac.org

---

1   This section is based upon a white paper, brochure that URAC published during the summer of 2004.

2   Please review documents and Web sites referenced in the "Resources" section of this document for specific policy and practice recommendations issued by the IOM and other patient safety organizations.

How to Use This Survey: Methodology and Template
David H. Reiter, J.D.

In this version of *The Utilization Management Guide*, URAC has again included a summary of health UM statutes and regulations for every U.S. state and major U.S. Territories. These summaries follow a standard outline that touches on most of the major facets of these laws and regulations. Along with its survey of health UM laws and regulations, URAC also has included a similar survey of Worker's Compensation utilization management regulations. The information was assembled by the law firm Blank Rome L.L.P.

In addition, this publication includes URAC's Health Utilization Management Standards and Workers' Compensation UM Standards. This should enable the reader to compare a particular state's requirement to a related provision in URAC's Standards. For instance, in the states' outlines there is a section titled "Telephone Access Standards." If you wish to know any given state's telephone access standards (i.e., the minimum requirements set by a state for telephone access to the utilization management organization or reviewer), simply turn to that state's entry and look at that specific section. The summaries for each state are arranged alphabetically.

Also, *The Utilization Management Guide* includes a summary chart as a quick reference in Section 3.0, "General Findings of State Laws and Regulations." This should provide the reader with a general snapshot of UM regulation in the states. Please note that the summary information in the chart is not as comprehensive or detailed as that found in the outline for each state.

Equally important to remember is that this publication provides only an overview of state and federal regulatory UM requirements. URAC strongly advises medical and compliance staff affiliated with various health care organizations (and other interested readers) to review the laws of each jurisdiction in which they operate and to contact the appropriate state and federal regulators for definitive answers to questions about UM requirements. Regulatory contact information can be found in Section II of each state's summary and in Appendix E, "State Regulatory Contacts. It also may be appropriate to consult with legal counsel.

The information obtained in these surveys is for reference use only and does not constitute the rendering of legal, financial, or other professional advice on the part of URAC. The state summaries found in Appendices B and C are current as of July 1, 2004.

Survey Methodology

In preparing the information that follows, URAC staff first referred to the state summaries prepared for URAC's *The Utilization Management Guide: Second Edition*. After reviewing that information, this research was updated through a series of searches on electronic legal databases such as Westlaw™, along with a review of each particular state's legislative and/or regulatory agency web site. Once the entire survey was compiled, each state's insurance regulatory agency was given a copy of their respective state for further comment and review. URAC incorporated the regulators' responses in the final summaries included in this document. Most of the state surveys were returned, and URAC expresses its deep appreciation to all these state regulators for their comments and assistance.

Simultaneously, URAC staff revised the template (Template for State Utilization Management Law Analysis) used in the earlier publication. In revising that template, URAC incorporated a number of suggestions made by helpful past readers of URAC's *The Utilization Management Guide: Second Edition*. Please note that the template does not include every issue addressed in state laws and regulations for UM. Rather, URAC designed the template to address those issues that are most important from a compliance or policy perspective. For instance, the template does not address administrative penalties a state can levy against utilization management organizations, even though many states devote a substantial amount of attention to this issue. By contrast, *The Utilization Management Guide* continues to include the subject of "same-state licensure" for clinical reviewers in the template. This policy question continues to be a focus of policy debates in the states and can be a compliance obstacle for utilization management organizations. As such, questions of state licensure in terms of compliance should always be addressed to the organization's legal offices.

Definitions

Terminology related to utilization review or UM varies from state-to-state as well as in the health and workers' compensation contexts. The definitions found at the back of URAC's Health Utilization Management Standards, (Appendix D) and URAC's Workers' Compensation Utilization Management Standards, (Appendix E) reflect the way URAC has used these terms for purposes of this publication. Here are several of the more commonly used terms a reader of *The Utilization Management Guide* may encounter:

➤ **Adverse Determination.** A determination that a specified service or treatment is not medically necessary. Sometimes referred to as a "denial" or "adverse decision."

➤ **Appeal.** A formal process by which a patient or provider can seek reconsideration of an adverse determination. Sometimes referred to as a "grievance."

➤ **Attending Provider.** The health care provider with primary responsibility for the treatment of a patient and typically responsible for recommending the treatment or service subject to UM. Sometimes referred to as the "treating provider," "ordering provider," or the "provider of record."

➤ **Expedited Appeal.** An appeal made available in circumstances where delay in a review determination may interfere with the provision of timely care to a patient. States vary in their requirements for the availability of an expedited appeal process.

➤ **External review.** This is defined as a level of independent review taken by a dissatisfied plan participant or provider when their internal review options within the managed care organization are exhausted. External reviews are conducted by an independent external review organization.

➤ **Independent or External Review Organizations.** Normally these are separate private companies who are independent of the managed care organization. They provide independent, expert medical reviews of benefit determinations where the medical service has been denied to plan participant.

➤ **Internal reviews.** Those series of initial review of benefit determinations by the managed care organization. There may be one or sometimes two levels of internal review.

➤ **Patient.** An individual who is eligible for coverage under a health benefits plan and for whom medical service or treatment is subject to UR. Sometimes referred to as "enrollee," "covered person," or "member."

➤ **N/A.** Means "not applicable."

➤ **Third-party payer.** An entity that bears the financial risk of paying for health and medical services as part of a health benefit plan. This term includes, but is not limited to, health maintenance organizations and insurers. This is sometimes referred to as "carrier" or "health carrier."

➤ **Utilization Review or UR.** A process, performed by or on behalf of a third-party payer that evaluates the medical necessity, appropriateness, and efficiency of the use of health care services, procedures, and facilities.

Note: The term "utilization review" always includes prospective and concurrent review. States vary in whether the term includes retrospective review. Refer to the appropriate section in each state's outline to see if retrospective review is included that state's definition. In many settings, "utilization management" has supplanted the term "utilization review." As URAC has seen a trend toward using "utilization management," that is the term used primarily in this publication.

➤ **Working days.** The days of the week, excluding Saturday, Sunday, and legal holidays, sometimes also referred to as "business days."

Points to Remember

Similar to the last edition of *The Utilization Management Guide*, URAC's research covers UM regulatory requirements in the workers' compensation (WC) context as well as the health sector. Some states apply the same requirements to both general health UM and WC UM. In contrast, other states have separate administrative or regulatory schemes for workers' compensation. To the degree that URAC has been able to identify the separate administrative or regulatory schemes, *The Utilization Management Guide* includes a separate summary, following the same template, for WC UM.

In preparing this survey, URAC focused on state laws and regulations that affect UR or UM in the health and workers' compensation contexts. Out of necessity, URAC did not try to address in detail every law or regulation (state or federal) that might apply to a particular managed care organization. For example, most every state has an HMO act, and HMO's in particular are especially likely to be subject to additional state requirements. Managed care organizations and others should consult applicable state laws and contact the appropriate government officials for definitive answers to regulatory questions.

Template for State Utilization Management Law Analysis.

(Note: this format and numbering is followed generally with some exceptions)

State

I. Scope and Applicability

A. **Who is subject to the state's utilization review laws? What types of entities fall within the scope of the state's utilization review requirements? What exemptions are provided, if any?**

1. **HMO's?** Are HMO's subject to the state's utilization review laws? If no, what are the requirements of the applicable HMO Act with respect to utilization **review?**

2. **Insurers?** Are health care insurers subject to the state's utilization review laws? Are domestic insurers, when conducting UR on their own members, subject to the UR laws? Are non-domestic insurers subject to the state's UR laws when conducting UR on their own members residing in the state?

3. **Utilization Review Organizations?** Are utilization review organizations subject to the state's utilization review laws?

4. **Retrospective Review?** Do these laws and regulations apply to retrospective review? (In many states, the law applies only to prospective and concurrent utilization review.)

B. **What term does the state use to refer to regulated entities?** Many states use different terms to refer to utilization review organizations – i.e., utilization management organizations, utilization review entities, private review agents, etc. [Include statutory/regulatory definition and citation.]

C. **What activities does the state include in its definition of utilization review?** How does this state define utilization review (or utilization management) and what is included? [Include statutory/regulatory definition and citation.]

II. Regulatory information

Which state agency is responsible for regulating utilization review? Who is the person to contact regarding utilization review regulation in the state? What are the citations for the applicable laws and regulations? For states that do not regulate utilization review, the contact listed is the person familiar with any plans or initiatives for the state to regulate utilization review.

B. **Responsible state agency.**

C. **Contact Information.**
   1. Name and Title.
   2. Address.
   3. Phone and Facsimile.
   4. E-mail.
   5. Web site.

III. Licensure/Certification Requirements

A. **What entities are required to obtain a license in the state to conduct utilization review for residents of the state?**
   1. HMOs?
   2. Insurers?

B. **How often must licensure/certification be renewed?** How often, and by what date, must utilization review licensures and certificates be renewed?

C. **Licensure fees (initial and renewal).** What is the fee charged by the state for a utilization review certificate or license? Is there a different fee to renew the certificate or license? If so, what is the renewal fee?

D. **Documentation required for licensure.** Generally, what types of documents must a utilization review organization submit with an application for licensure or certification?

E. **Exemptions from licensure.** Are out-of-state organizations, including HMO's, insurers, and utilization review organizations, granted an exemption from the state's licensure and certification requirements if they are duly licensed and/or certified in the state in which they are domiciled?

IV. Program Requirements

A. **Clinical review criteria.** How are utilization review criteria to be reviewed and updated? Are there requirements for the disclosure of criteria?

B. **Prohibitions against financial incentives.** Does the state prohibit financial incentives for utilization review reviewers or utilization review organizations?

C. **Telephone access standards.** What minimum requirements does the state set for telephone access?

D. **Quality assurance program.** Does the state require the utilization review organization to have a quality assurance program? If so, what are the requirements for such programs?

E. **Delegation of utilization review functions.** Does the state establish requirements for delegation of utilization review functions? If so, what are the requirements?

F. **Confidentiality.** What requirements does the state establish for the confidentiality of medical information used during the utilization review process?

V. Reviewer Qualifications

A. **Qualifications of reviewers that render utilization review determinations (at each level of utilization review, if applicable)?** What, if any, medical qualifications are necessary for the individual who makes the review determinations? If the state provides for more than one level of review or appeal, what are the required professional qualifications at each level?

B. **Requirements for medical director.** Is the utilization review organization required to have a medical director? If so, must the medical director be a physician or other health professional?

C. **Requirements for "same-state" licensure.** Must reviewers be licensed in the same state as the utilization review organization conducts business? Some states require reviewers to be licensed in their state.

VI. Reviews and Appeals

A. **Review determination and notice to patients/providers.** Does the state specify that the utilization review organization should notify patients and providers of review determinations?

1. **Time frame for determination.** How soon must the utilization review organization send notifications of determinations?

2. **Contents of notice of adverse determinations.** What information must be included in the notices of adverse determinations, i.e. determinations not to certify?

a. **Reasons for adverse determination.** Must notices of adverse determinations include an explanation of why the service was not approved? Must such notices include the clinical review criteria (or related material) upon which the decision was based?

b. **Notice of appeal rights.** Must notices of adverse determinations include information about how to initiate an appeal?

B. **Appeals requirements.** Must utilization review organizations offer an appeal of adverse determinations? (See Section V.A. for a description of the required qualifications of reviewers that render appeals determinations.) What decisions may be the subject of an internal appeal?

1. **Time frame for determination.** How soon must internal appeal considerations be completed for regular appeals? Are there requirements for expedited appeals?

2. **External appeals.** Does the state require access to an external appeal considered by an individual that is not affiliated with the utilization review organization?

C. **Emergency Services.** Are there specific provisions that deal with review of emergency services?

VII. Recognition of URAC Accreditation Status

A. **Does the state recognize URAC accreditation?** Has the state adopted laws or regulations that "give credit" to utilization review organizations that are accredited by URAC?

B. **Which of the state's requirements are waived for URAC-accredited organizations?** What benefits does URAC accreditation confer on a utilization review organization in this state?

VIII. Miscellaneous

Are there any other significant provisions in the state's utilization review laws that are not covered? (This section is optional and is only included if the state has additional provisions not covered by the standard summary.)

Alabama

I. Scope and Applicability

A. Who is subject to the state's utilization review laws? Any person or entity performing utilization review, including the State of Alabama. ALA. CODE § 27-3A-3(5) (2004).

1. **HMO's?** Yes, but only to extent of providing utilization review for the HMO's own members.
2. **Insurers?** Yes.
3. **Utilization review organizations?** Yes.
4. **Retrospective review?** No.

ALA. CODE § 27-3A-3(5) (2004).

B. What exemptions are provided?

1. An agency of the federal government.
2. An agent acting on behalf of the federal government, but only to the extent that the agent is providing services to the federal government.
3. The internal quality assurance program of a hospital.
4. An employee of a utilization review agent.
5. Health maintenance organizations licensed and regulated by the state, but only to the extent of providing a utilization review to their own members.
6. Any entity that has a current accreditation from the Utilization Review Accreditation Commission (URAC). However, entities with current URAC accreditation shall file a URAC certification with the department annually.
7. An entity performing utilization reviews or bill audits, or both, exclusively for workers' compensation claims pursuant to Section 25-5-312. If an entity also performs services for claims other than workers' compensation, it shall be considered a private review agent subject to this chapter for those claims.
8. An entity performing utilization reviews or bill audits, or both, exclusively for the Medicaid Agency.
9. A person performing utilization reviews or bill audits, or both, exclusively for their company's health plan, independent of a utilization review company.
10. An insurance company licensed by the State of Alabama performing utilization reviews or bill audits, or both, exclusively for their company's health plan, independent of a utilization review company.
11. The Peer Review Committee of the Alabama State Chiropractic Association. ALA. CODE § 27-3A-3(5) (2004).

C. What term does the state use to refer to regulated entities? A "Utilization Review Agent" is any person or entity, including the State of Alabama that performs utilization review, with the exceptions listed. ALA. CODE § 27-3A-3(5)(2004).

D. What activities does the state include in its definition of utilization review? "Utilization review" is defined as, "A system for prospective and concurrent review of the necessity and appropriateness in the allocation of health care resources and services given or proposed to be given to an individual within this state. The term does not include elective requests for clarification of coverage." ALA. CODE § 27-3A-3(4) (2004).

II. Regulatory Information

A. Responsible state agency. Alabama Department of Public Health, Division of Managed Care Compliance.

B. Contact Information.

1. **Name and Title:** Michelle Williams, Director, Division of Managed Care Compliance.
2. **Addres:** Alabama Department of Public Health, The RSA Tower, 201 Monroe Street, Suite 750, Montgomery, AL 36104.
3. **Phone and Facsimile:** (334) 206-5351; facsimile (334) 206-5303.
4. **E-mail:** mwilliams@adph.state.al.us.
5. **Web site:** http://www.adph.org/mcc/

III. Licensure/Certification Requirements

A. What entities are required to obtain a license in the state to conduct utilization review for residents of the state? Those defined as a utilization review agent under ALA. CODE § 27-3A-3(5) (2004).

B. How often must licensure be renewed? Annually, by July 1.

C. Licensure fees (initial and renewal). $1,000 per year, payable to the Alabama Department of Public Health.

D. Documentation required for licensure.

1. The utilization review agent must certify in writing to the Alabama Department of Public Health that it is in compliance with ALA. CODE § 27-3A-5 (2004). Certification is to be made annually on or before July 1st of each calendar year.

2. In addition, the agent must file: the name; address; telephone number; and normal business hours of the utilization review agent. The name and telephone number of a person for the department to contact. A description of the appeal procedures for utilization review determinations.

3. Any material changes in the information filed in accordance with this section shall be filed with the State Health Officer within 30 days of the change. ALA. CODE § 27-3A-4 (2004).

E. **Exemptions from licensure.** Out-of-state organizations are not granted an exemption from Alabama's licensure and certification requirements even if they are duly licensed and/or certified in their state of domicile.

IV. Program Requirements

A. **Clinical review criteria.** A physician must approve utilization review standards and guideline. ALA. CODE § 27-3A-5(a)(2) (2004).

B. **Prohibitions against financial incentives.** No provision.

C. **Telephone access standards.** Utilization review agent staff must be available by toll-free telephone at least 40 hours per week during normal business hours. Utilization review agents must have telephone systems capable of accepting or recording calls during non-business hours, and must respond to these calls within 2 working days. ALA. CODE § 27-3A-5(a)(5)-(6) (2004).

D. **Quality assurance program.** No provision.

E. **Delegation of utilization review functions.** No provision.

F. **Confidentiality.** Utilization review agents shall comply with all applicable laws to protect the confidentiality of individual medical records. ALA. CODE § 27-3A-5(a)(7) (2004).

V. Reviewer Qualifications

A. **Qualifications of reviewers that render utilization review determinations (at each level of utilization review, if applicable)?**

1. A licensed physician must review all review determinations or make determinations in accordance with standards or guidelines approved by a physician. ALA. CODE § 27-3A-5(a)(2) (2004).

2. Appeals must be considered by licensed physicians in the same or similar specialty as typically manages the medical condition under review. ALA. CODE § 27-3A-5(a)(4)a (2004).

3. Appeals of chiropractic services must be reviewed by a licensed chiropractor. ALA. CODE § 27-3A-5(a)(4)a (2004).

B. **Requirements for medical director.** Physicians, chiropractors, or psychologists making utilization review determinations shall have current licenses from a state licensing agency in the United States. ALA. CODE § 27-3A-5(a)(8) (2004).

C. **Requirement for "same-state" licensure.** No provision.

VI. Reviews and Appeals

A. **Review determinations and notice to patients/providers.**

1. **Time frame for determination.** Notification must be mailed or otherwise communicated to the provider of record within 2 business days of the receipt of the request for determination and the receipt of all information necessary to complete the review. ALA. CODE § 27-3A-5(a)(1) (2004).

2. **Contents of notice of adverse determination.**

   a. **Reasons for adverse determination.** Notification shall include principal reason for such a determination. ALA. CODE§ 27-3A-5(a)(2) (2004)

   b. **Notice of Appeal Rights.** Yes.

      i. **Appeals requirements.** All determinations not to certify an admission, service, or procedure as being necessary or appropriate are the subject of an internal appeal. ALA. CODE§ 27-3A-5(a)(4)a. (2004).

      ii. **Time frame for determination.** Appeals generally must be conducted within 30 days from receipt of all information necessary to consider the appeal. ALA. CODE§ 27-3A-5(a)(4)b. (2004).

      iii. **Are there requirements for expedited appeals?** Yes. Expedited appeals, made before or during a continuing service requiring review, must be completed within 48 hours of receipt of all information necessary to consider the appeal. ALA. CODE§ 27-3A-5(a)(4)c. (2004).

3. **External appeals.** No provision.

B. **Emergency Services.** Utilization review agents must allow a minimum of 24 hours after an emergency admission, service, or procedure for the patient (or representative) to request certification for continuing treatment. ALA. CODE § 27-3A-5(a)(9) (2004).

VII. Recognition of URAC Accreditation Status

A. **Does the state recognize URAC accreditation?** Yes.

B. **Which of the state's requirements are waived for URAC-accredited organizations?** URAC-accredited organizations are not defined as "Utilization Review Agents" under ALA. CODE § 27-3A-3(5) (2004). However, URAC-accredited organizations must initially file basic demographic information and evidence of their URAC certification and must annually file evidence of their URAC certification. ALA. CODE § 27-3A-3(5)f. (2004). In addition, the annual licensure fee is waived. ALA. CODE § 27-3A-4(d) (2004).

Alaska

I. Scope and Applicability

A. **Who is subject to the state's utilization review laws?** Alaska does not currently regulate utilization review organizations specifically. They do, however, regulate utilization review by managed care plans. ALASKA STAT. § 21.07.020(4)(2004).

   1. **HMO's?** Yes.
   2. **Insurers?** Yes.
   3. **Utilization review organizations?** Yes, but through requirements of managed care plans.
   4. **Retrospective review?** Yes.

B. **What term does the state use to refer to regulated entities?** No provision.

C. **What activities does the state include in its definition of utilization review?** "Utilization review" means a system of reviewing the medical necessity, appropriateness, or quality of health care services and supplies provided under a group managed care plan using specified guidelines, including preadmission certification, the application of practice guidelines, continued stay review, discharge planning, preauthorization of ambulatory procedures, and retrospective review. ALASKA STAT. § 21.07.250(16) (2004).

II. Regulatory Information

A. **Responsible state agency.** Department of Commerce and Economic Development, Division of Insurance

B. **Contact Information.**
   1. **Name and Title:** Linda Brunett, Program Coordinator, Alaska Division of Insurance
   2. **Address:** PO BOX 110805, Juneau, AK 99811-0805.
   3. **Phone and Facsimile:** (907) 465-2545; facsimile: (907) 465-2816.
   4. **E-mail:** linda_brunette@dced.state.ak.us
   5. **Web:** www.dced.state.ak.us/insurance.

III. Program Requirements

A. **Clinical review criteria.** No provision.
B. **Prohibitions against financial incentives.** No provision.
C. **Telephone access standards.** No provision.
D. **Quality assurance program.** No provision.
E. **Delegation of utilization review functions.** No provision.
F. **Confidentiality.** Medical and financial information in the possession of a managed care entity regarding an applicant or a current or former person covered by a managed care plan is confidential and is not subject to public disclosure. ALASKA STAT. § 21.07.040(a) (2004).

IV. Reviewer Qualifications

A. **Qualifications of reviewers that render utilization review determinations (at each level of utilization review, if applicable)?**

   1. Under Alaska's health maintenance organization (HMO) statute, a utilization review decision to deny, reduce, or terminate a health care benefit or to deny payment for a health care service because that service is not medically necessary may only be made by a health care provider trained in that specialty or subspecialty and licensed to practice in Alaska after consultation with the covered person's health care provider. ALASKA STAT. § 21.86.150(j)(2004).

   2. Utilization review by managed care plans that deny, reduce, or terminate a health care benefit or to deny payment for a health care service because that service is not medically necessary shall be made by an employee or agent of the managed care entity who is a licensed health care provider. ALASKA STAT. § 21.07.020(4)(B) (2004).

   3. Appeals decisions must be made by an employee or agent of the managed care entity who holds the same professional license as the health care provider who is treating the covered person. ALASKA STAT. § 21.07.020(5)(B) (2004).

V. Reviews and Appeals

A. **Review determinations and notice to patients/providers.**

   1. **Time frame for determination.** Utilization review decisions by managed care plans must be made within 72 hours after receiving the request for preapproval for nonemergency situations; for emergency situations, utilization review decisions for care following emergency services must be made as soon as is practicable but in any event no later than 24 hours after receiving the request for preapproval or for coverage determination. ALASKA STAT. § 21.07.020(4)(A) (2004).

2. Contents of notice of adverse determination.

   a. **Notice of Appeal Rights.** Managed care plans must disclose the existence of the right to an external appeal of a utilization review decision made by a managed care entity. ALASKA STAT. § 21.07.020(7) (2004).

   b. **Appeals requirements.** Managed care plans must provide for an internal appeal mechanism for a covered person who disagrees with a utilization review decision made by a managed care entity. This appeal mechanism must provide for a written decision. ALASKA STAT. § 21.07.020(5) (2004).

   c. **Time frame for determination.** Internal appeal decisions must be made within 18 working days after the date written notice of appeal is received. ALASKA STAT. § 21.07.020(5)(A) (2004).

   d. **Are there requirements for expedited appeals?** Yes. Managed care plans must provide for an internal appeal mechanism for a covered person who disagrees with a utilization review decision made by a managed care entity in any case in which delay would, in the written opinion of the treating provider, jeopardize the covered person's life or materially jeopardize the covered person's health. The managed care entity shall decide an appeal described in this paragraph within 72 hours after receiving the appeal. The decision must be in writing and by an employee or agent of the managed care entity who holds the same professional license as the health care provider who is treating the covered person. ALASKA STAT. § 21.07.020(6) (2004).

3. **External appeals.** A managed care entity offering group health insurance coverage shall provide for an external appeal process that meets the requirements of this section in the case of an externally appealable decision for which a timely appeal is made in writing either by the managed care entity or by the enrollee. ALASKA STAT. § 21.07.050(a) (2004).

   a. External review may be conditioned on the completion of internal appeal.

   b. External appeal decisions must be made in accordance with the medical exigencies of the case involved, but in no event later than 21 working days after the appeal is filed, or, in the case of an expedited appeal, 72 hours after the time of requesting an external appeal of the managed care entity's decision. ALASKA STAT. § 21.07.050(d)(8)(B) (2004).

   c. An external appeal agency qualifies to consider external appeals if, with respect to a group health plan, the agency is certified by a qualified private standard-setting organization approved by the director or by a health insurer operating in this state as meeting the requirements imposed under the law. ALASKA STAT. § 21.07.060(a) (2004).

VI. Miscellaneous

Qualis Health, a company accredited by URAC, provides utilization review services for Alaska's Medicaid clients under a contract awarded by the Alaska Department of Health and Social Services, Division of Medical Assistance.

A. As a condition for participation in the medical assistance programs, hospitals must have in effect a utilization review plan approved by the U.S. Department of Health and Human Services if utilization review is performed by a federally contracted professional review organization (PRO).

   1. The written plan submitted by the hospital or the PRO on behalf of the hospital must include detailed provisions described in 42 C.F.R. 456.50 - 456.145.

   2. The approved utilization review plan must be implemented through the PRO or a hospital that has been delegated review authority by the PRO.

   3. As a condition for participation in the medical assistance programs, hospitals shall participate in an assessment of health care services to program recipients. The division or its representative will conduct an annual on-site assessment. The assessment will be planned in advance and in coordination with the hospital.

   ALASKA ADMIN. CODE tit. 7, § 43.430 (2004).

American Samoa

I.   Scope and Applicability

URAC has found no statutes, regulations, or case law pertaining to utilization review/utilization management in American Samoa.

II.   Regulatory Information

A.   **Responsible state agency.** Office of the Insurance Commissioner, Office of the Governor

B.   **Contact Information.**

    1.   **Name and Title:** Elisara T. Togiai, Commissioner of Insurance

    2.   **Address:** American Samoa Government, Pago Pago, P.O. Box 485, American Samoa 96799

    3.   **Phone and Facsimile:** 011 (684) 633-4116/4009; facsimile 011 (684) 633-2269

    4.   **E-mail:** Not known.

    5.   **Web site:** www.asg.gov.com

III.   Recognition of URAC Accreditation Status

A.   Does the state recognize URAC accreditation? No.

B.   Which of the state's requirements are waived for URAC-accredited organizations? Not applicable.

Arizona

I. Scope and Applicability

A. **Who is subject to the state's utilization review laws?** A person or entity that performs utilization review. This includes any health care insurer whose utilization review plan includes the direct or indirect denial of requested medical or health care services or the denial of claims, but does not include a governmental agency, an agent that acts on behalf of the governmental agency, or an employee of a utilization review agent. ARIZ. REV. STAT. ANN. §§ 20-2501 and 20-2503 (2004).

   1. **HMOs?** Yes.
   2. **Insurers?** Yes.
   3. **Utilization review organizations?** Yes.
   4. **Retrospective review?** Yes.

A utilization review agent shall not conduct utilization review in Arizona unless the utilization review agent meets or is exempt from statutory regulation.

B. **What exemptions are provided, if any?** A person or entity is exempt from the provisions of this article if the person:

   1. Is accredited by the Utilization Review Accreditation Commission (URAC), the national committee for quality assurance or any other nationally recognized accreditation process recognized by the director.
   2. Conducts internal utilization review for hospitals, home health agencies, clinics, private offices or other health facilities or entities if the review does not result in the approval or denial of payment for hospital or medical services.
   3. Conducts utilization review activities exclusively for work related injuries and illnesses covered under the workers' compensation laws in title 23.
   4. Conducts utilization review activities exclusively for a self-funded or self-insured employee benefit plan if the regulation of that plan is preempted by § 514(b) of the Employee Retirement Income Security Act of 1974, 29 United States Code § 1144(b). ARIZ. REV. STAT. ANN. §§ 20-2502 and 20-2503 (2004).

C. **What term does the state use?** Utilization review agent is defined as a person or entity that performs utilization review. This includes any health care insurer whose utilization review plan includes the direct or indirect denial of requested medical or health care services or the denial of claims, but does not include a governmental agency, an agent that acts on behalf of the governmental agency, or an employee of a utilization review agent. ARIZ. REV. STAT. ANN. §§ 20-2501 and 20-2503 (2004).

D. **What activities does the state include in its definition of utilization review?** "Utilization review" is defined as "a system for reviewing the appropriate and efficient allocation of inpatient hospital resources, inpatient medical services and outpatient surgery services that are being given or are proposed to be given to a patient, and of any medical, surgical and health care services or claims for services that may be covered by a health care insurer depending on determinable contingencies, including without limitation outpatient services, in-office consultations with medical specialists, specialized diagnostic testing, mental health services, emergency care and inpatient and outpatient hospital services. Utilization review does not include elective requests for the clarification of coverage." ARIZ. REV. STAT. ANN. § 20-2501(A)(12)(2004).

E. **Application of Utilization Review Standards:** The utilization review standards established in this chapter apply to prospective, concurrent and retrospective utilization review for:

   1. Inpatient admissions to hospitals and other inpatient facilities.
   2. Outpatient admissions to surgical facilities.
   3. Outpatient surgical services provided in a health care provider's office.
   4. Medical, surgical and health care services that may be covered by a health care insurer depending on determinable contingencies, including without limitation outpatient services, in-office consultations with medical specialists, specialized diagnostic testing, mental health services, emergency care and inpatient and outpatient hospital services. For purposes of this law "inpatient admissions" includes inpatient admissions to all acute medical, surgical, obstetrical, and psychiatric and chemical dependency inpatient services at a licensed hospital or other inpatient facility. ARIZ. REV. STAT. ANN. §§20-2503 and 20-2531 (2004).

F. **Requirements:** Each utilization review agent and each health care insurer operating in this state

---

whose utilization review system includes the power to affect the direct or indirect denial of requested medical or health care services or claims for medical or health care services shall adopt written utilization review standards and criteria and processes for the review, reconsideration and appeal of denials. A utilization review agent shall conduct utilization review in accordance with the agent's utilization review plan that is on file with the Department of Insurance.

1. Exceptions are made for Utilization Review:
   a. Performed under contract with the federal government for utilization review of patients eligible for all services under title XVIII of the social security act.
   b. Performed by a self-insured or self-funded employee benefit plan or a multiemployer employee benefit plan created in accordance with and pursuant to 29 United States Code § 186(c) if the regulation of that plan is preempted by § 514(b) of the employee retirement income security act of 1974 (29 United States Code § 1144(b)), but these requirements do apply to a health care insurer that provides coverage for services as part of an employee benefit plan.
   c. Of work related injuries and illnesses covered under the workers' compensation laws in title 23.
   d. Performed under the terms of a policy that pays benefits based on the health status of the insured and does not reimburse the cost of or provide covered services.
   e. Performed under the terms of a long-term care insurance policy.
   f. Performed under the terms of a medicare supplement policy as defined by the Department of Insurance. ARIZ. REV. STAT. ANN. § 20-2531 (2004).

II. Regulatory Information

A. **Responsible state agency:** Department of Insurance, Life & Health Division.

B. **Contact Information.**
   1. **Name and Title:** Ms. Dolly Coleman, Health Utilization Administrator Analyst, Health Department of Insurance, Life & Health Division

   2. **Address:** 2910 North 44th Street, Suite 210, Phoenix, AZ 85018-7256.
   3. **Phone and Facsimile:** (602) 912-8460; facsimile (602) 912-8453.
   4. **E-mail:** dcoleman@id.state.az.us
   5. **Web site:** www.state.az.us/id.

III. Licensure/Certification Requirements

A. **How often must licensure be renewed?** Every 3 years. ARIZ. REV. STAT. ANN. § 20-2507 (2004).

B. **Examination fees (initial and renewal).** No actual amount stated, *see* ARIZ. REV. STAT. ANN. § 20-2506 (2004).

C. **Documentation required for licensure.** The utilization review agent must file a signed and notarized application as proscribed by the Health Department of Insurance, ARIZ. REV. STAT. ANN. § 20-2504 (2004), and the following information:
   1. A utilization review plan that includes a summary description of review guidelines, protocols and procedures, standards and criteria to be used in evaluating covered patient care made by the utilization review agent.
   2. The professional qualifications either of the personnel employed or under contract to perform the utilization review.
   3. A description of the policies and procedures that ensure that a representative of the utilization review agent is available to receive and send the notice and acknowledgments.
   4. A description of the policies and procedures that ensure that the utilization review agent will follow applicable state and federal laws to protect the confidentiality of individual medical records.
   5. A copy of the materials or a description of the procedure designed to inform patients and providers, as appropriate, of the requirements of the utilization review plan.

ARIZ. REV. STAT. ANN. § 20-2505 (2004).

In addition, standards and criteria must be objective, clinically valid and compatible with established principles of health care, established with input from physician advisors who represent major medical specialties and who are certified or board eligible under the standards of the appropriate American Medical Specialty Board, and include a process for prompt initial reconsideration of an adverse decision and a process for appeals that meet the requirements of this article (does not apply to utilization review activities limited to retrospective claims review). ARIZ. REV. STAT. ANN. § 20-2532(A) (2004).

IV. Program Requirements

A. **Clinical review criteria.** Standards and criteria must be objective, clinically valid and compatible with established principles of health care, established with input from physician advisors who represent major medical specialties and who are certified or board eligible under the standards of the appropriate American Medical Specialty Board, and include a process for prompt initial reconsideration of an adverse decision and a process for appeals that meet the requirements of this article (does not apply to utilization review activities limited to retrospective claims review). Deviations from the criteria are permitted when the patient would benefit from advances in medical treatment made since the criteria were adopted (does not apply to utilization review activities limited to retrospective claims review). ARIZ. REV. STAT. ANN. § 20-2532 (2004).

B. **Prohibitions against financial incentives.** No provision.

C. **Telephone access standards.** The utilization review agent must maintain a toll-free telephone line (or accept long-distance collect calls) for forty hours each week during normal business hours. ARIZ. REV. STAT. ANN. § 20-2505 (2004).

D. **Quality assurance program.** No provision.

E. **Delegation of utilization review functions.** Health care insurers who use outside utilization review agents shall adopt a utilization review plan pursuant to the statutory mandated criteria for utilization review plans. Health care insurers that delegate to a utilization review agent are responsible for the utilization review agent's acts on its behalf. ARIZ. REV. STAT. ANN. § 20-2532 (2004).

F. **Confidentiality.** Utilization review agents shall file written procedures for assuring patient information is maintained as confidential in accordance with applicable federal and state laws, is used only for purposes of utilization review, quality assurance, discharge planning and catastrophic case management, and is shared only with agencies authorized by the patient in writing. Utilization review agents shall comply with all applicable state and federal laws relating to the confidentiality of medical records. ARIZ. REV. STAT. ANN. § 20-2509 (2004).

V. Reviewer Qualifications

A. **Qualifications of reviewers that render utilization review determinations (at each level of utilization review, if applicable).**

1. Personnel conducting utilization review shall have current licenses that are in good standing and without restrictions from a state health care professional licensing agency in the United States and may be a member of a profession that practices inpatient hospital or outpatient surgical care. ARIZ. REV. STAT. ANN. § 20-2505 (2004).

2. Appeals of an issue of medical necessity, not whether the claim or service is covered, the informal reconsideration shall be performed by a licensed health care professional.

3. Expedited or formal reviews must be conducted by a physician or other health care professional who is licensed, or an out of state provider, physician or other health care professional who is licensed in another state and who is not licensed in this state and who typically manages the medical condition under review.

4. External, independent reviews must be conducted by a physician, provider, or other health professional who typically manages the medical condition under review and who is board-certified or eligible, and who shall not have a substantial interest in the member, provider or health care insurer involved in the particular case under review or any other conflict of interest that will preclude the reviewer from making a fair and impartial decision. The individual reviewer shall not be a policyholder or insured member of a company whose case is being reviewed. ARIZ. REV. STAT. ANN. §§ 20-2533 and 20-2538 (2004).

B. **Requirements for medical director.** Must hold an active unrestricted license to practice medicine in Arizona. ARIZ. REV. STAT. ANN. § 20-2510 (2004).

C. **Requirement for "same-state" licensure.** The law expressly permits out-of-state, licensed health professionals to conduct utilization review as well as external, independent reviews.

VI. Reviews and Appeals

A. **Review determinations and notice to patients/providers.** Any member who is denied a covered service or whose claim for a service is denied may pursue the applicable review process. ARIZ. REV. STAT. ANN. § 20-2533 (2004).

B. **Appeals requirements.** At the time of issuing a denial, the health care insurer shall notify the member of the right to appeal under this article. ARIZ. REV. STAT. ANN. §

20-2534 (2004). The utilization review agent must provide for four different types of appeals: 1) an expedited medical review; 2) an informal reconsideration; 3) a formal appeal process; and 4) an external independent review. A patient (or health insurer) who disagrees with the final decision of the external independent reviewer may seek judicial review. (A health care insurer may offer additional levels of review other than the levels prescribed as long as the additional levels of review do not increase the time period limitations prescribed by statute). ARIZ. REV. STAT. ANN. § 20-2533 (2004).

C. **Time frame for determination.** The first level or expedited medical reviews must be completed within one business day. ARIZ. REV. STAT. ANN. § 20-2534. The second level or informal reconsiderations must be completed within 30 days. ARIZ. REV. STAT. ANN. § 20-2535. The third level or formal appeals must be completed within 30 days for denied services not yet provided and within 60 days for denied claims. ARIZ. REV. STAT. ANN. § 20-2536 (2004).

D. **External appeals.** If the utilization review agent denies the member's request for a covered service or claim for a covered service at both the informal reconsideration level and the formal appeal level, or at the expedited medical review level, the member may initiate an external independent review. ARIZ. REV. STAT. ANN. § 20-2537 (2004).

E. The Department of Insurance maintains a list of Utilization Review Agents authorized to do business in Arizona. To access this list go to: http://www.id.state.az.us/publications/ur_list_arizona_national_ur_agents.pdf

F. **Emergency Services.** A health care services plan engaging in utilization review to determine whether any emergency services rendered by a provider were medically necessary and in accordance with this chapter shall consider the following factors:
1. Current emergency medical literature and standards of care.
2. Clinical information reasonably available to the provider at the time of the ARIZ. REV. STAT. ANN. §20-2804 (2004).

VII. Recognition of URAC Accreditation Status

A. Does the state recognize URAC accreditation? Yes.

B. Which of the state's requirements are waived for URAC-accredited organizations?
1. Having met URAC standards, a URAC accredited organization is exempt from the state application process. However, all utilization review agents must submit all required notices and comply with the provisions in Article 2 (health care appeals) in ARIZ. REV. STAT. ANN. §§ 20-2530 to 20-2539 (2004).
2. A health care insurer that proposes to provide coverage of inpatient hospital and medical benefits, outpatient surgical benefits or any medical, surgical or health care service for residents of Arizona with utilization review of those benefits can satisfy the state's requirements by attaining accreditation by URAC. ARIZ. REV. STAT. ANN. § 20-2510 (2004).

Arkansas

I. Scope and Applicability

A. **Who is subject to the state's utilization review laws?** A private review agent who approves or denies payment or who recommends approval or denial of payment for hospital or medical services or whose review results in approval or denial of payment for hospital or medical services on a case-by-case basis may not conduct utilization review in this state unless the State Board of Health has granted the private review agent a certificate. ARK. CODE ANN § 20-9-903 (2004).

1. HMO's? Yes.
2. Insurers? Yes.
3. Utilization review organizations? Yes.
4. Workers' Compensation? Yes.
5. Retrospective review? Yes.

B. **What exemptions are provided, if any?**

1. No certificate is required for a private review agent in connection with a contract with the federal government for utilization review of patients eligible for hospital and medical services under the Social Security Act.

2. No certificate is required for those private review agents conducting general in-house utilization review for hospitals, home health agencies, preferred provider organizations, other managed care entities, clinics, private offices, or any other health facilities or entities, so long as the review does not result in the approval or denial of payment for hospital or medical services for a particular case. Such general in-house utilization review is completely exempt from the provisions of this requiring a state certificate.

3. No certificate is required for utilization review by any Arkansas-licensed pharmacist or pharmacy, or organizations of either, while engaged in the practice of pharmacy, including, but not limited to, dispensing of drugs, participation in drug utilization reviews, and monitoring patient drug therapy. ARK. CODE ANN § 20-9-904 (2004).

C. **What term does the state use to refer to regulated entities?** "Private review agent" means a non hospital-affiliated person or entity performing utilization review on behalf of: 1) An employer of employees in the State of Arkansas; 2) or a third party that provides or administers hospital and medical benefits to citizens of this state. This includes a health maintenance organization issued a certificate of authority under and by virtue of the laws of the State of Arkansas, and a health insurer, nonprofit health service plan, health insurance service organization, or preferred provider organization or other entity offering health insurance policies, contracts, or benefits in this state; and the term "private review agent" does not include automobile, homeowner, or casualty and commercial liability. ARK. CODE ANN § 20-9-902(c)(1) (2004).

D. **What activities does the state include in its definition of utilization review?** "Utilization review" means a system for review which reviews the appropriate and efficient allocation of hospital resources and medical services given or proposed to be given to a patient or group of patients; and "Utilization review plan" means a description of the utilization review procedures of a private review agent.

II. Regulatory Information

A. **Responsible state agency:** Arkansas Department of Health, Division of Health Resources

B. **Contact Information.**

1. **Name and Title:** Mary Fuller, Director, Utilization Review Certification Program
2. **Address:** 5800 West 10th Street, Suite 400, Little Rock, AR, 72204
3. **Phone and Facsimile:** (501) 661-2771; facsimile (501) 661-2165; email: mfuller@healthyarkansas.com
4. **Web site:** http://www.healthyarkansas.com/

III. Licensure/Certification Requirements

A. **What entities are required to obtain a license in Arkansas to conduct utilization review for residents of the state?** Those entities included in the definition of "private review agent." ARK. CODE ANN § 20-9-903 (2004).

B. **How often must licensure be renewed?** Every 2 years. ARK. CODE ANN § 20-9-910 (2004).

C. **Licensure fees (initial and renewal).** $2,500.

D. **Documentation required for licensure.** Private review agents shall submit information that the State Board of Health requires, including:

1. A utilization review plan that includes: a) A description of review standards and

procedures to be used in evaluating proposed or delivered hospital and medical care; b) The provisions by which patients, physicians, or hospitals may seek reconsideration or appeal of adverse decisions by the private review agent;

2. The type and qualifications of the personnel either employed or under contract to perform the utilization review;

3. The procedures and policies to ensure that a representative of the private review agent is reasonably accessible to patients and providers 5 days a week during normal business hours in this state;

4. The policies and procedures to ensure that all applicable state and federal laws to protect the confidentiality of individual medical records are followed;

5. A copy of the materials designed to inform applicable patients and providers of the requirements of the utilization review plan; and

6. A list of the third party payors for which the private review agent is performing utilization review in this state.
ARK. CODE ANN § 20-9-909 (2004).

E. **Exemptions from licensure.** No certificate is required for a private review agent in connection with a contract with the federal government for utilization review of patients eligible for hospital services under Medicare and Medicaid. A private review agent does not need a certificate if conducting "in-house" utilization reviews for hospitals, home health agencies, PPO's, or other managed care entities, clinics, private offices, or any other health facility or entity as long as the review does not result in approval or denial of payment for hospital or medical services for a particular case. Any Arkansas-licensed pharmacist or pharmacy, or organization of either, does not need a certificate while engaged in the practice of pharmacy, which includes dispensing of drugs, participating in drug utilization reviews, and monitoring patient drug therapy.
ARK. CODE ANN § 20-9-904 (2004).

IV. Program Requirements

A. **Clinical review criteria.** A description of review standards and procedures to be used in evaluating proposed or delivered hospital and medical care. ARK. CODE ANN § 20-9-909 (2004).

B. **Prohibitions against financial incentives.** No provision.

C. **Telephone access standards.** The procedures and policies to ensure that a representative of the private review agent is reasonably accessible to patients and providers 5 days a week during normal business hours in Arkansas. ARK. CODE ANN § 20-9-909 (2004), *see also*, ARK. CODE ANN § 20-9-911 (2004).

D. **Quality assurance program.** Required by the Rules & Regulations for Utilization Review in Arkansas.

E. **Delegation of UR functions.** Any health insurer proposing to issue or deliver in this state a group or blanket health insurance policy or administer a health benefit program which provides for the coverage of hospital and medical benefits and the utilization review of such benefits shall have a certificate in accordance with the Arkansas Department of Health; or contract with a private review agent that has a certificate in accordance with the Arkansas Department of Health. ARK. CODE ANN § 20-9-907 (2004).

F. **Confidentiality.** A private review agent may not disclose or publish individual medical records or any other confidential medical information obtained in performing utilization review activities without appropriate procedures for protecting patient confidentiality. A private review agent may provide patient information to a third party with whom the private review agent is affiliated, under contract, or acting on behalf of. ARK. CODE ANN § 20-9-913 (2004).

V. Review Agent Qualifications

A. Qualifications:

1. Review Agents must have available the services of a sufficient number of qualified medical professionals supported and supervised by appropriate physicians to carry out its utilization review activities;

2. Meet any applicable regulations the board adopted under this subchapter relating to the qualifications of private review agents or the performance of utilization review; and

3. Provide assurances satisfactory to the board that:

   a. The procedure and policies of the private review agent will protect the confidentiality of medical records; and

   b. The review agent will be reasonably accessible to patients and providers for 5 working days a week during normal business hours in this state.

   ARK. CODE ANN § 20-9-911 (2004).

VI. Reviews and Appeals: Covered by the Arkansas External Review Regulation. Code of Arkansas Rules 054.00.077 et. seq. (2004); (Note: Reviews and Appeals fall under the Arkansas Department of Insurance exclusively and is therefore not subject to Arkansas Department of Health Utilization Review Certification Program oversight. *See*, ARK. CODE ANN § 23-99-414 (2004).)

A. Requirements:

1. A health care insurer issuing or delivering a managed care plan shall establish for those managed care plans a grievance procedure which provides covered persons with a prompt and meaningful review on the issue of denial, in whole or in part, of a health care treatment or service. ARK. CODE ANN § 23-99-410 (2004)

2. Every health benefit plan shall provide covered persons an external review process by an independent review organization to examine the health benefit plan's adverse determinations that meet the criteria specified in this regulation. Code of Arkansas Rules 054.00.077.76 (1)(B)(2004).

B. Review determinations and notice to patients/providers.

1. A health carrier shall notify the covered person and the covered person's treating health care professional in writing or via electronic media of the covered person's right to request an external review. Such notice shall include the appropriate statements and information at the time the health carrier sends written notice of an adverse determination and a final adverse determination. Code of Arkansas Rules 054.00.077.76 (4)(A)(2004).

2. For Standard External Review. At the time the health carrier receives a request for an external review, the health carrier shall assign an independent review organization, from the list of approved independent review organizations maintained by the commissioner pursuant to the Arkansas External Review Regulation, to conduct a preliminary review of the request to determine if:

   a. The request for external review meets the applicability standards, the covered person has exhausted the health carrier's internal grievance process, unless required differently by Arkansas Administrative Regulations, and the covered person has provided all the information and forms required to process an external review.

   b. Within 5 business days after receipt of the external review request, the independent review organization shall complete the preliminary review and notify the health carrier, the covered person and the covered person's treating health care professional in writing whether the request is complete; and the request has been accepted for external review.

   c. Within 45 calendar days after the date of receipt of the request for an external review, the assigned independent review organization shall provide written notice of its decision to uphold, reverse, or partially uphold or reverse the adverse determination or the final adverse determination to the covered person, the covered person's treating health care professional, and the health carrier.

   The notice must include: i) a general description of the reason for the request for external review; ii) the date the independent review organization received the assignment from the health carrier to conduct the preliminary review of the external review request; iii) the date the external review was conducted, if appropriate; iv) the date of its decision; v) the principal rationale, reason or reasons for its decision; vi) references to the evidence or documentation, including the practice guidelines.

   d. If the adverse determination involves a denial of coverage based on a determination that the recommended or requested health care services is "experimental" or "investigational," the independent review organization shall also consider whether there is sufficient evidence to demonstrate that the recommended or requested health care service or treatment is more likely than not to be more beneficial to the covered person than any available standard health care services or treatments and the adverse risks of the recommended or requested health care service or treatment would not be substantially increased over those of available standard health care services or treatments, and a description and analysis of any medical or scientific evidence, as that term is defined in the regulations, considered in reaching the opinion. Code of Arkansas Rules 054.00.077.76 (7) (2004).

3. For Expedited External Review: Can be made by the covered person after either an adverse determination or a final adverse determination where medical condition would seriously jeopardize the life or health of the covered person, or would jeopardize the covered person's ability to regain maximum function; or the final adverse determination concerns: an admission, availability of care, continued stay or health care service for which the covered person received emergency services, but has not been discharged from a facility; or a denial of coverage based on a determination that the recommended or requested health care service or treatment is experimental or investigational, and the covered person's treating physician certifies in writing and supports such certification with reasoning, rationale, or evidence that the recommended or requested health care service or treatment that is the subject of the request would be significantly less effective if not promptly initiated.

   a. As expeditiously as the covered person's medical condition or circumstances require, but in no event more than 72 hours after the date of receipt of the request for an expedited external review the assigned independent review organization shall: Make a decision to uphold or reverse the adverse determination or final adverse determination; and notify the covered person, the covered person's treating health care professional, and the health carrier of the decision.

   b. Upon receipt of a notice of adverse determination or final adverse determination, the health carrier immediately shall approve the coverage that was the subject of the adverse determination or final adverse determination.

   c. An expedited external review may not be provided for adverse or final adverse

determinations involving a retrospective review.
Code of Arkansas Rules 054.00.077.76 (8) (2004).

C. **Binding Decision:** An external review decision is binding on the health carrier except to the extent the health carrier has other remedies available under applicable federal or state law. An external review decision is binding on the covered person except to the extent the covered person has other remedies available under applicable federal or state law. A covered person may not file a subsequent request for external review involving the same adverse determination or final adverse determination for which the covered person has already received an external review decision pursuant to this regulation. Code of Arkansas Rules 054.00.077.76 (8) (2004).

VII. Recognition of URAC Accreditation Status

A. Does the state recognize URAC accreditation? No.

B. Which of the state's requirements are waived for URAC-accredited organizations? Not applicable.

California

I. Scope and Applicability

A. **Who is subject to the state's utilization review laws?** Every health care service plan and any entity with which it contracts for services that include utilization review or utilization management functions, that prospectively, retrospectively, or concurrently reviews and approves, modifies, delays, or denies, based in whole or in part on medical necessity, requests by providers prior to, retrospectively, or concurrent with the provision of health care services to enrollees, or that delegates these functions to medical groups or independent practice associations or to other contracting providers. CAL. HEALTH & SAFETY CODE § 1367.01(a) (2004).

   1. HMO's? Yes.
   2. Insurers? Yes.
   3. Utilization Review Organizations? No.
   4. Retrospective Review? Yes.

B. **What exemptions are provided, if any?** This section shall not apply to decisions made for the care or treatment of the sick who depend upon prayer or spiritual means for healing in the practice of religion as set forth in subdivision (a) of Section 1270. CAL. HEALTH & SAFETY CODE § 1367.01 (l) (2004)

C. **What term does the state use to refer to regulated entities?** Health care services plans as defined in section 1345 (f)(1)(2) of CAL. HEALTH & SAFETY CODE.

D. **What activities does the state include in its definition of utilization review?** "Utilization review" or "internal review" is the process by which health care service plans and disability insurers review, and approve, modify, or deny, requests for treatment of patients by physicians, and the legislature recognizes that it is an integral component of the total process by which consumers access health care services. *See* 1999 CAL. STAT., §1 c. 539.

II. Regulatory Information

A. **Responsible state agency.** Department of Managed Health Care

B. **Contact Information.**

   1. **Name and Title:** Warren Barnes, Assistant Deputy Director, Office of Legal Services.
   2. **Address:** Department of Managed Health Care, Office of Legal Services, 980 Ninth Street, Suite 500, Sacramento, CA 95814-2725

   3. **Phone and Facsimile:** (916) 322-6727; facsimile (916) 322-3968
   4. **E-mail:** khess@dmhc.ca.gov; cc: slayfayette@dmhc.ca.gov
   5. **Web site:** http://www.dmhc.ca.gov

III. Licensure/Certification Requirements

A. **What entities are required to obtain a license in the state to conduct utilization review for residents of the state?** Not applicable.

B. **How often must licensure/certification be renewed?** Not applicable.

C. **Licensure fees (initial and renewal).** Not applicable.

D. **Documents required for licensure.** Not applicable.

E. **Exemptions from licensure.** Not applicable.

IV. Program Requirements

A. **Clinical review criteria.**

   1. A health care service plan that is subject to UM regulation shall have written policies and procedures establishing the process by which the plan prospectively, retrospectively, or concurrently reviews and approves, modifies, delays, or denies, based in whole or in part on medical necessity, requests by providers of health care services for plan enrollees. These policies and procedures shall ensure that decisions based on the medical necessity of proposed health care services are consistent with criteria or guidelines that are supported by clinical principles and processes. These criteria and guidelines shall be developed pursuant to Section 1363.5. CAL. HEALTH & SAFETY CODE § 1367.01(b) (2004).

   2. The criteria or guidelines used by plans, or any entities with which plans contract for services that include utilization review or utilization management functions, to determine whether to authorize, modify, or deny health care services shall: a) Be developed with involvement from actively practicing health care providers. b) Be consistent with sound clinical principles and processes. c) Be evaluated, and updated if necessary, at least annually. d) If used as the basis of a decision to modify, delay, or deny services in a specified case under review, be disclosed to the provider and the enrollee in that specified case. e) Be available to the

THE UTILIZATION MANAGEMENT GUIDE

public upon request. A plan shall only be required to disclose the criteria or guidelines for the specific procedures or conditions requested. A plan may charge reasonable fees to cover administrative expenses related to disclosing criteria or guidelines pursuant to this paragraph, limited to copying and postage costs. The plan may also make the criteria or guidelines available through electronic communication means. CAL. HEALTH & SAFETY CODE § 1363.5(b) (2004).

3. These policies and procedures, and a description of the process by which the plan reviews and approves, modifies, delays, or denies requests by providers prior to, retrospectively, or concurrent with the provision of health care services to enrollees, shall be filed with the director for review and approval, and shall be disclosed by the plan to providers and enrollees upon request, and by the plan to the public upon request. CAL. HEALTH & SAFETY CODE § 1367.01(b) (2004).

4. Every health care service plan subject to this section shall employ or designate a medical director who holds an unrestricted license to practice medicine in the state of California pursuant to Section 2050 of the Business and Professions Code or pursuant to the Osteopathic Act, or, if the plan is a specialized health care service plan, a clinical director with California licensure in a clinical area appropriate to the type of care provided by the specialized health care service plan. The medical director or clinical director shall ensure that the process by which the plan reviews and approves, modifies, or denies, based in whole or in part on medical necessity, requests by providers prior to, retrospectively, or concurrent with the provision of health care services to enrollees, complies with the requirements of this section. CAL. HEALTH & SAFETY CODE § 1367.01(c) (2004).

B. **Prohibitions against financial incentives.** None specifically, though the KNOX-KEENE ACT has a general prohibition against financial incentives at CAL. HEALTH & SAFETY CODE § 1367(g) (2004), which applies generally to all aspects of a plan's operations. That provision states that plans must demonstrate to the Department that medical decisions are rendered by qualified medical providers, unhindered by fiscal and administrative management.

C. **Telephone access standards.** Every health care service plan shall maintain telephone access to providers to request authorization for health care services. CAL. HEALTH & SAFETY CODE § 1367.01(i) (2004).

D. **Quality assurance program.** Under CAL. HEALTH & SAFETY CODE § 1367.01(j) (2004), every health care service plan subject to this section that reviews requests by providers prior to, retrospectively, or concurrent with, the provision of health care services to enrollees shall establish, as part of the quality assurance program required by Section 1370, a process by which the plan's compliance is assessed and evaluated. The process shall include provisions for evaluation of complaints, assessment of trends, implementation of actions to correct identified problems, mechanisms to communicate actions and results to the appropriate health plan employees and contracting providers, and provisions for evaluation of any corrective action plan and measurements of performance.

E. **Delegation of utilization review functions.** Plans must have policies and procedures establishing the process by which plans or delegated utilization review entities undertake the utilization review function CAL. HEALTH & SAFETY CODE §§ 1367.01(a), 1367.01(b) (2004).

F. **Confidentiality.** Refer to Section 1364.5 (a) of CAL. HEALTH & SAFETY CODE.

V. **Reviewer Qualifications**

A. **Qualifications of reviewers that render utilization review determinations (at each level of utilization review, if applicable).** No individual, other than a licensed physician or a licensed health care professional who is competent to evaluate the specific clinical issues involved in the health care services requested by the provider, may deny or modify requests for authorization of health care services for an enrollee for reasons of medical necessity. CAL. HEALTH & SAFETY CODE § 1367.01(e) (2004).

B. **Requirements for medical director.** Every health care service plan shall employ or designate a medical director with an unrestricted California medical license issued pursuant to Section 2050 of the Business and Professions Code or osteopathic license. CAL. HEALTH & SAFETY CODE § 1367.01(c) (2004).

C. **Requirements for "same-state" licensure.** Must have California license.

VI. Reviews and Appeals

A. **Review determination and notice to patients/providers.**

1. If the health care service plan requests medical information from providers in order to determine whether to approve, modify, or deny requests for authorization, the plan shall request only the information reasonably necessary to make the determination. CAL. HEALTH & SAFETY CODE § 1367.01(g) (2004).

2. **Time frame of determination.**

   a. Decisions to approve, modify, or deny, based on non-emergency or non-life threatening medical matters shall be made in a timely fashion appropriate for the nature of the enrollee's condition, not to exceed 5 business days from the plan's receipt of the information reasonably necessary and requested by the plan to make the determination. In cases where the review is retrospective, the decision shall be communicated to the individual who received services, or to the individual's designee, within 30 days of the receipt of information that is reasonably necessary to make this determination, and shall be communicated to the provider in a manner that is consistent with current law. For purposes of this section, retrospective reviews shall be for care rendered on or after January 1, 2000. CAL. HEALTH & SAFETY CODE § 1367.01(h)(1) (2004).

   b. For emergency medical matters such that the enrollee faces an imminent and serious threat to his or her health including, but not limited to, the potential loss of life, limb, or other major bodily function, or the normal timeframe for the decision making process would be detrimental to the enrollee's life or health or could jeopardize the enrollee's ability to regain maximum function, decisions to approve, modify, or deny requests by providers prior to, or concurrent with, the provision of health care services to enrollees, shall be made in a timely fashion appropriate for the nature of the enrollee's condition, not to exceed 72 hours after the plan's receipt of the information reasonably necessary and

requested by the plan to make the determination. Nothing in this section shall be construed to alter the requirements of subdivision (b) of Section 1371.4. These requirements shall be applicable to all health plans and other entities conducting utilization review or utilization management. CAL. HEALTH & SAFETY CODE § 1367.01(h)(2) (2004).

   c. Decisions to approve, modify, or deny requests by providers for authorization prior to, or concurrent with, the provision of health care services to enrollees shall be communicated to the requesting provider within 24 hours of the decision. Except for concurrent review decisions pertaining to care that is underway, which shall be communicated to the enrollee's treating provider within 24 hours, decisions resulting in denial, delay, or modification of all or part of the requested health care service shall be communicated to the enrollee in writing within 2 business days of the decision. In the case of concurrent review, care shall not be discontinued until the enrollee's treating provider has been notified of the plan's decision, and a care plan has been agreed upon by the treating provider that is appropriate for the medical needs of that patient. CAL. HEALTH & SAFETY CODE § 1367.01(h)(3) (2004).

3. **Contents of notice of adverse determinations.** Communications to enrollees shall specify the specific health care service approved, communicated to the enrollee in writing, and to providers initially by telephone or facsimile, except with regard to decisions rendered retrospectively, and then in writing, and shall include a clear and concise explanation of the reasons for the plan's decision, a description of the criteria or guidelines used, and the clinical reasons for the decisions regarding medical necessity. Any written communication to a physician or other health care provider shall include the name and telephone number of the health care professional responsible for the denial, delay, or modification. The telephone number provided shall be a direct number or an extension, to allow the

physician or health care provider easily to contact the professional responsible for the denial, delay, or modification. Responses shall also include information as to how the enrollee may file a grievance with the plan pursuant to Section 1368, and in the case of Medi-Cal enrollees, shall explain how to request an administrative hearing and aid. CAL. HEALTH & SAFETY CODE § 1367.01(h)(4) (2004).

4. **Appeals requirements.**

a. All enrollee grievances involving a disputed health care service are eligible for review under the Independent Medical Review System if the requirements of this article are met. CAL. HEALTH & SAFETY CODE § 1374.30(d)(1) (2004).

b. "disputed health care service" means any health care service eligible for coverage and payment under a health care service plan contract that has been denied, modified, or delayed by a decision of the plan, or by one of its contracting providers, in whole or in part due to a finding that the service is not medically necessary. A decision regarding a disputed health care service relates to the practice of medicine and is not a coverage decision. CAL. HEALTH & SAFETY CODE § 1374.30(b) (2004). The Department shall be the final arbiter when there is a question as to whether an enrollee grievance is a disputed health care service or a coverage decision. CAL. HEALTH & SAFETY CODE § 1374.30(d)(3) (2004).

c. In any case in which an enrollee or provider asserts that a decision to deny, modify, or delay health care services was based, in whole or in part, on consideration of medical necessity, the department shall have the final authority to determine whether the grievance is more properly resolved pursuant to an independent medical review as provided under this article or pursuant to subdivision (b) of Section 1368. CAL. HEALTH & SAFETY CODE § 1374.30(d)(2) (2004).

d. Every health care service plan shall prominently display in every plan member handbook or relevant informational brochure, in every plan

contract, on enrollee evidence of coverage forms, on copies of plan procedures for resolving grievances, on letters of denials issued by either the plan or its contracting organization, on the grievance forms required under Section 1368, and on all written responses to grievances, information concerning the right of an enrollee to request an independent medical review in cases where the enrollee believes that health care services have been improperly denied, modified, or delayed by the plan, or by one of its contracting providers. CAL. HEALTH & SAFETY CODE § 1374.30(i) (2004).

B. **Time Frame for Independent Medical Review.** The enrollee must first present the disputed decision to the plan's internal grievance process. The dispute may be eligible for review if the plan upholds the decision or does not act on the grievance for 30 days. The enrollee shall not be required to participate in the plan's grievance process for more than 30 days. In the case of a grievance that requires expedited review, the enrollee shall not be required to participate in the plan's grievance process for more than three days. CAL. HEALTH & SAFETY CODE § 1374.30 (j)(3).

C. **Emergency services.** If there is an imminent and serious threat to the health of the enrollee, as specified in subdivision (c) of Section 1374.33, all necessary information and documents shall be delivered to an independent medical review organization within 24 hours of approval of the request for review. In reviewing a request for review, the department of insurance may waive the requirement that the enrollee follow the plan's grievance process in extraordinary and compelling cases, where the director finds that the enrollee has acted reasonably. CAL. HEALTH & SAFETY CODE § 1374.31(a) (2004).

VII. Recognition of URAC Accreditation Status

A. Does the state recognize URAC accreditation? No.

B. Which of the state's requirements are **waived** for URAC-accredited organizations? Not applicable.

Colorado

I. Scope and Applicability

A. **Who is subject to the state's utilization review laws?** A health coverage plan, meaning a policy, contract, certificate, or agreement entered into by, offered to, or issued by a carrier to provide, deliver, arrange for, pay for, or reimburse any of the costs of health care services. COLO. REV. STAT. § 10-16-102 (22.5) (2004). Carrier means any entity that provides health coverage in this state including a franchise insurance plan, a fraternal benefit society, a health maintenance organization, a nonprofit hospital and health service corporation, a sickness and accident insurance company, and any other entity providing a plan of health insurance or health benefits subject to the insurance laws and regulations of Colorado. COLO. REV. STAT. § 10-16-102 (8) (2004).

1. HMO's? Yes.
2. Insurers? Yes.
3. **Utilization review organizations?** No. Although the law does not apply directly to private utilization review organizations, any private utilization review organization providing services to an insurance carrier, nonprofit hospital and health care service corporation, or health maintenance organization regulated pursuant to the provisions of [article 16] is the direct representative of the insurance carrier, nonprofit hospital and health care service corporation, or health maintenance organization. Any insurance carrier, nonprofit hospital and health care service corporation, or health maintenance organization is responsible for the actions of any private utilization review organization acting within the scope of any contract and on its behalf within the scope of any contract which result in any violation of [Title 10] or any rules or regulations promulgated by the commissioner. COLO. REV. STAT. § 10-16-112 (2) (2004).
4. Retrospective review? Yes.

B. **What exemptions are provided, if any?** Private utilization review entity does not include a hospital or public reviewer following federal guidelines, which conducts utilization review. The definition of private utilization review organization also does not apply to any independent medical examination provided for in any policy of insurance. COLO. REV. STAT. § 10-16-112 (1)(a) (2004).

C. **What term does the state use to refer to regulated entities?** "Health coverage plan" means a policy, contract, certificate, or agreement entered into by, offered to, or issued by a carrier to provide, deliver, arrange for, pay for, or reimburse any of the costs of health care services. COLO. REV. STAT. § 10-16-102 (22.5) (2004).

D. **What activities does the state include in its definition of utilization review?** "Utilization review" means an evaluation of the necessity, appropriateness, and efficiency of the use of health care services, procedures, and facilities, but does not include any independent medical examination provided for in any policy of insurance. COLO. REV. STAT. § 10-16-112 (1)(b) (2004).

II. Regulatory Information

A. **Responsible state agency.** Department of Regulatory Agencies, Division of Insurance
B. **Contact Information.**
1. **Name and Title:** Kim Wells, Supervisor, Consumer Affairs/Life and Health, Colorado Insurance Division
2. **Address:** 1560 Broadway, Suite 850, Denver, CO 80202
3. **Phone and Facsimile:** 303-894-7748; facsimile: (303) 894-7455
4. **Web site:** www.dora.state.co.us/insurance

III. Licensure/Certification Requirements

A. **What entities are required to obtain a license in Colorado to conduct utilization review for residents of the state?** Colorado does not require a license specific to utilization review.
B. **How often must licensure be renewed?** Not Applicable.
C. **Licensure fees (initial and renewal).** Not Applicable.
D. **Documentation required for licensure.** Not Applicable.
E. **Exemptions from licensure.** Not Applicable.

IV. Program Requirements

A. **Clinical review criteria.** No Provision.
B. **Prohibitions against financial incentives.** A health plan shall ensure that a majority of the persons reviewing a grievance involving an

adverse determination [as part of the second-level appeal] do not have a direct financial interest in the outcome of the review. However, such persons may be part of the health coverage plan's provider network or employees of the health coverage plan. COLO. REV. STAT. § 10-16-113 (3)(b)(III) (2004).

C. **Telephone access standards.** No Provision.

D. **Quality assurance program.** No Provision.

E. **Delegation of UR functions.** Any insurance carrier, nonprofit hospital and health care service corporation, or health maintenance organization is responsible for the actions of any private utilization review organization acting within the scope of any contract and on its behalf within the scope of any contract which result in any violation of [Title 10] or any rules or regulations promulgated by the commissioner. COLO. REV. STAT. § 10-16-112 (2) (2004).

F. **Confidentiality.** No Provision.

V. Review Agent Qualifications

A. **Qualifications:**

1. All written denials or requests for covered benefits on the grounds that such benefits are not medically necessary, appropriate, effective, or efficient shall be signed by a licensed physician familiar with standards of care in Colorado. COLO. REV. STAT. § 10-16-113 (4) (2004).

2. The first-level appeal shall be a review by a physician who shall consult with an appropriate clinical peer or peers in the same or similar specialty as would typically manage the case being reviewed. The physician and clinical peer or peers shall not be involved in the initial denial. COLO. REV. STAT. § 10-16-113 (3)(b)(II) (2004).

3. The second-level appeal must be conducted by a panel consisting of at least three people. The panel may include employees of the health coverage plan who have appropriate professional expertise. A majority of the panel must include persons who were not previously involved in the grievance. However, a person who was previously involved with the grievance may be a member of the panel or appear before the panel to present information or answer questions. COLO. REV. STAT. § 10-16-113 (3)(b)(III) (2004).

VI. Reviews and Appeals

A. **Requirements:**

1. A health coverage plan must include in its written denial notification to the covered person that the covered person has a right to appeal the decision and the right to request an external review. COLO. REV. STAT. § 10-16-113 (3) (2004).

B. **Review determinations and notice to patients/providers.**

1. **Standard Utilization Review:**

   a. A health carrier shall make prospective review determinations and notify the covered person and the covered person's provider of the determination, whether the carrier certifies the provision of benefits or not, within a reasonable period of time appropriate to the covered person's medical condition, but in no event later than 15 days after the date the health carrier receives the request. 3 COLO. CODE REGS. § 702-4-2-17 Section 6 (B)(1)(a)(1) (2004). This time frame may be extended one time by the health carrier for up to 15 days, provided the health carrier:

      i. Determines that an extension is necessary due to matters beyond the health carrier's control, and

      ii. Notifies the covered person prior to the expiration of the initial 15-day time period, of the circumstances requiring the extension of time and the date by which the health carrier expects to make a determination. 3 COLO. CODE REGS. § 702-4-2-17 Section 6 (B)(1)(b) (2004).

      iii. If the extension is necessary due to the failure of the covered person to submit information necessary to reach a determination on the request, the notice of the extension must:

         ➢ Specifically describe the required information necessary to complete the request; and

         ➢ Give the covered person at least 45 days from the date of receipt of the notice to provide the specified information. 3 colo. code regs. § 702-4-2-17 Section 6 (B)(1)(c) (2004).

   b. For retrospective determinations, a health carrier shall make the determination and notify the covered person and the covered person's provider of the determination within a reasonable period of time, but in no event later than 30 days after the date of receiving the benefit request. 3 COLO. CODE REGS. § 702-4-2-17 Section 6 (C)(1)(a) (2004). This time frame may be extended one time by the health carrier for up to 15 days, provided the health carrier:

i. Determines that an extension is necessary due to matters beyond the health carrier's control, and

ii. Notifies the covered person prior to the expiration of the initial 30-day time period, of the circumstances requiring the extension of time and the date by which the health carrier expects to make a determination. 3 COLO. CODE REGS. § 702-4-2-17 Section 6 (C)(2)(a) (2004).

iii. If the extension is necessary due to the failure of the covered person to submit information necessary to reach a determination on the request, the notice of the extension must:

➤ Specifically describe the required information necessary to complete the request; and

➤ Give the covered person at least 30 days from the date of receipt of the notice to provide the specified information. 3 COLO. CODE REGS. § 702-4-2-17 Section 6 (B)(2)(b) (2004).

2. **Expedited Utilization Review:**

a. A health carrier shall provide that, in the case of a failure by a covered person to follow the health carrier's procedures for filing an urgent care request, the covered person shall be notified of the failure and the proper procedures to be following for filing the request. The notice must be in writing and provided to the covered person as soon as possible but not later than 24 hours after receipt of the request. 3 COLO. CODE REGS. § 702-4-2-17 Section 7 (A)(2) (2004).

b. For an urgent care request, the health carrier shall notify the covered person and the covered person's provider of the health carrier's determination with respect to the request, whether or not the determination is an adverse determination, as soon as possible,

taking into account the medical condition of the covered person, but in no event later than 72 hours after the receipt of the request by the health carrier. 3 COLO. CODE REGS. § 702-4-2-17 Section 7 (B)(1)(a) (2004).

c. If the covered person has failed to provide sufficient information for the health carrier to make a determination, the health carrier must notify the covered person either orally or, if requested by the covered person, in writing of this failure and state what specific information is needed as soon as possible, but in no event later than 24 hours after receipt of the request. 3 COLO. CODE REGS. § 702-4-2-17 Section 7 (B)(2)(a) (2004).

d. The health carrier shall provide the covered person a reasonable period of time to submit the necessary information, taking into account the circumstances, but in no event less than 48 hours after notifying the covered person of the failure to submit sufficient information. 3 COLO. CODE REGS. § 702-4-2-17 Section 7 (B)(2)(b) (2004).

e. The health carrier shall notify the covered person and the covered person's provider of its determination with respect to the urgent care request as soon as possible, but in no event more than 48 hours after the earlier of:

➤ The health carrier's receipt of the requested specified information; or

➤ The end of the period provider for the covered person is to submit the requested specified information. 3 COLO. CODE REGS. § 702-4-2-17 Section 7 (B)(2)(c) (2004).

f. For concurrent review urgent care requests involving a request by the covered person to extend the course of treatment beyond the initial period of time or the number of treatment, if the request is made at least 24 hours prior to the expiration of the prescribed period of time or number of treatments, the health carrier shall make a determination with respect to the request and notify the covered person and the covered person's provider of the determination, whether it is an adverse determination, or not, as soon as possible, taking into account the covered person's medical condition, but in no event more than 24 hours after the health carrier's receipt of the request. 3 COLO. CODE REGS. § 702-4-2-17 Section 7 (C)(1) (2004).

C. **Appeal Determinations.**

1. **First Level Review:**

    a. A covered person may file a grievance with the health carrier within 180 days after the date of receipt of a notice of an adverse determination. 3 COLO. CODE REGS. § 702-4-2-17 Section 10 (D) (2004).

    b. With respect to a request for a first level review of an adverse determination involving a prospective review request or a retrospective review request, the health carrier shall notify and issue a decision within a reasonable period of time that is appropriate given the covered person's medical condition, but no later than 30 days after the date of the health carrier's receipt of a request for the first level review. 3 COLO. CODE REGS. § 702-4-2-17 Section 10 (G) (2004).

2. **Voluntary Second Level Review:**

    a. A covered person may file a request for a voluntary second level review of an adverse determination within 30 days after the date of receipt of a notice of adverse determination. 3 COLO. CODE REGS. § 702-4-2-17 Section 11 (D) (2004).

    b. The review panel conducting the voluntary second level review must schedule and hold a meeting within 60 days of receiving a request from a covered person. The covered person must be notified in writing at least 20 days in advance of the review date. 3 COLO. CODE REGS. § 702-4-2-17 Section 11 (G)(1) (2004).

    c. The review panel, after private deliberation, shall issue a written decision to the covered person within 7 days of completing the review meeting. 3 COLO. CODE REGS. § 4-2-17 Section 11 (G)(5) (2004).

D. **External Review.**

1. **External Review Determinations:**

    a. A covered individual requesting an independent external review shall make such a request within 60 calendar days after receiving notification of a second-level appeal denial of coverage for such treatment or service. COLO. REV. STAT. § 10-16-113.5 (7) (2004).

    b. The certified independent external review entity shall submit the expert determination to the health coverage plan, the covered individual requesting independent external review, and the physician or other health care professional of the covered individual requesting an independent external review within 30 working days after the health coverage plan has received a request for external review. COLO. REV. STAT. § 10-16-113.5 (10)(a) (2004).

    c. Expedited external review: the independent external review entity must make a decision to uphold or reverse the carrier's final adverse determination within 7 working days. 3 COLO. CODE REGS. § 702-4-2-21 Section 9 (H) (2004).

2. **Binding Decision:** The determinations of the expert reviewer shall be binding on the health coverage plan and on the covered individual requesting independent review. COLO. REV. STAT. § 10-16-113.5 (11) (2004).

VII. Recognition of URAC Accreditation Status

A. **Does the state recognize URAC accreditation?** No.

B. **Which of the state's requirements are waived for URAC-accredited organizations?** Not Applicable.

Connecticut

I. Scope and Applicability

A. **Who is subject to the state's utilization review laws?** Any company, organization, or other entity performing utilization review. CONN. GEN. STAT. § 38a-226a(a) (2004); CONN. AGENCIES REGS. § 38a-226c-1 (2004).

   1. **HMO's?** Yes.
   2. **Insurers?** Yes.
   3. **Utilization review organizations?** Yes.
   4. **Retrospective review?** No. (By contrast, for the Department of Social Services, utilization review can be "conducted on a concurrent, prospective, or retrospective basis." *See, e.g.,* CONN. AGENCIES REGS. § 17b-262-338(44).)

B. **What exemptions are provided, if any?** An agency of the federal government; an agent acting on behalf of the federal government, but only to the extent that the agent is providing services to the federal government; any agency of the state of Connecticut; or a hospital's internal quality assurance program except if associated with a health care financing mechanism. CONN. GEN. STAT. § 38a-226(2) (2004).

C. **What term does the state use to refer to regulated entities?** "Utilization review company," which is "any company, organization, or other entity performing utilization review." CONN. GEN. STAT. § 38a-226(2) (2004).

D. **What activities does the state include in its definition of utilization review?** Utilization Review is defined as the prospective or concurrent assessment of the necessity and appropriateness of the allocation of health care resources and services given or proposed to be given to an individual within this state. Utilization review shall not include elective requests for clarification of coverage. CONN. GEN. STAT. § 38a-226(1) (2004).

II. Regulatory Information

A. **Responsible state agency.** Connecticut Insurance Department, Life & Health Division.

B. **Contact Information.**

   1. **Name and Title:** Patricia Levesque, Managed Care Program Manager, The Life & Health Division.
   2. **Address:** Connecticut Insurance Department, P.O. Box 816, Hartford, CT 06142-0816.
   3. **Phone and Facsimile:** (860) 297-3859; facsimile (860) 297-3941.
   4. **E-mail:** patricia.levesque@po.state.ct.us
   5. **Web site:** www.state.ct.us/cid.

III. Licensure/Certification Requirements

A. **What entities are required to obtain a license in the state to conduct utilization review for residents of the state?** No utilization review company may conduct utilization review in this state unless it is licensed by the commissioner. CONN. GEN. STAT. § 38a-226a(a) (2004); CONN. AGENCIES REGS. § 38a-226c-9 (2004).

B. **How often must licensure be renewed?** Annually. CONN. GEN. STAT. § 38a-226a(a) (2004).

C. **Licensure fees (initial and renewal).** $2,500 and shall be dedicated exclusively to the regulation of utilization review. CONN. GEN. STAT. § 38a-226a(b) (2004).

D. **Documentation required for licensure.**

   1. The request for licensure or renewal shall include the name, address, telephone number and normal business hours of the utilization review company, the name and telephone number of a person for the commissioner to contact, and evidence of compliance noted in the statutory provisions for requirements of Utilization Review organizations. Any material changes in the information filed in accordance with this subsection shall be filed with the commissioner within 30 days of the change. CONN. GEN. STAT. § 38a-226a(c) (2004).
   2. All utilization review companies shall annually file with the commissioner the names of all managed care organizations that the utilization review company services in Connecticut, any utilization review services for which the utilization review company has contracted out for services and the name of such company providing the services, and the number of utilization review determinations not to certify an admission, service, procedure or extension of stay and the outcome of such determination upon appeal within the utilization review company. Determinations related to mental or nervous conditions shall be reported separately from all other determinations reported. CONN. GEN. STAT. § 38a-226c(a)(12) (2004).

3. Each utilization review company shall maintain an audit trail, through a written control log or computer report, clearly evidencing the date and time a request for:
   a. utilization review;
   b. expedited utilization review;
   c. an appeal of an adverse determination; or
   d. an expedited appeal of an adverse determination was received, the dates, times and reasons for any subsequent requests for additional information required to complete any such review or appeal, the dates and times of the receipt of the additional information and the date and time of notification to the provider of record or the enrollee. CONN. AGENCIES REGS. § 38a-226c-7 (2004).

IV. Program Requirements: All utilization review companies must meet the following minimum standards:

A. **Review Criteria:** Each utilization review company shall utilize written clinical criteria and review procedures which are established and periodically evaluated and updated with appropriate involvement from practitioners. CONN. GEN. STAT. § 38a-226c(a)(5) (2004).

B. **Notification:** Each utilization review company shall maintain and make available procedures for providing notification of its determinations regarding certification in accordance with the following:
   1. Notification shall be mailed or otherwise communicated to the provider of record or the enrollee or other appropriate individual within 2 business days after the receipt of all information necessary to complete the review. Any determination not to certify an admission, service, procedure or extension of stay shall be in writing.
   2. Determinations that authorize an admission, service, procedure or extension of stay that are based on accurate information from the provider, and have been communicated to the appropriate individual, may not be reversed if such determination of admission, service, procedure or extension of stay has taken place in reliance on such determination.
   3. Notification of a concurrent determination shall be mailed or otherwise communicated to the provider of record within 2 business

days of receipt of all information necessary to complete the review. Any determination not to certify an admission, service, procedure or extension of stay shall be in writing.

4. The utilization review company shall not make a determination not to certify based on incomplete information unless it has clearly indicated, in writing, to the provider of record or the enrollee all the information that is needed to make such determination.

5. A utilization review company may give authorization orally, electronically or communicated other than in writing. If the determination is an approval for a request, the company shall provide a confirmation number corresponding to the authorization.

6. Any notice of a determination not to certify an admission, service, procedure or extension of stay shall include in writing:
   a. the principal reasons for the determination,
   b. the procedures to initiate an appeal of the determination or the name and telephone number of the person to contact with regard to an appeal pursuant to the provisions of this section, and
   c. the procedure to appeal to the insurance commissioner. CONN. GEN. STAT. § 38a-226c(a)(1) et seq. (2004).

7. Prohibitions against financial incentives. No utilization review company may give an employee any financial incentive-based on the number of denials or certifications such employee make. CONN. GEN. STAT. § 38a-226c (2004). See also CONN. AGENCIES REGS. § 38a-226c-5 (2004).

C. **Telephone access standards.**
   1. Each utilization review company shall make review staff available by toll-free telephone, at least 40 hours per week during normal business hours. CONN. GEN. STAT. § 38a-226c (2004).
   2. For expedited reviews to the utilization review company, each utilization review company shall make review staff available from 8:00 AM to 9:00 PM to process these types of requests. CONN. GEN. STAT. § 38a-226c(e) (2004).

D. **Quality assurance program.** No provision.

E. **Delegation of utilization review functions.** No provision.

1. **Confidentiality.** Each utilization review company shall comply with all applicable federal and state laws to protect the confidentiality of individual medical records. Summary and aggregate data shall not be considered confidential if it does not provide sufficient information to allow identification of individual patients. CONN. GEN. STAT. § 38a-226c(a)(9) (2004); CONN. AGENCIES REGS. § 38a-226c-6 (2004).

V. Reviewer Qualifications

A. **Qualifications of reviewers that render utilization review determinations (at each level of utilization review, if applicable).**

1. Any utilization review decision to initially deny services shall be made by a licensed health professional. CONN. GEN. STAT. § 38a-226c(a)(13) (2004).

2. Physicians, nurses and other licensed health professionals making utilization review decisions shall have current licenses from a state licensing agency in the United States or appropriate certification from a recognized accreditation agency in the United States. However, any final determination not to certify an admission, service, procedure or extension of stay for an enrollee within this state, except for a claims brought pursuant to Workers Compensation, shall be made by a physician, nurse or other licensed health professional under the authority of a physician, nurse or other licensed health professional who has a current Connecticut license from the Department of Public Health. CONN. GEN. STAT. § 38a-226c(a)(6) (2004).

3. In unsuccessful appeals to reverse a determination not to certify, each utilization review company shall assure that a practitioner in a specialty related to the condition is reasonably available to review the case. When the reason for the determination not to certify is based on medical necessity, including whether a treatment is experimental or investigational, each utilization review company shall have the case reviewed by a physician who is a specialist in the field related to the condition that is the subject of the appeal. Any such review, except for a claim brought pursuant to Workers Compensation, that upholds a final determination not to certify in the case of an enrollee within this state shall be conducted by such practitioner or physician under the authority of a practitioner or physician who has a current Connecticut license from the Department of Public Health. The review shall be completed within thirty days of the request for review. The utilization review company shall be financially responsible for the review and shall maintain, for the commissioner's verification, documentation of the review, including the name of the reviewing physician. CONN. GEN. STAT. § 38a-226c(a)(7) (2004).

B. **Requirements for medical director.** No provision.

C. **Requirement for "same-state" licensure.** Yes, for denials. *See* CONN. GEN. STAT. § 38a-226c(a)(6) (2004); CONN GEN. STAT. § 38a-226c(a)(7) (2004).

VI. Reviews and Appeals

A. **Review determinations and notice to patients/providers.** Must be mailed or otherwise communicated to the patient or provider of record. All determinations not to certify must be in writing. CONN. GEN. STAT. § 38a-226c(a)(1) (2004).

1. **Time frame for determination.** For prospective and concurrent determinations, notice must be sent within 2 business days of receipt of the information necessary to complete the review. CONN. GEN. STAT. § 38a-226c(a)(1) (2004).

2. **Contents of notice of adverse determination.**

   a. the principal reasons for the determination;

   b. the procedures to initiate an appeal of the determination or the name and telephone number of the person to contact with regard to an appeal pursuant to the provisions of this section; and

   c. the procedure to appeal to the insurance commissioner.
   CONN. GEN. STAT. § 38a-226c(a)(1) (2004).

B. **Appeals requirements.**

1. **Time frame for determination.** Each utilization review company shall notify in writing the enrollee and provider of record of its determination on the appeal as soon as practical, but in no case later than 30 days after receiving the required documentation

on the appeal. For emergency or life-threatening situations, an expedited appeal must be available. Expedited appeals must be completed within 2 business days of the receipt of information necessary to complete the appeal. CONN. GEN. STAT. § 38a-226c(a)(2) (A)(2004); CONN. GEN. STAT. § 38a-226c(a)(4) (2004).

2. **External appeals.** On or after January 1, 1998, any enrollee, or any provider acting on behalf of an enrollee with the enrollee's consent, who has exhausted the internal mechanisms provided by a managed care organization or utilization review company to appeal a determination not to certify an admission, service, procedure or extension of stay, may appeal such determination to the commissioner. CONN. GEN. STAT. § 38a-478n (2004). Public Act 04-157, effective October 1, 2004, extends the external appeals process mandated by §38a-478n to enrollees who have exhausted the internal appeals of a denial based on medical necessity regardless of whether such denial was made before, during, or after the admission, service, procedure or extension of stay. To appeal a decision under the provisions of this section, an enrollee or any provider acting on behalf of an enrollee shall, within 30 days from receiving a final written determination from the enrollee's managed care organization or utilization review company, file a written request with the commissioner. The Commissioner of Insurance will assign the appeal to an external review entity, which has 5 business days to determine whether the appeal is accepted or denied for full review. The external review entity has 30 business days to complete the full review and forward its recommendation to the Commissioner whose decision will be binding. CONN. GEN. STAT. § 38a-478n (2004). The Connecticut Insurance Department's "External Appeal Consumer Guide" is available at the Connecticut State of Insurance web site.

C. **Emergency Services.** Each utilization review company shall allow a minimum of twenty-four hours following an emergency admission, service or procedure for an enrollee or his representative to notify the utilization review company and request certification or continuing treatment for that condition. CONN. GEN. STAT. § 38a-226c(a)(10) (2004)

VII. Recognition of URAC Accreditation Status

A. **Does the state recognize URAC accreditation?** No. The Commissioner has not recognized any accreditation organizations. The law permits the Commissioner of Insurance to find that the state's requirements have been met if a utilization review company "has received approval or accreditation by a utilization review accreditation organization, or otherwise demonstrates to the commissioner that it adheres to standards which are substantially similar to the standards in section 38a-226c, provided such approval, accreditation or standards do not provide less protection to enrollees than is provided under said section 38a-226c." CONN. GEN. STAT. § 38a-226d (2004). In addition, The Commissioner of Insurance shall consult with the Commissioner of Public Health to adopt regulations pertaining to requirements for utilization review companies. The regulations shall include standards, "which may be based on the national standards of the American Accreditation Health Care [sic] Commission (now URAC), concerning the confidentiality of patient medical records." CONN. GEN. STAT. § 38a-226c(f) (2004).

Delaware

I. Scope and Applicability

A. **Who is subject to the state's utilization review laws?** Delaware does not currently regulate utilization review organizations. Delaware regulates the utilization review activities of managed care organizations (MCO's). Pursuant to the Delaware Code, the Secretary of the Department of Health and Social Services (DHSS) adopted regulations that address the utilization review activities of MCO's. DEL. CODE ANN. tit. 16, § 9124 (2004). (Note: There is a specific certification for utilization review organizations. However, the "certification" that is referred to in the statutes is specific to those utilization review organizations (URO's) that will be contracting with DHSS to perform Independent Utilization Review services for the Independent Healthcare Appeals Program (IHCAP). In order for an URO to provide these services, they must bid on a State Contract and be selected.)

1. **HMO's?** Yes.
2. **Insurers?** Yes.
3. **Utilization review organizations?** No.
4. **Retrospective Review?** Yes.

B. **What exemptions are provided, if any?** None listed.

C. **What term does the state use?** Delaware regulates the utilization review activities of "MCO's." Defined as a public or private organization, organized under the laws of any state, which: 1)provides or otherwise makes available to enrolled participants health care services, including at least the basic health services defined in 69.102; 2) is primarily compensated (except for co-payment) for the provision of basic health care services to the enrolled participants on a predetermined periodic rate basis; and 3) provides physician services directly through physicians who are either employees or partners of such organization, or through arrangements with individual physicians or one or more groups of physicians (organized on a group practice or individual practice basis). CODE DEL. REGS. § 40 700 035-69.132 (2004).

D. **What activities does the state include in its definition of utilization review?** "Utilization review" is defined as "a set of formal techniques designed to monitor the use of, or evaluate the clinical necessity, appropriateness, efficacy, or efficiency of health care services, procedures, or settings. Techniques may include ambulatory review, prospective review, second opinion, certification, concurrent review, case management, discharge planning, or retrospective review." CODE DEL. REGS. § 40 700 035-69.146 (2004).

II. Regulatory Information

A. **Responsible state agency.** Department of Health and Social Services, Division of Public Health, Office of Health Facilities Licensing and Certification.

B. **Contact Information.**
1. **Name and Title:** Ms. Judy Zumbo, RN, BSN, JD, Compliance Nurse
2. **Address:** Office of Health Facilities Licensing and Certification, Department of Health and Social Services, 2055 Limestone Road, Suite 200, Wilmington, DE 19808.
3. **Phone and Facsimile:** (302) 995-8521; facsimile: (302) 995-8529.
4. **E-mail:** judy.zumbo@state.de.us
5. **Web site:** www.state.de.us/dhss/dph

III. Licensure/Certification Requirements.

A. **What entities are required to obtain a license in the state to conduct utilization review for residents of the state?** Licensure not required.

B. **How often must licensure/certification be renewed?** Not applicable.

C. **Licensure fees (initial and renewal).** Not applicable.

D. **Documentation required for licensure.** Not applicable.

E. **Exemptions from licensure.** Licensure is not required.

F. **Certification for MCO's.** MCO's conduct utilization review. No person shall establish or operate an MCO in the state of Delaware or enter the state for the purposes of enrolling persons in an MCO without obtaining a Certificate of Authority under Chapter 91 of Title 16 of the Delaware Code. CODE DEL. REGS. § 40 700 035-69.201 (2004). All managed care organizations (MCO's) are regulated by the Department of Insurance (DOI) and the DHSS.

G. **Certification Fees.** Every MCO shall pay the fees in accordance with DEL. CODE ANN. tit. 16, § 9111 (2004). CODE DEL. REGS. § 40 700 035-69.318 (2004).

1. Certificate of Authority application filing fee: $375.
2. Annual report filing fee: $250.
   DEL. CODE ANN. tit. 16, § 9111 (2004).

IV. Program Requirements

The MCO shall establish and implement a comprehensive utilization management program to monitor access to and appropriate utilization of health care and services. The program shall be under the direction of a designated physician and shall be based on a written plan that is reviewed at least annually. The plan shall identify at least:

➤ Scope of utilization management activities;

➤ Procedures to evaluate clinical necessity, access, appropriateness, and efficacy of services;

➤ Mechanisms to detect under utilization;

➤ Clinical review criteria and protocols used in decision-making;

➤ Mechanisms to ensure consistent application of review criteria and uniform decisions;

➤ System for providers and enrollees to appeal utilization management determinations in accordance with the procedures set forth; and

➤ A mechanism to evaluate enrollee and provider satisfaction with the complaint and appeals systems set forth. Such evaluation shall be coordinated with the performance monitoring activities conducted pursuant to the continuous quality improvement program set forth. CODE DEL. REGS. § 40 700 035-69.403(A)(1) (2004).

A. **Clinical review criteria.** Utilization management determinations shall be based on written clinical criteria and protocols reviewed and approved by practicing physicians and other licensed health care providers within the network. These criteria and protocols shall be periodically reviewed and updated. With the exception of internal or proprietary quantitative thresholds, such criteria and protocols shall be readily available, upon request, to affected providers and enrollees. CODE DEL. REGS. § 40 700 035-69.403(A)(2) (2004).

B. **Prohibitions against financial incentives.** Compensation to persons providing utilization review services for a MCO shall not contain incentives, direct or indirect, for such persons to make inappropriate review decisions. Compensation may not be based, directly or indirectly, on the quantity or type of adverse determinations rendered. CODE DEL. REGS. § 40 700 035-69.403(A)(3) (2004).

C. **Telephone access standards.** At a minimum, appropriately qualified staff shall be immediately available by telephone, during routine provider work hours, to render utilization management determinations for providers. The MCO shall provide enrollees and providers with a toll free telephone number by which to contact customer service staff on at least a 5day, f40 hours a week basis. The MCO shall supply providers with a toll free telephone number by which to contact utilization management staff on at least a 5 days, 40 hours a week basis. The MCO must have policies and procedures addressing responses to inquiries concerning emergency or urgent care when a PCP or his/her authorized on call back up provider is unavailable. CODE DEL. REGS. § 40 700 035-69.403(B) (2004).

D. **Quality assurance program.** Under the direction of a medical director or his/her designated physician, the MCO shall have a system-wide continuous quality improvement program. The MCO shall coordinate its quality improvement with other performance monitoring activities, including utilization management and monitoring of enrollee and provider complaints. CODE DEL. REGS. § 40 700 035-69.405 (2004).

E. **Delegation of utilization review functions.** No provision.

F. **Confidentiality.** No provision.

V. Reviewer Qualifications

A. **Qualifications of reviewers that render utilization review determinations (at each level of utilization review, if applicable).** All determinations to authorize services shall be rendered by "appropriately qualified staff." All determinations to deny or limit an admission, service, procedure, or extension of stay shall be rendered by a physician under the clinical direction of the medical director responsible for medical services provided to the MCO's Delaware enrollees. Such determinations shall be made in accordance with clinical and medical criteria and standards, and shall take into account the individualized needs of the enrollee from whom the service, admission, procedure is requested. The MCO may not retroactively deny reimbursement. CODE DEL. REGS. § 40 700 035-69.403(C) (2004).

B. **Requirements for medical director.** The medical director and physicians designated to act on his behalf shall be Delaware licensed physicians. CODE DEL. REGS. § 40 700 035-69.306 (2004). The MCO's medical director shall supervise physicians making utilization management determinations. CODE DEL. REGS. § 40 700 035-69.403(C)(2) (2004).

C. **Requirements for "same-state" licensure.** No provision.

VI. Reviews and Appeals

A. **Review determination and notice to patient/providers.** An enrollee must receive upon request a written notice of all determinations to deny coverage or authorization for services required and the basis for the denial. CODE DEL. REGS. § 40 700 035-69.403(C)(5) (2004).

1. **Time frame for determination.** All determinations shall be made on a timely basis as required by the exigencies of the situation. CODE DEL. REGS. § 40 700 035-69.403(C)(3) (2004).

2. **Contents of notice of adverse determination.**

   a. **Reasons for adverse determination.** No provision.

   b. **Notice of appeal rights.** All enrollees and providers shall be provided with a written explanation of the appeal process upon enrollment, annually, upon request, and each time the appeal process is substantially changed. CODE DEL. REGS. § 40 700 035-69.404(B)(1) (2004).

B. **Appeals requirements.** MCO enrollees, or any provider acting on behalf of an enrollee with the enrollee's consent, may appeal any utilization management determination resulting in a denial, termination, or other limitation of covered health care services. The appeal process shall consist of the following stages: an internal review by the carrier (Stage 1 Appeal), a second subsequent internal review by the carrier (Stage 2 Appeal), and an external review (Stage 3 Appeal) by an independent utilization review organization. CODE DEL. REGS. § 40 700 035-69.404 (2004).

1. **Time frame for determination.** Stage 1 appeals shall be concluded as soon as possible in accordance with the medical exigencies of the case but no more than 5business days after receipt of the appeal. A carrier shall provide notice of the Stage 1 appeal determination to the appellant within 5 business days of receipt of the appeal. If such notice is provided verbally to the appellant, the carrier shall provide written notice of the determination to the appellant

within 5 business days of the verbal notice. Stage 2 appeals shall be concluded as soon as possible in accordance with the medical exigencies of the case but no more than 30 calendar days after receipt of the request for the Stage 2 appeal. The carrier may extend the Stage 2 appeal for up to an additional 30 calendar days for reasonable cause by submitting a written explanation for the delay to the Department within the original 30 calendar day review period. A carrier shall provide written notice of the Stage 2 appeal determination to the appellant within 5 business days of such determination. Neither Stage 1 nor Stage 2 appeals involving an imminent, emergent, or serious threat to the health of the enrollee shall exceed 72 hours. CODE DEL. REGS. § 40 700 035-69.404 (2004).

2. **External appeals.** An external Independent Health Care Appeals Program is governed by the Department of Health & Social Services. The program will include, at a minimum, a final step in the grievance process which provides for a review by an Independent Utilization Review Organization, hereafter referred to as "IURO," as specified in regulations promulgated by the Department. Upon receipt of an adverse determination any appellant who is dissatisfied with the results, shall have the opportunity to pursue her/his appeal before an independent utilization review organization. The appellant must file the request for appeal with the carrier within 60 calendar days of receipt of the adverse determination from the internal review process. Within 45 calendar days after the receipt of the request for external review, the assigned IURO shall provide written notice of its decision to uphold or reverse the adverse determination. *See* DEL. CODE ANN. tit. 16 § 9119 (2004); CODE DEL. REGS. § 40 700 035 et seq. (2004).

D. **Emergency Services.** Appeals involving an imminent, emergent or serious threat to the health of the enrollee shall be addressed within 72 hours. CODE DEL. REGS. § 40 700 035-69.404 (2004).

VII. Recognition of URAC Accreditation Status

A. **Does the state recognize URAC accreditation?** No.

B. **Which of the state's requirements are waived for URAC-accredited organizations?** Not applicable.

District of Columbia

I. Scope and Applicability

A. **Who is subject to the state's utilization review laws?** The District of Columbia does not regulate utilization review activities or utilization review organizations in the health insurance area. There are provisions that pertain to workers' compensation utilization review.

B. **What exemptions are provided, if any?** Not applicable.

C. **What term does the state use to refer to regulated entities?** Not applicable.

D. **What activities does the state include in its definition of utilization review?** Not defined for health insurance.

II. Regulatory Information.

A. **Responsible state agency.** Department of Insurance and Securities Regulation.

B. **Contact Information.**
1. **Name and Title:** Lawrence H. Mirel, Commissioner of Insurance and Securities Regulation.
2. **Address:** Department of Insurance and Securities Regulation, 810 First Street, N.E., Suite 701, Washington, DC 20002.
3. **Phone and Facsimile:** (202) 442-7773; facsimile (202) 535-1196.
4. **E-mail:** lhmirel-dcia@dcgov.org.
5. **Web site:** None

D. **Responsible state agency.** Department of Health.

E. **Contact Information.**
1. **Name and Title:** Patrick Kelly.
2. **Address:** Department of Health, 825 North Capitol Street, N.E., 4th Floor, Washington, DC 20002.
3. **Phone and Facsimile:** (202) 442-5979; facsimile (202) 442-4797.
4. **E-Mail:** pkelly@dchealth.com.
5. **Web site:** www.dchealth.dc.gov.

III. Miscellaneous

The District of Columbia has added language pertaining to how health maintenance organizations (HMO's) deal with utilization review in the context of maternity and newborn care. "No insurer may deselect, terminate the services of, require additional documentation from, require additional utilization review, reduce payments, or otherwise provide financial disincentives to any attending provider who orders care consistent with this chapter." D.C. CODE ANN. § 35-3802.01 (2003).

The Director of the Department of Health adopted new regulations promulgated under D.C. CODE ANN. § 32-571 et seq. on January 14, 2000. The new regulations, D.C. MUN. REGS. tit. 22, § 60, specify requirements for the establishment, operation, and maintenance of internal grievance and review procedures by health benefits plans and qualifications and procedures for independent review organizations to follow in conducting external reviews of decisions by health benefits plans. Each member (an individual enrolled in a health benefits plan) or his or her representative shall have the right to file a grievance with an insurer for a review of an "adverse decision." Each insurer's internal grievance system, detailed in § 6001, shall include an expedited grievance procedure for urgent or emergency medical conditions. Any member dissatisfied with an adverse decision shall have an opportunity to review the decision in an informal interview process with the insurer's medical director, physician, or other designee who rendered the decision. Any member or member representative dissatisfied with the decision from the informal internal review process may seek a formal internal review, with the opportunity for expedited review in emergency or urgent medical condition cases. A member or member representative must exhaust the insurer's internal grievance process before filing a request for external review with the Director of Health. Where external review is approved, the Director shall assign external review to certified independent review organizations.

Florida

I. Scope and Applicability

A. **Who is subject to the state's utilization review laws?** A private review agent conducting utilization review as to health care services performed or proposed to be performed in this state shall register with the agency in accordance with this section. FLA. STAT. ANN. § 395.0199(2) (2004).

   1. **HMO's?** No.
   2. **Insurers?** No, except that insurers may not knowingly contract with a private review agent that has not registered with the state.
   3. **Utilization review organizations?** Yes.
   4. **Retrospective review?** Yes.
       FLA. STAT. ANN. § 395.0199(1)(b)(2004).

B. **What exceptions are provided, if any?** There are exceptions for utilization review services provided under contract to the federal or state government for Medicaid or Medicare, but not for services provided for non-federally funded patients. There is another exception for persons who perform utilization review services for medically necessary hospital services provided to injured workers pursuant to the Workers' Compensation regulations and for self-insurance funds or service companies authorized under that chapter. FLA. STAT. ANN. §395.0199(8) (2004).

C. **What term does the state use to refer to regulated entities?** "Private review agent" is defined as "any person or entity which performs utilization review services for third-party payors on a contractual basis for outpatient or inpatient services." The term does not include "full-time employees, personnel, or staff of health insurers, health maintenance organizations, or hospitals, or wholly owned subsidiaries thereof or affiliates under common ownership, when performing utilization review for their respective hospitals, health maintenance organizations, or insureds of the same insurance group." FLA. STAT. ANN. § 395.002(25) (2004).

D. **What activities does the state include in its definition of utilization review?** "Utilization review" means a system for reviewing the medical necessity or appropriateness in the allocation of health care resources of hospital services given or proposed to be given to a patient or group of patients. FLA. STAT. ANN. § 395.002(31) (2004).

II. Regulatory Information

A. **Responsible states agency.** Florida Agency for Health Care Administration.

B. **Contact Information.**
   1. **Name and Title:** Ruby Schmigel & Susan Buchan, Regulatory Specialists II.
   2. **Address:** Florida Agency of Health Care Administration, Hospital & Outpatient Services Unit, 2727 Mahan Drive, MS #31 Tallahassee, FL 32308-5403
   3. **Phone and Facsimile:** (850) 487-2717; facsimile (850) 922-4351.
   4. **E-mail:** schmiger@fdhc.state.fl.us; buchans@fdhc.state.fl.us
   5. **Web site:** www.fdhc.state.fl.us. 6. http://www.fdhc.state.fl.us/MCHQ/Health_Facility_Regulation/Hospital_Outpatient/utilization.shtml

III. Registration Requirements

A. **What entities are required to obtain a registration in the state to conduct utilization review for residents of the state?** A private review agent conducting utilization review as to health care services performed or proposed to be performed in this state shall register with the agency in accordance with this section. FLA. STAT. ANN. § 395.0199(2) (2004).

B. **How often must registration be renewed?** Annually. FLA. STAT. ANN. § 395.0199(3) (2004).

C. **Registration fees (initial and renewal).** The fee shall be sufficient to pay for the administrative costs of registering the agent, but shall not exceed $250. The agency may also charge reasonable fees, reflecting actual costs, to persons requesting copies of registration. FLA. STAT. ANN. § 395.0199(3) (2004).

D. **Documentation required for Registration.** Registration shall include the following:
   1. A description of the review policies and procedures to be used in evaluating proposed or delivered hospital care.
   2. The name, address, and telephone number of the utilization review agent performing utilization review, who shall be at least a licensed practical nurse or licensed registered nurse, or other similarly qualified medical records or health care professionals, for performing initial review when information is necessary from the physician or hospital to determine the medical necessity or appropriateness of hospital

services; or, a licensed physician, or a licensed physician practicing in the field of psychiatry for review of mental health services, for an initial denial determination prior to a final denial determination by the health insurer and which shall include the written evaluation and findings of the reviewing physician.

3. A description of an appeal procedure for patients or health care providers whose services are under review, who may appeal an initial denial determination prior to a final determination by the health insurer with whom the private review agent has contracted.

4. A designation of the times when the staff of the utilization review agent will be available by toll-free telephone, which shall include at least 40 hours per week during the normal business hours of the agent.

5. An acknowledgment and agreement that any private review agent which, as a general business practice, fails to adhere to the policies, procedures, and representations made in its application for registration shall have its registration revoked.

6. Disclosure of any incentive payment provision or quota provision which is contained in the agent's contract with a health insurer and is based on reduction or denial of services, reduction of length of stay, or selection of treatment setting.

7. Updates of any material changes to review policies or procedures. FLA. STAT. ANN. § 395.0199(5) (2004). *See also* Registration requirements in FLA. ADMIN. CODE § 59A-15.004 (2004).

E. **Exemptions from registration.** Out-of-state organizations are not granted an exemption from Florida's registration requirements even if they are duly licensed and/or certified in their state of domicile.

IV. Program Requirements
A. **Clinical review criteria.** No provision.
B. **Prohibitions against financial incentives.** The private review agent must disclose any incentive payment provisions that are based on reduction or denial of services or treatment setting. FLA. STAT. ANN. § 395.0199(3) (2004).
C. **Telephone access standards.** Staff of a private review agent must be available by toll-free telephone at least 40 hours per week during

normal business hours. FLA. STAT. ANN. § 395.0199(5)(d) (2004).
D. **Quality assurance program.** No provision.
E. **Delegation of utilization review functions.** No provision. However, No insurer shall knowingly contract with or utilize a private review agent which has failed to register as required by this section or which has had a registration revoked by the agency. FLA. STAT. ANN. § 395.0199(7) (2004).
F. **Confidentiality.** Private review agents shall develop written policies and procedures to ensure the protection of personal and medical record information. FLA. ADMIN. CODE § 59A-15.009 (2004).

V. Reviewer Qualifications
A. **Qualifications of reviewers that render utilization review determinations (at each level of utilization review, if applicable).**
   1. Those agents performing Utilization Review must be at least; A licensed practical nurse or licensed registered nurse, or other similarly qualified medical records or health care professionals, for performing initial review when information is necessary from the physician or hospital to determine the medical necessity or appropriateness of hospital services; or;
   2. A licensed physician, or a licensed physician practicing in the field of psychiatry for review of mental health services, for an initial denial determination prior to a final denial determination by the health insurer and which shall include the written evaluation and findings of the reviewing physician.
   3. Licensed physicians (or licensed psychiatrists, for reviews of mental health services) must review appeals. FLA. STAT. ANN. § 395.0199(5)(b)(1) and (2) (2004).
B. **Requirements for medical director.** No provision.
C. **Requirement for "same-state" licensure.** No provision.

VI. Reviews and Appeals
A. **Review determinations and notice to patients/providers.** No provision.
B. **Time frame for determination.** Not applicable.
C. **Contents of notice of adverse determination.** Not applicable.
D. **Reasons for adverse determination.** Not applicable.
E. **Notice of Appeal Rights.** Not applicable.

F. **Appeals requirements.** The private review agent must provide the Agency for Health Care Administration with a description of an appeal procedure for patients or health care providers whose services are under review, who may appeal an initial denial determination before a final determination by the health insurer with whom the private review agent has contracted. A licensed physician (or a licensed psychiatrist, for reviews of mental health services) must review appeals. The appeal must include the written evaluation and findings of the reviewing physician. FLA. STAT. ANN. § 395.0199(c) (2004).

G. **Time frame for determination.** No provision.

H. **External appeals.** Florida has had an external review provision since 1985, *See* FLA. STAT. ANN. § 408.7056 (2004), as modified in 2003. This pertains to disputes involving "unresolved grievances" related to medical necessity, among other things, for "managed care entities," defined as HMO's, prepaid health clinics certified under state law, or exclusive provider organizations. This process requires the completion of internal appeals. Enrollees and health care providers may file an appeal. The review panel consists of staff of the Agency for Health Care Administration and the Department of Insurance. Those agencies have the option of contracting with independent reviewers for "additional technical expertise."

1. **External appeals process.** The Florida Agency for Health Care shall review all grievances within 60 days after receipt and make a determination whether the grievance shall be heard. Once notification to the appropriate parties is sent, the panel shall hear the grievance either in the network area or by teleconference no later than 120 days after the date the grievance was filed. The agency shall notify the parties, in writing, by facsimile transmission, or by phone, of the time and place of the hearing. The panel may take testimony under oath, request certified copies of documents, and take similar actions to collect information and documentation that will assist the panel in making findings of fact and a recommendation. The panel shall issue a written recommendation, supported by findings of fact, to the provider or subscriber, to the managed care entity, and to the agency or the office no later than 15 working days after hearing the grievance or after all documentation requested has been

provided to the panel. FLA. STAT. ANN. §§ 408.7056(2), 408.7056(3) (2004).

2. **Expedited appeals process.** Grievances that the Florida Agency for Health Care determine pose an immediate and serious threat to a subscriber's health must be given priority over other grievances. The panel may meet as quickly as possible but no later than 45 days after the date the grievance is filed, unless the panel receives a waiver of the time requirement from the subscriber. The panel shall issue a written recommendation, supported by findings of fact, to the office or the agency within 10 days after hearing the expedited grievance.

a. When the life of a subscriber is in imminent and emergent jeopardy, the chair of the panel may convene an emergency hearing, within 24 hours after notification to the managed care entity and to the subscriber. The grievance must be heard notwithstanding that the subscriber has not completed the internal grievance procedure of the managed care entity. The panel shall, upon hearing the grievance, issue a written emergency recommendation, supported by findings of fact, to the managed care entity, to the subscriber, and to the agency or the office for the purpose of deferring the imminent and emergent jeopardy to the subscriber's life. Within 24 hours after receipt of the panel's emergency recommendation, the agency or office may issue an emergency order to the managed care entity.

b. Post Agency Decision. After hearing a grievance, the panel shall make a recommendation to the agency or the office which may include specific actions the managed care entity must take to comply with state laws or rules regulating managed care entities. A managed care entity, subscriber, or provider that is affected by a panel recommendation may within 10 days after receipt of the panel's recommendation, or 72 hours after receipt of a recommendation in an expedited grievance, furnish to the agency or office written evidence in opposition to the recommendation or findings of fact of the panel. No later than 30 days after the issuance of the panel's recommendation and, for an expedited grievance, no later than 10 days after the issuance of the panel's recommendation, the agency or the office may adopt the panel's recommendation or findings of fact in a proposed order or an emergency order. The agency or the office may reject all or part of the panel's recommendation.

VII. Recognition of URAC Accreditation Status

A. Does the state recognize URAC accreditation? No.

B. Which of the state's requirements are waived for URAC-accredited organizations? Not applicable.

Georgia

I. Scope and Applicability

A. Who is subject to the state's utilization review laws? Private review agents who engage in utilization review with respect to health care services provided in Georgia. GA. CODE ANN. § 33-46-1(b) (2004). All managed care entities offering managed care plans in this state shall have a utilization review program which complies with the requirements of Title 33, Chapter 46 and the Rules and Regulations of the Office of Commissioner of Insurance Chapter 120-2-58. *See* GA. COMP. R. & REGS. r. 120-2-80-07(1) (2004).

  1. **HMO's?** Yes.
  2. **Insurers?** Yes.
  3. **Utilization review organizations?** Yes.
  4. **Retrospective review?** No.

B. What exemptions are provided, if any? There are exemptions for federal health programs as well as for claims arising under workers' compensation or malpractice insurance policies. GA. CODE ANN. § 33-46-1(b) (2004). No certificate is required for utilization review by any Georgia licensed pharmacist or pharmacy while engaged in the practice of pharmacy, including but not limited to review of the dispensing of drugs, participation in drug utilization review, and monitoring patient drug therapy. GA. CODE ANN. § 33-46-12 (2004).

C. What term does the state use to refer to regulated entities? A "private review agent" means "any person or entity which performs utilization review for: 1) an employer with employees who are treated by a health care provider in [Georgia]; 2) a payor; or 3) a claims administrator." GA. CODE ANN. § 33-46-2(9) (2004).

D. What activities does the state include in its definition of utilization review? "Utilization review" is "a system for reviewing the appropriate and efficient allocation or charges of hospital, outpatient, medical, or other health care services given or proposed to be given to a patient or group of patients for the purpose of advising the claims administrator who determines whether such services or the charges therefore should be covered, provided, or reimbursed by a payor according to the benefits plan." The definition explicitly does not include the review or adjustment of claims or the payment of benefits under liability, workers'

compensation, or malpractice insurance policies. GA. CODE ANN. § 33-46-2(11) (2004).

II. Regulatory Information

A. Responsible state agency. Office of Insurance and Safety Fire Commissioner, Life and Health Division.

B. Contact Information.

  1. **Name and Title:** Edith Johnson, Utilization Review Analyst.
  2. **Address:** Office of Insurance and Safety Fire Commissioner, Life and Health Division, 9th Floor, West Tower, Room 902, Floyd Building, 2 Martin Luther King, Jr. Drive, Atlanta, GA 30334.
  3. **Phone and Facsimile:** (404) 657-1705; facsimile: (404) 657-7679.
  4. **E-mail:** edith.johnson@mail.oci.state.ga.us.
  5. **Web site:** www.inscomm.state.ga.us.

III. Certification Requirements

A. What entities are required to obtain a license in the state to conduct utilization review for residents of the state? A private review agent may not conduct utilization review of health care provided in this state unless the Commissioner has granted the private review agent a certificate pursuant to this chapter. No individual conducting utilization review shall require certification if such utilization review is performed within the scope of such person's employment with an entity already certified. GA. CODE ANN. § 33-46-3(a) (2004). Any managed care entity or contractor providing utilization review services for a managed care plan must be certified as a Private Review Agent or otherwise deemed compliant by the Commissioner only if such entity or contractor is an applicant that has been accredited or certified by the Utilization Review Accreditation Commission (URAC) or the National Committee for Quality Assurance (NCQA). GA. COMP. R. & REGS. r. 120-2-80-07(1) (2004).

B. How often must certification be renewed? Every 2 years. GA. CODE ANN. § 33-46-3(a) (2004).

C. Certification fees (initial and renewal). Initial fee of $1,000; renewal fee of $500. GA. CODE ANN. § 33-8-1 (2004).

D. Documentation required for licensure. An applicant for a certificate shall submit an application on a form prescribed by the Commissioner and pay an application fee and a certificate fee. The application shall be signed and verified by the applicant. GA. CODE ANN. § 33-46-5(a) (2004).

1. In conjunction with the application, the private review agent shall submit such information that the Commissioner requires, including but not limited to: a) A utilization review plan; b) The type and qualifications of the personnel either employed or under contract to perform the utilization review; and c) A copy of the materials designed to inform applicable patients and health care providers of the requirements of the utilization review plan. GA. CODE ANN. § 33-46-5(b) (2004).

2. The information provided must demonstrate to the satisfaction of the Commissioner that the private review agent will comply with the requirements of this chapter. GA. CODE ANN. § 33-46-5(b) (2004).

3. Administrative Regulations require specifically: A utilization review plan; documentation that the private review agent has received full accreditation or certification by the Utilization Review Accreditation Commission (URAC) or the National Committee for Quality Assurance (NCQA). Reason or reasons should be stated if the organization is not presently fully accredited or certified by URAC or NCQA; The type, qualifications and number of the personnel to perform the utilization review; A copy of the materials designed to inform applicable patients and health care providers of the requirements of the utilization review plan; A written description of an ongoing quality assessment program; The written policies and procedures to ensure that an appropriate representative of the private review agent is reasonably accessible to patients and health care providers 5 days a week during normal business hours in this state; The written policies and procedures to ensure that information obtained in the course of utilization review is maintained in a confidential manner; The written policies and procedures establishing and maintaining a complaint system; and a sample John Doe copy of each type of contract or agreement to be executed between the private review agent and payor, employer, claim administrator, or other entity with certification that the private

review agent shall not enter into any incentive payment provision contained in a contract or agreement with a payor which is based on reduction of services or the charges thereof, reduction of length of stay, or utilization or alternative treatment settings to reduce amounts of necessary or appropriate medical care. GA. COMP. R. & REGS. r. 120-2-58-.03(6) (2004).

4. For initial certification, private review agents must submit all advertising materials to be used in Georgia. GA. COMP. R. & REGS. r. 120-2-58-.03(5) (2004).

E. **Exemptions from certification.** Out-of-state organizations are not granted an exemption from the state's licensure and certification requirements even if they are duly licensed and/or certified in their state of domicile.

IV. Program Requirements.

Georgia imposes minimum standards on private review agents who engage in utilization review with respect to health care services. Such standards include regulations concerning certification of private review agents, disclosure of utilization review standards and appeal procedures, minimum qualifications for utilization review personnel, minimum standards governing accessibility of utilization review, and such other standards, requirements, and rules or regulations promulgated by the Commissioner of Insurance. GA. CODE ANN. § 33-46-1(B) (2004).

A. **Clinical review criteria.** The medical protocols including reconsideration and appeal processes as well as other relevant medical issues used in the private review program shall be established with input from health care providers who are from a major area of specialty, and certified by the boards of the American medical specialties selected by a private review agency and shall be made available upon request of health care providers; or protocols, including reconsideration and appeal processes as well as other relevant health care issues used in the private review program, shall be established based on input from persons who are licensed in the appropriate health care provider's specialty recognized by a licensure agency of such a health care provider. GA. CODE ANN. § 33-46-4(1) (2004).

1. In any instances where the utilization review agent is questioning the medical necessity or appropriateness of care, the attending health care provider shall be able to discuss the plan

of treatment with an identified health care provider trained in a related specialty and no adverse determination shall be made by the utilization review agent until an effort has been made to discuss the patient's care with the patient's attending provider during normal working hours.

2. In the event of an adverse determination, notice to the provider and patient will specify the reasons for the review determination. GA. CODE ANN. § 33-46-4(5) (2004).

B. **Prohibitions against financial incentives.** A private review agent may not enter into any incentive payment provisions that are based on the reduction of services, reduction of length-of-stay, or use of alternative treatment settings. GA. CODE ANN. § 33-46-4(8) (2004).

C. **Telephone access standards.** An appropriate representative of the private review agent is reasonably accessible to patients and health care providers 5 days a week during normal business hours in Georgia. GA. COMP. R. & REGS. r. 120-2-58-.03(f) (2004). A private review agent shall provide access to its review staff by a toll free or collect call telephone line during normal business hours. A private review agent shall have an established procedure to review timely call backs from health care providers and shall establish written procedures for receiving after-hour calls, either in person or by recording. GA. COMP. R. & REGS. r. 120-2-58-.05(2) (2004).

D. **Quality assurance program.** Private review agents must maintain a continuing quality assessment program and must submit a written description with their certification for renewal. GA. COMP. R. & REGS. r. 120-2-58-.03(6)(e) (2004). *See also* GA. CODE ANN. § 33-28-5(3) (2004). A managed care plan must establish an ongoing quality assurance program for health care service it provides to enrollees. This quality assurance program shall provide for a utilization review program which stresses health outcomes, and provides for the establishment of written protocols for utilization review, based on current standards of the relevant health care profession. It should also provide review by physicians and appropriate health care providers of the process followed in the provision of such health care services and have mechanisms to detect both underutilization and over-utilization of services.

E. **Delegation of utilization review functions.** A managed care entity which uses a managed care contractor or contractors for its utilization review program must notify the Commissioner in its managed care plan certification application of all such contractors for all its managed care plans, and the extent to which each contractor conducts utilization review. The managed care entity must attest that each contractor either is certified as a Private Review Agent or is deemed compliant as a Private Review Agent by the Commissioner. GA. COMP. R. & REGS. r. 120-2-80-.07(3) (2004).

F. **Confidentiality.** Utilization review organizations must comply with all applicable laws to protect the confidentiality of individual medical records. Confidential information may only be shared with those agents that have authority to receive such information. Private review agents must adopt guidelines to prevent unauthorized release of individual health information to the public. Information collected for utilization review may be used solely for utilization review, quality management, discharge planning, and case management. GA. COMP. R. & REGS. r. 120-2-58-03(g) (2004).

V. **Reviewer Qualifications.**

The utilization review agent should respond promptly and efficiently to all requests including concurrent review in a timely method and a method for an expedited authorization process shall be available in the interest of efficient patient care. GA. CODE ANN. § 33-46-4(4) (2004).

A. **Qualifications of reviewers that render utilization review determinations (at each level of utilization review, if applicable).**

1. Private review agents shall have sufficient staff to facilitate review in accordance with review criteria and shall designate one or more individuals able to effectively communicate medical and clinical information. GA. COMP. R. & REGS. r. 120-2-58-05(1) (2004).

2. Attending health care providers shall have opportunity to discuss utilization review determination promptly by telephone with an identified health care provider representing the private review agent and trained in a related medical specialty. GA. CODE ANN. § 33-46-4(5) (2004).

3. In reconsideration, the utilization review agent shall make no adverse determination until making an effort to discuss the patient's care with the patient's attending provider. GA. CODE ANN. § 33-46-4(5) (2004).

4. Requirements for medical director. No provision.
5. Requirement for "same-state" licensure. No provision.
6. A managed care entity which uses a managed care contractor or contractors for its utilization review program must notify the Commissioner in its managed care plan certification application of all such contractors for all its managed care plans, and the extent to which each contractor conducts utilization review. The managed care entity must attest that each contractor either is certified as a Private Review Agent or is deemed compliant as a Private Review Agent by the Commissioner. GA. COMP. R. & REGS. r. 120-2-80-07(3) (2004).

VI. Reviews and Appeals

A. **Review determinations and notice to patients/providers.** 1) In the event a private review agent questions the medical necessity or appropriateness of care, the attending health care provider shall have the opportunity to discuss a utilization review determination promptly by telephone with an identified health care provider representing the private review agent and trained in a related medical specialty. 2) If the determination is made not to certify, an adverse determination exists. 3) The right to appeal an adverse determination shall be available to the enrollee and the attending physician or other ordering health care provider. 4) The enrollee or enrollee's representative shall be allowed a second review by another identified health care provider in an appropriate medical specialty who represents the private review agent.

B. **Notice and Time Frame for determination patients/providers.**
   1. When an initial determination is made to certify, notification shall be provided promptly either by telephone, in writing or electronic transmission to the attending health care provider, the facility rendering service as well as to the enrollee.
   2. Written notification shall be transmitted within 2 business days of the determination.
   3. When a determination is made not to certify, the attending physician and/or other ordering health care provider or facility rendering service shall:
      a. Be notified by telephone within 1 business day.

      b. Be sent a written notification within 1 business day, which also shall be sent to the enrollee.

C. **Contents of Notice.** The written notification shall include: principal reason(s) for the determination and instructions for initiating an appeal of the adverse determination.
   1. The private review agent shall establish procedures for appeals to be made in writing and by telephone. The private review agent shall notify the health care provider and enrollee in writing of its determination on the appeal as soon as possible, but in no case later than 60 days after receiving the required documentation to conduct the appeal. The appeals procedure does not preclude the right of an enrollee to pursue legal action.
   2. Reasons for adverse determination. Required.
   3. Notice of Appeal Rights. Required.
   GA. COMP. R. & REGS. r. 120-2-58-05(6) (2004).

D. **External Appeals and Independent Review.** Managed care plans must establish a grievance procedure which provides the enrollee with a prompt and meaningful hearing on the issue of denial, in whole or in part, of a health care treatment or service or claim therefore. Such hearing shall be conducted by a panel of not less than three persons, at least one member of which shall be a physician other than the medical director of the plan and at least one member of which shall be a health care provider competent by reason of training and licensure in the treatment or procedure which has been denied. The enrollee shall be provided prompt notice in writing of the outcome of the grievance procedure. In the event the outcome of the grievance is favorable to the enrollee, appropriate relief shall be granted without delay. In the event the outcome is adverse to the enrollee, the notice shall include specific findings related to the care, the policies and procedures relied upon in making the determination, the physician's and provider's recommendations, including any recommendations for alternative procedures or services, and a description of the procedures, if any, for reconsideration of the adverse decision. GA. CODE ANN. § 33-20A-5(3)(B)(ii) (2004).
   1. Enrollees entitled to Appeal to Independent Review. To be eligible for Independent Review the eligible enrollee must have received notice of an adverse outcome pursuant to a MCO's grievance procedure or

the managed care entity has not complied with the requirements or the MCO determines that a proposed treatment is excluded as experimental. GA. CODE ANN. § 33-20A-32 (2004).

2. Requirements. An eligible enrollee must submit the written request for independent review to the planning agency. Instructions on how to request independent review shall be given to all eligible enrollees with the written notice required by statutue together with instructions in simple, clear language as to what information, documentation, and procedure are required for independent review. GA. CODE ANN. § 33-20A-35(b) (2004). MCO pay costs for Independent Review. GA. CODE ANN. § 33-20A-35(e) (2004).

3. The expert reviewer of the independent review organization shall make a determination within 15 business days after expiration of all time limits set forth in this code section, but such time limits may be extended or shortened by mutual agreement between the eligible enrollee and the managed care entity. The determination shall be in writing and state the basis of the reviewer's decision. A copy of the decision shall be delivered to the managed care entity, the eligible enrollee, and the planning agency by at least first-class mail. GA. CODE ANN. § 33-20A-36(d) (2004).

4. A decision of the independent review organization in favor of the eligible enrollee shall be final and binding on the managed care entity and the appropriate relief shall be provided without delay. GA. CODE ANN. § 33-20A-37(a) (2004).

VII. Recognition of URAC Accreditation Status

A. Does the state recognize URAC accreditation? Yes.

B. Which of the state's requirements are waived for URAC-accredited organizations? In addition to meeting the state's requirements, a private review agent must submit documentation that the private review agent has received accreditation by URAC. If the private review agent is not presently fully accredited by URAC, the private review agent must provide the reason or reasons. GA. COMP. R. & REGS. r. 120-2-58-03 (2004).

Guam

I. Scope and Applicability

URAC has found no statutes, regulations, or case law pertaining to utilization review/utilization management in Guam. However, the Guam Code defines utilization review as "an organized review by peers designed to control or eliminate unnecessary admissions to hospitals, and unwarranted length of stays in hospitals." 10 GUAM CODE ANN. § 9102 (2004).

II. Regulatory Information

A. **Responsible state agency.** Department of Revenue and Taxation, Insurance, Securities, Banking and Real Estate Division.

B. **Contact Information.**

1. **Name and Title:** Artemio B. Ilagan, Commissioner of Insurance.

2. **Address:** Department of Revenue and Taxation, Insurance Branch, Government of Guam, Building 13-1 Mariner Avenue, Tiyan, Barrigada, Guam 96913.

3. **Phone and Facsimile:** 671 475-1843; facsimile 011 671 472-2643.

4. **E-mail:** jduenas@ns.ga.

5. **Web site:** http://ns.gov.gu/revtax/index.html.

III. Recognition of URAC Accreditation Status

A. **Does the state recognize URAC accreditation?** No.

B. **Which of the state's requirements are waived for URAC-accredited organizations?** Not applicable.

Hawaii (Insurance Code)

Note: Hawaii does not regulate utilization review organizations, but regulates utilization review in the areas of mental health, alcohol, and drug abuse treatment. Both the Insurance Code and Health Code address utilization review, creating a few differences in definitions and applications. There are separate summaries for the Insurance Code and Health Code because of the dual regulatory scheme and certain differences within each area.

I. Scope and Applicability

A. **Who is subject to the state's utilization review laws?** Providers of mental health, alcohol, and drug abuse treatment and most types of third party payors. Utilization review is required for these services. CODE HAW. R. § 16-16-2, -4, -5 (2004).

1. **HMO's?** Yes.
2. **Insurers?** Yes.
3. **Utilization review organizations?** No
4. **Retrospective review?** Yes.

B. **What exemptions are provided, if any?** While there are no specific exemptions listed in the insurance code, the applicability is limited to the defined payors, generally accident and sickness coverage. CODE HAW. R. § 16-16-5 (2004).

C. **What term does the state use?** "Providers" include licensed physicians, psychologists, hospitals, non-hospital facilities, facilities providing day treatment services, and mental health out-patient facilities that provide service to patients and are authorized to receive payment for the provision of such services. "Payors" include those entities responsible for payment for services on behalf of all individual and group accident and sickness insurance policies issued in Hawaii, individual or group hospital or medical service contracts, and nonprofit mutual benefit associations and health maintenance organizations. CODE HAW. R. § 16-16-2 (2004).

D. **What activities does the state include in its definition of utilization review?** "Utilization review" is defined as "the review of the diagnostic and evaluative findings regarding a patient, the review of a treatment plan, and the review of the extent to which treatment objectives are being achieved." CODE HAW. R. § 16-16-2 (2004).

II. Regulatory Information

A. **Responsible state agency.** Department of Commerce and Consumer Affairs, Insurance Division.

B. **Contact Information.**
1. **Name and Title:** Lloyd Lim, Health Insurance Branch Administrator.
2. **Address:** Department of Commerce and Consumer Affairs, Insurance Division, P.O. Box 3614, Honolulu, HI 96811.
3. **Phone and Facsimile:** (808) 586-2804; facsimile (808) 587-5379.
4. **E-mail:** llim@dcca.hawaii.gov
5. **Web site:** www.state.hi.us/dcca/divisions/ins.

III. Licensure/Certification Requirements

A. What entities are required to obtain a license in the state to conduct utilization review for residents of the state? No provision.
B. How often must licensure/certification be renewed? No provision.
C. Licensure fees (initial and renewal). No provision.
D. Documentation required for licensure. No provision.
E. Exemptions from licensure. No provision.

IV. Program Requirements

A. **Clinical review criteria.** There are detailed regulatory guidelines for admission for mental health, alcohol, and drug abuse treatment. *See* CODE HAW. R. § 16-16-10 – 16-16-41 (2004).
B. **Prohibitions against financial incentives.** No provision.
C. **Telephone access standards.** No provision.
D. **Quality assurance program.** No provision.
E. **Delegation of utilization review functions.** No provision.
F. **Confidentiality.** No provision specifically addressing utilization review. The State of Hawaii enacted H.B. 351, an act relating to privacy of health care information in 1999. *See* 1999 HAW. SESS. LAWS 87. This act includes provisions pertaining to individual rights, restrictions on use and disclosure, excepted uses and disclosures, and sanctions, and does include privacy protections for information associated with and obtained during "carrying out utilization management" functions.

V. Reviewer Qualifications

A. **Qualifications of reviewers that render utilization review determinations (at each level of utilization review, if applicable).** A licensed physician or psychologist shall review any denial of payment for benefits recommended by any utilization review procedure. CODE HAW. R. § 16-16-4 (2004).

B. **Requirements for medical director.** No provision.

C. **Requirements for "same-state" licensure.** No provision.

VI. Reviews and Appeals

A. **Review determination and notice to patients/providers.**

1. **Time frame for determination.** Any denial shall be "promptly" communicated to the patient and provider. CODE HAW. R. § 16-16-6(c) (2004). The payer shall make a reasonable attempt to notify the patient within 3 working days with a written notice of denial. CODE HAW. R. § 16-16-7(a) (2004).

2. **Contents of notice of adverse determinations.**

a. **Reasons for adverse determination.** The payer shall make a reasonable effort to contact the provider by verbal means to inform the provider of the intended denial and to elicit whether there may be any additional information which will bear upon the decision to deny payment. CODE HAW. R. § 16-16-6(a) (2004). If denial based on concurrent review, provision shall be made to allow for proper planning for discharge, transfer, or placement of a patient. CODE HAW. R. § 16-16-6(d) (2004). The written notice of denial shall include a list of the services for which payment has been denied and the reasons for such denial. CODE HAW. R. § 16-16-7(b) (2004).

b. **Notice of appeal rights.** The written notice of denial shall include notification of the right to appeal the denial to the payer and any applicable deadlines. CODE HAW. R. § 16-16-7(b)(3) (2004).

B. **Appeals requirements.**

1. **Time frame for determination.** Within 60 days of receipt of appeal, the payer shall submit a written report to the claimant, including the grounds for the initial denial of benefits and whether the denial is upheld or reversed. CODE HAW. R. § 16-16-7(e) (2004).

2. **External appeals.** The Director of the Department of Health has jurisdiction to review any denial of benefits. CODE HAW. R. § 16-16-7(h) (2004). Further, Hawaii has enacted an external appeal process for "managed care plans." Once a managed care enrollee has completed the internal appeals procedures, the enrollee may seek external review from a panel appointed by the Commissioner of Insurance.

C. **Emergency Services.** No provision.

VII. Recognition of URAC Accreditation Status

A. **Does the state recognize URAC accreditation?** Commissioner of Insurance has recognized URAC as an accreditation body for health plans. HAW. REV. STAT. § 432E-10(c) (Hawaii Patient Bill of Rights and Responsibilities Act). Haw. Ins. Memo. 2000-15(H) (Oct. 31, 2000).Haw. Ins. Memo. 2000-15(H) (Oct. 31, 2000).

B. **Which of the state's requirements are waived for URAC-accredited organizations?** Not applicable.

Hawaii (Health Code)

Note: Hawaii does not regulate utilization review organizations, but regulates utilization review in the areas of mental health, alcohol, and drug abuse treatment. Both the Insurance Code and Health Code address utilization review, creating a few differences in definitions and applications. There are separate summaries for the Insurance Code and Health Code because of the dual regulatory scheme and certain differences within each area.

I. Scope and Applicability

A. **Who is subject to the state's utilization review laws?** Hospitals or nonhospital-affiliated persons or entities performing utilization review affiliated with Hawaiian business entities or third parties that provide or administer hospital, medical, psychological, or other health care benefits. HAW. REV. STAT. ANN. § 334B-2 (2003).

1. **HMO's?** Yes.
2. **Insurers?** Yes.
3. **Utilization Review Organizations?** No.
4. **Retrospective Review?** Yes.

B. **What exemptions are provided, if any?** The utilization review laws do not apply to review agents with a contract with the federal government to provide utilization review for Medicaid, Medicare, or the Civilian Health and

Medical Program of the Uniformed Services (CHAMPUS). HAW. REV. STAT. ANN. § 334B-4 (2003).

C. **What term does the state use?** A "review agent" is a "hospital or nonhospital-affiliated person or entity performing utilization review or managed care that is either affiliated with, under contract with, or acting on behalf of: 1) A business entity in this state; or 2) A third party that provides or administers hospital, medical, psychological, or other health care benefits to citizens of this State, including a health insurer, nonprofit health service plan, health insurance service organization, health maintenance organization, or preferred provider organization authorized to offer health insurance policies or contracts in this State." HAW. REV. STAT. ANN. § 334B-2 (2003).

D. **What activities does the state include in its definition of utilization review?** "Utilization review," used interchangeably with "managed care," is defined as "a system for reviewing the appropriate and efficient allocation of mental health, alcohol, or drug abuse treatment services given or proposed to be given to a patient or group of patients for the purpose of recommending or determining whether such services should be reimbursed, covered, or provided by an insurer, plan or other entity or person." HAW. REV. STAT. ANN. § 334B-2 (2003).

II. Regulatory Information.

A. **Responsible state agency.** Department of Health.

B. **Contact Information.**
1. **Name and Title:** Anita Swanson, Deputy Director for Behavioral Health.
2. **Address:** Hawaii State Department of Health, 1250 Punchbowl Street, Honolulu, HI 96813.
3. **Phone and Facsimile:** 808-586-4416; facsimile (808) 586-4444.
4. **E-mail:** Not known.
5. **Web site:** www.state.hi.us/health.

III. Licensure/Certification Requirements

A. **What entities are required to obtain a license in the state to conduct utilization review for residents of the state?** No provision.

B. **How often must licensure/certification be renewed?** No provision.

C. **Licensure fees (initial and renewal).** No provision.

D. **Documentation required for licensure.** No provision.

E. **Exemptions from licensure.** No provision.

IV. Program Requirements

A. **Clinical review criteria.** The Director of Health shall develop rules requiring a review agent to provide patients and providers with its utilization review or managed care plan, including the specific review criteria and standards, procedures, and methods to be used in evaluating proposed or delivered mental health, alcohol, or drug abuse treatment services. HAW. REV. STAT. ANN. § 334B-3(c)(1) (2003).

B. **Prohibitions against financial incentives.** The Director of Health shall develop rules prohibiting contract provisions between or among any combination of the review agent, provider, business entity, or third-party payer that may constitute a conflict of interest. HAW. REV. STAT. ANN. § 334B-3(c)(10) (2003).

C. **Telephone access standards.** The Director of Health shall develop rules requiring a review agent to be reasonably accessible to patients, patients' families, and providers at least 5 days per week during normal business hours. HAW. REV. STAT. ANN. § 334B-3(c)(6) (2003).

D. **Quality assurance program.** No provision.

E. **Delegation of utilization review functions.** No provision.

F. **Confidentiality.** "A review agent may not disclose or publish individual medical or psychological records or any other confidential medical or psychological information obtained in the performance of utilization review or managed care activities." HAW. REV. STAT. ANN. § 334B-5 (2003). The Director of Health shall develop policies and procedures to ensure the following of all applicable state and federal laws protecting the confidentiality of individual medical records. HAW. REV. STAT. ANN. § 334B-3(c)(7) (2003). In addition, last year, the State of Hawaii enacted H.B. 351, an act relating to privacy of health care information. *See* 1999 HAW. SESS. LAWS 87. This act includes provisions pertaining to individual rights, restrictions on use and disclosure, excepted uses and disclosures, and sanctions, and does include privacy protections for information associated with and obtained during "carrying out utilization management" functions.

V. Reviewer Qualifications

A. **Qualifications of reviewers that render utilization review determinations (at each level of utilization review, if applicable)?** A licensed physician or psychologist shall review any denial of payment for benefits recommended by any utilization review procedure. CODE HAW. R. § 16-16-6(b) (2004).

B. Requirements for medical director. No provision.

C. Requirements for "same-state" licensure. No provision.

VI. Reviews and Appeals

A. Review determination and notice to patients/providers.

1. Time frame for determination. Not specified beyond a "timely manner," HAW. REV. STAT. ANN. § 334B-3(c)(9) (2003), and "promptly communicated," CODE HAW. R. § 16-16-6(c) (Weil 2004).

2. Contents of notice of adverse determinations.

a. Reasons for adverse determination. Any notice of denial of payments shall be promptly communicated by the payer in writing to the patient and provider. Payers are required to make reasonable efforts to contact the provider by verbal means to inform the provider of the intended denial and to elicit whether there may be any additional information bearing on the decision to deny payment. CODE HAW. R. § 16-16-6(a), (c) (2004).

b. Notice of appeal rights. If a payer denies a claim for benefits, in whole or part, the payer shall make a reasonable effort to notify the patient within 3 working days in writing with reasons for denial and notification of right to appeal. CODE HAW. R. § 16-16-7(a) (2004).

B. Appeals requirements.

1. Time frame for determination. Within 60 days of receipt of appeal, the payer shall submit a written report to the claimant, including the grounds for the initial denial of benefits and whether the denial is upheld or reversed. CODE HAW. R. § 16-16-7(e) (2004).

2. External appeals. The Director of Health has jurisdiction to review any denial of benefits. CODE HAW. R. § 16-16-7(h) (2004). Further, Hawaii has enacted an external appeal process for "managed care plans." Once a managed care enrollee has completed the internal appeals procedures, the enrollee may seek external review from a panel appointed by the Commissioner of Insurance.

C. Emergency Services. No provision.

VII. Recognition of URAC Accreditation Status

A. Does the state recognize URAC accreditation? No.

B. Which of the state's requirements are waived for URAC-accredited organizations? Not applicable.

Idaho

I. Scope and Applicability

A. **Who is subject to the state's utilization review laws?** All managed care organizations performing utilization management or contracting with third parties for the performance of utilization management. IDAHO CODE § 41-3930(1) (2004).

1. HMO's? Yes.
2. Insurers? Yes.
3. Utilization review organizations? No.
4. Retrospective review? Yes.

B. **What exemptions are provided, if any?** None specified.

C. **What term does the state use to refer to regulated entities?** "Managed care organization" means a public or private person or organization which offers a managed care plan. Unless otherwise specifically stated, the provisions of this chapter shall apply to any person or organization offering a managed care plan, whether or not a certificate of authority to offer the plan is required under this chapter. IDAHO CODE § 41-3903(14) (2004).

D. **What activities does the state include in its definition of utilization review?** "Utilization management program" means "a system of reviewing the medical necessity, appropriateness, or quality of health care services and supplies provided under a managed care plan using specified guidelines. Such a system may include, but is not limited to, preadmission certification, the application of practice guidelines, continued stay review, discharge planning, preauthorization of ambulatory procedures and retrospective review." IDAHO CODE § 41-3903(19) (2004).

II. Regulatory Information

A. **Responsible state agency.** Department of Insurance.

B. **Contact Information.**

1. **Name and Title:** Joan Krosch, Health Insurance Specialist.
2. **Address:** Department of Insurance, 700 W. State Street, 3rd Floor, Boise, ID 83720-0043.
3. **Phone and Facsimile:** (208) 334-4300; facsimile: (208) 334-4398.
4. **E-mail:** JKrosch@doi.state.id.us.
5. **Web site:** www.doi.state.id.us.

III. Licensure/Certification Requirements

A. **What entities are required to obtain a license in the state to conduct utilization review for residents of the state?** While utilization review organizations are not required to obtain a license or certificate, if utilization review is used, the regulated entity shall conduct utilization review activities in accordance with the Idaho Code.

B. **How often must licensure be renewed?** Not applicable.

C. **Licensure fees (initial and renewal).** Not applicable.

D. **Documentation required for licensure.** Not applicable.

E. **Exemptions from licensure.** Not applicable.

IV. Program Requirements

A. **Clinical review criteria.** Utilization management criteria must be based on sound patient care and scientific principles developed in cooperation with licensed physicians and other providers as deemed appropriate by the managed care organization. Such criteria shall be sufficiently flexible to allow deviations from norms when justified on a case-by-case basis. IDAHO CODE § 41-3930(1)(a) (2004). Criteria must contain procedures for a timely review by a licensed physician, peer provider or peer review panel when a claim has been denied as not medically necessary or as experimental. The procedure shall provide for a written statement of the reasons the service was denied and transmittal of that information to the appropriate provider for inclusion in the member's permanent medical record. IDAHO CODE § 41-3930(1)(b) (2004).

B. **Prohibitions against financial incentives.** No provision, but incentives to withhold care are prohibited under IDAHO CODE § 41-3928(1) (2004).

C. **Telephone access standards.** Qualified medical personnel shall be available by telephone during normal business hours for inquiries about medical necessity, including certification of continued length of stay. IDAHO CODE § 41-3930(2) (2004).

D. **Quality assurance program.** No provision specifically for utilization review, but to qualify for a certificate of authority, a managed care plan must establish and maintain reasonable and adequate procedures to monitor the quality of health care provided, including a reasonable system of internal peer review of diagnosis and treatment of member's health conditions. *See* IDAHO CODE §§ 41-3905(6)(a) (2004).

E. **Delegation of utilization review functions.** No provision.

F. **Confidentiality.** Upon enrollment, managed care organizations shall require members to provide written authorization for the release of medical information to the managed care organization. IDAHO CODE § 41-3930(1)(c) (2004). Utilization review organizations must also adopt procedures to protect the confidentiality of patient health records. IDAHO CODE § 41-3930(1)(d) (2004).

V. Reviewer Qualifications

A. **Qualifications of reviewers that render utilization review determinations (at each level of utilization review, if applicable).** Licensed physician, peer provider, or peer review panel must provide a timely review when a claim has been denied as not medically necessary or as experimental. IDAHO CODE § 41-3930(1)(b) (2004).

B. **Requirements for medical director.** No provision.

C. **Requirement for "same-state" licensure.** No provision.

VI. Reviews and Appeals

A. **Review determinations and notice to patients/providers.**

1. **Time frame for determination.** For prior authorization of nonemergency service, a managed care organization shall respond to member or provider requests within two business days of receipt of information necessary to conduct the review. "Exceptional circumstances" may warrant a longer period to evaluate a request. IDAHO CODE § 41-3930(2) (2004).

2. **Contents of notice of adverse determination.**

   a. **Reasons for adverse determination.** The notice must include a written statement of the reasons why the services were denied. IDAHO CODE § 41-3930(1)(b) (2004).

   b. **Notice of Appeal Rights.** No provision. *But see* IDAHO CODE §§ 41-3914(1)(d) (2004), every managed care organization must provide to its enrollees a clear and understandable description of the managed care

organization's method of resolving member grievances

B. **Appeals requirements.** No provision, but managed care organizations are required to have grievance systems. *See* IDAHO CODE § 41-3918(1) (2004), every managed care organization shall establish a grievance system to resolve grievances initiated by members concerning health care services.

1. **Time frame for determination.** Not applicable.

2. **External appeals.** Not applicable.

C. **Emergency Services.** No managed care organization shall require prior authorization for emergency services, if offered. IDAHO CODE § 41-3930(2) (2004).

VII. Recognition of URAC Accreditation Status

A. **Does the state recognize URAC accreditation?** No.

B. **Which of the state's requirements are waived for URAC-accredited organizations?** Not applicable.

VIII. Miscellaneous

When prior approval of covered services has been granted, the managed care organization may not rescind the approval after the covered service has been provided, except in cases of fraud or misrepresentation, nonpayment of premium, exhaustion of benefits, or if the member for whom the prior approval was granted is not enrolled at the time the covered service is provided. IDAHO CODE § 41-3930(3) (2004).

Illinois

I. Scope and Applicability

A. **Who is subject to the state's utilization review laws?** Any entities who conduct utilization review programs in Illinois. 215 ILL. COMP. STAT. ANN. 134/85(a) (2004).
1. HMO's? Yes.
2. Insurers? Yes.
3. Utilization Review Organizations? Yes.
4. Retrospective Review? Yes.

B. **What exemptions are provided, if any?** The utilization review provisions of this act do not apply to persons providing utilization review program services only to the federal government; self-insured health plans under the Employee Retirement Income Security Act of 1974, but does apply to persons conducting utilization review programs on behalf of these health plans. Also exempt are hospitals and medical groups performing utilization review activities for internal purposes unless conducted for another person. 215 ILL. COMP. STAT. ANN. 134/85(c) (2004).

C. **What term does the state use to refer to regulated entities?** Persons (corporations, associations, partnerships, limited liability companies, sole proprietorships, or any other legal entities) conducting utilization review programs. 215 ILL. COMP. STAT. ANN. 134/10 (2004), and 215 ILL. COMP. STAT. ANN. 134/85(a) (2004).

D. **What activities does the state include in its definition of utilization review?** "Utilization review" means the evaluation of the medical necessity, appropriateness, and efficiency of the use of health care services, procedures, and facilities. 215 ILL. COMP. STAT. ANN. 134/10 (2004), and ILL. ADMIN. CODE tit. 50, §5420.30 (2004).

II. Regulatory Information

A. **Responsible state agency.** Illinois Department of Financial and Professional Regulation Division of Insurance.

B. **Contact Information.**
1. **Name and Title:** Kelly Reim, Insurance Analyst
2. **Address:** Illinois Department of Financial and Professional Regulation Division of Insurance, 320 W. Washington Street, Springfield, IL 62767-0001.
3. **Phone and Facsimile:** (217) 558-2309; 558-2310; facsimile (217) 558-2083

4. **E-mail:** kelly_reim@ins.state.il.us
5. **Web site:** www.ins.state.il.us.

III. Licensure/Certification Requirements

A. **What entities are required to obtain a license in the state to conduct utilization review for residents of the state?** Persons (corporations, associations, partnerships, limited liability companies, sole proprietorships, or any other legal entities) conducting utilization review programs. 215 ILL. COMP. STAT. ANN. 134/10 (2004), and 215 ILL. COMP. STAT. ANN. 134/85(a) (2004). No person may conduct a utilization review program in Illinois unless once every 2 years the person registers the utilization review program with the Department and certifies compliance with URAC standards sufficient to achieve URAC accreditation, or submits evidence of accreditation by URAC for its Health Utilization Management Standards. 215 ILL. COMP. STAT. ANN. 134/85(a) (2004). In addition, the Director of the Department of Insurance, in consultation with the Director of the Department of Public Health, may certify alternative utilization review standards of national accreditation organizations or entities in order for plans to comply with the requirements in 215 ILL. COMP. STAT. ANN. 134/85(a). Any alternative utilization review standards shall meet or exceed those standards required. 215 ILL. COMP. STAT. ANN. 134/85(b) (2004).

B. **How often must licensure/certification be renewed?** Bi-annually. 215 ILL. COMP. STAT. ANN. 134/85(a) (2004).

C. **Licensure fees (initial and renewal).** $3,000, unless accredited by URAC, the National Committee for Quality Assurance, or the Joint Commission on Accreditation of Healthcare Organizations, in which case the fee is $1,500.

D. **Documentation required for licensure.** The registration shall include submission of the following information: name, address, and telephone number of the utilization review program; organization and governing structure of the program; number of lives for which utilization review is conducted by each program; hours of operation of each program; description of grievance process for each program; number of covered lives for which utilization review was conducted for previous calendar year; and written policies and procedures for protecting confidential information. 215 ILL. COMP. STAT.

ANN. 134/85(d) (2004), and ILL. ADMIN. CODE tit. 50, §5420 EXH. D (2004).

E. **Exemptions from licensure.** The statute does not exempt out-of-state organizations from registration with the Illinois Department of Insurance.

IV. Program Requirements

A. **Clinical review criteria.** When making prospective, concurrent, and retrospective determinations, utilization review programs shall collect only information necessary to make the determinations and shall not routinely require health care providers to code numerically diagnoses or procedures, unless required under state or federal rules or regulations. During prospective or concurrent review, copies of medical records shall only be required when necessary to verify that the health care services subject to review are medically necessary. 215 ILL. COMP. STAT. ANN. 134/85(e)(3) and (4) (2004),

B. **Prohibitions against financial incentives.** Yes. *See* 215 ILL. COMP. STAT. ANN. 134/30(a) (2004).

C. **Telephone access standards.** Yes.

D. **Quality assurance program.** Health care plans shall develop and implement a quality assessment and improvement strategy.

1. The strategy should be designed to identify and evaluate accessibility, continuity, and quality of care.

2. Specific Requirements for Quality Assurance Program include: a) an ongoing, written, internal quality assessment program; b) specific written guidelines for monitoring and evaluating the quality and appropriateness of care and services provided to enrollees requiring the health care plan to assess: i) the accessibility to health care providers; ii) appropriateness of utilization; iii) concerns identified by the health care plan's medical or administrative staff and enrollees; and iv) other aspects of care and service directly related to the improvement of quality of care; c) a procedure for remedial action to correct quality problems that have been verified in accordance with the written plan's methodology and criteria, including written procedures for taking appropriate corrective action; d) follow-up measures implemented to evaluate the effectiveness of the action plan.
215 ILL. COMP. STAT. ANN. 134/80(a) (2004).

3. The Department of Public Health shall accept evidence of accreditation with regard to the health care network quality management and performance improvement standards of the National Commission on Quality Assurance (NCQA); URAC, the Joint Commission on Accreditation of Healthcare Organizations (JCAHO); or any other entity that the Director of Public Health deems has substantially similar or more stringent standards. 215 ILL. COMP. STAT. ANN. 134/80(e) (2004).

E. **Delegation of utilization review functions.** Permitted. Nothing prohibits a health care plan or other entity from contractually requiring an entity to adhere to the utilization review program requirements of Illinois. 215 ILL. COMP. STAT. ANN. 134/85(c)(3) (2004).

F. **Confidentiality.** A utilization review program shall have written procedures for assuring that patient-specific information obtained during a utilization review process shall be kept confidential in accordance with applicable state and federal laws and shared only with the enrollee, the enrollee's designee, and the enrollee's health care provider, and those who are authorized by law to receive the information. 215 ILL. COMP. STAT. ANN. 134/85(e)(1) (2004).

V. Reviewer Qualifications

A. **Qualifications of reviewers that render utilization review determinations (at each level of utilization review, if applicable)?** Only a health care professional may make determinations regarding the medical necessity of health care services during the course of utilization review. 215 ILL. COMP. STAT. ANN. 134/85(e)(3) (2004).

B. **Requirements for medical director.** No.

C. **Requirements for "same-state" licensure.** No.

VI. Reviews and Appeals

A. **Review determination and notice to patients/providers.** A health care plan shall establish and maintain an appeals procedure. 215 ILL. COMP. STAT. ANN. 134/45(a) (2004). No one reviewing an appeal may have had any involvement in the initial determination that is the subject of the appeal. 215 ILL. COMP. STAT. ANN. 134/45(d) (2004).

B. **Notice and Time Frame for determination.**

1. When an appeal concerns a decision or action by a health care plan, its employees, or its subcontractors that relates to: health

care services which could significantly increase the risk to an enrollee's health; or a treatment referral, service, procedure, or other health care service, the denial of which could significantly increase the risk to an enrollee's health, the health care plan must allow for the filing of an appeal either orally or in writing.

    a. Upon submission of the appeal, a health care plan must notify the party filing the appeal, as soon as possible, but in no event more than 24 hours after the submission of the appeal, of all information that the plan requires to evaluate the appeal. The health care plan shall render a decision on the appeal within 24 hours after receipt of the required information.

    b. The health care plan shall notify the party filing the appeal and the enrollee, enrollee's primary care physician, and any health care provider who recommended the health care service involved in the appeal of its decision orally followed-up by a written notice of the determination. 215 ILL. COMP. STAT. ANN. 134/45(a) (2004).

2. For all appeals not related to those that significantly increase the risk to an enrollee's health, the health care plan shall establish a procedure for the filing of such appeals.

    a. Upon submission of an appeal under this subsection, a health care plan must notify the party filing an appeal, within 3 business days, of all information that the plan requires to evaluate the appeal. The health care plan shall render a decision on the appeal within 15 business days after receipt of the required information.

    b. The health care plan shall notify the party filing the appeal, the enrollee, the enrollee's primary care physician, and any health care provider who recommended the health care service involved in the appeal orally of its decision followed-up by a written notice of the determination. 215 ILL. COMP. STAT. ANN. 134/45(b) (2004).

    c. Contents of notice of adverse determinations. The written notice of determination shall include: (i) clear and detailed reasons for the determination; (ii) the medical or clinical criteria for the determination, which shall be based upon sound clinical evidence and reviewed on a periodic basis; and (iii) in the case of an adverse determination, the procedures for requesting an external independent review. 215 ILL. COMP. STAT. ANN. 134/45(d) (2004).

    d. External Review. If an appeal filed is denied for a reason including, but not limited to, the service, procedure, or treatment is not viewed as medically necessary, denial of specific tests or procedures, denial of referral to specialist physicians or denial of hospitalization requests or length of stay requests, any involved party may request an external independent review. 215 ILL. COMP. STAT. ANN. 134/45(e) (2004).

C. **External Review requirements.**

1. Enrollees seeking external independent review must notify the health care plan.

2. The health care plan shall seek to resolve all external independent reviews in the most expeditious manner and shall make a determination and provide notice of the determination no more than 24 hours after the receipt of all necessary information when a delay would significantly increase the risk to an enrollee's health or when extended health care services for an enrollee undergoing a course of treatment prescribed by a health care provider are at issue.

3. Within 30 days after the enrollee receives written notice of an adverse determination, if the enrollee decides to initiate an external independent review, the enrollee shall send to the health care plan a written request for an external independent review, including any information or documentation to support the enrollee's request for the covered service or claim for a covered service.

4. Within 30 days after the health care plan receives a request for an external independent review from an enrollee, the health care plan shall: provide a mechanism for joint selection of an external independent reviewer by the enrollee, the enrollee's physician or other health care provider, and the health care plan; and forward to the independent reviewer all

medical records and supporting documentation pertaining to the case, a summary description of the applicable issues including a statement of the health care plan's decision, the criteria used, and the medical and clinical reasons for that decision.

5. Within 5 days after receipt of all necessary information, the independent reviewer shall evaluate and analyze the case and render a decision that is based on whether or not the health care service or claim for the health care service is medically appropriate. The decision by the independent reviewer is final.

6. The health care plan shall be solely responsible for paying the fees of the external independent reviewer who is selected to perform the review.

215 ILL. COMP. STAT. ANN. 134/45(f) (2004).

VII. Recognition of URAC Accreditation Status

A. Does the state recognize URAC accreditation? Yes.

B. **Which of the state's requirements are waived for URAC-accredited organizations?** No one may conduct a utilization review program in Illinois unless registered with the Department of Insurance and either accredited by URAC or certified to be in compliance with URAC's accreditation standards sufficient to achieve URAC accreditation. Health care plans or subcontractors are not required to receive URAC accreditation.

VIII. Miscellaneous

"Any preferred provider organization providing hospital, medical or dental services must include a program of utilization review." 215 ILL. COMP. STAT. ANN. 5/370n (2004).

Indiana

I. Scope and Applicability

A. **Who is subject to the state's utilization review laws?** Any entity performing utilization review. IND. CODE ANN. § 27-8-17-9(a) (2004).

  1. **HMO's?** Yes.
  2. **Insurers?** Yes.
  3. **Utilization review organizations?** Yes.
  4. **Retrospective review?** Yes.

B. **What exemptions are provided, if any?** There are exceptions for an agency of the state or federal government, an agent acting on behalf of the federal or state government, entities conducting general in-house utilization review for hospitals, home health agencies, health maintenance organizations, preferred provider organizations, or other managed care entities, clinics, private offices, or any other health facility, as long as such review does not result in the approval or denial of an enrollee's coverage for hospital or medical services. IND. CODE ANN. § 27-8-17-7(a) (2004).

  1. However, an agent acting on behalf of the federal or state government who performs utilization review for a person other than the federal or state government is a utilization review agent and subject to the requirements of this chapter. IND. CODE ANN. § 27-8-17-7(b) (2004).

C. **What term does the state use to refer to regulated entities?** A "utilization review agent" is any entity performing utilization review. IND. CODE ANN. § 27-8-17-7(a) (2004).

D. **What activities does the state include in its definition of utilization review?** "Utilization review" is defined as "a system for prospective, concurrent, or retrospective review of the medical necessity and appropriateness of health care services provided or proposed to be provided to a covered individual." The term does not include "Elective requests for clarification of coverage, eligibility, or benefits verification" or "Medical claims review." IND. CODE ANN. § 27-8-17-6(a) (2004). "Utilization review determination" means the rendering of a decision based on utilization review that denies or affirms either the necessity or appropriateness of the allocation of resources, or the provision or proposed provision of health care services to a covered individual. The term does not include the identification of alternative, optional medical care that requires the approval of the covered individual, and does not affect coverage or benefits if rejected by the covered individual. IND. CODE ANN. § 27-8-17-8(a) and (b) (2004).

E. **What term does the state use to refer to regulated entities?** A "utilization review agent" is any entity performing utilization review. IND. CODE ANN. § 27-8-17-7(a) (2004).

II. Regulatory Information

A. **Responsible state agency.** Indiana Department of Insurance, Utilization Review/Medical Claims Review.

B. **Contact Information.**
  1. **Name and Title:** Angela Dailey, Secretary & UR/MCR Coordinator.
  2. **Address:** Indiana Department of Insurance, 311 W. Washington Street, Suite 300, Indianapolis, IN 46204-2787
  3. **Phone and Facsimile:** (317) 232-2390; facsimile (317) 232-5251.
  4. **E-mail:** adailey@doi.state.in.us
  5. **Web site:** www.in.gov/idoi

C. **Licensure/Certification Requirements**
  1. **What entities are required to obtain a license in the state to conduct utilization review for residents of the state?** A utilization review agent may not conduct utilization review in Indiana unless the utilization review agent holds a certificate of registration issued by the Department of Insurance. IND. CODE ANN.. § 27-8-17-9(a) (2004).
  2. **How often must licensure be renewed?** Annually, by June 30th. IND. CODE ANN.. § 27-8-17-10(a) (2004).
  3. **Licensure fees (initial and renewal).** The application for registration must be accompanied by the fee: $150 for initial and $100 for renewal. IND. CODE ANN. § 27-8-17-10(a) (2004); IND. ADMIN. CODE tit. 760, r. 1-46-11(2004). If not received prior to June 30th, must submit a new application with new application fee of $150. IND. ADMIN. CODE tit. 760, r. 1-46-3(g) (2004)
  4. **Documentation required for licensure.** An application containing the name, address, telephone number, and normal business hours of the utilization review agent, the name and telephone number of a person that the department may contact concerning the information in the application, and all documentation necessary for the department to determine that the utilization review agent is capable of satisfying the minimum statutory requirements. IND. CODE ANN.. § 27-8-17-9(b) (2004). Further, an application submitted under this section must be signed and verified by the applicant, accompanied by an application fee and provided with a signed statement of a physician employed by or under contract to the utilization review agent verifying that determinations made by the utilization review agent as to the necessity or appropriateness of admissions, services, and

procedures are reviewed by a physician or determined in accordance with standards or guidelines approved by a physician. IND. CODE ANN. § 27-8-17-9(c) (2004) and § 27-8-17-13 (2004). *See also* IND. ADMIN. CODE tit. 760, r. 1-46-3(c) (2004).

5. An application for certification of a utilization review agent must be filed with the Department of Insurance at 311 West Washington Street, Suite 300, Indianapolis, Indiana 46204. A copy may be obtained from the Department of Insurance, 311 West Washington Street, Suite 300, Indianapolis, Indiana 46204. IND. ADMIN. CODE tit. 760, r. 1-46-3(a) & (b) (2004).

III. Program Requirements

All utilization review agents must develop a utilization review plan and file a summary of the plan with the Department of Insurance. IND. CODE ANN § 27-8-17-11(11) (2004); IND. ADMIN. CODE tit. 760, r. 1-46-4(1) (2004).

A. **Clinical review criteria.** Each utilization review agent must use written screening criteria and review procedures. Criteria for review determinations must be developed and periodically updated with input from appropriate health care providers and approved by a physician. Criteria shall be available for inspection by the Department of Insurance. Every utilization review determination as to the necessity or appropriateness of an admission, a service, or a procedure must be reviewed by a physician, or determined in accordance with standards or guidelines approved by a physician. IND. CODE ANN. § 27-8-17-11(7) (2004). *See also* IND. CODE ANN § 27-8-17-13 (2004). Utilization review plan must provide a period of at least 48 hours following an emergency admission, service, or procedure during which an enrollee, or the representative of an enrollee, may notify the utilization review agent and request certification or continuing treatment. IND. CODE ANN. § 27-8-17-11(9) (2004).

B. **Telephone access standards.** Utilization review agents must provide toll free telephone access at least 40 hours each week during normal business hours. They must maintain a telephone call recording system capable of accepting or recording incoming telephone calls or providing instructions during hours other than normal business hours. Response to recorded messages is to be within 2 business days after receiving the call. IND. CODE ANN. § 27-8-17-11-(1), (2) and (3) (2004); IND. ADMIN. CODE tit. 760, r. 1-46-7 (2004).

C. **Time Frame and Notice.** Within 2 business days after receiving a request for a utilization review determination that includes all information necessary to complete the utilization review determination, the review agent must notify the enrollee or the provider of record of the utilization review determination by mail or another means of communication. Notifications to enrollees and providers of determination not to certify an admission, a service, or a procedure must include the principal reason for that determination, and the procedures to initiate an appeal of the determination. IND. CODE ANN. § 27-8-17-11(5) and (6) (2004).

D. **Prohibitions against financial incentives.** Compensation to utilization review agents may not be based on the extent to which certifications are denied or the amount by which claims are reduced for payment. IND. CODE ANN § 27-8-17-19 (2004).

E. **Quality assurance program.** No provision specifically for utilization review agents. However, a health maintenance organization shall establish procedures based on professionally recognized standards to assess and monitor the health care services provided to enrollees of the organization. *See* IND. CODE ANN. § 27-13-6-1 (2004), IND. CODE ANN. § 27-13-6-2 (2004) (Internal Quality Management Program), IND. CODE ANN. § 27-13-6-3 (2004) (Program Requirements).

F. **Delegation of utilization review functions.** No provision.

G. **Confidentiality.** Utilization review agents must protect the confidentiality of individual medical records in accordance with state and federal laws; must be used for purposes of utilization review, quality assurance, discharge planning, and catastrophic case management; shared with only those agencies that have authority to receive such information; must, when contacting a health care provider's office or hospital, provide its certification number and the caller's name to the provider's named utilization review representative in the health care provider's office. Medical records must be kept in a secure area with access limited only to utilization review personnel. Information generated and obtained shall be retained for at least 2 years. IND. CODE ANN. § 27-8-17-11 (4) (2004); IND. ADMIN. CODE tit. 760, r. 1-46-8 (2004); IND. ADMIN. CODE tit. 760, r. 1-46-3(c) (3) (2004); IND. ADMIN. CODE tit. 760, r. 1-46-4 (1) (H) (2004).

IV. Reviewer Qualifications

A. **Qualifications of reviewers that render utilization review determinations (at each level of utilization review, if applicable).** All utilization review determinations must be reviewed by a licensed physician or determined in accordance with standards or guidelines approved by a physician. On appeal, a health care provider licensed in the same discipline as the treating provider must consider the adverse determination. IND. CODE ANN. § 27-8-17-11(7)

(2004); IND. CODE ANN. § 27-8-17-12(B) (1) (2004).

B. **Requirements for medical director.** No provision.

C. **Requirement for "same-state" licensure.** Every physician making a utilization review determination for the utilization review agent has a current license issued by a state licensing agency in the United States. IND. CODE ANN. § 27-8-17-11(8) (2004).

V. Reviews and Appeals

A. **Review determinations and notice to patients/providers.** A utilization review agent shall make available to an enrollee, and to a provider of record upon request, at the time an adverse utilization review determination is made both:

1. A written description of the appeals procedure by which an enrollee or a provider of record may appeal the utilization review determination by the utilization review agent; and

2. In the case of an enrollee covered under an accident and sickness policy or a health maintenance organization contract notice that the enrollee has the right to appeal the utilization review determination, and the toll free telephone number that the enrollee may call to request a review of the determination or obtain further information about the right to appeal. IND. CODE ANN. § 27-8-17-12(a) (2004).

B. **Time frame for initial review determination.** The utilization review agent must notify the patient or treating provider within 2 days of receiving the information necessary to complete the review. IND. CODE ANN. § 27-8-17-11(5) (2004).

C. **Contents of notice of adverse determination.**

1. **Reasons for adverse determination.** In a notification of a utilization review determination not to certify an admission, service, or procedure, must include principal reason if based on medical necessity or appropriateness.

2. **Notice of Appeal Rights.** Contents must also include procedures to initiate an appeal. In addition, upon request, a utilization review agent shall make available a written description of the appeals procedure. IND. CODE ANN. § 27-8-17-12 (2004); IND. CODE ANN. § 27-8-17-11 (6) (2004).

D. **Appeals requirements.**

1. **Time frame for determination.** Appeals must be completed within 30 days of filing the appeal and receiving all information necessary to consider the appeal. IND. CODE ANN. § 27-8-17-12(b) (2) (2004).

2. On appeal, the determination not to certify an admission, a service, or a procedure as necessary or appropriate must be made by a health care provider licensed in the same discipline as the provider of record. IND. CODE ANN. § 27-8-17-12(b) (1) (2004).

3. **Expedited Appeals.** A utilization review agent shall provide an expedited appeals process for emergency or life-threatening situations. A physician shall complete a determination of an expedited appeal within 48 hours of the initiation of the appeal and the receipt of all information necessary to consider the appeal. IND. CODE ANN. § 27-8-17-12(c) (2004).

E. **External appeals.** No provision specifically for utilization review agents. Each HMO doing business in Indiana must establish and maintain an external grievance procedure pursuant to IND. CODE ANN. § 27-13-10.1-1 (2004) This procedure will be used to resolve grievances regarding adverse utilization review determinations, adverse determinations of medical necessity, or determinations that a proposed service is experimental or investigational. The Department of Insurance is required to establish and maintain a process for annual certification of independent review organizations (IRO's) and to maintain a list of certified IRO's to be used by HMO's. IND. CODE ANN. § 27-13-10.1-8 (2004).

VI. Recognition of URAC Accreditation Status

A. **Does the state recognize URAC accreditation?** Yes.

B. **Which of the state's requirements are waived for URAC-accredited organizations?** URAC-accredited companies are considered to have met most of the state's requirements for utilization review. See IND. CODE ANN. § 27-8-17-14(a) (2004). However, all utilization review agents must submit an annual licensure application and fee to the Department of Insurance.

VII. Miscellaneous

The Department of Insurance's Web site includes an application for utilization review agents, various checklists, information about URAC accreditation, and the pertinent utilization review statute and rules. See Web site at: http://www.in.gov/idoi/companyinfo/forms/index.html. Indiana treats separately "medical claims review," "medical claims review agents," and "medical claims review consultants." See IND. CODE ANN. § 27-8-16 et seq. (2004), IND. ADMIN. CODE tit. 760, r. 1-49-1 (2004) "Medical claims review" explicitly does not include "prospective, concurrent, or retrospective utilization review of health care services." IND. CODE ANN. § 27-8-16-4 (2004)

Iowa

I. Scope and Applicability

A. **Who is subject to the state's utilization review laws?** The provisions apply to a "third-party payors" who provides health benefits to a covered individual residing in this state. IOWA CODE ANN. § 514F.4(1) (2004); IOWA ADMIN. CODE r. 191-70.3(1) (2004).

   1. **HMO's?** Yes.

   2. **Insurers?** Yes.

   3. **Utilization review organizations?** Yes, but indirectly. The regulation directly affects third-party payors that delegate utilization review functions.

   4. **Retrospective review?** Yes.

B. **What exemptions are provided, if any?** Does not apply to utilization review performed solely under contract with the federal government for Medicare, the Civilian Health and Medical Program of the Uniformed Services (CHAMPUS), or any other federal employee health benefit plan." IOWA CODE ANN. § 514F.4(2) (2004); IOWA ADMIN. CODE r. 191-70.3(3) (2004).

C. **What term does the state use to refer to regulated entities?** "Third-party payors," which provide health benefits to a covered individual residing in this state shall not conduct utilization review, either directly or indirectly, under a contract with a third-party who does not meet the requirements established for accreditation by the utilization review accreditation commission, national committee on quality assurance, or another national accreditation entity recognized and approved by the commissioner.

   1. Third part-payors include insurers, health service corporations, health maintenance organizations, preferred provider arrangements, multiple employer welfare arrangements, third-party administrators, fraternal benefit societies, and any other benefit programs providing payment, reimbursement, or indemnification for health care costs for an enrollee or an enrollee's eligible dependents. IOWA CODE ANN. § 514F.4 (2004); IOWA ADMIN. CODE r. 191-70.2 (2004).

D. **What activities does the state include in its definition of utilization review?** Utilization review is defined as a program or process by which an evaluation is made of the necessity, appropriateness, and efficiency of the use of health care services, procedures, or facilities given or proposed to be given to an individual within this state. It does not apply to requests by an individual or provider for a clarification, guarantee, or statement of an individual's health insurance coverage or benefits provided under a health insurance policy, nor to claims adjudication. Unless it is specifically stated, verification of benefits, preauthorization, or a prospective or concurrent utilization review program or process shall not be construed as a guarantee or statement of insurance coverage or benefits for any individual under a health insurance policy. IOWA CODE ANN. § 514F.4 (2004); IOWA ADMIN. CODE r. 191-70.2.

II. Regulatory Information

A. **Responsible state agency.** Insurance Division, Iowa Department of Commerce.

B. **Contact Information.**

   1. **Name and Title:** Roger Strauss, Life & Health Bureau Chief.

   2. **Address:** Insurance Division, Iowa Department of Commerce, 330 E. Maple, Des Moines, IA 50319-0065.

   3. **Phone and Facsimile:** (515) 281-4222; facsimile (515) 281-5692.

   4. **E-mail:** Roger.Strauss@iid.state.ia.us

   5. **Web site:** www.iid.state.ia.us

III. Licensure/Certification Requirements

A. **What entities are required to obtain a license in the state to conduct utilization review for residents of the state?** No specific licensure is required. However, third-party payors who provides health benefits to a covered individuals residing in Iowa cannot conduct utilization review unless they meet the requirements established for accreditation by URAC, The National Committee on Quality Assurance, or another national accreditation entity recognized and approved by the commissioner. IOWA CODE ANN. § 514F.4(1) (2004); I IOWA ADMIN. CODE r. 191-70.3(1) (2004).

B. **How often must licensure/certification be renewed?** Not applicable.

C. **Licensure fees (initial and renewal).** Not applicable.

D. **Documentation required for licensure.** On or before March 1 each year, third-party payors must submit to the Commissioner of Insurance certain demographic information and an attestation that the payor complies with all regulations and will continually comply with all regulations. IOWA ADMIN. CODE r. 191-70.3(2) (2004).

E. **Exemptions from licensure.** Not applicable.

IV. Program Requirements

A. **Clinical review criteria.** No specific provisions. (*But see* IOWA ADMIN. CODE r. 191-70.4(2) (2004) For the purpose of certification and compliance, the most recently available utilization review standards adopted by URAC shall be used).

B. **Prohibitions against financial incentives.** No provision.

C. **Telephone access standards.** No provision.

D. **Quality assurance program.** No provision for utilization review, but each independent review entity shall have a quality assurance program that ensures the timeliness and quality of reviews, qualifications and independence of experts, and confidentiality of medical records and review materials. IOWA CODE ANN. § 514J.6(4) (2004);

E. **Delegation of utilization review functions.** A third party payor may only delegate utilization review functions to a utilization review organization that meets the most recent URAC accreditation standards or another national accreditation entity's standards, as long the Commissioner of Insurance has recognized and approved. IOWA CODE ANN. § 514F.4(1) (2004); IOWA ADMIN. CODE r. 191-70.3(1) (2004).

F. **Confidentiality.** Third-party payors shall require a contract utilization review agent to adhere to the same standards of patient medical record confidentiality as are directly applicable to the third-party payor. IOWA ADMIN. CODE r. 191-70.7 (2004).

V. Reviewer Qualifications

A. **Qualifications of reviewers that render utilization review determinations (at each level of utilization review, if applicable).** Individuals who are not licensed health care professionals, but who are otherwise qualified, may perform routine utilization review provided that they have received full orientation by the utilization review organization relating to administrative practices and policies, they have been fully trained in the application of the medical and/or benefit screening criteria established or endorsed by the utilization review organization, they are trained to refer review requests to licensed health care professionals when the required review exceeds their own expertise, when not addressed in the criteria established or endorsed by the

utilization review organization, or when requested by the provider, and they are under the direct supervision of a licensed health care professional. IOWA ADMIN. CODE r. 191-70.6(2) (2004).

B. **Requirements for medical director.** No provision.

C. **Requirement for "same-state" licensure.** No provision.

VI. Reviews and Appeals

A. **Review determinations and notice to patients/providers.** The regulations require notification of the attending physician and treatment facility as defined by URAC standards. IOWA ADMIN. CODE r. 191-70.6(1) (2004).

1. **Time frame for determination.** No provision.

2. **Contents of notice of adverse determination.** No provision.

3. **Reasons for adverse determination.** Not applicable.

4. **Notice of Appeal Rights.** Written notice to the enrollee of the right to have the coverage decision reviewed under the external review process.

Please Note: As the most recently available utilization review standards adopted by URAC are to be used in terms of compliance, URAC standards include procedures for Review and Appeals. *See* IOWA ADMIN. CODE r. 191-70.4(2) (2004).

B. **External Appeals requirements.**

1. **Time frame for determination.** Not applicable.

2. **Certification of Independent Review Entities.** For external appeals all Independent Review Entities must have as a minimum in order to be certified, a current unrestricted license to practice a health care profession in the United States, and a health care professional who is a medical physician shall also hold a certification by a recognized American medical specialty board. A health care professional who is not a medical physician shall also hold a current certification by the professional's respective licensing or specialty board if applicable. IOWA ADMIN. CODE r. 191-76.9(1) (2004).

3. **Notice:** When a claim is denied in whole or in part based on medical necessity, the carrier or organized delivery system shall provide a notice in writing to the enrollee of the internal appeal mechanism provided

under the carrier or organized delivery system's plan or policy. At the time of a coverage decision, the carrier or organized delivery system shall notify the enrollee in writing of the right to have the coverage decision reviewed under the external review process. IOWA CODE ANN. § 514J.3A (2004). The enrollee or the enrollee's treating health care provider acting on behalf of the enrollee must have exhausted all internal appeal mechanisms provided under the carrier's evidence of coverage. *See* IOWA ADMIN. CODE r. 191-76.3(3) (2004).

4. **Notice Requirements.** Notice must contain the following: The enrollee or the enrollee's treating health care provider must send the request for an external review within 60 days of receipt of the coverage decision from the carrier. The request shall be made to the Division of Insurance, 330 Maple Street, Des Moines, Iowa 50319. A copy of the carrier's coverage decision shall accompany the written request for an external review. A $25 filing fee is required unless the enrollee is requesting that the fee be waived. The check should be made payable to the Insurance Division. If a waiver is requested, the request shall include an explanation of why the enrollee is requesting that the fee be waived. IOWA ADMIN. CODE r. 191-76.3 (2004).

5. **Time Frame.** The independent review entity shall submit its external review decision as soon as possible, but not later than 30 days from the date the independent review entity received the information required under subsection 4 from the carrier or organized delivery system. The independent review entity, for good cause, may request an extension of time from the commissioner. The independent review entity's external review decision shall be mailed to the enrollee or the treating health care provider acting on behalf of the enrollee, the carrier or organized delivery system, and the commissioner. IOWA CODE ANN. § 514J.7(7) (2004).

6. **Confidentiality.** The confidentiality of any medical records submitted shall be maintained pursuant to applicable state and federal laws. IOWA CODE ANN. § 514J.7(8) (2004).

7. **Emergency Services.** An expedited review shall be conducted within 72 hours of

notification to the commissioner if the enrollee's treating health care provider states that delay would pose an imminent or serious threat to the enrollee. IOWA CODE ANN. § 514J.8 (2004).

VII. Recognition of URAC Accreditation Status

A. **Does the state recognize URAC accreditation?** Yes. Third-party payors may either perform or delegate utilization review functions. If the third-party payor performs utilization review, the third-party payor must meet the accreditation requirements set by URAC or other national accreditation organizations recognized and approved by the Commissioner of Insurance. If the third-party payor delegates utilization review, that other entity must meet the accreditation requirements set by URAC or other national accreditation organizations recognized and approved by the Commissioner. The Commissioner may approve a variance from URAC standards for good cause.

B. **Which of the state's requirements are waived for URAC-accredited organizations?** Not applicable.

VIII. Miscellaneous

When performing utilization review of inpatient hospital services related to maternity and newborn care, including but not limited to length of postdelivery stay and postdelivery follow-up care, a third-party payor shall not deselect, require additional documentation, require additional utilization review, terminate services to, reduce payment to, or in any manner provide a disincentive to an attending physician solely on the basis that the attending physician provided or directed the provision of services in compliance with those guidelines. This does not preclude a third-party payor from monitoring a patient's stay or making reasonable inquiries necessary to assess patient progress in accordance with the guidelines and to coordinate discharge planning or postdischarge care. IOWA ADMIN. CODE r. 191-70.8 (2004).

Kansas

I. Scope and Applicability

A. **Who is subject to the state's utilization review laws?** Any person or utilization review organization that performs utilization review activities in the state. KAN. STAT. ANN. § 40-22a07(a)(1) (2004).

    1. **HMO's?** Yes, except for federally-qualified HMOs, as noted above.

    2. **Insurers?** Yes.

    3. **Utilization review organizations?** Yes.

    4. **Retrospective review?** Yes.

B. **What exemptions are provided, if any?** Utilization review of health care services provided to patients under the authority of the Kansas Workers Compensation Act or any medical programs operated by the secretary of social and rehabilitation services or any entity to the extent it is acting under contract with the secretary. KAN. STAT. ANN. § 40-22a05(e) (2004).

C. The Commissioner of Insurance is responsible for adopting rules and regulations, with the advice of the advisory committee that govern the conduct of utilization review activities performed in the state or affecting residents of the state by utilization review organizations. KAN. STAT. ANN. § 40-22a04(a) (2004).

D. **What term does the state use to refer to regulated entities?** A "Utilization review organization" means "any entity which conducts utilization review and determines certification of an admission, extension of stay or other health care service." KAN. STAT. ANN. § 40-22a03(c) (2004).

E. **What activities does the state include in its definition of utilization review?** "Utilization review" is defined as "the evaluation of the necessity, appropriateness, and efficiency of the use of health care services, procedures, and facilities." KAN. STAT. ANN. § 40-22a03(b) (2004).

II. Regulatory Information

A. **Responsible state agency.** Kansas Insurance Department.

B. **Contact Information.**

    1. **Name and Title:** Julie Stell, Accident and Health Policy Examiner

    2. **Address:** Kansas Insurance Department, 420 SW 9th, Topeka, KS, 66612.

    3. **Phone and Facsimile:** (785) 296-7850; facsimile (785) 291-3034.

    4. **E-mail:** jstell@ksinsurance.org

    5. **Web site:** http://www.ksinsurance.org5.

III. Licensure/Certification Requirements

A. **What entities are required to obtain a license in the state to conduct utilization review for residents of the state?** Each organization offering utilization review services (prospective, concurrent, and retrospective) shall apply for a certificate from the Commissioner of Insurance. KAN. STAT. ANN. § 40-22a04(a) (2004).

B. **How often must licensure be renewed?** Annually (unless accredited by URAC).

C. **Licensure fees (initial and renewal).** $100 initial fee and $50 renewal fee. KAN. STAT. ANN. § 40-22a04(b)(5) (2004). (The application fee is not required for organizations accredited by URAC.)

D. **Documentation required for licensure.** An application form, a copy of the utilization review organization's articles of incorporation and bylaws, the location of the office(s) where utilization review will occur, and a summary of the qualifications and experience of persons performing utilization review. KAN. STAT. ANN. § 40-22a04(b)(1) et seq. (2004).

E. **Exemptions from licensure.** To perform utilization review activities in Kansas or affecting Kansas residents requires a certificate issued by the Kansas Insurance Department. However, no certificate is required for utilization review activities conducted by or on behalf of:

    1. an agency of the federal government;

    2. a person, agency or utilization review organization acting on behalf of the federal government, but only to the extent such person, agency or organization is providing services under federal regulation;

    3. a federally qualified health maintenance organization authorized to transact business in Kansas which is administering a quality assurance program and performing utilization review activities for its own members;

    4. a person employed or used by a utilization review organization authorized to perform utilization review in Kansas. (This exemption shall not apply with respect to individual persons performing utilization review activities in conjunction with any insurance contract or health benefit plan pursuant to a direct contractual relationship with a health maintenance organization, group-funded self-insurance plan or insurance company);

5. a health benefit plan that is self-insured and qualified under ERISA;

6. hospitals, home health agencies, clinics, private health care provider offices or any other authorized health care facility or entity conducting general, in-house utilization review unless such review is for the purpose of approving or denying payment for hospital or medical services in a particular case; or

7. Department of Insurance certificate requirements also do not apply to:

   a. Utilization review organizations accredited by and adhering to the national utilization review standards approved by the American Accreditation Health Care Commission (URAC); or

   b. Such other utilization review organizations as the advisory committee to the Commissioner of Insurance may recommend and the Commissioner approves. KAN. STAT. ANN. § 40-22a06(b) et seq. (2004).

IV. Program Requirements

A. **Clinical review criteria.** The utilization review organization must use clinically substantiated review criteria and clinical protocols that have been developed with the participation of health care providers contracting with the utilization review organization, including, as needed, one or more specialists who are board-certified or board-eligible and working toward certification in a specialty board approved by the American Board of Medical Specialists or the American Board of Osteopathy from the major areas of clinical services. The utilization review organization must periodically evaluate and update such criteria, which shall be made available to the attending health care provider on request. If copyright laws prohibit the utilization review organization from copying the criteria for providers, the utilization review organization shall supply the type of criteria being used. Utilization review organization must also use one or more peer clinical reviewers, who have a firm understanding of clinical practice, are familiar with current treatment guidelines, are able to access expert clinical opinions when necessary, and take into consideration any local specific issues as described by the attending health care

provider. KAN. ADMIN. REGS. 40-4-41f (2004); *See also* KAN. ADMIN. REGS. 40-4-41i (2004).

B. **Prohibitions against financial incentives.** Utilization review organizations (and individuals performing utilization review) may not be compensated based on the frequency of certification denials, costs avoided by denial, or reduction in claims payments. KAN. STAT. ANN. § 40-22a07(b) (2004).

C. **Telephone access standards.** Utilization review organizations must provide toll-free or collect call telephone access every normal business day from 9 AM to 4 PM Central Time. Utilization review organizations must also have procedures to handle off-hours calls. KAN. ADMIN. REGS.. 40-4-41g (2004).

D. **Quality assurance program.** Utilization review organizations must maintain written documentation of an active quality assurance program that promotes objective and systematic monitoring and evaluation of utilization review processes and services. It must provide management intervention as needed, and also support compliance with these standards. KAN. ADMIN. REGS. 40-4-41F (2004).

E. **Delegation of utilization review functions.** If utilization review organization delegates or subcontracts any of its utilization review functions, the utilization review organization shall exercise oversight of the delegated or subcontracted functions to ensure that these functions are performed in accordance with this regulation. The utilization review organization shall meet the following criteria:

   1. have a written contract with the subcontractor;

   2. periodically review the subcontractor's policies;

   3. monitor subcontractor's performance;

   4. subcontracted entity must be certified as a utilization review organization.

F. **Confidentiality.** Utilization review organizations must comply with all applicable state and federal laws to protect the confidentiality of individual medical records and limit the use of confidential information to utilization review, quality assurance, discharge planning, and case management. KAN. STAT. ANN. § 40-22a09 (2004); KAN. ADMIN. REGS. 40-4-41J (2004).

V. Reviewer Qualifications

A. **Qualifications of reviewers that render utilization review determinations (at each level of utilization review, if applicable).** Each utilization review organization shall have utilization review staff who are properly trained, qualified, supervised, and supported by written, clinically substantiated criteria and review procedures.

1. Nonclinical administrative staff to be used for data collection, intake screening, and scripted clinical screening.

2. Initial clinical review must be restricted to individuals who are health professionals, and posses a current and valid license or certificate in the state or states in which they work, be trained in the principles and procedures of utilization review. Initial clinical reviewers are to be supported by a doctor of osteopathic medicine or a clinical director who has an unrestricted license to practice medicine.

3. Peer clinical reviews shall be conducted by health professionals who directly support the utilization review activity, are oriented in the principles and procedures of utilization management and peer review. They must be qualified to render a clinical opinion about the medical condition, procedures, and treatment under review. Peer clinical reviewers must hold a current, unrestricted license in the same licensure category as that of the attending health care provider or other ordering provider, or for standard appeals, be in active practice. KAN. ADMIN. REGS. 40-4-41e (2004).

B. **Requirements for medical director.** The utilization review organization shall have a medical director or clinical director with professional post residency experience in direct patient care who holds an unrestricted license to practice medicine, and has a clinical specialty appropriate to the type of single service utilization management conducted.

C. **Requirement for "same-state" licensure.** No provision.

VI. Process Requirements

A. **Review determinations and notice to patients/providers.** The utilization review organization must notify the health care provider promptly by writing, telephone, or electronic transmission.

1. **Time frame for determination.** For prospective and concurrent reviews, the utilization review organization shall make its determinations within 2 working days of receipt of the information necessary to conduct the review. For retrospective review, 30 days are permitted. Decisions to extend a stay must be communicated by telephone or electronic means within 1 business day of receipt of required information. KAN. ADMIN. REGS. 40-4-41c (2004).

2. **Contents of notice of adverse determination.** When an initial determination is made to certify, the utilization review organization shall notify the attending health care provider or other ordering provider, facility rendering service, and enrollee or patient promptly in writing, by telephone, or by electronic transmission. When a prospective or concurrent review determination is made not to certify an admission or extension of an inpatient stay, course of treatment, or other service requiring a review determination, the decision shall be made by a peer clinical reviewer only after not less than 2 bona fide attempts have been made to contact and consult with the attending health care provider. KAN. ADMIN. REGS. 40-4-41c (2004).

3. **Reasons for adverse determination.** The written notification shall include the principal reasons for the determination and procedures to initiate an appeal of the determination. A determination not to certify may be based on a lack of adequate information to certify after a reasonable attempt has been made to contact the health care provider. Each of the letters to the provider, patient, and facility shall include a statement that the clinical rationale used in making the noncertification decision shall be provided in writing upon request. KAN. ADMIN. REGS. 40-4-41c(b)(4)(B) (2004).

4. **Notice of Appeal Rights.** The notice of adverse determination must include the procedures to initiate an appeal. The company's final adverse decision must include a notice of the right to pursue external review.

B. **Appeals procedures.** The right to appeal shall be available to the patient or enrollee, the representative of the patient or enrollee, and the attending health care provider, other ordering provider, or facility rendering service on behalf of the patient. Hospitals or other health care providers may assist in an appeal. Each utilization review organization shall have in place procedures for appeals of a determination not to certify an admission, procedure, service, or extension of stay. They must include procedures for an expedited and standard appeal.

1. **Expedited Appeal.** When an initial determination not to certify a health care service is made before or during an ongoing service requiring review, and the attending health care provider or other ordering provider believes that the determination warrants immediate appeal, the attending health care provider or other ordering provider shall have an opportunity to appeal that determination over the telephone or via facsimile on an expedited basis. Each utilization review organization shall provide reasonable access to a peer clinical reviewer, not to exceed one working day, by telephone or in person to discuss the determination with the attending health care provider or other ordering providers. The peer clinical reviewer shall be available for these appeals during normal business hours.

2. **Standard Appeal.** Each utilization review organization shall notify in writing the enrollee or patient, attending health care provider or other ordering provider, and claims administrator of its determination on the appeal as soon as practical, but never later than 30 days, in the absence of any contractual agreement, after receiving the required documentation for the appeal. The documentation required by the utilization review organization may include copies of part or all of the clinical record or a written statement from the attending health care provider or other ordering provider. KAN. ADMIN. REGS. 40-4-41d (2004).

C. **External appeals.** The insured, the treating physician or health care provider, or the insured's legal representative has the right to request an independent external review within 90 days of the receipt of an adverse decision by a health insurance plan or insurer.

1. The adverse decision shall be printed in clear, legible type and explain the procedure for initiating an external review. KAN. ADMIN. REGS. 40-4-42a (2004).

2. The insured must have exhausted all available internal review procedures provided by the health insurance plan or insurer, unless the insured has an emergency medical condition. Within 10 business days

after receiving the written request for external review and all necessary information, a preliminary determination shall be completed by the Commissioner of Insurance. KAN. ADMIN. REGS. 40-4-42b(a) (2004); *See also* KAN. STAT. ANN. § 40-22a14(b) (2004).

3. The insured may also request external review if a final decision from the insurer has not been received within 60 days of seeking an internal review. KAN. STAT. ANN. § 40-22a14 (2004).

4. Within 30 business days after the date of receipt of the request for external review, the assigned external review organization shall provide written notice of its decision to uphold or reverse the adverse decision. KAN. ADMIN. REGS. 40-4-42c(h) (2004).

5. Emergency Services. If an insured has an emergency medical condition, the insured can request an expedited external review through the Commissioner of Insurance. Insurers are required to provide or transmit all necessary documents and information considered in making the adverse decision to the assigned external review organization by 5 PM the next business day after receiving notification from the Commissioner. KAN. STAT. ANN. § 40-4-42d (2004).

VII. Recognition of URAC Accreditation Status

A. **Does the state recognize URAC accreditation?** Yes.

B. **Which of the state's requirements are waived for URAC-accredited organizations?** URAC-accredited utilization review organizations are exempt from all of the state's application requirements, including the certification fee. *See* KAN. STAT. ANN. § 40-22a06(b) et seq. (2004). An applicant for a certificate as a utilization review organization accredited by URAC need only file a copy of the certificate of accreditation and complete the certification and verification on the final page of the application form.

Kentucky

I. Scope and Applicability

A. **Who is subject to the state's utilization review laws?** Any insurer or its private review agent that provides or performs utilization review in connection with a health benefit plan, and any private review agent that performs utilization review functions on behalf of any person providing or administering health benefit plans. KY. REV. STAT. ANN. § 304.17A-605(1) (2004).

   1. HMOs? Yes.
   2. Insurers? Yes.
   3. Utilization review organizations? Yes.
   4. Retrospective review? Yes.

B. **What exceptions are provided, if any?** A private review agent does not include an "independent review entity" that performs external review of adverse determinations ('peer review organizations' that perform specialty reviews for an insurer may, under certain circumstances, be required to register as a private review agent). In addition, the registration requirements do not apply to a "private review agent that operates solely under contract with the federal government for utilization review or [sic] patients eligible for hospital services under Title XVIII of the Social Security Act…" KY. REV. STAT. ANN. § 304.17A-605(3) (2004).

C. **What term does the state use to refer to regulated entities?** A private review agent is defined as "a person or entity performing utilization review that is either affiliated with, under contract with, or acting on behalf of any insurer or other person providing or administering health benefits to citizens of [Kentucky]." KY. REV. STAT. ANN. § 304.17A-600 (2004).

D. **What activities does the state include in its definition of utilization review?** Utilization review is defined as "a review of the medical necessity and appropriateness of hospital resources and medical services given or proposed to be given to a covered person for purposes of determining the availability of payment. Areas of review include concurrent, prospective, and retrospective review." KY. REV. STAT. ANN. § 304.17A-600 (2004).

II. Regulatory Information

A. **Responsible state agency.** Kentucky Office of Insurance.

B. **Contact Information.**

   1. **Name and Title:** Lee Barnard, RN, Branch Manager of UR & Appeals Branch
   2. **Address:** Kentucky Office of Insurance, P.O. Box 517, 215 West Main Street, St. Frankfort, KY 40602.
   3. **Phone and Facsimile:** 1-800-595-6053 ext. 4345; facsimile (502) 564-2728.
   4. **E-mail:** lee.barnard@ky.gov.
   5. **Web site:** http://doi.ppr.ky.gov

III. Licensure/Certification Requirements

A. **What entities are required to obtain a license in the state to conduct utilization review for residents of the state?** An insurer or private review agent shall not provide or perform utilization reviews without being registered with the Kentucky Office of Insurance. KY. REV. STAT. ANN. § 304.17A-607 (2004).

B. **How often must licensure be renewed?** Registration expires on the second anniversary of the effective date unless renewed. KY. REV. STAT. ANN. § 304.17A-613(2) (2004).

C. **Licensure fees (initial and renewal).** $1000 for initial application and each renewal. KY. REV. STAT. ANN. § 304.17A-613 (2004).

D. **Documentation required for licensure.** An applicant must submit a utilization review plan, utilization review criteria, types and qualifications of personnel conducting utilization review, policies and procedures regarding accessibility during normal business hours, and policies and procedures regarding notice of review. KY. REV. STAT. ANN. § 304.17A-613 (2004).

E. **Exemptions from licensure.** Out-of-state organizations are not granted an exemption from Kentucky's registration requirements even if they are duly licensed and/or certified in their state of domicile.

IV. Program Requirements

A. **Clinical review criteria.** In promulgating emergency administrative regulations specifying the information required of insurers and private review agents, the Office of Insurance shall require descriptions and names of review criteria upon which utilization review decisions are based. KY. REV. STAT. ANN. § 304.17A-609 (2004).

B. **Prohibitions against financial incentives.** No provision.

C. **Telephone access standards.** A registered insurer or private review agent shall provide a toll-free telephone line for covered persons, authorized persons, and providers to contact the insurer or private review agent. That line must be accessible 40 hours per week, during normal business hours in Kentucky. Where an insurer, its agent, or private review agent provides or performs utilization review, be available to conduct utilization review during normal business hours and extended hours in this state on Monday and Friday through 6 PM., including federal holidays. (KRS 304.17A-607(1)(f), effective July 15, 2002). KY. REV. STAT. ANN. § 304.17A-607(1) (2004).

D. **Quality assurance program.** There is no provision in the utilization review requirements regarding quality assurance. However, KY. REV. STAT. ANN. § 304.17A-545(3) (2004) requires a managed care plan to have a quality assurance program.

E. **Delegation of utilization review functions.** An insurer or its agent shall be responsible for monitoring all utilization reviews and internal appeals carried out by or on behalf of the insurer and for ensuring that all requirements are met. KY. REV. STAT. ANN. § 304.17A-605(2)(a) (2004).

F. **Confidentiality.** Insurers or private review agents shall not disclose or publish individual medical records or any other confidential medical information in the performance of utilization review activities except as provided in the Health Insurance Portability and Accountability Act, related provisions in the Code of Federal Regulations, and other applicable laws and administrative regulations. KY. REV. STAT. ANN. § 304.17A-607(d) (2004). The Office of Insurance's emergency administrative regulations shall require insurers and private review agents to provide policies and procedures to ensure all applicable state and federal laws to protect the confidentiality of individual medical records. KY. REV. STAT. ANN. § 304.17A-609(5) (2004).

V. **Reviewer Qualifications**

A. **Qualifications of reviewers that render utilization review determinations (at each level of utilization review, if applicable).**

1. Only licensed physicians shall make a utilization review decision to deny, reduce, limit, or terminate a health care benefit or to deny or reduce payment for a health care

service because that service is not medically necessary, experimental, or investigational.

2. In the case of a health care service rendered by a chiropractor or optometrist the denial shall be made by a chiropractor or optometrist, respectively, duly licensed in Kentucky.

3. Only licensed physicians shall supervise "qualified personnel" (licensed physicians, registered nurses, licensed practical nurses, medical records technicians, or other licensed medical personnel) conducting case reviews.

4. Only a licensed physician who did not participate in the initial review and denial may conduct an internal appeal of an adverse determination. In the case of a review involving a medical or surgical specialty or subspecialty, if requested by a covered person, authorized person, or provider, the insurer or agent shall use a board eligible or certified physician in the appropriate specialty or subspecialty. KY. REV. STAT. ANN. §§ 304.17A-607 & 617 (2004).

B. **Requirements for medical director.** No provision specifically for utilization review. Under KY. REV. STAT. ANN. § 304.17A-545 (2004), a managed care plan shall appoint a medical director who is a physician licensed to practice in the state in which he or she is employed and who shall be responsible for treatment policies, protocols, quality assurance activities, and the plan's utilization management activities. (KRS 304.17A-545(1)(d) requires that any denial letter issued by a managed care plan required under KRS 304.17A-540 be signed by a Kentucky-licensed Medical Director.)

C. **Requirement for "same-state" licensure.** Chiropractors or optometrists making utilization review decisions and medical directors of managed care plans (HMOs) must be licensed in Kentucky. KY. REV. STAT. ANN. § 304.17A-607 (2004).

VI. **Reviews and Appeals**

A. **Review determinations and notice to patients/providers.** Review determinations must be sent to covered persons, authorized persons, and all providers. KY. REV. STAT. ANN. § 304.17A-607(1)(h) (2004).

1. **Time frame for determination.** Kentucky has adopted the timeframes found in the Department of Labor claims regulation 29

CFR Part 2560, with the following exceptions: Any request for preadmission review of a hospital admission or for preauthorization for outpatient surgery must be treated as urgent care. A determination on a retrospective review of an emergency admission where the covered person is still hospitalized at the time request is made must be provided within 24 hours of receipt of request. Must provide utilization review decision within 24 hours of receipt of request for review of a covered person's continued hospital stay and prior to the time when a previous authorization for hospital care will expire. KY. REV. STAT. ANN. § 304.17A-607(1)(h) (2004).

2. **Contents of notice of adverse determination.** An insurer or private review agent shall provide written notice of review decisions to the covered person, authorized person, and providers. An insurer or private review agent that denies coverage or reduces payment for a treatment, procedure, drug that requires prior approval, or device shall include certain information in the written notice. KY. REV. STAT. ANN. § 304.17A-607(j) (2004).

    a. **Reasons for adverse determination.** Must include statement of the specific medical and scientific reasons for denial or reduction of payment; name, state of licensure, medical license number, and title of reviewer making the determination; and, except for decisions on retrospective reviews, a description of alternative treatments, services, or supplies covered by the health benefit plan, if any. KY. REV. STAT. ANN. § 304.17A-607(j) (2004).

    b. **Notice of Appeal Rights.** Written notice shall include instructions for initiating or complying with the insurer's internal appeal procedure, stating at a minimum, whether the appeal shall be in writing, time limitations, or schedules for filing appeals, and the name and telephone number of a person to contact for additional information. KY. REV. STAT. ANN. § 304.17A-607(j) (2004).

B. **Appeals requirements.** Every insurer shall have an internal appeal process. The internal appeal process shall be disclosed to covered persons. The covered person, an authorized person, or a provider acting on behalf of the covered person may initiate the internal appeal, which shall include adequate and reasonable procedures for review and resolution of appeals concerning adverse determinations. There shall also be procedures for reviewing appeals from covered persons who required expedited review because of current hospitalization or because of medical conditions. KY. REV. STAT. ANN. § 304.17A-617 (2004).

1. **Time frame for determination.** Insurers or their designees shall provide decisions to covered persons, authorized persons, and providers on internal appeals of adverse determinations or coverage denials within 30 days of receipt of request for internal appeal. For an expedited appeal of an adverse determination or coverage denial, insurers or their designees shall render a decision within 3 business days of the request. KY. REV. STAT. ANN. § 304.17A-617(2) (2004). If the covered person, authorized person, or provider has new clinical information regarding the covered person's internal appeal, he or she shall provide that information to the insurer before initiating an external review. The insurer shall have 5 business days from receiving the new information to render a decision. KY. REV. STAT. ANN. § 304.17A-619(1) (2004).

2. **External appeals.** The Office of Insurance shall establish and maintain a system for receiving and reviewing requests for review of coverage denials, which does not include adverse determinations, from covered persons, authorized persons, and providers. In addition, under § 304.17A-621, the Independent External Review program is established in the Office of Insurance to provide covered persons with a formal, independent review to address disagreements between the covered person and the covered person's insurer regarding adverse determinations made by the insurer, its designee, or private review agent. KY. REV. STAT. ANN. § 304.17A-621 (2004). For expedited external review, the independent review entity shall make determinations within 24 hours of receipt of all information required from the insurer. KY. REV. STAT. ANN. § 304.17A-623(12) (2004). For those non-expedited external reviews, the independent review entity shall make determinations within 21 calendar days of

receiving all information required from the insurer. KY. REV. STAT. ANN. § 304.17A-623(13) (2004). In both cases, extensions are possible. *See* KY. REV. STAT. ANN. §§ 304.17A-623 (2004).

VII. Recognition of URAC Accreditation Status

A. **Does the state recognize URAC accreditation?** Yes. KY. REV. STAT. ANN. § 304.17A-609 (2004).

B. **Which of the state's requirements are waived for URAC-accredited organizations?** This varies, depending on which version of URAC's Health UM standards the company is accredited under (e.g, URAC Health UM Standards in 2002 and after). In lieu of disclosing a utilization review plan, an insurer or private review agent may instead submit to the Office of Insurance evidence of accreditation. KY. REV. STAT. ANN. § 304.17A-609(9) (2004).

Louisiana

I. Scope and Applicability

A. **Who is subject to the state's utilization review laws?** Any entity that determines what medical services or procedures will be covered under a health benefit plan based on medical necessity. LA. REV. STAT. ANN. § 22:3072 (2004).

   1. HMOs? Yes.

   2. Insurers? Yes.

   3. Utilization review organizations? Yes.

   4. Retrospective review? Yes.

B. **What exemptions are provided, if any?** There is an exemption for entities exempt from state regulation under the Employee Retirement Income Security Act of 1974 (ERISA). LA. REV. STAT. ANN. § 22:3071(26) (2004).

C. **What term does the state use?** "External review organization" and "medical necessity review organization" (MNRO). An external review organization is defined as "an entity that conducts independent external reviews of adverse determinations and final adverse determinations and whose accreditation or certification has been reviewed and approved by the Department of Insurance." LA. REV. STAT. ANN. § 22:3071(17) (2004). An MNRO is defined as "a health insurance issuer or other entity licensed or authorized pursuant to this Chapter to make medical necessity determinations for purposes other than the diagnosis and treatment of a medical condition." LA. REV. STAT. ANN. § 22:3071(27) (2004).

D. **What activities does the state include in its definition of utilization review?** LA. REV. STAT. ANN. § 22:3071 (2004) does not include a definition of "utilization review," but appears to include ambulatory review, case management, concurrent review, discharge planning, prospective review, retrospective review and second opinion. *See* LA. REV. STAT. ANN. § 22:3071 (2004).

II. Regulatory Information

A. **Responsible state agency.** Louisiana Department of Insurance.

B. **Contact Information.**

   1. **Name and Title:** Pamela Bollinger, Director, Division of Quality Assurance

   2. **Address:** 1702 N. Third St., Baton Rouge, LA, 70804.

   3. **Phone and Facsimile:** (225)219-8769; facsimile (225) 342-5711.

   4. **E-mail:** pbollinger@ldi.state.la.us.

   5. **Web site:** www.dhh.state.la.us.

III. Licensure/Certification Requirements

A. **What entities are required to obtain a license in the state to conduct utilization review for residents of the state?** Any entity acting as an MNRO for the purposes of determining medical necessity, appropriateness of care, the level of care needed, or other similar medical determinations. LA. REV. STAT. ANN. § 22:3072 (2004).

B. **How often must licensure/certification be renewed?** Every 2 years. LA. REV. STAT. ANN. § 22:3074(A) (2004).

C. **Licensure fees (initial and renewal).** $1,500 initial and renewal. LA. REV. STAT. ANN. § 22:3074(D) (2004).

D. **Documentation required for licensure.** Applicants for licensure shall submit an application to the Commissioner of Insurance and pay the initial licensure fee. Information required specified in LA. REV. STAT. ANN. § 22:3073 (2004).

E. **Exemptions from licensure.** Out-of-state organizations are not granted an exemption from the state's licensure and certification requirements even if they are duly licensed and/or certified in their state of domicile.

IV. Program Requirements

A. **Clinical review criteria.** The MNRO must have documented clinical review criteria that are based on sound clinical evidence and are evaluated periodically to assure continuing efficacy. An MNRO may develop its own clinical review criteria or it may purchase or license clinical review criteria from qualified vendors. An MNRO shall make available its clinical review criteria upon request to the Commissioner of Insurance. LA. REV. STAT. ANN. § 22:3076(A) (2004).

B. **Prohibitions against financial incentives.** Compensation may not contain incentives, direct or indirect, for those individuals performing the review to make inappropriate review determinations. Compensation to any such individuals shall not be based, directly or indirectly, on the quantity or type of adverse determinations rendered. LA. REV. STAT. ANN. § 22:3076(J) (2004).

C. **Telephone access standards.** An MNRO must provide health care providers with access to its review staff by a toll-free number that is operational for any period of time that an authorization, certification, or approval of coverage is required. LA. REV. STAT. ANN. § 22:3076(H) (2004). Independent review organizations must establish a toll-free telephone service to receive information related to external reviews on a 24 hour-a-day, seven day-a-week basis that is capable of accepting, recording, or providing appropriate instruction to incoming telephone callers during other than normal business hours. LA. REV. STAT. ANN. § 22:3086(A)(3) (2004).

D. **Quality assurance program.** Required. At least annually, an MNRO shall routinely assess the effectiveness and efficiency of its medical necessity determination program and report any deficiencies or changes to the Commissioner of Insurance. LA. REV. STAT. ANN. § 22:3076(D) (2004).

E. **Delegation of utilization review functions.** If delegated, the entity must obtain a license. LA. REV. STAT. ANN. § 22:3072 (2004).

F. **Confidentiality.** An MNRO shall annually provide written certification to the commissioner that its program for determining medical necessity complies with all applicable state and federal laws establishing confidentiality and reporting requirements. LA. REV. STAT. ANN. § 22:3089 (2004).

V. Reviewer Qualifications

A. **Qualifications of reviewers that render utilization review determinations (at each level of utilization review, if applicable).** Informal reconsideration, Standard Appeal, Second Level Review and External Review all have their own standards in reference to reviewer requirements. LA. REV. STAT. ANN. § 22:3078 – 3087.

1. The medical director shall administer the program and oversee all review decisions.
2. Only a duly licensed physician or clinical peer shall make adverse determinations.
3. An adverse determination made by an MNRO in the second level review shall become final only when a clinical peer has evaluated and concurred with such determination. LA. REV. STAT. ANN. § 22:3076(B) (2004).

B. **Requirements for medical director.** An MNRO must have a duly licensed physician as the medical director. LA. REV. STAT. ANN. § 22:3076(B) (2004).

C. **Requirements for "same-state" licensure.** No provision.

VI. Reviews and Appeals

A. **Review determinations and notice to patients/providers.**

1. **Time frame for determination.** An MNRO shall issue determination decisions in a timely manner. LA. REV. STAT. ANN. § 22:3077(B)(C) (2004). 80% of determinations shall be made within 2 working days of obtaining appropriate medical information. In no instance shall any determination of medical necessity be made later than 30 days from receipt of the request unless there is an agreed upon extension. For concurrent review, determinations of medical necessity shall be made within one working day. LA. REV. STAT. ANN. § 22:3077 (2004).

2. **Contents of notice of adverse determination.**

   a. **Reasons for adverse determination.** A written notification of an adverse determination shall include the principal reason or reasons for the determination and the instructions for requesting a written statement of the clinical rationale, including the clinical review criteria used to make the determination. LA. REV. STAT. ANN. § 22:3077(E) -3084(2004).

   b. **Notice of Appeal Rights.** The instructions for initiating an appeal or reconsideration of the determination are required. LA. REV. STAT. ANN. § 22:3077 - 3084 (2004).

B. **Appeals requirements.**

1. **Time frame for determination.** The MNRO must have a procedure for informal reconsideration that gives the provider rendering the service an opportunity to request on behalf of the covered person a reconsideration of an adverse determination by the physician or clinical peer making the adverse determination. Such informal review shall occur within 1 working day. LA. REV. STAT. ANN. § 22:3078 (2004). Standard appeals must be completed within 30 days of the receipt of all necessary information. LA. REV. STAT. ANN. § 22:3079 (2004). Expedited appeals must be completed within 72 hours of the receipt of all necessary information. LA. REV. STAT. ANN. § 22:3083 (2004).

Second level reviews are required and must be completed within 45 days. LA. REV. STAT. ANN. § 22:3080 (2004).

2. **External appeals.** Each health benefit plan shall provide an independent review process to examine the plan's coverage decisions based on medical necessity. A covered person, with the concurrence of the treating health care provider, may request an external review of an adverse determination made in a second level appeal. Covered persons may pursue a standard or expedited external appeal. LA. REV. STAT. ANN. § 22:3081 (2004).

C. **Emergency Services.** When conducting medical necessity determinations for emergency services, an MNRO shall not disapprove emergency services necessary to screen and stabilize a covered person and shall not require prior authorization of such services if a prudent lay person acting reasonably would have believed that an emergency medical condition existed. LA. REV. STAT. ANN. § 22:3088 and 3084 (B)(2004).

VII. Recognition of URAC Accreditation Status

A. Does the state recognize URAC accreditation? No.

B. Which of the state's requirements are waived for URAC-accredited organizations? Not applicable.

Maine

I. Scope and Applicability

A. **Who is subject to the state's utilization review laws?** A person, partnership or corporation, other than an insurer, nonprofit service organization, health maintenance organization, preferred provider organization or employee of those exempt organizations, that performs medical utilization review services on behalf of commercial insurers, nonprofit service organizations, third-party administrators, health maintenance organizations, preferred provider organizations ME. REV. STAT. ANN. tit. 24-A, § 2771(1) (2004).

   1. **HMO's?** Yes.
   2. **Insurers?** Yes.
   3. **Utilization review organizations?** Yes.
   4. **Retrospective review?** Yes.

B. **What exemptions are provided, if any?** Does not include services that are performed solely for research purposes and are not used in any way in connection with the payment of claims. Also does not include services performed solely under Medicaid, Medicare, Civilian Health and Medical Program of the United States (CHAMPUS), or any other federal program. ME. REV. STAT. ANN. tit. 24-A, § 2771 (1) (2004).

C. **What term does the state use to refer to regulated entities?** "Utilization review entity" means "an entity that conducts utilization review, other than a health carrier performing review for its own health plans." CODE ME. R. § 02-031-850 (2004).

D. **What activities does the state include in its definition of utilization review?** "Utilization review services" or "medical utilization review services" means "a program or process by which a person, partnership or corporation, on behalf of an insurer, nonprofit service organization, third-party administrator, health maintenance organization (HMO), preferred provider organization (PPO), or employer that is a payor for or that arranges for payment of medical services, seeks to review the utilization, appropriateness or quality of medical services provided to a person whose medical services are paid for, partially or entirely, by that insurer, nonprofit service organization, third-party administrator, HMO, PPO or employer. The terms include these programs or processes whether they apply prospectively or retrospectively to medical services." Utilization review services include second opinion programs, prehospital admission certification, preinpatient service eligibility certification, and concurrent hospital review to determinate appropriate length of stay." ME. REV. STAT. ANN. tit. 24-A, § 2773 (2004).

II. Regulatory Information

A. **Responsible state agency.** Department of Professional and Financial Regulation, Bureau of Insurance, Consumer Health Care Division.

B. **Contact Information.**
   1. **Name and Title:** Patty Woods, Claims Examiner
   2. **Address:** 34 State House Station, Augusta, ME 04333-0034.
   3. **Phone and Facsimile:** (207) 624-8459; facsimile (207) 624-8599.
   4. **E-mail:** patricia.a.woods@maine.gov
   5. **Web site:** www.state.me.us/pfr/ins/inshome2.htm.

III. Licensure/Certification Requirements

A. **What entities are required to obtain a license in the state to conduct utilization review for residents of the state?** A person, partnership or corporation that performs medical utilization review services on behalf of commercial insurers, nonprofit service organizations, third-party administrators, HMO's, PPO's, or employers. ME. REV. STAT. ANN. tit. 24-A, § 2771(1) (2004).

B. **How often must licensure be renewed?** Annually on or before April 1st. ME. REV. STAT. ANN. tit. 24-A, § 2771(3) (2004).

C. **Licensure fees (initial and renewal).** $400 application fee; $100 initial license fee; $100 license renewal fee. ME. REV. STAT. ANN. tit. 24-A, § 2771(1) (2004).

D. **Documentation required for licensure.** Utilization review entities (URE's)must submit an application that includes: a description of the process by which utilization review is conducted, the process used by the entity for addressing beneficiary or provider complaints, the types of utilization review programs offered by the entity (i.e. second opinion programs, prehospital admission certification, preinpatient service eligibility determination, concurrent hospital review), and the process chosen by the entity to preserve beneficiary confidentiality of medical information. As part of its initial application, the entity shall submit copies of all materials to be used to inform beneficiaries and providers of the requirements of its utilization review plans and their rights and responsibilities under the plan. ME. REV. STAT. ANN. tit. 24-A, § 2771(3) (2004).

E. **Exemptions from licensure.** Out-of-state organizations are not granted an exemption from Maine's licensure and certification requirements even if they are duly licensed and/or certified in their state of domicile.

IV. Program Requirements

A. **Clinical review criteria.** The licensee must have written medical utilization review criteria to be employed in the review process. ME. REV. STAT. ANN. tit. 24-A, § 2772(3-A) (2004). A utilization review program shall use documented clinical review criteria that are based on published sound clinical evidence and which are evaluated periodically to assure ongoing efficacy. A health carrier or the carrier's designated URE may develop its own clinical review criteria or may purchase or license clinical review criteria from qualified vendors. Upon request, a health carrier or the carrier's designated URE shall make available its clinical review criteria to the Superintendent and the Commissioner of the Department of Human Services. Review criteria must be available for inspection by the Bureau of Insurance. CODE ME. R. § 02-031-850 Sec.8(D)(1) (2004).

B. **Prohibitions against financial incentives.** Compensation may not be based on the quantity of adverse determinations rendered, or otherwise include incentive for reviewers to render inappropriate decisions. Utilization review entities must also ensure that an employee does not perform utilization review services involving a health care provider or facility in which that employee has a financial interest. See CODE ME. R. § 02-031-850 Sec.8(D)(9) (2004); ME. REV. STAT. ANN. tit. 24-A, § 2772(6) (2004).

C. **Telephone access standards.** Utilization review entities must provide a toll-free or collect call telephone line. Telephone lines must be adequately staffed to provide sufficient access. ME. REV. STAT. ANN. tit. 24-A, § 2772(3) (2004); CODE ME. R. § 02-031-850 Sec.8(D)(7) (2004).

D. **Quality assurance program.** Utilization review entities must routinely assess the effectiveness and efficacy of the utilization review program.

E. **Delegation of utilization review functions.** Third-party payers, such as HMO's and insurance companies, are responsible for monitoring utilization review activities that they delegate to another entity. If a health carrier delegates any utilization review activities to a utilization review entity, adequate oversight includes a written description of the utilization review entity's activities and responsibilities; evidence of formal approval of the utilization review entity by the health carrier; and a process by which the health carrier evaluates the utilization review entity. See CODE ME. R. § 02-031-850 Sec.8(D)(6) (2004).

F. **Confidentiality.** As part of the application, the utilization review entity must submit the process by which it will maintain confidentiality of medical information. Confidentiality must be maintained in accordance with state and federal laws. See ME. REV. STAT. ANN. tit. 24-A, § 2771(3)(D) (2004); ME. REV. STAT. ANN. tit. 24-A, § 2772(4) (2004)

V. Reviewer Qualifications

A. **Qualifications of reviewers that render utilization review determinations (at each level of utilization review, if applicable).** Qualified health care professionals shall administer the utilization review program and oversee review decisions. A clinical peer shall evaluate the clinical appropriateness of adverse determinations. CODE ME. R. § 02-031-850 §8(D)(2) (2004). Clinical peers must evaluate all adverse determinations. Code Me. R. § 02-031-850 Sec.8(F)(2) (2004). Appeals must be considered by clinical peers who were not involved in the original adverse determination. CODE ME. R. § 02-031-850 Sec.8(G)(1)(b) (2004).

B. **Requirements for medical director.** No provision specifically for utilization review entities, but under ME. REV. STAT. ANN. tit. 24-A, § 4304(1), a carrier must appoint a medical director "who is responsible for reviewing and approving the carrier's policies governing the clinical aspects of coverage determinations by any health plan that it offers."

C. **Requirement for "same-state" licensure.** As part of the application (see Section III.C., above), utilization review entities must report if the health professionals performing utilization review are licensed in Maine.

VI. Reviews and Appeals

A. **Review determinations and notice to patients/providers.**

1. **Time frame for determination.** For prospective determinations, within 2 business days of obtaining all information necessary to make a review determination.

For concurrent determinations, within 1 business day of obtaining all information necessary to make a review determination. For retrospective determinations, within 30 business days of obtaining all information necessary to make a review determination. CODE ME. R. § 02-031-850 Sec.8(E) (2004).

2. **Contents of notice of adverse determination.** A written notification of an adverse determination shall include the principal reasons or reasons for the determination, the instructions for initiating an appeal or reconsideration of the determination, and the instructions for requesting a written statement of the clinical rationale, including the clinical review criteria used to make the determination. The notification must include a phone number the covered person may call for information on and assistance with initiating an appeal or reconsideration and/or requesting clinical rationale and review criteria. The carrier or the carrier's designated URE shall respond expeditiously to such written requests. CODE ME. R. § 02-031-850 Sec.8(D)(5) (2004).

3. **Reconsideration.** The reconsideration shall occur within 1 working day of the receipt of the request and shall be conducted between the provider rendering the service and the reviewer who made the adverse determination or a clinical peer designated by the reviewer if the reviewer who made the adverse determination cannot be available within 1 working day. CODE ME. R. § 02-031-850 Sec.8(F)(2) (2004).

B. **Appeals requirements.** Utilization review entities must make available both standard and expedited appeals. Health carriers shall establish a first-level grievance process and a second-level grievance process.

1. **Standard Appeal.** Appeals shall be evaluated by an appropriate clinical peer or peers. The clinical peer(s) shall not have been involved in the initial adverse determination, unless the appeal presents additional information the decision maker was unaware of at the time of rendering the initial adverse determination. For standard appeals, the health carrier or the carrier's designated URE shall notify in writing both the covered person and the attending or ordering provider of the decision within 20 working days following the request for an appeal.

The reviewers' decision in clear terms and the clinical rationale in sufficient detail for the covered person to respond further to the health carrier's position. CODE ME. R. § 02-031-850 Sec.8(G)(1) (2004).

2. **Expedited Appeal.** Involves a situation where the time frame of the standard review procedures would seriously jeopardize the life or health of a covered person or would jeopardize the covered person's ability to regain maximum function. Expedited appeals shall be evaluated by an appropriate clinical peer or peers. The clinical peer(s) shall not have been involved in the initial adverse determination. A health carrier or the carrier's designated URE shall make a decision and notify the covered person and the provider acting on behalf of the covered person via telephone as expeditiously as the covered person's medical condition requires, but in no event more than 72 hours after the review is initiated. CODE ME. R. § 02-031-850 Sec.8(G)(2) (2004).

3. **Emergency Services.** A utilization review entity may not render an adverse determination, or require prior authorization, for emergency services necessary to screen and stabilize a patient. Utilization review entities must have a reviewer available 24 hours a day, 7 days a week to evaluate post-stabilization services or services shall be provided without liability to the covered person until an authorized representative is available. CODE ME. R. § 02-031-850 Sec.8(H) (2004).

4. **External appeals.** An enrollee has the right to an independent external review of a carrier's adverse health care treatment decision made by or on behalf of a carrier offering a health plan in accordance with the requirements of this section. An enrollee's failure to obtain authorization prior to receiving an otherwise covered service may not preclude an enrollee from exercising the enrollee's rights under this section. ME. REV. STAT. ANN. tit. 24-A, § 4312 (2004).

a. An enrollee or the enrollee's authorized representative shall make a written request for external review of an adverse health care treatment decision to the bureau of insurance.

b. An external review decision must be made as expeditiously as an enrollee's medical condition requires but in no

event more than 72 hours after receipt of a completed request for external review if the time frame for review required under paragraph C would seriously jeopardize the life or health of the enrollee or would jeopardize the enrollee's ability to regain maximum function.
ME. REV. STAT. ANN. tit. 24-A, § 4312(5)(2004).

VII. Recognition of URAC Accreditation Status

A. **Does the state recognize URAC accreditation?** Yes.

B. **Which of the state's requirements are waived for URAC-accredited organizations?** "A [health] carrier accredited by a nationally recognized accrediting organization may seek a waiver from the requirements of any or all of the standards of subsections E through G [pertaining to procedures for review decisions, requests for reconsideration, and appeals for adverse determinations]." *See* CODE ME. R. § 02-031-850 Sec.8 (2004). In addition, "A [health] carrier accredited by a nationally recognized accrediting organization may seek a waiver from the requirements of any or all of the standards of subsections C and D of this section [pertaining to procedures for first level grievance review and second level grievance review]. *See* CODE ME. R. §02-031-850 Sec. 9 (2004). The Maine Bureau of Insurance interprets the waiver provisions in these sections, which are considered on a case-by-case basis, to apply to health carriers and to utilization review entities that perform utilization review functions on a carrier's behalf or employer's behalf. For purposes of these sections, the Bureau of Insurance recognizes URAC's Health Utilization Management Standards.

VIII. Miscellaneous

The Bureau of Insurance's Web site provides a list of "Medical Utilization Review License Holders." This information is available at:
www.state.me.us/pfr/ins/insmedur.htm.

Maryland

I. Scope and Applicability

A. **Who is subject to the state's utilization review laws?** applies to entities that propose to issue or deliver individual, group, or blanket health insurance policies or contracts in the State or to administer health benefit programs that provide for the coverage of health care services and the utilization review of those services. MD. CODE ANN. [INS.] § 15-1001 (2004).

1. **HMO's?** Yes.
2. **Insurers?** Yes.
3. **Utilization review organizations?** Yes
4. **Retrospective review?** Yes.

B. **What exemptions are provided, if any?** Requirements may be waived for private review agents that operate solely under federal contract for utilization review of patients eligible for hospital services under Medicaid or Medicare.

C. **What term does the state use to refer to regulated entities?** "Private review agent" means: a nonhospital-affiliated person or entity performing utilization review that is either affiliated with, under contract with, or acting on behalf of a Maryland business entity or a third party that provides or administers hospital benefits to Maryland citizens, including a health maintenance organization (HMO), or a health insurer, nonprofit health service plan, health insurance service organization, or preferred provider organization (PPO) authorized to offer health insurance policies or contracts in Maryland, or any person or entity including a hospital-affiliated person performing utilization review for the purpose of making claims or payment decisions on behalf of the employer's or labor union's health insurance plan under an employee assistance program for employees other than the employees employed by the hospital or employed by a business wholly owned by the hospital. MD. CODE ANN. [INS.] § 15-10B-01(k) (2004).

D. **What activities does the state include in its definition of utilization review?** "Utilization review" means "a system for reviewing the appropriate and efficient allocation of health care services given or proposed to be given to a patient or group of patients. MD. CODE ANN. [INS.] § 15-10B-01(m) (2004). For purposes of MD. CODE ANN. [INS.] § 15-10B-06 (2004), pertaining to review of services for treatment of alcoholism, drug abuse, or mental illness,

"utilization review" means "a system for reviewing the appropriate and efficient allocation of health care resources and services given or proposed to be given to a patient or group of patients by a health care provider, including a hospital or an intermediate care facility…"

II. Regulatory Information

A. **Responsible state agency.** Maryland Insurance Administration.

B. **Contact Information.**
1. **Name and Title:** Ellen Woodall, Director, Medical Director/Private Review Agent Certification.
2. **Address:** 525 St. Paul Place, Baltimore, MD 21202-2272.
3. **Phone and Facsimile:** (410) 468-2226; facsimile: (410) 468-2270.
4. **E-mail:** ewoodall@mdinsurance.state.md.us
5. **Web site:** http://www.mdinsurance.state.md.us.

C. **Citations for Laws and Regulations.** MD. CODE ANN. [INS.] § 15-10B (2004); MD. REGS. CODE tit. 31, §10.21 (2004).

III. Licensure/Certification Requirements

A. **What entities are required to obtain a license in the state to conduct utilization review for residents of the state?** A private review agent may not conduct utilization review in this state unless the Commissioner has granted the private review agent a certificate. MD. CODE ANN. [INS.] § 15-10B-03(a) (2004).

B. **How often must certification be renewed?** Every 2 years.

C. **Certification fees (initial and renewal).** $1,500.

D. **Documentation required for licensure.** Private review agents must submit an application and documentation of compliance with the state's requirements. Documentation must include a utilization review plan that shows:
1. the specific criteria and standards to be used in conducting utilization review of proposed or delivered health care services;
2. those circumstances, if any, under which utilization review may be delegated;
3. any provisions by which patients, physicians, or hospitals may seek reconsideration;
4. the type and qualifications of the personnel either employed or under contract to perform the utilization review;

5. a copy of the private review agent's internal grievance process if a carrier delegates its internal grievance process to the private review agent;

6. the procedures and policies to ensure that a representative of the private review agent is reasonably accessible to patients and health care providers 7 days a week, 24 hours a day in this state;

7. the policies and procedures that ensure all applicable state,federal and confidentiality laws are followed;

8. a copy of a notice to inform applicable patients and providers of the requirements of the utilization review plan;

9. a list of the third party payors for which the private review agent is performing utilization review in this state;

10. the policies and procedures to ensure that the private review agent has a formal program for the orientation and training of the personnel either employed or under contract to perform the utilization review;

11. a list of the persons involved in establishing the specific criteria and standards to be used in conducting utilization review;

12. and certification by the private review agent that the criteria and standards to be used in conducting utilization review are:

    a. objective;
    b. clinically valid;
    c. compatible with established principles of health care; and
    d. flexible enough to allow deviations from norms when justified on a case by case basis.
    MD. CODE ANN. [INS.] § 15-10B-05(a) (2004). *See also* MD. REGS. CODE tit. 31, § 10.21.02 (2004) which lists the information required in the application for certification.

E. **Exemptions from licensure.** Out-of-state organizations are not granted an exemption from the state's licensure and certification requirements even if duly licensed and/or certified in their state of domicile. In addition, the Commissioner may consider an applicant as having met a particular certification requirement under this subtitle if the applicant has obtained utilization management accreditation from an approved accrediting organization as determined by the Commissioner, the approved accrediting organization has requirements that meet or

exceed the particular requirement in this subtitle, and the applicant demonstrates that the applicant meets or exceeds the particular requirement under this subtitle. MD. CODE ANN. [INS.] § 15-10B-03(d) (2004).

IV. **Program Requirements**

A. **Clinical review criteria.** Review criteria must be objective, clinically valid, compatible with established principles of health care, and flexible enough to allow deviations when justified on a case-by-case-basis. Specific criteria must be released as part of an appeals determination. MD. REGS. CODE tit. 31, § 10.21.02(B)10 (2004); *See also* MD. CODE ANN. [INS.] § 15-10B-11(8) (2004).

B. **Prohibitions against financial incentives.** Physicians who consider appeals may not be compensated in a manner that provides an incentive to deny or reduce covered health care services. MD. CODE ANN. [INS.] § 15-10B-7(b) (2004). *See also* MD. CODE ANN. [INS.] § 15-10B-17(b)(1) (2004) (A private review agent or any individual who is either affiliated with, under contract with, or acting on behalf of a private review agent may not refer a patient who has undergone utilization review by the private review agent to a health care facility in which the private review agent owns a significant beneficial interest, or the private review agent's own health care practice.

C. **Telephone access standards.** For certification, private review agents must submit to the Commissioner policies and procedures to ensure that a representative of a private review agent is reasonably accessible to patients and providers 7 days a week, 24 hours a day in Maryland. MD. REGS. CODE tit. 31, § 10.21.02(B)(3) (2004); MD. CODE ANN. [INS.] § 15-10B-05(a)(4) (2004).

D. **Quality assurance program.** No provision.

E. **Delegation of utilization review functions.** No provision.

F. **Confidentiality.** Private review agents must comply with all applicable laws to protect the confidentiality of individual medical records in accordance with applicable state and federal laws. MD. CODE ANN. [INS.] § 15-10B-05(a)(5) (2004).

V. **Reviewer Qualifications**

A. **Qualifications of reviewers that render utilization review determinations (at each level of utilization review, if applicable).**

    1. The type and qualifications either of personnel employed or under contract to perform utilization review include registered nurses, medical records technicians or

similar personnel supported and supervised by physicians as may be required, physicians, or other appropriate health care providers. MD. REGS. CODE tit. 31, § 10.21.02(B)(2) (2004).

2. Private review agents must have adequate numbers of qualified health professionals to carry out review activities.

3. All adverse decisions shall be made by a physician, or a panel of other appropriate health care service reviewers with at least one physician on the panel who is board certified or eligible in the same specialty as the treatment under review. MD. CODE ANN. [INS.] § 15-10B-07(a)(1) (2004).

4. Appeals must be considered by a physician (or a panel that includes a physician) who is board-certified or board-eligible in same specialty as the treatment under review. For dental services, appeals must be considered by a dentist.

B. **Requirements for medical director.** To be certified as a medical director under this subtitle, an applicant shall submit an application to the Commissioner on the form required by the Commissioner; and pay to the Commissioner an application fee of no more than $100 established by the Commissioner by regulation. The application shall include a description of the applicant's professional qualifications, including medical education information and, if appropriate, board certifications and licensure status, the utilization management procedures and policies to be used by the health maintenance organization. MD. CODE ANN. [INS.] § 15-10C-03 (2004).

C. **Requirement for "same-state" licensure.** No provision.

VI. Reviews and Appeals

A. **Review determinations and notice to patients/providers.**

1. **Time frame for determination.** A private review agent must make all initial determinations on whether to authorize or certify a non-emergency course of treatment for a patient within two working days of receipt of the necessary information. For concurrent review, the decision must be made within 1 working day of receipt of the information. MD. CODE ANN. [INS.] § 15-10B-06 (2004).

B. **Contents of notice of adverse determination.**

1. **Reasons for adverse determination.** Required. In addition, the notice of adverse determination must state in detail in clear, understandable language the specific factual basis for the decision; refer to the specific criteria and standards, including interpretive guidelines, used to make the decision; and state the name, business address, and business phone number of the medical director who made the decision if the carrier or private review agent is an HMO or designated employee or representative of the carrier or private review agent who has responsibility for the carrier's or private review agent's internal grievance process if the carrier or private review agent is not an HMO. MD. REGS. CODE tit. 31, § 10.18.04(B) (2004).

2. **Notice of Appeal Rights.** Required. The notice shall give written details of the internal grievance process and procedures. The notice must also include a statement that the member or provider may file a complaint with the Insurance Commissioner within 30 working days after receipt of the grievance decision. A complaint may also be filed without satisfying the internal grievance process if the member or health care provider can demonstrate a compelling reason to do so as determined by the Commissioner. The notice must provide the name, address, telephone and facsimile number for the Insurance Commissioner as well as information about the Health Education and Advocacy Unit of the Maryland Consumer Protection Division. HMO. MD. REGS. CODE tit. 31, § 10.18.04(B) (2004).

B. **Appeals requirements.** Private review agents must provide for emergency and non-emergency cases.

1. **Time frame for determination.** Appeals must generally be completed within 30 working days after the appeal is filed, with the following exceptions. Appeals regarding emergency cases must be completed within 24 hours after the appeal is filed. Appeals regarding retrospective reviews must be completed within 45 days after the appeal is filed. MD. CODE ANN. [INS.] § 15-10A-02(b)(2) (2004).

2. **External appeals.** In addition to the private review agent's internal appeals process, a patient may also file a complaint with the Insurance Commissioner. In the course of considering the complaint, the Commissioner may consult with an "independent review organization" or "medical expert." MD. REGS. CODE tit. 31, § 10.18.13 (2004). The Commissioner shall make a final decision within 30 working days after a complaint is filed regarding a pending health care service and within 45 working days after a complaint is filed regarding a retrospective denial of services. MD. REGS. CODE tit. 31, §10.19.07(A) (2004).

C. **Emergency Services.** An expedited review of an adverse decision in accordance with this regulation is required if:

1. the adverse decision is rendered for health care services that are proposed but have not been delivered; and

2. Services are necessary to treat a condition or illness that, without immediate medical attention, would seriously jeopardize the life or health of the member or the member's ability to regain maximum function, or cause the member to be in danger to self or others.

3. If an adverse decision is rendered for prospective services and the condition or illness, without immediate medical attention, would seriously jeopardize the life or health of the member or the member's ability to regain maximum function or cause the member to be in danger to self or others, an expedited review is required. For an emergency case, within one day after oral communication of a decision to the member or health care provider, the carrier shall send written notice of any adverse decision or grievance decision. A carrier shall render a final decision on a grievance involving an emergency case within 24 hours after filing under internal grievance process. MD. REGS. CODE tit. 31, §10.18.05(A) (2004).

VII. Recognition of URAC Accreditation Status

A. Does the state recognize URAC accreditation? No.

B. Which of the state's requirements are waived for URAC-accredited organizations? Not applicable.

Massachusetts

I. Scope and Applicability

A. **Who is subject to the state's utilization review laws?** Massachusetts does not currently regulate utilization review organizations. They do regulate the utilization review activities of health carriers that offer for sale, provide or arrange for the provision of a defined set of health care services to insureds through affiliated and contracting providers or employ utilization review in making decisions about whether services are covered benefits under a health benefit plan. A carrier that provides coverage for limited health services only, that provides specified services through a workers' compensation preferred provider arrangement, or that does not provide services through a network or through participating providers shall be subject to those requirements as deemed appropriate by the Commissioner of Insurance in a manner consistent with a duly filed application for accreditation. MASS. REGS. CODE tit. 211, § 52.04(1) (2004).

   1. **HMO's?** Yes.
   2. **Insurers?** Yes.
   3. **Utilization review organizations?** No.
   4. **Retrospective review?** Yes.

B. **What exemptions are provided, if any?** A carrier shall be exempt from Managed Care Consumer Protections and Accreditation Carriers regulations if in the written opinion of the Attorney General, the Commissioner of Insurance and the Commissioner of Public Health, the health and safety of health care consumers would be materially jeopardized by requiring accreditation of the carrier. MASS. REGS. CODE tit. 211, § 52.04(3) (2004).

C. **What term does the state use to refer to regulated entities?** Utilization review organization (URO) is an entity that conducts utilization review under contract with or on behalf of a carrier, but does not include a carrier performing utilization review for its own health benefit plans. MASS. REGS. CODE tit. 211, § 52.03 (2004).

D. **What activities does the state include in its definition of utilization review?** A set of formal techniques designed to monitor the use of, or evaluate the clinical necessity, appropriateness, efficacy, or efficiency of, health care services, procedures or settings. Such techniques may include, but are not limited to, ambulatory review, prospective review, second opinion, certification, concurrent review, case management, discharge planning or retrospective review. MASS. REGS. CODE tit. 211, § 52.03 (2004).

II. Regulatory Information

A. **Responsible state agency.**

B. **Contact Information.** Bureau of Managed Care.
   1. **Name and Title:** Nancy Scwartz, Director, Bureau of Managed Care.
   2. **Address:** Division of Insurance, One South Station, Boston, MA 02110.
   3. **Phone/Facsimile:** (617) 521-7347/(617) 521-7773.
   4. **E-mail:** nancy.schwartz@state.ma.us.
   5. **Web site:** www.state.ma.us/doi.

III. Accreditation Requirements

A. **What entities are required to be accredited in the state to conduct utilization review for residents of the state?** A carrier must be accredited according to the requirements set forth in 211 CMR 52.00 in order to offer for sale, provide, or arrange for the provision of a defined set of health care services to insureds through affiliated and contracting providers or employ utilization review in making decisions about whether services are covered benefits under a health benefit plan. MASS. REGS. CODE tit. 211, § 52.04(1) (2004).

B. **How often must accreditation be renewed?** Every 12 months. MASS. REGS. CODE tit. 211, § 52.06(1) (2004).

C. **Accreditation fees (initial and renewal).** $500.00. MASS. REGS. CODE tit. 211, § 52.06(3)(a) and 52.06(4)(a) (2004).

D. **Documentation required for accreditation.** Initial application must include a filing fee and:
   1. A complete description of the carrier's utilization review policies and procedures;
   2. A written attestation to the Commissioner that the utilization review program of the carrier or its designee complies with all applicable state and federal laws concerning confidentiality and reporting requirements;
   3. A copy of the most recent existing survey described in 211 CMR 52.08(10) (2004);
   4. A complete description of the carrier's internal grievance procedures and the external review process.
   5. A complete description of the carrier's process to establish guidelines for medical necessity, a description of the carrier's quality management and improvement

policies and procedures, a description of the carrier's credentialing policies and procedures, and the carrier's policies and procedures for providing or arranging for the provision of preventive health services;

6. A sample of every provider contract used by the carrier or the organization with which the carrier contracts;

7. A statement that advises the Bureau of Managed Care whether or not the carrier has issued new contracts, revised existing contracts, or after July 1, 2001, made revisions to fee schedules in any existing contract with a physician or physician group that impose financial risk on such physician or physician group for the costs of medical care, services or equipment provided or authorized by another physician or health care provider;

8. A copy of every provider directory used by the carrier;

9. The evidence of coverage for every product offered by the carrier;

10. A copy of disclosures issued to insured as mandated by the regulations;

11. A written attestation that the carrier has provided the proper documentation to The Office of Patient Protection; and

12. Any additional information as deemed necessary by the Commissioner. MASS. REGS. CODE tit. 211, § 52.06(3) (2004).

E. **Deeming.** A carrier may apply for deemed accreditation so long as they are in compliance with the standards set forth in the Managed Care Regulations and may be so accredited by the Bureau if it meets the following requirements: It must be accredited by JCAHO, NCQA or URAC. MASS. REGS. CODE tit. 211, § 52.05(1)(a) (2004).

IV. Program Requirements

A. **Clinical review criteria.**

1. A carrier's application will be reviewed for compliance with those NCQA accreditation standards MASS. REGS. CODE tit. 211, § 52.08(1) (2004).

2. Utilization review conducted by a carrier or utilization review organization shall be conducted pursuant to a written plan, under the supervision of a physician and staffed by appropriately trained and qualified personnel, and shall include a documented process to review and evaluate the plan's

effectiveness, ensure the consistent application of utilization review criteria, and ensure the timeliness of utilization review determinations. A carrier or utilization review organization shall adopt utilization review criteria and conduct all utilization review activities pursuant to said criteria.

3. The utilization criteria shall be developed with the input of participating physicians, consistent with the development of medical necessity criteria.

4. Utilization review criteria shall be applied consistently. MASS. REGS. CODE tit. 211, § 52.08(2) (2004).

5. Prohibitions against financial incentives. For External Review entities. *See* MASS. REGS. CODE tit. 105, § 128.309 (2004).

B. **Telephone access standards.** Must establish toll-free numbers that will enable consumers to determine the status or outcome of utilization review decisions. MASS. REGS. CODE tit. 211, § 52.13(1)(n) (2004).

C. **Quality assurance program.** A carrier or utilization review organization shall conduct an annual survey of insureds to assess satisfaction with access to specialist services, ancillary services, hospitalization services, durable medical equipment and other covered services. MASS. REGS. CODE tit. 211, § 52.08(10) (2004).

D. **Delegation of utilization review functions.** Any carrier that contracts with another organization to perform any of the functions specified in 211 CMR 52.00 is responsible for collecting and submitting all of the materials from the contracting organization. MASS. REGS. CODE tit. 211 CMR 52.06(3) and (4) (2004).

E. **Confidentiality.** In the initial and renewal applications, a carrier must provide a written attestation to the Commissioner that the utilization review program of the carrier or its designee complies with all applicable state and federal laws concerning confidentiality and reporting requirements. MASS. REGS. CODE tit. 211, § 52.06 (3)(c) and 52.06(4)(b) (2004).

V. Reviewer Qualifications

A. **Qualifications of reviewers that render utilization review determinations (at each level of utilization review, if applicable).**

1. The type and qualifications either of personnel employed or under contract to perform utilization review include registered nurses, medical records technicians or similar personnel supported and supervised

by physicians as may be required, physicians, or other appropriate health care providers. MASS. REGS. CODE tit. 211, § 52.03 (2004).

2. Adverse determinations rendered by a program of utilization review, or other denials of requests for health services, shall be made by a person licensed in the appropriate specialty related to such health service and, where applicable, by a provider in the same licensure category as the ordering provider, and shall explain the reason for any denial, including the specific utilization review criteria or benefits provisions used in the determination, and all appeal rights applicable to the denial. MASS. REGS. CODE tit. 211, § 52.08(3)(c) (2004).

B. **Requirements for medical director.** No specific provision.

C. **Requirement for "same-state" licensure.** Clinical Peer Reviewers must be Massachusetts-licensed providers according to MASS. REGS. CODE tit. 211, § 52.03 and 52.08(7) (2004).

VI. Reviews and Appeals

A. **Review determinations and notice to patients/providers.**

1. Time frame for determination. Initial determination regarding a proposed admission, procedure or service. A carrier or utilization review organization shall make an initial determination regarding a proposed admission, procedure or service that requires such a determination within 2 working days of obtaining all necessary information. MASS. REGS. CODE tit. 211, § 52.08(4) (2004).

2. In the case of a determination to approve an admission, procedure or service, the carrier or utilization review organization shall notify the provider rendering the service by telephone within 24 hours, and shall send written or electronic confirmation of the telephone notification to the insured and the provider within 2 working days thereafter. MASS. REGS. CODE tit. 211, § 52.08(4)(b) (2004).

3. In the case of an adverse determination, the carrier or the utilization review organization shall notify the provider rendering the service by telephone within 24 hours, and shall send written or electronic confirmation of the telephone notification to the insured and the provider within 1 working day

thereafter. MASS. REGS. CODE tit. 211, § 52.08(4)(c) (2004).

4. Concurrent reviews shall be made within 1 day of obtaining all information. MASS. REGS. CODE tit. 211, § 52.08(5) (2004).

5. In the case of a determination to approve an extended stay or additional services, the carrier or utilization review organization shall notify the provider rendering the service by telephone within 24 hours, and shall send written or electronic confirmation of the telephone notification to the insured and the provider within one working day thereafter. A written or electronic notification shall include the number of extended days or the next review date, the new number of total days or services approved, and the date of admission or initiation of services. MASS. REGS. CODE tit. 211, § 52.08(5)(a) (2004).

6. In the case of an adverse determination, the carrier or the utilization review organization shall notify the provider rendering the service by telephone within 24 hours, and shall send written or electronic confirmation of the telephone notification to the insured and the provider within 1 working day thereafter. The service will be continued without liability to the insured until the insured has been notified of the adverse determination. MASS. REGS. CODE tit. 211, § 52.08(5)(b) (2004).

B. **Contents of notice of adverse determination.**

1. Reasons for adverse determination. The written notification of an adverse determination shall include a substantive clinical justification that is consistent with generally accepted principles of professional medical practice.

2. Notifications shall, at a minimum, identify the information upon which the decision was based, the specific reasons why the medical evidence fails to meet the relevant medical review criteria, specify alternate treatment plan, include a clear, concise and complete description of the carrier's formal internal grievance process and the procedures for obtaining external review. MASS. REGS. CODE tit. 211, § 52.08(6) (2004).

C. **Appeals requirements.** A carrier or utilization review organization shall give a provider treating an insured an opportunity to seek reconsideration of an adverse determination from a clinical peer reviewer in any case involving an initial determination or a concurrent review determination. MASS. REGS. CODE tit. 211, § 52.08(7) (2004). If the adverse determination is not reversed by the reconsideration process, the insured, or the provider on behalf of the insured, may pursue the grievance process established, MASS. REGS. CODE tit. 211, § 52.08(7)(b) (2004), however, the reconsideration process shall not be a prerequisite to the internal grievance process or an expedited appeal. MASS. REGS. CODE tit. 211, § 52.08(7)(c) (2004).

D. **Time frame for determination.** The reconsideration process shall occur within 1 working day of the receipt of the request and shall be conducted between the provider rendering the service and the clinical peer reviewer or a clinical peer designated by the clinical peer reviewer if the reviewer cannot be available within 1 working day. MASS. REGS. CODE tit. 211, § 52.08(7)(a) (2004).

E. **External Appeals.** Any insured or authorized representative of an insured who is aggrieved by a final adverse determination issued by a carrier or utilization review organization may request an external review by filing a request in writing with the Office of Patient Protection within 45 days of the insured's receipt of written notice of the final adverse determination. MASS. REGS. CODE tit. 105, § 128.400 (2004).

1. **Conflict of Interest.** External review agencies shall insure that clinical reviewers assigned to any external review shall have no material, professional, familial affiliation with any party that is the subject of said review; shall have no material professional affiliation, material family affiliation or financial affiliation with any party that participated in the delivery of health care to the insured who is the subject of the review; and shall not have participated as a clinical reviewer in connection with any medical necessity determination with respect to the insured who is the subject of the review. MASS. REGS. CODE tit. 105, § 128.309 (2004).

F. **Expedited External Appeals.** An insured or the insured's authorized representative, if any, may request to have his or her request for review processed as an expedited external review. Any request for an expedited external review shall contain a certification, in writing, from a physician, that delay in the providing or continuation of health care services that are the subject of a final adverse determination, would pose a serious and immediate threat to the health of the insured. Upon a finding that a serious and immediate threat to the insured exists, the Office of Patient Protection shall qualify such request as eligible for an expedited external review. MASS. REGS. CODE tit. 105, § 128.400 (2004).

VII. Recognition of URAC Accreditation Status

A. **Does the state recognize URAC accreditation?** Yes.

B. **Which of the state's requirements are waived for URAC-accredited organizations?** A carrier may apply for deemed accreditation so long as they are in compliance with the standards set forth in the Managed Care Regulations and may be so accredited by the Bureau if it meets the following requirements: It must be accredited by JCAHO, NCQA or URAC. MASS. REGS. CODE tit. 211, § 52.05(1)(a) (2004).

Michigan

I. Scope and Applicability

A. **Who is subject to the state's utilization review laws?** Michigan does not currently regulate utilization review organizations.

Note: However, In Michigan "health carriers" are subject to the "Patient's Right to Independent Review Act." MICH. COMP. LAWS ANN. § 550.1905(1) (2000). Under this Act, health carriers are defined as an entity subject to the insurance laws and regulations of this state, or subject to the jurisdiction of the commissioner, that contracts or offers to contract to provide, deliver, arrange for, pay for, or reimburse any of the costs of health care services, including a sickness and accident insurance company, a health maintenance organization, a nonprofit health care corporation, or any other entity providing a plan of health insurance, health benefits, or health services. Health carrier does not include a state department or agency. MICH. COMP. LAWS ANN. § 550.1903(s) (2000).

(** The "Patient's Right to Independent Review Act" took effect October of 2000. It established internal grievance procedures for participants so that they could challenge "adverse determinations" made by a health carrier or its designee utilization review organization. However, the participant must first exhaust the health carrier's internal grievance process before seeking external review unless there is some basis for expedited review. The request is made to the Commissioner of the Office of Financial and Insurance Services (OFIS) who will then decide whether to assign the request to an IRO. After the IRO's decision the Commissioner is required to review it. **)

B. **What term does the state use to refer to regulated entities?** A utilization review organization (URO) is not defined for regulating URO's under "Patient's Right to Independent Review Act." Under this Act, URO's are defined as an entity that conducts utilization review, other than a health carrier performing a review for its own health plans. MICH. COMP. LAWS ANN. § 550.1903(aa) (2000)

C. **What activities does the state include in its definition of utilization review?** Under the "Patient's Right to Independent Review Act," utilization review is defined as a set of formal techniques designed to monitor the use of, or evaluate the clinical necessity, appropriateness, efficacy, or efficiency of, health care services, procedures, or settings. Techniques may include ambulatory review, prospective review, second opinion, certification, concurrent review, case management, discharge planning, or retrospective review. MICH. COMP. LAWS ANN. § 550.1903(z) (2000).

D. **The Patient's Right to Independent Review Act's Operation and Timelines.** MICH. COMP. LAWS ANN. § 550.1917 Sec. 17. (1) (2000). The Commissioner of the Office of Financial and Insurance Services (OFIS) shall approve independent review organizations eligible to be assigned to conduct external reviews under this act to ensure that an independent review organization satisfies the minimum standards established under the Act.

E. Specific requirements for those organizations that are contracted with the OFIS to participate in the Patient Review Act are listed under MICH. COMP. LAWS ANN. § 550.1919 (2000).

1. Once a utilization review decision is made, health carriers are expected to provide written notice to a covered person in plain English of the internal grievance and external review processes at the time the health carrier sends written notice of an adverse determination. MICH. COMP. LAWS ANN. § 550.1907(1) (2000).

2. Should an insured request an external review they must first complete the health carrier's internal grievance process. MICH. COMP. LAWS ANN. § 550.1907(2) (2000). The request must be filed no later than 60 days after the adverse decision, MICH. COMP. LAWS ANN. § 550.1911(1) (2000), and the independent review organization shall provide its recommendation to the Commissioner not later than 14 days after the assignment by the Commissioner of the request for an external review. MICH. COMP. LAWS ANN. § 550.1911(14) (2000).

3. For expedited external reviews, a covered person or the covered person's authorized representative may make a request for an expedited external review with the Commissioner within 10 days after the covered person receives an adverse determination. For expedited reviews the assigned independent review organization shall provide its recommendation to the Commissioner as expeditiously as the covered person's medical condition or

circumstances require, but in no event more than 36 hours. *See* MICH. COMP. LAWS ANN. § 550.1913 (2000).

4. An external review decision and an expedited external review decision are the final administrative remedies available under this act. A person aggrieved by an external review decision or an expedited external review decision may seek judicial review no later than 60 days from the date of the decision in the circuit court for the county where the covered person resides or in the circuit court of Ingham county. MICH. COMP. LAWS ANN. § 550.1915 (2000).

II. Recognition of URAC Accreditation Status

A. Does the state recognize URAC accreditation? No

B. Which of the state's requirements are waived for URAC-accredited organizations? Not applicable.

Minnesota

I. Scope and Applicability

A. **Who is subject to the state's utilization review laws?** Insurance companies, health service plans, health maintenance organizations (HMO's), community integrated service networks, accountable providers, fraternal benefit societies, joint self-insurance employee health benefit plans, multiple employer welfare arrangements, third party administrators, and "any entity performing utilization review that is affiliated with, under contract with, or conducting utilization review on behalf of, a business entity in [Minnesota]." MINN. STAT. ANN. § 62M.01(2) (2004).

1. **HMO's?** Yes.
2. **Insurers?** Yes.
3. **Utilization review organizations?** Yes.
4. **Retrospective review?** Yes.

B. **What exemptions are provided, if any?** None specified.

C. **What term does the state use to refer to regulated entities?** A "utilization review organization" is any entity that "conducts utilization review and determines certification of an admission, extension of stay, or other health care services for a Minnesota resident; or any entity performing utilization review that is affiliated with, under contract with, or conducting utilization review on behalf of, a business entity in this state." MINN. STAT. ANN. § 62M.02(21) (2004).

D. **What activities does the state include in its definition of utilization review?** "Utilization review" is defined as "the evaluation of the necessity, appropriateness, and efficacy of the use of health care services, procedures, and facilities, by a person or entity other than the attending health care professional, for the purpose of determining the medical necessity of the service or admission." In addition, it "includes review conducted after the admission of the enrollee" and "situations where the enrollee is unconscious or otherwise unable to provide advance notification." The definition "does not include a referral or participation in a referral process by a participating provider unless the provider is acting as a utilization review organization." MINN. STAT. ANN. § 62M.02(20) (2004).

II. Regulatory Information

A. **Responsible state agency.** Minnesota Department of Commerce.

B. **Contact Information.**
1. **Name and Title:** Susan Schmidt
2. **Address:** 85 7th Place East, Suite 500, St. Paul, MN 55101-2198.
3. **Phone and Facsimile:** (651) 297-1351; facsimile (651) 296-9434.
4. **E-mail:** susan.e.schmidt@state.mn.us
5. **Web site:** www.state.mn.us/cgi-bin/portal/mn/jsp/home.do?agency=Commerce

III. Licensure/Certification Requirements

A. **What entities are required to obtain a license in the state to conduct utilization review for residents of the state?** Any organization that meets the definition of utilization review organization in MINN. STAT. ANN. § 62M.02 must be licensed or registered. MINN. STAT. ANN. § 62M.03(1) (2004). Any organization that meets that definition that is not licensed in Minnesota that performs utilization review for Minnesota residents must certify compliance with MINN. STAT. ANN. §§ 62M.01-62M.16. MINN. STAT. ANN. § 62M.03 (2) (2004).

B. **How often must registration be renewed?** Registration is effective for 2 years and may be renewed for another 2 years by written request. MINN. STAT. ANN. § 62M.03(2) (2004).

C. **Licensure fees (initial and renewal).** $1,000 initial fee and $1,000 for each renewal. MINN. STAT. ANN. § 62M.03(2) (2004).

D. **Documentation required for licensure.** None specified. (Contact Department of Commerce for more information.) The Department of Commerce must approve an application before certifying a utilization review organization.

E. **Exemptions from licensure.** Out-of-state organizations are not exempt from Minnesota's licensure and ertification requirements if they are licensed and/or certified in their state of domicile.

IV. Program Requirements

A. **Clinical review criteria.** Utilization review organizations must use written clinical criteria and review procedures.

1. A utilization review organization must have written procedures for providing notification of its determinations on all certifications.

---

2. The criteria must be evaluated and updated annually based on sound clinical principles.

3. Utilization review organizations must have written procedures to ensure reviews are conducted in accordance with all statutory and regulatory requirements.

4. Clinical criteria and review procedures must be established with appropriate involvement from actively practicing physicians.

5. A utilization review organization must use written clinical criteria, as required, for determining the appropriateness of the certification request.

6. The utilization review organization must have a procedure for ensuring, at a minimum, the annual evaluation and updating of the written criteria based on sound clinical principles. MINN. STAT. ANN. § 62M.03(2) (2004); MINN. STAT. ANN. § 62M.09(5) (2004).

B. **Prohibitions against financial incentives.** No individual performing utilization review may receive any financial incentive based on number of denials or certifications. Utilization review organizations may establish medically appropriate performance standards. Prohibition on financial incentives does not apply to those between health plan companies and providers. MINN. STAT. ANN. § 62M.12 (2004).

C. **Telephone access standards.** A utilization review organization must provide access to its review staff by a toll-free or collect call telephone line during normal business hours. MINN. STAT. ANN. § 62M.10(1) (2004).

31. A utilization review organization must also have an established procedure to receive timely callbacks from providers and must establish written procedures for receiving after-hour calls, either in person or by recording. A utilization review organization must conduct its telephone reviews, on-site reviews, and hospital communications during reasonable and normal business hours, unless otherwise mutually agreed. MINN. STAT. ANN. § 62M.10(2) (2004).

E. **Quality assurance program.** Utilization review organizations must maintain documentation of an active quality assessment program. MINN. STAT. ANN. § 62M.09(8) (2004).

F. **Delegation of utilization review functions.** The regulated utilization review organization is accountable for the delegated utilization review activities of the clinic or health care system. MINN. STAT. ANN. § 62M.02(21) (2004).

G. **Confidentiality.** Utilization review organizations must have written procedures for ensuring patient-specific information obtained during process of utilization review will be kept confidential in accordance with applicable federal and state laws, used solely for purposes of utilization review, quality assurance, discharge planning, and case management; and shared only with those organizations or persons that have authority to receive such information. MINN. STAT. ANN. § 62.08(1) (2004).

V. Reviewer Qualifications

A. **Qualifications of reviewers that render utilization review determinations (at each level of utilization review, if applicable).**

1. Utilization review organization shall have utilization review staff who are properly trained, qualified, and supervised.

2. Nurses, physicians, and other licensed health professionals conducting reviews of medical services and other clinical reviewers conducting specialized reviews in their area of specialty must be currently licensed or certified by an approved state licensing agency in Unites States.

3. Physicians must review all cases in which utilization review organizations have concluded determination not to certify for clinical reasons is appropriate. The physician should be reasonably available by telephone to discuss the determination with the attending health care professional.

4. Peers of treating mental health or substance abuse providers or physicians must review requests for outpatient services in which utilization review organizations have concluded determination not to certify mental health or substance abuse service for clinical reasons is appropriate. Any final determination not to certify treatment must be made by psychiatrists certified by American Board of Psychiatry and Neurology and appropriately licensed in states in which psychiatrists reside.

5. Dentists must review all appeals in which utilization review organizations concluded that determination not to certify a dental service or procedure for clinical reasons is appropriate.

6. Chiropractors must review all appeals where utilization review organization has concluded determination not to certify a

chiropractic service or procedure for clinical reasons is appropriate.

7. Utilization review organizations must use physician consultants in appeal process and should include specialists who are board-certified or board-eligible and working toward certification in a specialty board approved by American Board of Medial Specialists or American Board of Osteopathy. MINN. STAT. ANN. § 62.09 et seq. (2004).

B. **Requirements for medical director.** No provision.

C. **Requirement for "same-state" licensure.** No provision.

VI. Reviews and Appeals

A. **Review determinations and notice to patients/providers.** A utilization review organization must have written procedures. An initial determination on all requests for utilization review must be communicated to provider and enrollee. MINN. STAT. ANN. § 62M.05(1) (2004).

1. **Time frame for determination.**

   a. **Standard Reviews.** Initial determination shall be made within 10 business days of request provided utilization review organization has all information reasonably necessary to make a determination on the request. Initial determination not to certify shall be communicated by telephone within 1 working day to attending health care professional and hospital and written notice sent to hospital, attending health care professional, and enrollee. MINN. STAT. ANN. § 62M.05(3a) (2004).

   b. **Expedited Reviews.** Notification of an expedited initial determination to either certify or not to certify must be provided to the hospital, the attending health care professional, and the enrollee as expeditiously as the enrollee's medical condition requires, but no later than 72 hours from the initial request. MINN. STAT. ANN. § 62M.05(3b)(b) (2004).

2. **Contents of notice of adverse determination.**

   a. **Reasons for adverse determination.** Required. Written notice must include principal reason or reasons for determination and process for initiating

an appeal. Upon request, utilization review organization shall provide provider or enrollee with criteria used to determine necessity, appropriateness, and efficacy of health care service and identify database, professional treatment parameter, or other basis for criteria. MINN. STAT. ANN. § 62M.05(3a)(c) (2004).

   b. **Notice of Appeal Rights.** Required. When an initial determination is made not to certify, written notification must inform enrollee and attending health care professional of right to submit an appeal to internal appeals process and procedure for initiating internal appeal. Notice of expedited initial determination to certify must be provided to hospital, attending health care professional and enrollee as expeditiously as medical condition requires, but not later than 72 hours from initial request. MINN. STAT. ANN. § 62M.05(3a)(d) (2004).

B. **Appeals requirements.** Utilization review organizations must provide for both standard and expedited appeals. Utilization review organization must establish procedures for standard appeals to be made either in writing or by telephone. An expedited determination must be used if attending health care professional believes an expedited determination is warranted. MINN. STAT. ANN. § 62M.06(1) (2004).

1. **Time frame for determination.** A utilization review organization shall notify enrollee, attending health care professional, and claims administrator in writing of determination on appeal within 30 days of receipt of notice of appeal. Utilization review organization may take up to 14 more days because of circumstances beyond such organization's control. Expedited appeals must be conducted telephonically and the utilization review organization shall notify enrollee and attending health care professional as expeditiously as medical condition requires, but no later than 72 hours after receiving expedited appeal. MINN. STAT. ANN. § 62M.06(2) (2004); MINN. STAT. ANN. § 62M.06(3) (2004).

2. **External appeals.** If determination not to certify is not reversed through expedited or standard appeal, utilization review

organization must include in notification right to submit appeal to external appeal process described in MINN. STAT. ANN. §§ 62Q.73 and procedure for initiating process. Information must be provided to enrollee and attending health care professional in writing as soon as practical. An enrollee may file complaint regarding determination not to certify directly to Commissioner of Commerce or Commissioner of Health. MINN. STAT. ANN. § 62M.06(2)(c) (2004); MINN. STAT. ANN. § 62M.06(3)(g) (2004).

C. **Emergency Services/Prior Authorization.** Utilization review organizations may not conduct or require prior authorization for emergency confinement or emergency treatment. Enrollee or enrollee's authorized representative may be required to notify health plan company, claims administrator, or utilization review organization as soon as reasonably possible after beginning of emergency confinement or treatment. MINN. STAT. ANN. § 62M.06(2)(c) (2004).

VII. Recognition of URAC Accreditation Status

A. Does the state recognize URAC accreditation? No.

B. Which of the state's requirements are waived for URAC-accredited organizations? Not applicable.

VIII. Miscellaneous

At the Web site: (http://www.state.mn.us/mn/externalDocs/URO_Application_031403110952_UROapplication.pdf) for the Department of Commerce, Insurance Bureau, one can find an application for registration by nonlicensed utilization review organizations. This form allows such organizations to certify compliance with MINN. STAT. ANN. §§ 62M.01-62M.16 (2004).

The Minnesota Utilization Review Act of 1992, as amended (MINN. STAT. ANN. §§ 62M.01-62M.16), contains a number of provisions limiting and specifying the data that utilization review organizations may collect during the utilization review process. *See* MINN. STAT. ANN. § 62M.04 *et seq.* (2004).

Mississippi

I. Scope and Applicability

A. **Who is subject to the state's utilization review laws?** Any private review agent (i.e., a nonhospital-affiliated person or entity performing utilization review) who approves or denies payment or who recommends approval or denial of payment for hospital or medical services or whose review results in approval or denial of payment for hospital or medical services on a case by case basis. MISS. CODE ANN. § 41-83-3(1) (2004); MISS. CODE ANN. § 41-83-1(b) (2004).

    1. HMO's? Yes.

    2. Insurers? Yes.

    3. Utilization review organizations? Yes.

    4. Retrospective review? Yes.

B. **What exemptions are provided, if any?** Exceptions are provided for general in-house utilization review conducted by hospitals, home health agencies, preferred provider organizations, or other managed care entities, clinics, private physician offices, or any other health facility or entity so long as the review does not result in the approval or denial of payment for hospital or medical services. MISS. CODE ANN. § 41-83-5 (2004). The Director of the Division of Health Facilities Licensure and Certification of the Mississippi State Department of Health may waive rules and regulations for a private review agent that operates solely under contract with the federal government for utilization review of patients eligible for hospital services under Medicare and Medicaid.

C. **What term does the state use to refer to regulated entities?** "Private review agent" means a nonhospital-affiliated person or entity performing utilization review on behalf of:

    1. An employer or employees in the state of Mississippi; or

    2. A third party that provides or administers hospital and medical benefits to citizens of this state, including: a health maintenance organization issued a certificate of authority under and by virtue of the laws of the state of Mississippi; or a health insurer, nonprofit health service plan, health insurance service organization, or preferred provider organization or other entity offering health insurance policies, contracts or benefits in this state. MISS. CODE ANN. § 41-83-1(b) (2004)

D. **What activities does the state include in its definition of utilization review?** "Utilization review" is defined as "a system for reviewing the appropriate and efficient allocation of hospital resources and medical services given or proposed to be given to a patient or group of patients as to necessity for the purpose of determining whether such service should be covered or provided by an insurer plan or other entity." MISS. CODE ANN. § 41-83-1(a) (2004).

II. Regulatory Information

A. **Responsible state agency.** Mississippi State Department of Health, Health Facilities Licensure & Certification.

B. **Contact Information.**

    1. **Name and Title:** Sherry Hofmister & Linda Trigg

    2. **Address:** Mississippi State Department of Health, Health Facilities Licensure and Certification, 570 East Woodrow Wilson, Ste. 200, P.O. Box 1700, Jackson, MS 39215-1700.

    3. **Phone and Facsimile:** (601) 576-7329; 601-5767328 facsimile (601) 576-7350.

    4. **E-mail:** shofmister@msdh.state.ms.us; ltrigg@msdh.state.ms.us

    5. **Web site:** www.msdh.state.ms.us.

III. Licensure/Certification Requirements

A. **What entities are required to obtain a license in the state to conduct utilization review for residents of the state?** "A private review agent who approves or denies payment or who recommends approval or denial of payment for hospital or medical services or whose review results in approval or denial of payment for hospital or medical services on a case by case basis" must receive a certificate from the Mississippi State Department of Health to conduct utilization review in the state. MISS. CODE ANN. § 41-83-3(1) (2004).

    1. No certificate is required for those private review agents conducting general in-house utilization review for hospitals, home health agencies, preferred provider organizations or other managed care entities, clinics, private physician offices or any other health facility or entity, so long as the review does not result in the approval or denial of payment for hospital or medical services for a particular case. Such general in-house utilization review is completely exempt.

MISS. CODE ANN. § 41-83-5 (2004). No certificate is required for utilization review by any Mississippi-licensed pharmacist, pharmacy, or organizations of either while engaged in the practice of "pharmacy" in Mississippi.

B. **How often must licensure be renewed?** Every 2 years. MISS. CODE ANN. § 41-83-11(1) (2004).

C. **Licensure fees (initial and renewal).** Fees of $1,000 for initial and renewal certification.

D. **Documentation required for licensure.** Private review agents must submit an application to the Mississippi Department of Health. MISS. CODE ANN. § 41-83-7 (2004). They must also submit the following:

1. A utilization review plan that includes a description of review criteria, standards and procedures to be used in evaluating proposed or delivered hospital and medical care and the provisions by which patients, physicians or hospitals may seek reconsideration or appeal of adverse decisions by the private review agent;

2. The type and qualifications of the personnel either employed or under contract to perform the utilization review;

3. The procedures and policies to insure that a representative of the private review agent is reasonably accessible to patients and providers at all times in this state;

4. The policies and procedures to insure that all applicable state and federal laws to protect the confidentiality of individual medical records are followed;

5. A copy of the materials designed to inform applicable patients and providers of the requirements of the utilization review plan; and

6. A list of the third party payors for which the private review agent is performing utilization review in this state. MISS. CODE ANN. § 41-83-9 (2004).

E. **Exemptions from licensure.** Out-of-state organizations are not exempt from the state's licensure requirements even if duly licensed in their state of domicile.

IV. **Program Requirements**

A. **Clinical review criteria.** Private review agents must provide examples of review criteria to the Department of Health. MISS. CODE ANN. § 41-83-9 (2004). Private review agents should use written clinical criteria to determine the

appropriateness of certification. Such criteria should be periodically evaluated and revised.

B. **Prohibitions against financial incentives.** No provision.

C. **Telephone access standards.** A representative of the private review agent must be reasonably accessible to patients and providers for five working days a week during normal business hours (9 AM-5 PM). MISS. CODE ANN. § 41-83-13(c) (2004). A free telephone number must be provided with adequate lines available and manned. There should be a specific procedure for handling after-hours inquiries.

D. **Quality assurance program.** A private review agent shall have written documentation of an active quality assessment program. MISS. CODE ANN. § 41-83-15 (2004).

E. **Delegation of utilization review functions.** No provision.

F. **Confidentiality.** Private review agents must comply with all applicable state and federal laws to protect the confidentiality of individual medical records. A private review agent may not disclose or publish individual medical records or other confidential medical information obtained during a utilization review without patient's authorization or court order. MISS. CODE ANN. § 41-83-13(c) (2004).

V. **Reviewer Qualifications**

A. **Qualifications of reviewers that render utilization review determinations (at each level of UR, if applicable).**

B. Upon request by the treating physician, a physician in the relevant specialty or subspecialty must review the case.

C. Each private review agent shall have utilization review staff who are properly trained, qualified, supervised, and supported by written clinical criteria and review procedures.

D. Nurses, physicians, and other licensed health professionals conducting reviews of medical services and other clinical reviewers conducting specialized reviews in their area of specialty shall be currently licensed or certified by an approved state licensing agency.

E. **Requirements for medical director.** No provision.

F. **Requirement for "same-state" licensure.** No determination adverse to a patient or to any affected health care provider shall be made on any question relating to the necessity or justification for any form of hospital, medical or other health care services without prior evaluation and concurrence in the adverse determination by a physician licensed to practice in Mississippi. MISS. CODE ANN. § 41-83-31(a) (2004). However, the physician who makes the evaluation and concurrence in the adverse determination must be licensed to practice in Mississippi shall not apply to the Comprehensive Health Insurance Risk Pool Association or its policyholders and shall not apply to any utilization review company which reviews fewer than 10 persons residing in the State of Mississippi. MISS. CODE ANN. § 41-83-31(c) (2004).

VI. Reviews and Appeals

A. Review determinations and notice to patients/providers.

1. **Time frame for determination.** Approvals must be communicated in writing within 2 working days. Adverse determinations must be communicated within 1 working day. A physician who made an adverse determination shall discuss the reason for any adverse determination with the affected health care provider, if requested, within 14 days of being notified of a request.

2. **Contents of notice of adverse determination.**

   a. **Reasons for adverse determination.** Required. Any determination regarding hospital, medical, or other health care services rendered to a patient that may result in denial of third-party reimbursement or denial of precertification shall include the evaluation, findings, and concurrence of a physician trained in the relevant specialty or subspecialty.

   b. **Notice of Appeal Rights.** Required to have provisions for expedited and standard appeals.

B. **Appeals requirements.** The treating physician may request a reconsideration of an adverse determination.

1. **Time frame for determination.** For a standard appeal, a private review agent shall notify in writing the patient, provider, and claims administrator of a decision as soon as practical, but no later than 60 days after receiving required documentation.

2. **External appeals.** No External Review per se. However, "Any person aggrieved by a final decision of the department or a private review agent in a contested case … shall have the right of judicial appeal to the chancery court of the county of the residence of the aggrieved person. MISS. CODE ANN. § 41-83-23 (2004).

C. **Emergency Services.** If a licensed physician certifies in writing within 72 hours of an admission that the patient was in need of immediate hospital care, the care shall be assumed to have been medically necessary. To overcome this, the private review agent must clearly demonstrate that the patient was not in need of immediate hospital care. MISS. CODE ANN. § 41-83-21 (2004).

VII. Recognition of URAC Accreditation Status

A. **Does the state recognize URAC accreditation?** No.

B. **Which of the state's requirements are waived for URAC-accredited organizations?** Not applicable.

Missouri

I. Scope and Applicability

A. **Who is subject to the state's utilization review laws?** A utilization review agent may not conduct utilization review in this state unless the Missouri department of insurance has granted the utilization review agent a certificate. MO. REV. STAT. § 374. 503.1 (2004).

   1. **HMO's?** Yes.
   2. **Insurers?** Yes.
   3. **Utilization review organizations?** Yes.
   4. **Retrospective review?** Yes.

B. **What exemptions are provided, if any?** No certificate is required for those review agents conducting general in-house utilization review for hospitals, home health agencies, clinics, private offices or any other health facility or entity, so long as the review does not result in the approval or denial of payment for hospital or medical services for a particular case. MO. REV. STAT. § 374. 503.2 (2004).

C. **What term does the state use to refer to regulated entities?** A "utilization review agent" is "any person or entity performing utilization review," except an agency of the federal government, an agent acting on behalf of the federal government, an individual employed or used by a utilization review agent, an employee health benefit plan that is self insured, a property-casualty insurer, and a health carrier performing a review of its own health plan. MO. REV. STAT. § 374. 500(6) (2004).

D. **What activities does the state include in its definition of utilization review?** "Utilization review" is "a set of formal techniques designed to monitor the use of, or evaluate the clinical necessity, appropriateness, efficacy, or efficiency of, health care services, procedures, or settings. Techniques may include ambulatory review, prospective review, second opinion, certification, concurrent review, case management, discharge planning or retrospective review." The definition does not include elective requests for clarification of coverage. MO. REV. STAT. § 374.500(5) (2004).

II. Regulatory Information

A. **Responsible state agency.** Missouri Department of Insurance, Life and Health Section.

B. **Contact Information.**

   1. **Name and Title:** Jane Knight, Insurance Product Analyst II
   2. **Address:** 301 West High Street, P.O. Box 690, Jefferson City, MO 65102-0690.
   3. **Phone and Facsimile:** (573) 751-8354; facsimile (573) 526-6075.
   4. **E-mail:** Jane.Knight@insurance.mo.gov
   5. **Web site:** insurance.mo.gov

III. Licensure/Certification Requirements

A. **What entities are required to obtain a license in the state to conduct utilization review for residents of the state?** Utilization review agents must receive a certificate from the Missouri Department of Insurance. Utilization review agents do not need a certificate for conducting general in-house utilization review for hospitals, home health agencies, clinics, private offices, or any other health facility or entity, if the review does not result in the approval or denial of payment for hospital or medical services. MO. REV. STAT. § 374. 503(1) (2004).

B. **How often must licensure be renewed?** Annually.

C. **Licensure fees (initial and renewal).** $1,000 initial fee; $500 renewal fee.

D. **Documentation required for licensure.** An applicant for a certificate shall: 1) Submit an application to the department of insurance; and 2) Pay to the department of insurance the application fee established by the department through regulation. The application shall: 1) Be on a form and accompanied by any reasonably related supporting documentation that the department of insurance requires; and 2) Be signed and verified by the applicant. MO. REV. STAT. § 374. 505.1 (2004).

E. **Exemptions from licensure.** Out-of-state organizations are not granted an exemption from the state's licensure and certification requirements even if they are duly licensed or certified in their state of domicile.

IV. Program Requirements

A. **Clinical review criteria.** A health carrier that conducts utilization review shall implement a written utilization review program that describes all review activities, both delegated and nondelegated, for covered services provided and shall file an annual report of its utilization review activities with the Commissioner. MO. REV. STAT. § 376.1359 (2004).

   1. A utilization review program shall use documented clinical review criteria that are based on sound clinical evidence and are evaluated periodically to assure ongoing efficacy. A health carrier may develop its

own clinical review criteria, or it may purchase or license clinical review criteria from qualified vendors. A health carrier shall make available its clinical review criteria upon request by either the director of the department of health and senior services or the director of the department of insurance. MO. REV. STAT. § 376.1361.1 (2004).

2. A health carrier shall issue utilization review decisions in a timely manner.

3. A health carrier shall obtain all information required to make a utilization review decision, including pertinent clinical information.

4. A health carrier shall have a process to ensure that utilization reviewers apply clinical review criteria consistently. MO. REV. STAT. § 376. 1361.2 (2004); MO. REV. STAT. § 376. 1361.3 (2004).

B. **Prohibitions against financial incentives.** Compensation to persons making utilization review determinations may not be based on the quantity or type of adverse determinations rendered and may not provide any incentive for medically inappropriate decisions. MO. REV. STAT. § 376. 1361.9 (2004)

C. **Telephone access standards.** Health carriers must provide timely access to review staff by a toll-free number. MO. REV. STAT. § 376. 1361.7 (2004)

D. **Quality assurance program.** Health carrier shall coordinate utilization review program with other medical management activities, such as quality assurance. MO. REV. STAT. § 376. 1361.6 (2004).

E. **Delegation of utilization review functions.** Health carriers are responsible for monitoring all utilization review activities carried out on their behalf. Oversight of delegated utilization review activities must include a formal initial review and continuing evaluation. MO. REV. STAT. § 376. 1353 (2004); MO. REV. STAT. § 376. 1361.5 (2004).

F. **Confidentiality.** Health carriers must submit an annual written certification to the Director of Insurance showing that the utilization review program of the carrier or designee complies with all applicable state and federal laws establishing confidentiality and reporting requirements. MO. REV. STAT. § 376. 1361.2 (2004)

V. Reviewer Qualifications

A. **Qualifications of reviewers that render utilization review determinations (at each level of utilization review, if applicable).** A licensed clinical peer must evaluate the appropriateness of adverse determinations. MO. REV. STAT. § 376. 1361.2 (2004)

B. **Requirements for medical director.** Any medical director who administers the utilization review program or oversees the review decisions shall be a qualified health care professional licensed in the state of Missouri. MO. REV. STAT. § 376. 1361.2 (2004)

C. **Requirement for "same-state" licensure.** The medical director must be licensed in Missouri. MO. REV. STAT. § 376. 1361.2 (2004)

VI. Reviews and Appeals

A. **Review determinations and notice to patients/providers.**

1. **Time frame for determination.** A health carrier shall issue utilization review decisions in a "timely manner." MO. REV. STAT. § 376.1361.3 (2003).

   a. Initial (prospective) determinations must be made within two working days of obtaining all necessary information, communicated by telephone within 24 hours, and followed up by written or electronic confirmation within 1 working day. MO. REV. STAT. § 376.1363.2(2) (2003).

   b. Concurrent determinations must be made within 1 working day of obtaining all necessary information. In the case of an adverse determination, the carrier shall notify by telephone the provider rendering the service within 24 hours of making the adverse determination, and provide written or electronic notification to the enrollee and the provider within one working day of the telephone notification. In the case of a determination to certify an extended stay or additional services the carrier must notify by telephone the provider rendering the services within 1 working day of making the certification and provide written or electronic confirmation to the enrollee and provider within 1 working day. MO. REV. STAT. § 376.1363.3 (2003).

   c. Retrospective determinations must be made within 30 days of obtaining all necessary information. A carrier shall provide notice in writing within 10 working days of making the

determination. MO. REV. STAT. §
376.1363.4 (2003).

2. **Reasons for adverse determination.** Written notice of an adverse   determination shall include principal reason or reasons, instructions for initiating an appeal or reconsideration, and instructions for requesting a written statement of the clinical rationale, including the clinical review criteria. MO. REV. STAT. § 376.1363.5 (2003).

3. **Notice of Appeal Rights.** Required in written notification.

B. **Appeals requirements.** Health carriers that offer managed care plans shall have a first level and second level grievance review process for managed care plans. MO. REV. STAT. § 376.1382.1 (2003); *See* MO. REV. STAT. § 376.1375 et seq. (2003) for specific grievance procedure filing requirements.

1. Time frame for determination. Upon request for a first level grievance, a health carrier shall acknowledge receipt in writing within 10 days, conduct a complete investigation within 20 days after receipt, have a party not involved in grievance or investigation decide upon appropriate resolution within 5 days after completing investigation, and notify the enrollee in writing within 15 days of completing the decision of the resolution and the right to file a second-level appeal. MO. REV. STAT. § 376.1382 et seq. (2003).

2. A health carrier shall submit a request for a second-level review to a "grievance advisory panel" consisting of other enrollee, and representatives of the health carrier that were not involved in the circumstances giving rise to the grievance. MO. REV. STAT. § 376.1385.1 (2004). The grievance advisory panel shall follow the same time frames as for first-level review. A health carrier shall establish written procedures for expedited review of grievances where there is serious jeopardy to the life or health of an enrollee's ability to regain maximum function. MO. REV. STAT. § 376.1385.2 (2004). A health carrier shall orally notify an enrollee within 72 hours of receiving such a request for expedited review and shall provide written confirmation within three working days of providing notification. MO. REV. STAT. § 376.1389.2 (2004).

3. External appeals. The Director of Insurance shall resolve any grievance regarding an adverse determination as to covered services appealed by an enrollee or health carrier or plan sponsor. If unresolved after completion of the Department of Insurance's consumer complaint process, the Director shall refer the grievance to an independent review organization. MO. REV. STAT. § 376.1387 (2004); MO. CODE REGS tit. 20, § 100-5.020 (2004).

C. **Emergency Services.** A health carrier must cover emergency services to screen and stabilize a patient. If the patient requires immediate post-evaluation or post-stabilization services, the carrier must render an authorization decision within 60 minutes of receiving a request. If the authorization decision is not made within 30 minutes, such services shall be deemed approved. Coverage of emergency services shall be subject to applicable cost-sharing requirements MO. REV. STAT. § 376.1367 (2004).

VII. Recognition of URAC Accreditation Status

A. **Does the state recognize URAC accreditation?** Yes.

B. **Which of the state's requirements are waived for URAC-accredited organizations?** A health carrier may satisfy the requirement for a written utilization review program by implementing the most recent utilization review program it has submitted to URAC, if that program reflects current policies, processes, and procedures, and is supplemented to address any Missouri requirements not in the URAC accreditation standards. MO. CODE REGS. tit. 20, § 400-10.010 (2004).

VIII. Miscellaneous

There are additional requirements for review of prescription drugs. Health carriers must provide coverage for prescription drugs and for any drug that has been approved by the Food and Drug Administration for at least one indication or is recognized for treatment of the covered indication in one of the standard reference compendia or in peer-reviewed medical literature. *See* MO. REV. STAT. § 376.1361.11 (2004).

A health carrier may not retract an authorization for medical services unless such authorization was based on material misrepresentation or omission about the patient's condition or the patient was not enrolled at the time of the service. MO. CODE REGS. tit. 20, § 400-10.200 (2004).

Montana

I. Scope and Applicability

A. **Who is subject to the state's utilization review laws?** Any entity that conducts utilization review that is or is affiliated with a Montana business entity; a third party that providers or administers health care benefits to a Montana citizen; a health insurer, nonprofit health service plan, health service corporation, employees' health and welfare fund, or preferred provider organization authorized to offer health insurance policies or contracts; a health maintenance organization (HMO); or a state agency. MONT. CODE ANN. § 33-32-105(1) (2004).
   1. HMO's? Yes.
   2. Insurers? Yes.
   3. Utilization review organizations? Yes.
   4. Retrospective review? Yes.

B. **What exemptions are provided, if any?** Exemptions are provided for in-house utilization review activities, including those for a long-term care facility and those required by Medicaid and Medicare, that do not result in payment decisions and for peer review procedures conducted by a professional society or association of providers. MONT. CODE ANN. § 33-32-105(2) (2004).

C. **What term does the state use to refer to regulated entities?** A person or entity performing utilization review of health care services provided or to be provided to a patient covered under a contract or plan for health care services issued in Montana. MONT. CODE ANN. § 33-32-103(1) (2004).

D. **What activities does the state include in its definition of utilization review?** "Utilization review" means "a system for review of health care services for a patient to determine the necessity or appropriateness of services, whether that review is prospective, concurrent, or retrospective, when the review will be utilized directly or indirectly in order to determine whether the health care services will be paid, covered, or provided." The definition does not include "routine claim administration or determination that does not include determinations of medical necessity or appropriateness." MONT. CODE ANN. § 33-32-102(4)(a) (2004).

II. Regulatory Information

A. **Responsible state agency.** Montana Insurance Division, State Auditor's Office.

B. **Contact Information.**
   1. **Name and Title:** Pam Forsman, Forms Analyst.
   2. **Address:** Montana Insurance Division, State Auditor's Office, 840 Helena Avenue, Helena, MT 59601.
   3. **Phone and Facsimile:** (406) 444-9751; facsimile (406) 444-3497.
   4. **E-mail:** pforsman@state.mt.us
   5. **Web site:** http://sao.state.mt.us/sao/insurance/index.html

III. Licensure/Certification Requirements

A. **What entities are required to obtain a license in the state to conduct utilization review for residents of the state?** Montana does not require a license or certificate but does require the filing of specific documents. MONT. CODE ANN. § 33-32-103(1) (2004).

B. **How often must licensure be renewed?** Not applicable.

C. **Licensure fees (initial and renewal).** Not applicable.

D. **Documentation required.** "A person may not conduct a utilization review of health care services provided or to be provided to a patient covered under a contract or plan for health care services issued in [Montana] unless that person, at all times, maintains with the [C]ommissioner [of Insurance] a current utilization review plan…" MONT. CODE ANN. § 33-32-103 (2004).

E. **Exemption from licensure.** Out-of-state organizations are not granted an exemption from Montana's licensure and certification requirements even if they are duly licensed and/or certified in their state of domicile.

IV. Program Requirements

A. **Clinical review criteria.** Utilization review plan must include review criteria, standards, and procedures to be used in evaluating proposed or delivered health care services that, to the extent possible, must:
   1. be based on nationally recognized criteria, standards, and procedures;
   2. reflect community standards of care, except that a utilization review plan for health care services under the Medicaid program provided for in Title 53 need not reflect community standards of care;
   3. ensure quality of care; and
   4. ensure access to needed health care services;

5. the provisions by which patients or providers may seek reconsideration or appeal of adverse decisions by the person conducting the utilization review;

6. the type and qualifications of the personnel either employed or under contract to perform the utilization review;

7. policies and procedures to ensure that a representative of the person conducting the utilization review is reasonably accessible to patients and health care providers at all times;

8. policies and procedures to ensure compliance with all applicable state and federal laws to protect the confidentiality of individual medical records;

9. a copy of the materials designed to inform applicable patients and health care providers of the requirements of the utilization review plan.
MONT. CODE ANN. § 33-32-103 (2004).

B. **Prohibitions against financial incentives.** No provision.

C. **Telephone access standards.** Utilization review plan shall ensure that a representative of person conducting utilization review is "reasonably accessible to patients and health care providers at all times." MONT. CODE ANN. § 33-32-103(4) (2004).

D. **Quality assurance program.** No provision.

E. **Delegation of utilization review functions.** No provision.

F. **Confidentiality.** Utilization review plan must include policies and procedures to ensure compliance with all applicable state and federal laws protecting the confidentiality of individual medical records. When a utilization review requires disclosure of personal information regarding the patient or client, including personal and family history or current and past symptoms of a mental disorder, then the identity of that individual must be concealed from anyone having access that information so patient or client may remain anonymous. *See* MONT. CODE ANN. § 33-32-103(5) (2004); MONT. CODE ANN. § 33-32-201(1) (2004); MONT. CODE ANN. § 33-32-201(2) (2004).

V. **Reviewer Qualifications**
A. Qualifications of reviewers that render utilization review determinations (at each level of utilization review, if applicable).

B. Adverse determinations must be evaluated by a health professional trained in the relevant area of

health care. MONT. CODE ANN. § 33-32-201(3) (2004).

C. If the treating provider is a licensed social worker, licensed professional counselor, licensed psychiatric nurse, licensed psychiatrist, or licensed psychologist, the review must be conducted by a person trained in the same field as the provider. MONT. CODE ANN. § 33-32-201(5) (2004).

D. **Requirements for medical director.** Each managed care organization shall employ or contract with a physician who must be licensed in the state pursuant to Title 37, chapter 3, to serve as medical director. MONT. CODE ANN. § 33-37-110 (2004).

E. **Requirement for "same-state" licensure.** No provision.

VI. **Reviews and Appeals**
A. **Review determinations and notice to patients/providers.**
1. A determination that is made on appeal or reconsideration as provided in 33-32-203 and that is adverse to a patient or to an affected health care provider may not be made on a question relating to the necessity or appropriateness of a health care service without prior written findings, evaluation, and concurrence in the adverse determination by a health care professional trained in the relevant area of health care. Copies of the written findings, evaluation, and concurrence must be provided to the patient on request. MONT. CODE ANN. § 33-32-201(3) (2004).

2. A determination made on appeal or reconsideration, as provided in 33-32- 203, that health care services rendered or to be rendered are medically inappropriate may not be made unless the health care professional performing the utilization review has made a reasonable attempt to consult with the patient's attending health care provider concerning the necessity or appropriateness of the health care service. MONT. CODE ANN. § 33-32-201(4) (2004).

3. For services provided by a a health care provider who is a licensed social worker, licensed professional counselor, licensed psychiatric nurse, licensed psychiatrist, or a licensed psychologist, the patient may, at the patient's expense, request an independent review of the patient's or the provider's records by a health care provider licensed in

the field of the provider that rendered the health care service and may require that review to be considered by the insurer in reaching its decision. If the initial adverse determination of medical necessity or appropriateness is reversed, the insurer shall bear the expense of the independent review. MONT. CODE ANN. § 33-32-201(5)(b) (2004).

4. Time frame for determination. A managed care entity shall notify an enrollee and health care provider of any adverse determination within 10 calendar days from date of decision, if decision involves routine medical care. If the decision involves a medical care determination that qualifies for expedited review, a managed care entity shall notify an enrollee and health care provider within 48 hours from the date of decision, excluding Sundays and holidays. MONT. ADMIN. R. 37.108.310(1) (2004).

5. Reasons for adverse determination. Notice shall explain reasons for adverse determination. MONT. ADMIN. R. 37.108.310(2)(c) (2004).

6. Notice of Appeal Rights. Notice shall include an explanation of enrollee's right to appeal adverse determination or to submit adverse determination for an independent review and provide instructions on initiating an appeal or independent review. MONT. ADMIN. R. 37.108.310(2)(d) (2004).

B. **Appeals requirements.** A patient or provider affected by a utilization review decision has at least 30 days to file an appeal or to seek reconsideration of the adverse decision. MONT. CODE ANN. § 33-32-203(1) (2004). Copies of written findings, evaluation, and concurrence on a question relating to the necessity or appropriateness of a health care service must be provided to the patient on request. Before seeking an independent review, an enrollee or authorized representative must exhaust the managed care entity's internal appeals unless the internal appeals process is not completed within 60 calendar or if serious threat to health or life involved. MONT. ADMIN. R. 37.108.315(1) (2004).

C. **Time frame for determination.** A final decision on appeal or reconsideration must be made within 60 days of receipt of all relevant medical information. MONT. CODE ANN. § 33-32-201(5)(b) (2004).

D. **External appeals.** A health carrier or managed care entity or an agent of a health carrier or managed care entity, other than a health carrier or other managed care entity providing medicaid-funded services or any other publicly funded health care-related services authorized under Title 50, 52, or 53, shall permit any party whose appeal of an adverse determination is denied by the health carrier, the managed care entity, or the agent of the health carrier or managed care entity to seek independent review of that determination by a peer or, if the health carrier or managed care entity does not maintain an appeals process, permit any party receiving an adverse determination to seek independent review of that determination. MONT. CODE ANN. § 33-37-102 (2004). During the course of an appeal, the patient may, at the patient's expense, request an independent review by a health care provider licensed in the same field as the treating provider. If the adverse determination is reversed, the insurer shall bear the cost of the independent review. In the case of routine health care decisions, the peer or independent review organization shall notify managed care entity, enrollee, and health care provider of decision within 30 calendar days of receiving case file. In the case of an expedited review, the peer or independent review organization shall notify the managed care entity, enrollee, and health care provider within 72 hours. MONT. ADMIN. R. 37.108.305(4) (2004).

E. **Emergency Services.** Under the new rules for independent review, if a health care treatment decision results in a serious threat to the health or life of the enrollee, upon certification by health care provider, the internal appeals process can be bypassed and the matter immediately submitted for expedited review. MONT. ADMIN. R. 37.108.315(1)(b) (2004).

VII. Recognition of URAC Accreditation Status
A. Does the state recognize URAC accreditation? No
B. Which of the state's requirements are waived for URAC-accredited organizations? Not applicable.

Nebraska

I. Scope and Applicability

A. **Who is subject to the state's utilization review laws?** Any person, company health carrier, organization or other entity that performs utilization review. NEB. REV. STAT. § 44-5418(31) (2004).

1. HMO's? Yes.
2. Insurers? Yes.
3. Utilization review organizations? Yes.
4. Retrospective review? Yes.

B. **What exceptions are provided, if any?** Exceptions are provided for agencies of the state or federal government; internal quality assurance programs conducted by hospitals, home health agencies, preferred provider organizations (PPO's), health maintenance organizations (HMO's), other managed care entities, clinics, or private offices for purposes other than claims payment; Nebraska licensed pharmacists, pharmacies, or organizations engaged in the practice of pharmacy; any person performing utilization review of workers' compensation benefits; or any employee benefit plan exempt from state regulation under the Employee Retirement Income Security Act of 1974 (ERISA). NEB. REV. STAT. § 44-5418(31) (2004).

C. **What term does the state use to refer to regulated entities?** A "utilization review agent" is "any person, company, health carrier, organization, or other entity performing utilization review." NEB. REV. STAT. § 44-5418(31) (2004).

D. **What activities does the state include in its definition of utilization review?** "Utilization review" means "a set of formal techniques designed to monitor the use of, or evaluate the clinical necessity, appropriateness, efficacy, or efficiency of, health care services, procedures, or facilities." Envisioned techniques include "ambulatory review, prospective review, second opinion, certification, concurrent review, case management, discharge planning, or retrospective review." The definition does not include "elective requests for clarification of coverage." NEB. REV. STAT. § 44-5418(30) (2004).

II. Regulatory Information

A. **Responsible state agency.** Nebraska Department of Insurance, Licensing Division.

B. **Contact Information.**

1. **Name and Title:** Beverly Creager, Administrator.

2. **Address:** Nebraska Department of Insurance, Licensing Division, 941 "O" Street, Suite 400, Lincoln, NE 68508.

3. **Phone and Facsimile:** (402) 471-4707; facsimile (402) 471-6559.

4. **E-mail:** bcreager@doi.state.ne.us.

5. **Web site:** www.nol.org/home/ndoi.

III. Licensure/Certification Requirements

A. **What entities are required to obtain a license in the state to conduct utilization review for residents of the state?** A utilization review agent may not conduct utilization review upon a covered person in this state unless the agent is granted a certificate by the director. NEB. REV. STAT. § 44-5419 (2004).

B. **How often must licensure be renewed?** Every 2 years. NEB. REV. STAT. § 44-5419 (2004).

C. **Licensure fees (initial and renewal).** $300 initial application fee; $100 renewal. NEB. REV. STAT. § 44-5420(1) (2004).

D. **Documentation required for licensure.** Utilization review agents must submit an application form, documentation that they have been accredited by URAC (or a similar organization with substantially similar standards, which the Director of Insurance has approved), and other reasonable information or documentation required by the Department of Insurance. NEB. REV. STAT. § 44-5420(2) (2004).

E. **Exemptions from licensure.** Out-of-state organizations are not granted an exemption from the state's licensure and certification requirements even if they are duly licensed and/or certified in their state of domicile.

IV. Program Requirements

A. **Clinical review criteria.** A utilization review program shall use documented clinical review criteria that are based on sound clinical evidence and periodically evaluated to assure continuing efficacy. A health carrier may develop its own clinical review criteria or it may purchase or license clinical review criteria from qualified vendors. A health carrier shall make available its clinical review criteria upon request to authorized government agencies. NEB. REV. STAT. § 44-5426 (2004).

B. **Prohibitions against financial incentives.** A utilization review agent may not refer a patient to a health care facility in which the agent has a significant beneficial interest or a utilization review agent's own health care practice. This does not apply to HMO's or PPO in-network referrals. A utilization review agent may not offer compensation based directly on the number of adverse determinations. NEB. REV. STAT. § 44-5422 (2004).

C. **Telephone access standards.** No provision specifically for utilization review entities, but a health carrier shall print on its membership cards a toll-free telephone number to call for utilization review decisions. NEB. REV. STAT. § 44-5420(2)(a) (2004).

D. **Quality assurance program.** A health carrier that issues a closed plan or a combination plan having a closed component shall develop and maintain the internal structures and activities necessary to improve quality as required. NEB. REV. STAT. § 44-7207 (2004).

E. **Delegation of utilization review functions.** A health carrier shall be responsible for monitoring all utilization review activities carried out by, or on behalf of, the health carrier and for ensuring that all requirements of the Utilization Review Act and applicable rules and regulations are met. The health carrier shall also ensure that appropriate personnel have operational responsibility for the conduct of the health carrier's utilization review program.

F. **Confidentiality.** No provision.

V. Reviewer Qualifications

A. **Qualifications of reviewers that render utilization review determinations (at each level of utilization review, if applicable).** During a final appeal of a decision not to certify or approve for clinical reasons, a utilization review agent shall assure that a physician is reasonably available to review the case, except that if the health care services were provided or authorized by a provider other than a physician, such appeal may be reviewed by a nonphysician provider whose scope of practice includes the treatment or services. NEB. REV. STAT. § 44-5422(f) (2004).

B. **Requirements for medical director.** No provision.

C. **Requirement for "same-state" licensure.** No provision.

VI. Reviews and Appeals

A. **Review determinations and notice to patients/providers.**

B. **Time frame for determination.** No provision.

C. **Reasons for adverse determination.** A covered person or attending physician on behalf of a covered person shall, upon request, have timely access to the clinical basis for the decision,

including any criteria, standards, or clinical indicators used as a basis for such recommendation or decision. NEB. REV. STAT. § 44-5422(e) (2004). For first level grievance review under the Health Carrier Grievance Procedure Act, if a covered person makes a request to a health carrier for a health care service and the request is denied, the health carrier shall provide the covered person with an explanation of the reasons for the denial, a written notice of how to submit a grievance, and the telephone number to call for information and assistance. NEB. REV. STAT. § 44-7308(1) (2004).

D. **Notice of Appeal Rights.** No specific provision, however, NEB. REV. STAT. § 44-7307(1) (2004) requires a description of the grievance procedure for health carriers to be set forth in the policy, certificate, membership booklet, outline of coverage, or other evidence of coverage provide to the covered person.

E. **Appeals requirements.** No specific provision for utilization review agents, but health carriers must offer covered persons a first-level grievance review, a second-level grievance review, and expedited reviews. *See* NEB. REV. STAT. § 44-7308 (2004); NEB. REV. STAT. § 44-7309 (2004); NEB. REV. STAT. § 44-7310 (2004), NEB. REV. STAT. § 44-7311 (2004).

F. **Time frame for determination.** Standard reviews shall be completed in writing within 15 working days of the request for a review. NEB. REV. STAT. § 44-7310 (3)(2004).

G. **External appeals.** No provision, though a covered person may contact the Director of Insurance for assistance at any time with a grievance against a health carrier.

H. **Emergency Services.** A utilization review agent must allow a minimum of 24 hours following an emergency admission or service for the patient to request certification. Expedited reviews of a grievance involving a situation in which the timeframe explained above would seriously jeopardize the life or health of a covered person's ability to regain maximum function shall be handled as expeditiously as the condition requires, but no later than 72 hours after commencing the review. NEB. REV. STAT. § 44-5422(1)(d) (2004).

VII. Recognition of URAC Accreditation Status

A. **Does the state recognize URAC accreditation?** Yes.

B. **Which of the state's requirements are waived for URAC-accredited organizations?** No provisions are waived, but to be certified in Nebraska, a utilization review agent must submit with their application documentation that the applicant has received approval or accreditation by the American Accreditation HealthCare Commission/URAC, or a similar organization which has standards for utilization review agents that are substantially similar to the standards of the American Accreditation HealthCare Commission/URAC, and which has been approved by the Director. NEB. REV. STAT. § 44-5420(2)(a) (2004).

VIII. Miscellaneous

Nebraska has enacted the Health Carrier Grievance Procedure Act (*see* NEB. REV. STAT. §§ 44-7303 through 44-7315). This act applies to health carriers that offer managed care plans. For purposes of this act, an "adverse determination" is "a determination by a health carrier or its designee utilization review agent that an admission, availability of care, continued stay, or other health care service has been reviewed and, based upon the information provided, does not meet the health carrier's requirements for medical necessity, appropriateness, health care setting, level of care, or effectiveness, and the requested health care service is therefor denied, reduced, or terminated." NEB. REV. STAT. § 44-7303(1).

Nevada

I. Scope and Applicability

A. **Who is subject to the state's utilization review laws?** Any entity that performs utilization review.

   1. **HMO's?** No. The Nevada Health Maintenance Organization Act, NEV. REV. STAT. ANN. §§ 695C.010 et seq. (2004), does not explicitly address utilization review.

   2. **Insurers?** No.

   3. **Utilization review organizations?** Yes.

   4. **Retrospective review?** Yes.

B. **What exemptions are provided, if any?** There are exemptions for entities performing utilization review on behalf of the federal government. Nevada's statute applies to third parties that perform utilization review and exempts authorized insurers; fraternal benefit societies; nonprofit corporations for hospital, medical, or dental services; health maintenance organizations (HMO's); and organizations for dental care that perform their own utilization review. NEV. REV. STAT. ANN. § 683A.377 (2004)

C. **What term does the state use to refer to regulated entities?** An "agent who performs utilization review" is "any person who performs such review except a person acting on behalf of the Federal Government, but only to the extent that the person provides the service for the Federal Government or an agency thereof." NEV. REV. STAT. ANN. § 683A.376(1) (2004).

D. **What activities does the state include in its definition of utilization review?** "Utilization review" is defined as "a system that provides, at a minimum, for review of the necessity and appropriateness of the allocation of health care resources and services provided or proposed to be provided to an insured. The term does not include responding to requests made by an insured for clarification of his coverage." NEV. REV. STAT. ANN. § 683A.376(3) (2004).

II. Regulatory Information

A. **Responsible state agency.** Department of Business and Industry, Division of Insurance.

B. **Contact Information.**

   1. **Name and Title:** Kristin Kinsley & Lou Roggensack, Administrative Officer/ Medical Relations.

   2. **Address:** Nevada Division of Insurance, 788 Fairview Drive, Suite 300, Carson City, NV 89701.

   3. **Phone and Facsimile:** (775) 687-4270; facsimile (775) 687-3937.

   4. **E-mail:** kkinsley@doi.state.nv.us & roggen@doi.state.nv.us

   5. **Web site:** http://www.doi.state.nv.us.

III. Licensure/Certification Requirements

A. **What entities are required to obtain a license in the state to conduct utilization review for residents of the state?** A person shall not conduct utilization review unless he is registered with the commissioner as an agent who performs utilization review and has a medical director who is a physician or, in the case of an agent who reviews dental services, a dentist, licensed in any state, or employed by a registered agent who performs utilization review. NEV. REV. STAT. ANN. § 683A.378 (2004).

B. **How often must license/certification be renewed?** Annually, before March 1.

C. **Registration fees (initial and renewal).** $250 for initial and renewal fee. NEV. REV. STAT. ANN. § 683A.378(2) (2004).

D. **Documentation required for registration.** The following is required: The applicant's name, address, telephone number and normal business hours. The name and telephone number of a person the commissioner may contact for information concerning the applicant. The name of the medical director of the applicant and the state in which he is licensed to practice medicine or dentistry; and a summary of the plan for utilization review, including procedures for appealing determinations made through utilization review. NEV. REV. STAT. ANN. § 683A.378(2) (2004). The application form (Application for Certificate of Registration for Utilization Review) is available on the Division of Insurance's Web site (www.doi.state.nv.us).

E. **Exemptions from licensure.** Out-of-state organizations are not granted an exemption from the state's licensure and certification requirements even if they are duly licensed and/or certified in their state of domicile.

IV. Program Requirements

A. **Clinical review criteria.** No provision.

B. **Prohibitions against financial incentives.** No provision. HMO's may not allow a health care provider who has a financial interest of more than 10 percent in a delivery system intermediary to participate on a utilization review committee or taking any action to change an authorization made by the utilization review committee or an authorized physician. NEV. ADMIN. CODE ch. 695 §505(13) (2004).

C. **Quality assurance program.** No provision.

D. **Delegation of utilization review functions.** No provision, though under NEV. REV. STAT. ANN. § 695G.120 (2004), each managed care organization shall require any person with whom it subcontracts to provide utilization review to use the same written policies and procedures.

E. **Confidentiality.** No provision.

V. Reviewer Qualifications

A. **Qualifications of reviewers that render utilization review determinations (at each level of utilization review, if applicable).** No provision.

B. **Requirements for medical director.** The agent must have a medical director who is a licensed physician. For agents that review dental services, the medical director must be a licensed dentist. NEV. REV. STAT. ANN. § 683A.378(2)(c) (2004).

C. **Requirement for "same-state" licensure.** No provision.

VI. Reviews and Appeals

A. **Review determinations and notice to patients/providers.** No provision.

B. **Time frame for determination.** Not applicable.

C. **Contents of notice of adverse determination.** Not applicable.

D. **Reasons for adverse determination.** Not applicable.

E. **Notice of Appeal Rights.** Not applicable.

F. **Appeals requirements.** The utilization review plan must include procedures for appealing utilization review determinations.

G. **Time frame for determination.** No provision.

H. **External appeals.** An external review organization shall not conduct an external review of a final adverse determination unless the external review organization is certified in accordance with regulations adopted by the Commissioner. NEV. REV. STAT. ANN. § 683A.371(1) (2004). (Enacted July 1st, 2004). This new statute has brand new requirements such as an external review organization must demonstrate to the Commissioner of Insurance, without limitation, proof that the external review organization employs, contracts with or otherwise retains only persons who are qualified because of their education, training, professional licensing and experience to perform the duties assigned to those persons. NEV. REV. STAT. ANN. § 683A.371(1)3(a) (2004).

I. **Emergency Services.** No provision.

VII. Recognition of URAC Accreditation Status

A. **Does the state recognize URAC accreditation?** No.

B. **Which of the state's requirements are waived for URAC-accredited organizations?** Not applicable.

VIII. Miscellaneous

Each managed care plan shall have a policy for resolving complaints of insureds, including adverse determinations made through utilization review. *See* NEV. REV. STAT. ANN. § 695G.200(1)(b) (2004).

New Hampshire

I. Scope and Applicability

A. **Who is subject to the state's utilization review laws?** Any person, partnership or corporation, other than an insurer, nonprofit service organization, health maintenance organization, or an employee of those exempt organizations, that performs medical utilization review services on behalf of commercial insurers, nonprofit service organizations, health maintenance organizations, third-party administrators or employers. N.H. REV. STAT. ANN. § 420-E:2(I) (2004).

   1. **HMO's?** Yes, except for utilization review licensure requirement. HMO's that do not contract with a utilization review entity are exempt from licensure as a utilization review entity, but shall conform to URAC's standards and all applicable rules issued by the Insurance Commissioner. N.H. REV. STAT. ANN. §§ 420-J:6(I) (2004).

   2. **Insurers?** Yes, except for utilization review licensure requirement.

   3. **Utilization review organizations?** Yes.

   4. **Retrospective review?** Yes.

B. **What exemptions are provided, if any?** Any organization that performs medical utilization review activities solely for research purposes or solely for Medicaid, Medicare, or the Civilian Health and Medical Program of the United States (CHAMPUS) is exempt. In addition, insurers, nonprofit service organizations, HMO's, or an employee of such organizations that do not contract with a utilization review entity are exempt from licensure as a utilization review entity. Note: Such organizations shall conform to either URAC's or National Committee for Quality Assurance's (NCQA) standards and all applicable rules issued by Insurance Commissioner. N.H. REV. STAT. ANN. § 420-E:2(I) (2004).

C. **What term does the state use to refer to regulated entities?** A "medical utilization review entity" or "utilization review entity" is "any person, partnership, or corporation which provides utilization review services." N.H. CODE ADMIN. R. [INS.] 2001.03(10) (2004); N.H. REV. STAT. ANN. § 420-E:2(I) (2004).

D. **What activities does the state include in its definition of utilization review?** "Utilization review" is defined as "a system for reviewing the appropriate and efficient allocation of hospital, medical or other health care services given to a patient or group of patients as to necessity, for the purpose of recommending or determining whether such services should be covered or provided by an insurer, nonprofit service organization, [HMO], third-party administrator or employer. The terms include those programs or processes whether they apply prospectively or retrospectively to medical services." The definition includes "second opinion programs; prehospital admission certification; preinpatient service eligiblity certification; and concurrent hospital review to determine appropriate length of stay." The definition does not include "claims review or decisions." N.H. REV. STAT. ANN. §§ 420-E:1(IV) (2004).

II. Regulatory Information

A. **Responsible state agency.** New Hampshire Insurance Department, Examination Division.

B. **Contact Information.**

   1. **Name and Title:** Mary Verville, Examination Division

   2. **Address:** New Hampshire Insurance Department, Examination Division

   3. 21 South Fruit Street, Suite 14

   4. Concord, NH 03301.

   5. **Phone and Facsimile:** (603) 271-7973 facsimile (603) 271-0248

   6. **E-mail:** mary.verville@ins.nh.gov

   7. **Web site:** www.nh.gov/insurance

III. Licensure Requirements

A. **What entities are required to obtain a license in the state to conduct utilization review for residents of the state?** Any person, partnership or corporation, other than an insurer, nonprofit service organization, health maintenance organization, or an employee of those exempt organizations, that performs medical utilization review services on behalf of commercial insurers, nonprofit service organizations, health maintenance organizations, third-party administrators or employers. N.H. REV. STAT. ANN. § 420-E:2(I) (2004).

B. **How often must licensure be renewed?** Annually, on or before April 1. N.H. REV. STAT. ANN. § 420-E:3(I) (2004).

C. **Licensure fees (initial and renewal).** $500 initial and $100 renewal. There is a $25 fee for changing a name on the license.

D. **Documentation required for licensure.** The process used by the entity to carry out its utilization review services, including the categories of health care personnel that perform utilization review activities and whether or not such individuals are licensed in this state.

  1. The process used by the entity for addressing beneficiary or provider complaints.

  2. The types of utilization review programs offered by the entity, including, but not limited to: a) Second opinion programs. b) Prehospital admission certification. c) Preinpatient service eligibility determination. d) Concurrent hospital review to determine appropriate length of stay.

  3. The process used by the entity to preserve beneficiary confidentiality of medical information. N.H. REV. STAT. ANN. § 420-E:3(I) (2004).

E. **Exemption from licensure.** Out-of-state organizations are not granted an exemption from the state's licensure and certification requirements even if they are duly licensed and/or certified in their state of domicile.

IV. Program Requirements

A. **Clinical review criteria.** Clinical criteria must be:

  1. Developed with input from appropriate actively practicing practitioners in the carrier or other licensed entity's service area;

  2. Updated at least biennially and as new treatments, applications, and technologies emerge;

  3. Developed in accordance with the standards of national accreditation entities;

  4. Based on current, nationally accepted standards of medical practice; and

  5. If practicable, evidence-based. N.H. REV. STAT. ANN. § 420-E:4(III) (2004).

B. **Standards.** Each person, partnership, or corporation licensed under this chapter shall adopt as the minimal acceptable standards for licensure either the Utilization Review Accreditation Commission (URAC) standards, the National Committee for Quality Assurance (NCQA) standards, or other similar standards acceptable to the commissioner, unless stricter standards are adopted. N.H. REV. STAT. ANN. § 420-E:3(II) (2004).

C. **Prohibitions against financial incentives.** No provision.

D. **Telephone access standards.** The licensee shall maintain a toll-free telephone number to ensure that a representative of the licensee shall be accessible by telephone to insureds, patients, and providers 7 days a week during normal working hours in the provider's local time zone. N.H. REV. STAT. ANN. § 420-E:4(I) (2004); N.H. CODE ADMIN. R. [INS.] 2001.12 (2004)

E. **Quality assurance program.** No provision, but under N.H. REV. STAT. ANN. § 420-J:9(II) (2004), a health carrier shall establish and maintain a written quality assessment program and quality improvement program.

F. **Delegation of utilization review functions.** No provision

G. **Confidentiality.** Medical utilization review entities must comply with all applicable state and federal laws protecting the confidentiality of individual medical records. N.H. REV. STAT. ANN. § 420-E:4(VI) (2004).

V. Reviewer Qualifications

A. **Qualifications of reviewers that render utilization review determinations (at each level of utilization review, if applicable).**

  1. Licensed or certified health care providers shall make initial review determinations. N.H. REV. STAT. ANN. § 420-E:4(II) (2004).

  2. All communications on the part of a medical utilization review entity or exempt organization with either a beneficiary or provider, other than communications carried out for the purpose of collecting and recording demographic data, shall be conducted by personnel who are licensed health care providers. N.H. CODE ADMIN. R. [INS.] 2001.16(b) (2004)

  3. On reconsideration, persons of the same or similar specialty as the patient's health care provider shall make utilization review determinations. N.H. REV. STAT. ANN. § 420-J:5(II)(a) (2004); N.H.

  4. URAC standards also apply.

B. **Requirements for medical director.** Every medical utilization review entity licensed by the department under this chapter shall employ a medical director who is licensed by New Hampshire. N.H. REV. STAT. ANN. § 420-E:2a (2004); N.H. CODE ADMIN. R. [INS.] 2001.16(c) (2004)

C. **Requirement for "same-state" licensure.** No provision.

VI. Reviews and Appeals

A. **Review determinations and notice to patients/providers.**

  1. Time frame for determination.

a. **Urgent Claims.** The determination of a claim involving urgent care shall be made as soon as possible, taking into account the medical exigencies, but in no event later than 72 hours after receipt of the claim, unless the claimant or claimant's representative fails to provide sufficient information to determine whether, or to what extent, benefits are covered or payable. N.H. REV. STAT. ANN. § 420-E:4(IV)(a) (2004).

b. **Standard Claims.** The determination of all other claims for preservice benefits shall be made within a reasonable time period appropriate to the medical circumstances, but in no event more than 15 days after receipt of the claim. This period may be extended one time by the licensee for up to 15 days; provided, that the licensee both determines that such an extension is necessary due to matters beyond the control of the licensee and notifies the claimant or claimant's representative, prior to the expiration of the initial 15-day period, of the circumstances requiring the extension of time and the date by which the licensee expects to render a decision. N.H. REV. STAT. ANN. § 420-E:4(IV)(c) (2004).

c. **Retrospective Claims.** The determination of a post service claim shall be made within 30 days of the date of filing. N.H. REV. STAT. ANN. § 420-E:4(IV)(d) (2004).

2. **Contents of notice of adverse determination.** Notice to the claimant or their representative must be in writing. N.H. REV. STAT. ANN. § 420-E:4(V)(a) (2004).

3. **Reasons for adverse determination.** The notification shall state the specific reason or reasons for the determination and shall refer to the specific provision of the policy or plan on which the determination is based. N.H. REV. STAT. ANN. § 420-E:4(V)(b) (2004).

4. **Notice of Appeal Rights.** The notification shall include a statement of the claimant's right or the right of the claimant's representative to access the internal grievance process and the process for obtaining external review. N.H. REV. STAT. ANN. § 420-E:4(V)(c) (2004).

B. **Appeals requirements.**
1. **Internal Grievance Procedure.** Every carrier or other licensed entity shall establish and shall maintain a written procedure by which a claimant or a representative of the claimant, shall have a reasonable opportunity to appeal a claim denial to the carrier or other licensed entity, and under which there shall be a full and fair review of the claim denial. N.H. REV. STAT. ANN. § 420-J:5 (2004).

a. The persons reviewing the grievance shall not be the same person or persons making the initial determination, and shall not be subordinate to or the supervisor of the person making the initial determination.

b. The person reviewing the grievance on a first or second level appeal have appropriate medical and professional expertise and credentialing to competently render a determination on appeal. The claimant shall have at least 180 days following receipt of a notification of a claim denial to appeal; N.H. REV. STAT. ANN. § 420-J:5 (I)(2004).

c. For urgent care claims, the determination of the appeal not more than 72 hours after the submission of the request for appeal. N.H. REV. STAT. ANN. § 420-J:5 (II)(2004).

d. In the case of nonexpedited appeal of a pre-service claim or post-service claim, the determination on appeal shall be made within a reasonable time appropriate to the medical circumstances, but in no event more than 30 days after receipt by the carrier or other licensed entity of the claimant's appeal. N.H. REV. STAT. ANN. § 420-J:5 (III)(2004).

2. **External Review.** A covered person shall have the right to independent external review of a determination by a health carrier or its designee utilization review entity when all of the following conditions apply:

a. There must be an adverse determination;

b. The covered person has completed the internal review procedures provided by the carrier, or the covered person has requested a first or second level standard or expedited review and has not received a decision by the carrier within the required time frames;

c. The request for external review has been made within 180 days of the carriers second level denial;

d. The cost of service is equal to or exceeds $400 dollars;

e. The service is not excluded form those designated for external review;

f. The claim is not based on malpractice or negligence. N.H. REV. STAT. ANN. § 420-J:5-a(I)(2004).

3. **Time frame for External Review determination.**

a. For standard reviews it must be within 20 days of the date that any new or additional information from the covered person is due. N.H. REV. STAT. ANN. § 420-J:5-b(X)(2004).

b. For expedited review it must be within 72 hours. N.H. REV. STAT. ANN. § 420-J:5-c(VI)(2004).

VII. Recognition of URAC Accreditation Status

A. **Does the state recognize URAC accreditation?** Yes.

B. **Which of the state's requirements are waived for URAC-accredited organizations?** URAC's or NCQA's standards are the minimum acceptable standards for licensure unless the Insurance Commissioner adopts rules establishing stricter standards. N.H. REV. STAT. ANN. §§ 420-E:3 (2004). In addition, each health carrier that does not contract with a utilization review entity shall establish written procedures for carrying out its utilization review processes and shall conform to URAC's or NCQA's standards.

New Jersey

I. Scope and Applicability

A. **Who is subject to the state's utilization review laws?** In New Jersey UM organizations are not directly regulated, but UM activities by HMO's, organized delivery systems, health carriers, and health plans are covered by specific statutory provisions. The New Jersey's Health Care Quality Act covers UM activities or components of UM, by, and on behalf of, carriers (insurance companies authorized to do business in N.J.), and certified/licensed organized delivery systems (Under the Organized Delivery Systems Act). N.J. ADMIN CODE tit. 8 § 38A-3.4 (2004). Managed care plans that constitute HMO's who engage in UM activities are covered under N.J. ADMIN CODE tit. 8 § 38A-8.1 (2004). Organized Delivery Systems (organizations that contract with carriers to provide for the provision of health care) who engage in UM are covered under N.J. ADMIN CODE tit. 8 § 38B-3.7 (2004).

  1. **HMO's?** Yes.
  2. **Insurers?** Yes
  3. **Utilization review organizations?** No

B. **What term does the state use to refer to regulated entities?** N.A.

C. **What activities does the state include in its definition of utilization review?** "Utilization management" is "a system for reviewing the appropriate and efficient allocation of health care services under a health benefits plan according to specified guidelines, in order to recommend or determine whether, or to what extent, a health care service given or proposed to be given to a covered person should or will be reimbursed, covered, paid for, or otherwise provided under the health benefits plan." This may include "preadmission certification, the application of practice guidelines, continued stay review, discharge planning, preauthorization of ambulatory care procedures and retrospective review." N.J. STAT. ANN. § 26:2S-2 (2004); *see also* N.J. ADMIN CODE tit. 8 § 38A-1.2 (2004); N.J. ADMIN CODE tit. 8 § 38-1.2 (2004); N.J. ADMIN CODE tit. 8 § 38B-1.2 (2004).

II. Regulatory Information

A. **Responsible state agency.** Department of Health and Senior Services, Office of Managed Care.

B. **Contact Information.**

  1. **Name and Title:** Sylvia Allen-Ware, Director.

  2. **Address:** Department of Health and Senior Services, Office of Managed Care, P.O. Box 360, Trenton, NJ 08625.

  3. **Phone and Facsimile:** (609) 633-0660; facsimile (609) 633-0807.

  4. **E-mail:** Sylvia.allen-ware@doh.state.nj.us.

  5. **Web site:** www.state.nj.us/health.

C. **Responsible State Agency:** New Jersey Department of Banking and Insurance, Managed Care Bureau, Life and Health division.

III. Licensure Requirements

A. **What entities are required to obtain a license in the state to conduct utilization review for residents of the state?** New Jersey does not certify or license utilization management. However, for most health carriers, organized delivery systems, and health plans that include UM as part of their services (or delegated to another entity), that entity would have to be either licensed by the Department of Banking and Insurance, or certified by the Department of Health and Senior Services. If the entity involved in UM activities is one that assumes financial risk, licensure must come from the Department of Banking and Insurance. If the entity involved in UM activities is one that does not assume financial risk, certification must come from the Department of Health and Senior Services. (Please Note). If a carrier delegates UM activities they will still be responsible for compliance with the Health Care Quality Act. The entity that has been delegated these functions as an organized delivery system (ODS) will themselves be responsible for their compliance with the Health Care Quality Act as well.

IV. Program Requirements.

HMO's shall implement a UM program under the direction of a Medical Director or his designee. N.J. ADMIN CODE tit. 8 § 8:38-8.1 (2004). A carrier's or ODS' UM program shall be under the direction of the medical director, or his or her designee (who shall be a physician licensed to practice medicine in the State of New Jersey), and shall be based on a written plan, reviewed annually by the carrier, and available for review by the Department. *See* N.J. ADMIN CODE tit. 8 § 8:38A-3.4 (2004); N.J. ADMIN CODE tit. 8 § 8:38B-3.7 (2004).

A. **Clinical review criteria.** Carriers shall ensure that UM determinations are based on written clinical criteria and protocols developed with involvement from practicing physicians and other licensed health care providers and based upon generally accepted medical standards. The carrier shall periodically review (no less than annually) and update these criteria as necessary. The carrier shall make the criteria readily available, upon request, to covered persons and interested providers except that internal or proprietary quantitative thresholds for UM is not required to be released to covered persons or providers. N.J. ADMIN CODE tit. 8 § 8:38A-3.4(b) (2004)(Carriers); *see* N.J. ADMIN CODE tit. 8 § 8:38B-3.7(a)2 (2004)(ODS); N.J. ADMIN CODE tit. 8 § 8:38-8.1(b) (2004)(HMO's)

B. **Prohibitions against financial incentives.** No provision.

C. **Telephone access standards.** For routine utilization-related inquiries, covered persons and providers shall have access to UM staff on, at a minimum, a five-day, 40 hours a week basis through a toll-free telephone number. If the carrier requires preauthorization for use of emergency departments or for reimbursement of services rendered under an emergency or urgent situation, the carrier shall have a registered professional nurse or physician immediately available by phone seven days a week, 24 hours a day to render UM determinations to providers. N.J. ADMIN CODE tit. 8 § 8:38-8.2 (2004)(for HMO's); N.J. ADMIN CODE tit. 8 § 8:38A-3.4(c) (2004)(Carriers).

D. **Quality assurance program.** Not specifically for UM organizations. However, HMO's shall have a system-wide continuous quality improvement program to monitor the quality and appropriateness of care and services provided to members. N.J. ADMIN CODE tit. 8 § 8:38-7.1(a) (2004). Carriers shall have or employ a CQI program to monitor the quality of their UM program. N.J. ADMIN CODE tit. 8., § 8:38A-3.8(a)(2004); *see also* N.J. ADMIN CODE tit. 8 § 8:38B-3.10 (2004) (ODS).

E. **Confidentiality.** All Carriers shall set forth its system for its CQI program in a plan reviewable upon request by the Department specifying its confidentiality policies and procedures. N.J. ADMIN CODE tit. 8 § 8:38A-3.8(b)5 (2004). HMO's and ODS are under similar requirements of confidentiality.

V. **Reviewer Qualifications**

A. **Qualifications of reviewers that render utilization review determinations (at each level of utilization review, if applicable).**

1. All determinations by Carriers to deny or limit an admission, service, procedure or

extension of stay, or benefits therefor, shall be made in accordance with the clinical and medical necessity criteria, and rendered by a physician under the clinical direction of the medical director. N.J. ADMIN CODE tit. 8 § 8:38A-3.4(d)1 (2004); N.J. ADMIN CODE tit. 8 § 8:38-8.3(b) (2004)(HMO).

B. **Requirements for medical director.** UM programs should be under the direction of a Medical Director or his designee.

C. **Requirement for "same-state" licensure.** Medical directors must be licensed in New Jersey.

VI. **Reviews and Appeals.**

A. **Review determinations and notice to patients/providers.**

B. **For HMO's.** All determinations shall be made on a timely basis, as required by the exigencies of the situation. N.J. ADMIN CODE tit. 8 § 8:38-8.3(c) (2004).

1. **Stage 1 appeal.** Each HMO shall establish and maintain an informal internal appeal process (stage 1 appeal) whereby any member, or any provider acting on behalf of a member, shall have the opportunity to speak to and appeal that determination with the HMO medical director and/or physician designee who rendered the determination. All such stage 1 appeals shall be concluded as soon as possible in accordance with the medical exigencies of the case, which in no event shall exceed 72 hours in the case of appeals from determinations regarding urgent or emergency care (including all situations in which the member is confined as an inpatient), and five business days in the case of all other appeals. If the appeal is not resolved to the satisfaction of the member at this level, the HMO shall provide the member and/or the provider with a written explanation of his or her right to proceed to a stage 2 appeal, including the applicable time limits, if any, for making the appeal, and to whom the appeal should be addressed. N.J. ADMIN CODE tit. 8 § 8:38-8.5 (2004).

2. **Stage 2 appeal.** Members or providers dissatisfied with State 1 appeals shall have the opportunity to pursue his or her appeal before a panel of physicians and/or other health care professionals selected by the HMO who have not been involved in the utilization management determination at issue. The formal internal utilization management appeal panel shall have available consultant practitioners who are trained or who practice in the same specialty as would typically manage the case at issue or such other

licensed health care professional as may be mutually agreed upon by the parties. In no event, however, shall the consulting practitioner or professional have been involved in the utilization management determination at issue. All such stage 2 appeals shall be acknowledged by the HMO, in writing, to the member or provider filing the appeal within 10 business days of receipt.

   a. All such stage 2 appeals shall be concluded as soon as possible after receipt by the HMO in accordance with the medical exigencies of the case, which in no event shall exceed 72 hours in the case of appeals from determinations regarding urgent or emergent care (including all situations in which the member is confined as an inpatient) and, except as set forth in (e) below, 20 business days in the case of all other appeals.

   b.   The HMO may extend the review for up to an additional 20 business days where it can demonstrate reasonable cause for the delay beyond its control and where it provides a written progress report and explanation for the delay to the satisfaction of the Department, with notice to the member and/or provider within the original 20 business day review period. N.J. ADMIN CODE tit. 8 § 8:38-8.6 (2004).

3. **External appeal.** Any HMO member or provider will have a right to appeal the HMO's internal Stage 1 and Stage 2 review processes contingent on compliance with

both processes. The appeal can be made to an independent utilization review organization within 60 days of the determination by the Stage 2 appeal by filing a written demand to the Department of Health and Senior Services, Office of Managed Care. The independent review decision is to be made within 30 business days from receipt of all the documentation necessary for the review, but may be extended if deemed necessary but no longer than 90 days following receipt of the completed application. N.J. ADMIN CODE tit. 8 § 8:38-8.7 (2004).

4. **For Carriers and Organized Delivery Systems.** A carrier shall establish an appeal process whereby a covered person or a provider acting on behalf of the covered person, with the covered person's consent, may appeal any UM decision resulting in a denial, termination or limitation of services or the payment of benefits therefor covered under the contract or policy. N.J. ADMIN CODE tit. 8 § 8:38A-3.5 (2004). (The internal appeals process and external appeals process follow the same procedures that are required for HMO appeals). *See* N.J. ADMIN CODE tit. 8 § 8:38A-3.5 et seq.(2004). The same is true for Organized Delivery Systems. N.J. ADMIN CODE tit. 8 § 8:38B-3.9 (2004).

VII. Recognition of URAC Accreditation Status

   A. Does the state recognize URAC accreditation? No.

   B. Which of the state's requirements are waived for URAC accredited organizations? Not applicable.

New Mexico

I. Scope and Applicability

A. **Who is subject to the state's utilization review laws?** State laws governing utilization review programs apply to all managed health care plans. N.M. STAT. ANN. § 59A-57-2 and § 59A-57-4 (2004). Under the New Mexico Patient Protection Act, N.M. STAT. ANN. § 59A-57-1, *et. seq.* (2004), the term "managed health care plan" (MHCP) is defined to include "a health care insurer or a provider service network when offering a benefit that either requires a covered person to use, or creates incentives, including financial incentives, for a covered person to use health care providers managed, owned, under contract with or employed by the health care insurer or provider service network." N.M. STAT. ANN. § 59A-57-3(J) (2004). The statute specifically excludes from the scope of the term managed health care plan any "plan that does not include a health care insurer or provider service network offering a traditional fee-for-service indemnity benefit or a benefit that covers only short-term travel, accident-only, limited benefit, student health plan or specified disease policies." *Id.*

B. **What term does the state use to refer to regulated entities?** New Mexico does not regulate utilization review organizations, but does oversee the utilization review activities of "managed health care plans." N.M. STAT. ANN. § 59A-57-3(J) (2004).

C. **What activities does the state include in its definition of utilization review?** "Utilization review" means a system for reviewing the appropriate and efficient allocation of health care services given or proposed to be given to a patient or group of patients. N.M. STAT. ANN. § 59A-57-3(O) (2004).

II. Regulatory Information.

A. **Responsible state agency.** New Mexico Public Regulation Commission, Insurance Division, Managed Health Care Ombudsman Bureau.

B. **Contact Information**
  1. Names and Titles:
     Linda Grisham, Manager
     (Linda.Grisham@state,nm.us);
     Vacant, External Reviews (as of August 5, 2004); Kathi Padilla, Internal Reviews and Complaints (Kathy.Padilla@state.nm.us);

Patricia Torres, Compliance Plans and Provider Complaints
(Patricia.Torres@state.nm.us)
  2. **Address:** New Mexico Department of Insurance, P.O. Box 1269, Santa Fe, NM 87504-1269.
  3. **Phone and Facsimile:** (505) 827-4468; facsimile (505) 827-4734.
  4. **Web site:** www.nmprc.state.nm.us/insurance/inshm.htm.

III. Licensure/Certification Requirements

A. **What entities are required to obtain a license in the state to conduct utilization review for residents of the state?** Not applicable.

B. **How often must licensure/certification be renewed?** Not applicable.

C. **Licensure fees (initial and renewal).** Not applicable.

D. **Documentation required for licensure.** Not applicable.

E. **Exemptions from licensure.** Not applicable.

IV. Program Requirements

A. **Clinical review criteria.** Must be based on written clinical criteria and protocols developed with involvement from practicing physicians and other health professionals and providers within the MHCP's network. The criteria and protocols shall be periodically reviewed and updated, and shall, with the exception of internal or proprietary quantitative thresholds for utilization management, be readily available, upon request, to affected providers and enrollees.

B. **Prohibitions against financial incentives.** No provision.

C. **Telephone access standards.** For MHCPs' utilization review programs, a registered professional nurse or physician shall be immediately available by telephone seven days a week, 24 hours per day, to render utilization management determinations for providers. MHCP's shall provide all enrollees and providers with a toll-free telephone number to contact utilization management staff 5 days and 40 hours per week.

D. **Quality assurance program.** MHCP's shall have a continuous quality improvement program.

E. **Delegation of utilization review functions.** Not applicable.

F. **Confidentiality.** MHCP's shall ensure the confidentiality of patient specific information.

V. Reviewer Qualifications

A. **Qualifications of reviewers that render utilization review determinations (at each level of utilization review, if applicable)?** Physicians, registered professional nurses, or other qualified health professionals shall render all determinations to authorize an admission, service, procedure, or extension of stay. Physicians, under the clinical direction of the medical director, shall render all determinations to deny or limit an admission, service, procedure, or extension of stay.

B. **Requirements for medical director.** The MHCP's utilization management program shall be under the direction of a medical director responsible for the medical services provided by the MHCP in New Mexico.

C. **Requirements for "same-state" licensure.** The medical director must be a licensed physician in New Mexico.

VI. Reviews and Appeals

A. **Review determination and notice to patients/providers.**

1. **Time frame for determination.** Determinations by a MHCP shall be made in a "timely manner" as required by the needs of the situation which shall not exceed 24 hours for emergency care and 7 days for all other determinations.

2. **Contents of notice of adverse determinations.**

   a. **Reasons for adverse determination.** The reason for denial of coverage or authorization must be included in a written notice.

   b. **Notice of appeal rights.** The notice shall describe the procedures necessary for commencing an internal review of the determination.

B. **Appeals requirements.**

1. **Time frame for determination.** All informal internal grievance procedures (stage 1 reviews) shall be concluded as soon as possible in accordance with medical exigencies of case, but no later than 48 hours in cases involving urgent or emergency care and 7 days in the case of other grievances. The MHCP shall provide a written decision containing required information. Each MHCP shall maintain a formal internal review process (stage 2 reviews) for any enrollee or provider acting on behalf of enrollee. MHCP's shall acknowledge all stage 2 reviews in 7 days and shall conclude review for urgent or emergency cases in 48 hours and 30 days in all other grievances.

2. **External appeals.** If the enrollee has complied with the 2-stage internal review process, an MHCP enrollee or provider acting on behalf of an enrollee may seek review by an independent utilization review board. To initiate an external review, an enrollee or provider shall file a written request with the Department of Insurance.

C. **Emergency Services.** Enrollees must have 24-hour, 7-day a week access to either their primary care physician or the utilization management staff for emergency or urgent care.

VII. Recognition of URAC Accreditation Status

A. **Does the state recognize URAC accreditation?** No.

B. **Which of the state's requirements are waived for URAC-accredited organizations?** Not applicable, though if the MHCP seeks to meet the requirements through accreditation by a private accrediting entity, the MHCP must submit certain information to the Department. The Department may recognize and approve accreditation by outside entities.

New York

I. Scope and Applicability

A. **Who is subject to the state's utilization review laws?** Any "utilization review agent." Under the New York Public Health Law ("Public Health Law"), this means any entity performing utilization review. Under the New York Insurance Law ("Insurance Law"), this means any insurer subject to Article 32 or 43 of the Insurance Law that performs utilization review and any independent utilization review agent under contract with such an insurer.

B. **What exemptions are provided, if any?** Under the Public Health Law, there are exemptions for: a federal agency; an agent of the federal government to the extent the agent is acting on behalf of the federal government; an agent acting on behalf of the state and local government for services provided under title XIX of the Social Security Act; a hospital's internal quality assurance program except if associated with a health care financing mechanism; or any insurer subject to Article 32 or Article 43 of the New York Insurance Law and any independent utilization review agent performing utilization review under a contract with such insurer, which shall be subject to Article 49 of the New York Insurance Law. The utilization review activities of ERISA plans are not governed by New York law. N.Y. [PUB. HEALTH] LAW § 4908 (2004).

1. HMO's? Yes.
2. Insurers? Yes.
3. Utilization review organizations? Yes.
4. Workers' Compensation? Yes.
5. Retrospective review? Yes.

B. **What term does the state use to refer to regulated entities?** The Public Health Law defines the term "utilization review agent" as "any company, organization or other entity performing utilization review," except 1) a federal agency; 2) an agent of the federal government to the extent the agent is acting on behalf of the federal government; 3) an agent acting on behalf of the state and local government for services provided under title XIX of the federal social security act; 4) a hospital's internal quality assurance program except if associated with a health care financing mechanism; or 5) any insurer subject to Article 32 or Article 43 of the New York Insurance Law and any independent utilization review agent performing utilization review under a contract with such insurer, which shall be subject to

Article 49 of the New York Insurance Law. N.Y. [PUB. HEALTH] LAW § 4900(9) (2004). The Insurance Law uses identical nomenclature. N.Y. [INS.] LAW § 4900(i) (2004).

C. **What activities does the state include in its definition of utilization review?** "Utilization review" is defined as "the review to determine whether health care services that have been provided, are being provided or are proposed to be provided to a patient, whether undertaken prior to, concurrent with or subsequent to the delivery of such services are medically necessary." The definition does not include "denials based on a failure to obtain health care services from a designated or approved health care provider as required under a contract;" review of the appropriateness of a particular coding; any issues related to determination of amount or extent of payment; or determination of any coverage issues beyond whether health care services were medically necessary. N.Y. [PUB. HEALTH] LAW § 4900(8) (2004); *see also* N.Y. [INS.] LAW § 4900(h) (2004).

II. Regulatory Information.

A. **Responsible state agency.** New York State Department of Health, Bureau of Managed Care Certification and Surveillance. Note: Oversees utilization review activities by managed care entities.

B. **Contact Information**
1. **Name and Title:** Jeanette M. Hill, Project Manager, Utilization Review.
2. **Address:** New York State Department of Health, Bureau of Managed Care Certification and Surveillance, Corning Tower, Room 1911, Albany, NY 12237.
3. **Phone and Facsimile:** (518) 474-4156; facsimile (518) 473-3583.
4. **E-mail:** jmh30@health.state.ny.us.
5. **Web site:** www.health.state.ny.us/

C. **Responsible state agency:** New York State Insurance Department, Health Bureau. Note: Oversees utilization review activities by insurers.

D. **Contact Information.**
1. **Name and Title:** Deborah Kozemko, JD, Associate Insurance Attorney.
2. **Address:** New York State Insurance Department, Agency Building One, Empire State Plaza, Albany, NY 12257.
3. **Phone and Facsimile:** (518) 474-4098; facsimile (518) 473-4600.

    4.   E-mail: dkozemko@ins.state.ny.us.

    5.   Web site: www.ins.state.ny.us.

III. Registration Requirements

A. **What entities are required to obtain a license in the state to conduct utilization review for residents of the state?** Every utilization review agent who conducts the practice of utilization review.

B. **How often must registration be renewed?** Every 2 years.

C. **Registration fees (initial and renewal).** No fee.

D. **Documentation required for licensure.** Utilization review agents must submit an application form that includes a utilization review plan that documents compliance with state requirements and a list of managed care organizations and/or insurers for which the agent provides utilization review services.

E. **Exemptions for licensure.** Out-of-state organizations are not granted an exemption from the state's registration and certification requirements even if they are duly licensed and/or certified in their state of domicile and/or have URAC accreditation.
N.Y. [PUB. HEALTH] LAW § 490 (2004)1. N.Y. [INS.] LAW § 4901 (2004).

IV. Program Requirements

A. **Clinical review criteria.** Clinical review criteria must be established according to the utilization review plan.

B. **Prohibitions against financial incentives.** A utilization review agent may not offer compensation based on a percentage of the amount of reduction or any other method that encourages the rendering of adverse determinations.

C. **Telephone access standards.** The utilization review agent must make review staff reasonably available by toll-free telephone at least 40 hours per week during normal business hours. The utilization review agent must also be able to accept after-hours calls, including requests for expedited reviews, and return those calls no later than the next business day after the calls were received.

D. **Quality assurance program.** No provision, though HMO's must have a quality assurance program under N.Y. COMP. CODES R. & REGS. tit. 10, § 98-1.12 (2004).

E. **Delegation of utilization review functions.** The application for registration must document the circumstances under which utilization review could be delegated. The utilization review agent must implement mechanisms ensuring that all sub-contractors adhere to state requirements.

F. **Confidentiality.** Utilization review agents must comply with all applicable state and federal laws protecting the confidentiality of individual medical records.
N.Y. [PUB. HEALTH] LAW §§ 4902, 4903 and 4915 (2004). N.Y. [INS.] LAW §§ 4902, 4903 and 4915 (2004).

V. Reviewer Qualifications

A. **Qualifications of reviewers that render utilization review determinations (at each level of utilization review, if applicable).**
Health care professionals conducting utilization review must be appropriately licensed, registered, or certified and trained in the utilization review agent's procedures. Only clinical peer reviewers may render adverse determinations. Different clinical peer reviewers than ones who rendered initial adverse determinations shall conduct appeals.

B. **Requirements for medical director.** A licensed physician must be responsible for oversight of the utilization review process. However, a specialty utilization review agent may appoint a clinical director licensed in the appropriate specialty.

C. **Requirement for "same-state" licensure.** No provision.
N.Y. [PUB. HEALTH] LAW § 4912 (2004). N.Y. [INS.] LAW § 4912 (2004).

VI. Reviews and Appeals

A. **Review determinations and notice to patients/providers.**
    1.   **Time frame for determination.** Prospective review determinations must be communicated to the patient and attending provider within 3 working days of receipt of the information necessary to complete the review. Concurrent review determinations must be communicated to the patient and attending provider within 1 working day of receipt of the information necessary to complete the review. Retrospective review determinations must be made within thirty days of receipt of the information necessary to complete the review. If an adverse determination is rendered without attempting to discuss such matter with the health care provider, the health care provider shall have the opportunity to request a reconsideration of the adverse determination. Except in cases of

retrospective reviews, such reconsideration shall occur within 1 business day of receipt of the request and shall be conducted to the clinical peer reviewer making the initial determination.

2. **Contents of notice of adverse determination.**

   a. **Reasons for adverse determination.** Required, including reasons for the determination and clinical rationale, if any, as well as appeal rights, and availability upon request by insured or insured's designee or clinical review criteria.

   b. **Notice of Appeal Rights.** The notice must include instructions on how to initiate standard appeals, expedited appeals, and external appeal; however, the external appeal is available at the time of the final adverse determination. The external appeal forms and instructions are sent to the enrollee at that time.

B. **Appeals requirements.** A utilization review agent shall establish a standard appeal process which includes procedures for appeals to be filed in writing or by telephone.

   1. **Time frame for determination.** Standard appeal determinations must be rendered within 60 days of the receipt of the necessary information to conduct the appeal. Expedited appeal determinations must be rendered within 2 working days of the receipt of the necessary information to conduct the appeal.

   2. **External appeals.** Enrollees and insureds have a right to an external appeal of a final adverse determination by a managed care organization or insurer. An enrollee, insured, or, in the case of retrospective reviews, the enrollee's or insured's provider, may request a review by an independent "external appeal agent" certified by the Superintendent of Insurance and/or Commissioner of Health. An external appeal must be requested within 45 days after receipt of the notice of the final adverse determination or after both the plan and enrollee or the insurer and insured have jointly agreed to waive any internal appeal. *See* N.Y. [INS.] LAW § 4914(b)(1) (2004) and N.Y. [PUB. HEALTH] LAW § 4914(2)(a) (2004).

C. **Emergency Services.** A utilization review agent may not require prior authorization for services necessary to stabilize or treat an emergency condition. In addition, a utilization review agent shall not deny reimbursement for such service on retrospective review, provided that such services were medically necessary to stabilize or treat an emergency condition.
N.Y. [PUB. HEALTH] LAW §§ 4904, 4910 and 4914(2004). N.Y. [INS.] LAW §§ 4904, 4910 and 4914 (2004).

VII. Recognition of URAC Accreditation Status

A. **Does the state recognize URAC accreditation?** No, but see following summary for recognition of URAC accreditation for workers' compensation preferred provider organizations.

B. **Which of the state's requirements are waived for URAC-accredited organizations?** Not applicable.

VIII. Miscellaneous

The New York State Insurance Department's Web site, which is at www.ins.state.ny.us/extappaqa.htm, includes information on the external review program, including "Frequently Asked Questions and Related Forms and Instructions Regarding External Review." To request an external review, New York consumers must complete an application and send it to the Department. The instructions and application are also available on the Web site.

The Web site also features the "1999 New York Consumer Guide to Health Insurers," published by the New York State Insurance Department. This guide includes a chapter on "Utilization Review Appeals," showing appeals filed and their resolution for HMO's, non-profit indemnity insurers, and commercial insurers. There is also an appendix on "How to File an External Appeal."

North Carolina

I. Scope and Applicability

A. **Who is subject to the state's utilization review laws?** North Carolina does not regulate utilization review organizations, but does regulate the activities of all entities that perform utilization review in connection with a health benefits plan. In addition, all insurers shall monitor all utilization review carried out by or on behalf of the insurer and ensure compliance with this section. An insurer shall ensure that appropriate personnel have operational responsibility for the conduct of the insurer's utilization review program. N.C. GEN. STAT. § 58-50-61(b) and (d) (2004).

1. **HMO's?** Yes.
2. **Insurers?** Yes.
3. **Utilization review organizations?** Not directly, but insurers must monitor the utilization review organizations with which they contract to ensure compliance. N.C. GEN. STAT. § 58-50-61(b) (2004).
4. **Retrospective review?** Yes.

B. **What exemptions are provided, if any?** None listed.

C. **What term does the state use to refer to regulated entities?** A "utilization review organization" is defined as "an entity that conducts utilization review under a managed care plan, but does not mean an insurer performing utilization review for its own health benefit plan." N.C. GEN. STAT. § 58-50-61(a)(18) (2004).

D. **What activities does the state include in its definition of utilization review?** "Utilization review" means "a set of formal techniques designed to monitor the use of or evaluate the clinical necessity, appropriateness, efficacy or efficiency of health care services, procedures, providers, or facilities." The definition includes: ambulatory review, case management, certification, concurrent review, discharge planning, prospective review, retrospective review, and second opinion. N.C. GEN. STAT. § 58-50-61(a)(17) (2004).

II. Regulatory Information

A. **Responsible state agency.** North Carolina Department of Insurance, Managed Care and Health Benefits Division.

B. **Contact Information.**
1. **Name and Title:** Nancy O'Dowd, Deputy Commissioner.
2. **Address:** P.O. Box 26387, 111 Seaboard Avenue, Raleigh, NC 27611.
3. **Phone and Facsimile:** (919) 715-0526; facsimile (919) 715-0198.
4. **E-mail:** nodowd@ncdoi.com
5. **Website:** www.ncdoi.com

III. Licensure/Certification Requirements

A. **What entities are required to obtain a license in the state to conduct utilization review for residents of the state?** North Carolina does not require specific licensure for utilization review organizations or activities.

B. **How often must licensure be renewed?** Not applicable.

C. **Licensure fees (initial and renewal).** Not applicable.

D. **Documentation required for licensure.** Not applicable. However, North Carolina requires every insurer that performs or delegates utilization review in a health benefit plan to prepare and maintain a utilization review program document that describes all delegated and nondelegated review functions for covered services including:

1. Procedures to evaluate the clinical necessity, appropriateness, efficacy, or efficiency of health services.
2. Data sources and clinical review criteria used in decision-making.
3. The process for conducting appeals of noncertifications.
4. Mechanisms to ensure consistent application of review criteria and compatible decisions.
5. Data collection processes and analytical methods used in assessing utilization of health care services.
6. Provisions for assuring confidentiality of clinical and patient information in accordance with State and federal law.
7. The organizational structure (e.g., utilization review committee, quality assurance, or other committee) that periodically assesses utilization review activities and reports to the insurer's governing body.
8. The staff position functionally responsible for day-to-day program management.
9. The methods of collection and assessment of data about underutilization and overutilization of health care services and how the assessment is used to evaluate and

improve procedures and criteria for utilization review. N.C. GEN. STAT. § 58-50-61(c) (2004).

E. **Exemption from licensure.** Not applicable.

IV. Program Requirements

A. **Clinical review criteria.** In every utilization review program, an insurer or utilization review organization shall use documented clinical review criteria based on sound clinical evidence, which is periodically evaluated to ensure continuing efficacy. An insurer may develop its own clinical review criteria or purchase or license such criteria. Criteria for determining when a patient needs to be placed in a substance abuse treatment program shall be either the diagnostic criteria contained in the most recent revision of the American Society of Addiction Medicine Patient Placement Criteria for the Treatment of Substance-Related Disorders or criteria adopted by the insurer or its URO. The department, in consultation with the Department of Health and Human Services, may require proof of compliance with this subsection by a plan or URO. N.C. GEN. STAT. § 58-50-61 (a)(2) and (d) (2004).

B. **Prohibitions against financial incentives.** Compensation to utilization reviewers may not be based directly or indirectly on making any particular utilization review decision. N.C. GEN. STAT. § 58-50-61(d) (2004). In addition, HMO's are required to ensure that the person conducting utilization review does not have a direct or indirect financial interest in the provider of services. N.C. ADMIN. CODE tit. 11, r. 20.0508.

C. **Telephone access standards.** Provide covered persons and their providers with access to its review staff by a toll-free or collect call telephone number whenever any provider is required to be available to provide services which may require prior certification to any plan enrollee. Every insurer shall establish standards for telephone accessibility and monitor telephone service as indicated by average speed of answer and call abandonment rate, on at least a month-by-month basis, to ensure that telephone service is adequate, and take corrective action when necessary. N.C. GEN. STAT. § 58-50-61(e)(3) (2004).

D. **Quality assurance program.** An insurer must routinely assess the effectiveness and efficacy of its utilization review program and coordinate utilization review with other medical management activity, including quality assurance. N.C. GEN. STAT. § 58-50-61(e)(2) (2004).

E. **Delegation of utilization review functions.** Insurers shall monitor all utilization review carried out by or on behalf of the insurer and ensure compliance with N.C. GEN. STAT. § 58-50-61(b) (2004). Such monitoring shall include a written description of the utilization review organization's activities and responsibilities, evidence of formal approval of the utilization review organization program by the insurer, and a process by which the insurer evaluates the utilization review organization's performance. N.C. GEN. STAT. § 58-50-61(c) (2004).

F. **Confidentiality.** Insurers must adopt provisions for assuring confidentiality of clinical and patient information in accordance with State and federal law. N.C. GEN. STAT. § 58-50-61(c)(6) and 58-67-180 (2004).

V. Reviewer Qualifications

A. **Qualifications of reviewers that render utilization review determinations (at each level of utilization review, if applicable).**

1. Qualified health professionals must administer the utilization review program and oversee review decisions. N.C. GEN. STAT. § 58-50-61(d) (2004).

2. A medical doctor licensed in North Carolina must evaluate all noncertifications. N.C. GEN. STAT. § 58-50-61(d) (2004).

3. Second-level appeals must be heard by a panel comprised of persons not previously involved in the review who are not employees of the insurer and who have no financial interest in the outcome. The panel must include appropriate clinical expertise.

B. **Requirements for medical director.** The utilization review program must operate under the direction of a medical doctor.

C. **Requirement for "same-state" licensure.** Only the medical doctor who evaluates the clinical appropriateness of noncertifications must be licensed in North Carolina.

VI. Reviews and Appeals

A. **Review determinations and notice to patients/providers.**

1. **Time frame for determination.** For prospective and concurrent review, the insurer must render a determination within 3 business days after obtaining all necessary information. For retrospective reviews, the insurer must render a determination within

30 days of receiving all necessary information.

    a. **Contents of notice of adverse determination.** A written notification of a noncertification shall include all reasons for the noncertification, including the clinical rationale, the instructions for initiating a voluntary appeal or reconsideration of the noncertification, and the instructions for requesting a written statement of the clinical review criteria used to make the noncertification. An insurer shall provide the clinical review criteria used to make the noncertification to any person who received the notification of the noncertification and who follows the procedures for a request. An insurer shall also inform the covered person in writing about the availability of assistance from the Managed Care Patient Assistance Program, including the telephone number and address of the Program and of the covered person's right to request an external review. N.C. GEN. STAT. § 58-50-61(h) (2004) and 58-50-77.

    b. **Notice of Appeal Rights.** Required. An insurer shall notify the covered person in writing of the covered person's right to request an external review. N.C. GEN. STAT. § 58-50-77(a) (2004).

B. **Appeals requirements.**

  1. Time frame for determination. Every insurer shall establish and maintain procedures to ensure that covered persons have an opportunity to pursue appropriate resolutions of grievances, including first- and second-level reviews of grievances. If the insurer does not have a procedure for informal consideration or if an informal consideration does not resolve the grievance, the grievance process shall provide for first- and second-level reviews of grievances. N.C. GEN. STAT. § 58-50-62(e)(2) (2004).

  2. For first level grievance review, the insurer must render a decision within 30 days of receiving the appeal. N.C. GEN. STAT. § 58-50-62(e)(2) (2004).

  3. For second level grievance review, an insurer shall issue a written decision to the covered person and, if applicable, to the covered person's provider, within 7 business days after completing the review meeting. N.C. GEN. STAT. § 58-50-62(h) (2004).

  4. Expedited second level reviews must be completed no more than 4 days after receiving the information necessary to justify the expedited review. In addition to the appeal, insurers must also make available to patients a formal grievance procedure for second-level appeal of utilization review decisions. N.C. GEN. STAT. § 58-50-62(i) (2004).

  5. External appeals. Available to assure that covered persons have the opportunity for an independent review of an appeal decision upholding a noncertification or a second-level grievance review decision upholding a noncertification. External appeals are available only after exhaustion of the internal grievance process. N.C. GEN. STAT. § 58-50-75 and 58-50-79 (2004). It applies to all insurers that offer a health benefit plan and provide or perform utilization review. N.C. GEN. STAT. § 58-50-75(b) (2004). If the covered person has a medical condition where the time frame for completion of an expedited review would seriously jeopardize the person's health, he or she may file a request for an expedited external review at the same time the covered person files a request for an expedited review of a grievance review. N.C. GEN. STAT. § 58-50-77(c) (2004). Standard external review decisions must be made in within 45 days after the date of receipt by the Commissioner of the request for external review. N.C. GEN. STAT. § 58-50-80(j) (2004). Expedited external review decisions must be made as expeditiously as the covered person's medical condition or circumstances require, but not more than four days after the date of receipt of the request for an expedited external review. N.C. GEN. STAT. § 58-50-80(e) (2004). The Department assigns the review to an independent review organization approved under N.C. GEN. STAT. § 58-50-85. The panel must include providers with appropriate expertise. N.C. GEN. STAT. § 58-50-87 (b)

C. **Emergency Services.** North Carolina uses the "prudent layperson" standard for emergency services. Payment of claims for emergency services shall be based on the retrospective review of the presenting history and symptoms of the covered person. N.C. GEN. STAT. § 58-3-190 (a).

VII. Recognition of URAC Accreditation Status

A. **Does the state recognize URAC accreditation?** Not for health utilization management, but for independent review organizations. N.C. GEN. STAT. § 58-50-85 (c).

B. **Which of the state's requirements are waived for URAC-accredited organizations?** If accredited by URAC, the Commissioner of Insurance shall deem a health care purchasing alliance as meeting the regulatory requirements for utilization management. N.C. GEN. STAT. § 143-629(b) (2004).

VIII. Miscellaneous

The North Carolina Department of Health and Human Services, Division of Medical Assistance regulates managed care products for the Medicaid program. The Division's medical policy/utilization control mission is "to structure medical benefits and service coverages available to Medicaid clients in a manner that promotes access to medically appropriate and cost effective care." See the agency's Web site at www.dhhs.state.nc.us/dma/mp.htm.

North Dakota

I. Scope and Applicability

A. **Who is subject to the state's utilization review laws?** Utilization review agents defined as any person or entity performing utilization review in the allocation of health care resources and services that are subject to state insurance regulations. N.D. CENT. CODE § 26.1-26.4-01(2) (2004); N.D. CENT. CODE § 26.1-26.4-03 (2004).
   1. HMO's? Yes.
   2. Insurers? Yes.
   3. Utilization review organizations? Yes.
   4. Retrospective review? Yes.

B. **What exemptions are provided, if any?** There are exceptions for an agency or agent of the federal government or an agent providing services to the North Dakota Department of Human Services. N.D. CENT. CODE § 26.1-26.4-02(9) (2004).

C. **What term does the state use to refer to regulated entities?** A "utilization review agent" is "any person or entity performing utilization review," with the exceptions noted above in Section I.A. N.D. CENT. CODE § 26.1-26.4-02(9) (2004).

D. **What activities does the state include in its definition of utilization review?** "Utilization review" is defined as "a system for prospective, retrospective, and concurrent review of the necessity and appropriateness in the allocation of health care resources and services that are subject to state insurance regulation and which are given or proposed to be given to an individual within this state. Utilization review does not include elective requests for clarification of coverage. N.D. CENT. CODE § 26.1-26.4-02(8) (2004).

II. Regulatory Information

A. **Responsible state agency.** North Dakota Department of Insurance.

B. **Contact Information.**
   1. **Name and Title:** Leona Ziegler(records/applications); Laurie Wolf (legal)
   2. **Address:** North Dakota Department of Insurance, 600 East Boulevard Avenue, Dept. 401, Bismarck, ND 58505-0320.
   3. **Phone and Facsimile:** (701) 328-3548; facsimile (701) 328-4880.
   4. **E-mail:** lziegler@state.nd.us
   5. **Web site:** http://www.state.nd.us/ndins.

III. Licensure/Certification Requirements

A. **What entities are required to obtain a license in the state to conduct utilization review for residents of the state?** A utilization review agent may not conduct utilization review in this state unless the utilization review agent has certified to the Commissioner of Insurance in writing that the agent is in compliance with North Dakota's minimum requirements for review agents. N.D. CENT. CODE § 26.1-26.4-03 (2004).

B. **How often must certification be renewed?** Annually, by March 1. N.D. CENT. CODE § 26.1-26.4-03 (2004).

C. **Certification fees (initial and renewal).** $10.

D. **Documentation required for certification.** The utilization review agent must submit a certification that it is in compliance with the state's requirements. In addition, it must submit:
   1. The name, address, telephone number, and normal business hours of the utilization review agent.
   2. The name and telephone number of a person for the commissioner to contact.
   3. A description of the appeal procedures for utilization review determinations.
   4. A list of the third-party payers for whom the private review agent is performing utilization review in the state. N.D. CENT. CODE § 26.1-26.4-03 (2004).

E. **Exemptions from licensure.** Out-of-state organizations are not granted an exemption from the state's licensure and certification requirements even if they are duly licensed and/or certified in their state of domicile.

IV. Program Requirements

A. **Clinical review criteria.** A provider may request that a utilization review agent furnish the provider with the medical review criteria to be used in evaluating health care services. N.D. CENT. CODE § 26.1-26.4-03 (2004).

B. **Prohibitions against financial incentives.** No individual or organization may be compensated for utilization review where compensation is contingent on a denial or reduction in payment for hospital, medical, or other health care services. N.D. CENT. CODE § 26.1-26.4-04.1 (2004).

C. **Telephone access standards.** Utilization review agents shall have utilization review staff available by toll-free telephone at least 40 hours per week during normal business hours. N.D. CENT. CODE

§ 26.1-26.4-04(5) (2004). In addition, utilization review agents shall have a mechanism to accept or record off-hours calls and shall respond to such calls within 2 working days. N.D. CENT. CODE § 26.1-26.4-04(6) (2004).

D. **Quality assurance program.** No provision.

E. **Delegation of utilization review functions.** A health care insurer that contracts with another entity to perform utilization review on its behalf remains responsible to ensure that all the requirements of N.D. CENT. CODE § 26.1-26.4 are met to the same extent the health care insurer would be if it performed the utilization review itself. N.D. CENT. CODE § 26.1-26.4-04.2 (2004).

F. **Confidentiality.** Utilization review agents shall comply with all applicable laws protecting the confidentiality of individual medical records. N.D. CENT. CODE § 26.1-26.4-04(7) (2004).

V. Reviewer Qualifications

A. **Qualifications of reviewers that render utilization review determinations (at each level of utilization review, if applicable).**

1. A licensed physician or, if appropriate, a licensed psychologist, shall review all initial determinations. In the alternative, the review determination can be made in accordance with standards or guidelines approved by a physician or licensed psychologist. N.D. CENT. CODE § 26.1-26.4-04(2) (2004).

2. A licensed physician, or, if appropriate, a licensed psychologist shall consider all appeals. N.D. CENT. CODE § 26.1-26.4-04(4)(a) (2004).

3. When an initial appeal to reverse a determination is unsuccessful, a subsequent determination regarding hospital, medical, or other health care services provided or to be provided to a patient which may result in a denial of third-party reimbursement or a denial of precertification for that service must include the evaluation, findings, and concurrence of a physician trained in the relevant specialty to make a final determination that care provided or to be provided was, is, or may be medically inappropriate. N.D. CENT. CODE § 26.1-26.4-04(10) (2004).

4. The Commissioner of Insurance may find that the minimum standards have been met if the utilization review agent has received approval or accreditation by a utilization review accreditation organization. N.D. CENT. CODE § 26.1-26.4-04 (2004).

B. **Requirements for medical director.** No provision.

C. **Requirement for "same-state" licensure.** Psychologists making utilization review determinations shall have current licenses from the state board of psychologist examiners. Physicians making utilization review determinations shall have current licenses from the state board of medical examiners. N.D. CENT. CODE § 26.1-26.4-04(8) (2004).

VI. Reviews and Appeals

A. **Review determinations and notice to patients/providers.** Required. N.D. CENT. CODE § 26.1-26.4-04(3) (2004).

B. **Time frame for determination.** The notification of a utilization review determination must be mailed or otherwise communicated within 2 days of receipt of all necessary information. *See* N.D. CENT. CODE § 26.1-26.4-04(4)(b) (2004).

C. **Contents of notice of adverse determination.**

1. **Reasons for adverse determination.** Must include principal reasons for adverse determination. N.D. CENT. CODE § 26.1-26.4-04(3) (2004).

2. **Notice of Appeal Rights.** Must include procedures to initiate an appeal of the adverse determination. N.D. CENT. CODE § 26.1-26.4-04(4) (2004).

D. **Appeals requirements.** Utilization review agents must provide for both standard and expedited appeals. Expedited appeals must be available for emergency or life-threatening situations. After the initial appeal is conducted, the patient has a right to a final determination.

1. **Time frame for determination.** Standard appeals must be completed within 30 days from the receipt of all necessary information. Expedited appeals must be completed within 48 hours of the receipt of all information necessary to consider the appeal. N.D. CENT. CODE § 26.1-26.4-04(4)(b) (2004).

2. **External appeals.** No provision.

E. **Emergency Services.** Utilization review agents must allow a minimum of 24 hours following an emergency admission for the patient to notify them and request certification for continuing treatment. A utilization review agent may not deny coverage for emergency services and may not require prior authorization of such services. N.D. CENT. CODE § 26.1-26.4-04(4)(c) (2004).

VII. Recognition of URAC Accreditation Status

A. Does the state recognize URAC accreditation? Yes.

B. Which of the state's requirements are waived for URAC-accredited organizations? The Commissioner of Insurance may find that a URAC-accredited utilization review agent complies with most of North Dakota's utilization review requirements at N.D. CENT. CODE § 26.1-26.4-04 (2204).

Ohio

I. Scope and Applicability

A. **Who is subject to the state's utilization review laws?** Any health insuring corporation that provides or performs utilization review services in connection with its policies, contracts, and agreements covering basic health care services and to any designee of the health insuring corporation, or to any utilization review organization that performs utilization review functions on behalf of the health insuring corporation in connection with policies, contracts, or agreements of the health insuring corporation covering basic health care services. OHIO REV. CODE ANN. § 1751.78(A)(1) (2004).

   1. **HMO's?** Yes.

   2. **Insurers?** Yes, as long as the health insuring corporation provides or performs utilization review services in connection with its policies, contracts, and agreements covering basic health care services.

   3. **Utilization review organizations?** Yes.

   4. **Retrospective review?** Yes.

B. **What exemptions are provided, if any?** Health insuring corporations are not required to provide or perform utilization review services. OHIO REV. CODE ANN. § 1751.78(A)(2) (2004).

C. **What term does the state use to refer to regulated entities?** "Health insuring corporations" are health maintenance organizations (HMO's), preferred provider organizations (PPO's), and other managed care organizations. "Utilization review organization" means an entity that conducts utilization review, other than a health insuring corporation performing a review of its own health care plans. OHIO REV. CODE ANN. § 1751.77(P) (2004).

D. **What activities does the state include in its definition of utilization review?** "Utilization review" means "a process used to monitor the use of, or evaluate the clinical necessity, appropriateness, efficacy, or efficiency of, health care services, procedures, or settings. Areas of review may include ambulatory review, prospective review, second opinion, certification, concurrent review, case management, discharge planning, or retrospective review." OHIO REV. CODE ANN. § 1751.77(P) (2004).

II. Regulatory Information

A. **Responsible state agency.** Department of Insurance, Office of Life, Health, and Managed Care Services.

B. **Contact Information.**

   1. **Name and Title:** Mary Richardson , Senior Insurance Contract Analyst.

   2. **Address:** 2100 Stella Court, Columbus, OH 43215-1067

   3. **Phone and Facsimile:** (614) 728-1756; facsimile (614) 719-1673.

   4. **E-mail:** mary.richardson@ins.state.oh.us

   5. **Web site:** http://www.ohioinsurance.gov/

III. Licensure/Certification Requirements

A. **What entities are required to obtain a license in the state to conduct utilization review for residents of the state?** While a license is not required, a health insuring corporation shall file annually a certification of compliance.

B. **How often must licensure be renewed?** File certificate annually.

C. **Licensure fees (initial and renewal).** Not applicable.

D. **Documentation required for licensure.** Certificate of compliance. OHIO REV. CODE ANN. § 1751.823 (2004). Further, a health insuring corporation that conducts utilization review shall prepare a written utilization review program that describes all review activities, both delegated and nondelegated, for covered health care services provided. OHIO REV. CODE ANN. § 1751.79 (2004). The program must describe procedures to evaluate the clinical necessity, appropriateness, efficacy or efficiency of health care services, mechanisms to ensure consistent application or criteria, data collection processes, along with mechanisms for assuring confidentiality.

E. **Exemptions from licensure.** Not applicable.

IV. Program Requirements

A. **Clinical review criteria.** The program shall use documented clinical review criteria that are based on sound clinical evidence and are evaluated periodically to assure ongoing efficacy. A health insuring corporation may develop its own clinical review criteria or may purchase or license such criteria from qualified vendors. OHIO REV. CODE ANN. § 1751.80(A) (2004).

B. **Accreditation.** A health insuring corporation may present evidence of compliance by submitting evidence to the superintendent of insurance of its accreditation by an independent, private accrediting organization, such as the national committee on quality assurance, the National Quality Health Council, the Joint

Commission on Accreditation of Health Care Organizations, or the American Accreditation Healthcare Commission/Utilization Review Accreditation Commission (URAC). The superintendent, upon review of the organization's accreditation process, may determine that such accreditation constitutes compliance by the health insuring corporation with the requirements of these sections. OHIO REV. CODE ANN. § 1751.821 (2004).

C. **Prohibitions against financial incentives.** Compensation to individuals or organizations conducting utilization review may not contain any incentives for inappropriate review decisions. OHIO REV. CODE ANN. § 1751.80(G) (2004). For external reviewers, *see* OHIO REV. CODE ANN. § 1751.84(D)(2) (2004).

D. **Telephone access standards.** The health insuring corporation or its designee utilization review organization shall provide enrollees and participating providers with access to its review staff by means of a toll-free telephone number or collect-call telephone line. OHIO REV. CODE ANN. § 1751.80(E) (2004).

E. **Quality assurance program.** Health insuring corporations and utilization review organizations must conduct periodic assessments of utilization review activities. OHIO REV. CODE ANN. § 1751.79(F) (2004).

F. **Delegation of utilization review functions.** Health insuring corporations are responsible for monitoring all utilization review activities conducted on their behalf, and for ensuring that state requirements are met. OHIO REV. CODE ANN. § 1751.78(B)(2) (2004). Health insuring corporations must document a formal process by which they select and oversee utilization review organizations. OHIO REV. CODE ANN. § 1751.80(D) (2004).

G. **Confidentiality.** Health insuring corporations and utilization review organizations must have mechanisms to protect the confidentiality of clinical and proprietary information. OHIO REV. CODE ANN. § 1751.79(E) (2004).

V. Reviewer Qualifications

A. Qualifications of reviewers that render utilization review determinations (at each level of utilization review, if applicable). Qualified providers shall administer the program and oversee review determinations. A clinical peer in the same, or in a similar, specialty as typically manages the medical condition, procedure, or treatment under review shall evaluate the clinical

appropriateness of adverse determinations that are the subject of an appeal. OHIO REV. CODE ANN. § 1751.80(B) (2004).

B. Independent review organizations shall use the services of clinical peers who have expertise in the treatment of the medical condition of the enrollee condition and knowledgeable about the recommended or requested therapy. Each clinical peer assigned by an independent review organization to conduct external reviews shall have expertise in treating the enrollee's medical condition in the past 3 years, hold a license that is not restricted in the state issuing it, not been disciplined or sanctioned by a hospital or government entity based on the quality of care provided by the clinical peer, and in the case of physician, be certified by a nationally recognized medical specialty board in the area that is the subject of review. OHIO REV. CODE ANN. § 3901.81 (2004).

C. **Requirements for medical director.** No specific provision.

D. **Requirement for "same-state" licensure.** No provision.

VI. Reviews and Appeals

A. **Review determinations and notice to patients/providers.**

1. **Time frame for determination.** Prospective review determinations must be made within 2 business days of obtaining the information necessary to conduct the review. OHIO REV. CODE ANN. § 1751.81(C) (2004). Concurrent review determinations must be made within 1 business day of obtaining the information necessary to conduct the review. OHIO REV. CODE ANN. § 1751.81(D) (2004). Retrospective review determinations must be made within 30 business days of obtaining the information necessary to conduct the review. If warranted by the patient's medical condition, review determinations must be completed in less than the time frames listed above. OHIO REV. CODE ANN. § 1751.81(D) (2004).

2. **Contents of notice of adverse determination.**

   a. **Reasons for adverse determination.** A written notification of an adverse determination shall include the principal reason or reasons for the determination, and instructions for requesting a written statement of the clinical rationale used to make the determination. A health insuring corporation shall provide the clinical rationale for an adverse determination in writing to any party who received notice of the adverse determination and who follows the instructions for a request. OHIO REV. CODE ANN. § 1751.81(G) (2004).

    b. **Notice of Appeal Rights.** Required. A written notification of an adverse determination shall include instructions for initiating a reconsideration of the determination or an internal review. OHIO REV. CODE ANN. § 1751.81(G) (2004).

B. **Appeals requirements.** Health insuring corporations and utilization review organizations must provide for standard and expedited appeals. Health insuring corporations shall establish and maintain independent review.

C. **Internal Review.** A health insuring corporation shall establish and maintain an internal review system that has been approved by the superintendent of insurance. The system shall provide for review by a clinical peer and include adequate and reasonable procedures for review and resolution of appeals from enrollees concerning adverse determinations including procedures for verifying and reviewing appeals from enrollees whose medical conditions require expedited review. OHIO REV. CODE ANN. § 1751.83 (2004).

D. **External appeals.**

    1. In lieu of conducting a prospective, concurrent, or retrospective review providing a reconsideration, or conducting an internal review, a health insuring corporation may afford an enrollee an opportunity for an external review. If an external review is conducted, the health insuring corporation is not required to afford the enrollee an opportunity for any of the reviews that were disregarded pursuant, including the external review that may have resulted from a review that was disregarded pursuant to this section, unless new clinical information is submitted to the health insuring corporation. OHIO REV. CODE ANN. § 1751.811 (2004).

    2. Reconsideration is not a prerequisite to an internal or external review of an adverse determination. OHIO REV. CODE ANN. § 1751.82(C) (2004).

    3. OHIO REV. CODE ANN. § 1751.84 (2004) provides details on the external review process and the involvement of independent review organizations (IRO's) and OHIO REV. CODE ANN. § 1751.85 (2004) provides details on external, independent review of coverage for enrollees with terminal conditions.

    4. Time frame for determination. No provision. 60 days after receipt of standard requests/ 7 days after receipt of expedited requests. OHIO REV. CODE ANN. § 1751.84(B)(9)(a) (2004)

E. **Emergency Services.** No specific provision in the utilization review section of the law, *see* OHIO REV. CODE ANN. § 1753.28 (2004), but a 3-day period for reconsideration of an initial determination or concurrent review determination shall not apply if the seriousness of the medical condition requires a more expedited reconsideration.

VII. Recognition of URAC Accreditation Status

A. **Does the state recognize URAC accreditation?** Yes. Health insuring corporations and utilization review organizations may document compliance by submitting evidence of accreditation by an independent, private accrediting organization. URAC is one of the acceptable accrediting organizations. OHIO REV. CODE ANN. § 1751.821 (2004).

B. **Which of the state's requirements are waived for URAC-accredited organizations?** Upon review of the accreditation process, the Superintendent of Insurance may determine that such accreditation constitutes compliance by a health insuring corporation with the requirements of OHIO REV. CODE ANN. §§ 1751.77 to 1751.86. The Superintendent may deem URAC-accredited organizations to be in compliance in those areas where URAC standards meet or exceed Ohio's requirements. OHIO REV. CODE ANN. § 1751.821 (2004).

VIII. Miscellaneous

In response to inquiries from the State Medical Board of Ohio, Betty D. Montgomery, the Ohio Attorney General, offered an opinion on several issues related to utilization review. The Attorney General wrote: 1) Rendering of an opinion as to the medical necessity of physician medical services for purposes of utilization review is not considered to be the practice of medicine and does not come within the regulatory, investigatory, or enforcement authority of the State Medical Board; 2) Rendering of an opinion as to the medical necessity of physician medical services during an appeal of an adverse determination is not considered to be the practice of medicine and does not come within the regulatory, investigatory, or enforcement authority of the State Medical Board; and 3) A physician's rendering of a medical necessity opinion during the course of utilization review is not considered the practice of medicine and is not subject to review by the State Medical Board as an act of medical practice, but the physician remains subject to the jurisdiction of the State Medical Board in other respects. 99-044 Op. Att'y Gen.8-9 (Aug. 31, 1999).

Oklahoma

I. Scope and Applicability

A. **Who is subject to the state's utilization review laws?** A private review agent who approves or denies payment or who recommends approval or denial of payment for hospital or medical services or whose review results in approval or denial of payment for hospital or medical services on a case-by-case basis. OKLA. STAT. ANN. tit. 36, § 6553(A) (2004).

   1. **HMO's?** Yes, except for: federally qualified health maintenance organizations (HMO's) that have their utilization review plan on file with the Oklahoma State Department of Health; or HMO's that contract with certified private review agents.

   2. **Insurers?** Yes, except for insurers that contract with certified private review agents or perform in-house utilization review.

   3. **Utilization review organizations?** Yes.

   4. **Retrospective review?** Yes.

B. **What exemptions are provided, if any?** Exemptions are provided for the State and Education Employees Group Insurance Board, state and federal health programs, and in-house utilization review programs that do not result in payment decisions. OKLA. STAT. ANN. tit. 36, § 6553(B) (2004); OKLA. STAT. ANN. tit. 36, § 6553(c) (2004).

C. **What term does the state use to refer to regulated entities?** "Private review agent" is an entity or person who performs utilization review on behalf of an Oklahoma employer or a third party that providers or administers hospital and medical benefits to Oklahoma citizens, including, but not limited to, HMO's, unless federally regulated and licensed with a plan of utilization review on file with the Oklahoma Department of Health, or a health insurer, not-for-profit hospital service or medical plan, health insurance service organization, or preferred provider organization, or other entity offering health insurance policies, contracts, or benefits in Oklahoma. OKLA. STAT. ANN. tit. 36, § 6552(2) (2004).

D. **What activities does the state include in its definition of utilization review?** As used in the "Hospital and Medical Services Utilization Review Act" (OKLA. STAT. ANN. tit. 36, § 6551 et seq. (2004)), "utilization review" is "a system for prospectively, concurrently and retrospectively reviewing the appropriate and efficient allocation of hospital resources and medical services given or proposed to be given to a patient or group of patients." The definition does not include "an insurer's normal claim review process to determine compliance with the specific terms and conditions of the insurance policy." OKLA. STAT. ANN. tit. 36, § 6552(1) (2004).

II. Regulatory Information

A. **Responsible state agency.** Oklahoma Insurance Department.

B. **Contact Information.**

   1. **Name and Title:** Dalora Schafer, Director of Life Accident and Health, UR

   2. **Address:** PO Box 524408, Oklahoma City, OK, 73152

   3. **Phone and Facsimile:** (405) 521-3541; facsimile (405) 522-1860.

   4. **E-mail:** daloraschafer@insurance.state.ok.us.

   5. **Web site:** www.oid.state.ok.us.

III. Licensure/Certification Requirements

A. **What entities are required to obtain a license in the state to conduct utilization review for residents of the state?** A private review agent who approves or denies payment, recommends approval or denial of payment for hospital or medical services, or whose review results in approval or denial of payment for hospital or medical services on a case-by-case basis shall not conduct utilization review unless granted a certificate by the Insurance Commissioner. OKLA. STAT. ANN. tit. 36, § 6553(A) (2004). Every health insurance plan which proposes to administer a health benefits program that provides for the coverage of hospital and/or medical benefits and the utilization review of those benefits shall be certified in accordance with the Hospital and Medical Services Utilization Review Act. OKLA. STAT. ANN. tit. 36, § 6556(1) (2004).

   1. Requirements are waived for private review agents engaged in reviews of patients eligible under Social Security, and the conducting on in-house utilization review. OKLA. STAT. ANN. tit. 36, § 6554 (2004).

B. **How often must licensure be renewed?** Annually. A certificate expires on the first anniversary of its effective date. OKLA. STAT. ANN. tit. 36, § 6560 (2004).

C. **Licensure fees (initial and renewal).** Initial and renewal fees are $500. OKLA. STAT. ANN. tit. 36, § 6557 (2004). Insurance companies that provide for in-house utilization review shall pay an annual fee to the Insurance Commissioner of $500. OKLA. STAT. ANN. tit. 36, § 6559(B) (2004).

D. **Documentation required for licensure.** The private review agent must submit an application and documentation that includes:

1. a utilization review plan that demonstrates compliance with the state's requirements,

2. the type and qualification of personnel either employed or under contract to perform the utilization review,

3. policies and procedures that show agents are accessible to patients and providers, policies and procedures to ensure that all state and federal laws regarding confidentiality are followed,

4. documentation used to inform patients and providers of the plan's requirements,

5. a list of the third-party payers whom utilization review services are rendered,

6. and procedures for handling complaints. OKLA. STAT. ANN. tit. 36, § 6558 (2004).

E. The application and annual renewal forms are at http://www.oid.state.ok.us. Look under Agent & Broker tab then in the Life, Accident and Health publications.

F. **Exemptions from licensure.** Out-of-state organizations are not granted an exemption from the state's licensure and certification requirements even if they are duly licensed and/or certified in their state of domicile.

IV. Program Requirements

A. **Clinical review criteria.** Review criteria must be established with input from health care providers representing major areas of specialty and certified by the boards of the various American medical specialties. OKLA. STAT. ANN. tit. 36, § 6558(1)(b) (2004).

B. **Prohibitions against financial incentives.** No provision.

C. **Telephone access standards.** In-state private review agents must be accessible by toll-free telephone 5 days a week during normal business hours. Out-of-state private review agents shall be accessible by toll-free telephone at least 40 hours per week during normal business hours, shall be capable of accepting or recording off-hours calls, and shall respond to such calls within 2 working days. OKLA. STAT. ANN. tit. 36, § 6558(3) (2004).

D. **Quality assurance program.** No specifics. However, review agents must submit to the Commissioner in their application procedures for receiving and handling complaints by

patients and health care providers concerning utilization review. OKLA. STAT. ANN. tit. 36, § 6558(8) (2004).

E. **Delegation of utilization review functions.** No provision, but those health insurance plans which propose to administer a health benefits program that provides for coverage of hospital and/or medical benefits and the utilization review of those benefits shall contract with a private review agent who is certified in accordance with the Hospital Services Utilization Review Act. OKLA. STAT. ANN. tit. 36, § 6556(2) (2004).

F. **Confidentiality.** Private review agents must comply with all applicable state and federal laws protecting the confidentiality of individual medical records. OKLA. STAT. ANN. tit. 36, § 6558(4) (2004). A private review agent shall not disclose or publish individual medical records or any other confidential medical information obtained in the performance of utilization review activities without the appropriate procedures for protecting the patient's confidentiality. OKLA. STAT. ANN. tit. 36, § 6562 (2004).

V. Reviewer Qualifications

A. **Qualifications of reviewers that render utilization review determinations (at each level of utilization review, if applicable).** No provision.

B. **Requirements for medical director.** No provision.

C. **Requirement for "same-state" licensure.** Yes. Required for denial for medical necessity appeals and for health professionals supervising utilization review activities.

VI. Reviews and Appeals

A. **Review determinations and notice to patients/providers.**

1. Time frame for determination. No provision.

2. Contents of notice of adverse determination. After a request for medical evaluation, treatment, or procedures has been rejected in whole or in part and in the event a copy of the report on said rejection is requested, a copy of the report of a private review agent concerning the rejection shall be mailed by the insurer, postage prepaid, to the ill or injured person, the treating health care provider or to the person financially responsible for the patient's bill within 15 days after receipt of the request for the

report. OKLA. STAT. ANN. tit. 36, § 6558(9) (2004).

3. Reasons for adverse determination. No provision.

4. Notice of appeal rights. No provision.

5. Note: Every health benefit plan subject to the provisions of the Oklahoma Managed Care External Review Act shall establish internal appeals procedures in accordance with rules promulgated by the state regulatory entity of the health benefit plan. The State Board of Health and the Insurance Commissioner shall respectively promulgate rules for internal review procedures for the health benefit plans subject to licensure or regulation by the State Department of Health or the Insurance Department as applicable. The rules shall include but not be limited to provisions for expedited internal review procedures in emergency situations. OKLA. STAT. ANN. tit. 63, § 2528.4(B) (2004).

   a. Upon the request of an insured person or the representative of an insured person, every health benefit plan shall provide the requester with clear information about the terms, conditions and procedures of the internal review process and the external review process. OKLA. STAT. ANN. tit. 63, § 2528.4(C) (2004).

B. **Appeals requirements.** Private review agents must have a process by which patients or health care providers may seek reconsideration or appeal of adverse decisions concerning requests for medical evaluation, treatment, or procedures. OKLA. STAT. ANN. tit. 36, § 6558(1)(c) (2004).

1. Time frame for determination. No provision.

2. External appeals. An insured person shall have the right to an external review by an independent review organization of a decision under a health benefit plan to deny coverage of or reimbursement for a medical treatment or service to the insured person that is otherwise a covered benefit when:

   a. All applicable internal appeals procedures established by the health benefit plan have been exhausted;

   b. The denial is based on a determination by the health benefit plan that the service or treatment is not medically necessary, medically appropriate, or medically effective;

   c. The usual, customary and reasonable charge or allowable charge, as shown in the health benefit plan's fee schedule, of the service or treatment for which coverage or reimbursement was denied by the health benefit plan exceeds $1,000.00;

   d. The insured person or the designee of the insured person agrees to the terms and conditions of external review as provided in Section 5 of this act. OKLA. STAT. ANN. tit. 63, § 2528.3 (2004).

   e. Every health benefit plan that is offered issued or renewed after February 1, 2000, shall provide for an external review process by an independent review organization in accordance with the provisions of the Oklahoma Managed Care External Review Act. OKLA. STAT. ANN. tit. 63, § 2528.4(A) (2004). This does not include health benefit plans that do not use a primary care physician-based prior authorization system and that have written procedures that permit external review, health benefit plans and care provided under the Social Security Act, and worker's compensation benefits; and

   f. An insured person or the designee of an insured person shall be required to pay $50.00 to the health benefit plan toward the cost of an external review. OKLA. STAT. ANN. tit. 63, § 2528.5(A) (2004).

C. **Emergency Services.** Internal appeals procedures must provide for expedited internal review procedures in emergency situation. OKLA. STAT. ANN. tit. 63, § 2528.4(B) (2004).

VII. Recognition of URAC Accreditation Status

A. **Does the state recognize URAC accreditation?** No.

B. **Which of the state's requirements are waived for URAC-accredited organizations?** Not applicable.

Oregon

I. Scope and Applicability

A. **Who is subject to the state's utilization review laws?** All insurers offering a health benefit plan in this state that provide utilization review or have utilization review provided on their behalf. OR. REV. STAT. § 743.807(1) (2004).
   1. HMO's? Yes.
   2. Insurers? Yes.
   3. Utilization review organizations? Yes.
   4. Retrospective review? Yes.

B. **What exemptions are provided, if any?** The definition of health benefit plans do not include coverage for accident only, specific disease or condition only, credit, disability income, coverage of Medicare services pursuant to contracts with the federal government, Medicare supplement insurance policies, coverage of CHAMPUS services pursuant to contracts with the federal government, benefits delivered through a flexible spending arrangement when the benefits are provided in addition to a group health benefit plan, long term care insurance, hospital indemnity only, short term health insurance policies (the duration of which does not exceed 6 months including renewals), student accident and health insurance policies, dental only, vision only, a policy of stop-loss coverage, coverage issued as a supplement to liability insurance, insurance arising out of a workers' compensation or similar law, automobile medical payment insurance or insurance under which benefits are payable with or without regard to fault and that is statutorily required to be contained in any liability insurance policy or equivalent self-insurance. Nothing in this subsection shall be construed to regulate any employee welfare benefit plan that is exempt from state regulation because of the federal Employee Retirement Income Security Act of 1974, as amended. OR. REV. STAT. § 743.730(18)(b) (2004).

C. **What term does the state use to refer to regulated entities?** Comprehensive health benefit plans

D. **What activities does the state include in its definition of utilization review?** "Utilization review" is defined as "a set of formal techniques used by an insurer or delegated by the insurer designed to monitor the use of or evaluate the medical necessity, appropriateness, efficacy or efficiency of health care services, procedures or settings." OR. REV. STAT. § 743.730(15) (2004).

II. Regulatory Information

A. **Responsible state agency.** Department of Consumer and Business Services, Insurance Division.

B. **Contact Information.**
   1. **Name and Title:** Carol Simila, Consumer Advocate Liaison.
   2. **Address:** 350 Winter Street NE, 4th Floor, P.O. Box 14480, Salem, OR 97309-0405.
   3. **Phone and Facsimile:** (503) 947-7629; facsimile (503) 378-4351.
   4. **E-mail:** carol.r.simila@state.or.us
   5. **Web site:** www.cbs.state.or.us/external/ins.

III. Licensure/Certification Requirements

A. **What entities are required to obtain a license in the state to conduct utilization review for residents of the state?** Oregon does not require utilization review organizations to obtain a licensure or certification.

B. **How often must licensure be renewed?** Not applicable.

C. **Licensure fees (initial and renewal).** Not applicable.

D. **Documentation required.** All insurers offering a health benefit plan in this state that provide utilization review or have utilization review provided on their behalf shall file an annual summary with the Department of Consumer and Business Services that describes all utilization review policies, including delegated utilization review functions, and documents the insurer's procedures for monitoring of utilization review activities. OR. REV. STAT. § 743.807(1) (2004).

E. **Exemption from licensure.** Not applicable.

IV. Program Requirements

A. **Clinical review criteria.** For all utilization review performed pursuant to a medical services contract to which an insurer is not a party, and all insurers offering a health benefit plan, the criteria used in the review process and the method of development of the criteria shall be made available for review upon request to a party, to medical service contracts, and to contracting providers. OR. REV. STAT. § 743.806(1) (2004); OR. REV. STAT. § 743.807(1) (2004).

B. **Prohibitions against financial incentives.** No provision.

C. **Telephone access standards.** Qualified health care personnel must be available for same-day telephone responses to inquiries concerning certification of continued length of stay. OR. REV. STAT. § 743.806(4) (2004); OR. REV. STAT. § 743.807(2)(d) (2004).

D. **Quality assurance program.** No specific UM provisions. However, all insurers offering managed health insurance in this state shall have a quality assessment program that enables the insurer to evaluate maintain and improve the quality of health services provided to enrollees. OR. REV. STAT. § 743.814(1) (2004).

E. **Delegation of utilization review functions.** Annual summary must document insurer's procedures for monitoring delegated utilization review activities. OR. REV. STAT. § 743.807(1) (2004).

F. **Confidentiality.** Utilization review organizations must comply with all applicable laws protecting the confidentiality of individual medical records. *See* OR. REV. STAT. § 743.839 (2004).

V. Reviewer Qualifications

A. **Qualifications of reviewers that render utilization review determinations (at each level of utilization review, if applicable).** An Oregon-licensed doctor of medicine or osteopathy must be responsible for all final recommendations regarding utilization review determinations, and must consult with appropriate medical and mental health specialists in making such recommendations. OR. REV. STAT. § 743.806(2) (2004); OR. REV. STAT. § 743.807(2)(b) (2004).

B. **Requirements for medical director.** No provision.

C. **Requirement for "same-state" licensure.** An Oregon-licensed doctor of medicine or osteopathy shall be responsible for all final recommendations regarding utilization review determinations and shall consult as appropriate with medical and mental health specialists in making such recommendations. OR. REV. STAT. § 743.806(2)(d) (2004); OR. REV. STAT. § 743.807(2)(b) (2004).

VI. Reviews and Appeals

A. **Review determinations and notice to patients/providers.**

B. **Time frame for determination.** Requests for prior authorization (prospective review) of nonemergency service must be answered within 2 business days. Requests for certification of continued length of stay (concurrent review) must be answered the same day. OR. REV. STAT. § 743.806(4) (2004); OR. REV. STAT. § 743.807(2)(d) (2004).

1. **Contents of notice of adverse determination.** No provision.
2. **Reasons for adverse determination.** No provision.
3. **Notice of Appeal Rights.** No provision.

C. **Appeals requirements.** Patients or providers who are subject to an adverse determination (not medically necessary or experimental) must be provided an opportunity for a timely appeal before an appropriate medical consultant or peer review committee. OR. REV. STAT. § 743.806(3) (2004); OR. REV. STAT. § 743.807(2)(c) (2004).

1. **Time frame for determination.** A patient or provider shall have an opportunity for "timely appeal." OR. REV. STAT. § 743.807(2)(c) (2004). Insurer shall acknowledge receipt of notice of appeal not later than 7 days after receiving notice and appropriate medical consultant or peer review committee shall review and decide appeal not later than 30 days after receiving notice. OR. ADMIN. R. 836-053-1140 (2004).

2. **Internal reviews.** All insurers offering a health benefit plan in Oregon shall have an appeal process for grievances that includes at least the following:

   a. Three levels of review, the second of which shall be by persons not previously involved in the dispute and the third of which shall provide external review pursuant to an external review program.

   b. Opportunity for enrollees and any representatives of the enrollees to appear before a review panel at either the first or second level of review.

   c. Written decisions in plain language justifying appeal determinations, including specific references to relevant provisions of the health benefit plan and related written corporate practices. OR. REV. STAT. § 743.804(3)(f) (2004).

3. **External appeals.** An insurer offering health benefit plans in this state shall have an external review program. Each insurer shall provide the external review through an independent review organization that is under contract with the Director of the Department of Consumer and Business Services to provide external review. Each health benefit plan must allow an enrollee, by applying to the insurer, to obtain review by an independent review organization of a dispute relating to an adverse decision by the insurer on one or more of the following:

a. Whether a course or plan of treatment is medically necessary.

b. Whether a course or plan of treatment is experimental or investigational.

c. Whether a course or plan of treatment that an enrollee is undergoing is an active course of treatment for purposes of continuity of care.
OR. REV. STAT. § 743.857(1) (2004).

D. **Emergency Services.** An insurer shall expedite an enrollee's case of external review if a provider with an established clinical relationship to the enrollee certifies in writing and provides supporting documentation that the ordinary time period for external review would seriously jeopardize the life or health of the enrollee or the enrollee's ability to regain maximum function. OR. REV. STAT. § 743.857(4) (2004).

VII. Recognition of URAC Accreditation Status

A. **Does the state recognize URAC accreditation?** No.

B. **Which of the state's requirements are waived for URAC-accredited organizations?** Not applicable.

VIII. Miscellaneous

The Office of Medical Assistance Program, Oregon Department of Human Services, administers the Medicaid program in Oregon and has prepared the "Prioritized List of Health Services." In addition to using this to rank health services from the most important to least important based on the comparative benefit to the population to be served to determine the benefit package under the Medicaid demonstration, the Office for Oregon Health Plan Policy and Research Oregon Health Plan conducts utilization review of services of health care facilities. OR. REV. STAT. § 442.420 (2004).

Pennsylvania

I. Scope and Applicability

A. **Who is subject to the state's utilization review laws?** Any entity conducting utilization review for managed care plans must be certified by the Department of Health, except as otherwise noted below. PA. STAT. ANN. tit. 40, § 991.2151(a). Any entity interested in placement on the Department of Health's list of approved organizations to conduct external grievance appeals will also require certification. An entity can become certified for both activities.

1. **HMO's?** Yes, except that HMO's do not need to obtain a utilization review certificate.

2. **Insurers?** Yes, if conducting utilization review on behalf of managed care plans.

3. **Utilization review organizations?** Yes, if conducting utilization review on behalf of managed care plans.

4. **Retrospective review?** Yes.

B. **What exemptions are provided, if any?** Licensed entities such as health maintenance organizations (HMO's), and gatekeeper preferred provider organizations (PPO's) do not need UR certification from the Department of Health, but must provide information to the Department during licensure and on an ongoing basis to demonstrate compliance with Act 68 [PA. STAT. ANN. tit. 40, §§ 991.2001-991.2361]. Note: Act 68 only applies to health insurance products and does not apply to automobile or workers' compensation insurance activities. Also exempt from Act 68 are plans covered under the Employee Retirement Income Security Act of 1974, non-gatekeeper PPO's, and other nonmanaged care plans.

C. **What term does the state use to refer to regulated entities?** A "utilization review entity" is "Any entity certified pursuant to PA. STAT. ANN. tit. 40, §§ 991.2151 and 991.2152 that performs utilization review on behalf of a managed care plan." PA. STAT. ANN. tit. 40, § 991.2102 .

D. **What activities does the state include in its definition of utilization review?** "Utilization review" is defined as a "system of prospective, concurrent or retrospective utilization review performed by a utilization review entity of the medical necessity and appropriateness of health care services prescribed, provided or proposed to be provided to an enrollee." This definition does not include requests for clarification of coverage, eligibility, or health care service verification and does not include a health care provider's internal quality assurance or utilization review process unless such review results in the denial of payment for a health care service. PA. STAT. ANN. tit. 40, § 991.2102 .

II. Regulatory Information

A. **Responsible state agency.** Department of Health, Bureau of Managed Care.

B. **Contact Information.**

1. **Name and Title:** William Wiegmann, Director, Division of Certification.

2. **Address:** P.O. Box 90, Harrisburg, PA 17108 - 0090.

3. **Phone and Facsimile:** (717) 787-5193; facsimile (717) 705-0947.

4. **E-mail:** wwiegmann@state.pa.us.

5. **Web site:** www.health.state.pa.us.

III. Certification Requirements

A. **What entities are required to obtain a license in the state to conduct utilization review for residents of the state?** Any entity must be certified to perform utilization review if conducting utilization review for managed care plans.

B. **How often must certification be renewed?** Every 3 years.

C. **Certification fees (initial and renewal).** $1000 initial fee to conduct utilization review on behalf of managed care plans; $2000 to conduct external grievance appeal reviews. Renewals, $500 for each. 28 PA. CODE § 9.746.

D. **Documentation required for certification.** An application for certification as a utilization review entity is available at the Department of Health's Web site at: www.health.state.pa.us. Utilization review entities that wish to pursue the option to conduct external grievance reviews of enrollee appeals (all grievance appeals or only behavioral health appeals, such as mental health and drug- and alcohol-related) must also complete this form, and answer additional questions. 28 PA. CODE § 9.743 (2004).

E. **Exemptions from license.** Out-of-state utilization review entities conducting utilization review on behalf of Pennsylvania managed care plans are not granted an exemption from Pennsylvania's licensure and certification requirements even if they are duly licensed and/or certified in their state of domicile.

IV. Program Requirements

A. **Clinical review criteria.** Information is requested regarding the clinical criteria utilized, frequency of updates to criteria, input of physicians, etc. Providers may request the criteria for an adverse determination.

B. **Prohibitions against financial incentives.** Compensation to any entity or person conducting utilization review may not contain direct or indirect incentives to approve or deny payment for the delivery of any health care service.

C. **Telephone access standards.** Utilization review entities must provide access by toll-free telephone at least 40 hours per week during normal business hours and must maintain a system to receive calls during nonbusiness hours. Utilization review entities must respond to calls received during nonbusiness hours within 1 working day after the receipt of the call.

D. **Quality assurance program.** No provision.

E. **Delegation of utilization review functions.** No provision.

F. **Confidentiality.** Utilization review entities and managed care plans shall adopt and maintain procedures to ensure the adequate protection of all identifiable information regarding enrollee health, diagnosis, and treatment and keep confidential in compliance with all applicable federal and state laws, regulations, and professional ethical standards. PA. STAT. ANN. tit. 40, § 991.2131(2004). Applicants must submit procedures and policies to demonstrate this. PA. STAT. ANN. tit. 40, § 991.2152 (2004).

V. Reviewer Qualifications

A. **Qualifications of reviewers that render utilization review determinations (at each level of utilization review, if applicable).**
   1. All individuals conducting utilization review must have health care licenses in good standing, or other appropriate credentials.
   2. A licensed physician (in Pennsylvania, an M.D. or a D.O.) must make all adverse determinations, except that qualified psychologists may review adverse determinations for services within psychologists' scope of practice (excluding denials of payment for inpatient care or prescription drugs).
   3. Grievance appeal reviews, including external grievance review decisions, must include a licensed physician in the same or similar specialty as typically manages the condition

under review, or, if appropriate, a licensed psychologist.
   4. A person who was not previously involved in the adverse determination must conduct appeal reviews.
   5. A panel of at least 3 people, none of whom were previously involved, must consider second-level appeals in the adverse determination of initial appeal.

B. **Requirements for medical director.** No provision.

C. **Requirement for "same-state" licensure.** Yes, regulations require a managed care organization's medical director responsible for overseeing utilization review and quality assurance to be licensed to practice in Pennsylvania.

VI. Reviews and Appeals

A. **Review determinations and notice to patients/providers.**
   1. **Time frame for determination.** Prospective review decisions must be made and communicated verbally within 2 working days after receiving the information necessary to complete the review. 28 PA. CODE § 9.753(b) (2004). Then, the decision must be communicated in writing or electronically within an additional 2 working days. Concurrent review determinations must be made and communicated within 1 working day after receiving the information necessary to complete the review, and in writing within 1 additional working day. 28 PA. CODE § 9.753(a) (2004). Retrospective review determinations must be made and communicated within 30 days after receiving the information necessary to complete the review and in writing within another 15 working days. 28 PA. CODE § 9.753(c) (2004).
   2. **Contents of notice of adverse determination.**
      a. **Reasons for adverse determination.** Required in writing, including the contractual basis and clinical rationale for the decision.
      b. **Notice of Appeal Rights.** Required. Must include the procedures, address and timeframe to appeal decision.

B. **Appeals requirements.** Managed care plans must provide for both standard and expedited appeals. 28 PA. CODE § 9.504(b) (2004). A certified utilization review entity may be delegated the appeal process by a managed care plan but must be approved by the Department to conduct appeals. A "grievance" is "a request by an enrollee or a health care provider, with the written consent of the enrollee, to have a managed care plan or utilization review entity review the denial of a health care service based on medical necessity and appropriateness.") Plans must have 2 levels of appeals. A certified utilization review entity may be approved to conduct one or both levels of appeal.

1. **Time frame for determination.** Standard appeals must be completed within 30 days after the appeal is filed. Second-level appeals must be completed within 45 days after a request for second-level review. Expedited appeals must be completed within 48 hours after the appeal is filed.

2. **External appeals.** In addition to the internal grievance process, there is also an external appeal process. External appeals are conducted by utilization review entities certified and selected by the Department of Health. Such external review entity shall issue a written decision within 60 days of the filing of the external grievance and inform the managed care plan, enrollee, and health care provider of the basis and clinical rationale for the decision. The external review decision shall be subject to appeal to a court of competent jurisdiction within 60 days of receipt of notice of decision. If approved by the Department of Health, written contracts between managed care plans and health care providers may provide an alternative dispute resolution system to the external grievance system.

C. **Emergency Services.** Utilization review entities must use the "prudent layperson" standard when evaluating emergency services. Emergency services do not require pre-certification.

VII. Recognition of URAC Accreditation Status

A. **Does the state recognize URAC accreditation?** No. The Department of Health recognizes national accrediting organizations and standards and may accept such accreditation in lieu of an on-site inspection. PA. STAT. ANN. tit. 40, § 991.2151(c) (2004).

B. **Which of the state's requirements are waived for URAC-accredited organizations?** None, but the Department of Health may use a nationally-recognized accrediting body acceptable to the Department to support an applicant's compliance (and to verify continued compliance) as a certified utilization review entity.

VIII. Miscellaneous

A licensed insurer or a managed care plan with a certificate of authority shall comply with the standards and procedures of the Commonwealth's insurance law governing utilization review, but shall not be required to obtain separate certification as a utilization review entity. PA. STAT. ANN. tit. 40, § 991.2151(e) (2004).

Puerto Rico

I.   Scope and Applicability

At this time, there are no statutes, regulations or case law pertaining to utilization review or to utilization management in the Commonwealth of Puerto Rico.

II.   Regulatory Information

   A.   **Responsible state agency.** Office of the Commissioner of Insurance, Commonwealth of Puerto Rico

   B.   **Contact Information**
   1.   **Name and Title:** Aurea López, Deputy Commissioner of Supervision & Compliance.
   2.   **Address:** P.O. Box 8330, Fernández Juncos Station, Santurce, PR 00910-8330.
   3.   **Phone and Facsimile:** (787) 722-8686 or (787) 722-8782; facsimile (787) 722-4400.
   4.   **E-mail:** alopez@ocs.gobierno.pr.
   5.   **Web site:** www.ocs.gobierno.pr.

III.   Recognition of URAC Accreditation Status

   A.   **Does the state recognize URAC accreditation?** URAC accreditation is not formally recognized by the government of Puerto Rico. Nonetheless, URAC accreditation is recognized by the healthcare industry in Puerto Rico and its standards are often included in requirements set forth in contracts between healthcare providers.

   B.   **Which of the state's requirements are waived for URAC-accredited organizations?** Not applicable at this time.

Rhode Island

I. Scope and Applicability

A. **Who is subject to the state's utilization review laws?** Any review agent conducting utilization review in the state of Rhode Island. R.I. GEN. LAWS § 23-17.12-3(a) (2004). **What exemptions are provided, if any?** The Department of Health shall waive certification requirements for activities of review agents conducted for federal programs such as Medicaid, Medicare, and the Civilian Health and Medical Program of the Uniformed Services (CHAMPUS) only when a direct conflict exists. Also, URAC-accredited review agencies that do not perform reviews related to mental health/substance abuse are waived from certain sections of the R.I. GEN. LAWS § 23-17.12 .

1. HMO's? Yes.
2. Insurers? Yes.
3. Utilization review organizations? Yes.
4. Retrospective review? Yes.

B. **What term does the state use to refer to regulated entities?** A "review agent" is defined as a "person or entity or insurer performing utilization review that is either employed by, affiliated with, under contract with, or acting on behalf of: 1) A business entity doing business in this state; or 2) A party that provides or administers health care benefits to citizens of this state, including a health insurer, self-insured plan, non-profit health service plan, health insurance service organization, preferred provider organization or health maintenance organization authorized to offer health insurance policies or contracts or pay for the delivery of health care services or treatment in this state; or 3) A provider." R.I. GEN. LAWS § 23-17.12-2(9) (2004).

C. **What activities does the state include in its definition of utilization review?** "Utilization review" is defined as "the prospective, concurrent, or retrospective assessment of the necessity and appropriateness of the allocation of health care services of a provider, given or proposed to be given to a patient or group of patients." The definition does not mean 1) elective requests for the clarification of coverage; 2) claims review that does not include the assessment of the medical necessity and appropriateness; 3) a provider's internal quality assurance program except if it is associated with a health care financing mechanism; 4) the therapeutic interchange of drugs or devices by a pharmacy operating as part of a licensed inpatient health care facility; and 5) the assessment by a licensed pharmacist in a pharmacy operating as part of a licensed inpatient health care facility in the interpretation, evaluation and implementation of medical orders, including assessments and/or comparisons involving formularies and medical orders. R.I. GEN. LAWS § 23-17.12-2(11) (2004).

II. Regulatory Information

A. **Responsible state agency.** Rhode Island Department of Health, Division of Health Services Regulation, Office of Managed Care Regulation.

B. **Contact Information.**
1. **Name and Title:** Fernanda da Costa, MPH, Chief, Office of Managed Care Regulation .
2. **Address:** 3 Capitol Hill, Room 410, Providence, RI 02908-5097.
3. **Phone and Facsimile:** (401) 222-6015; facsimile (401) 222-3017.
4. **E-mail:** fernl@doh.state.ri.us.
5. **Web site:** www.health.ri.gov.

III. Licensure/Certification Requirements

A. **What entities are required to obtain a license in the state to conduct utilization review for residents of the state?** All "review agents." R.I. GEN. LAWS § 23-17.12-3(a) (2004). Individuals are not required to hold separate certification under the Rhode Island Utilization Review Act when acting as either an employee of, an affiliate of, a contractor for, or otherwise acting on behalf of a certified review agent. R.I. GEN. LAWS § 23-17.12-3(c) (2004).

B. **How often must licensure be renewed?** Certification is required every 2 years. R.I. GEN. LAWS § 23-17.12-5 (2004).

C. **Licensure fees (initial and renewal).** In addition to an initial $500 application certification fee, the Rhode Island Department of Health bills the utilization review agencies monthly for time spent on activities related to maintaining certification. R.I. GEN. LAWS § 23-17.12-3 (14) (h) (2004).(2004).

D. **Documentation required for licensure.** Review agents must submit an application, utilization review plan, and written policies and procedures that document compliance with state requirements as set forth in R.I. GEN. LAWS § 23-17.12-4 (2004).

E. Exemption from licensure. N/A

IV. Program Requirements

A. **Clinical review criteria.** Criteria must be established and periodically updated with appropriate consultation with the Medical Directors of each Rhode Island licensed hospital, and at least 5 Rhode Island-licensed providers, including those providers in the same specialty as would typically order the services subject to the criteria.

B. **Prohibitions against financial incentives.** No employee of or other individual rendering an adverse determination for a review agent may receive any financial incentives based on the number of denials of certification. No appeals reviewers may receive a bonus or incentive based on making or upholding an adverse determination.

C. **Telephone access standards.** A representative of the review agent must be reasonably available to patients and providers 5 days a week during normal business hours in the State of Rhode Island and during the agent's review operations. If the review agency performs concurrent review, it must maintain an acceptable mechanism to conduct such concurrent review after the agency's normal business hours.

D. **Quality assurance program.** Review agents must have quality assurance program to monitor and evaluate the implementation of administrative and operational policies on an annual basis.

E. **Delegation of utilization review functions.** Review agents must describe the circumstances under which utilization review may be delegated and demonstrate that entities performing delegated utilization review functions are certified in Rhode Island.

F. **Confidentiality.** Review agents must comply with all applicable state and federal laws protecting the confidentiality of individual medical records and health care information.

V. Reviewer Qualifications

A. **Qualifications of reviewers that render utilization review determinations (at each level of utilization review, if applicable).**

1. Only a licensed physician, dentist, or other practitioner with the same licensure status as the ordering practitioner shall make adverse determinations.

2. Only a licensed practitioner with the same licensing status as the treating provider or a licensed physician in the same or similar general specialty as typically manages the medical condition under review may consider second level appeals.

B. **Requirements for medical director.** No provision.

C. **Requirement for "same-state" licensure.** No provision.

VI. Reviews and Appeals

A. **Review determinations and notice to patients/providers.**

1. **Time frame for determination.** Review agents shall notify providers and patients of prospective determinations within 1 business day of receipt of all necessary information, except for non-urgent or non-emergent cases which must be communicated within 7 business days of receipt of all necessary information or prior to the proposed date of service if more than 7 days. Notification of concurrent adverse determinations shall be communicated to the patient and the provider of record prior to the end of the current certified period. Notification of retrospective adverse determinations must be communicated within 30 business days of receipt of a request for payment and all supporting documentation for the covered benefit being reviewed.

B. **Contents of notice of adverse determination.**

1. **Reasons for adverse determination.** Required. Notice of determination not to certify shall include principal reasons for adverse determination.

2. **Notice of Appeal Rights.** Required. Such notice shall include procedures to initiate an appeal, telephone number of contact person, and reasonable period of time in which to file appeal.

C. **Appeals requirements.** Review agents shall maintain and make available to enrollees and providers a written description of appeal procedure by which patient or provider may seek review of determinations not to certify. Review agents shall assure licensed practitioner with same licensure status as ordering practitioner or licensed physician in the same or similar specialty conducts the next level of review. R.I. CODE R. 23-17-6.4 UR (2004). No reviewer who has been involved in prior reviews at either the adverse determination or appeal level may participate in subsequent reviews.

1. **Time frame for determination.** For first and second level appeals, determinations for concurrent and prospective reviews must be communicated to the patient and provider within 15 business days of the receipt of required documentation. Determinations in retrospective reviews shall be communicated within 30 business days. For first and second level appeals, if appeal notice is verbal and provided within the required timeframes, written notification to the patient and provider may be given within 6 business days of verbal notice. Review agents shall complete adjudication of expedited appeals within 2 business days of the receipt of all necessary information.

2. **External appeals.** The Rhode Island Department of Health may review an internal appeal regarding any adverse determination in response to a written complaint. Where the second level of appeal is unsuccessful, the review agent shall provide an external appeal by an "unrelated and objective appeal agency," R.I. GEN. LAWS § 23-17.12-10(a) (2004), selected by the Director of Health. Neutral physicians, dentists, or other practitioners in the same or similar general specialty shall make external appeal decisions. The review agent and patient share equally the cost of the external appeal, but if the decision of the review agent is overturned, the review agent shall reimburse the appealing party. The decision of an external appeal agency is binding, but any aggrieved person who has exhausted all administrative remedies or is aggrieved by a final decision of the external appeals agency is entitled to judicial review.

D. **Emergency Services.** The review agent must provide immediate treatment for any condition that the treating provider has determined to be an emergency.

VII. Recognition of URAC Accreditation Status

A. **Does the state recognize URAC accreditation?** Yes, but there is an exception for utilization review activities performed to determine the necessity and appropriateness of substance abuse and mental health care, treatment, or services.

B. **Which of the state's requirements are waived for URAC-accredited organizations?** The Rhode Island Department of Health determines the waiver of the requirements of URAC accredited review agencies. Except for review agencies that do not perform reviews related to mental health/substance abuse and except for requirements related to sections 23-17.12-9, 23-17.12-12 and 23-17.12-14 of the of the R.I. GEN. LAWS § 23-17.12, URAC accredited review agencies may be waived from requirements of the of the R.I. GEN. LAWS § 23-17.12 (2004).

VIII. Miscellaneous.

Utilization review agencies are required to provide reports to the Rhode Island Department of Health on a quarterly basis to the Rhode Island Department of Health.

South Carolina

I. Scope and Applicability

A. **Who is subject to the state's utilization review laws?** Private Review Agents, insurance companies, administrators of insurance benefit plans and health maintenance organizations must comply with the laws governing utilization review. S.C. CODE ANN. §38-70-15 (2004).

   1. **HMO's?** No. HMO's licensed and regulated by the Department of Insurance that perform utilization review are not required to obtain a certificate. However, these HMOs must comply with such provisions as procedures for utilization review determinations, appeals process, information upon which utilization review is conducted, retrospective review, accessibility, staff and program qualifications, and confidentiality. S.C. CODE ANN. REGS. 69-47 §II(H)(2) (2004).

   2. **Insurers?** Insurance companies licensed and regulated by the Department of Insurance that perform utilization review are not required to obtain a certificate. However, these insurers must comply with such provisions as procedures for utilization review determinations, appeals process, information upon which utilization review is conducted, retrospective review, accessibility, staff and program qualifications, and confidentiality. S.C. CODE ANN. REGS. 69-47 §II (H)(2) (2004).

   3. **Utilization review organizations?** Yes

   4. **Retrospective review?** Yes.

B. **What exemptions are provided, if any?** Insurance companies, administrators of insurance benefit plans, and health maintenance organizations (HMO's) licensed and regulated by the South Carolina Department of Insurance, must comply with the substantive provisions of the law, but are exempt from the certification requirements for private review agents. Private review agents performing utilization reviews only for single employer, self-insured employee health benefit plans or pursuant to federal law are not required to obtain a certificate. S.C. CODE ANN. REGS. 69-47 §II(H) (2004).

C. **What term does the state use to refer to regulated entities?** "Private review agent" is used interchangeably with "utilization review agent." A private review agent is defined as "a person performing utilization reviews who is either under contract with or acting on behalf of, but not employed by: 1) a South Carolina business entity; 2) the State of South Carolina; or 3) a hospital." S.C. CODE ANN. § 38-70-10(2) (2004).

D. **What activities does the state include in its definition of utilization review?** "Utilization review" is "a system for reviewing the necessary, appropriate, and efficient allocation of health care resources and services given or proposed to be given to a patient or group of patients." S.C. CODE ANN. § 38-70-10(1) (2004).

II. Regulatory Information

A. **Responsible state agency.** Department of Insurance, Licensing & Education Services Division.

B. **Contact Information.**
   1. **Name and Title:** Willie C. Seawright, Licensing Coordinator.
   2. **Address:** P.O. Box 100105, 300 Arbor Lake Drive, Suite 12000, Columbia, SC 29223.
   3. **Phone and Facsimile:** (803) 737-6134; facsimile (803) 737-6100.
   4. **E-mail:** wseawright@doi.state.sc.us.
   5. **Web site:** www.doi.state.sc.us/

III. Certification Requirements

A. **What entities are required to obtain a license in the state to conduct utilization review for residents of the state?** All private review agents shall receive a certificate to conduct utilization reviews in South Carolina.

B. **How often must licensure/certification be renewed?** Every 2 years, beginning on July 1 of even-numbered years. S.C. CODE ANN. REGS. 69-47 §III (2004).

C. **Licensure fees (initial and renewal).** Application fee of $400. Biennial certificate fee of $800 (renewal). S.C. CODE ANN. REGS. 69-47 §III (2004).

D. **Documentation required for licensure.** Private review agents must submit an application including the source of the utilization criteria (the written policies, rules, medical protocols, or guides used by the private review agent to review, grant or deny certification), and a written utilization review program. S.C. CODE ANN. REGS. 69-47 §III (2004).

E. **Exemption from licensure.** Out-of-state organizations are not granted an exemption from the state's licensure and certification requirements even if they are duly licensed and/or certified in their state of domicile.

IV. Program Requirements

A. **Clinical review criteria.** Utilization criteria, the written policies, rules, medical protocols, or guides used by the private review agent to review, grant or deny certification must be established under the direct supervision of a health care provider licensed in the same profession and practicing in the same or similar specialty as typically manages the medical condition, procedure, or treatment. S.C. CODE ANN. REGS. 69-47 §IX (B)(1) (2004). "Certification" is defined as a determination by a utilization review organization that an admission, extension of stay, or other health care services has been reviewed and, based on the information provided, meets the clinical requirements for medical necessity, appropriateness, level of care or effectiveness under the applicable health benefit plan. S.C. CODE ANN. REGS. § 69-47 §II(C) (2004).

B. **Prohibitions against financial incentives.** No provision.

C. **Telephone access standards.** A representative of the private review agent must be accessible by toll-free telephone at least 40 hours per week during normal business hours. S.C. Code Ann. §38-70-20(C)(3) (2004). Private review agents must provide sufficient telephone lines to ensure a reasonable response time (not more than a 90-second wait) to inquiries. S.C. CODE ANN. REGS. 69-47(VIII) (A) and (B) (2004).

D. **Quality assurance program.** Private review agents must develop and use an internal, continuing, written quality assessment program. S.C. CODE ANN. REGS. 69-47 §IX(2) (2004).

E. **Delegation of utilization review functions.** No provision.

F. **Confidentiality.** The utilization review program shall follow all applicable state and federal laws to protect the confidentiality of individual medical records. Private review agents must have written procedures for assuring that patient-specific information obtained during utilization reviews will be kept confidential and used only for utilization reviews, internal quality assurance, discharge planning, case management, or claims payment. S.C. CODE ANN. REGS. 69-47 §X (2004).

V. Reviewer Qualifications

A. **Qualifications of reviewers that render utilization review determinations (at each level of utilization review, if applicable).** The private review agent must have sufficient numbers of properly trained and qualified health professionals, supervised by appropriate health care providers, to carry out its utilization review activities. Health care providers conducting utilization reviews must be licensed as health care providers by an approved state licensing agency in the United States. S.C. CODE ANN. REGS. 69-47 §IX(A) (2004).

B. **Requirements for medical director.** No provision.

C. **Requirement for "same-state" licensure.** No provision.

VI. Reviews and Appeals

A. **Review determinations and notice to patients/providers.**

1. **Time frame for determination.** Private review agents must make a certification determination within 2 working days of receipt of the necessary information. With respect to concurrent review, private review agents must make a certification determination of an extended stay or additional service within one working day of receipt of the necessary information, including second opinion, but may not routinely conduct daily review on all such stays. S.C. CODE ANN. REGS. 69-47 §IV(A) (2004).

2. **Time Frame for Notice.** Private review agents must make a certification determination within 2 working days of receiving all necessary information. For an extended stay or additional service, private review agents must make a certification determination within 1 working day of receiving all necessary information. When a determination is made to deny certification, private review agent must provide notice immediately either by telephone or electronic copier to person or entity who initiated request or patient, enrollee, insured, or other designated party. S.C. CODE ANN. REGS. 69-47 §IV(B) (2004).

3. **Contents of notice of adverse determination.**

   a. **Reasons for adverse determination.** Written notification must include principal reason(s) for denial of certification and procedure for appealing denial of certification. S.C. CODE ANN. REGS. 69-47 §IV(B)(2) (2004).

   b. **Notice of Appeal Rights.** Required.

B. **Appeals requirements.** Private review agents must provide for standard and expedited appeal of adverse determinations. Right to appeal must be available to person or entity that initiated the request or to patient, enrollee, insured, or other designee. Right to appeal must include right to request that health care provider performing review must practice same profession as attending health care provider and right to request review be performed by a health care provider who did not make initial denial of certification. Appeal procedure may require filing of an appeal within a specified period, which may not be less than 60 days of denial of certification. S.C. CODE ANN. REGS. 69-47 §V (2004).

   1. **Time frame for determination.** For standard appeal, the private review agent must notify in writing person or entity who initiated request or patient, enrollee, insured, or designee as soon as practical, but no later than 30 days after receiving all necessary information. If the appeal is denied, the notification must contain justification for denial. In extraordinary circumstances, the 30-day period may be extended to 60 days.

   2. For an expedited appeal, when the person or entity who initiated the request or the patient, enrollee, insured, or designee believes the determination warrants immediate appeal, a telephone appeal must be available. A decision by telephone must be communicated within two working days of receiving all necessary information. An appellant may resubmit through the standard appeal process an expedited appeal which does not resolve a difference of opinion. S.C. CODE ANN. REGS. 69-47 §V (2004).

   3. **External appeals.** No provision.

C. **Emergency Services.** No provision.

VII. Recognition of URAC Accreditation Status

A. Does the state recognize URAC accreditation? No.

B. Which of the state's requirements are waived for URAC-accredited organizations? Not applicable.

South Dakota

I. Scope and Applicability

A. **Who is subject to the state's utilization review requirements?** Any health carrier that provides or performs utilization review services and any designee of the health carrier or utilization review organization that performs utilization review functions on behalf of the carrier.

1. **HMO's?** Yes.

2. **Insurers?** Yes.

3. **Utilization review organizations?** Yes.

4. **Workers' Compensation?** Yes. However, the requirements of S.D. CODIFIED LAWS ANN. §§ 58-17C-34 through 58-17C-57 (2004) only apply to certain health carriers. The provisions of S.D. CODIFIED LAWS ANN 58-17D apply.

5. **Retrospective review?** Yes.

B. **What exemptions are provided, if any?** The utilization review provisions do not apply to dental only, vision only, accident only, school accident, travel, or specified disease plans or plans that primarily provide a fixed daily, fixed occurrence, or fixed per procedure benefit without regard to expenses incurred. S.D. CODIFIED LAWS ANN. § 58-17C-55 (2004).

C. **What term does the state use to refer to regulated entities?** All health carriers which perform utilization review and utilization review organizations. A utilization review organization is "an entity that conducts utilization review" other than a health carrier performing utilization review for its own health benefit plans. S.D. CODIFIED LAWS ANN. § 58-17C-1(40) (2004).

D. **What activities does the state include in its definition of utilization review?** "Utilization review" is "a set of formal techniques used by a managed care plan or utilization review organization to monitor and evaluate the clinical necessity, appropriateness, and efficiency of health care services and procedures." The definition includes "ambulatory review, prospective review, second opinion, certification, concurrent review, case management, discharge planning, and retrospective review." S.D. CODIFIED LAWS ANN. § 58-17C-1(39) (2004).

II. Regulatory Information

A. **Responsible state agency.** South Dakota Division of Insurance.

B. **Contact Information.**

1. **Name and Title:** Ellen Blauert, Managed Care Analyst.

2. **Address:** 445 East Capitol Avenue, Pierre, SD 57501.

3. **Phone and Facsimile:** (605) 773-3563; facsimile (605) 773-5369.

4. **E-mail:** Ellen.Blauert@state.sd.us.

5. **Web site:** www.state.sd.us/dcr2/insurance.www.state.sd.us/drr2/reg/insurance

III. Registration Requirements

A. **What entities are required to obtain a license in the state to conduct utilization review for residents of the state?** Any utilization review organization that engages in utilization review in South Dakota shall register with the Division of Insurance before conducting business in the state. S.D. CODIFIED LAWS ANN. § 58-17C-64 and 67 (2004).

B. **How often must registration be renewed?** Annually. S S.D. CODIFIED LAWS ANN. § 58-17C-65 (2004).

C. **Licensure fees (initial and renewal).** Initial and annual registration fee of $250. S.D. CODIFIED LAWS ANN. § 58-17C-68 (2004).

D. **Documentation required for registration.** Utilization review organizations are required to submit the information outlined in S.D. CODIFIED LAWS ANN. § 58-17C-64 (2004). Forms available on the website.

E. **Exemptions from licensure.** Health carriers do not need separate utilization review organization registration if they are performing review for their own plans, but must comply with the provisions of the statute.

IV. Program Requirements

A. **Clinical review criteria.** A utilization review program shall use documented clinical review criteria based on sound clinical evidence and updated periodically to assure continuing efficacy. A health carrier may develop its own clinical review criteria or may purchase or license clinical review criteria from qualified vendors. A health carrier shall make available its clinical review criteria upon request to authorize government agencies including the Division of Insurance and Department of Health. S.D. CODIFIED LAWS ANN. § 58-17C-38 (2004).

B. **Prohibitions against financial incentives.** Persons providing utilization review services for a health carrier shall not receive incentives, direct or indirect, to make inappropriate review decisions. Such compensation may not be based, directly or indirectly, on the quantity or type of adverse determinations rendered. S.D. CODIFIED LAWS ANN. § 58-17C-47 (2004).

C. **Telephone access standards.** A health carrier shall provide 24-hour per day, 7-day per week access to an authorized representative to facilitate review or otherwise provide coverage for immediately required post-evaluation or post-stabilization services. South Dakota does not set minimum requirements for telephone access for utilization review, but a health carrier shall print on its membership cards a toll-free telephone number to call for utilization review decisions. S.D. CODIFIED LAWS ANN. § 58-17C-30 (2004).

D. **Quality assurance program.** A health carrier shall coordinate the utilization review program with other medical management activity conducted by the carrier, such as quality assurance, credentialing, provider contracting data reporting, grievance procedures, processes for assessing member satisfaction, and risk management. S.D. CODIFIED LAWS ANN. § 58-17C-44 (2004).

E. **Delegation of utilization review functions.** If a health carrier delegates any utilization review activities to a utilization review organization, the health carrier shall maintain responsibility for ensuring that all regulatory requirements are met and that appropriate personnel have operational responsibility for conduct of the carriers utilization review program. S.D. CODIFIED LAWS ANN. § 58-17C-35 (2004).

F. **Confidentiality.** When conducting utilization review, a health carrier shall collect only information necessary to certify the admission, procedure or treatment, length of stay, frequency, and duration of services. S.D. CODIFIED LAWS ANN. § 58-17C-46 (2004).

V. Reviewer Qualifications

A. **Qualifications of reviewers that render utilization review determinations (at each level of utilization review, if applicable)?** Qualified licensed health care professionals shall administer the utilization review program and oversee review decisions. Any adverse determination shall be evaluated by an appropriately licensed and clinically qualified health care provider. S.D. CODIFIED LAWS ANN. § 58-17C-39 (2004). If a grievance is filed, each managed care plan or utilization review organization shall provide for a review of services or treatment in the case of a grievance by a similarly licensed peer whose scope of treatment

includes the services or treatment under review and who shall not have been involved in the initial adverse determination. S.D. CODIFIED LAWS ANN. § 58-17C-83 (2004).

B. **Requirements for medical director.** A managed care plan shall appoint a medical director who has an unrestricted license to practice medicine. A managed care plan that specializes in a specific healing art shall appoint a director who has an unrestricted license to practice that healing art. The director is responsible for oversight of the managed care plan's treatment policies, protocols, quality assurance activities and utilization management decisions. S.D. CODIFIED LAWS ANN. §58-17C-2 (2004). Nothing in §58-17C-2 (2004) applies to dental only, accident only, school accident, travel, or specified disease plans or plans that primarily provide a fixed daily, fixed occurrence, or fixed per procedure benefit without regard to expenses incurred.

C. **Requirements for "same-state" licensure.** Not applicable.

VI. Reviews and Appeals

A. **Review determination and notice to patients/providers.**

1. **Time frame for determination.** For a prospective determination, a health carrier shall make the determination within 15 working days of obtaining all necessary information about a proposed admission, procedure, or service. S.D. CODIFIED LAWS ANN. § 58-7C-49 (2004). For concurrent review determinations, a health carrier shall make the determination and notify the covered person at a time sufficiently in advance of the reduction or termination to permit that person to file a grievance before the benefit is reduced or terminated. S.D. CODIFIED LAWS ANN. § 58-7C-50 (2004). For retrospective review determinations, the managed care plan or utilization review organization shall provide the covered person, his or her representative, provider, and facility rendering service a written decision with 30 days following request. S.D. CODIFIED LAWS ANN. § 58-7C-51 (2004). Urgent concurrent determinations must be made and notification provided more than 24 hours prior to reduction or termination of the benefit. S.D. CODIFIED LAWS ANN. § 58-7C-77 (2004).

2. Contents of notice of adverse determinations.

   a. **Reasons for adverse determination.** Any written notice of an adverse determination shall include the principal reason or reasons for the determination, instructions for initiating an appeal, grievance, or reconsideration, and instructions for requesting a written statement of the clinical rationale used in making the determination. A health carrier shall provide the clinical rationale in writing to any party who received notice of the adverse determination and followed the procedures for a request. The clinical rationale shall contain sufficient detail to allow the covered person to understand the basis of the adverse determination. S.D. CODIFIED LAWS ANN. § 58-17C-52 (2004).

   b. **Notice of appeal rights.** Required in written notice of any adverse determination.

B. **Appeals requirements.** There is a standard and expedited review process for grievances.

   1. **Time frame for determination.** If a grievance is based on an adverse determination and the time frame of a standard review would seriously jeopardize the life or health of a covered person or would jeopardize the person's ability to regain maximum function, a managed care plan or utilization review organization shall provide for expedited review. The process must include telephone notification to the attending physician or ordering provider within 72 hours of beginning review and written notice of certification or noncertification within 2 business days. S.D. CODIFIED LAWS ANN. § 58-17C-72 (2004).

   2. **External appeals.** Not applicable.

C. **Emergency Services.** Provision for expedited review.

VII. Recognition of URAC Accreditation Status

A. **Does the state recognize URAC accreditation?** No.

B. **Which of the state's requirements are waived for URAC-accredited organizations?** Not applicable.

Tennessee

I. Scope and Applicability

A. **Who is subject to the state's utilization review laws?** A person or entity performing utilization review. " TENN. CODE ANN. § 56-6-704 (2004).

    1. **HMO's?** HMO's have their own utilization review requirements. HMO's can "enforce reasonable peer review or utilization review protocols." TENN. CODE ANN. § 56-32-230(b) (2004).

    2. **Insurers?** Yes.

    3. **Utilization review organizations?** Yes.

    4. **Retrospective review?** No.

B. **What exemptions are provided, if any?** There are exceptions for an agency of the federal government, a hospital's internal quality assurance program, and health maintenance organizations (HMO's) licensed and regulated by the (Insurance) Commissioner providing utilization review to their own members. TENN. CODE ANN. § 56-6-703(5)(2004).

C. **What term does the state use to refer to regulated entities?** A "utilization review agent" is "any person or entity, including the state of Tennessee, performing utilization review, except: 1) An agency of the federal government; 2) An agent acting on behalf of the federal government, but only to the extent that the agent is providing services to the federal government; 3) A hospital's internal quality assurance program; 4) An employee of a utilization review agent; or 5) [HMO's] licensed and regulated by the [Commissioner of Commerce and Industry], but only to the extent of providing utilization review to their own members." TENN. CODE ANN. § 56-6-703(5) (2004).

D. **What activities does the state include in its definition of utilization review?** "Utilization review" is defined as "a system for prospective and concurrent review of the necessity and appropriateness in the allocation of health care resources and services given or proposed to be given to an individual within [Tennessee]." The definition does not include "elective requests for clarification of coverage." TENN. CODE ANN. § 56-6-703(4)(A) and (B) (2004).

II. Regulatory Information

A. **Responsible state agency.** Department of Commerce and Insurance.

B. **Contact Information.**

    1. **Name and Title:** Howard Magill, Director, Life, Accident, and Health Actuarial Section.

    2. **Address:** Davy Crockett Tower, Suite 500, Nashville, TN 37243-0565.

    3. **Phone and Facsimile:** (615) 741-2825; facsimile (615) 741-0648.

    4. **E-mail:** Howard.magill@state.tn.us

    5. **Web site:** www.state.tn.us/commerce/insurance/index.html

III. Licensure/Certification Requirements

A. **What entities are required to obtain a license in the state to conduct utilization review for residents of the state?** All utilization review agents that perform utilization review, with specified exceptions. TENN. CODE ANN. § 56-6-704(b) (2004).

B. **How often must licensure be renewed?** Annually (from July 1 to June 30).

C. **Licensure fees (initial and renewal).** $1,000 annually, but the Commissioner shall exempt from payment of the annual fee any utilization review agent which has received accredittion by the Utilization Review Accreditation Commission (URAC) TENN. CODE ANN. § 56-6-704(c) (2004).

E. **Documentation required for licensure.** Utilization review agents must certify to the Commissioner that they are in compliance with the state's requirements at TENN. CODE ANN. § 56-6-705 (2004) along with contact information and a description of their appeals procedures. Additionally, utilization review programs for mental health and chemical dependency care shall make available to a provider submitting patient utilization review information a description of utilization review standards and procedures applicable to that provider. TENN. CODE ANN. § 56-6-704(b) (2004).

F. **Exemptions from licensure.** Agencies of the federal government, hospital internal quality assurance program, and health maintenance organizations (HMO's) licensed and regulated by the (Insurance) Commissioner providing utilization review to their own members." TENN. CODE ANN. § 56-6-703(5) (2004).

IV. Program Requirements

A. **Clinical review criteria.** Any determination by a utilization review agent as to the necessity or appropriateness of an admission, service or procedure shall be reviewed by a physician or determined in accordance with standards or guidelines approved by a physician. TENN. CODE ANN. § 56-6-705(a)(2) (2004).

B. **Prohibitions against financial incentives.** No provision.

C. **Telephone access standards.** Utilization review staff must be available by toll-free telephone at least 40 hours per week during normal business hours. The utilization review agent must be capable of accepting or recording off-hours calls, and must respond to these calls within 2 working days. TENN. CODE ANN. § 56-6-705(a)(5) (2004).

D. **Quality assurance program.** No provision.

E. **Delegation of utilization review functions.** No provision.

F. **Confidentiality.** Utilization review agents must comply with all applicable laws protecting the confidentiality of individual medical records. TENN. CODE ANN. § 56-6-705(a)(7), including HIPAA. TENN. CODE ANN. § 56-6-704(a) (2004).

V. Reviewer Qualifications

A. **Qualifications of reviewers that render utilization review determinations (at each level of utilization review, if applicable).**

1. A physician must review all determinations by a utilization review agent or all determinations must be made in accordance with standards or guidelines approved by a physician. TENN. CODE ANN. § 56-6-705(a)(2) (2004).

2. Physicians or psychologists making review determinations must have current licenses from a state licensing agency in the United States. TENN. CODE ANN. § 56-6-705(a)(8) (2004).

3. On appeal, all determinations not to certify an admission, service, or procedure as being necessary or appropriate shall be made by a physician in same or similar general specialty as typically manages the medical condition, procedure, or treatment under discussion as mutually deemed appropriate. For mental health and chemical dependency care, the person performing the utilization review in these appeal determinations must be both licensed at the independent practice level and in an appropriate mental health or chemical dependency discipline like that of the provider seeking authorization for the care denied. TENN. CODE ANN. § 56-6-705(a)(4)(A) (2004).

B. **Requirements for medical director.** No provision.

C. **Requirement for "same-state" licensure.** The statute specifically provides that physicians or psychologists making utilization review decisions shall have current licenses from a state licensing agency in the United States. TENN. CODE ANN. § 56-6-705(a)(8) (2004).

VI. Reviews and Appeals

A. **Review determinations and notice to patients/providers.**

1. **Time frame for determination.** Notification of a determination must be mailed or otherwise communicated to the provider, enrollee, or other appropriate person within 2 business days of receipt the request for determination and the receipt of all necessary information to complete the review. TENN. CODE ANN. § 56-6-705(a)(1) (2004).

2. **Contents of notice of adverse determination.**

a. **Reasons for adverse determination.** Notice of determination not to certify an admission, service, or procedure must include principal reason for determination. TENN. CODE ANN. § 56-6-705(a)(3) (2004).

b. **Notice of Appeal Rights.** Notice of determination not to certify must include procedures to initiate an appeal. TENN. CODE ANN. § 56-6-705(a)(3) (2004).

B. **Appeals requirements.** Utilization review agencits shall complete the adjudication of appeals of determinations not to certify admissions, services, and procedures no later than 30 days from the date the appeal is filed and the receipt of all information necessary to complete the appeal. When an initial determination not to certify a health care service is made prior to or during an ongoing service requiring review, and the attending physican believes that the determination warrants immediate appeal, the attending physician shall have an opportunity to appeal an initial determination by telephone on an expedited basis when the attending physician believes such a process is necessary. TENN. CODE ANN. § 56-6-705(a)(4)(C) (2004).

1. **Time frame for determination.** Standard appeals must be completed within 30 days of the receipt of all necessary information. TENN. CODE ANN. § 56-6-705(a)(4)(B) (2004). Expedited appeals must be completed within 48 hours of the receipt of all

necessary information. TENN. CODE ANN. § 56-6-705(a)(4)(C) (2004).

2. **External appeals.** No provision.

C. **Emergency Services.** Utilization review agents must allow a minimum of 24 hours after an emergency admission or service for a patient to notify them and request certification or continuing treatment for that condition.

VII. **Recognition of URAC Accreditation Status**

A. **Does the state recognize URAC accreditation?** Yes.

B. **Which of the state's requirements are waived for URAC-accredited organizations?** Utilization review agents accredited by URAC are exempt from the annual certification fee of $1,000. TENN. CODE ANN N. § 56-6-704(c) (2004). In addition, utilization review agents accredited by URAC are exempt from the minimum standards, including notification of determinations by utilization review agents, review of determinations by physicians, written description of appeal procedures, qualifications of reviewers on appeal, adjudication of appeals, expedited appeals, availability of staff and telephone lines, etc. TENN. CODE ANN. § 56-6-705 (2004).

Teas

I. Scope and Applicability

A. **Who is subject to the state's utilization review laws?** Insurance companies, health maintenance organizations (HMO's) and utilization review agents (URA's) performing utilization review for those entities. A URA, including an HMO or insurer that performs utilization review for other than its own enrollees or insured must be certified as a utilization review agent to perform utilization review as defined by Texas Insurance Code art. 21.58A. TEX. INS. CODE ANN. art. 21.58A §§3(a), (g), (h), (i), and (j) (2004).

1. **HMO's?** An HMO that performs utilization review for other than its own enrollees must be certified as an URA. However, if the HMO only performs utilization review for its own enrollees, it must comply with the statute as a condition of licensure. The HMO must also register with the department and submit evidence of compliance. In the latter event, the HMO does not pay an application fee. TEX. INS. CODE ANN. art. 21.58A §3(g) and (i).

2. **Insurers?** An insurer that performs utilization review for other than its own insureds must be certified as a URA. However, if the insurer only performs utilization review for its own insureds, it must comply with the statute as a condition of licensure. The insurer must also register with the department and submit evidence of compliance. In the latter event, the insurer does not pay an application fee. TEX. INS. CODE ANN. art. 21.58A §3(h) and (j).

3. **Utilization review agents?** Yes.

4. **Retrospective review?** When a retrospective review of the medical necessity and appropriateness of health care service is made under a health insurance policy or plan: a) such retrospective review shall be based on written screening criteria established and periodically updated with appropriate involvement from physicians, including practicing physicians, and other heath care providers; and b) the payor's system for such retrospective review of medical necessity and appropriateness shall be under the direction of a physician. When an adverse determination is made based on a retrospective review of the medical necessity and appropriateness of the allocation of health care resources and services, the payor must afford the health care providers the opportunity to appeal the determination. TEX. INS. CODE ANN. art t. 21.58A §11 (2004). *See also* TEX. ADMIN. CODE .Title 28, §§19.1715 (2004) and 19.2015.

5. **What exemptions are there, if any?** The statutory provisions regarding utilization review do not apply to any contract with the federal government for utilization review of patients eligible for services under Medicaid and Medicare, Texas Medicaid program, chronically ill and disabled children's services program, any program of the Texas Department of Mental Health and Mental Retardation, any program of the Texas Department of Criminal Justice, utilization review of health care services provided under an automobile insurance policy or contract, and terms and benefits of employee welfare plans defined in Employee Retirement Income Security Act of 1974. TEX. INS. CODE ANN. art. 21.58A §14(b), (d), and (e) (2004).

B. **What term does the state use to refer to regulated entities?** A "utilization review agent" is defined as "an entity that conducts utilization review for: 1) an employer with employees in this state who are covered under a health benefit plan or health insurance policy; 2) a payor; or 3) an administrator." TEX. INS. CODE ANN. art. 21.58A§2(21) (2004). "A specialty utilization review agent" means "a utilization review agent that conducts utilization review for specialty health care services, including but not limited to dentistry, chiropractic, or physical therapy." TEX. INS. CODE ANN. art. 21.58A §14(j) (2004).

C. **What activities does the state include in its definition of utilization review?** "Utilization review" is defined as "a system for prospective or concurrent review of the medical necessity and appropriateness of health care services being provided or proposed to be provided to an individual within this state." The definition does not include "elective requests for clarification of coverage." TEX. INS. CODE ANN. art. 21.58A §2(20) (2004).

II. Regulatory Information

A. **Responsible state agency.** Texas Department of Insurance, HMO/URA Division.

B. **Contact Information.**

1. **Name and Title:** Dina Bonugli, Insurance Specialist.

2. **Address:** P.O. Box 149104, 333 Guadalupe Street, Austin, TX 78714-9104.

3. **Phone and Facsimile:** (512) 322-4266; facsimile (512) 490-1011322-4260.

4. **E-mail:** Dina.bonugli@tdi.state.tx.us.

5. **Web site:** www.tdi.state.tx.us.

III. Licensure/Certification Requirements

A. **What entities are required to obtain a license in the state to conduct utilization review for residents of the state?** All utilization review agents must receive a certificate from the Commissioner of Insurance to conduct utilization review of health care provided in Texas. TEX. INS. CODE ANN. art. 21.58A §3(a) (2004).

B. **How often must licensure be renewed?** Every 2 years from date of certification. TEX. INS. CODE ANN. art. 21.58A §3(d) (2004).

C. **Licensure fees (initial and renewal).** $2,150 initial; $545 renewal.

D. **Documentation required for licensure.** Utilization review agents must submit an application that includes approximately 20 exhibits. Each exhibit represents a specific requirement under the statute and/or department rule. The exhibits include, among others, including and a summary of their utilization review plan and policies and procedures (excluding proprietary details) that documents compliance with the state's requirements; notification requirements, personnel categories that will perform utilization review; the procedure for appeal of an adverse determination; the procedure for handling oral and written complaints by enrollees, patients or health care providers, and requirements related to independent review by an independent review organization. TEX. INS. CODE ANN. art. 21.58A §3(e) (2004).

E. **Exemption from licensure.** See response under Section I.A.6. under Scope and Applicability. A utilization review agent may not conduct utilization review of health care in Texas unless the Commissioner has granted a certificate pursuant to the statute. TEX. INS. CODE ANN. art. 21.58A §3(a) (2004). The Commissioner may only issue a certificate to an applicant that has met all the requirements of this article and all applicable rules and regulations of the commissioner. TEX. INS. CODE ANN. art. 21.58A §3(b) (2004). Therefore, out-of-state organizations are not granted an exemption from the state's licensure and certification requirements even if they are duly licensed and/or certified in their state of domicile.

IV. Program Requirements

A. **Clinical review criteria.** Each utilization review agent shall utilize written medically acceptable screening criteria and review procedures which are established and periodically evaluated and updated with appropriate involvment from physicians, including practicing physicians, dentists, and other health care providers. Utilization review decisions shall be made in accordance with currently accepted medical or health care practices, taking into account special circumstances of each case that may require deviation from the norm stated in the screening criteria. Screening criteria must be objective, clinically valid, compatible with established principles of health care, and flexible enough to allow deviations from the norms when justified on a case-by-case basis. Screening criteria must be used to determine only whether to approve the requested treatment. Such written screening criteria and review procedures shall be available for review and inspection to determine appropriateness and compliance as deemed necessary by the commissioner..." TEX. INS. CODE ANN. art. 21.58A §4(i) (2004).

B. **Prohibitions against financial incentives.** A utilization review agent may not permit or provide compensation or any thing of value to its employees or agents, condition employment of its employee or agent evaluations, or set its employee or agent performance standards, based on the amount or volume of adverse determinations, reductions or limitations on lengths of stay, benefits, services, or charges or on the number or frequency of telephone calls or other contacts with health care providers or patients, which are inconsistent with the provisions of this statute. TEX. INS. CODE ANN. art. 21.58A §4(f) (2004).

C. **Telephone access standards.** Appropriate personnel must be available by toll-free telephone at least 40 hours per week during normal business hours in Texas. The utilization review agent must also have a system to accept or record off-hour calls and shall respond to such calls within 2 working days. TEX. INS. CODE ANN. art. 21.58A§7(a) and (b) (2004). In relation to HMO's and PPO carriers that have contracting providers, the following requirements apply: an HMO or preferred provider carrier shall have appropriate personnel reasonably available at a toll-free telephone number to provide the determination between 6:00 AM and 6:00 PM central time Monday through Friday on each day that is not a legal holiday and between 9:00 AM and noon central time on Saturday, Sunday, and legal holidays. An HMO or preferred provider carrier must have a telephone system capable of accepting or recording incoming inquiries after 6:00 PM central time Monday through Friday and after noon central time on Saturday, Sunday, and legal holidays and must acknowledge each of those calls not later than 24 hours after the call is received. TEX. ADMIN. CODE Title 28 §19.1723(e).

D. **Delegation of utilization review functions.** Utilization review agents may delegate utilization review to qualified personnel in the hospital or health facility in which services are to be provided. However, the utilization review agent is still responsible for compliance with the state's utilization review requirements, including the conduct of those to whom utilization review has been delegated.

E. **Confidentiality.** Utilization review agents must comply with all applicable laws protecting the confidentiality of individual medical records. Generally, utilization review agents may not release individual medical information without prior consent from the patient. The utilization review agent must adopt appropriate safeguards to protect the confidentiality of medical information.

V. Reviewer Qualifications

A. **Qualifications of reviewers that render utilization review determinations (at each level of utilization review, if applicable).**

1. Utilization review personnel (who are not physicians or dentists) who obtain information regarding a patient's specific medical condition, diagnosis and treatment options or protocols directly from the attending provider must be nurses, physician's assistants, or health care providers. TEX. INS. CODE ANN. art. 21.58A §4(c).

2. Denials must be referred to an appropriate physician, dentist, or other health care provider to determine medical necessity. TEX. INS. CODE ANN. art. 21.58A §4(i).

3. If the appeal is denied and within 10 working days the health care provider sets forth in writing good cause for having a particular type of a specialty provider review the case, the denial shall be reviewed by a

health care provider in the same or similar specialty as typically manages the medical, dental, or specialty condition, procedure, or treatment under discussion for review of the adverse determination. TEX. INS. CODE ANN. art. 21.58A §6(b)(3).

4. Expedited appeals for emergency care denials, denials of care for life-threatening conditions, and denials of continued stays for hospitalized patients must be reviewed by a health care provider who has not previously reviewed the case and who is of the same or a similar specialty as typically manages the medical condition, procedure, or treatment under review. TEX. INS. CODE ANN. art. 21.58A §6(b)(4).

B. **Requirements for medical director.** A licensed physician must direct the conduct of utilization review for a utilization review agent. A health care provider of the same specialty who is licensed or otherwise authorized shall direct the conduct of utilization review for a specialty utilization review agent. TEX. INS. CODE ANN. art. 21.58A §4(h).

C. **Requirement for "same-state" licensure.** No provision.

VI. Reviews and Appeals

A. **Review determinations and notice to patients/providers.**

1. **Time frame for determination.** Review determinations must be mailed or otherwise transmitted within 2 working days after receipt of all information necessary to conduct the review. Adverse determinations must be provided: within 1 working day by telephone or electronic transmission in the case of a patient who is hospitalized at the time of the adverse determination; within 3 working days if the patient is not hospitalized at the time of the adverse determination; and within 1 hour from notification when denying post-stabilization care subsequent to emergency treatment as requested by a treating physician or provider. In such circumstances, notification shall be provided to the treating physician or health care provider. TEX. INS. CODE ANN. art.§21.58A(5) (2004). In relation to HMO's and PPO carriers that have contracting providers, the following requirements apply: a) for services not concurrent hospitalization or post-stabilization treatment, the HMO or

preferred provider carrier must issue the determination not later than the third calendar day after the date the request is received by the HMO or preferred provider carrier. If the request is received outside of the period requiring the availability of appropriate personnel, the determination must be issued and transmitted within 3 calendar days from the beginning of the next time period requiring such personnel; b) for concurrent hospitalization care, the HMO or preferred provider carrier must issue the determination within 24 hours of receipt of the request. If the request is received outside of the period requiring the availability of appropriate personnel, the determination must be issued and transmitted within 24 hours from the beginning of the next time period requiring such personnel; and c) for services involving post-stabilization treatment, or a life-threatening condition, the HMO or preferred provider carrier must issue the determination no later than one hour from receipt of the request. If the request is received outside of the period requiring the availability of appropriate personnel, the determination must be issued within one hour from the beginning of the next time period requiring such personnel. TEX. ADMIN. CODE Title 28 §19.1723.

2. **Contents of notice of adverse determination.**
   a. **Reasons for adverse determination.** Required, including the clinical basis and the principal reasons for the determination, a description of the screening criteria, a description of the procedure for the complaint and appeal process, and the independent review notification and form.
   b. **Notice of Appeal Rights.** Required.

B. **Appeals requirements.** The utilization review agent must provide both standard and expedited appeals. For life-threatening situations, the patient is entitled to immediate appeal to an independent review organization (*see* VI.B.2. below).

1. **Time frame for determination.** Standard appeals must be completed within 30 days after the utilization review agent receives the appeal. If the appeal is denied, the treating provider may request a secondspecialty appeal to be considered by an appropriate specialist physician. Such specialist review

must be completed within 15 working days of the request. Expedited appeals must be completed no later than 1 working day from the receipt of the information necessary to complete the appeal. TEX. INS. CODE ANN. art. 21.58A §6.

2. **External appeals.** Any person whose appeal to the utilization review agent is denied may seek review of the determination by an independent review organization. The utilization review agent is responsible for the cost of the independent review and for supplying the information necessary for the independent review organization to make its determination. The utilization review agent is bound by the independent review organization's determination regarding medical necessity. TEX. INS. CODE ANN. art. 21.58A §6A.

C. **Emergency Services.** The utilization review agent's utilization review plan must include procedures for responding to requests for post-stabilization care subsequent to emergency treatment. When an enrollee has a "life-threatening condition" (a "disease or other medical condition, with respect to which death is probable unless the course of the disease or condition is interrupted"), the enrollee has a right to immediate review of an adverse decision in utilization review by an independent review organization. Such an enrollee does not have to comply with procedures for internal review of the utilization review agent's adverse determination. TEX. INS. CODE ANN. art. 21.58A(6)(c) (2004).

VII. Recognition of URAC Accreditation Status

A. **Does the state recognize URAC accreditation?** Although the Texas Department of Insurance recognizes the value of URAC accreditation, it still requires certification and compliance with state requirements related to utilization review.

B. **Which of the state's requirements are waived for URAC-accredited organizations?** Not applicable.

VIII. Miscellaneous

A physician must approve the utilization review plan, including reconsideration and appeal requirements. For a specialty utilization review agent, a health care provider of the appropriate specialty shall approve the utilization review plan. The utilization review plan must be conducted in accordance with standards developed with input from appropriate health care providers.

UM TEXAS

The Texas Department of Insurance maintains a list of certified/registered utilization review agents. This information is available on the Web site at www.tdi.state.tx.us/apps/perlroot/u-lh-ura/uralist.html.

Utah

I. Scope and Applicability

While Utah does not directly regulate utilization management or review, it specifically requires health insurance policies, health maintenance organization contracts and income replacement or disability income policies to have a process for the internal review of adverse benefit determinations and the independent review if the adverse benefit determination involves payment of a claim or denial of coverage regarding medical necessity. UTAH CODE ANN. §31A-22-629 (2004).

Adverse benefit determination is defined to mean the denial of a benefit; reduction of a benefit; termination of a benefit; or failure to provide or make payment, in whole or in part, for a benefit resulting from the application of a utilization review. UTAH CODE ANN. §31A-22-629 (2004).

The Insurance Department regulations governing health maintenance organizations also require each HMO to develop a quality assurance plan which is subject to external review. The quality assurance plan "shall be designed to systematically monitor and evaluate the quality and appropriateness of patient care, pursue opportunities to improve patient care, and resolve identified problems." Therefore, external review of the HMO's quality assurance plan includes review of the utilization review practices.

The external review and certification of the quality assurance plan must occur no later than 18 months after receipt of the HMO's certificate of authority and every 3 years thereafter unless the certifying entity requires a shorter time frame. URAC is specifically identified as an approved entity for certification of HMO quality assurance plans. UTAH ADMIN. R. 590-76-9 (2004).

II. Regulatory Information

A. **Responsible state agency.** Utah Insurance Department.

B. **Contact Information.**
1. **Name and Title:** Suzette Green-Wright, Director, Health Insurance Division and Office of Consumer Health Assistance.
2. **Address:** State Office Building, Room 3110, Salt Lake City, UT 84114-1201.
3. **Phone and Facsimile:** (801) 538-9674; facsimile (801) 538-3829.
4. **E-mail:** sgreenwright@utah.gov
5. **Web site:** www.insurance.state.ut.us.

Vermont

Part 1 – Mental Health (Only)

I. Scope and Applicability

A. **Who is subject to the state's utilization review laws?** Any entity performing mental health utilization review on behalf of a business entity or a third party who provides or administers mental health care benefits to citizens of Vermont, including a health insurer, nonprofit health service plan, health service organization, health maintenance organization or preferred provider organization, including organizations that rely upon primary care physicians to coordinate delivery of services, authorized to offer health insurance policies or contracts in Vermont. VT. STAT. ANN. tit. 8, § 4089a(b)(4) (2004).

1. HMO's? Yes.
2. Insurers? Yes.
3. Utilization review organizations? Yes.
4. Retrospective review? Yes.
5. What exemptions are provided, if any? Pertains only to mental health services.

B. **What term does the state use to refer to regulated entities?** A "review agent" is defined as "a person or entity performing service review activities who is either affiliated with, under contract with, or acting on behalf of a business entity in [Vermont]; or a third party who provides or administers mental health care benefits to citizens of Vermont, including a health insurer, nonprofit health service plan, health service organization, health maintenance organization or preferred provider organization, including organizations that rely upon primary care physicians to coordinate delivery of services, authorized to offer health insurance policies or contracts in Vermont." VT. STAT. ANN. tit. 8, § 4089a(b)(4) (2004).

C. **What activities does the state include in its definition of utilization review?** "Service review" is defined as "any system for reviewing the appropriate and efficient allocations of mental health care services given or proposed to be given to a patient or group of patients for the purpose of recommending or determining whether such services should be reimbursed, covered or provided by an insurer, plan or other entity or person and includes activities of utilization review and managed care, but does not include professional peer review which does not affect

reimbursement for or provision of services." VT. STAT. ANN. § 4087a(b)(5) (2004).

II. Regulatory Information

A. **Responsible state agency.** Division of Health Care Administration, Department of Banking, Insurance, Securities, and Health Care Administration.

B. **Contact Information.**

1. **Name and Title:** Robert Aiken, Health Care Administrator.
2. **Address:** 89 Main Street, Drawer 20, Montpelier, VT 05620.
3. **Phone and Facsimile:** (802) 828-2900 ext. 2905; facsimile (802) 828-2949.
4. **E-mail:** baiken@bishca.state.vt.us.
5. **Web site:** www.bishca.state.vt.us.

III. Licensure/Certification Requirements

A. **What entities are required to obtain a license in the state to conduct utilization review for residents of the state?** Any person who meets the definition of review agent. VT. STAT. ANN. § 4089a(c) (2004).

B. **How often must licensure be renewed?** Biennially. Vt. R.95-2§5 (2004)

C. **Licensure fees (initial and renewal).** License fee of $200 for registration and renewal. A review agent shall also pay any additional expenses incurred to examine and investigate an application or amendment. VT. STAT. ANN. § 4089a(h) (2004).

D. **Documentation required for licensure.** An application; an organizational chart; review criteria; procedures, policies and procedures for appeals; and other information detailed at VT. CODE R. 95-2, § 6 (2004).

E. **Exemption from licensure.** Out-of-state organizations are not granted an exemption from Vermont's licensure and certification requirements even if they are duly licensed and/or certified in their state of domicile.

IV. Program Requirements

A. **Clinical review criteria.** Criteria must be compatible with accepted medical practice and developed and periodically updated with appropriate involvement from mental health providers. Criteria must allow for unique or special circumstances for a particular case. Upon request, the review agent must make available the specific criteria used to evaluate proposed mental health services Vt. R. 95-2, § 7 and 8, and § 10(A)(1) (2004).

B. **Prohibitions against financial incentives.** Compensation to review agents may not include incentives or contingent fees based on the reduction of mental health services, reduction of length of stay, reduction of treatment, or treatment setting selected. VT. STAT. ANN. § 4089a(c)(10) (2004).

C. **Telephone access standards.** The review agent must provide 24-hour access by telephone at no charge to the patient or provider. VT. CODE R. 95-2, § 10 (2004).

D. **Quality assurance program.** No provision.

E. **Delegation of utilization review functions.** No provision.

F. **Confidentiality.** Review agents must comply with all applicable state and federal laws protecting the confidentiality of individual medical records. The regulations also provide for numerous additional requirements regarding confidentiality. VT. CODE R. 95-2, § 9 (2004).

V. Reviewer Qualifications

A. **Qualifications of reviewers that render utilization review determinations (at each level of utilization review, if applicable).**

1. Licensed mental health professionals must conduct all utilization review services. VT. CODE R. 95-2, § 8 (2004).

2. Any adverse decision must include the evaluation, findings and concurrence of a mental health professional whose training and expertise is at least comparable to that of the treating clinician. VT. STAT. ANN. § 4089a(c)(3) (2004).

3. Upon request, the review agent must make available the credentials of reviewing health professionals. VT. CODE R. 95-2, § 10(A)(1) (2004).

B. **Requirements for medical director.** No provision.

C. **Requirement for "same-state" licensure.** Vermont law provides for an Independent Panel of Mental Health Care Providers to conduct procedures for the reconsideration of adverse decisions by a review agent. The members of the Independent Panel must have current Vermont licenses. VT. CODE R. 95-2, § 13(D) (2004). No similar requirement exists for review agents.

VI. Reviews and Appeals

A. **Review determinations and notice to patients/providers.**

1. **Time frame for determination.** The review agent must notify the attending provider of an adverse determination within 2 business days of receiving the information necessary to conduct the review. VT. CODE R. 95-2, § 7(B)(6) (2004).

2. **Contents of notice of adverse determination.** The notice must include: a)the identity of the person responsible for receiving appeals and other consumer complaints and a toll-free telephone access number;b) a summary of the appeal procedure for review of adverse cessions; c) a notice that a client or patient may appeal a final adverse decision of the review agent to the Independent Panel of Mental Health Care Providers. VT. CODE R. 95-2, § 10(A)(2) (2004).

   a. **Reasons for adverse determination.** Disclosure must include the specific review criteria and standards, interpretative guidelines, credentials of the reviewing mental health care providers, and procedures and methods used or to be used in evaluating proposed or delivered mental health care services. VT. CODE R. 95-2, § 10(A)(1) (2004).

   b. **Notice of Appeal Rights.** The notice regarding service review activities must include notice that a client/patient may appeal a final adverse decision of the review agent. VT. CODE R. 95-2, § 10(A)(2)(c) (2004).

B. **Appeals requirements.** The review agent must provide for standard and expedited internal appeals.

1. **Time frame for determination.** Standard appeals must be completed within 10 days of the request for an appeal. Expedited appeals in emergency situations must be completed within 24 hours of the request for an appeal. VT. CODE R. 95-2, § 12 (2004).

2. **External appeals.** The review agent must inform the client/patient of the right to have prompt reconsideration of an appeal decision before an independent, seven-member panel of mental health professionals (Independent Panel of Mental Health Care Providers). VT. CODE R. 95-2, § 12 (2004). The Commissioner of Banking, Insurance, Securities, and Health Care Administration appoints the members of that panel.

C. **Emergency Services.** If prospective or concurrent utilization review is conducted for emergency care, the review agent must provide for review during non-business hours. The review agent must make expedited appeals available for emergencies.

Vermont

Part 2 – General Health (excluding mental health)

I. Scope and Applicability

A. **Who is subject to the state's utilization review laws?** "Each managed care law shall be responsible for monitoring all utilization review activities carried out by or on its behalf..." HCA RULE, § 10.203(B)(1) (2004).

1. HMO's? Yes.
2. Insurers? Yes.
3. Utilization review organizations? Yes.
4. Retrospective review? Yes.

B. **What term does the state use to refer to regulated entities?** The regulations are applicable to "managed care plans." HCA RULE, § 10.103(WW) (2004). A "utilization review organization" is "an entity that conducts utilization review, other than a managed care plan performing a review for its own members." HCA RULE, § 10.103(WW) (2004).

C. **What activities does the state include in its definition of utilization review?** "Utilization management" is "the set of organizational functions and related policies, procedures, criteria, standards, protocols and measures used by a managed care plan to ensure that it is appropriately managing access to and the quality and cost of health care services provided to its members." HCA RULE, § 10.103(TT) (2004). "Utilization review" is "a set of formal techniques designed to monitor the use of, or evaluate the clinical necessity, appropriateness, efficacy, or efficiency of, health care services, procedures, or settings. Techniques may include ambulatory review, prospective review, second opinion, certification, concurrent review, case management, discharge planning or retrospective review." HCA RULE, § 10.103(UU) (2004).

II. Regulatory Information

A. **Responsible state agency.** Division of Health Care Administration, Department of Banking, Insurance, Securities, and Health Care Administration.

VII. Recognition of URAC Accreditation Status

A. **Does the state recognize URAC accreditation?** No.

B. **Which of the state's requirements are waived for URAC-accredited organizations?** Not applicable.

B. **Contact Information.**

1. **Name and Title:** Susan Gretkowski, JD, Deputy Commissioner of Health Care Administration.
2. **Address:** 89 Main Street, Drawer 20, Montpelier, VT 05620.
3. **Phone and Facsimile:** (802) 828-2900; facsimile (802) 828-2949.
4. **E-mail:** sgretkowski@bishca.state.vt.us.
5. **Web site:** www.bishca-state-vt.us.

III. Licensure/Certification Requirements

A. **What entities are required to obtain a license in the state to conduct utilization review for residents of the state?** The State of Vermont does not separately license utilization review organizations. However, the Commissioner's annual and triennial reviews of managed care organizations include a review of utilization review and management. HCA RULE, § 10.302 and 10.303 (2004).

B. **How often must licensure be renewed?** Not applicable.

C. **Licensure fees (initial and renewal).** Not applicable.

D. **Documentation required for licensure.** Not applicable.

E. **Exemption from license.** Not applicable.

IV. Program Requirements

A. **Clinical review criteria.** Each managed care plan shall base its clinical review criteria on sound clinical evidence and shall evaluate the criteria periodically. To ensure their ongoing efficacy using practicing physicians and other health care providers within the plan's network. A managed care plan may develop its own clinical review criteria, or it may purchase such criteria from qualified vendors. The criteria shall be periodically reviewed and updated by the plan. Clinical review criteria must be provided to participating providers and managed care plan members on request. HCA RULE, § 10.203(B)(4) (2004).

B. **Prohibitions against financial incentives.** Compensation to persons providing utilization review services may not contain incentives, direct or indirect, for those persons to limit medically necessary care, and may not be based on the quantity or type of adverse determinations rendered. HCA RULE, § 10.203(B)(14) (2004).

C. **Telephone access standards.** Managed care plans must provide access to its review staff by toll-free or collect-call telephone line. HCA RULE, § 10.203(B)(12) (2004). Managed care plans must have a registered nurse or physician available by telephone 7 days a week, 24 hours a day, to render utilization review determinations to its providers. HCA RULE, § 10.203(B)(5) (2004).

D. **Quality assurance program.** Managed care plans should routinely assess the effectiveness and efficiency of its utilization review program and shall coordinate utilization review with its quality assurance program. HCA RULE, § 10.203(B)(11) (2004).

E. **Delegation of utilization review functions.** If a managed care plan delegates utilization review functions to a utilization review organization, the managed care plan must maintain "effective oversight of those activities." HCA RULE, § 10.203(B)(10) (2004).

F. **Confidentiality.** Each managed care plan shall take appropriate steps necessary to ensure that information gathered by it in its quality assurance activities shall be confidential and privileged. HCA RULE, § 10.205(A) (2004).

V. Reviewer Qualifications

A. **Qualifications of reviewers that render utilization review determinations (at each level of utilization review, if applicable).**
   1. Physicians must render all adverse decisions. HCA RULE, § 10.203(B)(5) (2004).
   2. A clinical peer of the attending provider who was not involved with the initial adverse determination must consider appeals. HCA RULE, § 10.203(D)(1) (2004).

B. **Requirements for medical director.** The medical director must be a health care provider who is board-certified or board-eligible in his specialty. HCA RULE, § 10.103(AA) (2004).

C. **Requirement for "same-state" licensure.** The medical director must be licensed in Vermont. HCA RULE, § 10.202(G)(4) (2004).

VI. Reviews and Appeals

A. **Review determinations and notice to patients/providers.**

   1. **Time frame for determination.** For prospective and concurrent review, managed care plans must render a review decision within 3 working days of receiving all necessary information and notify the treating provider by telephone. HCA RULE, § 10.203(C)(2) (2004). Managed care plans shall establish procedures to expedite initial and concurrent review determinations in cases involving urgently-needed care and shall make such determinations in 24 hours. HCA RULE, § 10.203(C)(2)(b) (2004). For retrospective review, the managed care plan must render a decision within 30 days of receiving all necessary information. HCA RULE § 10.203(C)(3) (2004).

   2. **Contents of notice of adverse determination.**
      a. **Notice of Appeal Rights and Reasons for adverse determination.** Written notification of an adverse determination shall include the principal reasons for the determination, instructions for giving the determination, a written statement of the clinical rationale for the determination and an explanation of the relevant clinical review criteria. Upon request, the plan shall make available the actual clinical criteria. HCA RULE, § 10.203(C)(4) (2004).

B. **Appeals requirements.** Managed care plans must provide for both standard and expedited grievances. Patients who are not satisfied with the initial resolution of their grievance may request a second review of the appeal.

   1. **Time frame for determination.** Plans must respond to grievances related to emergency services on urgent case no more than 3 days after receipt of the necessary information. HCA RULE, § 10.203(D)(2)(a) (2004). Standard appeals must be completed within 15 days of receipt of the information necessary to consider the appeal. Second reviews of the appeal must generally be completed in 30 days, except for reviews that involve emergency services, which must be completed in 2 days. HCA RULE, § 10.203(D)(5) (2004).

   2. **External appeals.** Within 90 days of exhausting the internal appeals process, an insured may request independent external review of an insurer's decision to deny, reduce, or terminate health care coverage or to deny payment for a covered health care

service. An insured must file such a request for an appeal with the Division of Health Care Administration. After a review, the Division will forward to an independent review organization. HCA RULE, § H-99-1§6 (2004).

C. **Emergency Services.** Managed care plans may not require prior authorization of screening and stabilization services for emergency medical conditions. HCA RULE, § 10.203(E)(2) (2004).

VII. Recognition of URAC Accreditation Status

A. Does the state recognize URAC accreditation? No.

B. Which of the state's requirements are waived for URAC-accredited organizations? Not applicable.

VIII. Miscellaneous

A. Managed care plans are required to maintain detailed utilization review program documents.

B. Where these requirements come into conflict with the requirements for mental health utilization review (*see* Part 1 -- Mental Health), the mental health regulations take precedence.

Virgin Islands

I.   Scope and Applicability

URAC has found no statutes, regulations, or case law pertaining to utilization review/utilization management in the Virgin Islands.

II.   Regulatory Information

A.   **Responsible state agency.** Office of the Lieutenant Governor, Division of Banking and Insurance.

B.   **Contact Information.**

1.   **Name and Title:** Vargrave A. Richards, Lieutenant Governor/Commissioner.

2.   **Address:** Office of the Lieutenant Governor, Division of Banking and Insurance, 1131 King Street, Suite 101, Christiansted, St. Croix, VI 00820.

3.   **Phone and Facsimile:** (340) 774-7166; facsimile (340) 773-6953.

4.   **E-mail:** Not known.

5.   **Web site:** Not known.

III.   Recognition of URAC Accreditation Status

A.   Does the state recognize URAC accreditation? No.

B.   Which of the state's requirements are waived for URAC-accredited organizations? Not applicable.

Virginia

Note: The Virginia Department of Health has oversight for "private review agents" as well as for "managed care health insurance plans" (MCHIP's), both of which are "Utilization Review Entities" but are regulated under different statutory and regulatory provisions. The Bureau of Insurance of the Virginia State Corporation Commission has oversight for independent external review of final adverse utilization review decisions.

I. Scope and Applicability

A. **Who is subject to the state's utilization review laws?** Utilization Review Entities which are persons or entities that perform utilization review. "Private review agents" must be granted a certificate of registration to conduct utilization review in Virginia. 12 VA. ADMIN. CODE § 5-405-30 (2004). In addition, MCHIP's shall have a utilization review and management process that complies with the requirements of VA. ADMIN. CODE. §§ 32.1-137.7 through 32.1-137.17 (2004) and 12 VA. ADMIN. CODE § 5-408-10 et seq. (2004).

B. **What exemptions are provided, if any?** MCHIP's do not require a certificate of registration if such entities perform utilization review solely for subscribers, policyholders, members, or enrollees. Such exemptions from registration include health maintenance organizations (HMO's), health insurers, hospital service corporations, health services plans, or preferred provider organization (PPO) plans authorized to offer health benefits in Virginia. The requirements for registration also do not apply for any private review agent that operates under contract with the federal government for utilization review for hospital services under Medicare or plans exempt from state regulation under the Employee Retirement Income Security Act of 1974 (ERISA). 12 VA. ADMIN. CODE § 5-405-30 (2004).

1. **HMO's?** MCHIP licensees (the definition of MCHIP includes HMO's) must follow the requirements of VA. CODE. ANN. §§ 32.1-137.7 through 32.1-137.17 (2004) and 12 VA. ADMIN. CODE § 5-408-360 (2004). In developing a utilization review program, MCHIP's shall use URAC's accreditation standards, the National Committee for Quality Assurance's or other nationally recognized accrediting with comparable standards for utilization review accepted by the department.

2. **Insurers?** MCHIP licensees must follow the requirements of VA. CODE. ANN. §§ 32.1-137.7 through 32.1-137.17 (2004).

3. **Utilization review organizations?** Private Review Agents may not conduct utilization reviews in Virginia without a certificate of registration. VA. CODE. ANN. § 32.1-138.7 (2004).

4. **Retrospective review?** Yes.

C. **What term does the state use to refer to regulated entities?** "Private review agent" is "a person or entity performing utilization review, except that the term shall not include the following entities or any employees of any entity so long as they conduct utilization reviews solely for subscribers, policy holders, members or enrollees." VA. CODE. ANN. § 32.1-137.7 (2004). This term includes MCHIP's and utilization review entities. VA. CODE. ANN. § 32.1-138.6 (2004).

D. **What activities does the state include in its definition of utilization review?** "Utilization review" means "a system for reviewing the necessity, appropriateness, and efficiency of hospital, medical or other health care services rendered or proposed to be rendered to a patient or group of patients for the purpose of determining whether such services should be covered or provided by an insurer, health services plan, managed care health insurance plan licensee, or other entity or person." The term includes "preadmission, concurrent and retrospective medical necessity determination, and review related to the appropriateness of the site at which services were or are to be delivered." The definition does not include: 1) review of issues concerning insurance contract coverage or contractual restrictions on facilities to be used for the provision of services, 2) any review of patient information by an employee of or consultant to any licensed hospital for patients of such hospital, or 3) any determination by an insurer as to the reasonableness and necessity of services for the treatment and care of an injury suffered by an insured for which reimbursement is claimed under a contract of insurance covering any classes of insurance defined in [various provisions of the Code of Virginia]. VA. CODE. ANN. § 32.1-137.7 (2004).

II. Regulatory Information.

A. **Responsible state agency.** Virginia Department of Health, Center for Quality Health Care Services and Consumer Protection. (**Note:** As mentioned, the Department of Health oversees private review agents and MCHIP's.)

B. **Contact Information.**

1. **Name and Title:** Harry Armstrong, Managed Care Health Insurance Plan Supervisor.

2. **Address:** Virginia Department of Health, 3600 West Broad Street, Suite 216, Richmond, VA 23230.

3. **Phone and Facsimile:** (804) 367-2102; facsimile (804) 367-2149.

4. **E-mail:** harry.armstrong@vdh.virginia.gov

5. **Web site:** www.vdh.state.va.us

III. Licensure/Certification Requirements

A. **What entities are required to obtain a license in the state to conduct utilization review for residents of the state?** Private review agents, except for those exempted from compliance (i.e., a private review agent that operates under contract with the federal government for utilization review or Medicaid patients or under contract with a plan exempt under ERISA), must obtain a certificate of registration to conduct utilization review in the Commonwealth of Virginia. VA. CODE. ANN. § 32.1-138.7 (2004). MCHIP's are required to comply with utilization review standards as a condition of licensure. VA. CODE. ANN. § 32.1-137.8 (2004).

B. **How often must licensure be renewed?** Private review agents must renew the certificate of registration every 2 years. VA. CODE. ANN. § 32.1-138.10 (2004).

C. **Licensure fees (initial and renewal).** Initial and renewal fee of $500.

D. **Documentation required for licensure.** Private review agents must submit an application that includes:

1. A description of the procedures to be used in evaluating proposed or delivered hospital, medical or other health care services;

2. The procedures by which patients or providers may seek reconsideration of determinations by private review agents;

3. The type and qualifications of the staff either employed or under contract to perform the utilization review;

4. Procedures and policies which ensure that patient-specific medical records and information shall be kept strictly

confidential except as authorized by the patient or by 12 VA. ADMIN. CODE §5-405-100 (2004); and

5. Assurances that reviewers will be readily accessible by telephone to patients and providers at least 40 hours per week during normal business hours.

E. **Exemption from licensure.** The Department shall waive the certificate requirement for utilization review entities that contract with the federal government for the review of hospital services under Medicare or with an ERISA plan. VA. CODE. ANN. § 32.1-138.12 (2004).

IV. Program Requirements

A. **Clinical review criteria.** Utilization review entities shall establish reasonable and prudent standards and criteria with input from physician advisors representing major areas of specialty and certified by boards of various American medical specialties. Such standards shall be "objective, clinically valid, and compatible with established principles of health care." VA. CODE. ANN. § 32.1-137.9 (2004).

B. **Prohibitions against financial incentives.** No provision.

C. **Telephone access standards.** Utilization review entities must provide for access by free telephone at least 40 hours per week during normal business hours. Utilization review entities must also have the capacity to accept and record calls outside of normal business hours. VA. CODE. ANN. § 32.1-138.9 (2004).

D. **Quality assurance program.** No provision specifically for utilization review entities, but MCHIP's must have a quality assurance program.

E. **Delegation of utilization review functions.** MCHIP's may delegate "utilization management" but must retain accountability for oversight of such services. 12 VA. ADMIN. CODE § 5-408-320 (2004). The written plan shall include guidelines for delegation of utilization review to external entities and expectations for that delegation.

F. **Confidentiality.** Private review agents must comply with all applicable laws protecting the confidentiality of individual medical records and shall have policies and procedures which ensure that patient specific medical records and information shall be kept strictly confidential except as authorized by the patient or regulations. VA. CODE. ANN. § 32.1-138.9 (2004).

V. Reviewer Qualifications

A. Qualifications of reviewers that render utilization review determinations (at each level of utilization review, if applicable).

1. Review staff must be properly qualified, trained, and supervised.

2. Utilization review entities must make arrangements for access on an "as needed" basis to a peer and/or physician advisors who are specialists in the various categories of health care.

3. Standard appeals shall be rendered by a physician advisor or a peer of the treating health care provider who shall be board-certified or board-eligible, and shall specialize in a pertinent discipline. 12 VA. ADMIN. CODE § 5-405-70 (2004).

4. With the exception of adverse decisions made on the basis of retrospective review, prior to the issuance of an adverse decision, and if requested by the provider, the case in question must be reviewed either by a physician advisor or by a peer of the provider proposing the care. In addition, to the extent appropriate, the case in question must be reviewed in consultation with a physician advisor with experience in the same field of practice as the attending physician. The physician advisor or peer must be on the staff of the private review agent. 12 VA. ADMIN. CODE § 5-405-80(A) (2004).

5. Any case under appeal shall be rendered by a physician advisor, peer of the treating health care provider, or panel of other appropriate health care providers with at least one physician advisor on the panel. Chiropractic appeals shall be reviewed by a chiropractor with the exception of expedited appeals. Physician advisors who review cases under appeal must be board certified or board eligible in a discipline pertinent to the issue under review. 12 VA. ADMIN. CODE § 5-450-90 (2004).

6. Physician advisors who render appeals determinations shall not have been involved in the original determination, shall not be employed by or a director of the utilization entity; and shall be licensed in Virginia or under a comparable state licensing law as a peer of the treating health care provider. VA. CODE. ANN. § 32.1-138.6 (2004).

B. Requirements for medical director. No provision.

C. Requirement for "same-state" licensure. Individuals who render appeals determinations must be licensed in Virginia or under a comparable state licensing law. VA. CODE. ANN. § 32.1-138.6 (2004).

VI. Reviews and Appeals

A. Review determinations and notice to patients/providers.

1. Time frame for determination. Utilization review entities shall communicate review decisions no later than 2 business days after receiving all necessary information. There shall be an expedited review of no more than 24 hours for review determinations related to prescriptions for alleviating cancer pain, including oral notification by telephone of treating provider within 24 hours of any adverse decision. VA. CODE. ANN. § 32.1-137.13 (2004).

2. Contents of notice of adverse determination.

a. Reasons for adverse determination. Prior to a determination, the treating provider shall be entitled to review the issue of medical necessity with a physician advisor or peer of the treating health care provider. VA. CODE. ANN. § 32.1-137.13 (2004).

b. Notice of Appeal Rights. A utilization review entity shall have a process for reconsideration. On reconsideration, the utilization review entity shall notify the treating provider of the determination, including the criteria used, clinical reason for the adverse decision, and alternate length of treatment of alternative treatment setting or settings. VA. CODE. ANN. 32.1-137.14 (2004). A utilization review entity shall notify covered persons of the review process, including the appeals process.

B. Appeals requirements. A utilization review entity must provide for standard and expedited appeals. The appellant shall have an opportunity to present additional evidence. VA. CODE. ANN. § 32.1-137.15 (2004).

1. Time frame for determination. Standard appeals must be completed within 60 working days after receiving the information necessary to consider the appeal. Expedited appeals must be completed within 4 working days after receipt of the necessary information, but a treating health care provider shall be able to appeal immediately

by telephone adverse decision or adverse reconsideration involving a prescription alleviating cancer pain. A utilization review entity shall decide such an expedited appeal within 1 business after receiving all necessary information. VA. CODE. ANN. § 32.1-137.15 (2004).

2. **External appeals.** Notification of denial of appeal shall include clear and understandable description of right to appeal final adverse decisions to Bureau of Insurance, procedures for making appeal, and binding nature and effect of such appeal. The Bureau of Insurance shall contract with one or more impartial health entities, such as medical peer review organizations and independent utilization review companies, to perform the review of final adverse decisions. The Office of the Managed Care Ombudsman in the Bureau of Insurance shall assist consumers with understanding rights and processes and provide information. *See* VA. CODE. ANN. § 38.2-5900 *et seq.* (2004) and 14 VA. ADMIN. CODE § 5-215-10 et seq. (2004).

C. **Emergency Services.** For emergency health care, a covered person, representative, or provider may request authorization within 48 hours of or by end of first business day following the rendering of the emergency care, whichever is later. A utilization review entity shall promptly review a request for an extension of the original approved duration of health care or hospitalization.

VII. Recognition of URAC Accreditation Status

A. **Does the state recognize URAC accreditation?** Not for private review agents, but yes for MCHIP's.

B. **Which of the state's requirements are waived for URAC-accredited organizations?** Not applicable for private review agents. In developing its utilization review program, an MCHIP shall use URAC's Health Utilization Management Standards, Version 3.0, or another accreditation organization's standards. These are the criteria for determining compliance with the utilization management and review requirements except where Virginia law or regulation is more stringent.

VIII. Miscellaneous

Under VA. CODE. ANN. § 38.2-5900 *et seq.* (2004), the Bureau of Insurance has a new Office of the Managed Care Ombudsman. This office cannot investigate or resolve complaints, but can assist people in navigating the internal appeal process provided their MCHIP or in directing to the appropriate regulatory authority. The Bureau of Insurance handles any complaint that questions the application of Virginia insurance law or regulation. The Office of the Managed Care Ombudsman performs other functions described in more detail in the Bureau of Insurance's Web site.

The Virginia Department of Health handles any complaint that involves the quality of health care delivered to patients. Statutory and regulatory requirements of MCHIP's that address utilization review, grievance procedures, credentialing, subscriber rights, access to and availability of care, quality improvement programs, delegation of services, and complaints encompassing these areas should be addressed to the Department of Health. The Department's complaint hotline is (1-800-955-1819) or local (804) 367-2106.

Washington

I. Scope and Applicability

A. **Who is subject to the state's utilization review laws?** The State of Washington requires all health carriers to maintain a documented utilization review program description and written utilization review criteria based on reasonable medical evidence. The program must include a method for reviewing and updating criteria. Carriers shall make clinical protocols, medical management standards and other review criteria available upon request to participating providers. WASH. REV. CODE §48.43.520. Health carrier is defined to mean a disability insurer, health care service contractor or a health maintenance organization. WASH. REV. CODE §48.43.005. Washington State does not regulate independent utilization review organizations.

1. HMO's? Yes.
2. Insurers? Yes.
3. Utilization review organizations? No
4. Retrospective review? Yes.

B. **What exemptions are provided, if any?** None cited.

C. **What term does the state use to refer to regulated entities?** Health Carriers. WASH. REV. CODE §48.43.520 (2004).

D. **What activities does the state include in its definition of utilization review?** "Utilization review means the prospective, concurrent, or retrospective assessment of the necessity and appropriateness of the allocation of health care resources and services of a provider or facility, given or proposed to be given to an enrollee or a group of enrollees." WASH. REV. CODE §48.43.005 (2004).

II. Regulatory Information

A. **Responsible state agency.** Washington State Office of the Insurance Commissioner.

B. **Contact Information.**
1. **Name and Title:** John Conniff, Deputy Commissioner of Managed Health Care.
2. **Address:** P.O. Box 40255, Olympia, WA 78504-0255.
3. **Phone and Facsimile:** (360) 664-3786; facsimile (360) 586-3535.
4. **E-mail:** JohnC@oic.wa.gov.
5. **Web site:** www.insurance.wa.gov.

III. Licensure/Certification Requirements

A. **What entities are required to obtain a license in the state to conduct utilization review for residents of the state?** Washington State does not separately license utilization review. Health carriers shall maintain a documented utilization review program that meets the national certification standards set by the Insurance Commissioner. WASH. ADMIN. CODE § 284-43-410 (2004).

B. **How often must licensure be renewed?** No provision.

C. **Licensure fees (initial and renewal).** No provision.

D. **Documentation required for licensure.** Health carriers are required to maintain a documented utilization review program description and written utilization review criteria based on reasonable medical evidence. The program must include a method for reviewing and updating criteria. Carriers shall make clinical protocols, medical management standards and other review criteria available upon request to participating providers. WASH. REV. CODE §48.43.520 (2004).

E. **Exemptions from licensure.** None cited.

IV. Program Requirements

A. **Clinical review criteria.** Health carriers are required to maintain a documented utilization review program description and written utilization review criteria based on reasonable medical evidence. The program must include a method for reviewing and updating criteria. Carriers shall make clinical protocols, medical management standards and other review criteria available upon request to participating providers. WASH. REV. CODE §48.43.520 (2004).

B. **Prohibitions against financial incentives.** Not applicable.

C. **Telephone access standards.** Not applicable.

D. **Quality assurance program.** Not applicable.

E. **Delegation of utilization review functions.** The statute and regulation do not preclude.

F. **Confidentiality.** Not applicable.

Each carrier when conducting utilization review shall:

1. Accept information from any reasonably reliable source that will assist in the certification process;
2. Collect only the information or portions of the medical record necessary to certify the admission, procedure or treatment, length of stay or frequency or duration of services; for prospective and concurrent review;

3. Base review determinations solely on the medical information obtained by the carrier at the time of the review determination;

4. For retrospective review, base review determinations solely on the medical information available to the attending physician or order provider at the time the health service was provided;

5. Not retrospectively deny coverage for emergency and non-emergency care that had prior authorization at the time the care was rendered unless the prior authorization was based upon a material misrepresentation by the provider;

6. Not retrospectively deny coverage for coverage or payment based upon standards or protocols not communicated to the provider or facility within a sufficient time period for the provider or facility to modify care in accordance with such standard or protocol; and,

7. Reverse its certification determination only when information provided to the carrier is materially different from that which was reasonably available at the time of the original determination. WASH. ADMIN. CODE § 284-43-410 (2004).

V. **Reviewer Qualifications.** No qualifications for initial utilization review other than reference to national standards.

A. **Qualifications of reviewers that render utilization review determinations (at each level of utilization review, if applicable).** Appeals of adverse determinations shall be evaluated by health care providers who were not involved in the initial decision and who have appropriate expertise in the field of medicine that encompasses the covered person's condition or disease. WASH. ADMIN. CODE § 284-43-620 (2004).

B. **Requirements for medical director.** Any carrier and any self-insured health plan shall designate a medical director who is licensed in Washington. Dental only plans shall designate a dental director who is a dentist licensed in Washington State or in a state that has been determined by the dental quality assurance commission to have substantially equivalent licensing standards to those in Washington. WASH. REV. CODE §48.43.540 (2004).

C. **Requirement for "same-state" licensure.** For medical director. WASH. REV. CODE §48.43.540 (2004).

VI. **Process Requirements**
A. Review determinations and notice to patients/providers.
1. Time frame for determination.
   a. For prospective peview, determinations must be made within 2 business days for receipt of necessary information on a proposed admission or service requiring a review determination.
   b. For retrospective review, determinations must be completed within 30 days of receipt of the necessary information. WASH. ADMIN. CODE § 284-43-410(5) (2004).

2. Contents of notice of adverse determination.
   a. Notification of the determination shall be provided to the attending physician, or ordering provider or facility and to the covered person within 2 days of the determination and shall be provided within one day of concurrent review determination. Notification shall include the number of extended days, the next anticipated review point, the new total number of days or services approved, and the date of admission or onset of services. WASH. ADMIN. CODE § 284-43-410(5) (2004).
   b. Reasons for adverse determination. No provision.
   c. Notice of Appeal Rights. A covered person or the covered person's representative, including the treating provider may appeal an adverse determination in writing. The carrier must reconsider the adverse determination and notify the covered person of its decision within 14 days of receipt of the appeal unless the carrier notifies the covered person that an extension is necessary to complete the appeal; however, the extension cannot delay the decision beyond 3 days of the request for appeal, without the informed written consent of the average person. WASH. ADMIN. CODE § 284-43-620(1) (2004).
   d. Grievances. The carrier must implement procedures for registering to oral and written grievances in a timely manner. WASH. ADMIN. CODE § 284-43-615(2)(d) (2004).

B. **Appeals requirements.** Each carrier must adopt and implement a comprehensive process for the resolution of covered person's grievances and appeals of adverse determinations. This process shall meet accepted national certification standards. WASH. ADMIN. CODE § 284-43-615(1) (2004).

   1. **Time frame for determination.** No provisions.

   2. **External appeals.** A covered person may seek review by a certified independent review organization of an adverse decision after exhausting the carrier's grievance process and receiving a decision that is unfavorable to the covered person, or after the carrier has exceeded the timelines for grievances without good cause and without reaching a decision. A carrier may establish a process to bypass the carrier's internal grievance process and allow for the direct appeal to a certified independent review organization for certain classes of adverse determinations. WASH. ADMIN. CODE § 284-43-630(1) (2004).

      The medical reviewers from a certified independent review organization shall make determinations regarding the medical necessity or appropriateness of, and the application of health plan coverage provisions to, health care services for a covered person. The medical reviewer's determinations must be based upon their expert medical judgment, after consideration of the relevant medical scientific and cost-effectiveness evidence, and medical standards of practice in the state of Washington. The certified independent review organization must ensure that determinations are consistent with the scope of covered benefits. Medical reviewers may override the health plan's medical necessity or appropriateness standards if the standards are determined upon review to be unreasonable or inconsistent with sound, evidence-based medical practice. WASH. ADMIN. CODE § 284-43-630(3) (2004).

C. **Emergency Services.** Whenever a health carrier makes an adverse determination and delay would jeopardize the covered person's life or materially jeopardize the covered person's health, the carrier shall expedite and process either a written or an oral appeal and issue a decision no later than 72 hours after receipt of the appeal. If the treating health care provider determines that delay could jeopardize the covered person's health or ability to regain maximum function, the carrier shall presume the need for expeditious review, including the need for an expeditious determination in any independent review. WASH. ADMIN. CODE § 284-43-620(2).

VII. Recognition of URAC Accreditation Status

   A. **Does the state recognize URAC accreditation?** Yes. For UR for medical treatment for offenders (RFP no. CR FP 5627, March 2002).

   B. **Which of the state's requirements are waived for URAC-accredited organizations?** Not applicable.

West Virginia

I. Scope and Applicability

A. Who is subject to the state's utilization review laws? The State of West Virginia regulates utilization management as a component of quality assurance programs of health maintenance organizations and prepaid limited health service organizations. Collectively, West Virginia law refers to HMO's and prepaid limited health service organizations as "managed care plans." W. VA. CODE ST. R. § 114-58-2.13 (2004).

1. **HMO's?** Utilization management is regulated by the Insurance Commissioner pursuant to the Health Maintenance Organization Act (*see* W. VA. CODE ST. R. § 114-51-1 *et seq.* (2004)).

2. **Insurers?** Prepaid Limited Health Service Organizations. W. VA. CODE § 33-25D-19(a)(2) (2004).

3. **Utilization Review Organizations?** No.

4. **Retrospective Review?** Yes.

5. **What exemptions are provided, if any?** Not applicable.

B. What term does the state use to refer to regulated entities? For purposes of utilization management, West Virginia regulates health maintenance organizations, limited prepaid health service organizations and external review organizations.

C. What activities does the state include in its definition of utilization review? Under the Health Maintenance Organization Act, "utilization management" is defined as "a system for the evaluation of the necessity, appropriateness and efficiency of the use of health care services, procedures and facilities." W. VA. CODE § 33-25A-2(27) (2004); W. VA. CODE ST. R. § 114-51-2.7 (2004). The regulations for prepaid limited health service organizations use the same definition. W. VA. CODE ST. R. § 114-56-2 (2004).

II. Regulatory Information

A. Responsible state agency. West Virginia Insurance Commission.

B. Contact Information.

1. **Name and Title:** Charles Dunn, Director of the Office of Advocacy.

2. **Address:** Consumer Advocate Division, P.O. Box 50540, Charleston, WV 25305-0540.

3. **Phone and Fax:** (304) 558-3864; facsimile (304) 558-2381.

4. **E-mail:** charleydunn@wvinsurance.gov.

5. **Web site:** http://www.wvinsurance.gov/

III. Licensure/Certification Requirements

A. What entities are required to obtain a license in the state to conduct utilization review for residents of the state? HMO's and limited health services organizations, as part of the process for issuance of a certificate of authority. W. VA. CODE § 33-25A-4(1)(b) (2004)(HMO's); W. VA. CODE §33-25D-5(a)(2) (2004). External Review Organizations as mandated by the Patient Bill of Rights. W. VA. CODE §33-25C-6 (2004); W. VA. CODE ST. R. §114-58-1 et. seq. (2004).

B. How often must licensure/certification be renewed? Not applicable.

C. Licensure fees (initial and renewal). Not applicable.

D. Documentation required for licensure. Not applicable.

E. Exemptions from licensure. Not applicable.

IV. Program Requirements

A. Clinical review criteria. The utilization management program of an HMO shall use written utilization management decision protocols based on reasonable medical evidence. Among other things, an HMO shall clearly document and make available, upon request, to participating physicians, its criteria for appropriateness of medical services; shall establish a mechanism for checking the consistency of application of criteria used by reviewers; and shall establish a mechanism for periodically updating review criteria. W. VA. CODE ST. R. § 114-51-4.6 (2004). The UM program shall have professionally accepted, pre-established criteria for preauthorization of medical services and concurrent review of admissions. W. VA. CODE ST. R. § 114-51-4.7 (2004).

B. Prohibitions against financial incentives. None.

C. Telephone access standards. None.

D. Quality assurance program. For managed care plans, a utilization management program is a component of the quality assurance program. W. VA. CODE § 33-25A-4(1)(b) (2004) (HMO's); W. VA. CODE e §33-25D-5(a)(2) (2004); (Prepaid Limited Health Service Organizations).

E. Delegation of utilization review functions. If an HMO delegates any utilization management function, there shall be evidence of oversight of the contracted entity. The health maintenance organization shall maintain evidence of: 1) the approval of the contractor's UM program; and 2) evaluation of regular UM reports of the contractors. W. VA. CODE ST. R. § 114-51-4.4 (2004). The HMO shall be responsible for monitoring the activities of the entity to which it delegates utilization management activities and for ensuring that the requirements of W. VA. CODE ST. R. § 114-51-1 et seq. (2004) are met.

F. **Confidentiality.** Any data or information pertaining to the diagnosis, treatment or health of any enrollee or applicant obtained from that person or from any provider by any health maintenance organization shall be held in confidence and shall not be disclosed to any person except: 1) as necessary for quality assurance or grievance purposes; 2) upon the express written consent of the enrollee; 3) pursuant to statute or court order; 4) in the event of claim or litigation between that person the HMO where the data or information is pertinent; or 5) to a department or division of the state. W. VA. CODE §33-25A-26 (2004).

V. Reviewer Qualifications

A. **Qualifications of reviewers that render utilization review determinations (at each level of utilization review, if applicable)?** For the utilization management program of any HMO, qualified medical professionals shall review decisions for preauthorization of medical services and concurrent review of admissions; a duly licensed physician shall conduct a review of medical appropriateness on any denial of medical services; and at any point during the review process, a licensed physician consultant specially trained in the area of medicine in question shall be available to provide his or her expert opinion regarding medical appropriateness and necessity of medical services. W. VA. CODE ST. R. § 114-51-4.7 (2004).

B. **Requirements for medical directors.** No.

C. **Requirements for "same-state" licensure.** No.

VI. Reviews and Appeals

A. **Review determination and notice to patients/providers.**
   1. **Time frame for determination.** For HMO's, "decisions regarding provision of medical services shall be made in a timely manner depending upon the urgency of the situation." W. VA. CODE ST. R. § 114-51-4.8 (2004). HMO's shall establish "medically appropriate time frames for urgent,

emergency and planned care cases." W. VA. CODE ST. R. § 114-51-4.8(a) (2004).
   2. **Contents of notice of adverse determinations.**
      a. **Reasons for adverse determination.** HMO's shall send written notices of denial "immediately" to all parties, including subscriber, primary care physician, and facility. Such written notice shall include reason for denial and explanation of the internal review process. W. VA. CODE ST. R §114-51-4.8b (2004). Once the internal process is exhausted, and the managed care issues an adverse determination, the managed care plan must also notify the enrollee in writing of the enrollee's right to request an external review and shall include in the required notice: i) the specific criteria and standards on which the adverse determination was based; ii) a description of both the standards and expedited external review procedures; iii) the circumstances under which the enrollee may use either procedure. W. VA. CODE ST. R. §114-58-3.1 (2004).
      b. **Notice of appeal rights.** Yes.

B. **External Appeals requirements.** For determinations of whether a health care service is medically necessary, or determinations of whether a health care service is experimental, an enrollee may seek review by a certified external review organization of a managed care plan's decision to deny, modify, reduce or terminate coverage of or payment for a health care service, after exhausting the managed care plan's internal grievance process and receiving a decision that is unfavorable to the enrollee or after the managed care plan has exceeded the time periods for grievances. W. VA. CODE ST. R §33-26C-6(a) (2004). The right to external review is available only if the adverse determination would result in payment of at least $1,000 if the health care services were paid for any the enrollee. W. VA. CODE ST. R. §114-58-4.1 (2004). The request for external review must be made in writing to the managed care plan and the commissioner within 60 days of receipt of notice of the adverse determination. W. VA. CODE ST. R. §114-58-4.2-4.3 (2004).
   1. **Time frame for determination.** Standard review in 45 days. W. Va. Code St. R. §114-58-5.14 (2004); Expedited external review must be assigned to the external review organization within 2 days of receipt by the

Commissioner and the external review organization must notify the enrollee of its decision to uphold or reverse the adverse determination within 7 days. W. VA. CODE ST. R. §114-58-6.12 (2004).

C. **Emergency Services.** HMO shall establish "medically appropriate" time frames" for "urgent" and "emergency" matters. W. VA. CODE ST. R. § 114-51-4.8a (2004).

VII. Recognition of URAC Accreditation Status. A
managed care plan may be exempted from the requirements for external review upon showing that it has an established external review procedure in place, that it is fully accredited and that the accreditation includes external review. W. VA. CODE §33-25C-2 (2004); W. VA. CODE ST. R. §114-58-12 (2004).

A. **Does the state recognize URAC accreditation?** No.

B. **Which of the state's requirements are waived for URAC-accredited organizations?** Not applicable.

VIII. Miscellaneous
Within the Department of Health and Human Resources, the Bureau for Medical Services operates the Office of Surveillance and Utilization Review. This office reviews participating providers, using post-payment review techniques, to determine compliance with regulations.

Wisconsin

I. Scope and Applicability

The State of Wisconsin does not currently regulate utilization review organizations or activities. However, Wisconsin requires all insurers offering health care plans or health benefit plans, including limited service health organizations and specified disease policies, to have an internal and expedited grievance processes. Insurers offering health benefit plans including specified disease plans are also required to provide insureds with the right to independent review of adverse determinations and experimental treatment determinations. Typically the right to independent review follows exhaustion of internal grievance processes, however, there are provisions in law for both an expedited independent review and the ability to seek independent review without exhaustion of internal review when both the insured and insurer agree. WIS. STAT. § 632.83 and 632.835 (1999), WIS. ADM. CODE INS. § 3.67, § 18.03 , et. seq. and § 18.10 (2000 and 2001, respectively).

II. Regulatory Information

A. **Responsible state agency.** Office of the Commissioner of Insurance.

B. **Contact Information.**
1. **Name and Title:** Jorge Gomez, Commissioner of Insurance.
2. **Address:** P.O. Box 7873, 125 South Webster Street, Madison, WI 53707-7873.
3. **Phone and Facsimile:** (608) 267-1233; facsimile (608) 261-8579.
4. **E-mail:** information@oci.state.wi.us.
5. **Web site:** http://oci.wi.gov/oci_home.htm

III. Program Requirements

A. **Review determinations and notice to patients/providers.** An insurer offering a health care plan or a health benefit plan shall develop an internal grievance and expedited grievance procedure that shall be described in each policy and certificate issued to insureds at the time of enrollment or issuance. WIS. ADM. CODE INS. § 3.67 (4), (2000) 18.03(1)(b) (2001).

1. **Time frame for determination.** Insurers are required to timely pay claims within 30 days of receipt of the claim unless otherwise documented. WIS. STAT. § 628.46.

2. **Notification of right to appeal.** Each time an insurer offering a health benefit plan denies a claim or benefit or initiates disenrollment proceedings, the insurer offering the health benefit plan shall notify the affected insured of the right to file a grievance. WIS. ADM. CODE INS. § 3.67 (4)(b)

and § 18.03(2)(a) (2001). The notification shall either direct the insured to the policy or certificate section that delineates the procedure for filing a grievance or shall describe, in detail, the grievance procedure to the insured. WIS. ADM. CODE INS. § 3.67 (4)(f) and § 18.03(2)(b) (2004). Additionally, by definition an insured may file a grievance regarding any dissatisfaction with the provision of services or claim practices of an insurer offering a health benefit plan that is expressed in writing to the insurer by, or on behalf of, an insured. WIS. ADM. CODE INS. §3.67 (1)(b) 18.01 (4).

3. **Reasons for claim determination.** The notification shall state the specific reason for the denial, determination or initiation of disenrollment. WIS. ADM. CODE INS. § 18.03(2)(b) (2001).

4. **Grievance Review Procedure.** The grievance procedure shall include a method whereby the insured has a right to appear in person before the grievance panel to present written or oral information. The insurer shall permit the grievant to submit written questions to the person or persons responsible for making the determination that resulted in the denial or determination in the absence of a meeting with the decision maker. WIS. ADM. CODE INS. § 3.67 (4)(a) and § 18.03(3)(a) (2001).

5. **Composition of Hearing Panel.** The grievance panel shall not include the person who ultimately made the initial determination. If the panel consists of at least 3 persons, no more than one shall be a subordinate of the ultimate initial determination-maker. WIS. STAT. § 632.83 (3) (b) and WIS. ADM. CODE INS. § 18.03 (3) (d).

6. **Time Frame for Grievance.** An insurer shall resolve a grievance within 30 days of receiving it, but may extend the period up to another 30 calendar days. WIS. ADM. CODE INS. § 3.67 (4)(d) and § 18.03(6)(b) (2001). An insurer shall also have a separate expedited grievance procedure which shall resolve the grievance as expeditiously as the insured's health condition requires, but not more than 72 hours after receipt of the grievance. For expedited grievances, 72

hours. WIS. ADM. CODE INS. § 3.67 (4)(e) and § 18.05
WIS. ADM. CODE INS. § 18.10 (2001).

B. Reviews and Appeals
1. **Independent Review procedures.** Every health benefit plan shall establish an independent review procedure, whereby an insured may directly request and obtain an independent review of an adverse determination or experimental treatment determination. The health benefit plan shall provide notice of the independent review after resolution of the integral grievance process. The insured, with the agreement of the insurer may also bypass the internal grievance process and proceed to the independent review. In order for the insured to have the right to a grievance, the cost of the treatment denied must exceed $250 or as adjusted annually by the CPI Index and posted to the OCI's website. WIS. STAT. §632.835 (1999), and WIS. ADM. CODE INS. § 18.11, 18.11 (2) (a) 6., (2001).

2. **Expedited Appeal.** The insured may bypass the internal grievance process if requiring the insured to use the internal grievance procedure before proceeding to independent review would jeopardize the life or health of the insured or the insured's ability to regain maximum function. WIS. STAT. §632.835(2)(d)(2) (1999) and WIS. ADM. CODE INS. § 18.11 (3) (d) (2001).

3. **Reviewer Qualifications.** A clinical peer reviewer who conducts a review on behalf of a certified independent review organization must satisfy all of the following requirements: (a) be a health care provider who is expert in treating the medical condition that is the subject of the review and who is knowledgeable about the treatment that is the subject of the review through current, actual experience; (b) hold a credential license, certificate, registration or permit that authorizes or qualifies the health care provider to perform acts substantially the same as those acts authorized by a licensed health care provider in Wisconsin; (c) if a physician, hold a current certification by a recognized American medical specialty board in the area or areas appropriate to the subject of the review; and (d) have no history of disciplinary sanctions. WIS. STAT.

§632.835(6m) (1999) and WIS. ADM. CODE INS. § 18.12 (4).

4. **Conflict of Interest.** The independent review organization and clinical peer review assigned to conduct an independent review may not have a material professional, familial or financial interest in: a) the health benefit plan or any officer, director or management employee thereof; b) the health care provider, group or facility that recommended or provided the care under review; c) the developer of the procedure, equipment, drug or device that is the subject of the review; or d) the insured or his or her representative. WIS. STAT. §632.835(5)(b) (1999) and WIS. ADM. CODE INS. § 18.12 (5).

IV. Miscellaneous.
The regulations governing certification of independent review organizations are found at WIS. ADM. CODE INS. § 18.10, et seq. (2001), and WIS. STAT. § 632.835 (1999), and include requirements for telephone access and medical director credentials.

Wyoming

I. Scope and Applicability

The State of Wyoming does not currently regulate utilization review activities or utilization review organizations.

II. Regulatory Information

   A. **Responsible state agency.** Wyoming Insurance Department.

   B. **Contact Information.**

   1. **Name and Title:** Teri Green, Medicaid Policy Manager.

   2. **Address:** 6101 Yellowstone Road, Suite 210, Cheyenne, WY 82002.

   3. **Phone and Facsimile:** (307) 777-7908; facsimile (307) 777-6964.

   4. **E-mail:** Tgreen1@state.wy.us.

   5. **Web site:** http://insurance.state.wy.us/

III. Miscellaneous

There are a few, scattered references to "utilization review" in Wyoming's statutes and regulations. While not defined in the Small Employer Health Insurance Availability Act, there is a description of utilization review as a "cost containment" feature, including "review of medical necessity of hospital and physician services." WYO. STAT. § 26-19-308(c)(i)(A) (2003).

Alabama

Note: The surveys of Workers' Compensation UM laws & regulations were completed by the law firm Blank Rome, LLP.

I. Scope and Applicability

A. **Who is subject to the state's utilization review laws?** Alabama has a separate administrative scheme for utilization review for workers' compensation. "All insurers, claims adjusters, self-administered employees, and any entity involved in the administration or payments of worker's compensation claims may, but are not required to, implement utilization review and bill screening/or (worker's compensation) health services . . . " This provision also provides that "(U)tilization review and bill screening shall be performed by qualified individuals or entities to ensure the integrity of the services and the quality of cost containment." ALA. CODE § 25-5-293(g) (2004). "(A)ny and all utilization review, bill screening, medical necessity determinations . . . shall only be conducted in accordance with policies, guidelines or regulations . . . " ALA. CODE § 25-5-293(k) (2004).

B. **What exemptions are provided, if any?** None listed.

   1. **HMO's?** Yes.
   2. **Insurers?** Yes.
   3. **Utilization review organizations?** Yes.
   4. **Workers' Compensation?** Yes.
   5. **Retrospective review?** Yes, for emergency cases.

C. **What term does the state use to refer to regulated entities?** A "utilization review entity" is a "private utilization review vendor, a carrier or its affiliate, a self-insured employer, a third-party administrator, or a group fund that provides utilization review." ALA. ADMIN. CODE r. 480-5-5.02(70) (2004).

D. **What activities does the state include in its definition of utilization review?** "Utilization management" is a "comprehensive set of integrated components including: pre-certification review, admission review, continued stay review, retrospective review, discharge planning, bill screening and individual medical case management as required." ALA. ADMIN. CODE r. 480-5-5.02(67) (2004). "Utilization review" is a "determination of medical necessity for medical and surgical in-hospital, outpatient, and alternative settings treatments for acute and rehabilitation care. It includes precertification for elective treatments. Concurrent review and, if necessary, retrospective review are required for

emergency cases." ALA. ADMIN. CODE § 480-5-5.02(68) (2004)

II. Regulatory Information

A. **Responsible state agency.** Department of Industrial Relations, Workers' Compensation Division.

B. **Contact Information.**

   1. **Name and Title:** Trevor A. Perry, Administrative Analyst
   2. **Address:** "Department of Industrial Relations, Workers' Compensation Division, 649 Monroe Street, Montgomery, AL 36131
   3. **Phone and Facsimile:** (334) 353-0540; facsimile (334) 353-8228.
   4. **E-mail:** tperry@dir.state.al.us.
   5. **Web:** http://dir.Alabama.gov/wc/

III. Licensure/Certification Requirements

A. **How often must licensure be renewed?** Every 2 years. ALA. ADMIN. CODE r. 480-5-5-.06 7(f) (2004).

B. **Licensure fees (initial and renewal).** No provision.

C. **Documentation required for licensure.** Application (WC Form 50 or most current version). ALA. ADMIN. CODE r. 480-5-5.06(7)(b) (2004).

D. **Exemptions from licensure.** Out-of-state organizations are not granted an exemption from Alabama's licensure and certification requirements even if they are duly licensed and/or certified in their state of domicile. ALA. ADMIN. CODE r. 480-5-5.06(7)(d) (2004).

IV. Program Requirements

A. **Clinical review criteria.** Any prevailing and generally accepted medical policies, rules, medical protocols, guides and standards which may include, but are not limited to, criteria set out in the Intensity/Severity/Discharge Manual; the nomenclature and rules set out in the latest edition of Physicians' Current Procedural Terminology (CPT-4) publication; the nomenclature and rules set out in the latest edition of International Classification of Diseases; the nomenclature and rules set out in the latest edition of the American Society of Anesthesiologist Relative Value Guide; rules and nomenclature set out in the latest edition of Global Service Data for Orthopaedic Surgery published by the American Academy of

Orthopaedic Surgeons; criteria established by the Commission on Accreditation of Rehabilitation Facilities (CARF); rules, nomenclature and standards established by the National Association of Rehabilitation Professionals in the Private Sector (NARPPS); rules, nomenclature and standards established by the latest edition of the Health Care Finance Administration Finance Common Procedure Coding Systems (HCPCS); rules and criteria as described in the Professional Activity Study; and prevailing rules, nomenclature and standards established by peer review committees established by medical provider associations used by the utilization review entity to determine certification of medical services; or any other professional groups as recognized by the Alabama Workers' Compensation Medical Services Board. ALA. ADMIN. CODE r. 480-5-5.02(14) (2004).

B. **Prohibitions against financial incentives.** No provision.

C. **Telephone access standards.** Utilization review entities must be reasonably accessible to injured workers and providers Monday through Friday, except legal holidays, during normal business hours. ALA. ADMIN. CODE r. 480-5-5-.06(7)(g)(2) (2004). A physician or medical director performing second level clinical review shall be reasonably available by phone or in person to discuss determinations with ordering providers. ALA. ADMIN. CODE r. 480-5-5-.07(4)(b) (2004). When a decision is made to deny certification and the provider feels immediate appeal is necessary, the provider may appeal the determination over the phone on an expedited basis. ALA. ADMIN. CODE r. 480-5-5-.07(5)(2) (2004).

D. **Quality assurance program.** No provision.

E. **Delegation of utilization review functions.** UR may be performed by the insurance carrier, employer/agent, self-insured employee or group insurance fund. There is no requirement to hire an outside URE. ALA. ADMIN. CODE r. 480-5-5-.07(i) (2004).

F. **Confidentiality.** According to the application, utilization review entities must protect the confidentiality of medical records. ALA. ADMIN. CODE r. 480-5-5-.067)(g)(2) (2004). *See also* ALA. ADMIN. CODE r. 480-5-5-.06(7)(g)(2) (2004) and ALA. CODE r. § 25-5-294 (2004).

V. Reviewer Qualifications
ALA. ADMIN. CODE r. 580-5-5-.06 (2004).

A. **Qualifications of reviewers that render utilization review determinations (at each level of utilization review, if applicable)?**

1. Nurses and other licensed or similarly certified medical professionals conducting First Level Clinical Review shall possess current and valid license or certificate from appropriate licensure agency; be familiar with principles and procedures of utilization review and rules; and be supported by an available physician with a nonrestricted license to practice medicine. ALA. ADMIN. CODE r. 480-5-5-.06(2)(2) (2004).

2. Physicians or medical directors who directly support the utilization review activity of an employer/agent or utilization review entity shall perform Second Level Clinical Review and shall hold a current, nonrestricted license to practice medicine or a health profession in the United States; be oriented to the principles and procedures of utilization review, peer review, and these rules; review cases in which a clinical determination to certify cannot be made by the first level clinical review; and review all cases in which the utilization review process has concluded a determination not to certify is clinically appropriate. ALA. ADMIN. CODE r. 480-5-5-.06(3)(2) (2004).

3. Third Level Clinical Reviewers shall be providers who serve as peer consultants or peer advisers and render peer clinical review determination and shall demonstrate their competency and currency by being in active practice or holding a current, unrestricted license to practice medicine or a health profession in the United States; be board-certified in the same or similar specialty approved by the American Board of Medical Specialists or Advisory Board of Osteopathic Specialists; and be familiar with the practices and procedures of utilization review, peer review, and these rules. ALA. ADMIN. CODE r. 480-5-5-.06(4)(1) (2004).

B. **Requirements for medical director.** No provision.

C. **Requirement for "same-state" licensure.** U.S. licensure. ALA. ADMIN. CODE r. 480-5-5-.06(3)(a) (2004).

VI. Reviews and Appeals

A. **Review determinations and notice to patients/providers.** Alabama provides for 4 levels of review, the first being a "technical review" followed by 3 levels of clinical review. ALA. ADMIN. CODE r. 480-5-5-.06 (2004).

1. **Time frame for determination.** Initial determination is not specified, but the physician or medical director performing second level clinical review shall be reasonably available by telephone or in person to discuss the determination within one business day. ALA. ADMIN. CODE r. 480-5-5-.07(4)(6) (2004).

2. **Contents of notice of adverse determination.** The denial letter shall contain the following elements: employee's name, social security number, and address; date of service; date of injury; name of provider and facility; pre-certification number; reason for denial and the appeals process. ALA. ADMIN. CODE r. 480-5-5-.10(7) (2004).

   a. **Reasons for adverse determination.** Notification shall include principal reason for such a determination. ALA. ADMIN. CODE r. 480-5-5-.10(7) (2004).

   b. **Notice of Appeal Rights.** Yes. ALA. ADMIN. CODE r. 480-5-5-.10(7) (2004).

B. **Appeals requirements.** A utilization review entity shall establish procedures for appeals in writing or by telephone. All utilization review entities or employers/agents shall have in place an appeal process through peer clinical review (third level clinical review) when an adverse decision is rendered. ALA. ADMIN. CODE r. 480-5-5-.23 (2004).

1. **Time frame for determination.** On appeal, the reviewer shall make a decision within 30 calendar days, unless an expedited appeal pursuant to ALA. ADMIN. CODE r. 480-5-5-.07 (2004) is required. If the decision is reversal of noncertification or denial, provider must be immediately notified by phone. If the decision upholds denial, the adjudicator must verbally notify the provider. ALA. ADMIN. CODE r. 480-5-5-.23(1)(2)(3) (2004). Are there requirements for expedited appeals? Yes. Each qualified utilization review entity shall provide for reasonable access to its consulting peer clinical review providers by telephone. ALA. ADMIN. CODE r. 480-5-5-.07(s)(a) (2004). However, an expedited appeal is provided only when the provider and U.R.E. mutually agree that it is necessary. ALA. ADMIN. CODE r. 480-5-5-.230 (2004).

2. **External appeals.** Any party may request an administrative appeal by filing a letter of request with the Workers' Compensation Division. Any party may submit an adverse decision resulting from the peer clinical review to medical dispute resolution, which an ombudsman may decide through alternative dispute resolution within 60 days of a hearing. A party to an unresolved medical dispute, after a review of medical services, may petition the Alabama circuit court for relief.

C. **Emergency Services.** Not applicable.

VII. Recognition of URAC Accreditation Status

A. **Does the state recognize URAC accreditation?** Yes. ALA. ADMIN. CODE r. 480-5-5-.06(7)(d) (2004).

B. **Which of the state's requirements are waived for URAC-accredited organizations?** Any utilization review entity accredited by URAC (or the Alabama Department of Public Health) shall be deemed to be qualified and shall be issued a certificate by the Department of Industrial Relations upon receipt of such certification.

Arkansas

I. Scope and Applicability

A. **Who is subject to the state's utilization review laws?** Worker's compensation plans, which include managed care organizations (MCO's)and workers' compensation carriers. Managed care organizations must implement a utilization review program which includes concurrent and retrospective review. The MCO utilization review program must meet the requirements of ARK. CODE ANN. §§ 20-9-902 (2004), the rules and regulations for Utilization Review in Arkansas, and must be certified with the Arkansas Department of Health Utilization Review Certification programs as a Private Review Agent. ARK. WORKERS' COMP. COMM. R. 33, VII 16(7)(e) (1990).

B. **What exemptions are provided, if any?** None specifically in the workers' compensation context.
   1. HMO's? Yes.
   2. Insurers? Yes.
   3. Utilization review organizations? Yes.
   4. Workers' Compensation? Yes.
   5. Retrospective review? Yes.

C. **What term does the state use to refer to regulated entities?** ARK. WORKERS' COMP. COMM. R. 33 provides for the certification, administration, evaluation, and enforcement of managed care organizations (MCO's), which are certified entities that provide for the delivery and management of treatment to injured employees, and internal managed care systems (IMCS), which are certified and established and operated by an insurance carrier, employer, or self-insured employer. ARK. WORKERS' COMP. COMM. R. 30 provides requirements pertaining to utilization review activity by worker's compensation carriers. ARK. WORKERS' COMP. COMM. R. 30, IV A (1990).

D. **What activities does the state include in its definition of utilization review?** ARK. WORKERS' COMP. COMM. R. 30, IV (B)(3) (1990) lists the following activities as part of utilization review: review of medical bills to identify over utilization of services and improper billing, procedure coding, reduction of bills to the maximum allocable payment for that procedure, and reference to the Workers' Compensation Commission providers whose billing practices indicate over-utilization.

II. Regulatory Information

A. **Responsible state agency.** Arkansas Workers' Compensation Commission

B. **Contact Information.**
   1. **Name and Title:** Pat Capps Hannah, Division Head, Medical Cost Containment
   2. **Address:** Arkansas Workers' Compensation Commission, 324 Spring St. P.O. Box 950, Little Rock, AR 72203-0950.
   3. **Phone and Facsimile:** (501) 682-3930; facsimile (501) 682-1790.
   4. **E-mail:** pcapps@awcc.state.ar.us
   5. **Web site:** www.awcc.state.ar.us.

III. Licensure/Certification Requirements

A. **What entities are required to obtain a license in Arkansas to conduct utilization review for residents of the state?** The workers' compensation MCO utilization review program must meet the requirements of ARK. CODE ANN. § 20-9-902 et seq. (2004) and must have certification from the Ark. Dept. of Health as a private review agent. ARK. WORKERS' COMP. COMM. R. 33, VII 1 b(7) (1990)

B. **How often must licensure be renewed?** Every 2 years. Ark. Code Ann. § 20-9-909 (2004).

C. **Licensure fees (initial and renewal).** $500 for I.M.C.S. ARK. WORKERS' COMP. COMM. R 33, VIII 3 (1990).

D. **Documentation required for licensure.** Private review agents must submit an application; a utilization review plan that includes a description of review standards and procedures, appeals processes; and documentation of compliance with the state's requirements. ARK. CODE ANN. § 20-9-909 (2004). MCO's and IMCS' must apply pursuant to ARK. WORKERS' COMP. COMM. R. 33 (1990).

E. **Exemptions from licensure.** Out-of-state organizations are not granted an exemption from Arkansas' licensure and certification requirements even if they are duly licensed and/or certified in their state of domicile. ARK. CODE ANN. § 20-9-903 (2004). However, the State Board of Health may waive certification requirements for private review agents in connection with contracts with the federal government for utilization review of patients eligible for services under the Social Security Act. In-house utilization review is exempt so long as it does not result in approval or denial of payment for services and no certificate is needed for utilization review by any Arkansas-licensed pharmacist or pharmacy while engaged in the practice of pharmacy. ARK. CODE ANN. § 20-9-904 (2004).

IV. Program Requirements

A. **Clinical review criteria.** No provision in workers' compensation context.

B. **Prohibitions against financial incentives.** No provision.

C. **Telephone access standards.** No provision in workers' compensation context.

D. **Quality assurance program.** For certification as an MCO, must describe quality assurance program, which includes internal dispute resolution program, medical peer review program, pre-admission review program, second surgical opinion program, utilization review program, and technical and professional review programs. ARK. WORKERS' COMP. COMM. R. 33, VII 1 b(7) (1990).

E. **Delegation of UR functions.** A carrier may have another certified entity perform utilization review activities on its behalf. ARK. WORKERS' COMP. COMM. R. 30, IV B3(c) (1990). However, that carrier maintains full responsibility for compliance regardless of delegation. ARK. WORKERS' COMP. COMM. R. 30 IV B7 (1990).

F. **Confidentiality.** Private review agents must protect patients' confidentiality but may provide patient information to third parties with whom the private review agent is affiliated, under contract, or working on behalf of ARK. CODE ANN. § 20-9-913 (2004). *See also* ARK. CODE ANN. § 20-9-906 (2004).

V. Reviewer Qualifications

A. **Qualifications of reviewers that render utilization review determinations (at each level of UR, if applicable).** Review must be conducted by licensed, registered, or certified reliable professionals with suitable occupational injury or disease expertise to render an informed medical judgment. ARK. WORKERS' COMP. COMM. R. 30 (1990).

B. **Requirements for medical director.** Medical director can be a medical case manager, Arkansas physician, certified case manager, registered nurse or licensed practical nurse. ARK. WORKERS' COMP. COMM. R 33, vii, 1d(3) (1990).

C. **Requirement for "same-state" licensure.** No provision in workers' compensation context.

VI. Reviews and Appeals – ARK. WORKERS' COMP. COMM. R 33, XI

A. **Review determinations and notice to patients/providers.** Disputes arising on a issue related to managed care, such as the question of inappropriate, excessive, or not medically necessary treatment, shall be processed without charge to the employee or health care provider through the MCO's or IMCS's dispute resolution process. Disputes must be in writing and filed within 30 days of the dispute. ARK. WORKERS' COMP. COMM. R. 33, XI (1990).

1. **Time frame for determination.** Within 30 days of receipt of written request.

2. **Contents of notice of adverse determination.**

   a. **Reasons for adverse determination.** Not applicable.

   b. **Notice of Appeal Rights.** Not applicable.

B. **Appeals requirements.** If the dispute cannot be resolved or one of the parties makes a written request, the Administrator of the Medical Cost Containment Dept. of the Ark. Workers' Comp. Comm. may assist in resolving. Request for administrative review must be made in writing within 90 days of the disputed action. All parties will have 30 days from date of receipt of notification to submit further evidence, documentation, or clarification to the Administrator. ARK. WORKERS' COMP. COMM. R. 33, XI, 2(a) (1990).

1. **Time frame for determination.** Administrator or designee shall issue order or award within 30 days of review, which may include a hearing. Rehearing may be requested within 10 days in writing. Any aggrieved party may have 10 days to appeal in writing to an administrative law judge of the Arkansas Workers' Compensation Commission. ARK. WORKERS' COMP. COMM. R. 33, XI, 2 (d) and (e) (1990).

2. **External appeals.** Order or award of administrative law judge can be appealed to full Arkansas Workers' Compensation Commission. Order or award of the Arkansas Workers' Compensation Commission can be appealed to the Arkansas Court of Appeals. ARK. WORKERS' COMP. COMM. R. 33, XI, 2(f) (1990).

C. **Emergency Services.** Non-participating providers may provide emergency medical treatment. ARK. WORKERS' COMP. COMM. R. 33 (1990).

VII. Recognition of URAC Accreditation Status

    A.   Does the state recognize URAC accreditation?
No.

    B.   Which of the state's requirements are waived for
URAC-accredited organizations? Not
applicable.

California

I. Scope and Applicability

A. **Who is subject to the state's utilization review laws?** Every employer shall establish a utilization review process in compliance with the CAL. LAB. CODE § 4610 (2004), either directly or through its insurer. The Administrative Director of the Division of Workers' Compensation has adopted regulations setting forth utilization review standards applicable to workers' compensation insurers and self-insured employers. *See* CAL. CODE REGS. tit. 8, § 9792.6 (2004). Insurers and self-insured employers which implement or maintain a system of utilization review of the medical treatment provided to injured employees to manage costs and improve care had to comply with these standards CAL. CODE REGS. tit. 8, § 9792.6(b) (2004). The regulations pertain to insurers, including self-insured employers. The insurers may delegate (contract with) others, including health maintenance organizations (HMO's) or other managed care organizations, to perform utilization review services. The insurers are then responsible for ensuring that their contractors comply with the regulations.

B. **What exemptions are provided, if any?** Entities that do not perform utilization review are exempt from the minimum standards.
   1. **HMO's?** Yes. There is no direct regulation of HMO utilization review.
   2. **Insurers?** Yes, for workers' compensation insurers.
   3. **Utilization review organizations?** No. (Not directly. See above.)
   4. **Workers' Compensation?** Yes.
   5. **Retrospective review?** Yes.

C. **What term does the state use to refer to regulated entities?** The utilization review activities of workers' compensation insurers and self-insured employers are subject to minimum standards.

D. **What activities does the state include in its definition of utilization review?** "Utilization review" is "a system used to manage costs and improve patient care and decision making through case by case assessments of the frequency, duration, level and appropriateness of medical care and services to determine whether medical treatment is or was reasonably required to cure or relieve the effects of the injury." The definition includes "review of requests for authorization, and the review of bills for medical services for the purpose of determining whether medical services provided were reasonably required to cure or relieve the injury." The definition does not include "bill review for the purpose of determining whether the medical services rendered were accurately billed, and does not include any system, program, or activity in connection with making decisions concerning whether a person has sustained an injury which is compensable under Division 4 (commencing with section 3200) of the Labor Code (that is, one compensable by another source)." CAL. CODE REGS. tit. 8, § 9792.6(a)(5) (2004).

II. Regulatory Information

A. **Responsible state agency.** California Department of Industrial Relations, Division of Workers' Compensation.

B. **Contact Information.**
   1. **Name and Title:** Andrea Hoch, Administrative Director, Division of Workers' Compensation.
   2. **Address:** California Department of Industrial Relations, 455 Golden Gate Ave., 9th Floor, San Francisco, CA 94102-3660.
   3. **Phone and Facsimile:** (415) 703-4600
   4. **Web site:** www.dir.ca.gov/dwc.

III. Licensure/Certification Requirements

A. **What entities are required to obtain a license in the state to conduct utilization review for residents of the state?** No license is required. Insurers and self-insured employers are not required to implement or maintain a utilization review system. If the Administrator Director finds that an insurer has implemented or maintained a utilization review system that does not comply with CAL. CODE REGS. tit. 8, § 9792.6(c)(4)(e) (2004), the Administrative Director shall notify the insurer in writing and provide up to 90 days to correct any noted deficiency.

B. **How often must licensure be renewed?** Not applicable.

C. **Licensure fees (initial and renewal).** Not applicable.

D. **Documentation required for licensure.** Any insurer that implements or maintains a system of utilization review shall maintain and make available to the Administrative Director upon request a written summary of the insurer's utilization review system. Such summary shall include a description of the review process; a description of the specific criteria used in the review and throughout the decision-making process, including treatment protocols or standards used in the process; and a description of the qualifications and manner of involvement of the utilization review personnel. CAL. CODE REGS. tit. 8, § 9792.6(b) (2004).

E. **Exemptions from licensure.** Not applicable.

IV. Program Requirements

A. **Clinical review criteria.** Only medically-based criteria shall be used in utilization review and decision making process. Such criteria shall be based on professionally-recognized standards; developed using sound clinical principles and processes; developed by physicians, with the involvement of actively practicing health care providers, and undergo peer review; evaluated annually and updated, if necessary; and signed CAL. LAB. CODE and dated by the physicians who developed them. CAL. CODE REGS. tit. 8, § 9792.6(c)(3) (2004). *See also* CAL. LAB. CODE § 4610(f) (2004).

B. **Prohibitions against financial incentives.** No provision.

C. **Telephone access standards.** Workers' compensation insurer, third-party administrator, or other entity that requires a treating physician to obtain utilization review shall ensure availability of services from 9 AM to 5:30 PM Pacific time on business days. CAL. LAB. CODE § 4600.4 (2004). Also, if the insurer denies authorization, it must provide the name and phone number of the reviewer and his or her hours of availability. CAL. CODE REGS. tit. 8, § 9792.6(c)(4) (2004).

D. **Quality assurance program.** Every organization shall establish procedures for continuously reviewing the quality of care, performance of medical personnel, utilization of services and facilities and costs. CAL. LAB. CODE 4600.6(k) (2004).

E. **Delegation of utilization review function.** Insurers and self-insured employers who contract with others to handle claims administration or utilization review are responsible for ensuring that those with whom they contract comply with the utilization review standards.

F. **Confidentiality.** Not applicable.

V. Reviewer Qualifications

A. **Qualifications of reviewers that render utilization review determinations (at each level of utilization review, if applicable).**

1. Non-physician reviewer may initially apply medically-based criteria to requests for authorization or to bills for medical services.

2. Only physician with unrestricted license from his or her licensing board with pertinent education, training, expertise, and experience for specific clinical issues or services under review can deny request for authorization or deny or reduce request for payment.

3. Under no circumstance may a registered nurse make an appeal decision.

B. **Requirements for medical director.** Medical directors must have an unrestricted license to practice medicine in California. CAL. LAB. CODE 4610(d) (2004).

C. **Requirement for "same-state" licensure.** Medical directors must have an unrestricted license to practice medicine in this state. CAL. LAB. CODE 4610(d) (2004).

VI. Reviews and Appeals

A. **Review determinations and notice to patients/providers.**

1. Time frame for determination. Upon receipt of written request for authorization, an insurer shall issue a written authorization, denial, or notice of delay of decision to the health care provider. Decision shall be transmitted or mailed no later than 7 working days after insurer's receipt of request and any supporting information. A notice of delay shall include what additional information is required and when a decision will be made. CAL. CODE REGS. tit. 8, § 9792.6(c)(1) (2004).

2. If the decision cannot be made within the required timeframes either because the employer or other entity lacks the information reasonably necessary and requested, because employer requires an expert opinion or has asked for additional testing consistent with good medical practice, the employee and physician must be notified in writing. CAL. LAB. CODE § 4610(g)(4) (2004).

3. Prospective or concurrent decisions must be made no more than 5 working days from the receipt of information reasonably necessary to make the determination but no later than 14 days from the date of medical treatment or recommendation by the physician. If the employee's condition poses a serious or imminent danger to his or her health,

prospective or concurrent review must be made in a timely way not to exceed 72 hours after the relevant information is received. Retrospective decisions must be made within 30 days of receipt of information necessary to make a determination. CAL. LAB. CODE § 4610(g)(1) and § 4610(g)(2) (2004). Determinations must be communicated within 24 hours of such decisions. CAL. LAB. CODE § 4610(g)(3)(A) (2004).

4. Contents of notice of adverse determination. The authorization, denial, or notice of delay shall include some means of identification of the request and shall include the name and phone number of a responsible contact person. CAL. CODE REGS. tit. 8, § 9792.6(c)(A) (2004) a notice of delay shall

   a. **Reasons for adverse determination.** If an insurer denies a request for authorization or denies or reduces a bill for medical services on the basis that the services were not reasonably necessary, the insurer must submit to the health care provider a written explanation of the basis of the denial or reduction. Such explanation shall include the name of the reviewer, telephone number and hours of availability of the reviewer, and medical criteria upon which the denial was based.

   b. **Notice of Appeal Rights.** The regulations neither require nor prohibit an internal appeals process. Note: Disputed medical issues in workers' compensation cases can be taken to the Workers' Compensation Appeals Board.

B. **Appeals requirements.** Under rules in Labor Code, Division 4, disputes can be taken to the Workers' Compensation Appeals Board. Among other things, there is a right to an expedited hearing in cases related to medical treatment. If requests are not granted in full, disputes will be resolved according to CAL. LAB. CODE 4062 (2004).

   1. **Time frame for determination.** No provision.

   2. **External appeals.** Workers Compensation Appeals Board.

C. **Emergency Services.** In emergency situations, a timely decision must be rendered no more than 72 hours after receipt of information reasonably necessary to make the determination CAL. LAB. CODE 4610(g)(2) (2004).

VII. Recognition of URAC Accreditation Status
A. Does the state recognize URAC accreditation? No.
B. Which of the state's requirements are waived for URAC-accredited organizations? Not applicable.

Colorado

I. Scope and Applicability

A. **Who is subject to the state's utilization review laws?** The Colorado Division of Workers' Compensation performs utilization review in individual cases, using a three-member review panel tailored to the type of claim being made. Those who desire utilization review must request it. COL. REV. STAT. §8-43-501(3)(b) (2004). *See also* 7 COLO. CODE REGS.1101-3, R. XV G (2004). The division does not directly regulate entities that perform utilization review. Colorado law does not directly regulate internal UM processes of worker's compensation carriers or of employers, but delegates external UM to the state. Id.

B. **What term does the state use to refer to regulated entities?** Not applicable.

C. **What activities does the state include in its definition of utilization review?** The purpose of the utilization review program is to "provide a mechanism to review medical care or health care services rendered pursuant to this article that may not be reasonably necessary or reasonably appropriate according to accepted professional standards and to provide a mechanism to prevent such health care providers from providing medical care or health care services." COL. REV. STAT. § 8-43-503(1). *See also* 7 COLO. CODE REGS.1101-3, R. XV A(1) (2004).

II. Regulatory Information

A. **Responsible state agency.** Department of Labor and Employment, Division of Workers' Compensation.

B. **Contact Information.**
   1. **Name and Title:** Debra Northrup, RN, Medical Policy Specialist
   2. **Address:** Division of Workers' Compensation, 1515 Arapahoe, Tower 2, Suite 640, Denver, CO 80202-2117.
   3. **Phone and Facsimile:** (303) 318-8761; facsimile (303)318-8758.
   4. **Email:** debra.northrup@state.co.us.
   5. **Web site:** www.coworkforce.com/DWC.

III. Licensure/Certification Requirements

A. **What entities are required to obtain a license in the state to conduct utilization review for residents of the state?** Not applicable.

B. **How often must licensure be renewed?** Not applicable.

C. **Licensure fees (initial and renewal).** Not applicable.

D. **Documentation required for licensure.** Not applicable.

E. **Exemptions from licensure.** Not applicable.

IV. Program Requirements

A. **Clinical review criteria.** Members of medical utilization review committees shall consider all applicable medical treatment guidelines. The Division of Workers' Compensation shall provide copies of appropriate guidelines to committee upon request. 7 COLO. CODE REGS. 1101-3, R. XV H(2) (2004).

B. **Prohibitions against financial incentives.** Health professionals that serve on second-level appeals panels may not have a financial interest in the case under review.

C. **Telephone access standards.** No provision.

D. **Quality assurance program.** No provision.

E. **Delegation of utilization review functions.** The medical director may contract with an appropriate private organization meeting the definition of a utilization and quarterly control peer review organization under 42 U.S.C. §1320(c)-1(1)(A) or (1)(B) and conduct peer review activities and recommend whether adverse action is warranted. COL. REV. STAT. §8-42-101 (2004).

F. **Confidentiality.** The Division of Workers' Compensation maintains a special file for utilization review cases. Only interested parties in a utilization review case shall have access to such file. Members of utilization review committees shall not engage in communication regarding the utilization review with any other person except Division Staff, with limited exceptions. 7 COLO. CODE REGS. 1101-3, R. XV F(5) (2004).

V. Reviewer Qualifications

A. **Qualifications of reviewers that render utilization review determinations (at each level of utilization review, if applicable).** 7 COLO. CODE REGS.1101-3, R. XV, F., G. (2004).
   1. Director of Workers' Compensation will appoint appropriate peer professionals to serve on utilization review committees for 3 years.
   2. Provider may not serve on a utilization review committee unless his or her professional license or certificate is current, active, and unrestricted.
   3. Joints/Musculoskeletal Committee shall include 2 practitioners licensed in same

discipline of care as provider under review and one occupational medicine practitioner (M.D. or D.O) with specified years of experience.

4. Dental Committee shall include 3 dentists.

5. Pyschiatry Committee shall include one occupational medicine practitioner (M.D. or D.O.) and 2 psychiatrists.

B. **Requirements for medical director.** Director must be a medical doctor licensed to practice in Colorado with experience in occupational medicine. COL. REV. STAT. §8-42-101(3)(n) (2004).

C. **Requirement for "same-state" licensure.** No provision.

VI. Reviews and Appeals

A. **Review determinations and notice to patients/providers.** The report of each member of the utilization review committee shall be restricted to the specific questions submitted by the division and shall include a written narrative demonstrating how the answers were determined. 7 COLO. CODE REGS.1101-3, R. XV H(3)(a) and (b) (2004).

    1. **Time frame for determination.** Not known.

    2. **Contents of notice of adverse determination.**

    a. **Reasons for adverse determination.** Not known.

    b. **Notice of Appeal Rights.** Appeal form prescribed by Division of Workers' Compensation.

B. **Appeals requirements.** Appealing party shall complete the appeal form prescribed by the Division of Workers' Compensation. The form is to be filed with the medical utilization review coordinator. The appeal form includes instructions for scheduling a de novo hearing, if the appealing party is entitled to one. 7 COLO. CODE REGS. 1101-3, R. XV J. (2004) Claimants, providers, and insurers can request reviews of records by administrative law judges. COL. REV. STAT. §8-43-501(s)(2) (2004).

    1. **Time frame for determination.** Not specified.

    2. **External appeals.** Can appeal administrative law judge's decision to Industrial Claims Appeals Plan and then to Colorado Court of Appeals. COL. REV. STAT. §8 43 301 (2004).

C. **Emergency Services.** No provision.

VII. Recognition of URAC Accreditation Status

A. **Does the state recognize URAC accreditation?** No.

B. **Which of the state's requirements are waived for URAC-accredited organizations?** Not applicable.

Connecticut

I. Scope and Applicability

A. **Who is subject to the state's utilization review laws?** Any employer or insurer acting on behalf of an employer that establishes a plan, subject to the approval of the chairman of the Workers' Compensation Commission, for the provision of medical care provided by the employer for treatment of any injury or illness under Chapter 568 (Workers' Compensation Act) shall include a description of how the quality and quantity of medical care will be managed. CONN. GEN. STAT. § 31-279(c)(1)(D) (2004). Any medical care plan which engages directly in utilization review and any utilization review contractor which performs on behalf of any medical care plea shall according to law, be licensed by the Commissioner of Insurance as a Utilization Review Company. CONN. AGENCIES REGS. §31-279-10(h)(7) (2004).

B. **What exemptions are provided, if any?** Exceptions for those entities that are not defined as a utilization review company: an agency of the federal government, an agent acting on behalf of the federal government, any Connecticut agency and a hospital's internal quality assurance program. In the case of practitioners on the approved list who are not employees or contract providers and who are not providing medical and health care services pursuant to an employee's election to obtain their services rather than the services of a plan provider, the service utilization review and dispute resolution provision of CONN. AGENCIES REGS. §31-279-10 (2004) shall not apply.

1. **HMO's?** Yes.
2. **Insurers?** Yes.
3. **Utilization review organizations?** Yes.
4. **Workers' Compensation?** Yes.
5. **Retrospective review?** No. (By contrast, for the Department of Social Services, utilization review can be "conducted on a concurrent, prospective, or retrospective basis." *See, e.g.,* CONN. AGENCIES REGS. § 17b-262-338(44) (2004).

C. **What term does the state use to refer to regulated entities?** "Medical care plans," CONN. AGENCIES REGS. 31-279-10 (2004), and "Utilization Review Companies." CONN. GEN. STAT. § 38a-226(a) (2004).

D. **What activities does the state include in its definition of Workers' Comp. utilization review?** Utilization review provides "a method to evaluate the necessity and appropriateness of medical and health care services recommended by a provider, and a means of dispute resolution if payment for such medical and health care services is denied." CONN. AGENCIES REGS. § 31-279-10(e) (2004).

II. Regulatory Information

A. **Responsible state agency.** Connecticut Workers' Compensation Commission.

B. **Contact Information.**
1. **Name and Title:** Marilou Lang.
2. **Address:** Connecticut Workers' Compensation Commission, Capitol Place, 21 Oak Street, Fourth Floor, Hartford, CT 06106.
3. **Phone and Facsimile:** (860) 493-1559; facsimile (860) 247-1361.
4. **E-mail:** marilou.lang@po.state.ct.us.
5. **Web site:** wcc.state.ct.us.

III. Licensure/Certification Requirements

A. **What entities are required to obtain a license in the state to conduct utilization review for residents of the state?** No utilization review company may conduct utilization review in Connecticut unless licensed by the Commissioner of Insurance under CONN. GEN. STAT. § 38a-226a (2004). Any medical care plan engaging directly in utilization review and any utilization review contractor performing utilization review on behalf of a plan shall be licensed. CONN. AGENCIES REGS. § 31-279-10(h)(7) (2004).

B. **How often must licensure be renewed?** Annually.

C. **Licensure fees (initial and renewal).** $2,500. CONN. GEN. STAT. §38a-226a (2004).

D. **Documentation required for licensure.** Demographic information about the utilization review company and **documentation of compliance with the state's requirements.**

E. **Exemptions from licensure.** Certain organizations, as shown above in I.A., are exempt.

IV. Program Requirements

A. **Clinical review criteria.** Each utilization review company shall use written clinical criteria and review procedures that are established and periodically evaluated and updated with appropriate involvement from practitioners. CONN. AGENCIES REGS. §31-279-10(e)(2) (2004).

B. **Prohibitions against financial incentives.** "No utilization review professional may receive any financial incentive based on the number of denials of certification made by such professional." CONN. AGENCIES REGS. § 31-279-10(h)(6) (2004).

C. **Telephone access standards.** Utilization review staff shall be available by toll-free telephone at least 40 hours per week during regular business hours. CONN. AGENCIES REGS. §1-279-10(h)(2) (2004).

D. **Quality assurance program.** No separate provision.

E. **Delegation of UR functions.** No separate provision.

F. **Confidentiality.** Each utilization review professional shall comply with all applicable state and federal laws to protect the confidentiality of individual medical records; summary and aggregate data shall not be considered confidential if there is insufficient information to allow identification of individual patients. CONN. AGENCIES REGS. § 31-279-10(h)(3) (2004).

V. Reviewer Qualifications

A. **Qualifications of reviewers that render utilization review determinations (at each level of utilization review, if applicable).**

1. Nurses and other health professionals, other than physicians, making utilization review recommendations and decisions shall have current and valid licenses from a state licensing agency in the United States. CONN. AGENCIES REGS. §31-279-10(h)(1) (2004).

2. Physicians making utilization review recommendations and decisions shall have current and valid licenses from Connecticut. CONN. AGENCIES REGS. §31-279-10(h)(1) (2004).

B. **Requirements for medical director.** No separate provision.

C. **Requirement for "same-state" licensure.** Physicians must have Connecticut license, but nurses and other health professionals, making utilization review recommendations need valid licenses from any state licensing agency in the U.S. CONN. AGENCIES REGS. §31-279-10(h)(1) (2004).

VI. Reviews and Appeals

A. **Review determinations and notice to patients/providers.** Each medical care plan shall include a means of dispute resolution if payment for medical and health care services is denied. Any written notice of a determination not to certify an admission, service, procedures, or extension of stay shall include reasons and name and telephone number of person to contact regarding an appeal. Provider and employee shall receive copy of written review and appeal procedures. CONN. AGENCIES REGS. §31-279-10(e)(3) (2004).

B. **Time frame for determination.** Within 2 business days of receiving all information, plan shall provide written notice to provider and employee of determination regarding recommended treatment.

1. **Contents of notice of adverse determination.**

   a. **Reasons for adverse determination.** Written notice of a determination not to certify shall include reason for such determination. CONN. AGENCIES REGS. §31-279-10(e)(3) (2004).

   b. **Notice of Appeal Rights.** Yes. Written determination must include name and telephone number of contact person regarding an appeal. CONN. AGENCIES REGS. §31-279-10(e)(3) (2004).

C. **Appeals requirements.** Within 15 days of written notice of determination, a provider or employee may notify the plan of intent to appeal. Upon such appeal, plan shall provide a practitioner in a specialty relating to the employee's condition to review the plan's initial decision. CONN. AGENCIES REGS. §31-279-10(e)(4) and (5) (2004).

1. **Time frame for determination.** Within 15 days of request for such review and submission of any further documentation, the reviewing practitioner shall submit opinion to medical director of medical care plan who has 15 days to render a written decision. The employee, provider, or employer may request a further review of the medical director's written decision within 15 days in writing. The chief executive officer of the medical plan shall issue a final written decision within 30 days of later of date of submission of written request or conclusion of hearing requested as part of such review. CONN. AGENCIES REGS. §31-279-10(e)(6) (2004).

2. **External appeals.** After exhausting plan's utilization review and dispute resolution review and appeal procedures, *see*, CONN. AGENCIES REGS. § 31-279-10(e) (2004), a Workers' Compensation commissioner may review necessity and appropriateness of

medical and health care services recommended by providers. Commissioner may only modify decision of chief executive officer of plan upon showing that decision was unreasonable, arbitrary, or capricious. CONN. AGENCIES REGS. §31-279-10(f) (2004).

D. **Emergency Services.** Employee or representative shall have minimum of 24 hours after an emergency admission, service, or procedure to request certification and continuing treatment. Upon a determination not to provide continuing treatment, if employee or representative, provider, or employer requests review, the medical director shall render final decision within 2 days. CONN. AGENCIES REGS. §31-279-10(e)(8) (2004).

VII. Recognition of URAC Accreditation Status

A. Does the state recognize URAC accreditation? No.

B. Which of the state's requirements are waived for URAC-accredited organizations? Not applicable.

District of Columbia

I. Scope and Applicability

A. **Who is subject to the state's utilization review laws?** The District of Columbia does not regulate utilization review organizations or activities, but any medical care or service furnished or scheduled to be furnished under the Worker's Compensation Act is subject to utilization review, which may be performed before, during or after the medical service is provided. D.C. CODE ANN. § 7-119.1 (2004). D.C. MUN. REGS. tit. 7, §232.1.

B. **What exemptions are provided if any?** Not applicable.
   1. **HMOs?** Not applicable.
   2. **Insurers?** Not applicable.
   3. **Utilization Review Organizations?** Not applicable.
   4. **Workers' Compensation?** Yes.
   5. **Retrospective Review?** Yes.

C. **What term does the state use to refer to regulated entities?** Utilization review organization or individual.

D. **What activities does the state include in its definition of utilization review?** "Utilization review" is defined as "the evaluation of the necessity, character, and sufficiency of both the level and quality of medically related services provided an injured employee based upon medically related standards." D.C. CODE ANN. § 32-1501(18)(A) (2004).

II. Regulatory Information

A. **Responsible state agency.** Department of Employment Services, Office of Labor Standards.

B. **Contact Information**
   1. **Name and Title:** Charles L. Green, Associate Director for Workers' Compensation.
   2. **Address:** 64 New York Ave., N.E., Washington, DC 20002.
   3. **Phone and Facsimile:** 202) 671-1055; facsimile (202) 671-1929.
   4. **E-mail:** charles.green@d.c.gov.
   5. **Web site:** www.does.dc.gov/does/cwp/view.asp?a=123 2&Q=537428.

III. Licensure/Certification Requirements

A. **What entities are required to obtain a license in the state to conduct utilization review for residents of the state?** A utilization review organization or individual used pursuant to the Worker's Compensation Act shall be certified by the URAC, but no license is required. D.C. MUN. REGS. tit.7, §1-232.2 (2004).

B. **How often must licensure/certification be renewed?** Not applicable.

C. **Licensure fees (initial and renewal).** Not applicable.

D. **Documentation required for licensure.** Not applicable.

E. **Exemptions from licensure.** Not applicable as licensure is not required.

IV. Program Requirements

A. **Clinical review criteria.** No provision.

B. **Prohibitions against financial incentives.** No provision.

C. **Telephone access standards.** No provision.

D. **Quality assurance program.** No provision.

E. **Delegation of utilization review functions.** No provision.

F. **Confidentiality.** Any publication by a medical utilization review committee shall keep patient identity confidential. D.C. CODE ANN.§46-804 (2004).

V. Reviewer Qualifications

A. **Qualifications of reviewers that render utilization review determinations (at each level of utilization review, if applicable)?** No provision.

B. **Requirements for medical director.** No provision.

C. **Requirements for "same-state" licensure.** No provision.

VI. Reviews and Appeals

A. **Review determination and notice to patients/providers.** The report of the review shall specify medical records considered and shall set forth rational medical evidence to support each finding. The utilization review individual or officer of the utilization review organization shall provide report to the employee, employer and Office of Employment Benefits. D.C. MUN. REGS. tit. §1-232.4, D.C. CODE ANN.§ 7-119.4.
   1. **Time frame for determination.** No provision.
   2. **Contents of notice of adverse determinations.**
   a. **Reasons for adverse determination.** The report shall set forth rational medical evidence to support each finding.
   b. **Notice of appeal rights.** No provision.

B. **Appeals requirements.** If the medical care provider disagrees with the opinion of the utilization review organization or individual, such provider may submit a written request for reconsideration. Such request shall contain reasonable medical justification for the request and shall be made within 60 days of the receipt of the utilization review report. D.C. CODE ANN § 7-119.6. (2004).

   1. **Time frame for determination.** No provision.

   2. **External appeals.** In the event of a dispute between the medical care provider, the employee, or the Department of Employment Services on the issue of necessity, character, or sufficiency of the medical care or service or fees charged to the medical provider, the Director of the Department of Employment Services shall resolve the dispute upon application for a hearing. Any party adversely affected by the Director's decision may appeal to the D.C. Court of Appeals. D.C. CODE ANN. § 7-119.7, D.C. MUN. REGS. tit. 7 § 232.7. The decision of the Director may also be reviewed by the Superior Court of D.C. without appeal to the Employee's Compensation Appeals Board. D.C. CODE ANN.119.7 (2004)

C. **Emergency Services.** No provision.

VII. Recognition of URAC Accreditation Status

A. **Does the state recognize URAC accreditation?** Yes.

B. **Which of the state's requirements are waived for URAC-accredited organizations?** Any organization or individual performing workers' compensation utilization review shall be accredited by URAC.

Georgia

I. Scope and Applicability

A. **Who is subject to the state's workers' compensation utilization review laws?** Utilization review, quality assurance, and peer review activities performed by health care providers or groups of medical service providers certified to offer managed care to injured employees (WC/MCO's) are subject to the review of the State Workers' Compensation Board. GA. CODE ANN. § 34-9-208(f) (2004)).

B. **What term does the state use to refer to regulated entities?** Workers' Compensation/Managed Care Organization (WC/MCO).

C. **What activities does the state include in its definition of utilization review?** Each WC/MCO must implement a plan for utilization review, which must include the collection, review, and analysis of group data to improve overall quality of care, efficient use of resources, and duration of disability. GA. COMP. R & REGS. r. 208(g)(2) (2003). Peer review is the procedure by which disputes concerning the necessity of services and reasonableness of fees are resolved. GA. COMP. R & REGS. r. 200.1(d)(12) (2003).

II. Regulatory Information

A. **Responsible state agency.** Georgia State Board of Worker's Compensation.

B. **Contact Information.**

1. **Name and Title:** Deborah Krotenberg, Division Director, Managed Care and Rehabilitation Division, Georgia State Board of Workers' Compensation

2. **Address:** 270 Peachtree Street, NW. Atlanta, GA 30303-1299

3. **Phone and Facsimile:** (404)656-0849; facsimile (404) 463-0310.

4. **E-mail:** krotenbe@sbwc.state.ga.us

5. **Web site:** http://sbwc.georgia.gov

III. Certification Requirements

A. **What entities are required to obtain a license in the state to conduct utilization review for residents of the state?** WC/MCO's.

B. **How often must certification be renewed?** In order to maintain certification, each WC/MCO shall provide the following information in the form of a certified annual report on the first working day following each anniversary of initial certification: information regarding all organization personnel and licenses; a summary of all sanctions and punitive actions taken by the WC/MCO against any participating providers; a report summarizing peer review, utilization review, supplier profiles, reported complaints, and dispute resolution proceedings; and an audited financial statement for the most recent fiscal year. GA. COMP. R & REGS. r. 208(c)(2) (2003).

C. **Certification fees (initial and renewal).** For initial certification, an organization must pay a non-refundable fee of $1,000. GA. COMP. R & REGS. r. 208(a)(1) (2003). To have certification renewed annually, an existing WC/MCO must pay a non-refundable fee of $500. GA. COMP. R & REGS. r. 208(c)(2)(E) (2003).

D. **Documentation required for licensure.** To become certified as a WC/MCO, each entity must provide the State Board of Workers' Compensation with the following: audited financial statement; information regarding organization personnel; list of provisions of quality services; description of its proposed geographic service area; list of minority providers; sample agreements with providers; statement that all licensing requirements for providers and managers are current; referrals; procedures to notify employees of their rights, for approval of services outside the managed care plan, for peer review and utilization, and for internal dispute resolution; information for employees regarding all choices of medical services provided within the plan; and a description of how medical case management will be provided for injured employees. GA. COMP. R & REGS. r. 208(a) (2003).

E. **Exemptions from certification.** All WC/MCO's providing services in the state of Georgia must meet the certification requirements of the State Board of Workers' Compensation.

IV. Program Requirements

The state of Georgia does not mandate any specific program requirements for utilization review. Instead, when a WC/MCO applies to the State Board of Workers' Compensation for certification, it is required to include a proposed procedure for peer review and utilization. A peer review system will be approved by the Board provided it will improve patient care and cost effectiveness, it includes a majority of health care providers of the same discipline being reviewed, it is designed to evaluate the quality of care given by a health care provider to a patient, and it describes how providers will be selected for review, the nature of the review, and how the results will be used. GA. COMP. R & REGS. r. 208(g)(1) (2003). The WC/MCO's plan for utilization review will attain Board approval provided it profiles each medical supplier, includes the collection, review, and analysis of group data to improve overall quality of care, efficient use of resources, and duration of disability, and specifies the data to be collected, how the data will be analyzed, and how the results will be applied to improve patient care and increase the cost effectiveness of treatment. GA. COMP. R & REGS. R. 208(g)(2) (2003). Therefore, each WC/MCO may have different clinical review criteria, telephone access standards, quality assurance programs, and the like, so long as the overall peer and utilization review processes meet Board standards for certification.

A. **Prohibitions against financial incentives.** Each WC/MCO must provide appropriate financial incentives to reduce service costs and utilization without sacrificing the quality of service. GA. COMP. R & REGS. r. 208(a)(1)(C) (2003).

B. **Delegation of utilization review functions.** According to the State Board of Workers' Compensation, a WC/MCO may contract out any of its responsibilities required for certification, including utilization review, provided the contract is granted Board approval. GA. COMP. R & REGS. r. 208(a)(1)(B)(6) (2003).

C. **Confidentiality.** Data generated in connection with utilization review, quality assurance, and peer review activities, including written reports, notes, or records of such activities, or of the board's review thereof, shall be confidential and not disclosed except as considered necessary by the Board. GA. CODE ANN. § 34-9-208(f) (1994).

V. Reviewer Qualifications

Like program requirements, Georgia does not have any strict mandates concerning reviewer qualifications so long as reviewers are capable of satisfying the Board's standards for peer and utilization review outlined in GA. COMP. R & REGS. r. 208(g) (2003).

A. **Qualifications of reviewers that render utilization review determinations (at each level of utilization review, if applicable).** Peer review must include a majority of health care providers of the same discipline as that being reviewed and must be designed to evaluate the quality of care given by a provider. GA. COMP. R & REGS. r. 208(g)(1) (2003).

B. **Requirements for medical director.** Medical case management for an employee covered by a WC/MCO must be provided by one of the following licensed registered health care

professionals: Certified Rehabilitation Registered Nurse; Certified Case Manager; Certified Occupational Health Nurse or Specialist; Certified Disability Management Specialist, Certified Rehabilitation Counselor; Work Adjustment/Vocational Evaluation Specialist; or Licensed Professional Counselor. Case managers must have at least 1 year of experience in workers' compensation. GA. COMP. R & REGS. r. 208(h)(2) (2003).

VI. Reviews and Appeals

A. **Review determinations and notice to patients/providers.** Georgia does not mandate specific requirements for review determinations outside of the peer and utilization review proposals required for certification as a WC/MCO.

1. **Time frame for determination.** For charges not contained in the fee schedule established by the Board of Workers' Compensation and are disputed as not being the usual, customary, and reasonable charges prevailing in Georgia, the employer, insurer, or physician shall file a request for peer review with a peer review organization authorized by the Board within 30 days of the receipt of charges. GA. COMP. R & REGS. r. 203(c)(2) (2003).

2. **Notice of adverse determination.** If a utilization review results in a determination unfavorable to a party, that party must first proceed through the WC/MCO's internal dispute resolution process, which must be completed within 30 days of written notice. If the dispute cannot be resolved in this manner, the WC/MCO must notify the aggrieved party of its right to appeal the determination to the State Board of Workers' Compensation. GA. COMP. R & REGS. r. 208(f) (2003). A physician whose fee has been reduced by the peer review committee shall have 30 days from the date that the recommendation is mailed to request a hearing. GA. COMP. R & REGS. r. 203(c)(6) (2003).

B. **Emergency Services.** In emergency situations, a health care provider who is not a participating provider may provide medical services to an employee covered by a WC/MCO. GA. COMP. R & REGS. r. 208(e)(1) (2003).

VII. Recognition of URAC Accreditation Status

All WC/MCO's must obtain certification in Georgia regardless of their status in other states or URAC certification.

VIII. Miscellaneous

Georgia requires WC/MCO's to be certified in the state and to provide utilization and peer review, but the State Board of Workers' Compensation does not specify the precise qualifications required of reviewers or the procedures they are required to use. These details are left to each WC/MCO, though the organization must obtain approval of the Board during the certification and renewal process.

WCUM KANSAS

Kansas

I. Scope and Applicability

A. **Who is subject to the state's utilization review laws?** The Kansas Division of Workers' Compensation, Department of Human Resources, does not regulate the utilization review activities of utilization review organizations, insurers, or carriers, but does administer a utilization review program. KAN. STAT. ANN. § 44-510(d)(1) (2004). For this purpose, the Division contracts with an outside peer review organization to review all referred workers' compensation cases.

B. **What term does the state use to refer to regulated entities?** Not applicable.

C. **What activities does the state include in its definition of utilization review?** "Utilization review" is defined as "the initial evaluation of appropriateness in terms of both the level and the quality of health care and health services provided a patient, based on accepted standards of the health care profession involved. Such evaluation is accomplished by means of a system which identifies the utilization of health care services above the usual range of utilization range of utilization for such services, which is based on accepted standards of the health care profession involved, and which refers instances of possible inappropriate utilization to the director for referral to a peer review committee." KAN. STAT. ANN. § 44-508(m) (2004).

II. Regulatory Information

A. **Responsible state agency.** Kansas Department of Human Resources, Division of Workers Compensation.

B. **Contact Information.**

1. **Name and Title:** Terry Tracy, MD, Director, Medical Services Section, Kansas Workers' Compensation, Department of Human Resources.

2. **Address:** 800 SW Jackson Street, Suite 600, Topeka, KS 66612-1227.

3. **Phone and Facsimile:** (785)296-0846; facsimile (785) 296-4215.

4. **E-mail:** ttracy@hr.state.ks.us.

5. **Web site:** www.dol.ks.gov/wc/html/wc_ALL.html.

III. Miscellaneous

Among other things, the Medical Services Section, Division of Workers Compensation, administers a plan for health care services utilization and peer review. The section reviews disputed services or charges rendered by health care providers.

The Director of Worker's Compensation may delegate utilization review functions. Prior to a formal hearing, the director may conduct utilization review concerning disputed bills. Utilization review shall result in a report to the director concerning whether a provider improperly utilized or ordered services or whether fees were excessive. This report must be provided to all parties within 20 days prior to the formal hearing. With regard to confidentiality, all records and findings related to utilization review are privileged. KAN. STAT. ANN. § 44-510j (2004).

Kentucky

I. Scope and Applicability

A. **Who is subject to the state's utilization review laws?** All insurance carriers with workers' compensation insurance in Kentucky, individual self-insured employers, and group self-insurance funds shall implement a utilization review and medical bill audit program. KY REV. STAT. ANN § 42.035(5); 803 KY ADMIN. REGS. 25:190 (2004).

B. Workers compensation managed health care systems shall establish procedures for utilization review of medical services to assure that: a course of treatment is reasonably necessary; diagnostic procedures not unnecessarily duplicated; the frequent scope and duration of treatment is appropriate; pharmaceuticals are not unnecessarily prescribed; and that ongoing and proposed treatment is not experimental, cost-ineffective or harmful to the employee. KY REV. STAT. ANN § 342.020 (4)(f) (2004).

C. **What exemptions are provided, if any?** None listed.
   1. **HMOs?** Yes.
   2. **Insurers?** Yes.
   3. **Utilization Review Organizations?** Yes.
   4. **Workers' Compensation?** Yes.
   5. **Retrospective Review?** Yes.

D. **What term does the state use to refer to regulated entities?** Workers' Compensation Managed Health Care Systems as defined above.

E. **What activities does the state include in its definition of utilization review?** In the workers' compensation context, "utilization review" is defined as "a review of the medical necessity and appropriateness of medical care and services for purposes of recommending payments for compensable injuries or disease." 803 KY ADMIN. REGS. 25:190 § 1(6) (2004).

II. Regulatory Information.

A. **Responsible state agency.** Department of Workers Claims.

B. **Contact Information.**
   1. **Name and Title:** Shari Lafoe, Medical Cost Containment Section.
   2. **Address:** Perimeter Park West, Building C, 1270 Louisville Road, Frankfort, KY 40601.
   3. **Phone and Facsimile:** (502) 564-5550 ext. 4487; facsimile (502) 564-5741.
   4. **E-mail:** shari.lafoe@ky.gov.
   5. **Web site:** www.labor.ky.gov/dwc/ur.htm.

III. Licensure/Certification Requirements

A. **What entities are required to obtain a license in the state to conduct utilization review for residents of the state?** In addition, an insurance carrier, individual self-insured employer, and group self-insurer shall fully implement and maintain a written utilization review and medical bill audit plan, which the Commissioner of the Department of Workers Claims shall approve. KY ADMIN. REGS. § 25:190(3) (2004). Workers' Compensation Managed Health Care Services Plans are certified under 803 KY ADMIN. REGS. 25:110 (2004).

B. **How often must licensure/certification be renewed?** Utilization Review Plans for carriers shall be valid for up to 4 years. 803 KY ADMIN. REGS. § 25:190:3(5) (2004). A certificate for a managed care services plan shall be valid for 2 years. 803 KY ADMIN. REGS. § 25:110 § 5(2) (2004).

C. **Licensure fees (initial and renewal).** $500 initial and renewal fees, as noted above. There are no fees associated with the necessary plan approval from the Department of Workers Claims.

D. **Documentation required for licensure.** A written utilization and medical bill audit plan must be submitted. The submission must describe the process, policies, and procedures for making decisions. The submission must include a description of: the specific criteria used in the decision-making process; the specific medical guidelines used as a resource to confirm the medical diagnosis and to provide consistent criteria and practice standards against which care quality and related costs are measured; the selection criteria for review; the qualifications of internal and consulting personnel; the process to assure that a treatment plan shall be obtained for review by qualified medical personnel; the process for designating a physician when required; the process for notifying the provider and employee of the decision; and the reconsideration process. § 4 of 803 KY ADMIN. REGS. 25:190 (2004) and 803 KY ADMIN. REGS. 25:110 § 4 (2004) for worker's compensation managed health care plans.

E. **Exemptions from licensure.** There are no exemptions from licensure/approval with the Department of Workers Claims.

IV. Program Requirements

A. **Clinical review criteria.** Medical guidelines adopted by the Commissioner shall be incorporated in a utilization review plan including treatment standards upon which utilization review decisions shall be based (including low back symptoms and injuries to the upper extremities and knees) assuring quality care in accordance with prevailing communing medical standards. KY ADMIN. REGS. 25:110 § 4(5)(a) (2004).

B. **Prohibitions against financial incentives.** None listed.

C. **Telephone access standards.** Toll-free line shall be provided for employees or medical providers to contact the utilization reviewer. The reviewer or a representative shall be reasonably accessible at least 5 days per week, 40 hours per week, during normal business hours. 803 KY ADMIN. REGS. 25:140 § 4(10) (2004).

D. **Quality assurance program.** None listed.

E. **Delegation of utilization review functions.** An insurance carrier, individual self-insured employer, and group self-insurer that contracts with an approved vendor for utilization review or medical bill audit services shall notify the Commissioner of that arrangement.

F. **Confidentiality.** There shall be policies and procedures to protect the confidentiality of patient information.

V. Reviewer Qualifications

A. **Qualifications of reviewers that render utilization review determinations (at each level of utilization review, if applicable)?**

1. A utilization reviewer should be "appropriately qualified." 803 KY ADMIN. REGS. 25:190 § 2 (2004).

2. Utilization review personnel shall have education, training, and experience necessary for evaluating clinical issues and services under review. A licensed physician, registered nurse, licensed practical nurse, medical records technician, or other personnel who is qualified to issue decisions on medical necessity or appropriateness shall issue the initial utilization review approval. 803 KY ADMIN. REGS. 25:190 § 6(1) (2004).

3. A licensed physician shall issue an initial utilization review denial. A licensed physician shall supervise utilization review personnel in making recommendations. Personnel shall hold the license required by the jurisdiction where they are employed. 803 KY ADMIN. REGS. 25:190 § 6(2) and (3) (2004).

4. Reconsideration requires a different reviewer of at least the same qualifications as the initial reviewer. 803 KY ADMIN. REGS. 25:190 § 8(1)(b) (2004).

B. **Requirements for medical director.** A licensed physician shall supervise utilization review personnel in making utilization review recommendations.

C. **Requirements for "same-state" licensure.** No provision, but a "specialty match" for chiropractic care – a chiropractor qualified pursuant to KY REV. STAT. ANN. § 312.200(3) (2004) and 201 KY ADMIN. REGS. 21:095 (2004) – must be used. In effect, this statute and regulation require the chiropractor to be licensed in Kentucky. 25:190 § 8(2)(a).

VI. Reviews and Appeals

A. **Review determination and notice to patients/providers.** Yes.

1. **Time frame for determination.** If preauthorization requested, the initial utilization review determination shall be provided to the medical provider and employee within 2 working days of the initiation of the review process. 803 KY ADMIN. REGS. § 25:190 § 5(2)(a)(1). If retrospective utilization review occurs, the initial utilization review decision shall be provided to medical provider and employee within 10 days of initiation of process. 803 KY ADMIN. REGS. § 25:190 § 7(1)(a) (2004).

2. **Contents of notice of adverse determinations.**

   a. **Reasons for adverse determination.** A written notice of denial shall be issued to both treating physician and employee no more than 10 days after initiation of review process. Notice shall contain statement of medical reasons for denial, and name, state of licensure, and medical license number of reviewer. 803 KY ADMIN. REGS. § 25:190 § 7(1)(c)(1) and (2) (2004).

   b. **Notice of appeal rights.** Such notice shall also contain an explanation of reconsideration rights. 803 KY ADMIN. REGS. 25:190 § 7(c)(3) (2004).

B. **Appeals requirements.** There shall be a reconsideration process to appeal an initial decision. Reconsideration shall be requested within 14 days of receipt of the notice of denial.

803 KY ADMIN. REGS. 25:190 § 8 (2004). If a utilization review denial is upheld on reconsideration and a board eligible or certified physician in the appropriate specialty or subspecialty or chiropractor has not previously reviewed the matter, an aggrieved party may request further review by a board eligible or board certified physician in the appropriate specialty or subspecialty or a chiropractor. 803 KY ADMIN. REGS. 25:190 § 8(2)(a) (2004).

1. **Time frame for determination.** The reconsideration decision shall be written and shall be rendered within 10 days of receipt of request. If there is a request for specialty reconsideration, a written decision shall be rendered within 10 days of that request. 803 KY ADMIN. REGS. 25:190 § 8(2)(b) (2004).

2. **External appeals.** None listed.

C. **Emergency Services.** A medical provider may request an expedited utilization review determination for proposed medical treatment or services where serious physical or mental disability or death could result. An expedited utilization review determination is due in 24 hours. *Id.*

VII. Recognition of URAC Accreditation Status

A. **Does the state recognize URAC accreditation?** No. The Department of Workers Claims must approve the utilization review plan.

B. **Which of the state's requirements are waived for URAC-accredited organizations?** Not applicable.

VIII. Miscellaneous

The Department of Workers Claims publishes a list of approved vendors for utilization review and medical bill audit. This list is available at the Department's Web site. The Web site also includes a report on utilization review and related issues in the workers' compensation context in Kentucky.

Maine

I. Scope and Applicability

A. **Who is subject to the state's utilization review laws?** Utilization review must be performed by an insurance carrier, self-insurer or group self-insurer pursuant to a system established by the (Workers' Compensation) board that identifies the rays of utilization of health care and health services. ME. REV. STAT. ANN. tit 39A, § 210(3) (2004).

B. **What exemptions are provided, if any?** None.
   1. HMOs? Yes.
   2. Insurers? Yes.
   3. Utilization review organizations? Yes.
   4. Workers' Compensation? Yes.
   5. Retrospective review? Yes.

C. **What term does the state use to refer to regulated entities?** A "utilization review agent" is "Any person or entity, including insurance carriers, self-insurers, and group self-insurers, certified by the [Workers' Compensation] Board, to perform utilization review activities." CODE ME. R. §90-351-007 (2004).

D. **What activities does the state include in its definition of utilization review?** "Utilization review" means "the initial prospective, concurrent or retrospective evaluation by an insurance carrier, self-insurer or group self-insurer of the appropriateness in terms of both the level and the quality of health care and health services provided an injured employee, based on medically accepted standards. Utilization review requires the acquisition of necessary records, medical bills and other information concerning any health care or health services." ME. REV. STAT. ANN. tit. 39-A, § 210(2) (2004).

II. Regulatory Information

A. **Responsible state agency.** Maine Workers' Compensation Board, Office of Medical/Rehabilitation Services.

B. **Contact Information.**
   1. **Name and Title:** Elizabeth Inman, Deputy Director
   2. **Address:** "Medical and Rehabilitation Services, Workers' Compensation Board, 106 Hogan Road, Bangor, ME 04401".
   3. **Phone and Facsimile:** (207)941-4557; facsimile (207) 941-4509.
   4. **E-mail:** betty.inman@maine.gov.
   5. **Web site:** www.state.me.us/wcb.

III. Licensure/Certification Requirements

A. **What entities are required to obtain a license in the state to conduct utilization review for residents of the state?** Any person or entity, including insurance carriers, self insurers, and group self insurers, performing utilization review activities.

B. **How often must licensure be renewed?** Annually.

C. **Licensure fees (initial and renewal).** None.

D. **Documentation required for licensure.** To be certified by the Workers' Compensation Board, an applicant must submit an application for conditional or unconditional certification. Unconditional certification is granted to any entity accredited under URAC's National Workers' Compensation Utilization Management Standards. Conditional certification is available to entities that have applied for URAC accreditation. CODE ME. R. § 90-351-007-1 (2004).

E. **Exemptions from licensure.** Out-of-state organizations are not granted an exemption from Maine's licensure and certification requirements even if they are duly licensed and/or certified in their state of domicile.

IV. Program Requirements

A. **Clinical review criteria.** Utilization review agents providing or performing utilization review services shall use treatment guidelines approved by the Workers' Compensation Board. The Board has approved several guidelines and incorporated by reference at CODE ME. R. §90-351-007-2.

B. **Prohibitions against financial incentives.** No provision.

C. **Telephone access standards.** No provision.

D. **Quality assurance program.** No provision.

E. **Delegation of utilization review functions.** If delegated, the insurer, self insurer or group self insurer maintains full responsibility for compliance with Maine workers' compensation law and Board rules.

F. **Confidentiality.** No provision.

V. Reviewer Qualifications

A. **Qualifications of reviewers that render utilization review determinations (at each level of utilization review, if applicable).** No provision.

B. **Requirements for medical director.** No provision.

C.   Requirement for "same-state" licensure. No provision.

VI. Reviews and Appeals

When an employee/insurer requests utilization review the employer/insurer must notify the injured employee that it intends to initiate utilization review. CODE ME. R. § 90-351 §7-3 (2004).

A.   **Review determinations and notice to patients/providers.** CODE ME. R. § 90-351 §7-3 (2004).

    1.   **Time frame for determination.** Within 1 business day of completion of the review.

    2.   **Contents of notice of adverse determination.**

        a.   **Reasons for adverse determination.** The notice must include, at a minimum, the determination and the reasons for that determination.

        b.   **Notice of Appeal Rights.** The determination must advise the injured employee that he can send a letter to the utilization review agent, within 10 days, contesting the decision.

B.   **Appeals requirements.**

    1.   **Time frame for determination.** Within 1 day of the completion of the final level of utilization review, the utilization review agent shall serve a report to the injured employee, the affected health care provider, and the employer/insurer. The report must include, at a minimum, the utilization review Agent's determination and, the reasons therefore. *Id.*

    2.   **External appeals.** If a health care provider or injured employee disagrees with the determination rendered in the utilization review process, that party may appeal to the Board by submitting a copy of the notification not to certify. *Id.*

C.   **Emergency Services.** No provision.

VII. Recognition of URAC Accreditation Status

A.   **Does the state recognize URAC accreditation?** Yes.

B.   **Which of the state's requirements are waived for URAC-accredited organizations?** An entity may only perform utilization review if it is accredited by URAC or has applied for accreditation from URAC.

VIII. Miscellaneous

The Bureau of Workers' Compensation Board includes a list of "Certified URAC UR Providers" on its Web site.

This information is available at: www.janus.state.me.us/wcb/departments/omrs/ur.htm.

Massachusetts

I. Scope and Applicability.

A. **Who is subject to the state's utilization review laws?** All workers' compensation insurers, self-insurers, and self-insured groups are required to undertake utilization review either by contracting with agents who provide utilization review services in programs approved by the Commonwealth or by developing their own utilization review programs for both outpatient and inpatient health care services with similar approval. MASS. REGS. CODE tit. 452 § 6.04(1) (2004).

B. **What exemptions are provided, if any?** Does not apply to agency of the federal government or agent acting on behalf of the federal government or to certain activities of the Commonwealth's cities, towns, and municipalities.

 1. **HMOs?** No.
 2. **Insurers?** Yes.
 3. **Utilization Review Organizations?** Yes.
 4. **Workers' Compensation?** Yes.
 5. **Retrospective Review?** Yes.

C. **What term does the state use to refer to regulated entities?** "Utilization review agent" is defined as "any person or entity, including the Commonwealth of Massachusetts or any insurer which has developed its own utilization program, performing utilization review." MASS. REGS. CODE tit. 452, § 6.02 (2004).

D. **What activities does the state include in its definition of utilization review?** "Utilization review" is defined as a "system for reviewing the appropriate and efficient allocation of health care services given to a patient or group of patients as to necessity, for the purpose of recommending of determining whether such services should be covered or provided by an insurer, provider, nonprofit service organization, third-party administrator or employer." The definition includes "programs or processes whether they apply prospectively, concurrently, or retrospectively to health care services." In addition, "utilization review services" include, but are not limited to "second opinion programs; pre-hospital admission certification; pre-inpatient service eligibility certification; and concurrent hospital review to determine appropriate length of stay." MASS. REGS. CODE tit. 452, § 6.02 (2004).

II. Regulatory Information.

A. **Responsible state agency.** Massachusetts Department of Industrial Accidents.

B. **Contact Information.**

 1. **Name and Title:** Catherine Farnam, Executive Director and Director, Office of Health Policy.
 2. **Address:** Massachusetts Department of Industrial Accidents, 600 Washington Street, 7th Floor, Boston, MA 02111.
 3. **Phone and Facsimile:** (617) 727-4900 ext. 574; facsimile (617) 292-7708.
 4. **E-mail:** cathyf@dia.state.ma.us.
 5. **Web site:** www.state.ma.us/dia.

III. Licensure/Certification Requirements

A. **What entities are required to obtain a license in the state to conduct utilization review for residents of the state?** To conduct utilization review in the Commonwealth of Massachusetts, a utilization review agent must request approval of its utilization review program from the Commissioner of the Department of Industrial Accidents in writing and shall file certain information. Health Maintenance Organizations licensed and regulated by The Department of Insurance are exempt to the extent they provide UR to their own members. MASS. REGS. CODE tit. 452, § 6.04 (2004). Definition of Utilization Review Agent MASS. REGS. CODE tit. 452, § 6.02 (2004).

B. **How often must licensure/certification be renewed?** The Department of Industrial Accidents will annually publish the list of approved utilization review agents and the nature of the utilization review programs.

C. **Licensure fees (initial and renewal).** None required.

D. **Documentation required for licensure.** A utilization review agent shall file name, address, telephone number, contact person, normal business hours for utilization review agent; information on review criteria; current professional licenses for all providers rendering utilization review decisions; detailed description of appeal procedures; and disclosure of any economic incentive for reviewers in the utilization review program. MASS. REGS. CODE tit. 452, §604(2) (2004).

E. **Exemptions from licensure.** Out-of-state organizations are not exempt from Massachusett's registration requirements even if duly licensed and/or certified in their state of domicile. Health maintenance organizations are exempt under the Definition of Utilization Review Agent.

IV. Program Requirements

A. **Clinical review criteria.** The utilization review agent shall file with the Department of Industrial Accidents sources of review criteria, types of criteria, (i.e., diagnostic, treatment), process for and frequency of revisions, protocols and/or decision rules for utilization review determinations, and public availability of criteria. At least annually, the Health Care Services Board will review and update treatment guidelines. For each treatment guideline, the Department of Industrial Accidents shall create and develop utilization review criteria to be applied to each guideline. MASS. REGS. CODE tit. 452, § 6.04(2)(b) (2004).

B. **Prohibitions against financial incentives.** The utilization review agent shall disclose any economic incentives for reviewers in the utilization review program. MASS. REGS. CODE tit. 452, § 6.04(2)(e) (2004).

C. **Telephone access standards.** Staff of utilization review agents shall be available by toll-free telephone at least 40 hours per week between the hours of 9 AM-5 PM Eastern. Utilization review agents shall have a telephone system capable of accepting or recording telephone calls during other than normal business hours and shall respond to such calls within 2 business days. If the utilization review agent maintains a pre-certification program, there shall be 24-hour per day telephone contact. MASS. REGS. CODE tit. 452, § 6.04(4)(d)and(e) (2004).

D. **Quality assurance program.** Applicants for approval of a utilization review program must provide the state with a description of the quality assessment program(s) each will maintain.

E. **Delegation of utilization review functions.** Insurers who do not wish to obtain the state's approval to conduct utilization review may delegate the regulatory obligation to conduct utilization review to licensed utilization review agents. MASS. REGS. CODE tit. 452, § 6.04(1) (2004).

F. **Confidentiality.** Utilization review agents shall comply with all applicable laws to protect the confidentiality of medical records and where necessary shall obtain a medical release. MASS. REGS. CODE tit. 452, § 6.04(4)(f) (2004).

V. Reviewer Qualifications

A. **Qualifications of reviewers that render utilization review determinations (at each level of utilization review, if applicable)?** Utilization review programs approved by the state must use registered nurses, at a minimum, to conduct first level (initial) utilization reviews and practitioners (physicians or dentists) of the same school as the practitioner ordering the specific medical services under review to review all adverse determinations. MASS. REGS. CODE tit. 452, § 6.04(4)(a) (2004).

B. **Requirements for medical director.** No.

C. **Requirements for "same-state" licensure.** Licensure from "appropriate state agency" could be integrated to require state licensure. MASS. REGS. CODE tit. 452, § 6.04(2)(c) (2004).

VI. Reviews and Appeals

A. **Review determination and notice to patients/providers.** Utilization review agent must communicate all adverse determinations to provider of record and injured employee or other appropriate individual in writing. MASS. REGS. CODE tit. 452, § 6.04(4)(b) (2004).

1. **Time frame for determination.** For prospective review, notice of adverse determination must occur within 2 business days of receipt of request for determination and receipt of all information necessary to complete review. For concurrent review, notification shall be within 1 day before implementation (i.e., discharge). For retrospective review, notification shall be within 10 days of adverse determination.

2. **Contents of notice of adverse determinations.**

   a. **Reasons for adverse determination.** Any notification to provider and injured employee must include the review criteria and all reasons for the determination.

   b. **Notice of appeal rights.** Such notification to provider and injured employee must include procedure to initiate an appeal of determination. MASS. REGS. CODE tit. 452, § 6.04(4)(c) (2004).

B. **Appeals requirements.** Utilization review agents shall maintain and make available a written description of appeal procedure by which attending practitioner and/or injured employee may seek review of determination by utilization review agent. When an adverse determination not to approve a health care service is made before or during a continuing service requiring review, and the injured employee and/or provider believes that determination warrants immediate appeal, injured employee and/or provider shall have opportunity to appeal determination over telephone to utilization review agent, with "the right to speak to speak to a practitioner of the same school on an expedited basis, said appeal to occur not later than 30 days from the date of receipt of notice of adverse determination."

1. **Time frame for determination.** Utilization review agents shall complete adjudication of appeal on an expedited basis, but at least within two business days of date of appeal. Utilization review agents shall complete adjudication of all other appeals of adverse determinations no later than 20 days from date the appeal is filed.

2. **Are there requirements for expedited appeals?** Injured employee and/or provider has right to speak to practitioner of same school on expedited basis. MASS. REGS. CODE tit. 452, § 6.04(4)(c)(1) (2004).

3. **External appeals.** After exhaustion of process in MASS. REGS. CODE tit. 452, § 6.04(4)(c) (2004) to appeal the determination of utilization review agent, a party may file a claim or complaint with the Department of Industrial Accidents in accordance with MASS. REGS. CODE tit. 452, § 1.07. (2004) and MASS. REGS. CODE tit. 452, § 6.04(5) (2004).

C. **Emergency Services.** Utilization review agents shall allow a minimum of 24 hours after an emergency admission, service, or procedure for an injured employee or injured employee's representative to notify utilization review agent and request approval for treatment. MASS. REGS. CODE tit. 452, § 6.04(4) (2004).

VII. Recognition of URAC Accreditation Status

A. **Does the state recognize URAC accreditation?** No.

B. **Which of the state's requirements are waived for URAC-accredited organizations?** Not applicable.

Montana

I. Scope and Applicability

While Montana law does not separately regulate utilization management in the worker's compensation context, a health care provider or managed care organization may apply to be certified to provide managed care to injured workers. MONT. CODE. ANN. §39-71-1105. To be certified, the provider or managed care organization must meet standards set by the Department of Labor and Industry, including those providing for utilization review.

II. Regulatory Information

A. **Responsible state agency.** Montana Department of Labor and Industry, Worker's Compensation Regulation Bureau

B. **Contact Information.**

   1. **Name and Title:** Debra Blossom and Wade Wilkison, Administrative Officers in Medical Regulations

   2. **Address:** 1805 Prospect Avenue, P.O. Box 8011, Helena MT 59624-8011

   3. **Phone and Facsimile:** (406)444-7732 or (406)444-6562; Facsimile (406) 444-3465

   4. **E-mail:** dblossom@state.tx.us; wwilkison@state.mt.us

   5. **Web site:** http://dli.state.mt.us/.

III. Licensure/Certification Requirements

A. **What entities are required to obtain a license in the state to conduct utilization review for workers compensation claims in Montana?** Health care providers or managed care organizations that are certified by the Department of Labor and Industry.

Oregon

I. Scope and Applicability

A. **Who is subject to the state's utilization review laws?** Oregon does not regulate workers' compensation utilization management directly. However, the Labor and Industrial Relations Code includes certification procedures for managed health care providers for workers' compensation. The Director of the Department of Consumer and Business Services shall certify a health care provider or group of medical service providers to provide managed care under a plan if the Director finds the plan, among other things, provides "adequate methods" of "service utilization review." OR. REV. STAT. § 656.260(4)(d) (2004). Service utilization review "means evaluation and determination of the reasonableness, necessity and appropriateness of a worker's use of medical care resources and the provision of any needed assistance to clinician or member, or both, to ensure appropriate use of resources." This includes "prior authorization, concurrent review, retrospective review, discharge planning and case management activities." OR. REV. STAT. § 656.260(4)(d)(B) (2004).

II. Miscellaneous

The Office of Medical Assistance Program, Oregon Department of Human Services, administers the Medicaid program in Oregon and has prepared the "Prioritized List of Health Services." In addition to using this to rank health services from the most important to least important based on the comparative benefit to the population to be served to determine the benefit package under the Medicaid demonstration, the Office for Oregon Health Plan Policy and Research Oregon Health Plan conducts utilization review of services of health care facilities. OR. REV. STAT. § 442.420 (2004). For further information, contact Lynn Read, Director, Office of Medical Assistance Programs, at (503) 945-5772.

South Dakota

I. Scope and Applicability

A. **Who is subject to the state's utilization review requirements?** South Dakota doesn't regulate workers' compensation utilization management directly. However, under S.D. CODIFIED LAWS § 58-20-24, every policy issued for workers' compensation purposes must contain a case management plan that meets certain requirements. To be certified, a plan must provide "methods of utilization review to prevent inappropriate, excessive or medically unnecessary medical services." S.D. ADMIN. R. § 47:03:04:03 (2004).

B. **What activities does the state include in its definition of utilization review?** Utilization review is defined as the "objective evaluation of the necessity, appropriateness, efficiency, and quality of medical services provided to an injured or disabled employee." S.D. ADMIN. R. § 47:03:04:01(14) (2004).

Utah

I. Scope and Applicability

While Utah does not directly regulate utilization management or review, it specifically requires health insurance policies, health maintenance organization contracts and income replacement or disability income policies to have a process for the internal review of adverse benefit determinations and the independent review if the adverse benefit determination involves payment of a claim or denial of coverage regarding medical necessity. UTAH CODE ANN. §31A-22-629 (2004).

Adverse benefit determination is defined to mean the denial of a benefit; reduction of a benefit; termination of a benefit; or failure to provide or make payment, in whole or in part, for a benefit resulting from the application of a utilization review. UTAH CODE ANN. §31A-22-629 (2004).

The Insurance Department regulations governing health maintenance organizations also require each HMO to develop a quality assurance plan which is subject to external review. The quality assurance plan "shall be designed to systematically monitor and evaluate the quality and appropriateness of patient care, pursue opportunities to improve patient care, and resolve identified problems." Therefore, external review of the HMO's quality assurance plan includes review of the utilization review practices.

The external review and certification of the quality assurance plan must occur no later than 18 months after receipt of the HMO's certificate of authority and every 3 years thereafter unless the certifying entity requires a shorter time frame. URAC is specifically identified as an approved entity for certification of HMO quality assurance plans. UTAH ADMIN. R. 590-76-9 (2004).

II. Regulatory Information

    A. **Responsible state agency.** Utah Insurance Department.

    B. **Contact Information.**

        1. **Name and Title:** Suzette Green-Wright, Director, Health Insurance Division and Office of Consumer Health Assistance.

        2. **Address:** State Office Building, Room 3110, Salt Lake City, UT 84114-1201.

        3. **Phone and Facsimile:** (801) 538-9674; facsimile (801) 538-3829.

        4. **E-mail:** sgreenwright@utah.gov

        5. **Web site:** www.insurance.state.ut.us.

Virginia

I. Scope and Applicability

A. **Who is subject to the state's utilization review laws?** The Commonwealth of Virginia does not regulate workers' compensation utilization review organizations.

B. **What term does the state use to refer to regulated entities?** Not applicable.

C. **What activities does the state include in its definition of utilization review?** "Utilization review" means "the initial evaluation of appropriateness, in terms of the level, quality and duration of health care and health services provided a patient based on medically accepted standards. Such evaluation shall be accompanied by means of a system which identifies any utilization of medical services above the usual range of utilization for such services based on medically accepted standards." VA. CODE ANN. § 65.2-1300 (2004).

II. Regulatory Information.

A. **Responsible state agency.** Virginia Workers' Compensation Commission.

B. **Contact Information.**

1. **Name and Title:** James Szablewicz, Chief Deputy Commissioner, VA Worker's Compensation Commission.

2. **Address:** 1000 DMV Drive, Richmond, VA 23220.

3. **Phone and Facsimile:** (877) 664-2566; facsimile (804) 367-9740.

4. **E-mail:** Not known.

5. **Web site:** www.vwc.state.va.us/index.htm

III. Miscellaneous

Under the Virginia Workers' Compensation Act, the Statewide Coordinating Committee shall develop utilization review programs for services rendered by physicians. VA. CODE ANN. § 65.2-1304 (2004). The Statewide Coordinating Committee shall establish a regional peer review committee in each health systems area; each regional peer review committee shall be composed of 5 physicians appointed by the Statewide Coordinating Committee from nominations submitted by the Medical Society of Virginia; and each committee member shall practice in the health systems area and have patients the costs of whose treatment is reimbursed in whole or in part under the Workers' Compensation Act. VA. CODE ANN. § 65.2-1303 (2004). Each regional peer review committee will develop its own utilization review program.

URAC Core Standards
Version 1.1

This document is intended to provide a basic understanding of the URAC Core accreditation standards. It does not include interpretive information, scoring information, or other guidance necessary for a detailed understanding of the standards and the accreditation process. This information is contained in the Program Guide for this accreditation program, which may be purchased on URAC's Web site at www.urac.org. All URAC accredited organizations must comply with the Core Standards.

To achieve URAC Health Utilization Management Accreditation, an organization must comply with both URAC's Core Standards and Health Utilization Management Standards or Workers' Compensation Standards.

Organizational Structure

Standard CORE 1

The organization has a clearly defined organizational structure outlining direct and indirect oversight responsibility throughout the organization.

Standard CORE 2

Organization's documents address:

(a) Mission statement;
(b) Organizational framework for program;
(c) A description of the service delivery model;
(d) The population served; and
(e) Organizational oversight and reporting requirements of the program.

Policies and Procedures

Standard CORE 3

The organization:

(a) Maintains and complies with written policies and procedures that govern all aspects of its operations; and
(b) Maintains a master list of all such policies and procedures.

Standard CORE 4

The organization reviews policies and procedures no less than annually and revises as necessary.

Standard CORE 5

All policies and procedures include:

(a) Effective dates, including the date of the most recent revision; and
(b) Signature of reviewing and approval authority.

Inter-Departmental Coordination

Standard CORE 6

The organization establishes and implements mechanisms to promote collaboration, coordination, and communication across disciplines and departments within the organization, with emphasis on integrating administrative activities, quality improvement, and where present, clinical operations.

Information Management

Standard CORE 7

The organization implements information system(s) (electronic or paper) to collect, maintain, and analyze information necessary for organizational management that:

(a) Provides for data integrity;
(b) Provides for data confidentiality and security;
(c) Includes a disaster recovery plan; and
(d) Includes a plan for storage, maintenance, and destruction.

Business Relationships

Standard CORE 8

The organization maintains signed written agreements with all clients describing the scope of the business arrangement.

© 2005

Oversight of Delegated/Sub-Contracted Functions

Standard CORE 9
Prior to delegating functions to another entity, the organization conducts a review of the potential contractor's policies and procedures and capacity to perform delegated functions. The organization outlines and follows criteria and processes for approving contractors.

Standard CORE 10
The organization establishes and implements criteria and processes for an assessment prior to the delegation of functions.

Standard CORE 11
The organization enters into written agreements with contractors that:

(a) Specify those responsibilities delegated to the contractor and those retained by the organization;
(b) Require that services be performed in accordance with the organization's requirements and URAC standards;
(c) Require notification to the organization of any material change in the contractor's performance of delegated functions;
(d) Specify that the organization may conduct surveys of the contractor, as needed;
(e) Require that the contractor submit periodic reports to the organization regarding the performance of its delegated responsibilities;
(f) Specify recourse and/or sanctions if the contractor does not make corrections to identified problems within a specified period;
(g) Specify the circumstances under which activities may be further delegated by the contractor, including any requirements for obtaining permission from the organization before any further delegation; and
(h) Specify that, if the contractor further delegates organizational functions, those functions shall be subject to the terms of the written agreement between the contractor and the organization and in accordance with URAC standards.

Standard CORE 12
The organization implements an oversight mechanism for delegated functions that includes:

(a) A periodic review (no less than annually) of the contractor's policies and procedures and documentation of quality activities for related delegated functions;
(b) A process to verify (no less than annually) the contractor's compliance with contractual requirements and policies and procedures; and
(c) A mechanism to monitor financial incentives to ensure that quality of care or service is not compromised.

Staff Qualifications

Standard CORE 13
The organization has written job descriptions for staff that address:

(a) Required education, training, and/or professional experience;
(b) Expected professional competencies;
(c) Appropriate licensure/certification requirements; and
(d) Scope of role and responsibilities.

Standard CORE 14
Staff meets qualifications as outlined in written job descriptions.

Standard CORE 15
The organization implements a policy to:

(a) Verify the current licensure and credentials of licensed or certified personnel/consultants upon hire, and thereafter no less than every 3 years; and
(b) Implement corrective action in response to adverse changes in licensure or certification status.

Staff Management

Standard CORE 16
The organization has a training program that includes:

(a) Initial orientation and/or training for all staff before assuming assigned roles and responsibilities;
(b) Ongoing training as needed to maintain professional competency;
(c) Training in URAC Standards as appropriate to job functions;
(d) Training in state and regulatory requirements as related to job functions;

(e) Documentation of all training provided for staff;
(f) Conflict of interest;
(g) Confidentiality;
(h) Organizational structure; and
(i) Delegation oversight, if necessary.

Standard CORE 17

The organization provides staff with:

(a) Written operational policies and procedures appropriate to their jobs; and
(b) Clinical decision support tools as appropriate.

Standard CORE 18

The organization maintains a formal assessment program for individual staff members that includes an annual performance appraisal.

Clinical Oversight

Standard CORE 19

The organization designates at least one senior clinical staff person who has:

(a) Current, unrestricted clinical license(s) (or if the license is restricted, the organization has a process to ensure job functions do not violate the restrictions imposed by the State Board);
(b) Qualifications to perform clinical oversight for the services provided; and
(c) Post-graduate experience in direct patient care; and
(d) Board certification (if the senior clinical staff person is an M.D. or D.O.).

Standard CORE 20

The senior clinical staff person:

(a) Provides guidance for all clinical aspects of program;
(b) Is responsible for clinical aspects of program; and
(c) Has periodic consultation with practitioners in the field.

Regulatory Compliance

Standard CORE 21

The organization implements a regulatory compliance program that:

(a) Tracks applicable laws and regulations in the jurisdictions where the organization conducts business; and
(b) Ensures the organization's compliance with applicable laws and regulations.

Quality Management Program

Standards CORE 22

The organization maintains a quality management program that promotes objective and systematic monitoring and evaluation of consumer and client service and health care services.

Standard CORE 23

The organization employs staff and provides resources necessary to support the day-to-day operations of the qualitymanagement program.

Standard CORE 24

The organization has a written description for its quality management program that:

(a) Is approved by the organization's governing body;
(b) Defines the scope, objectives, activities, and structure of the quality management program;
(c) Is reviewed and updated by the quality management committee at least annually;
(d) Defines the roles and responsibilities of the quality management committee; and
(e) Designates a senior-level management member with the authority and responsibility for the overall operation of the quality management program and who serves on the Quality Management Committee.

Standard CORE 25

The organization has a mechanism to respond on an urgent basis to situations that pose an immediate threat to the health and safety of consumers.

Quality Management Committee

Standard CORE 26

The organization has a quality management committee that:

(a) Is granted authority for quality management by the organization's governing body;
(b) Is accountable to the organization's governing body;
(c) Meets at least quarterly;
(d) Maintains approved minutes of all committee meetings;
(e) If applicable, includes at least one participating provider or receives input from a participating provider committee (such as a Physician Advisory Group);
(f) Provides guidance to staff on quality management priorities and projects;
(g) Approves the quality improvement projects to undertake;
(h) Monitors progress in meeting quality improvement goals; and
(i) Evaluates the effectiveness of the quality management program.

Quality Management Documentation

Standard CORE 27

The organization, as part of its quality management program, provides written documentation of:

(a) Ongoing monitoring for compliance with URAC Standards;
(b) Objectives and approaches utilized in the monitoring and evaluation of activities;
(c) Identification of key indicators and measures of consumer and client service, which may include clinical care, complaint rates, and adverse events;
(d) The implementation of action plans to improve or correct identified problems;
(e) The mechanisms to communicate the results of such activities to staff;
(f) The mechanisms to communicate the results of such activities to the governing body or to corporate management; and
(g) Tracking and trending of data related to consumer and client service and health care services.

Quality Improvement Projects

Standard CORE 28

At any given time, the organization maintains at least two ongoing quality improvement projects that:

(a) Focus on consumers and/or clients;
(b) Relate to key indicators of quality as described in Standard 27(c); and
(c) Rely on data that is statistically valid, reliable, and comparable over time.

Standard CORE 29

If a quality improvement project is clinical in nature, then the organization involves a senior clinical staff person in judgments about clinical aspects of performance.

Standard CORE 30

For each quality improvement project, the organization utilizes statistically valid techniques to:

(a) Develop quantifiable measures;
(b) Measure its current level of performance; and
(c) Establish goals for quality improvement

Standard CORE 31

For each quality improvement project, the organization:

(a) Designs and implements strategies to improve performance; and
(b) Establishes projected timeframes for quality improvement.

Standard CORE 32

For each quality improvement project, the organization periodically measures progress in meeting quality improvement goals.

Financial Incentives

Standard CORE 33

If the organization has a system for reimbursement, bonuses, or incentives to staff or health care providers based directly on consumer utilization of health care services, then the organization implements mechanisms addressing how the organization will ensure that consumer health care is not compromised.

Communications

Standard CORE 34

The organization follows marketing and communication practices that include:

(a) Mechanisms to clearly and accurately communicate information about services to consumer and clients; and
(b) Safeguards against misrepresentations about the organization's services.

Standard CORE 35

The organization implements a communication plan to inform consumers and clients of their rights and responsibilities, including:

(a) How to obtain services; and
(b) Their rights to submit a grievance or appeal, and how to do so.

Satisfaction

Standard CORE 36

The organization implements a mechanism to collect or obtain information about consumer satisfaction with services provided by the organization.

Standard CORE 37

Consumer satisfaction results are shared with the Quality Management Committee (see Core 26).

Access to Services

Standard CORE 38

The organization establishes standards to assure that consumers and clients can obtain services.

Standard CORE 39

The organization defines and monitors its performance with respect to the requirements established under Core 38 and, as appropriate, acts to improve access to services.

Standard CORE 40

Information about the ability of consumers to access services is reported to the Quality Management Committee (*see* Core 26).

Complaints and Appeals

Standard CORE 41

The organization maintains a system to receive and respond in a timely manner to complaints and, when appropriate, inform consumers of their rights to submit an appeal.

Standard CORE 42

The organization maintains a formal appeal resolution process that includes:

(a) Written notice of final determination with an explanation of the reason for the determination;
(b) Notification of the process for seeking further review, if available; and
(c) A reasonable, specified timeframe for resolution and response.

Standard CORE 43

Analysis of the complaints and appeals is reported to the Quality Management Committee (*see* Core 26).

Health Utilization Management Standards
Version 4.2

This document is intended to provide a basic understanding of the Health Utilization Management accreditation standards. It does not include interpretive information, scoring information, or other guidance necessary for a detailed understanding of the standards and the accreditation process. This information is contained in the Program Guide for this accreditation program, which may be purchased on URAC's Web site at www.urac.org.

To achieve URAC Health Utilization Management Accreditation, an organization must comply with both URAC's Core Standards <u>and</u> Health Utilization Management Standards Standards.

Staff Qualifications and Oversight

Standard UM 1

The organization ensures that utilization management staff (including non-clinical administrative staff) is supported by explicit, written clinical review criteria and review procedures.

Standard UM 2

As part of the staff performance assessment required by Core 18, the organization reviews case files for each member of the utilization management staff.

Standard UM 3

The organization has a mechanism to ensure that the utilization management process, including decisions made by staff and reviewers, are not influenced by conflicts of interest.

Review Criteria

Standard UM 4

The organization utilizes explicit clinical review criteria or scripts for pre-review screening that are:

(a) Developed with involvement from appropriate providers with current knowledge relevant to the criteria or scripts under review;
(b) Based on current clinical principles and processes; and
(c) Evaluated at least annually by appropriate, actively practicing physicians and other providers with current knowledge relevant to the criteria or scripts under review, and updated if necessary.

Accessibility of Review Services

Standard UM 5

The organization provides access to its review staff by a toll free or collect telephone line at a minimum from 9:00 a.m. to 4:00 p.m. of each normal business day in each time zone where the organization conducts at least two percent of its review activities.

Standard UM 6

The organization maintains processes to:
(a) Receive communications from providers and patients during the business day and after business hours; and
(b) Respond to communications within one business day.

Standard UM 7

The organization conducts its outgoing communications related to utilization management during providers' reasonable and normal business hours, unless otherwise mutually agreed.

Standard UM 8

The organization:

(a) Requires utilization management staff to identify themselves by name, title, and organization name; and
(b) Upon request, verbally informs patients; facility personnel; the attending physician and other ordering providers; and health professionals of specific utilization management requirements and procedures.

Onsite Review Services

Standard UM 9

For on-site review services, the organization:

(a) Requires on-site reviewers to carry a picture ID with full name and the name of the organization; and
(b) Schedules reviews at least one business day in advance, unless otherwise agreed.

Standard UM 10

For on-site review services, the on-site reviewers follow reasonable hospital or facility procedures, including checking in with designated hospital or facility personnel.

Confidentiality

Standard UM 11

The organization implements mechanisms to ensure that patient-specific information obtained during the utilization management process will be:

(a) Kept confidential in accordance with applicable laws;
(b) Used solely for the purposes of utilization management, quality management, disease management, discharge planning, case management, and claims payment;
(c) Shared only with those entities who have authority to receive such information; and
(d) Shared only with those individuals who need access to such information in order to conduct utilization management and related processes.

Standard UM 12

If provider-specific data is to be released to the public, the organization implements policies to exercise due care in compiling and releasing data that address:

(a) How data is obtained and verified using valid methodologies;
(b) How the subjects of such disclosures are informed of the disclosures;
(c) How potential users of the information are informed about the uses and limitations of the data; and
(d) How the release of the data complies with applicable confidentiality laws and regulations.

Pre-Review Screening

Standard UM 13

For pre-review screening, the organization limits use of non-clinical administrative staff to:

(a) Performance of "review of service requests" for completeness of information;
(b) Collection and transfer of non-clinical data;
(c) Acquisition of structured clinical data; and
(d) Activities that do not require evaluation or interpretation of clinical information.

Standard UM 14

All scripts or algorithms used for pre-review screening are:

(a) Approved by the medical director or clinical director (or designate); and
(b) Reviewed (and updated if necessary) no less than annually.

Standard UM 15

Licensed health professionals monitor non-clinical administrative staff performing pre-review screening.

Standard UM 16

The organization does not issue non-certifications based on pre-review screening.

Initial Clinical Review

Standard UM 17

Individuals who conduct initial clinical review:

(a) Are health professionals; and
(b) Possess an active professional license or certificate.

Standard UM 18

Individuals who conduct initial clinical review have access to consultation with a:

(a) Licensed doctor of medicine or doctor of osteopathic medicine;
(b) Licensed health professional in the same licensure category as the ordering provider; or
(c) Health professional with the same clinical education as the ordering provider in clinical specialties where licensure is not issued.

Standard UM 19

The organization does not issue non-certifications based on initial clinical review.

Peer Clinical Review

Standards UM 20
The organization conducts peer clinical reviews for all cases where a certification is not issued through initial clinical review or pre-review screening.

Standard UM 21
Individuals who conduct peer clinical review:

(a) Are health professionals;
(b) Are qualified, as determined by the medical director or clinical director, to render a clinical opinion about the medical condition, procedures, and treatment under review; and
(c) Hold a current and valid license:
    (i)   In the same licensure category as the ordering provider;
    (ii) Or as a doctor of medicine or doctor of osteopathic medicine.

Peer-to-Peer Conversation

Standard UM 22
Health professionals that conduct peer clinical review are available, by telephone or in person, to discuss review determinations with attending physicians or other ordering providers.

Standard UM 23
When a determination is made to issue a non-certification and no peer-to-peer conversation has occurred, the organization provides, within one business day of a request by the attending physician or ordering provider, the opportunity to discuss the non-certification decision with the clinical peer reviewer making the initial determination (or with a different clinical peer), if the original clinical peer reviewer cannot be available within one business day.

Timeframes for Initial UM Decision

Standard UM 24
For prospective review, the organization issues a determination:

(a) As soon as possible based on the clinical situation, but in no case later than 72 hours of the receipt of request for a utilization management determination, if it is a case involving urgent care; or
(b) Within 15 calendar days of the receipt of request for a utilization management determination, if it is a non-urgent case. (This period may be extended one time by the organization for up to 15 calendar days provided that the organization determines that an extension is necessary because of matters beyond the control of the organization and notifies the patient, prior to the expiration of the initial 15 calendar day period of the circumstances requiring the extension and the date when the plan expects to make a decision. If a patient fails to submit necessary information to decide the case, the notice of extension must specifically describe the required information, and the patient must be given at least 45 calendar days from receipt of notice to respond to the plan request for more information.)

Standard UM 25
For retrospective review, the organization issues a determination within 30 calendar days of the request for a utilization management determination. (This period may be extended one time by the organization for up to 15 calendar days provided that the organization determines that an extension is necessary because of matters beyond the control of the organization and notifies the patient, prior to the expiration of the initial 15 day calendar day period of the circumstances requiring the extension and the date when the plan expects to make a decision. If a patient fails to submit necessary information to decide the case, the notice of extension must specifically describe the required information, and the patient must be given at least 45 calendar days from receipt of notice to respond to the plan request for more information.)

Standard UM 26
For concurrent review, the organization adheres to the following timeframes:

(a) For reductions or terminations in a previously approved course of treatment, the organization issues the determination far enough in advance of the reduction or termination to allow for an appeal of the determination to be completed; and
(b) For requests by a patient to extend a current course of treatment, the organization issues the determination within:
    (i)   24 hours of the request for a utilization management determination, if it is a case involving urgent care and the request for extension was received at least 24 hours before the expiration of the currently certified period or treatments; or

(ii) 72 hours of the request for a utilization management determination, if it is a case involving urgent care and the request for extension was received less than 24 hours before the expiration of the currently certified period or treatments.

Notice of Certification Decisions

Standard UM 27

For certifications, the organization provides notification to the attending physician or other ordering provider, facility rendering service, and patient.

Standard UM 28

Notices of certification include tracking information (such as a reference number) for the certification.

Standard UM 29

Upon request from the attending physician or other ordering provider, facility rendering service, or patient, the organization provides written notification of any certification.

Standard UM 30

Confirmation of certification for continued hospitalization or services includes the number of extended days or units of service, the next anticipated review point, the new total number of days or services approved, and the date of admission or onset of services.

Notice of Non-Certification Decisions

Standard UM 31

For non-certifications, the organization issues written notification of the non-certification decision to the patient and attending physician or other ordering provider or facility rendering service.

Standard UM 32

Written notification of a non-certification includes:

(a) The principal reasons for the determination not to certify;
(b) A statement that the clinical rationale used in making the non-certification decision will be provided, in writing, upon request; and
(c) Instructions for initiating an appeal of the non-certification.

Standard UM 33

Upon request from the patient, attending physician, or other ordering provider or facility rendering service, the organization provides the clinical rationale for the non-certification, including the specific clinical review criteria upon which the non-certification was based.

UM Procedures

Standard UM 34

The organization does not reverse a certification determination unless it receives new information that is relevant to the certification and that was not available at the time of the original certification.

Standard UM 35

The organization ensures that the frequency of reviews for the extension of initial determinations is based on the severity or complexity of the patient's condition or on necessary treatment and discharge planning activity (i.e., not routinely conducted on a daily basis).

Appeals Considerations

Standard UM 36

The organization maintains a formal process to consider appeals of non-certifications that includes:

(a) The availability of standard appeal for non-urgent cases and expedited appeal for cases involving urgent care; and
(b) Written policies and procedures that:
  (i) Clearly describe the appeal process, including the patient's, provider's, or facility rendering service's right to appeal;
  (ii) Provide for explicit timeframes for each stage of the appeal resolution process; and
  (iii) Are available, upon request, to any patient, provider, or facility rendering service.

Standard UM 37

The organization allows the patient, provider, or facility rendering services at least 180 calendar days after the receipt of a notice of non-certification to initiate the appeals process by telephone or written notification.

Standard UM 38

As part of the appeals process, the organization provides the patient, provider, or facility rendering service the opportunity to submit written comments, documents, records, and other information relating to the case.

Standard UM 39

As part of the appeals process, the organization and individuals considering the appeal take into account all documents, records, or other information submitted by the patient, provider, or facility rendering service relating to the case, without regard to whether such information was submitted or considered in the initial consideration of the case.

Standard UM 40

Appeals considerations are conducted by health professionals who:

(a) Are clinical peers;
(b) Hold an active, unrestricted license to practice medicine or a health profession;
(c) Are board-certified (if applicable) by:
   (i) A specialty board approved by the American Board of Medical Specialties (doctors of medicine); or
   (ii) The Advisory Board of Osteopathic Specialists from the major areas of clinical services (doctors of osteopathic medicine);
(d) Are in the same profession and in a similar specialty as typically manages the medical condition, procedure, or treatment as mutually deemed appropriate; and
(e) Are neither the individual who made the original non-certification, nor the subordinate of such an individual.

Standard UM 41

The organization observes the following timeframes for appeal:

(a) Expedited appeals are completed (i.e., written notification of the appeal decision issued) as soon as possible, and no later than 72 hours after the initiation of the appeal process;
(b) Standard appeals are completed (i.e., written notification of the appeal decision issued) within 30 calendar days of the initiation of the appeal process

Standard UM 42

Written notification of adverse appeals determinations includes:

(a) The principal reasons for the determination to uphold the non-certification;
(b) A statement that the clinical rationale used in making the appeal decision will be provided, in writing, upon request; and
(c) In the case of expedited appeals, the method to initiate the standard appeal process.

Standard UM 43

The organization keeps a record for each appeal that includes:

(a) The name of the patient, provider, and/or facility rendering service;
(b) Copies of all correspondence from the patient, provider, or facility rendering service and the organization regarding the appeal;
(c) Dates of appeal reviews, documentation of actions taken, and final resolution; and
(d) Minutes or transcripts of appeal proceedings (if any).

Information Upon Which Utilization Management is Conducted

Standard UM 44

The organization, when conducting routine prospective review, concurrent review, or retrospective review:

(a) Accepts information from any reasonably reliable source that will assist in the certification process;
(b) Collects only the information necessary to certify the admission, procedure or treatment, length of stay, or frequency or duration of services
(c) Does not routinely require hospitals, physicians, and other providers to numerically code diagnoses or procedures to be considered for certification, but may request such codes, if available;
(d) Does not routinely request copies of all medical records on all patients reviewed;
(e) Requires only the section(s) of the medical record necessary in that specific case to certify medical necessity or appropriateness of the admission or extension of stay, frequency or duration of service, or length of anticipated inability to return to work; and

(f) Administers a process to share all clinical and demographic information on individual patients among its various clinical and administrative departments that have a need to know, to avoid duplicate requests for information from enrollees or providers.

Standard UM 45

For prospective review and concurrent review, the organization bases review determinations solely on the medical information obtained by the organization at the time of the review determination.

Standard UM 46

For retrospective review, the organization bases review determinations solely on the medical information available to the attending physician or ordering provider at the time the medical care was provided.

Standard UM 47

The organization implements policies and procedures to address situations in which it has insufficient information to conduct a review. Such policies and procedures provide for:

(a) Procedural timeframes that are appropriate to the clinical circumstances of the review (i.e., prospective, concurrent, retrospective reviews);

(b) Resolution of cases in which the necessary information is not provided to the organization within specified timeframes; and

(c) Processes by which the organization issues an administrative non-certification due to lack of information.

Standard UM 48

The organization, for review purposes other than an appeal or a legal request, reimburses reasonable costs of medical record duplication, unless otherwise provided for by contract or law.

Workers' Compensation Utilization Management Standards
Version 3.0

This document is intended to provide a basic understanding of the Workers' Compensation UM accreditation standards. It does not include interpretive information, scoring information, or other guidance necessary for a detailed understanding of the standards and the accreditation process. This information is contained in the Program Guide for this accreditation program, which may be purchased on URAC's Web site at www.urac.org, or by calling (202) 216-9010.

To achieve URAC Workers' Compensation Utilization Management Accreditation, an organization must comply with both URAC's Core Standards <u>and</u> Workers' Compensation UM Standards.

Staff Qualifications and Oversight

Standard WC 1
The organization ensures that utilization management staff (including non-clinical administrative staff) are supported by explicit, written clinical review criteria and review procedures.

Standard WC 2
As part of the staff performance assessment required by Core 18, the organization reviews case files for each member of the utilization management staff.

Standard WC 3
The organization has a mechanism to ensure that the utilization management process, including decisions made by staff and reviewers, are not influenced by conflicts of interest.

Review Criteria

Standard WC 4
The organization utilizes explicit clinical review criteria or scripts for pre-review screening that are:

(a) Developed with involvement from appropriate providers with current knowledge relevant to the criteria or scripts under review;

(b) Based on current clinical principles and processes; and

(c) Evaluated at least annually by appropriate, actively practicing physicians and other providers with current knowledge relevant to the criteria or scripts under review, and updated if necessary.

Accessibility of Review Services

Standard WC 5
The organization provides access to its review staff by a toll free or collect telephone line at a minimum from 9:00 a.m. to 4:00 p.m. of each normal business day in each time zone where the organization conducts at least two percent of its review activities.

Standard WC 6
The organization maintains processes to:

(a) Receive communications from providers and workers during the business day and after business hours; and

(b) Respond to communications within one business day.

Standard WC 7
The organization conducts its outgoing communications related to utilization management during providers' reasonable and normal business hours, unless otherwise mutually agreed.

Standard WC 8
The organization:

(a) Requires utilization management staff to identify themselves by name, title, and organization name; and

(b) Upon request, verbally informs workers; facility personnel; the attending physician and other ordering providers; and health professionals of specific utilization management requirements and procedures.

Onsite Review Services

Standard WC 9
For on-site review services, the organization:

(a) Requires on-site reviewers to carry a picture ID with full name and the name of the organization; and

(b) Schedules reviews at least one business day in advance, unless otherwise agreed.

Standard WC 10

For on-site review services, the on-site reviewers follow reasonable hospital or facility procedures, including checking in with designated hospital or facility personnel.

Confidentiality

Standard WC 11

The organization implements mechanisms to ensure that worker-specific and provider-specific information obtained during the utilization management process will be kept confidential in accordance with applicable laws.

Initiation of Review Process

Standard WC 12

The organization allows any appropriate person to initiate the certification review process, as determined by state law or regulation or by the workers' compensation insurer or claims administrator. Appropriate persons may include, but are not limited to the worker or a representative of the worker, the claims adjustor, the facility rendering service, the provider, or a state regulator.

Pre-Review Screening

Standard UM 13

For pre-review screening, the organization limits use of non-clinical administrative staff to:

(a) [This standard number is reserved to synchronize with URAC's Health Utilization Management Standards.]
(b) Collection and transfer of non-clinical data;
(c) Acquisition of structured clinical data; and
(d) Activities that do not require evaluation or interpretation of clinical information.

Standard WC 14

All scripts or algorithms used for pre-review screening are:

(a) Approved by the medical director or clinical director (or designate); and
(b) Reviewed (and updated if necessary) no less than annually.

Standard WC 15

Licensed health professionals monitor non-clinical administrative staff performing pre-review screening.

Standard WC 16

The organization does not issue non-certifications based on pre-review screening.

Initial Clinical Review

Standard WC 17

Individuals who conduct initial clinical review:

(a) Are health professionals; and
(b) Possess an active professional license or certificate.

Standard WC 18

Individuals who conduct initial clinical review have access to consultation with a:

(a) Licensed doctor of medicine or doctor of osteopathic medicine; Licensed health professional in the same licensure category as the ordering provider; or
(b) Health professional with the same clinical education as the ordering provider in clinical specialties where licensure is not issued.

Standard WC 19

The organization does not issue non-certifications based on initial clinical review.

Peer Clinical Review

Standards WC 20

The organization conducts peer clinical reviews for all cases where a certification is not issued through initial clinical review or pre-review screening.

Standard WC 21

Individuals who conduct peer clinical review:

(a) Are health professionals;

(b) Are qualified, as determined by the medical director or clinical director, to render a clinical opinion about the medical condition, procedures, and treatment under review; and

(c) Hold a current and valid license:

    (i) In the same licensure category as the ordering provider;

    (ii) Or as a doctor of medicine or doctor of osteopathic medicine.

Peer-to-Peer Conversation

Standard WC 22

Health professionals that conduct peer clinical review are available, by telephone or in person, to discuss review determinations with attending physicians or other ordering providers.

Standard WC 23

When a determination is made to issue a non-certification and no peer-to-peer conversation has occurred, the organization provides, within one business day of a request by the attending physician or ordering provider, the opportunity to discuss the non-certification decision with the clinical peer reviewer making the initial determination (or with a different clinical peer, if the original clinical peer reviewer cannot be available within one business day.)

Timeframes for Initial UM Decision

Standard WC 24

For prospective review, the organization issues a review determination within:

(a) 72 hours of the request for a utilization management determination, if it is a case involving urgent care; or

(b) 5 calendar days of the request for a utilization management determination, if it is a non-urgent case.

Standard WC 25

For retrospective review, the organization issues a review determination within 30 calendar days of the request for a utilization management determination. (This period may be extended one time by the organization for up to 15 calendar days, provided that such an extension is necessary due to matters beyond the control of the organization and notifies the consumer, prior to the expiration of the initial 30 calendar day period, of the circumstances requiring the extension of time and the date by which the organization expects to render a determination.)

Standard WC 26

For concurrent review, the organization issues a determination within:

(a) 24 hours of the request for a utilization management determination, if it is a case involving urgent care; or

(b) 4 calendar days of the request for a utilization management determination, if it is a non-urgent case.

Notice of Certification Decisions

Standard WC 27

For certifications, the organization provides notification to the attending physician or other ordering provider, facility rendering service, and worker.

Standard WC 28

Notices of certification include tracking information (such as a reference number) for the certification.

Standard WC 29

Upon request from the attending physician or other ordering provider, facility rendering service, or worker, the organization provides written notification of any certification.

Standard WC 30

Confirmation of certification for continued hospitalization or services includes the number of extended days or units of service, the next anticipated review point, the new total number of days or services approved, and the date of admission or onset of services.

Notice of Non-Certification Decisions

Standard WC 31

For non-certifications, the organization issues written notification of the non-certification decision to the worker and attending physician or other ordering provider or facility rendering service.

Standard WC 32

Written notification of a non-certification includes:

(a) The principal reasons for the determination not to certify;

(b) A statement that the clinical rationale used in making the non-certification decision will be provided, in writing, upon request; and

(c) Instructions for initiating an appeal of the non-certification.

Standard WC 33

Upon request from the worker, attending physician, or other ordering provider or facility rendering service, the organization provides the clinical rationale for the non-certification, including the specific clinical review criteria upon which the non-certification was based

UM Procedures

Standard WC 34

The organization does not reverse a certification determination unless it receives new information that is relevant to the certification and that was not available at the time of the original certification.

Standard WC 35

The organization ensures that the frequency of reviews for the extension of initial determinations is based on the severity or complexity of the worker's condition or on necessary treatment and discharge planning activity (i.e., not routinely conducted on a daily basis).

Appeals Considerations

Standard WC 36

The organization maintains a formal process to consider appeals of non-certifications that includes:

(a) The availability of standard appeal and expedited appeal processes;

(b) The right of the worker, provider, or facility rendering service to initiate the standard appeal process when the expedited appeal process does not resolve a difference of opinion regarding the non-certification; and

(c) Written policies and procedures that:

    (i) Clearly describe the appeal process, including the worker's, provider's, or facility rendering service's right to appeal;

    (ii) Provide for explicit timeframes for each stage of the appeal resolution process; and

    (iii) Are available, upon request, to any worker, provider, or facility rendering service.

Standard WC 37

The organization allows the worker, provider, or facility rendering services a reasonable period after the receipt of a notice of non-certification to initiate the appeal process by telephone or written notification.

Standard WC 38

When applicable, the organization coordinates its appeal activities with regulatory appeals processes, which may be available to the worker.

Standard WC 39

[This standard number is reserved to synchronize with URAC's Health Utilization Management Standards.]

Standard WC 40

Appeals considerations are conducted by health professionals who:

(a) Are clinical peers;

(b) Hold an active, unrestricted license to practice medicine or a health profession;

(c) Are board-certified (if applicable) by:

    (i) A specialty board approved by the American Board of Medical Specialties (doctors of medicine); or

    (ii) The Advisory Board of Osteopathic Specialists from the major areas of clinical services (doctors of osteopathic medicine);

(d) Are in the same profession and in a similar specialty as typically manages the medical condition, procedure, or treatment as mutually deemed appropriate; and

(e) Are neither the individual who made the original non-certification, nor the subordinate of such an individual.

Standard WC 41

The organization observes the following time frames for appeal:

(a) Expedited appeals are completed (i.e. written notification of the appeal decision issued) as soon as possible, and no later than 72 hours after the initiation of the appeal process;

(b) Standard appeals are completed (i.e. written notification of the appeal decision issued) within 30 calendar days of the initiation of the appeal process.

Standard WC 42

Written notification of adverse appeals determinations includes:

(a) The principal reasons for the determination to uphold the non-certification;
(b) A statement that the clinical rationale used in making the appeal decision will be provided, in writing, upon request; and
(c) In the case of expedited appeals, the method to initiate the standard appeals process.

Standard WC 43

The organization keeps a record for each appeal that includes:

(a) The name of the worker, provider, and/or facility rendering service;
(b) Copies of all correspondence from the worker, provider, or facility rendering service and the organization regarding the appeal;
(c) Dates of appeal reviews, documentation of actions taken, and final resolution; and
(d) Minutes or transcripts of appeal proceedings (if any).

Information Upon Which Utilization Management is Conducted

Standard WC 44

The organization, when conducting routine prospective review, concurrent review, or retrospective review:

(a) Accepts information from any reasonably reliable source that will assist in the certification process;
(b) Collects only the information necessary to certify the admission, procedure or treatment, length of stay, frequency or duration of services, or length of anticipated inability to return to work;
(c) [This standard number is reserved to synchronize with URAC's Health Utilization Management Standards.]
(d) [This standard number is reserved to synchronize with URAC's Health Utilization Management Standards.]
(e) Requires only the section(s) of the medical record necessary in that specific case to certify medical necessity or appropriateness of the admission or extension of stay, frequency or duration of service, or length of anticipated inability to return to work; and
(f) Administers a process to share all clinical and demographic information on individual workers among its various clinical and administrative departments that have a need to know, to avoid duplicate requests for information from workers or providers.

Standard WC 45

For prospective review and concurrent review, the organization bases review determinations solely on the medical information obtained by the organization at the time of the review determination.

Standard WC 46

For retrospective review, the organization bases review determinations solely on the medical information available to the attending physician or ordering provider at the time the medical care was provided.

Standard WC 47

The organization implements policies and procedures to address situations in which it has insufficient information to conduct a review. Such policies and procedures provide for:

(a) Procedural timeframes that are appropriate to the clinical circumstances of the review (i.e., prospective, concurrent, retrospective reviews);
(b) Resolution of cases in which the necessary information is not provided to the organization within specified timeframes; and
(c) Processes by which the organization issues an administrative non-certification due to lack of information.

Standard WC 48

The organization, for review purposes other than an appeal or a legal request, reimburses reasonable costs of medical record duplication, unless otherwise provided for by contract or law.

Health UM RegulatoryContacts

Alabama
Michele Williams, M.P.M.
Director, Division of Managed Care Compliance
Alabama Department of Public Health
The RSA Tower
201 Monroe Street, Suite 750
Montgomery, AL 36104.
Phone: (334) 206-5351
Fax: (334) 206-5303
mwilliams@adph.state.al.us
http://www.adph.org/mcc/Linda Brunett

Alaska
Linda Brunett
Program Coordinator
Alaska Division of Insurance
PO BOX 110805
Juneau, AK 99811-0805
Phone: (907) 465-2545
Fax: (907) 465-2816
linda_brunette@dced.state.ak.us
http://www.dced.state.ak.us/insurance

American Samoa
Elisara T. Togiai
Commissioner of Insurance
American Samoa Government
PO Box 485
Pago Pago, American Samoa 96799
Phone: 011 (684) 633-4116/4009
Fax: 011 (684) 633-2269
http://www.asg-gov.com/

Arizona
Dolly Coleman
Health Utilization Administrator Analyst, Life & Health
Division
Arizona Department of Insurance
2910 North 44th Street, Suite 210
Phoenix, AZ 85018-7256
Phone: (602) 912-8460
Fax: (602) 912-8453.
dcoleman@id.state.az.us
http://www.state.az.us/idMary Fuller

Arkansas
Mary Fuller
Director of UR
Utilization Review Cerification Program
Arkansas Department of Health
5800 West 10th Street, Suite 400
Little Rock, AR, 72204·
Phone: (501) 661-2771
Fax: (501) 661-2165
http://www.healthyarkansas.com/

California
Warren Barnes and Kimberlee Hess
Acting Assistant Deputy Director, Office of Legal Services
California Department of Managed Health Care
California HMO Help Center
980 Ninth Street, Suite 500
Sacramento, CA 95814-2725
Phone: (888) HMO-2219
Fax: (916) 229-0465
wbarnes@dmhc.ca.gov; cc:khess@dmhc.ca.gov
http://www.hmohelp.ca.gov

Colorado
Kim Wells
Supervisor , Life & Health of Consumer Affairs
Colorado Insurance Division
1560 Broadway, Suite 850
Denver, CO 80202
Phone: (303) 894-7748
Fax: (303) 894-7455
kwells@dora.state.co.us
http://www.dora.state.co.us/insurance

Connecticut
Patricia Levesque
Managed Care Program Manager, The Life & Health
Division
Connecticut Insurance Department
P.O. Box 816·Hartford, CT 06142-0816
Phone: (860) 297-3859
Fax: (860) 297-3941
patricia.levesque@po.state.ct.us
http://www.state.ct.us/cid

Delaware

Judy Zumbo
Compliance Nurse
Office of Health Facilities Licensing and Certification
Delaware Department of Health and Social Services
2055 Limestone Road, Suite 200
Wilmington, DE 19808
Phone: (302) 995-8521
Fax: (302) 995-8529
judy.zumbo@state.de.us
http://www.state.de.us/dhss/dph

District of Columbia

Patrick Kelly
Grievance & Appeals Coordinator
District of Columbia Department of Health
Office of the Grievance and Appeals Coordinator
825 North Capitol Street, NE, 4th Floor
Washington, DC 20002
Phone: (202) 442-5979
Fax: (202) 442-4979
patrick.kelly@dc.gov
http://dchealth.dc.gov/index.asp

Florida

Ruby Schmigel & Susan Buchan
Regulatory Specialists II
Florida Agency of Health Care Administration
Hospital & Outpatient Services Unit
2727 Mahan Drive, MS #31
Tallahassee, FL 32308-5403
Phone: (850) 487-2717
Fax: (850) 922-4351
schmiger@fdhc.state.fl.us;buchans@fdhc.state.fl.us
http://www.fdhc.state.fl.us

Georgia

Edith Johnson
Utilization Review Analyst
Georgia Insurance and Safety Fire Commissioner
Life and Health Division
9th Floor, West Tower, Room 902, Floyd Building,
2 Martin Luther King, Jr. Drive
Atlanta, GA 30334
Phone: (404) 657-1705
Fax: (404) 657-7679
edith.johnson@mail.oci.state.ga.us
www.inscomm.state.ga.us

Guam

Joseph T. Duenas
Commissioner of Insurance
Guam Department of Revenue and Taxation
Insurance Branch, Government of Guam
Building 13-3, 1st Floor, Mariner Avenue, Tiyan,
Barrigada, Guam 96913
Phone: 011 (671) 475-1801
Fax: 011 (671) 472-2643
jduenas@ns.ga

Hawaii

Diane Mokumur
Chief of the Office of Health Care Assurance
Hawaii Department of Health
1250 Punchbowl Street
Honolulu, HI 96813
Phone: (808)-586-4080
Fax: (808) 586-4444
dmokumur@mail.health.state.hi.us
www.state.hi.us/health

Idaho

Joan Krosch
Health Insurance Specialist
Idaho Department of Insurance
700 W. State Street, 3rd Floor
Boise, ID 83720-0043
Phone: (208) 334-4250
Fax: (208) 334-4298
JKrosch@doi.state.id.us
www.doi.state.id.us

Illinois

Kelly Reim
Insurance Analyst
Illinois Department of Financial & Professional
Regulation
320 W. Washington Street
Springfield, IL 62767-0001
Phone: (217) 558-2309
Fax: (217) 558-2083
kelly_reim@ins.state.il.us
www.ins.state.il.us

Indiana

Angela Dailey
Secretary for Financial Services Operations
Indiana Department of Insurance
311 W. Washington Street, Suite 300
Indianapolis, IN 46204-2787
Phone: (317) 232-2390
Fax: (317) 232-5251
adailey@doi.state.in.us
www.in.gov/idoi

Iowa
Roger Strauss
Life & Health Bureau Chief
Insurance Division
Iowa Department of Commerce
330 E. Maple
Des Moines, IA 50319-0065
Phone: (515) 281-4222
Fax: (515) 281-5692
Roger.Strauss@iid.state.ia.us
www.iid.state.ia.us

Kansas
Julie Stell
Accident and Health Policy Examiner
Kansas Insurance Department
420 SW 9th Street
Topeka, KS, 66612
Phone: (785) 296-7850
Fax: (785) 291-3034
jstell@ksinsurance.org
www.ksinsurance.org

Kentucky
Lee Barnard
Branch Manager of UR & Appeals
Kentucky Department of Insurance
P.O. Box 517, 215 West Main Street
Frankfort, KY 40602-0517
Phone: 1-800-595-6053, ext. 4345
Fax: (502) 564-2728
lee.barnard@ky.gov
www.doi.state.ky.us

Louisiana
Pamela Bollinger
Director, Division of Quality Assurance
Office of Health Insurance
Louisiana Department of Insurance
1702 N. 3rd Street
Baton Rouge, LA 70804
Phone: (225)219-8769
Fax: (225) 342-5711
pbollinger@ldi.state.la.us
www.dhh.state.la.us

Maine
Patty Woods
Claims Examiner
Maine Department of Professional & Financial Regulation
34 State House Station
Augusta, ME 04333-0034
Phone: (207) 624-8459
Fax: (207) 624-8599
patricia.a.woods@maine.gov
www.state.me.us/pfr/ins/inshome2.htm

Maryland
Ellen Woodall
Director, Medical Director/Private Review Agent
Certification
Maryland Insurance Administration
525 St. Paul Place
Baltimore, MD 21202-2272
Phone: (410) 468-2276
Fax: (410) 468-2270
ewoodall@mdinsurance.state.md.us
www.mdinsurance.state.md.us

Massachusetts
Nancy Schwartz
Director, Bureau of Managed Care
Massachusetts Division of Insurance
One South Station
Boston, MA 02110
Phone: (617) 521-7347
Fax: (617) 521-7773
nancy.schwartz@state.ma.us
www.state.ma.us/doi

Minnesota
Susan Schmidt
Minnesota Department of Commerce
85 7th Place East, Suite 500
St. Paul, MN 55101-2198
Phone: (651) 297-1351
Fax: (651) 296-9434
susan.e.schmidt@state.mn.us
http://www.state.mn.us/cgi-bin/portal/mn/jsp/home.do?agency=Commerce

Mississippi
Sherry Hofmister & Linda Trigg
Licensure and Certification
Mississippi State Department of Health
Health Facilities Licensure and Certification
421 West Pascagoula Street, P.O. Box 1700
Jackson, MS 39215-1700
Phone: (601) 576-7329; (601) 576-7328
Fax: (601) 354-7230
shofmister@msdh.state.ms.us;ltrigg@msdh.state.ms.us
www.msdh.state.ms.us

Missouri
Jane Knight
Insurance Product Analyst II, Life & Health Section
Missouri Department of Insurance
P.O. Box 690
Jefferson City, MO 65102-0690
Phone: (573) 751-8354
(573) 526-6075
jknight@mail.state.mo.us
www.insurance.state.mo.us

Montana

Pam Forsman
Forms Analyst
Montana Insurance Division
State Auditor's Office
840 Helena Avenue
Helena, MT 59601
Phone: (406) 444-9751
Fax: (406) 444-3497
pforsman@state.mt.us
http://sao.state.mt.us/

Nebraska

Beverly Creager
Administrator
Nebraska Department of Insurance
Licensing Division
941 O Street, Suite 400
Lincoln, NE 68508
Phone: (402) 471-4704
Fax: (402) 471-6559
bcreager@doi.state.ne.us
www.nol.org/home/ndoi

Nevada

Kristin Kinsley & Lou Roggensack
Licensing Contact & Actuary II
Nevada Division of Insurance
788 Fairview Drive, Suite 300
Carson City, NV 89701
Phone: (775) 687-4270 ext. 235 & 245
Fax: (775) 687-3937
kkinsley@doi.state.nv.us & roggen@doi.state.nv.us
http://doi.state.nv.us/

New Hampshire

Mary Verville
Examination Division
New Hampshire Insurance Department
56 Old Suncook Road
Concord, NH 03301
Phone: (603) 271-7973, ext.254
Fax: (603) 271-7029
mary.verville@ins.nh.gov
www.nh.gov/insurance

New Jersey

Sylvia Allen-Ware
Director of the Office of Managed Care
New Jersey Department of Health and Senior Services
Office of Managed Care
P.O. Box 360, Market & Warren Street
Trenton, NJ 08625
Phone: (609) 633-0660
Fax: (609) 633-0807
Sylvia.Allen-Ware@doh.state.nj.us
www.state.nj.us/health

New Mexico

Linda Grisham
Manager of Managed Health Care Bureau
New Mexico Department of Insurance
P.O. 1269,
Santa Fe, NM 87504-1269
Phone: (505) 827-4468
Fax: (505) 827-4734
linda.grisham@state.nm.us
http://www.nmprc.state.nm.us/insurance/inshm.htm

New York

Jeanette M. Hill
Project Manager, Utilization Review
New York State Department of Health
Bureau of Managed Care Certification and Surveillance
Corning Tower, Room 1911
Albany, NY 12237
Phone: (518) 474-4156
Fax: (518) 473-3583
jmh30@health.state.ny.us
www.health.state.ny.us

North Carolina

Nancy O'Dowd
Deputy Commissioner, Managed Care & Health Benefits Division
North Carolina Department of Insurance
P.O. Box 26387, 111 Seaboard Avenue
Raleigh, NC 27611
Phone: (919) 715-0526
Fax: (919) 715-0198
nodowd@ncdoi.net
www.ncdoi.com

North Dakota
Leona Ziegler(records/applications); Laurie Wolf (legal)
Company Administrators
North Dakota Department of Insurance
600 East Boulevard Avenue, Dept. 401
Bismarck, ND 58505-0320
Phone: (701) 328-3548 ext. 3
Fax: (701) 328-4880
lziegler@state.nd.us
http://www.state.nd.us/ndins

Ohio
Mary Richardson
Senior Insurance Contract Analyst
Ohio Department of Insurance
2100 Stella Court
Columbus, OH 43215-1067
Phone: (614) 728-1756
Fax: (614) 719-1673
mary.richardson@ins.state.oh.us
www.ohioinsurance.gov

Oklahoma
Dalora Schafer
Director of Life Accident and Health, UR
Oklahoma Insurance Department
2401 N.W. 23rd, Suite 28 (Shepherd Mall)
P.O. Box 53408
Oklahoma City, OK 73152-3408 (405) 521-3541
Phone: (405) 522-1860
daloraschafer@insurance.state.ok.us
www.oid.state.ok.us

Oregon
Carol Simila
Consumer Advocate Liason, Insurance Division
Oregon Department of Consumer & Business Services
350 Winter Street NE, 4th Floor
P.O. Box 14480
Salem, OR 97309-0405
Phone: (503)947-7269
Fax: (503) 378-4351
carol.r.simila@state.or.us
www.cbs.state.or.us/external/ins

Pennsylvania
William Wiegmann
Director, Division of Certification
Pennsylvania Department of Health
P.O. Box 90
Harrisburg, PA 17108-0090
Phone: (717) 787-5193
Fax: (717) 705-0947
wwiegmann@state.pa.us
www.health.state.pa.us/qa/hmo/default.htm

Puerto Rico
Dorelisse Juarbe
Commissioner of Insurance
Puerto Rico Insurance Department
P.O. Box 8330, Fernandez Juncos Station
Santurce, PR 00910-8330
Phone: (787) 722-8686
Fax: (787) 722-4400
djuarbe@ocs.gobierno.pr

Rhode Island
Donald Williams
Associate Chief
Rhode Island Department of Health
3 Capitol Hill, Room 410
Providence, RI 02908-5097
Phone: (401) 222-6015
Fax: (401) 222-3017
donw@doh.state.ri.us
www.health.state.ri.us

South Carolina
Willie C. Seawright
Licensing Coordinator
South Carolina Department of Insurance
P.O. Box 100105, 300 Arbor Lake Drive, Suite 12000
Columbia, SC 29223
Phone: (803) 737-6134
Fax: (803) 737-6100
wseawright@doi.state.sc.us
https://www.doi.state.sc.us/

South Dakota
Ellen Blauert
Managed Care Analyst
South Dakota Division of Insurance
445 East Capitol Avenue
Pierre, SD 57501
Phone: (605) 773-3563
Fax: (605) 773-5369
ellen.blauert@state.sd.us
www.state.sd.us/dcr/insurance

Tennessee
Howard L. Magill
Director, Life, Accident, and Health Actuarial Section
Tennessee Department of Commerce & Insurance
Davy Crockett Tower, Suite 500
Nashville, TN 37243-0565
Phone: (615) 741-2825
Fax: (615) 741-0648
Howard.magill@state.tn.us
http://www.state.tn.us/commerce/

Texas

Dina Bonugli
Insurance Specialist
Texas Department of Insurance
P.O. Box 149104, 333 Guadalupe Street
Austin, TX 78714-9104
Phone: (512) 322-4266
Fax: (512) 322-4260
dina.bonugli@tdi.state.tx.us
www.tdi.state.tx.us

Utah

Suzette Green-Wright
Director, Health Insurance Division and Office of
Consumer Health Assistance
Utah Insurance Department
State Office Building, Room 3110
Salt Lake City, UT 84114-1201
Phone: (801) 538-9674
Fax: (801) 538-3829
sgreenwright@utah.gov
www.insurance.state.ut.us

Vermont

Bob Aiken
Health Care Administrator
Vermont Department of Banking, Insurance, Securities &
Health Care Administration
89 Main Street, Drawer 20
Montpelier, VT 05620
Phone: (802) 828-2900 ext. 2905
Fax: (802) 828-2949
baiken@bishca.state.vt.us
www.bishca.state.vt.us

Virgin Islands

Gerard Luz Amwur James II
Lieutenant Governor/Commissioner
Virgin Islands Office of the Lieutenant Governor, Division
of Banking and Insurance
1131 King Street, Suite 101, Christiansted
St. Croix, VI 00820
Phone: (340) 773-6449
Fax: (340) 773-4052

Virginia

Harry Armstrong
Managed Care Health Insurance Supervisor
Virginia Department of Health
3600 West Broad Street, Suite 216
Richmond, VA 23230-4920
Phone: (804) 367-2102
Fax: (804) 367-2149
harry.armstrong@vdh.virginia.gov
www.vdh.state.va.us/quality/default.htm

West Virginia

Charles Dunn
Director of the Office of Advocacy
Consumer Advocate Division
West Virginia Insurance Commission
P.O. Box 50540
Charleston, WV 25305-0540
Phone: (304) 558-3864
Fax: (304) 558-2381
charlie.dunn@wvinsurance.gov
http://www.wvinsurance.gov/

Wisconsin

Jorge Gomez
Commissioner of Insurance
Wisconsin Office of the Commissioner of Insurance
P.O. Box 7873, 125 South Webster Street
Madison, WI 53707-7873
Phone: (608) 267-1233
Fax: (608) 261-8579
information@oci.state.wi.us
http://oci.wi.gov/oci_home.htm

Wyoming

Teri Green
Medicaid Policy Manager
Wyoming Insurance Department
6101 Yellowstone Road, Suite 210
Cheyenne, WY 82002
Phone: (307) 777-7908
Fax: (307) 777-6964
tgreen1@state.wy.us
http://insurance.state.wy.us/

Washington

John Coniff
Deputy Commissioner of Managed Health Care
Washington State Office of the Insurance Commissioner
P.O. Box 40255
Olympia, WA 78504-0255
Phone: (360)664-3786
Fax: (360)586-3535
JohnC@oic.wa.gov
www.insurance.wa.gov

Workers' Compensation Regulatory Contacts

Alabama

Trevor A. Perry
Administrative Analyst
Alabama Department of Industrial Relations
Workers' Compensation Division
649 Monroe Street
Montgomery, AL 36131
Phone: (334) 353-0540
Fax: (334) 353-8228tperry@dir.state.al.us
http://www.dir.state.al.us

Alaska

Paul F. Lisankie
Director, Division of Workers' Compensation
Alaska Division of Workers' Compensation
PO Box 25512
Juneau, AK 99802
Phone: (907)465-2790
Fax: (907)465-2797
paul_lisankie@labor.state.ak.us
www.labor.state.ak.us

Arkansas

Pat Hannah
Medical Cost Containment Administrator
Arkansas Workers' Compensation Commission
324 Spring St., PO Box 950
Little Rock, AR 72203-0950
Phone: (501)682-2549
Fax: (501)682-1790
pathannah@awcc.state.ar.us
http://www.awcc.state.ar.us/

California

Andrea Hoch
Administrative Director
California DIR, Division of Workers' Comp
455 Golden Gate Ave., 9th Floor
San Francisco, CA 94102
Phone: (415)703-4679
Fax: (415)703-4664
gshor@dir.ca.gov
http://www.dir.ca.gov/dwc

Colorado

Debra Northrup, RN
Medical Policy Specialist, Medical Policy Unit, Division of Workers' Compensation
Colorado Department of Labor and Employment
1515 Arapahoe, Tower 2, Suite 610
Denver, CO 80202-2117
Phone: (303) 318-8761
Fax: (303)318-8758
debra.northrup@state.co.us
www.coworkforce.com/DWC

Connecticut

Marilou Lang
Administration Hearing Specialist
Connecticut Workers' Compensation Commission
Capitol Place, 21 Oak Street, Fourth Floor
Hartford, CT, 06106
Phone: (860) 493-1559
Fax: (860) 247-1361
marilou.lang@po.state.ct.us
http://wcc.state.ct.us/

District of Columbia

Charles L. Green
Associate Director, Office of Worker's Compensation
District of Columbia Department of Employment Services
64 New York Avenue, NE, Room 2051
Washington, DC 20002
Phone: (202) 671-1055
Fax: (202) 671-1929
charles.green@dc.gov
http://www.does.dc.gov/does/cwp/view.asp?a=1232&Q=537428

Florida

Sam Willis
Unit Manager, Division of Managed Care & Health Quality, Bureau of Managed Health, Workers' Compensation Unit
Florida Agency of Health Care Administration
2727 Mahan Drive, MS #26
Tallahassee, FL 32308
Phone: (850) 922-6481
Fax: (850) 921-1004
williss@fdhc.state.fl.us
http://www.fldfs.com/WC/

Georgia

Deborah Krotenberg, Esq.
Director of Division of Managed Care and Rehabilitation
Georgia State Board of Workers' Compensation
270 Peachtree St., NW
Atlanta, GA 30303-1299
Phone: (404) 656-0849
Fax: (404) 463-0310
krotenbe@sbwc.state.ga.us
http://www.ganet.org/sbwc/

Hawaii

Clyde T. Imada, Chief of Workers' Compensation
Department of Commerce and Consumer Affairs
Hawaii Insurance Division
P.O. Box 3614
Honolulu, HI 96811
Phone: (808) 587-8782
Fax: 808) 586-2806
clyde.t.imada@hawaii.gov
http://dlir.state.hi.us/

Kentucky

Shari Lafoe
UR Coordinator, Department of Workers' Claims
Kentucky Office of Workers' Claims
657 Chamberlin Avenue
Frankfort, KY 40601
Phone: (502) 564-5550 ext. 4487
Fax: (502) 564-5741
shari.lafoe@ky.gov
www.labor.ky.gov/dwc/ur.htm

Louisiana

Judith Albarado
Manager of Medical Services
Louisiana Office of Workers' Compensation
Administration
P.O. Box 94094
1001 North 23rd Street
Baton Rouge, LA 70802
Phone: (225) 342-7559 or (800) 201-2494
Fax: (225) 342-9836
jalbarado@ldol.state.la.us
www.laworks.net

Maine

Elizabeth Inman
Deputy Director, Medical and Rehabilitation Services
State of Maine Workers' Compensation Board
106 Hogan Road
Bangor, ME 04401
Phone: (207)941-4557
Fax: (207) 941-4509
betty.inman@maine.gov
www.state.me.us/wcb

Massachusetts

Catherine Farnam
Director of the Office of Health Policy
Massachusetts Department of Industrial Accidents
600 Washington Street, 7th Floor
Boston, MA 02111
Phone: (617) 727-4900 ext. 574
Fax: (617) 292-7708
cathyf@dia.state.ma.us
www.state.ma.us/dia

Montana

Debra Blossom and Wade Wilkison
Administrative Officers of Medical Regulations
Montana Workers' Compensation Regulation Bureau
Employment Relations Division
PO Box 8011
Helena, MT 59604-8011
Phone: (406) 444-7732 or (406) 444-6562
Fax: (406) 444-3465
dblossom@state.tx.us; wwilkison@state.mt.us
http://dli.state.mt.us/

New Mexico

Ann Carrizales
Program Manager
New Mexico Workers' Compensation Administration
P.O. Box 27198
Albuquerque, NM 87125-7198
Phone: (505) 841-6844
Fax: (505) 841-6840
ann.carrizales@state.nm.us
www.state.nm.us/wca

New York

Joe Salamone
Director, Health Provider Administrator
New York State Workers' Compensation Board
20 Park Street
Albany, NY 12207
Phone: (518) 474-2686
Fax: (518) 473-6379
joe.salamone@wcb.state.ny.us
www.wcb.state.ny.us

North Carolina

Thomas Bolch
Commissioner of Insurance
North Carolina Industrial Commission
4336 Mail Service Center
Raleigh, NC 27699-4336
Phone: (919) 807-2519
Fax: (919) 715-0282/0283
bolcht@ind.commerce.state.nc.us
www.comp.state.nc.us/

North Dakota
Mary Selzler
Claims Program Manager
North Dakota Workforce Safety & Insurance
1600 East Century Avenue, Suite 1
Bismarck, ND 58503-0644
Phone: (701) 328-3851 or 1-800-440-3796 ext.3851
Fax: 1-888-777-5872
mselzler@wcb.state.nd.us
www.workforcesafety.com

Oklahoma
Ann Seibel
Director of Claims Administration
CompSource
PO Box 53505
Oklahoma City, OK 73152
Phone: (405) 962.3252
Fax: (405) 528.2165
ann_s@compsourceok.com
http://www.state.ok.us/~okdol/workcomp/

Pennsylvania
Eileen K. Wunsch, MS, CPIW, ARM
Chief, Health Care Services Review Division
Pennsylvania Bureau of Workers' Compensation
1171 S. Cameron Street, Room 310
Harrisburg, PA 17104-2501
Phone: (717) 772-1912
Fax: (717) 772-1919
ewunsch@state.pa.us
http://www.dli.state.pa.us/landi/cwp/view.asp?a=138&Q=
58929&landiPNav=|#1026

Tennessee
Bob Kirkpatrick, M.D.
Medical Director
Andrew Johnson Tower, 2nd Floor, 710 James Robertson
Parkway
Nashville, TN 37243-0661
Phone: (615) 532-8700
Fax: (615) 253-5265
www.state.tn.us/labor-wfd/wcomp.html

Texas
Blanca Guardiola
Research, Rules, and Analysis Program Specialist
Texas Workers' Compensation Commission
7551 Metro Center Drive, Suite 100
Austin, TX 78744-1609
Phone: (512) 804-4853
Fax: (512) 804-4801
blanca.guardiola@twcc.state.tx.us
http://www.twcc.state.tx.us/

Utah
Allan Colledge
Medical Director
Labor Commission of Utah
P.O. Box 146610
Salt Lake City, UT 84114-6610
Phone: (801) 361-7584
Fax: (801) 530-6804
acolledge@utah.gov
www.ind-com.state.ut.us/indacc/indacc.htm

Vermont
Laura Collins
Deputy Commissioner, Department of Labor & Industry
Vermont Department of Labor & Industry
National Life Building
Drawer 20
Montpelier, VT 05620-3401
Phone: (802) 828-5092
Fax: (802) 828-2195
laura.collins@labind.state.vt.us
http://www.state.vt.us/labind/wcindex.htm

Virginia
James Szablewicz
Chief Deputy Commissioner
The Virginia Workers' Compensation Commission
1000 DMV Drive
Richmond, VA 23220
Phone: 1-877-664-2566
Fax: (804) 367-9740
kathy.daniel@vwc.state.va.us
www.vwc.state.va.us/index.htm

Wyoming
Gary Child
Administrator
Wyoming Worker Safety & Compensation
1510 East Pershing Blvd.
Cheyenne, WY 82002
Phone: (307) 777-7159
Fax: (307) 777-5524
gchild@state.wy.us
http://wydoe.state.wy.us/doe.asp?ID=9

States That Recognize URAC Accreditation
November 2004

Alabama
- Health UM
- Work Comp UM

Arizona
- Health UM

Arkansas
- Independent Review

California
- Health Call Center

Delaware
- Independent Review

District of Columbia
- Work Comp UM

Florida
- Credentialing
- Health Plan

Georgia
- Health UM
- Health Network

Hawaii
- Health Network
- Health Plan

Illinois
- Health UM

Indiana
- Health Network
- Health UM

Iowa
- Health UM

Kansas
- Health Plan
- Health UM

Kentucky
- Health UM

Maine
- Health UM
- Work Comp UM

Massachusetts
- Health Network
- Health Plan
- Health UM

Michigan
- Health Plan

Missouri
- Health Plan
- Health UM

Nebraska
- Health UM

Nevada
- Health Plan
- Independent Review

New Hampshire
- Health UM
- Work Comp UM

New Jersey
- Health Network

New York
- Work Comp UM

North Carolina
- Health UM

North Dakota
- Health UM

Ohio
- Case Management
- Health Network
- Work Comp UM
- Provider Credentialing

Oklahoma
- Health Plan
- Work Comp Network

Rhode Island
- Health UM

South Carolina
- Health Plan

Tennessee
- Health UM
- Work Comp UM

Utah
- Health Plan

Vermont
- Case Management
- Health UM

Virginia
- Health Network
- Health Plan
- Health UM

Washington
- Health UM
- Independent Review
- Work Comp UM

West Virginia
- Health Plan

For more information, please check the URAC Web site at www.urac.org.

URAC Directory of Accredited Organizations

Please refer to the online directory on URAC's web site for the latest information on accredited companies. Visit www.urac.org, click on Programs and Services, then Directory.

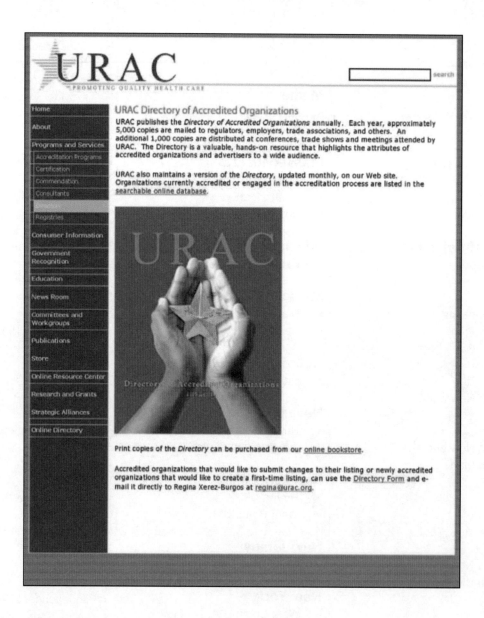

ACCREDITED
Health Utilization Management
Since July 1993

CERTIFIED
Utilization Management
Since May 2001

CERTIFIED
Credentialing and
Recredentialing
Since August 2001

ACCREDITED
Health Network
with Credentialing
Since October 2001

Quality has always been one of our strong points. But it seems we have a knack for quantity as well.

PHCS was the first national health care cost management company to be awarded NCQA certification and URAC accreditation for our network credentialing... and again for our utilization management services. And we're still the only one to win all of these impressive accolades.

But it's really our ongoing commitment to excellence, not our crowded trophy case, that enables you to choose PHCS with the utmost of confidence. Call 1-866-750-7427 or visit www.phcs.com today and see how we can put the exceptional quality of PHCS to work for you.

You put your time in. Would you want any of it going to waste?

At Preferred Health Systems, we've improved our efficiency to the point that less than 10 percent of your premium is used for our operating costs. But we're not stopping there. We're looking for additional ways to make the most of every premium dollar.

You can be a part of the solution, too. By reviewing your health insurance plan carefully and being aware of how various services are covered, you can ensure that you continue to benefit from high quality health care at a reasonable price.

Health plans that work.  **Preferred** Health Systems

PAT FORD HEALTHCARE CONSULTING
17207 76TH Avenue West
Edmonds, WA. 98026
Phone: 425.743.0576 ~ Fax: 425.787.2774
Email: pat@pfhc.com
Website: www.pfhc.com

Pat Ford HealthCare Consulting (PFHC) specializes in developing strategies, which address the changing healthcare environment. PFHC offers its customers an individualized process that focuses on strategies related to Quality Improvement (QI), Utilization Management/Care Management (UM), Case Management (CM), Credentialing Medical Records review, comprehensive accreditation and medical management services for URAC, Mock Survey, Clinical Peer Review Process, and Regulatory Compliance. PFHC has assisted several clients in achieving full URAC accreditation. Outsourcing some or all of this process will result in less disruption to your staff and the office's workflow.

PFHC will consult with you without the expense of onsite visits. Through the use of fax, phone, and email, we can review, revise, and make recommendations. PFHC will provide the highest quality consultant service at the most economical price. (If an onsite visit is requested or necessary, we will hold our travel costs to minimum.)

A telephonic Initial Assessment Interview is FREE. Call 425.743.0576 or email us at pat@pfhc.com.

URAC Trained Consultants are available for the following accreditation programs – Health Utilization Management, Case Management, Disease Management and External Review Organizations.

AMERICAN
WHOLEHEALTH SM
NETWORKS, INC.

American WholeHealth Networks, Inc. (AWHN) is a leading nationwide Complementary and Alternative Medicine (CAM) company, headquartered in Sterling, VA. AWHN's practitioner network offers more than 35 CAM specialties to health plans and managed care organizations nationwide, including massage therapy, acupuncture, and chiropractic, as well as yoga and Pilates, tai chi and qi gong, nutritional counseling, fitness centers, spas, and more. In addition to network management, the company also provides eligibility verification, utilization management, data reporting, credentialing, claims processing, provider relations, and member services. Network practitioners are supported through the company's professional website www.wholehealthpro.com, and health plan members receive information and resources through AWHN's award-winning member education website www.wholehealthmd.com.

The company has received full accreditation for URAC's Health Utilization Management Standards, and its credentialing process is modeled after NCQA, an independent, nonprofit organization that certifies credentials verification organizations, and accredits managed care organizations. AWHN is poised to assist managed care companies in becoming market leaders in the healthcare revolution through its unique and innovative CAM products and solutions. More information about the company can be found at www.americanwholehealth.com.

a nabn company
gateway
HEALTH MANAGEMENT SERVICES

*URAC accredited since 1994, NABN's subsidiary company, **Gateway Health Management Services (GHMS)**, performs comprehensive utilization and case management services. These services enhance the effectiveness and value of health care delivery to all the employers and employees we service. We work closely with the patient and the attending physician to offer support to the employee and family through the course of the treatment.*

To enhance our service and in response to our clients, NABN and its subsidiaries, with an operating history of over 40 years, have built and continue to refine their services to better manage their clients' health plan assets. In doing so, NABN has set itself apart from other TPAs and health insurers. The result is out Integrated Risk Management Model. It builds on and integrates systematically, the unique capabilities of our claims management, utilization management and under-writing management. With all of these tools at our fingertips, we are able to assist our clients to manage their health plans with great efficiency.

- NOTES -

- NOTES -